Professional Windows® PowerShell for Exchange Server 2007 Service Pack 1

Part I: PowerShell for Exchange Fundamentals

Part II: Working with Server Roles

Part III: Working with PowerShell in a Production Environment

(Continued)

Part IV: Automating Administration

Professional
Windows® PowerShell for Exchange Server 2007 Service Pack 1

Professional
Windows® PowerShell for Exchange Server 2007 Service Pack 1

Joezer Cookey-Gam

Brendan Keane

Jeffrey Rosen

Jonathan Runyon

Joel Stidley

WILEY

Wiley Publishing, Inc.

Professional Windows® PowerShell for Exchange Server 2007

Published by
Wiley Publishing, Inc.
10475 Crosspoint Boulevard
Indianapolis, IN 46256
www.wiley.com

Copyright © 2008 by Wiley Publishing, Inc., Indianapolis, Indiana

Published by Wiley Publishing, Inc., Indianapolis, Indiana

Published simultaneously in Canada

ISBN: 978-0-470-22644-5

Manufactured in the United States of America

10 9 8 7 6 5 4 3 2 1

For general information on our other products and services or to obtain technical support, please contact our Customer Care Department within the U.S. at (800) 762-2974, outside the U.S. at (317) 572-3993 or fax (317) 572-4002.

Library of Congress Cataloging-in-Publication Data is available from the publisher.

To my wife Isu for her support even while caring for our newborn daughter Hallel, also to Dad and Mum for stirring my interest on an Engineering career path, and most especially to Jehovah, my best friend, without which this would have been impossible.
—Joezer Cookey-Gam

Thanks to my wife for her support and to my friends and family for understanding my mumblings about .NET references, variables, and why this piece of code worked last time I used it. I would also like to thank Joel Stidley for providing this opportunity, mentorship, and for his friendship.
—Brendan Keane

To my wife, Christine, and our daughters, Madison and Isabel, I love you and thanks for the patience and support. Also thanks to Mom and Dad for everything. Thanks to Joel Stidley for offering me the chance to work on this book, as well as the co-authors, technical reviewers, and editors.
—Jeffrey Rosen

To Lisa and Evan. Thanks for giving me purpose.
—Jonathan Runyon

To my wife Andrea, and my children Ethan and Jaelyn for putting up with me for the last few months of extra work.
—Joel Stidley

About the Authors

Joezer Cookey-Gam holds a Bachelor of Technology degree in Electrical Engineering (Electronics Major) from the Rivers State University of Science and Technology in Nigeria. He is a Microsoft Certified Systems Engineer with focus on messaging. He began his IT career as a Network Engineer and Exchange administrator supporting medium to large Enterprise networks. In this role he provided solutions for LinkServe Limited, a leading Internet service provider in Nigeria. He joined Microsoft in 2001 and currently is a Support Escalation Engineer supporting enterprise Exchange customers

Brendan Keane is currently an information security principal specializing in Microsoft technologies. Brendan began his tenure with Exchange 5.5 and has enjoyed working more with each new release.

Jeffrey Rosen has a Masters of Business Administration from Case Western Reserve Weatherhead School of Management specializing in Information Systems. He is a Microsoft Certified Architect, an MCSE specializing in messaging and security, and a CISSP. He began his career working with Microsoft Mail and Novell Netware. Since then, Jeffrey has been working for Microsoft Consulting Services for nine years, working on large and complex Exchange deployments.

Jonathan Runyon has worked in the IT Industry for more than 17 years. He joined Microsoft in 2001 and has worked exclusively on Exchange Server support ever since. Jonathan recently contributed to the development of Exchange Server 2007 internal training for Microsoft Customer Service and Support. He is a Microsoft Certified Systems Engineer and MCSA, specializing in messaging.

Joel Stidley has been working with Microsoft Exchange since the Exchange Server 5.0 beta releases and hasn't missed deploying a release since. He has been working with the Microsoft Exchange JDP/TAP program since Exchange Server 2000 Service Pack 3, and has been running Exchange Server 2007 in production since 2005. Joel also founded ExchangeExchange.com, an Exchange-focused community website in 2004 where he blogs and provides forums for discussing Exchange and PowerShell information. Currently he is a Senior Solutions Engineer at Terremark Worldwide Inc where he works with a variety of storage, virtualization, and messaging technologies.

Credits

Executive Editor
Chris Webb

Development Editor
Sydney Jones

Technical Editor
Josh Maher

Production Editor
Elizabeth Ginns Britten

Copy Editor
Kim Cofer

Editorial Manager
Mary Beth Wakefield

Production Manager
Tim Tate

Vice President and Executive Group Publisher
Richard Swadley

Vice President and Executive Publisher
Joseph B. Wikert

Project Coordinator, Cover
Lynsey Stanford

Proofreader
Sossity Smith

Indexer
Jack Lewis

Contents

Contents

Contents

Contents

Contents

Contents

Contents

Contents

Contents

Acknowledgments

This book would not have been possible without all of the contributions of time and effort from the Wrox staff and the detailed work of the authors and editors.

First we have to thank Chris Webb for this opportunity to write, as well as his patience and persistence in getting this book written.

We would also like to thank Sydney Jones for doing an awesome job keeping the project running and Joshua Maher for turning around the technical edits quickly and accurately. Also, we would be remiss if we didn't thank Liz Britten and Kim Cofer for an amazing job with copy editing.

The authors all would like to thank our families for their support during the writing of this book. Writing a book always seems to take longer than you would expect, so having a dedicated and loving support team at home is essential to any successful project.

Joezer Cookey-Gam in particular would also like to thank David Santamaria, Bill Long, Austin Audu and Robert Zeigler, the phenomenal Exchange Escalation Engineers who allowed him to bounce off his ideas, questions and solutions.

Lastly, we have to thank the Microsoft Exchange product team for not listening to the nay-sayers (including some of us authors) and forging ahead with PowerShell as the management interface for Exchange Server and providing amazingly detailed documentation to get us started.

Introduction

Windows PowerShell is a new command-line administration tool that is a giant step forward from previous command-line tools. Often, each Microsoft product would develop separate tools for command-line management, and each of these tools usually had a very narrow feature list and varied command syntax. This would usually lead developers to have to use a variety of management APIs to accomplish even the simplest tasks. PowerShell is meant to create a unified management tool for all Microsoft products, and to simplify management.

The first major product to be released with Windows PowerShell as its management interface was Exchange Server 2007, a complete rewrite of the familiar Exchange management tools using PowerShell to provide all management functions. The GUI management tools were built on top of PowerShell and provide only a subset of the functions available from the command line.

Initial feedback during the beta releases was that providing a mostly PowerShell interface was not something even experienced administrators would embrace. As the beta releases of the product continued the Exchange Management Shell (the PowerShell-based management tool for Exchange Server 2007) continued to improve as did the Exchange Management Console (the GUI-based management tool).

Slowly, the Management Shell has begun to win over many of the opposers because it provides more functionality, it's often quicker, and it provides more power to the administrator. Many administrators now prefer to use the Exchange Management Shell over the Exchange Management Console for these reasons.

Although groundwork will be laid for new Exchange features, this book is tailored to current Exchange professionals wanting to take full advantage of the new Management shell, PowerShell, for deploying, configuring, managing, and maintaining an Exchange Server 2007 organization. Details for many of the PowerShell commands are provided along with real-world examples for using these commands.

Time is spent explaining many of the key commands along with details behind using them. Additional time is spent showing how to put these commands together to show Exchange administrators how to become comfortable with PowerShell and use PowerShell to manage and streamline their Exchange Server 2007 organization.

Who This Book Is For

This book in intended to for Exchange professionals who are looking to become comfortable with Windows PowerShell and want to use PowerShell to effectively manage, automate, and streamline their Exchange 2007 organization. Having some knowledge of Exchange Server 2007 is helpful but not required because we spend time discussing some of the new features and how they work.

What This Book Covers

The first two chapters cover the basics on using PowerShell, so those with little to no experience with PowerShell should be sure to read those chapters with keen interest.

After Chapter 2, the book takes a deeper dive into the Exchange PowerShell cmdlets and how to combine their use to simplify and automate with real-world examples.

How This Book Is Structured

The book is separated into four main parts. The first section helps the reader become familiar with Windows PowerShell and the Exchange Server 2007 Management Shell. Time is spent discussing the roots of PowerShell as well as the fundamentals for using PowerShell with Exchange.

The second section of the book focuses on working with the new Exchange server roles. The cmdlets and features that are specific to each of these roles are discussed and real examples are used to help identify the appropriate times that the cmdlets would be used.

The third section brings PowerShell into your environment, showing examples of how to work with users and groups. Also, time is spent working with clusters and troubleshooting with PowerShell.

The final section puts together all of the things that have been discussed previously. Time is spent with a number of examples, explaining how they work and providing a basis for you to modify the examples for your own environment.

What You Need to Use This Book

To be able to follow along in this book it would be beneficial to have a working Exchange organization with at least one Exchange Server 2007 computer. Microsoft provides a number of resources for this on its website. You can download a virtual hard disk (VHD) with Exchange Server 2007 already installed to be able to run on Microsoft Virtual Server, or you can also download a trial version of Exchange to install on your physical hardware.

> *You can download an Exchange Server 2007 virtual machine or obtain the trial software at* `http://technet.microsoft.com/en-us/exchange/bb330851.aspx`.

Chapter 17 has some C# code that can be run within Microsoft Visual Studio 2005. If you do not have Visual Studio 2005, you can download Visual Web Developer Express to run the examples in the chapter.

Conventions

To help you get the most from the text and keep track of what's happening, we've used a number of conventions throughout the book.

```
Boxes like this one hold important, not-to-be forgotten information that is
directly relevant to the surrounding text.
```

Notes, tips, hints, tricks, and asides to the current discussion are offset and placed in italics like this.

As for styles in the text:

❑   We *highlight* new terms and important words when we introduce them.

❑   We show keyboard strokes like this: Ctrl+A.

❑   We show filenames, URLs, and code within the text like so: `persistence.properties`.

❑   We present code in two different ways:

```
We use a monofont type with no highlighting for most code examples.
```

```
We use gray highlighting to emphasize code that's particularly important in the
present context.
```

Errata

We make every effort to ensure that there are no errors in the text or in the code. However, no one is perfect, and mistakes do occur. If you find an error in one of our books, like a spelling mistake or faulty piece of code, we would be very grateful for your feedback. By sending in errata you may save another reader hours of frustration and at the same time you will be helping us provide even higher quality information.

To find the errata page for this book, go to `http://www.wrox.com` and locate the title using the Search box or one of the title lists. Then, on the book details page, click the Book Errata link. On this page you can view all errata that has been submitted for this book and posted by Wrox editors. A complete book list including links to each book's errata is also available at `www.wrox.com/misc-pages/booklist.shtml`.

If you don't spot "your" error on the Book Errata page, go to `www.wrox.com/contact/techsupport.shtml` and complete the form there to send us the error you have found. We'll check the information and, if appropriate, post a message to the book's errata page and fix the problem in subsequent editions of the book.

p2p.wrox.com

For author and peer discussion, join the P2P forums at `p2p.wrox.com`. The forums are a Web-based system for you to post messages relating to Wrox books and related technologies and interact with other readers and technology users. The forums offer a subscription feature to e-mail you topics of interest of your choosing when new posts are made to the forums. Wrox authors, editors, other industry experts, and your fellow readers are present on these forums.

Introduction

At `http://p2p.wrox.com` you will find a number of different forums that will help you not only as you read this book, but also as you develop your own applications. To join the forums, just follow these steps:

1. Go to `p2p.wrox.com` and click the Register link.

2. Read the terms of use and click Agree.

3. Complete the required information to join as well as any optional information you wish to provide and click Submit.

4. You will receive an e-mail with information describing how to verify your account and complete the joining process.

> *You can read messages in the forums without joining P2P but in order to post your own messages, you must join.*

Once you join, you can post new messages and respond to messages other users post. You can read messages at any time on the Web. If you would like to have new messages from a particular forum e-mailed to you, click the Subscribe to this Forum icon by the forum name in the forum listing.

For more information about how to use the Wrox P2P, be sure to read the P2P FAQs for answers to questions about how the forum software works as well as many common questions specific to P2P and Wrox books. To read the FAQs, click the FAQ link on any P2P page.

Part I

PowerShell for Exchange Fundamentals

Getting Started with Windows PowerShell

Windows PowerShell is the next-generation command-line shell and scripting language for Windows. Exchange Server 2007 is the first Microsoft application to utilize Windows PowerShell for deployment and administration. This chapter introduces Windows PowerShell and explains the basic concepts you'll need to know to use Windows PowerShell effectively.

The first section, "What Is Windows PowerShell?" includes command shell history and describes the features that make Windows PowerShell the ideal management platform for Exchange Server 2007.

The section that follows, "Windows PowerShell Basics," covers the fundamentals of Windows PowerShell. This section describes the components of Windows PowerShell and how to find commands and then learn how to use them.

To understand Windows PowerShell and its benefit to Exchange administrators, this chapter covers the following key areas:

- ❑ Command shells vs. Graphical User Interfaces
- ❑ Windows PowerShell components
- ❑ Windows PowerShell built-in help
- ❑ Composing commands using pipelines

What Is Windows PowerShell?

Windows PowerShell is a new command-line shell and scripting language for Windows. It was designed by Microsoft specifically to give administrators an extensible command shell for managing Windows environments with greater control and flexibility. This section includes a brief discussion of some traditional administrative interfaces to help you understand why there is a need for an advanced interface like Windows PowerShell. What follows is a discussion of the main features that set Windows PowerShell apart from other management interfaces and make it the most powerful administrative interface that Microsoft has ever produced.

Shell History

Before there was the Graphical User Interface (GUI), there was the Command Line Interface (CLI). The CLI was born of a need to quickly interact with the operating system at a time when computers were mostly controlled using punch card or paper tape input. The first CLIs used teletype machines to enter commands directly into the computer for execution, with the results returned to the operator as printed output. Teletypes were later replaced with dedicated text-based CRT terminals that offered an even greater advantage in speed and the amount of information available to the operator.

All CLIs rely on a program that interprets textual commands entered on the command line and turns them into machine instructions. This program is known as a command-line interpreter or shell. Every major operating system includes some sort of shell interface. UNIX administrators may be familiar with several shells (SH, KSH, CSH, and BASH) as well as the text processing languages AWK and PERL. Windows users may also be familiar with cmd.exe, the Windows command-line interpreter and the Windows Script Host for running scripts.

All these shells make possible direct communication between the operating system and the user. They include built-in commands and provide an environment for running text-based applications and utilities.

When Shells Are Better than GUI Interfaces

GUI interfaces came later in computer development and opened the door to less-technically-advanced users looking for a more "comfortable" way to interact with the operating system. Although they provide a simple-to-use interface, GUI applications are prone to user error because their use requires direct interaction between the user and the interface through menus, controls, and fields. For each administrator in the organization to complete the same tasks as all other administrators, they must learn and then use the correct menu choices and controls in order to get consistent results.

GUI-based management programs also constrain administrators to predetermined properties and controls. They lack provisions for special or one-off tasks because they are designed and written with specific functionality that is appropriate for general purposes.

Shells offer a powerful solution for overcoming these GUI shortcomings by providing a method to gather commands into a batch file, also known as a script, and then run them as if they had been entered one at a time at the command line. Administrators create and run scripts to automate everyday tasks and resolve difficult issues GUI interfaces are not designed to handle. Scripts allow a reliable, sustainable method for administering an environment.

Once a script has been written and proven to work for its intended purpose, it can be distributed throughout an organization and used as needed by any administrator, with expected and consistent results. Examples of some common script solutions you might find in most organizations are used for unattended machine deployments, user account provisioning, and nightly database backups.

Common Shell Limitations

The traditional shells mentioned earlier offer an administrator greater control and flexibility for tackling everyday or even unusual management tasks, but they all suffer from significant drawbacks.

Command shells operate by executing built-in commands that run within the process of the shell, or by executing a command or application in a new process outside of the shell. Many applications lack command-line equivalents for controls found in their GUI management programs. And the number of built-in commands offered by most shells is usually small, requiring more applications and utilities to run outside the shell to accomplish critical tasks. Most organizations lack the resources to develop special applications and utilities on their own and may struggle to accomplish more complex tasks using available commands alone.

Another drawback shared by most shells is the way in which they handle information. The results of running a command or utility is returned as text to the command line. If you need to use this text as input for another command, which is common in scripting, it has to be parsed. Parsing is the process of evaluating text and extracting the meaningful values in a form that can then be properly interpreted by another command. Parsing is prone to error and can be time consuming because the format required for preparing the textual input can vary greatly between different commands, applications, and utilities.

One final limitation to consider is the lack of integration between a shell and the scripting languages you would use in that shell. For example, Windows Script Host provides a method for implementing a variety of scripting languages from the command line (via cmd.exe), but it is not integrated with cmd.exe and is thus not interactive. It also lacks readily accessible documentation from the command line as you would find in many other shells and scripting environments.

The Power Behind PowerShell

What sets Windows PowerShell apart from all other command shells is that it is built on top of .NET Framework version 2.0. Windows PowerShell exposes .NET classes as built-in commands. When these commands are executed they create a collection of one or more structured objects as output. Instead of text, all actions in Windows PowerShell are based on .NET objects.

Windows PowerShell objects have a specific type based on the class used to create them. They have properties (which are characteristics) and methods (which are actions you can take). Because objects have a defined structure, a collection of objects created by one command can be passed to another command as input without the need for parsing the data in-between.

Windows PowerShell includes a fully integrated and intuitive scripting language for managing .NET objects. The language is consistent with higher-level languages used in programming .NET. Those administrators familiar with the C# programming language will find many similarities in the grammar, syntax, and keywords used by the Windows PowerShell scripting language.

Windows PowerShell includes more than 130 built-in commands for performing the most common system administrative tasks. The commands are designed to be easy to understand and use because they share common naming and parameter conventions. Learning how to use one command makes it easy to understand how similar commands are also used.

Because Windows PowerShell is fully extensible, software developers can create their own custom built-in commands to handle those administrative tasks not already addressed in the default built-in command set. Exchange Management Shell is an example of Windows PowerShell extended to include more than 500 built-in commands.

Windows PowerShell not only allows access to the local disk drives as a file system, but it also exposes the local Registry, certificate store, and system environment variables and allows you to navigate them using the same familiar methods you would use for navigating a file system. Windows PowerShell also provides additional data stores for variables, functions, and alias definitions used inside the shell.

GUI management applications can be built on top of Windows PowerShell. Software developers can ensure that all administrative functions found in a GUI management application built on Windows PowerShell have a corresponding scriptable equivalent in the Windows PowerShell CLI. Exchange Management Console is an example of a GUI management application built on top of Windows PowerShell.

PowerShell Basics

You may be asking yourself why a book about Exchange Management Shell is spending so much time in the beginning talking about Windows PowerShell. Because Exchange Management Shell is built on top of Windows PowerShell, you need to understand the basic concepts and components of Windows PowerShell first.

The Command-Line Interface

Windows PowerShell operates within a hosting application. The default application is `powershell.exe`, a console application that presents a command line to the user. To start PowerShell from the Start menu select All Programs ⇨ Windows PowerShell 1.0 ⇨ Windows PowerShell. This opens Windows PowerShell with the default console application as shown in Figure 1-1.

Many first-time users of Exchange Management Shell may be confused when after opening the default Windows PowerShell console application that they are unable to run any Exchange-specific commands. This is because Exchange Management Shell is an extension of Windows PowerShell. The default Windows PowerShell hosting application does not include any Exchange-specific commands. Windows PowerShell is extended by the use of a component called a snap-in. A snap-in provides a method for loading custom PowerShell commands and functionality contained in an application extension file.

To start Exchange Management Shell from the Start menu, select All Programs ⇨ Exchange Server 2007 ⇨ Exchange Management Shell. The target definition for this program shortcut contains the following underlying command line:

```
C:\WINDOWS\system32\WindowsPowerShell\v1.0\PowerShell.exe -PSConsoleFile
"C:\Program Files\Microsoft\Exchange Server\bin\exshell.psc1" -noexit -command ".
'C:\Program Files\Microsoft\Exchange Server\bin\Exchange.ps1'"
```

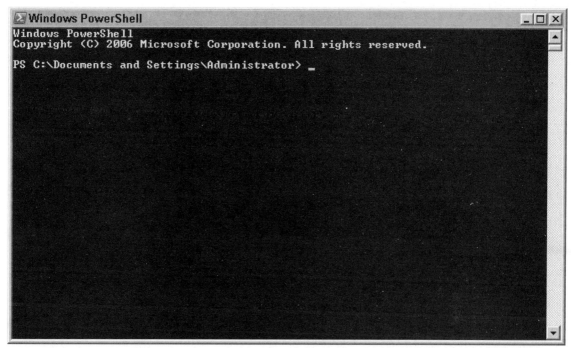

```
Windows PowerShell                                                    _ □ ×
Windows PowerShell
Copyright (C) 2006 Microsoft Corporation. All rights reserved.

PS C:\Documents and Settings\Administrator> _
```

Figure 1-1

While invoking Windows PowerShell, this command specifies a console definition file identified by the PSConsoleFile parameter. The exshell.psc1 file contains a pointer to the Exchange Management Shell snap-in definition stored in the Registry at HKEY_LOCAL_MACHINE\SOFTWARE\ Microsoft\PowerShell\1\PowerShellSnapIns\Microsoft.Exchange.Management .PowerShell.Admin.

The ModuleName value stored in this location contains the path to the application extension file Microsoft.Exchange.PowerShell.Configuration.dll, located in the %ProgramFiles%\ Microsoft\Exchange Server\Bin directory. Windows PowerShell loads this .dll file to make the Exchange commands available.

In addition to loading the snap-in for Exchange Management Shell, the underlying command also uses the command parameter to specify additional commands to run at startup, in this case the script file Exchange.ps1. This script file contains definitions for aliases, functions, and variables specific to

Exchange management. It also defines the appearance of the command-line prompt and the initial welcome banner shown in Figure 1-2.

As you can see, the appearance of the Exchange Management Shell is a bit different from the default Windows PowerShell console application, yet all the functionality of the core shell remains intact. Because Windows PowerShell is hosted in a console application, all the familiar properties and controls for a console application are available. Later in this section you learn how to set up your Exchange Management Shell for the best user experience when following the examples in this book.

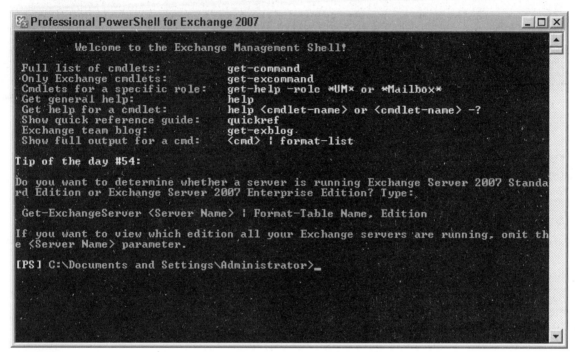

Figure 1-2

Cmdlets

The most basic component of Windows PowerShell is the built-in commands, called cmdlets (pronounced command-lets). Almost all the work done through Windows PowerShell is done through the use of cmdlets. Cmdlets are similar to built-in commands found in other shells; for example, the built-in command DIR found in cmd.exe. In Exchange Management Shell, cmdlets that perform a specific administrative function are often referred to as tasks.

All cmdlets share the same basic structure. They have a name and take one or more parameters as input. Entering the name of a cmdlet, followed by any necessary parameter names and values, will result in the execution of the cmdlet. For example, the cmdlet `Get-ExchangeServer` returns a list of all Exchange servers in the organization in a formatted list as shown in Figure 1-3.

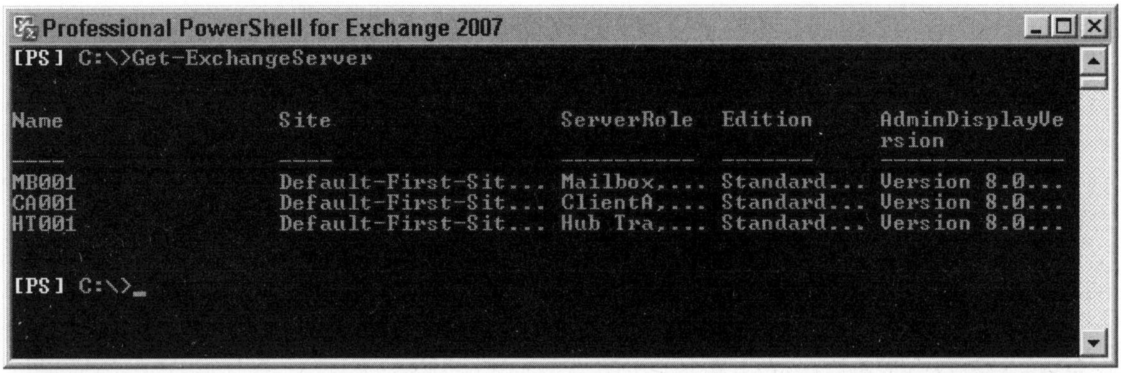

```
Professional PowerShell for Exchange 2007                                    _ □ X
[PS] C:\>Get-ExchangeServer

Name                    Site                ServerRole   Edition      AdminDisplayVe
                                                                       rsion
----                    ----                ----------   -------      --------------
MB001                   Default-First-Sit... Mailbox,....  Standard...  Version 8.0...
CA001                   Default-First-Sit... ClientA,....  Standard...  Version 8.0...
HT001                   Default-First-Sit... Hub Tra,....  Standard...  Version 8.0...


[PS] C:\>_
```

Figure 1-3

Windows PowerShell commands are case-insensitive. The examples given in this section use the default form of capitalizing the first letter of each distinct word in the command elements. Only spelling and syntax count when entering Windows PowerShell commands.

Cmdlet Names: The Verb-Noun Pair

Cmdlet names always take the form of two or more words, separated by a dash or hyphen (-). The first word is known as the verb and refers to an action the cmdlet will take. The second word or group of words is known as the noun, and refers to the target of the verb. The verb and noun describe the action and the target of the action. Using this convention for naming cmdlets makes discovering and learning cmdlets more intuitive.

Cmdlet nouns may contain multiple words but have no spaces between them.

Common Verb Names

Microsoft has produced a list of common verb names recommended for use by software programmers developing Windows PowerShell cmdlets. This helps maintain a well-known list of verb names an administrator needs to know when learning about cmdlets. Here are some common verb names used in Exchange Management Shell cmdlets and what they do:

❑   `Get`: The `Get` verb retrieves information about the target of the cmdlet. In the previous example, `Get-ExchangeServer`, the cmdlet retrieved information about Exchange servers.

❑   `Set`: The `Set` verb sets a condition or makes a configuration change to the cmdlet target.

❑   `New`: The `New` verb creates a new instance of the cmdlet target.

❑   `Remove`: The `Remove` verb deletes the cmdlet target.

The Get *verb is the most common verb used in Exchange Management Shell cmdlets. It is also known as the default verb. When a cmdlet noun name is entered without a verb, Windows PowerShell assumes that the* Get *verb was implied and runs that cmdlet. In the preceding example, entering* ExchangeServer *instead of* Get-ExchangeServer *would yield the same results.*

Noun Names

Nouns always represent the target of the cmdlet, in other words the thing on which the cmdlet will act. Noun names are usually straightforward and simply describe the target item. For example, consider the cmdlet Get-ClusteredMailboxServerStatus. From looking at this cmdlet's name you should be able to figure out that its purpose is to retrieve the status of Clustered Mailbox Servers. When you apply this logic to other cmdlet names you quickly begin to understand how easy it can be to discover and learn cmdlets.

Another concept of noun names you should understand is that many cmdlet names share the same noun. For example, there are 10 different cmdlets that all affect mailbox items. Here are examples of just a few of these cmdlets:

❑   Get-Mailbox is used to retrieve information about one or more mailbox-enabled users.

❑   Set-Mailbox is used to change configuration settings for one or more mailbox-enabled users.

❑   New-Mailbox is used to create a new mailbox-enabled user.

❑   Move-Mailbox is used to move one or more mailboxes from one mailbox database to another.

As you can see, these examples all use a common noun name, yet each cmdlet yields very different results when it is coupled with a different verb name.

Parameters

Parameter names are preceded by a dash or hyphen (-) and can be made up of a single word or multiple words with no spaces between them. Parameter names are typically followed by one or more values that are used either to provide input data for setting property values or to dictate the behavior of the cmdlet. Parameters that dictate behavior act as switches and typically do not require an input value.

Parameters have certain characteristics that determine how they are used. You can find out these characteristics via the built-in help information for each cmdlet that is readily available from the command line. Later this section covers how to get help and how to interpret that information to know how to use parameters effectively.

Parameter Input Values

Parameter input values are typically integer (numbers), string (words), or Boolean (true or false) data types. Other more specialized data types are also possible as defined by the class the cmdlet represents. For example, many cmdlets specific to Exchange Management Shell have data type input values specific to Exchange configuration components. The parameter data type is set when the cmdlet is defined. Windows PowerShell validates parameter input values as the cmdlet executes. If an invalid value is used or the format of the input data does not meet the cmdlet's specification, the cmdlet fails to execute. For example, if a parameter takes as input an integer value, but a string value is entered instead, the cmdlet fails with an error that states the wrong data type was used.

In Figure 1-4, the `Set-Mailbox` cmdlet is being used to set the `ProhibitSendQuota` attribute on mailbox-enabled user John Doe. The expected data input type for parameter `ProhibitSendQuota` is an integer value or integer value with a standard byte size abbreviation as a suffix. Because an alphanumeric string value (`somestring`) was entered instead, the command fails to execute and the error message shown describes the exact cause for the error. The solution is to provide the input value in the correct format, in this case 2GB to specify a `ProhibitSendQuota` value of 2,147,483,648 bytes.

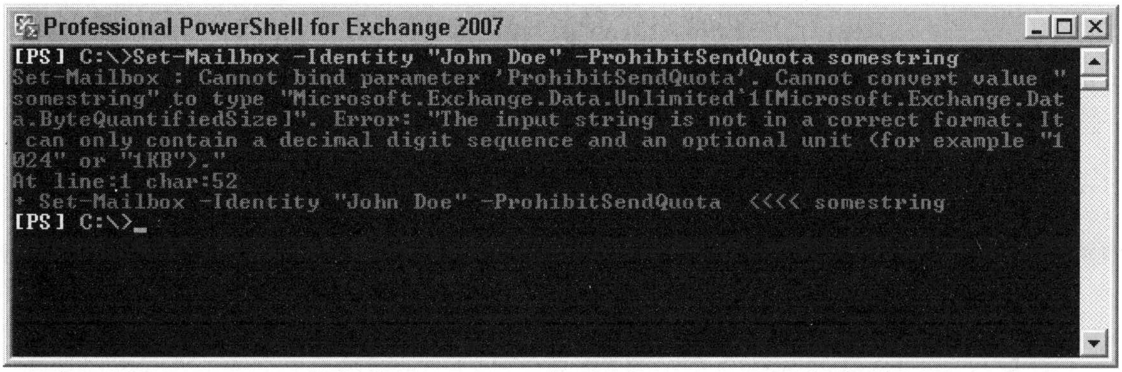

```
Professional PowerShell for Exchange 2007                                    _ □ ×
[PS] C:\>Set-Mailbox -Identity "John Doe" -ProhibitSendQuota somestring
Set-Mailbox : Cannot bind parameter 'ProhibitSendQuota'. Cannot convert value "
somestring" to type "Microsoft.Exchange.Data.Unlimited`1[Microsoft.Exchange.Dat
a.ByteQuantifiedSize]". Error: "The input string is not in a correct format. It
 can only contain a decimal digit sequence and an optional unit (for example "1
024" or "1KB")."
At line:1 char:52
+ Set-Mailbox -Identity "John Doe" -ProhibitSendQuota <<<< somestring
[PS] C:\>_
```

Figure 1-4

Single-word string values can be entered as is, but string values that contain multiple words with spaces must be encapsulated in single or double quotes. Some parameters take as input multiple values. Each value must be separated by commas. When entering multiple string values with spaces, encapsulate each value in quotes, and separate each value with commas.

In Figure 1-5, the `Set-User` cmdlet is being used to set the multi-valued attribute `OtherHomePhone` with two separate string values that both contain spaces.

```
Select Professional PowerShell for Exchange 2007                             _ □ ×
[PS] C:\>Set-User "John Doe" -OtherHomePhone "Home Office Line 1 - 555-1234", "H
ome Office Line 2 - 555-5678"
[PS] C:\>_
```

Figure 1-5

Some parameters support wildcards as input. Windows PowerShell handles wildcard matching so all cmdlets that accept wildcard input behave the same way. The most commonly known wildcard you will find useful is the asterisk or star (*). The asterisk wildcard can be used to stand for zero or more characters in a string.

For example, the `Get-Service` cmdlet is used to gather information about services and supports wildcards for the `Name` parameter used to identify those services. Using the asterisk wildcard you can generate a list of all services with names that match the given pattern, as shown in Figure 1-6 for services that begin with `Net`.

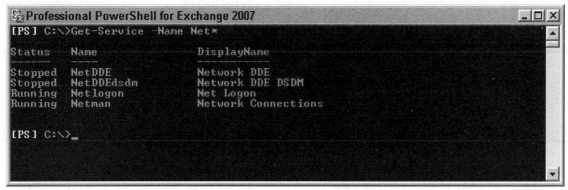

Figure 1-6

Most cmdlets that use the `Identity` parameter support wildcards as input. Also most cmdlets that use the `Get` verb and the `Identity` parameter support a default value of `*` for the `Identity` parameter. This means that when you enter the cmdlet name without any parameters or values, it is implied you want to gather information about all the possible matches.

For example, typing and entering `Get-Mailbox` returns information about all mailbox-enabled accounts. In large organizations this could result in thousands of matches so cmdlets like `Get-Mailbox` limit the results to 1,000 matches. This can be increased by including the `ResultSize` parameter with an appropriate higher value.

In Figure 1-7, `Get-Mailbox` is used to retrieve all mailboxes in the organization.

```
Professional PowerShell for Exchange 2007                          _ □ X
[PS ] C:\>Get-Mailbox

Name                     Alias                ServerName       ProhibitSendQuo
                                                               ta
----                     -----                ----------       ---------------
Administrator            Administrator        mb001            unlimited
John Doe                 johdoe               mb001            unlimited
Jane Doe                 jandoe               mb001            unlimited

[PS ] C:\>_
```

Figure 1-7

Optional and Required Parameters

Cmdlets may have some parameters that are not required to be used each time the cmdlet is run and are considered optional. You will find that most cmdlets have at least some optional parameters, especially cmdlets that modify items, because not all properties of an item require changing at the same time. This allows you to use only the optional parameters necessary to make the desired changes while leaving out all other optional parameters.

Then there are other parameters that must always be used when the cmdlet is run. You will find that most cmdlets that take an action such as creating, modifying, or removing items have at minimum one required parameter to identify the items on which to take action. If any required parameters are left out when running a cmdlet, Windows PowerShell prompts the user to enter an input value for each of the missing required parameters.

The Identity parameter is one of the most common required parameters, typically used by cmdlets that need as input the name of the object on which to take some action. For example, the Set-User cmdlet modifies attributes on an existing user account in the Active Directory directory service. The Identity parameter is required when using Set-User and is used to identify the user account on which the changes are to be made.

In Figure 1-8, the Set-User cmdlet is being used to set the Department attribute, but the Identity parameter was not used to name the target user so the shell prompts the operator for the missing value.

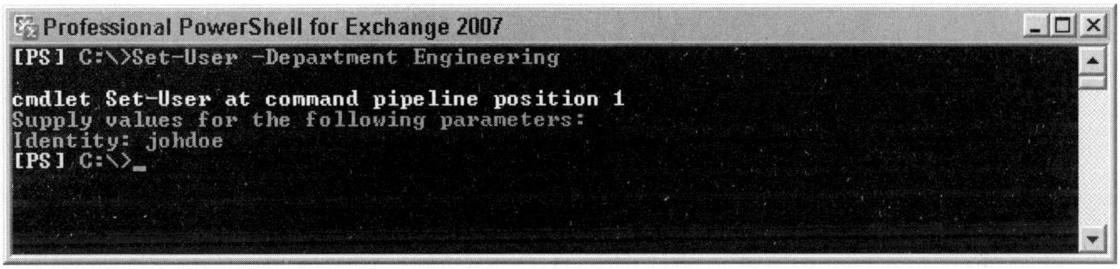

```
Professional PowerShell for Exchange 2007                                _ □ x
[PS] C:\>Set-User -Department Engineering

cmdlet Set-User at command pipeline position 1
Supply values for the following parameters:
Identity: johdoe
[PS] C:\>_
```

Figure 1-8

Positional and Named Parameters

Another parameter characteristic to consider is whether a parameter is positional or named. A positional parameter can be used without actually entering the parameter name, as long as the input value is in the position where the parameter name would normally have been used. Positional parameters are designated with a number, starting with position 1, then position 2, and so on. Using positional parameters effectively can be a real time-saving practice.

For example, the `Identity` parameter is typically a positional parameter used in position 1 after the cmdlet name. The `Get-Mailbox` cmdlet uses the `Identity` parameter in position 1 to identify the mailbox-enabled user for which to retrieve information. In Figure 1-9, you can see that the results of running the `Get-Mailbox` cmdlet with and without the `Identity` parameter name are identical as long as the input value is supplied in the first position after the cmdlet name.

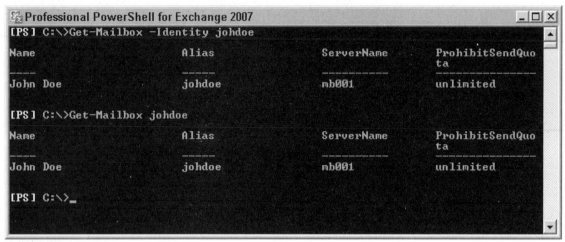

Figure 1-9

If a parameter is not positional, then it is named. To use a named parameter you must always enter the parameter name followed by the input value. The order in which you enter named parameters and their input value on the command line does not matter because the shell's command parser interprets the command in total before execution.

Parameter Shortcuts

Another time-saving feature you may find useful is parameter name shortcuts. When entering the name of a parameter, you need to supply only enough of a parameter's name to disambiguate it from any other parameter name. In the following example the first command uses the `Set-User` cmdlet to set the `Manager` attribute on user account `John Doe` to his manager `Jane Doe`. `-ma` is enough information for the shell to interpret the parameter name `Manager` so the command succeeds. In the second command, `-po` is being used to refer to the `PostalCode` parameter. However, `-po` is ambiguous and also matches parameter `PostOfficeBox`. In this case the command fails with the error shown Figure 1-10.

```
Professional PowerShell for Exchange 2007                    _ □ ×
[PS] C:\>Set-User -id "John Doe" -ma "Jane Doe"
[PS] C:\>Set-User -id "John Doe" -po 90120
Set-User : Parameter cannot be processed because the parameter name 'po' is amb
iguous. Possible matches include: -PostalCode -PostOfficeBox.
At line:1 char:9
+ Set-User  <<<< -id "John Doe" -po 90120
[PS] C:\>_
```

Figure 1-10

The solution is to provide enough of the parameter name to make it unique, in this case `posta` would be enough to disambiguate `PostalCode` from `PostOfficeBox`.

Discovering Commands and Getting Help

Now that you have learned the basic concept of using cmdlets, we'll discuss how to go about discovering cmdlets and learning how to use them.

Even with more than 500 cmdlets in Exchange Management Shell, finding the right cmdlet to accomplish a task is easier than you might think. Earlier in this section you learned that a cmdlet's name is typically descriptive of the cmdlet's purpose. Using this knowledge along with some simple commands, you can quickly and easily find any cmdlet.

Using Get-Help to Find Cmdlets

Windows PowerShell provides powerful built-in help information available directly from the command line. Most cmdlets have some level of help content stored in a cmdlet help file that can be accessed from the command line using the `Get-Help` cmdlet. You don't need to know where the help file is or how to get to help information for a specific cmdlet; PowerShell works out these details as part of built-in help.

Besides displaying cmdlet help information, `Get-Help` is a powerful tool for finding cmdlets based on ambiguous name matching. When supplied with a specific and unique cmdlet name as input to the `Name` parameter, `Get-Help` displays the help information for that cmdlet. But if the input is ambiguous, `Get-Help` displays a list of all cmdlets that are a close match.

Using this approach you simply need to supply enough of the possible cmdlet name to generate a list of cmdlets from which to choose. For example, say you would like to learn about cmdlets that are used for managing Exchange databases but you don't know the exact names, or even which cmdlets might be available. The command shown in Figure 1-11 generates a list of cmdlets that contain the word `database`.

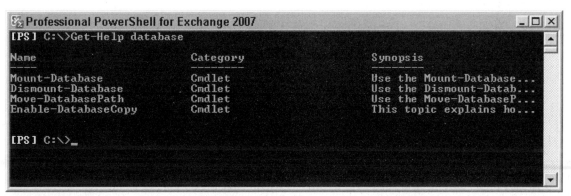

Figure 1-11

In this example for Get-Help *and for those that follow later in this section, input values are used without specifying the parameter* Name. *Because* Name *is a positional parameter (for position 1), it is not required to be named as long as the input value appears on the command line in the first position after* Get-Help.

Using the whole word database produces a list of cmdlets that have at least the word at the beginning of the noun name. But can you be sure that this is a list of every cmdlet possible that can be used to manage databases? Luckily, Get-Help supports the use of wildcards to search for matching cmdlet names. To display a list of cmdlets that have the word database anywhere in the cmdlet name, add the * wildcard to the beginning and end of the name. This causes Windows PowerShell to return a list of all possible matches as shown in Figure 1-12.

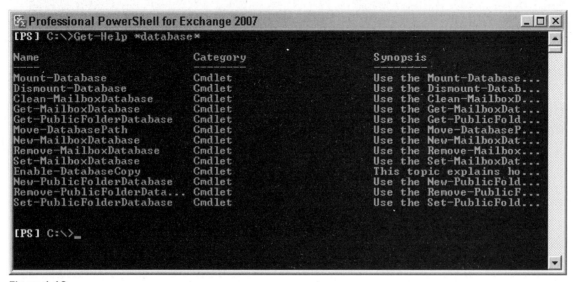

Figure 1-12

This produces a comprehensive list of all available cmdlets that deal with the management of Exchange databases. Now you would simply need to select the most likely cmdlet for accomplishing a given task based on how closely the cmdlet name describes what the cmdlet does, then access the help information for that cmdlet to learn how it is used. For example, if you want to learn how to create a mailbox database, the cmdlet New-MailboxDatabase is the most likely choice.

Another simple way to use Get-Help is with the Role parameter. Exchange Server 2007 architecture allows for the installation of different server roles on a given server to match the needs of an organization's messaging system. There are five server roles, and by specifying a wildcard role value with the Role parameter, Get-Help displays a list of all cmdlets used to manage that role. For example, to display all cmdlets used to manage the Mailbox server role, the command shown in Figure 1-13 would be used.

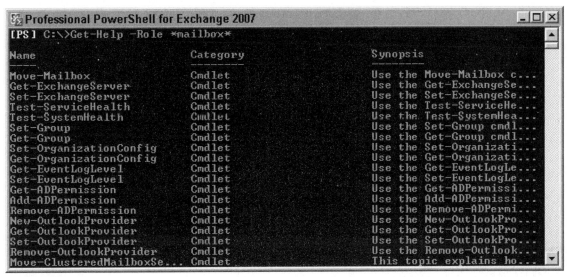

Figure 1-13

The other possible role values you can use with the Role parameter are:

❑   *client* for Client Access Server

❑   *hub* for Hub Transport server

❑   *um* for Unified Messaging server

❑   *edge* for Edge Transport server

Using Get-Command to Find Cmdlets

In addition to the Get-Help cmdlet, the Get-Command cmdlet is very useful for discovering cmdlets and other Windows PowerShell command elements such as functions, aliases, applications, and external scripts.

Running Get-Command without any parameters produces a list of every available cmdlet. With more than 500 available cmdlets in Exchange Management Shell, this extensive list is not very efficient for discovering individual cmdlets. The parameters for Get-Command allow you to refine the list into something comprehensive. Using the Name parameter you can supply enough of the cmdlet name with wildcards to create a list of ambiguous matches similar to the previous example using Get-Help.

The parameters Verb and Noun are used either alone or together to search for cmdlets with matching verb and noun names. Wildcards are permitted for both of these parameters. The Name parameter cannot be used in conjunction with either the Verb or Noun parameters. In Figure 1-14, Get-Command is used with the Verb and Noun parameters to return a list of matching cmdlets.

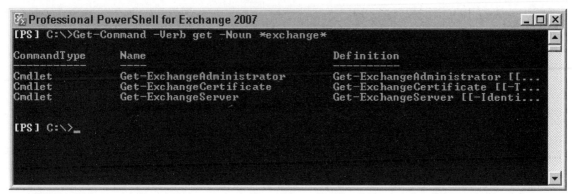

Figure 1-14

The CommandType parameter allows you to specify the type of command for which to return matches. Possible values are Alias, Function, Cmdlet, ExternalScript, Application, and All. Using Get-Command in this way allows you to find these additional command elements that are not exposed when searching for cmdlets using Get-Help. For example, the command in Figure 1-15 uses the CommandType parameter to find external scripts that contain the word database somewhere in their name.

```
Professional PowerShell for Exchange 2007                              _ |□| x |
[PS] C:\>Get-Command *database* -CommandType ExternalScript

CommandType        Name                           Definition
-----------        ----                           ----------
ExternalScript     GetDatabaseForSearchIndex.ps1  C:\Program Files\Microsoft\E...
ExternalScript     GetSearchIndexForDatabase.ps1  C:\Program Files\Microsoft\E...

[PS] C:\>_
```

Figure 1-15

ExternalScript command elements are Windows PowerShell scripts located in the %ProgramFiles%\ Microsoft\Exchange Server\Scripts directory. In this example two scripts included with Exchange Server 2007 match the search criteria for names that include database.

`Get-Command` can also be used to return detailed information about the syntax of a given cmdlet using the `Syntax` parameter. However, you may find the syntax information exposed in a cmdlet's help information to be more useful in the long run because it is accompanied by other help details.

Using Help Information Effectively

Cmdlet help information is very detailed and you may find it difficult to follow when you first start learning about a given cmdlet. Luckily `Get-Help` makes it possible to access specific areas of help information in varying degrees of detail. Using `Get-Help` effectively allows you to access the information you are interested in without displaying the entire help information available for a cmdlet.

There are three versions of `Get-Help` that display help information differently depending on how they are used:

❑   `Get-Help` displays help information without pausing when the console display is full. Parameters are used with `Get-Help` to determine the type of information and detail level displayed. The basic syntax is `Get-Help <cmdlet name><parameters>`.

❑   `Help` is a function based on `Get-Help` that displays help information one screenful at a time, pausing when the console screen is full to allow the operator to advance the display either one full page using the space bar, or one line using the Enter key. The parameters available for `Get-Help` also work with `Help`. The basic syntax is `Help <cmdlet name><parameters>`.

❑   `-?` is a pseudo-parameter that displays basic help information without pausing when the console display is full. `-?` takes no parameters as input like the other versions of `Get-Help`. The basic syntax is `<cmdlet name> -?`.

The information contained in cmdlet help files you will find most interesting is divided into six major topics. By using certain parameters with `Get-Help`, you can display each of these topics in varying degrees of detail:

❑   **Synopsis:** A brief description of the cmdlet and what it does.

❑   **Syntax:** One or more syntax diagrams that detail the use of the cmdlet and its input parameters.

❑   **Detailed Description:** A more detailed description than the synopsis.

❑   **Parameters:** A detailed description of each parameter and how they are used.

❑   **Examples:** One or more examples of how the cmdlet is executed.

❑   **Related Links:** The names of other cmdlets that may be related in some way to this cmdlet.

The command `Get-Help <cmdlet name>` without any parameters displays the Synopsis, Syntax, Detailed Description, and Related Links topics. This is the same information displayed when using the command `<cmdlet name> -?`.

The command `Get-Help <cmdlet name> -Detailed` displays additional information about the cmdlet including descriptions of each parameter (but not details) along with the Examples topic.

The command `Get-Help <cmdlet name> -Full` displays the entire contents of the help file for the cmdlet including detailed information about each parameter.

The command `Get-Help <cmdlet name> -Examples` displays the Examples topic along with the Synopsis topic.

The command `Get-Help <cmdlet name> -Parameter <parameter name>` displays the detailed information about the specified parameter. Wildcards are permitted.

Although the descriptions and examples included in the help files are useful, you may find that the most beneficial information for learning how to use a cmdlet are the details contained in the Syntax and Parameter topics.

Syntax Details

The information included in the Syntax topic contains one or more syntax diagrams showing how the cmdlet and its parameters are used. Some cmdlets can have more than one syntax diagram depending on how the parameters work in combination with each other.

For example, the `Get-PublicFolderDatabase` cmdlet has three distinct syntax diagrams in its help file. Each diagram shows a different way to run the cmdlet depending on the parameters being used:

```
Get-PublicFolderDatabase [-Identity <DatabaseIdParameter>] [-DomainControll
er <Fqdn>] [-IncludePreExchange2007 <SwitchParameter>] [-Status <SwitchPara
meter>] [<CommonParameters>]

Get-PublicFolderDatabase -Server <ServerIdParameter> [-DomainController <Fq
dn>] [-IncludePreExchange2007 <SwitchParameter>] [-Status <SwitchParameter>
] [<CommonParameters>]

Get-PublicFolderDatabase -StorageGroup <StorageGroupIdParameter> [-DomainCo
ntroller <Fqdn>] [-IncludePreExchange2007 <SwitchParameter>] [-Status <Swit
chParameter>] [<CommonParameters>]
```

The `Get-PublicFolderDatabase` can be used with the `Identity` parameter to identify a specific database, the `Server` parameter to specify the server where the database is located, and the `StorageGroup` parameter to specify the storage group that holds the database. Each of these parameters is exclusive and cannot be used in combination with one another, therefore the separate syntax diagrams are necessary to show how each is used.

Parameter Details

Two levels of parameter details can be displayed using `Get-Help`. The `Detailed` parameter causes the output to include the name and description of each parameter, but omits technical details. The `Full` parameter results in the display of all parameter details. To display the full details of a single given parameter, the `Parameter` parameter is used followed by the name of the parameter. The `Detail`, `Full`, and `Parameter` parameters cannot be used in conjunction with one another.

Parameter details describe whether the parameter is required or optional and if it is positional or named. They also describe whether the parameter has a default value and if it accepts pipeline input and wildcard characters. For example, the parameter details for the Identity parameter as used with the SetMailbox cmdlet contain the information displayed in Figure 1-16 using Get-Help and the Parameter parameter.

```
Professional PowerShell for Exchange 2007                              _ □ ✕
[PS] C:\>Get-Help Set-Mailbox -Parameter Identity

-Identity <MailboxIdParameter>
    The Identity parameter identifies the mailbox. You can use the following va
    lues:
    * GUID
    * ADObjectID
    * Distinguished name (DN)
    * Domain\Account
    * User principal name (UPN)
    * LegacyExchangeDN
    * SmtpAddress
    * Alias

    Required?                        true
    Position?                        1
    Default value
    Accept pipeline input?           True
    Accept wildcard characters?      false


[PS] C:\>_
```

Figure 1-16

As you can see in these details, the Identity parameter is required (true) and positional (for position 1), has no default value, and accepts pipeline input (true) but not wildcard characters (false).

Learning More

In addition to help information for individual cmdlets, there are several supplementary help files that cover conceptual topics related to using Windows PowerShell. The names of the individual help files by and large describe the topic they cover and are prefixed with the string about_. To see a complete list of available topics simply type the command shown in Figure 1-17.

To access the contents of one of these help files simply enter Get-Help about_<topic name>. For example, to read the help file that covers the usage of wildcards in Windows PowerShell, type Get-Help about_wildcard.

Using Tab Expansion to Enter Cmdlets and Parameters

At this point you may be asking yourself how you will ever be able to remember exact cmdlet names and type them in without making spelling mistakes. Fortunately that is not a problem once you understand how to use the tab expansion feature of Windows PowerShell.

```
Professional PowerShell for Exchange 2007                              _ □ ×
[PS] C:\>Get-Help about_

Name                         Category        Synopsis
────                         ────────        ────────
about_alias                  HelpFile        Using alternate names ...
about_arithmetic_operators   HelpFile        Operators that can be ...
about_array                  HelpFile        A compact data structu...
about_assignment_operators   HelpFile        Operators that can be ...
about_associative_array      HelpFile        A compact data structu...
about_automatic_variables    HelpFile        Variables automaticall...
about_break                  HelpFile        A statement for immedi...
about_command_search         HelpFile        How the Windows PowerS...
about_command_syntax         HelpFile        Command format in the ...
about_commonparameters       HelpFile        Parameters that every ...
about_comparison_operators   HelpFile        Operators that can be ...
about_continue               HelpFile        Immediately return to ...
about_core_commands          HelpFile        Windows PowerShell cor...
about_display.xml            HelpFile        Controlling how object...
about_environment_variable   HelpFile        How to access Windows ...
about_escape_character       HelpFile        Change how the Windows...
about_execution_environ...   HelpFile        Factors that affect ho...
about_filter                 HelpFile        Using the Where-Object...
about_flow_control           HelpFile        Using flow control sta...
about_for                    HelpFile        A language command for...
about_foreach                HelpFile        A language command for...
```

Figure 1-17

Most shells offer some form of automatic completion to take some of the drudgery and guesswork out of entering certain command elements. Even cmd.exe offers automatic completion using the tab key when typing directory paths and filenames. Windows PowerShell takes this feature to whole new levels of functionality by providing tab expansion of cmdlet and parameter names as well.

To use tab expansion when typing a cmdlet name, simply type the verb name followed by the hyphen, then the first few letters of the noun name. When you press the Tab key, Windows PowerShell automatically expands what you entered to the first matching cmdlet name. If there are other possible matches, pressing the Tab key repeatedly cycles through the available choices. Pressing the Tab key while holding down the Shift key causes Windows PowerShell to cycle backwards through the available choices. The more characters you enter before pressing the Tab key make the search more specific and narrows the number of possible matches.

For example, say you need to run the cmdlet Get-MailboxFolderStatistics. This cmdlet is useful for determining the size and number of items in given mailbox folders. Using tab expansion you can enter this long cmdlet name with no mistakes and a minimal number of keystrokes using the following procedure:

1. Type get-ma and press the Tab key. This expands to Get-Mailbox. Notice the name automatically changes to the standard form of uppercase first letters.

2. Now press the Tab key a second time. This time the cmdlet name expands to Get-MailboxCalendarSettings.

3. Press the Tab key again and the name expands to Get-MailboxDatabase.

4. Press the Tab key one last time to expand the name to Get-MailboxFolderStatistics. To continue at this point simply hit the space bar and continue typing the rest of the command.

Using this procedure you can enter complex, mistake-free cmdlet names using a minimal number of characters and Tab keystrokes. One major benefit of tab expansion is you don't have to remember exact cmdlet names as long as you can enter at least the verb name followed by a few letters of the noun name.

Tab expansion works for parameter names in the same manner. This works especially well when you don't know all the possible parameter names a cmdlet is using. To cycle through all the parameter names type a hyphen and press the Tab key repeatedly. When the correct parameter name appears, continue typing to enter the parameter value as applicable.

> *Be careful when using this procedure because Windows PowerShell does not validate the parameter names entered on the command line until the command is parsed at run time. Using tab expansion it is possible to inadvertently enter the same parameter name twice, causing the command to fail.*

Using Cmdlet Aliases

Windows PowerShell allows you to refer to cmdlets using a shorter, simpler name called an alias. The default installation of Windows PowerShell comes complete with several predefined alias names that approximate a similar function in other command shells.

You may have already noticed that Windows PowerShell accepts `dir` as a command to display items in the current location. There is no real cmdlet called `dir`, instead it is an alias for the underlying Windows PowerShell cmdlet `Get-ChildItem`. Several other familiar command names have been defined as alias names for the matching Windows PowerShell command. To see a list of all alias definitions, run `Get-Alias`.

Windows PowerShell also allows you to define your own alias definitions using the `New-Alias` cmdlet. The lifetime of alias definitions is linked to the lifetime of the current shell session. When the shell closes the definition is lost. To learn more about aliases, type `Get-Help about_Alias`.

Using Pipelines

As mentioned earlier in this chapter, the results of running a Windows PowerShell cmdlet is a collection of one or more .NET objects. These objects have a structure that describes the properties (attributes) of the objects and the states (current value) of these properties. This feature of Windows PowerShell makes it possible to take the results of one cmdlet and pass it via pipeline as input to another cmdlet for further processing. Using a pipeline to pass data from one cmdlet to another is known as *composition*.

The vertical pipeline operator (|) is used to instruct Windows PowerShell to pass the collected objects from the command just prior to the pipeline to the next command. Commands can be constructed using multiple pipelines to accomplish tasks too complex for a single cmdlet to accomplish alone.

Some cmdlets that use the `Get` verb provide a way to limit the collection of objects based on a parameter value that acts as a filter. The resulting collection can then be passed by pipeline to a cmdlet that uses the `Set` verb to modify one or more properties on each object. For example, the `Get-User` cmdlet includes the `OrganizationalUnit` parameter.

Say your organization has implemented Organizational Units as a way to contain all users located in the same geographical office. A need arises to change the fax number attribute for all user accounts in the same office. Using the `Get-User` cmdlet with the appropriate value for the `OrganizationalUnit` parameter you can create a collection of user objects limited to the users in the office. By passing this collection to the `Set-User` cmdlet along with the appropriate value for the `Fax` parameter you can change the fax number quickly and easily on every user account using a single command line.

Commands that use multiple cmdlets and pipelines on a single line are often referred to as "one-liners." The following one-line command demonstrates the previous example for changing the fax number for all users contained in the "`Denver`" organizational unit:

```
[PS] C:\>Get-User -OrganizationalUnit "CN=Denver,DC=exchangeexchange,DC=local" |
Set-User -Fax 555-1234
```

Whether there are 10 or 10,000 users in the organizational unit really does not matter in this example. By collecting the user objects based on their organizational unit container with the first cmdlet, we are able to modify the fax number on all users in bulk with the second cmdlet without additional complex programming.

Filtering Objects

Not all cmdlets may provide parameters for filtering objects like the one shown in the previous example. And though some cmdlets may provide a few filtering parameters, they may not provide a parameter for the specific property you may need to use as a filter condition. That's when you need to become familiar with the `Where-Object` filter cmdlet.

`Where-Object` allows you to filter objects out of the command stream based on one or more test conditions you specify in a script block. The test conditions are based on one or more of the objects' properties. Only the objects that meet the test conditions are passed on to the next command, while all others are discarded. The most basic syntax of `Where-Object` is easy to learn:

```
<command> | Where-Object { <test condition> } | <command>
```

`Where` and `"?"` are both shorthand alias names for the `Where-Object` cmdlet.

The test condition is an expression that resolves to either Boolean true or false. Only the objects that resolve true when tested are passed down the pipeline to the next command. The syntax of the test condition is made up of the following elements:

```
{ $_.<property name><comparison operator><value to test><conjunction> $_.<property
name><comparison operator><value to test> ...}
```

The first element `$_` is a special variable (called an automatic variable) and is used to refer to objects in the pipeline stream. Using a technique called dot notation a property name is appended to the `$_` variable to refer to the specific object property to which the test applies. For example, `$_.Identity` refers to an object's `Identity` property.

A comparison operator is used to set the condition of the test. Windows PowerShell supports a number of named comparison operators. The most frequently used operators for comparing whole property values are `eq` (equals), `ne` (not equals), `lt` (less than), and `gt` (greater than). The `like` and `notlike` operators are used to compare string values using wildcard rules. To see a complete list of all comparison operators type `Get-Help about_Comparison_Operators` at the command line.

The value to test must be of the same data type of the property being tested. For example, if the property data type is string, a string value enclosed in quotes must be used for the test. If the property data type is integer, a numeric value must be used for the test and so on.

While Windows PowerShell validates the syntax used inside the script block, the result of entering an unknown property name or an invalid data type is a failure to pass any objects down the pipeline without reporting any error to the operator.

Multiple test conditions can be used in the same script block as long as they are separated by one or more conjunctive or disjunctive operators:

❑ The and conjunction operator is used to compare the Boolean results of two or more test conditions to render a concluding Boolean value. If any of the test conditions are true, a true is returned.

❑ The or disjunctive operator is used to compare the Boolean results of only two test conditions. If either one or both test conditions are false, a false is returned.

❑ Conjunctive and disjunctive groups of test conditions can be used in the same script block as long as they are enclosed in parentheses.

Now let's look at a practical example of using Where-Object as a filter in the pipeline stream. Say that you need to change the Manager property for several users based on the department to which they belong (Engineering), and the office from which they work (the Dallas office) to show they report to manager John Doe. The command would look like this:

```
[PS] C:\>Get-User | Where-Object { $_.Office -eq "Dallas" -and $_.Department -eq
"Engineering" } | Set-User -Manager "John Doe"
```

After collecting all users with Get-User, the collection of objects is passed to Where-Object to apply the test conditions on each object one at a time. The first test checks for the Office property equal to "Dallas". The second condition checks the Department property equal to "Engineering". If both test conditions result in true, the object is passed to the next command. If one of the test conditions results in false, the object is disposed. After processing all objects in the stream, they are passed to Set-User for applying the modification.

Finding Property Names and Data Types

To use Where-Object effectively you need to know the available property names and data types for the objects being passed by a given cmdlet. By passing the results of any cmdlet that uses the Get verb to the Get-Member cmdlet you can generate a list of properties and their data type. For example, the command in Figure 1-18 sends the objects collected by the Get-Mailbox cmdlet to Get-Member and displays the objects' properties and their definition.

It is important to know the exact name of each property used in the Where-Object script block. Mistyping a property name results in a failure to pass any objects down the pipeline stream without reporting any error to the operator.

```
Professional PowerShell for Exchange 2007                                    _ □ ×
[PS ] C:\>Get-Mailbox | Get-Member -MemberType Property                         ▲


    TypeName: Microsoft.Exchange.Data.Directory.Management.Mailbox

Name                            MemberType  Definition
----                            ----------  ----------
AcceptMessagesOnlyFrom          Property    Microsoft.Exchange.Data.MultiU...
AcceptMessagesOnlyFromDLMembers Property    Microsoft.Exchange.Data.MultiU...
AddressListMembership           Property    Microsoft.Exchange.Data.MultiU...
Alias                           Property    System.String Alias {get;set;}
AntispamBypassEnabled           Property    System.Boolean AntispamBypassE...
CustomAttribute1                Property    System.String CustomAttribute1...
CustomAttribute10               Property    System.String CustomAttribute1...
CustomAttribute11               Property    System.String CustomAttribute1...
CustomAttribute12               Property    System.String CustomAttribute1...
CustomAttribute13               Property    System.String CustomAttribute1...
CustomAttribute14               Property    System.String CustomAttribute1...
CustomAttribute15               Property    System.String CustomAttribute1...
CustomAttribute2                Property    System.String CustomAttribute2...
CustomAttribute3                Property    System.String CustomAttribute3...
CustomAttribute4                Property    System.String CustomAttribute4...
CustomAttribute5                Property    System.String CustomAttribute5...
CustomAttribute6                Property    System.String CustomAttribute6...
CustomAttribute7                Property    System.String CustomAttribute7...  ▼
```

Figure 1-18

Controlling Output

When you run a cmdlet in Windows PowerShell, the type of data displayed as output, if any, is determined by the default format of the cmdlet. The output format is determined at the time the cmdlet is created. Most cmdlets that use the Get verb have some form of default display formatting that results in what the programmer determined the most useful information. For example, running the Get-Mailbox cmdlet for a specific user results in the output shown in Figure 1-19.

```
Professional PowerShell for Exchange 2007                                    _ □ ×
[PS ] C:\>Get-Mailbox jandoe                                                    ▲

Name                    Alias               ServerName          ProhibitSendQuo
                                                                ta
----                    -----               ----------          ---------------
Jane Doe                jandoe              mb001               unlimited

[PS ] C:\>_
                                                                                ▼
```

Figure 1-19

At times you need to see more specific information not included in the default format. By using the pipeline operator to pass objects to the Format-List and Format-Table cmdlets you can control a cmdlet's output to see either all properties or only those properties you specify.

Format-List

In the previous example Get-Mailbox displayed only those properties specified as default output for the cmdlet. By passing the object to Format-List (or its alias name fl) without any additional parameters, all properties are displayed in a list format as shown in Figure 1-20.

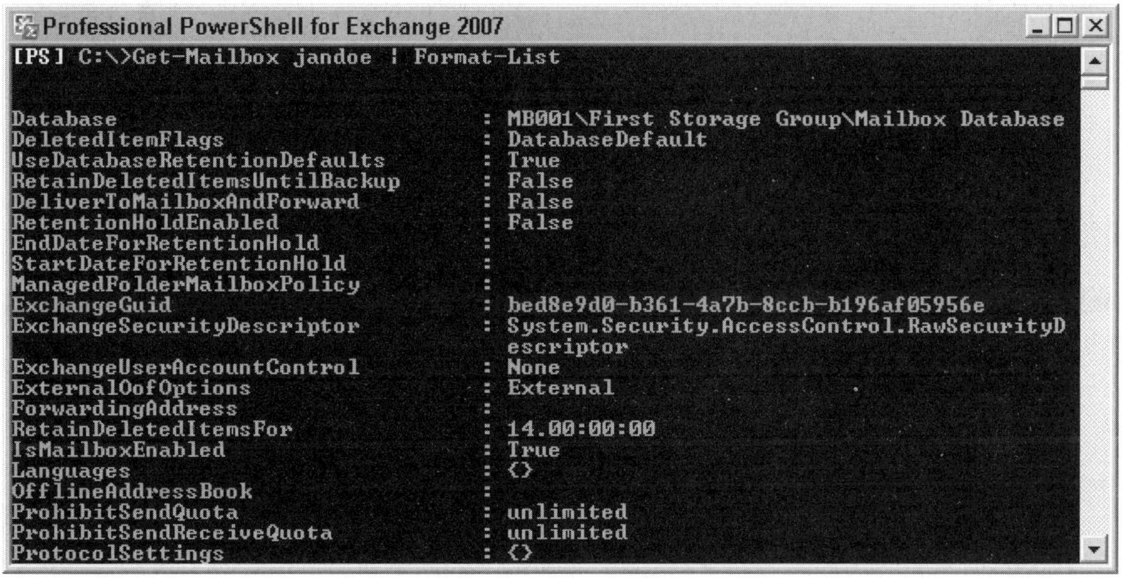

```
Professional PowerShell for Exchange 2007                                  _ □ ×
[PS] C:\>Get-Mailbox jandoe | Format-List

Database                        : MB001\First Storage Group\Mailbox Database
DeletedItemFlags                : DatabaseDefault
UseDatabaseRetentionDefaults    : True
RetainDeletedItemsUntilBackup   : False
DeliverToMailboxAndForward      : False
RetentionHoldEnabled            : False
EndDateForRetentionHold         :
StartDateForRetentionHold       :
ManagedFolderMailboxPolicy      :
ExchangeGuid                    : bed8e9d0-b361-4a7b-8ccb-b196af05956e
ExchangeSecurityDescriptor      : System.Security.AccessControl.RawSecurityD
                                  escriptor
ExchangeUserAccountControl      : None
ExternalOofOptions              : External
ForwardingAddress               :
RetainDeletedItemsFor           : 14.00:00:00
IsMailboxEnabled                : True
Languages                       : {}
OfflineAddressBook              :
ProhibitSendQuota               : unlimited
ProhibitSendReceiveQuota        : unlimited
ProtocolSettings                : {}
```

Figure 1-20

To display only specific properties, add the property names, separated by commas, after Format-List. For example, if you only want to see the Name, Alias, and PrimarySMTPAddress properties for user jandoe, you would then run the command shown in Figure 1-21.

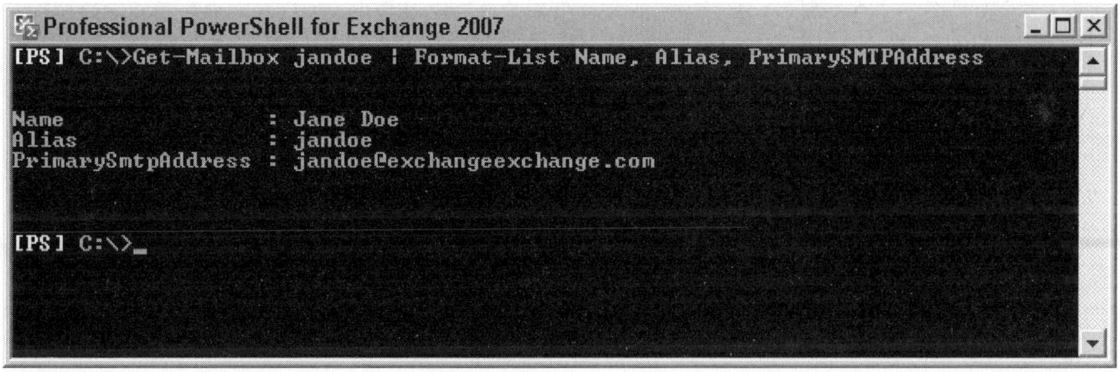

```
Professional PowerShell for Exchange 2007                                  _ □ ×
[PS] C:\>Get-Mailbox jandoe | Format-List Name, Alias, PrimarySMTPAddress

Name               : Jane Doe
Alias              : jandoe
PrimarySmtpAddress : jandoe@exchangeexchange.com


[PS] C:\>_
```

Figure 1-21

Format-Table

Format-Table (and its alias, ft) is similar to Format-List except it allows you to format output in table format. Unlike Format-List, passing objects to Format-Table without any additional parameters results in one of two displays. If the default format for displaying output is table format of select properties, the default format is used for display. If the default format is a list of all properties, Windows PowerShell attempts to display as many of the properties as possible in table format. This is usually very impractical so Format-Table is typically used with a list of properties to display.

If Format-Table is used in place of Format-List in the previous example, the resulting display would look like Figure 1-22.

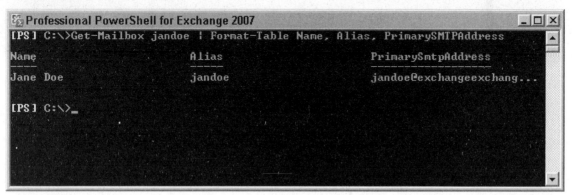

Figure 1-22

As more properties are specified, or if property values are longer than can be displayed on a single line, Windows PowerShell truncates the output with ellipses to indicate more information is available as shown in Figure 1-23 where the LegacyExchangeDN property has been added to the previous command.

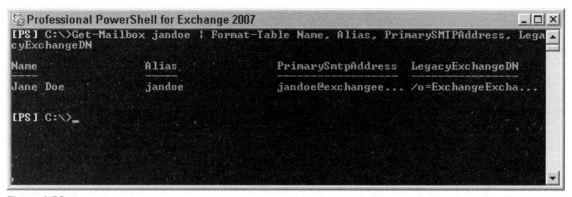

Figure 1-23

To change this behavior, add the `AutoSize` parameter to force `Format-Table` to change column widths to make the most of the console screen width, and the `Wrap` parameter to wrap long values that won't fit on a single line to the next line. The addition of these two parameters to the previous example yields the results shown in Figure 1-24.

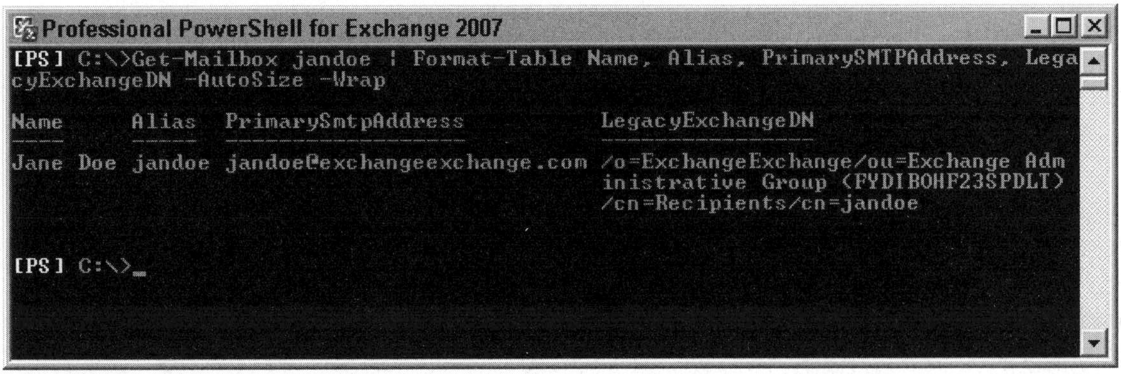

Figure 1-24

Running Scripts

As you learn to use Exchange Management Shell to manage your Exchange organization you will most likely identify several command sequences that you run on a regular basis to accomplish some task. Store these commands in a Windows PowerShell script file so you can run them all by simply executing the script file. Use your favorite text editing software to create and edit script files. Windows PowerShell script files use `.ps1` as the file extension name.

To run a script, type its name at the command line. You do not have to include the `.ps1` file extension. However, you do have to pay attention to the drive location where the script is stored and the current location from which the script is being run. You must supply the full path to the script file even if the script is stored in the current location. To tell Windows PowerShell the script is in the current directory, either type the full path or use a dot and backslash (`.\`) to indicate the current directory as shown in this example:

```
[PS] C:\scripts>.\myscript
```

Exchange Management Shell provides a default directory for storing several script files provided with Exchange Server 2007. You do not have to provide the full path name when running any script located in the `%ProgramFiles%\Microsoft\Exchange Server\scripts` directory because this path is stored in the Windows system variable path statement as part of Exchange Server installation. By placing your script files in this directory you can keep them in a known directory and run them from any drive location without providing the full path.

The chance that a script may include destructive code may raise security concerns among administrators. Windows PowerShell provides a method for applying a security policy for controlling which scripts are allowed to run on a machine. The execution policy determines whether or not scripts are allowed to run, and whether they must include a digital signature that verifies the origin of the script and if it has been tampered with in any way since it was digitally signed by its creator.

All scripts included with Exchange Server 2007 have been code signed by Microsoft to ensure the scripts comply with the execution policy model for ensuring scripts can be accounted for before execution. The default execution policy setting for Exchange Management Shell is RemoteSigned. This level allows you to run scripts you create locally and warns you when scripts provided by Microsoft have been altered.

To learn more about Windows PowerShell execution policies, type Get-Help about_signing.

Preparing Exchange Management Shell

Before continuing on to the rest of the book, take a moment to review the following procedure for customizing your Exchange Management Shell console application. You'll find these options convenient when trying the examples shown in the following chapters.

1. Navigate to the Exchange Management Shell shortcut: from the Start menu, select All Programs ⇨ Exchange Server 2007 and then right-click Exchange Management Shell and select Properties.

2. Select the Options tab and make the following modifications:

   a. To make it possible to select, copy, and paste text in the console screen, under Edit Options click to select the QuickEdit Mode checkbox. With this option selected, you can select text in the console window by dragging the left mouse button. Copy the selected text to the clipboard using the right mouse button or by pressing Enter.

   b. The Insert Mode checkbox is typically already selected, but make sure it is checked as well. This option allows you to paste text into the command line by positioning the cursor at the desired position, then using the right mouse button to paste the contents of the clipboard.

   c. Under Command History set the Buffer Size to at least 100. This number determines the number of commands stored in the console buffer. Previously entered commands can be recalled by using the up and down cursor keys. Click to select the Discard Old Duplicate checkbox to automatically discard any duplicate commands from the console buffer.

3. Select the Layout tab and make the following modifications:

   a. Under Screen Buffer Size change the Height setting to 9,999. This setting determines the number of lines of output held in the console buffer you can view using the console window scroll control.

   b. Under Window Size, set the Width setting to a number between 80 and 120. This setting determines the number of characters displayed across the console window. Though a higher number setting allows you to type more characters before wrapping to the next line, the default output format of most Exchange Management Shell cmdlets is based on an 80-character display. If you change this number, make sure the value for Width under Screen Buffer matches.

4. Click OK to commit these changes and close Properties. The changes take effect the next time Exchange Management Shell is started.

Summary

❏ Windows PowerShell is the next-generation command-line shell and scripting language for Windows. Exchange Server 2007 is the first Microsoft application to utilize Windows PowerShell for deployment and administration.

❏ Command shells provide a more flexible administrative interface compared to Graphical User Interfaces (GUIs). Administrators use scripts to automate everyday tasks and resolve issues GUI interfaces are not able to handle.

❏ Windows PowerShell is built on top of .NET Framework version 2.0 and exposes .NET classes as built-in commands. Actions in Windows PowerShell are based on .NET objects that carry their structure definition as well as the current state of their attributes. Windows PowerShell objects have properties (which are characteristics) and methods (which are actions that you can take) and can be passed from one command to another without the need for parsing.

❏ Exchange Management Shell extends Windows PowerShell to include more than 500 built-in commands. Exchange Management Console is a GUI management application built on top of Windows PowerShell.

❏ The most basic component of Windows PowerShell is the built-in commands called cmdlets. Cmdlet names are made up of a verb name that identifies the action to take and the noun name that identifies the object on which to take action. Cmdlets use named parameters to identify individual properties or control how the cmdlet executes.

❏ Windows PowerShell includes a powerful help system available directly from the command line that makes it easy to first discover and then learn how to use cmdlets.

❏ The Windows PowerShell tab expansion feature takes the drudgery and guesswork out of typing commands by allowing you to automatically complete partially entered cmdlet and parameter names using the Tab key.

❏ Windows PowerShell makes it possible to take the results of one cmdlet and pass it via pipeline as input to another cmdlet for further processing. Using a pipeline to pass data from one cmdlet to another is known as composition.

❏ Command sequences that are run on a regular basis can be stored in a Windows PowerShell script file for execution. Sharing these scripts between all administrators in an organization ensures consistent results.

Further Reading

If you want a more basic understanding of general Windows PowerShell usage outside of Exchange, explore another fine Wrox publication:

Professional Windows PowerShell; Andrew Watt; ISBN: 978-0-471-94693-9; Wrox, 2004.

## 2

Using Exchange Management Shell

The Exchange Management Shell is the best tool overall for controlling your Exchange Server 2007 organization. This chapter provides an overview of the management functionality it provides.

This chapter also explains why you should consider learning Exchange Management Shell an essential part of building your Exchange Server 2007 management skills.

The section "Shell versus Console" provides a comparison between the two interfaces in the context of the Exchange management functions they provide and when to choose the Exchange Management Shell.

The section "Working from the Command Line" provides some basic information for getting started using Exchange Management Shell. It covers navigation, using aliases and variables with Exchange cmdlets, and some general tips you'll find useful.

The final section, "Working with Windows," tells how to control services and processes, access the Windows Registry as a drive, and view Windows event logs.

In this chapter you learn:

- ❑ Exchange cmdlet sets
- ❑ Shell navigation
- ❑ Variables, aliases, and functions
- ❑ Profiles
- ❑ Process and service control
- ❑ Registry control
- ❑ Event log control

Why Learn Exchange Management Shell?

Because you are reading this book you have already taken steps to advance your knowledge of the Exchange Management Shell. Maybe you already realize that Exchange Management Shell is a vital part of Exchange Server 2007 management. Or maybe you are curious to find out just what this "shell thing" does. Either way, learning how to use Exchange Management Shell is essential for any Exchange administrator. For those of you that still may need some convincing, here are some points to consider:

❑ **Exclusive Operations:** Many operations available in Exchange Management Shell are not included in Exchange Management Console; therefore you are forced to use the shell. In these situations you have no other choice.

❑ **Bulk Operations:** Many of the operations available in the Exchange Management Console are singular, in other words you can take action on only one object at a time. Large organizations needing to perform changes to thousands of objects on a regular basis know that bulk operations save time and lessen the chance of operator error. Using the pipeline to pass objects from one cmdlet to another in Exchange Management Shell provides a quick and easy method for taking action on any number of objects from the command line.

❑ **Automation:** Exchange Management Console provides no way for automating even simple operations. Scripts run from the Exchange Management Shell ensure consistent results and can be used to work out complex administrative tasks.

Just how deeply you need to learn Exchange Management Shell depends a lot on your responsibilities. If you administrate a large organization with multiple server roles, it is likely Exchange Management Shell is used on a daily basis. Smaller organizations may not require as much use, but rest assured the shell is used from time to time.

Shell versus Console

When first learning Exchange Server 2007 administration, there may be times when you'll wonder which options are available to you when choosing between the console and the shell interfaces. Without knowledge of what you can accomplish from either interface, you may struggle to find the right path.

This section gives a comparison of operations available in the Exchange Management Console and in the Exchange Management Shell. It also describes the layout of the console and how this information can be used to understand the structure of cmdlets in the shell. Included is a summary of Exchange cmdlets and methods for categorizing these cmdlets based on administrative scope.

Direct Comparison

Each Exchange component has administrative functionality made available via cmdlets. That functionality is always available in the Exchange Management Shell and may be available in the Exchange Management Console. The availability of administrative functionality for a given Exchange component falls into one of three categories:

❑ **Parity:** There is complete parity between the functionality available from the shell and the console. Bulk operations and filtering are possible using shell commands but the console makes it possible to accomplish the same operations to at least one object at a time.

❑ **Mixed:** Most administrative functionality for a component is available using either the shell or the console, whereas some operations can be accomplished only via a shell cmdlet. Usually these cmdlets are used for configuration changes that an administrator would not make on a regular basis and therefore are not available from the console.

❑ **Exclusive:** All operations for certain components are available only from the shell and have no equivalent administrative functionality from the console.

Parity Functionality

When it comes to parity functionality, choosing the right interface depends on what you are trying to get done. You may find it just as easy to use the Exchange Management Console for one-off quick operations as opposed to using the Exchange Management Shell. For bulk operations you must use Exchange Management Shell because most all operations in Exchange Management Console do not allow the selection of more than one object at a time.

Mixed and Exclusive Functionality

For some mixed functionality and all exclusive functionality, you have no choice but to use the Exchange Management Shell. The following table lists by category the Exchange components that have at least some administrative operations that are available only via Exchange Management Shell.

Category	Role	Description
ActiveSync	Client Access	Most operations are available in the console, while gathering ActiveSync usage information is only possible using shell cmdlet `Export-ActiveSyncLog`.
Autodiscover	Client Access	Configuration of the Exchange Autodiscover feature is only possible using shell cmdlets.
Availability Service	General	Configuration of the Exchange Availability Service feature is only possible using shell cmdlets.
CAS Mailbox features	Client Access	Most operations are available in the console, while some granular configuration is only possible using shell cmdlet `Set-CASMailbox`.
CAS Virtual Directories	Client Access	Some configuration of features provided by individual virtual directories is possible through the console, while granular configuration of the virtual directories is only available from the shell.
Certificates	Client Access	Exchange certificates are managed using shell cmdlets only.
Clustered Mailbox Server	Mailbox	While some management features are available in the console, most operations are possible using shell cmdlets only.

Table continued on following page

Category	Role	Description
Edge Transport	Edge	Operations shared with Hub Transport are available from the console, while operations specific to the Edge role granular configuration are only available using shell cmdlets.
Exchange Server	General	While server roles have a presence in the console, some specific configuration settings are only possible via the shell.
File Distribution Service	Client Access	The File Distribution Service can only be updated using the `Update-FileDistributionService` cmdlet.
Mailbox	Mailbox	Most mailbox-related general configurations and operations are possible from the console, while granular configuration is only possible via the shell.
Messaging Records Management	Mailbox	All operations are handled by the console except for the Managed Folder Assistant, which can only be started and stopped via shell cmdlets.
Permissions	General	Full mailbox access permissions can be set via the console, but other rights can only be set via shell cmdlets. Active Directory permissions can also be set via shell cmdlets as well as traditional means.
Public Folders	Mailbox	Most public folder administration is made possible by the console, while granular configuration is only possible via the shell.
Resource Management	Mailbox	Some resource management operations are available from the console, while granular configuration is only possible via the shell.
Testing and Diagnostics	General	These cmdlets are used to test and confirm the functionality of Exchange and are exclusive to the shell.
Transport	Hub Transport	Most operations are available from the console, while granular configuration is only possible via the shell.
Unified Messaging	Unified Messaging	Most operations are available from the console, while granular configuration is only possible via the shell.

Exchange Management Console

The Exchange Management Console is based on Microsoft Management Console (MMC) 3.0. The MMC standard interface layout consists of a Tree pane for navigating the management elements, a Result pane for displaying objects based on the currently selected management element, and an Action pane to display the actions that can be taken on the currently selected objects in the Result pane.

The Tree pane is arranged in a hierarchical order of management elements for an Exchange organization. This arrangement provides a visual guide to aid the operator in finding and selecting a management operation. Figure 2-1 shows the console Tree view taken from an instance of Exchange Management Console installed with any combination of the four main server roles. Each node of the console tree constitutes a management element in order of precedence:

❑   The Organization Configuration node consists of operations that control Exchange Server 2007 at a global level. Each server role is used to categorize the elements that apply to that specific server role. For example, Address Lists are managed from the Mailbox selection and Accepted Domains are managed from the Hub Transport selection.

❑   The Server Configuration node consists of operations that control individual servers and their components. For example, from the Mailbox selection you can select a specific mailbox server and then select and take action on one of its mailbox databases, such as mounting or dismounting the database.

❑   The Recipient Configuration node is the most granular and provides access to the individual mail-enabled objects of the organization. From this node you can mailbox enable or disable a user, create contacts and distribution groups, and re-connect mailboxes to accounts in Active Directory.

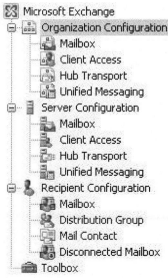

Figure 2-1

❑ The Toolbox node is not a true management element in the sense of the other nodes. It provides an interface for selecting management tools that run outside of the Exchange Management Console. These tools include the Exchange Best Practices Analyzer as well as tools for public folders, disaster recovery, mail flow analysis, and performance troubleshooting.

The Exchange Management Console is a well-thought-out management interface. Because this book is about Exchange Management Shell it may seem strange to cover the console interface at all. Actually, understanding the organization of the Exchange Management Console is very helpful for understanding the organization of Exchange Management Shell cmdlets.

Exchange cmdlets are organized into groups based on how they are used. Exchange Management Shell's command-line interface lacks a method for providing a visual representation of its command organization. Because Exchange Management Console is based on Exchange cmdlets, its visual arrangement of management elements actually represents the underlying cmdlet organization that cannot be represented in the shell. By learning this structure, you learn the basic organization of Exchange cmdlets.

Exchange Cmdlet Sets

Exchange Management Shell provides more than 500 cmdlets for administering your Exchange organization. Because Exchange Management Shell lacks the hierarchical command interface found in Exchange Management Console, you may find it easier to manage cmdlets by thinking of them as being organized into sets that share some commonality.

Chapter 1 discussed using the Get-Help cmdlet to find other cmdlets and learn how to use them. The Get-Help cmdlet includes the Role parameter that allows you to retrieve cmdlets grouped by the Exchange Server role with which they are used. Get-Help also provides the Component parameter to group cmdlets by the Exchange Server component they are used to administer, and the Functionality parameter to group cmdlets by the scope of their control. The scope can be on the organization level, the server level, or the user level. This is similar to the categorization used in the Exchange Management Console.

These parameters allow you to retrieve Exchange cmdlets in logical groupings. For example, to quickly find cmdlets used to control Clustered Mailbox Servers use the Component parameter with the value *cluster* as shown in this command:

```
[PS] C:\>Get-Help -Component *cluster*

Name                       Category            Synopsis
----                       --------            --------
Move-ClusteredMailboxSe... Cmdlet              This topic explains ho...
Start-ClusteredMailboxS... Cmdlet              This topic explains ho...
Get-ClusteredMailboxSer... Cmdlet              Use the Get-ClusteredM...
Stop-ClusteredMailboxSe... Cmdlet              This topic explains ho...
Enable-ContinuousReplic... Cmdlet              In the RTM version of ...
Test-ReplicationHealth     Cmdlet              Service Pack 1 introdu...
```

You cannot use these parameters in combination with each other. You may find the results of the `Role` and `Functionality` parameters are too broad to produce a comprehensive list of cmdlets, but the `Component` parameter can be used to produce a more focused list.

Keep in mind that there is a certain amount of overlap when retrieving cmdlet sets using `Get-Help`. For example, the cmdlets retrieved using the component value `*cluster*` in the previous command also appear in a list generated when using the component value `*highavailability*` because the Clustered Mailbox Server cmdlets also fall under the category of high-availability cmdlets.

The following table details the appropriate values and results when using `Get-Help` with the `Role` parameter.

Value 1	Value 2	Use to find:
`*client*`	`*ca*`	Client Access Server administrative cmdlets
`*edge*`	`*et*`	Edge Transport server administrative cmdlets
`*hub*`	`*ht*`	Hub Transport server administrative cmdlets
`*mail*`	`*mb*`	Mailbox server administrative cmdlets
`*unified*`	`*um*`	Unified Messaging server administrative cmdlets
`*org*`	`*oa*`	Exchange Organization administrative cmdlets
`*rpct*`	`*ra*`	Exchange Recipient administrative cmdlets
`*srv*`	`*sa*`	Exchange Server administrative cmdlets
`*win*`	`*wa*`	Windows administrative cmdlets
`*read*`	`*ro*`	Cmdlets that gather information without making changes

The following table details the appropriate values and results when using `Get-Help` with the `Component` parameter.

Value	Use to find:
`*addressing*`	Address List and E-Mail Address policy cmdlets
`*agent*`	Transport Agent, Content/Sender Filtering, IP Allow/Block, and Transport Rules cmdlets
`*antispam*`	IP Allow/Block, Content/Sender Filtering, and Anti Spam cmdlets
`*autoDiscover*`	Autodiscover cmdlets
`*calendaring*`	Availability configuration and Resource/Mailbox calendar setting cmdlets
`*certificate*`	Exchange SSL certificate cmdlets
`*classification*`	Message Classification and Transport Rule cmdlets

Table continued on following page

Value	Use to find:
client	Outlook Anywhere and CAS Mailbox cmdlets
cluster	Clustered Mailbox Server cmdlets
compliance	Transport Rule and Journal Rule cmdlets
delegate	Exchange Administrator delegation cmdlets
diagnostic	Message Queue cmdlets and cmdlets that test certain functionality
domain	Remote and Accepted Domain cmdlets
extensibility	Transport Agent and Web Services Virtual Directory cmdlets
freebusy	Availability Service configuration cmdlets
gal	Address List and Offline Address Book cmdlets
group	Group/Distribution Group/Dynamic Distribution Group cmdlets
highavailability	Clustered Mailbox Server and Local/Cluster Continuous Replication cmdlets
imap	IMAP and CAS Mailbox cmdlets
mailbox	Mailbox, UM Mailbox, and Mailbox Permission cmdlets
mailflow	Transport Agent, Message Queue, Accepted/Remote Domain, Receive/Send Connector, Edge Subscription, and Routing Group Connector cmdlets
managedfolder	Messaging Records Management cmdlets
mobility	ActiveSync cmdlets
oab	Offline Address Book cmdlets
outlook	Outlook Provider and Outlook Anywhere cmdlets
owa	OWA and Exchange Web Services Virtual Directory cmdlets
permission	Active Directory Permission and Mailbox Permission cmdlets
pop	POP3 cmdlets
publicfolder	Public Folder cmdlets
queuing	Message and Message Queue cmdlets
recipient	Mail-enabled object (mailbox, contact, user) cmdlets
routing	Accepted Domain, AD Site Link, and Routing Group Connector cmdlets
rule	Message Classification and Transport/Journal Rule cmdlets
search	Exchange Search cmdlets
server	Exchange Server cmdlets
statistics	Mailbox/Public Folder/Logon Statistic cmdlets
storage	Storage Group and Mailbox/Public Folder Database cmdlets
um	Unified Messaging cmdlets
virtualdirectory	Client Access Server Virtual Directory cmdlets

The following table details the appropriate values and results when using `Get-Help` with the `Functionality` parameter.

Value	Use to find:
Global	Cmdlets that administer objects on the organizational level
Server	Cmdlets that administer objects on a server level
User	Cmdlets that administer objects on the recipient level

Working from the Command Line

All action in the Exchange Management Shell starts at the command prompt. That is where the rubber meets the road so to speak. To use Exchange Management Shell effectively you must familiarize yourself with some basic concepts for navigation and control.

Getting Around

One of the first things with which you should become familiar is how to find your way around inside Windows PowerShell. If you are familiar with other shells like cmd.exe, you already understand the concept of file system navigation: named files and the hierarchical directories where these files are located.

In Windows PowerShell, this concept is expanded to include systems outside of the familiar file system. These other systems can be accessed and navigated from the command line in the same way you would navigate the file system. For example, you can navigate the Registry or certificate store on a server using the same commands for navigating the file drives.

Because other things besides files can be accessed from the command line, in Windows PowerShell all these things are referred to as *items*. Carrying this concept further, the place where an item can be found is referred to as a *location*.

After starting a default instance of the Exchange Management Shell, the command prompt is presented to the user with the current location set to the "home" file directory of the user context. The prompt is set to always display the current location, making it easier for the users to know where they are. For example, when logged on to a server as user exadmin, after starting Exchange Management Shell the following command prompt appears:

```
[PS] C:\Documents and Settings\exadmin>
```

To help users quickly learn how to get around Windows PowerShell, many related cmdlets have been given aliases matching the names of commands found in other command shells. Chances are you already know some of these common command names and can use many of them to get expected results without knowing the underlying Windows PowerShell command that makes them possible.

For example, you may be familiar with the cmd.exe commands cd and chdir, used for changing the current working directory. In Windows PowerShell the cmdlet Set-Location is used for setting the current location. Luckily you can use cd or chdir in the same way you would use Set-Location without really needing to learn any new command names.

Using the previous example, the following command uses the relative path notation backslash character to change the current location to the root of drive C:\:

```
[PS] C:\Documents and Settings\exadmin>cd \
```

Notice in this example the prompt is updated to show the current location after the command completes. Also notice the space used between the cd alias and the backslash character (\). Because of the way Windows PowerShell parses commands, there must be a space between a cmdlet or alias name and parameter values passed to the command as input. This is different from the way cd behaves when used in cmd.exe.

Other relative path notations recognized by Windows PowerShell include a single period (.) to represent the current location, and double periods (..) to represent the parent of the current location.

The following table describes the most common command names and the corresponding cmdlets you'll find useful for navigating locations and controlling items from the command line.

Common Command	Windows PowerShell Command (& Alias)	Description
CD CHDIR	Set-Location (sl)	Sets the current working location to a specified location.
PWD	Get-Location (gl)	Gets the current location.
POPD	Pop-Location	Restores the previous value of the location saved by Push-Location.
PUSHD	Push-Location	Saves the current location then changes to the specified location.
DIR LS	Get-ChildItem (gc)	Gets the items and child items in a specified location.
CLS CLEAR	Clear-Host	Clears the console screen.*
DEL ERASE RD RMDIR RM	Remove-Item (ri)	Deletes one or more specified items.
MOVE MV	Move-Item (mi)	Moves one or more items from one location to another location.
COPY CP	Copy-Item (cpi)	Copies one or more items from one location to another location.
RENAME REN	Rename-Item (rni)	Renames a specified item.

Common Command	Windows PowerShell Command (& Alias)	Description

MD
MKDIR
	`param([string[]]$paths);`
	`New-Item -type directory`
	`-path $paths`
		Creates a new item of file type directory.**

TYPE CAT	`Get-Content (gc)`	Gets the contents of an item at a specified location.

`*Clear-Host` is a function and not a true cmdlet.

`**MD` and `MKDIR` are functions that use cmdlet `New-Item` to make items of type `Directory`.

Windows PowerShell Drives

Windows PowerShell drives are local data stores exposed to the command line that you can access like a file system drive. Several drives are provided by default. To see a list of all available drives on a server use the `Get-PSDrive` cmdlet as shown in this example:

```
[PS] C:\>Get-PSDrive

Name       Provider      Root                          CurrentLocation
----       --------      ----                          ---------------
A          FileSystem    A:\
Alias      Alias
C          FileSystem    C:\
cert       Certificate   \
D          FileSystem    D:\
Env        Environment
Function   Function
HKCU       Registry      HKEY_CURRENT_USER
HKLM       Registry      HKEY_LOCAL_MACHINE
Variable   Variable
Z          FileSystem    Z:\
```

Windows PowerShell drives are exposed via providers, which are .NET programs that present the data from each store in a consistent format. The following table describes the default providers in a standard deployment of Exchange Management Shell.

Provider	Data Store	Description
Alias	Windows PowerShell Alias	Predefined and user-defined aliases
Certificate	X509 Certificates	Certificates used for digital signatures and data encryption
Environment	Windows Environment Variables	Operating system environment variables
FileSystem	File System Drives	Fixed, removable, and mapped drives

Table continued on following page

Provider	Data Store	Description
Function	Windows PowerShell Functions	Predefined and user-defined functions
Registry	Windows Registry	Both HKEY_CURRENT_USER and HKEY_LOCAL_MACHINE Registry keys
Variable	Windows PowerShell Variables	Predefined and user-defined variables

To access the data in any Windows PowerShell drive, simply provide a path that includes the drive name followed by a colon (:). For example, the following command is used to list the environment variables in the Env drive that start with the word User:

```
[PS] C:\>dir env:\user*

Name                          Value
----                          -----
USERDOMAIN                    EXCHEXCH
USERDNSDOMAIN                 EXCHANGEEXCHANGE.LOCAL
USERPROFILE                   C:\Documents and Settings\exadmin
USERNAME                      exadmin
```

To change from the current location to another drive, use the Set-Location command or one of its aliases followed by the full path as shown in this example that sets the location to the Services key:

```
[PS] C:\>cd HKLM:\SYSTEM\CurrentControlSet\Services
[PS] HKLM:\SYSTEM\CurrentControlSet\Services>
```

To navigate from any of the non-file drives back to a file drive, simply type the drive letter followed by a colon. Windows PowerShell has a set of predefined functions for each drive letter, with a definition of Set-Location <drive letter>. In the previous example, entering C: sets the current location back to the previous location at the root of drive C:\.

Navigating Windows PowerShell drives is not exactly as straightforward as navigating a file system drive. There are some distinctions you'll need to keep in mind to use them effectively. The items and structure of these drives differ greatly from file system items. The Alias, Environment, Function, and Variable drive spaces are all flat, with only a root level and no hierarchy. You will also find that some item cmdlets do not work as expected on certain drive items due to the way the items are defined.

Navigating the Certificate and Registry drives offers some additional challenges due to the somewhat complicated nature of the hierarchical structures and item properties. Working with the Windows Registry using the Registry drives is discussed in further detail later in this chapter.

Fortunately most Exchange administrative tasks can be handled by available cmdlets so you may never have to navigate the non-file drives. Users who need to handle more sophisticated tasks, especially those that are automated via scripting, may find it necessary to learn how to work directly with these drives.

Working with Output

You may have noticed that most everything you do in Windows PowerShell results in the output of some information to the screen. That is certainly true of all cmdlets that use the Get verb, and usually the case for cmdlets that have been designed to give some feedback to the user so you know the outcome of running the cmdlet.

Any cmdlet that produces output at the end of the pipeline stream passes that information to an unseen cmdlet called Out-Host. Anything at the end of the pipeline that is not redirected to another cmdlet is automatically handled by Out-Host. Out-Host does not have to be explicitly called because it is the default output handler. The output that appears on the screen can take one of two forms: raw and formatted.

❑   Raw output is just raw object information without any special formatting. All properties for the object are displayed along with their current values. If there are multiple objects in the stream, the property values for all objects are displayed. The information is displayed in "list" form, with each property on a single line.

❑   Formatted output is formatted to show what the cmdlet designer decided was the most interesting information in the most useful form. The information is typically in "table" form, with one or more properties for each object on a single line, with header labels at the top to identify each property.

Figure 2-2 shows an example of both raw and formatted output. The Get-TransportConfig cmdlet produces an output of all properties in list format and Get-TransportServer produces just three property values in table format.

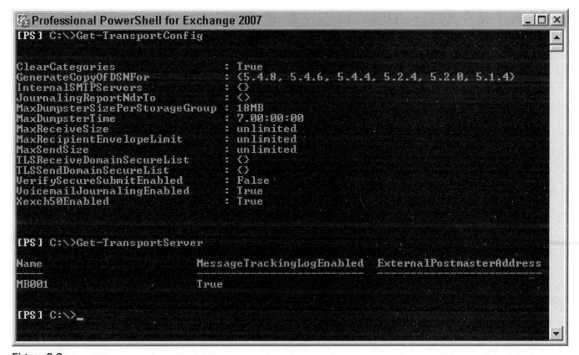

Figure 2-2

In most cases when using Exchange Management Shell you will see table-formatted output. The predefined formatting being used is specified in a file called `exchange.format.ps1xml` located in the `Exchange\bin` directory.

When it is necessary to see information that is not included in default output, Windows PowerShell provides several cmdlets that allow you to override the formatting to force the display of information after it is passed to `Out-Host`. The two cmdlets you will find most useful for this purpose are `Format-Table` and `Format-List`.

Consider the cmdlet `Get-Mailbox`. The standard output for this cmdlet is table format, with property values `Name`, `Alias`, `ServerName`, and `ProhibitSendQuota` as shown in the following example:

```
[PS] C:\>get-mailbox johdoe

Name                          Alias             ServerName        ProhibitSendQuo
                                                                  ta
----                          -----             ----------        ----------------
John Doe                      johdoe            mb001             unlimited
```

Suppose that you need to see different properties, such as `Database` and `PrimarySMTPAddress` instead of `ServerName` and `ProhibitSendQuota`. Using `Format-Table` (or its alias `ft`) you can override the default format by specifying the property names you want displayed separated by commas as shown in this example:

```
[PS] C:\>get-mailbox johdoe | Format-Table name, alias, database, primarysmtpadd
ress

Name                Alias           Database          PrimarySmtpAddress
----                -----           --------          ------------------
John Doe            johdoe          MB001\First Stor... johdoe@exchangee...
```

So now you see the information that you are looking for, but because the default behavior of table formatting is to truncate anything that cannot be displayed in the current column width and on one line, you don't get to see all the information. Notice there is some wasted space between columns. By adding the `AutoSize` parameter you can force `Format-List` to more efficiently use the entire width of the console screen as shown in this example:

```
[PS] C:\>get-mailbox johdoe | Format-Table name, alias, database, primarysmtpadd
ress -AutoSize

Name      Alias  Database                                   PrimarySmtpAddress
----      -----  --------                                   ------------------
John Doe  johdoe MB001\First Storage Group\Mailbox Database johdoe@exchangeex...
```

Now you can see more information, but notice that the `PrimarySMTPAddress` column is still truncated. By adding the `Wrap` parameter you can force `Format-List` to wrap values longer than one line to as many additional lines required to display the entire value as shown in this example:

```
[PS] C:\>get-mailbox johdoe | Format-Table name, alias, database, primarysmtpadd
ress -AutoSize -wrap

Name      Alias  Database                                    PrimarySmtpAddress
----      -----  --------                                    ------------------
John Doe  johdoe MB001\First Storage Group\Mailbox Database  johdoe@exchangeexcha
                                                             nge.com
```

The `Wrap` parameter can be used independent of the `AutoSize` parameter. `Format-Table` also supports wildcards when specifying property names.

At times you may find displaying information in table format unworkable, such as when the number of properties you want to display do not fit well in the width of the screen. Using `Format-List` (or its alias `fl`) you can change the default output of a cmdlet to list form and specify the property names to display. To change the information displayed in the preceding example to list form, use the command shown here:

```
[PS] C:\>get-mailbox johdoe | Format-List name, alias, database, primarysmtpaddr
ess

Name               : John Doe
Alias              : johdoe
Database           : MB001\First Storage Group\Mailbox Database
PrimarySmtpAddress : johdoe@exchangeexchange.com
```

`Format-List` also supports wildcards to specify property names. To display all properties use `Format-List` followed by `*`.

After applying formatting, you may want to direct output to a file for reporting purposes. Using `Out-File` at the end of the pipeline stream directs the output to the file specified by the `FilePath` parameter. To write the output of the information in the preceding example to a text file called `johndoembx.txt`, use the following command:

```
[PS] C:\>get-mailbox johdoe | Format-List name, alias, database, primarysmtpaddr
ess | Out-File -FilePath c:\johndoembx.txt
```

Notice that in this example the `Out-File` cmdlet "intercepted" the output and nothing is displayed on the screen. This is because the information was directed to `Out-File` and not `Out-Host`. Other parameters for `Out-File` include `Append` and `NoClobber`. Use the `Append` parameter to add the output stream to the end of the file specified by `FilePath`. The `NoClobber` parameter is used to prevent the command from overwriting an existing file with the same path name that is specified by `FilePath` parameter.

Using Variables, Aliases, and Functions

Windows PowerShell provides the ability to create user-defined command elements and store them in memory to make entering and running commands easier.

Variables

Windows PowerShell variables are basically named objects that you can use later in another command. Variable names begin with the $ character followed by any combination of alphanumeric characters. To create a variable simply enter the name at the command line. The variable is created but no value is assigned. To assign a value to a variable, enter the name followed by the equality symbol (=) and the value. The value can be a literal value such as an integer or string value, or it can be the results of a cmdlet. For example, to create a variable called $exservers and assign it the value of all Exchange servers in the organization, use the following command:

```
[PS] C:\>$exservers = Get-ExchangeServer
```

Notice there is no feedback to indicate the command completed successfully. There is no feedback unless the command fails. To see the values stored in the variable, simply enter the name:

```
[PS] C:\>$exservers

Name              Site              ServerRole  Edition    AdminDisplayVe
                                                           rsion
----              ----              ----------  -------    --------------
MB001             Default-First-Sit... Mailbox,... Standard... Version 8.0...
```

Typing the name of the variable $exservers results in the redirection of its contents to the screen. The output in this case is the same information that would have been displayed if the command used to define the variable was run instead, so it retains the output format specified to the cmdlet.

Once an object it stored in a variable, it can be used as input to any cmdlet that takes that object type. Keep in mind that the variable is storing an object's properties as well. This allows you to dereference individual property values by using dot notation. For example, the following command displays the values stored in the ServerRole property:

```
[PS] C:\>$exservers.ServerRole
Mailbox, ClientAccess, HubTransport
```

To see all the possible properties that you can dereference from a user-defined variable, use the Get-Member cmdlet followed by the InputObject parameter to specify the variable and the MemberType parameter to specify Property as shown in this example:

```
[PS] C:\>get-member -InputObject $exservers -MemberType Property

   TypeName: Microsoft.Exchange.Data.Directory.Management.ExchangeServer
```

```
Name                            MemberType Definition
----                            ---------- ----------
AdminDisplayVersion             Property   Microsoft.Exchange.Data.ServerV...
CurrentConfigDomainController   Property   System.String CurrentConfigDoma...
CurrentDomainControllers        Property   Microsoft.Exchange.Data.MultiVa...
...
```

User-Defined Variable Lifetime

User-defined variables have a lifetime of the current shell session. Once the shell is closed, the variable definition held in memory is lost. To have user-defined variables persist, add them to the Windows PowerShell profile to be loaded each time the shell is started. Profiles are covered in greater detail later in this chapter.

Automatic Variables

Windows PowerShell includes a set of predefined variable definitions known as automatic variables. *Automatic variables* are either dynamic or static, but always set automatically by the shell. For example, the $PID variable stores the current process ID for the current shell session. This is a unique value set each time the shell is started. The $PSHome variable stores the directory path where Windows PowerShell is installed. This value is static and never changes.

To see a list of all variables and their values, enter dir variables:.

Exchange Variables

Exchange Management Sell includes a set of Exchange-specific variables defined when the Exchange.ps1 script file is loaded during startup. These variables provide an easy way to supply useful file system path values to the command line. The three variables are $exbin (Exchange binary file directory), $exinstall (Exchange install base directory), and $exscripts (Exchange scripts directory).

You can use any of these variables in place of the underlying value they store. For example, to change the current location to the Exchange bin directory, simply enter cd $exbin.

Aliases

As you have already seen, aliases provide a convenient method for substituting a shorter or easier to remember name for an underlying cmdlet. Windows PowerShell includes a host of predefined aliases. To see a list of all aliases, simply enter dir alias: to list the contents of the Variable drive. This list includes the alias names and their definition (the cmdlet they are tied to).

You can add your own alias definitions using the New-Alias and Set-Alias cmdlets. There are a few simple rules to follow when creating your alias definitions:

❑ Some predefined aliases are read-only, so you cannot redefine them or make a new alias using the same name. You can, however, safely redefine any aliases you create.

❑ Alias definitions only allow for the name of a cmdlet, so you cannot include any parameters or values. Use functions to define more complex commands.

❑ Alias names must start with a letter, but the rest of the name can contain any combination of alphanumeric characters.

To create a new alias, use `New-Alias` or `Set-Alias` followed by the name of the alias and the name of the cmdlet it represents as shown in this example for creating an alias called `setweb` for the cmdlet `Set-WebServicesVirtualDirectory` cmdlet:

```
[PS] C:\>Set-Alias setweb Set-WebServicesVirtualDirectory
```

There is no feedback to tell you the command completed successfully. Use the `Get-Alias` cmdlet to confirm an alias's definition:

```
[PS] C:\>Get-Alias setweb

CommandType      Name          Definition
-----------      ----          ----------
Alias            setweb        Set-WebServicesVirtualDirectory
```

Like user-defined variables, user-defined aliases persist only as long as the current shell session. You need to add their definitions to the user profile to have them available each time the shell is started.

Functions

A Windows PowerShell function is a named block of code containing one or more commands that can be run as a single command by entering the name of the function. Functions can be created as input directly at the command line or included as part of a script. Use functions to accomplish more complex tasks without the monotony of entering the same command elements over and over.

Function definition begins with the keyword `Function`, followed by the name of the function and a block of code enclosed in curly braces: `{}`. A function can contain a single or multiple commands, and the definition can span multiple lines as long as opening brace is entered on the first line and the closing brace is entered on the last line.

Functions can take as input from the command line one or more arguments entered at the time the function is run. By providing input values to the function as parameters, you can create flexible command structures that provide the functionality you need without being limited to static values embedded in the function itself.

For example, the `Get-Mailbox` cmdlet by default displays results as `Name`, `Alias`, `ServerName`, and `ProhibitSendQuota` values in a table format. These may not be the most interesting values for your needs, so you would like to have another cmdlet that displays a different set of values by default. Creating a function that uses the `Get-Mailbox` cmdlet with customized output formatting is a quick and easy way to get the results you need. Entering this function at the command line looks like this:

```
[PS] C:\>Function get-mailbox2
>> {
>> param($name)
>> Get-Mailbox $name | Format-List Name, Database, OrganizationalUnit
>> }
>>
```

The results of running this function along with a valid mailbox-enabled account identity as input looks like this:

```
[PS] C:\>get-mailbox2 johdoe

Name              : John Doe
Database          : MB001\First Storage Group\Mailbox Database
OrganizationalUnit : exchangeexchange.local/Users
```

The definition of the function in this example starts with the Function keyword, followed by a unique name, in this case Get-Mailbox2. Be careful when choosing a name because Windows PowerShell does no validation to prevent you from entering the name of an existing cmdlet. Names can contain any alphanumeric character, but must always start with a letter.

When you press Enter at the end of the first line, Windows PowerShell expects more instructions are to be entered and drops to the next input line. The two greater than characters (>>) on the input line prompt the user that Windows PowerShell is expecting more input. The script block then starts with entering the left curly brace ({).

The input parameter definition is very simple, using the keyword param followed by a variable name enclosed in parentheses, in this case $name. This parameter will be used for inputting the identity of the mailbox-enabled account for which the function gets information. Multiple parameter variable names can be defined, separated by commas. The use of input parameters is optional, but their use extends the usefulness of a function by allowing you to enter dynamic information at the time the function is run.

The next line comprises the main command for this function. This command uses Get-Mailbox to get information about the mailbox-enabled account identified by the $name parameter, then passes that object to the Format-List cmdlet to output its Name, Database, and OrganizationalUnit properties in list format.

The script block is ended by entering the right curly brace (}) on a line by itself. Pressing Enter on the blank last line ends function definition and writes it to memory. The command-line prompt then returns to normal.

Windows PowerShell does some limited validation of a function definition entered from the command line before it is saved to memory. Any code in the script block that would cause a processing error, such as divide by zero, is brought to the user's attention and identified by the line and the character position where the faulty code is located. If you make this type of mistake when entering a function from the command line, the function is not saved to memory and the definition fails.

There is no validation for cmdlet elements entered as part of a function definition. For example, the misspelling or misuse of a cmdlet or parameter name is only exposed when the function is run. Function definitions can be changed by re-entering the definition at the command line.

Entering a function containing more than a few lines of code at the command line can be somewhat frustrating; if you make any mistakes you have to start over. You may find it more useful to work out and proof each individual element as a "stand alone" command before committing to their use together in the script block.

Functions are stored in memory and exposed by the Function provider in the form of the `function:\` drive. To view functions, access the `function:\` drive by either changing the current location or by getting a function's information using the `Get-Item` cmdlet as shown in this example:

```
[PS] C:\>Get-Item function:\get-mailbox2 | Format-list Definition

Definition : param($name) Get-Mailbox $name | Format-List Name, Database, Organ
             izationalUnit
```

Function definitions entered at the command line last only as long as the current shell session from which they were entered. To have a function available for use each time the shell is started, add the function definition to the user profile.

Using Profiles

When you create user-defined aliases, variables, and functions, their definitions last only as long as the current Windows PowerShell session used to create them. Because they are stored in memory, closing the shell purges them and they are lost.

To have these aliases, variables, and function definitions available for your use each time you start Exchange Management Shell, create a Windows PowerShell profile script file and add these custom definitions. Each time the shell is started these definitions are read from the profile script and loaded into memory.

Four types of profiles can be defined for use, but for Exchange Management Shell you will probably be interested in just two of them: a profile that affects only the current user and a profile that affects all users. The location of the profile script file determines the profile type:

❑ **Current User:** `%userprofile%\My Documents\WindowsPowerShell\Microsoft .PowerShell_profile.ps1`

❑ **All Users:** `windir%\system32\windowspowershell\v1.0\Microsoft.PowerShell profile.ps1`

When Windows PowerShell starts, it checks these locations and loads the `Microsoft.PowerShell_ profile.ps1` script files if found; the all users profile is loaded first followed by the current user profile. By loading the all users profile script, all users have access to the same custom command elements contained in the script. Additional elements can then be added to the current user profile script for more specific command elements each individual user requires.

Command elements loaded by the current user profile script override command elements of the same name loaded by the all users profile script.

To create your own current user `Microsoft.PowerShell_profile.ps1` script file and open it in Notepad for editing, run the following commands:

```
[PS] C:\>New-Item -Path $profile -ItemType file -Force

    Directory: Microsoft.PowerShell.Core\FileSystem::C:\Documents and Settings\
    Administrator\My Documents\WindowsPowerShell

Mode                 LastWriteTime       Length Name
----                 -------------       ------ ----
-a---        8/4/2007  12:25 PM              0 Microsoft.PowerShell_profile.ps1

[PS] C:\>Notepad $profile
```

The `New-Item` cmdlet is used to create a new item of type file in the location specified by the `Path` parameter, in this case `$profile`. Windows PowerShell provides the automatic variable `$profile`, which always points to the path for the current user profile file. This makes it easy to create and edit the profile file because this variable is always set according to the current user context. The new file is opened for editing by invoking `Notepad` followed by the path to the profile file, again provided by the `$profile` variable.

To add function, alias, and variable definitions to the profile file, simply add them as if you were entering them from the command line. The following example adds the function definition from a previous example, an alias definition, and a variable definition:

```
#Administrator's current user profile
#updated 07-12-07: added variable definition

#Functions

Function get-mailbox2
{
param($name)
Get-Mailbox $name | Format-List Name, Database, OrganizationalUnit
}

#Aliases

Set-Alias getmbx Get-Mailbox

#Variables
$mb001 = (Get-ExchangeServer MB001)
```

Use the pound character (#) to add comments to your profile file and keep it organized. Other command elements can also be loaded by the profile script file. You can include any command as well as other script files to load and run.

One command you may find very useful when added to your profile script is `Start-Transcript`. The `Start-Transcript` cmdlet creates a complete record of all actions from a shell session by writing each command entered at the command line and each output displayed to the console screen to a transcript log file. By default the transcript file is stored in the `%UserProfile%\My Documents` directory of the current user. Each time `Start-Transcript` runs it creates a new transcript file named `PowerShell_transcript.<timestamp>.txt`. You can override the default file path location using the `Path` parameter.

Working with Windows

Windows PowerShell provides a powerful administrative interface for managing the Windows operating system. From the command line you can determine and change the status of processes and services, read and change Registry values, and access diagnostic information. This section covers Windows PowerShell features you'll find useful for managing your Windows servers.

Controlling Processes

At any given time there are dozens of processes active on an Exchange Server 2007 computer. Traditionally administrators have used tools such as Windows Task Manager to determine the current status of each active process. By default from Task Manager you can view the process name, the user context under which it is running, the percentage of total CPU utilization, and the memory being used by the process. This is all useful information to an administrator investigating certain issues like performance or unexpected behavior.

Windows PowerShell makes it possible to investigate these issues through the `Get-Process` cmdlet. Using `Get-Process` you can collect detailed information about any processes running on an Exchange Server 2007 computer. For example, to see the current state for the `store.exe` process, the following command is used:

```
[PS] C:\>get-process store

Handles  NPM(K)    PM(K)      WS(K) VM(M)   CPU(s)     Id ProcessName
-------  ------    -----      ----- -----   ------     -- -----------
   1098     207   101504      40132   371     6.02   1764 store
```

The default output for `Get-Process` displays the current number of Handles opened by the process, the Non-Paged Memory (NPM(K)) used by the process in kilobytes, the Paged memory (PM(K)) used by the process in kilobytes, the size of the Working Set (WS(K)) in kilobytes, the Virtual Memory (VM(M)) used by the process in megabytes, the CPU(s) time used by the process total in seconds, the Process Identifier number (ID), and the Process Name.

Additional details for a process can be displayed by piping the results of `Get-Process` to the `Format-List` cmdlet along with the names of properties of interest. Use the wildcard * character to display all properties. Using these additional properties administrators can determine and confirm such important details as file version, image path, process start time, and loaded modules to name a few.

Administrators can end processes using the `Stop-Process` cmdlet along with the Process Identifier. In the following example the `Get-Process` cmdlet is used to get all processes for the application Notepad, and then the `Stop-Process` cmdlet is used to stop one of them:

```
[PS] C:\>Get-Process notepad

Handles  NPM(K)    PM(K)      WS(K) VM(M)   CPU(s)     Id ProcessName
-------  ------    -----      ----- -----   ------     -- -----------
     62       2      868       3608    27     0.91   1020 notepad
     62       2      848       3600    27     0.29   2556 notepad
```

```
[PS] C:\>Stop-Process 1020
[PS] C:\>Get-Process notepad

Handles  NPM(K)    PM(K)      WS(K) VM(M)   CPU(s)     Id ProcessName
-------  ------    -----      ----- -----   ------     -- -----------
     62       2      848       3600    27     0.29   2556 notepad
```

In this example the Process Identifier for both Notepad processes are returned by `Get-Process`. By passing the Process Identifier 1020 to `Stop-Process`, the first instance of Notepad is ended and only the second instance remains as confirmed by running `Get-Process` a second time.

Ending a process using `Stop-Process` *may cause unexpected results. Use* `Stop-Process` *only after confirming the process to be stopped is properly identified and the process cannot be stopped programmatically.*

Controlling Services

Administrators typically manage services from the Services administrative tool provided as part of a basic Windows operating system installation. Windows PowerShell provides a host of cmdlets for managing Windows services from the command line. Using these cmdlets you can confirm the current status of services as well as start, stop, pause, and resume them.

To see a list of all services use the `Get-Service` cmdlet with no other arguments. On a typical Exchange Server 2007 computer this can produce a list of more than 100 services. To display services in which you are probably more interested, use the specific service name or wildcards to produce a list that includes a particular keyword. For example, to see all services that include the word "Exchange," use the following command:

```
[PS] C:\>Get-Service *exchange*

Status    Name              DisplayName
------    ----              -----------
Running   MSExchangeADTop... Microsoft Exchange Active Directory...
Running   MSExchangeAntis... Microsoft Exchange Anti-spam Update
Running   MSExchangeEdgeSync Microsoft Exchange EdgeSync
Running   MSExchangeFDS      Microsoft Exchange File Distribution
Stopped   MSExchangeImap4    Microsoft Exchange IMAP4
Running   MSExchangeIS       Microsoft Exchange Information Store
Running   MSExchangeMailb... Microsoft Exchange Mailbox Assistants
Running   MSExchangeMailS... Microsoft Exchange Mail Submission
Stopped   MSExchangeMonit... Microsoft Exchange Monitoring
```

(continued)

(continued)

```
Stopped  MSExchangePop3     Microsoft Exchange POP3
Running  MSExchangeRepl     Microsoft Exchange Replication Service
Running  MSExchangeSA       Microsoft Exchange System Attendant
Running  MSExchangeSearch   Microsoft Exchange Search Indexer
Running  MSExchangeServi... Microsoft Exchange Service Host
Running  MSExchangeTrans... Microsoft Exchange Transport
Running  MSExchangeTrans... Microsoft Exchange Transport Log Se...
Running  msftesql-Exchange  Microsoft Search  (Exchange)
```

This narrows down the list quite a bit, but to see specific information about a service, provide the service name and pipe the results to the `Format-List` cmdlet to display all properties as shown in this example:

```
[PS] C:\>Get-Service MSExchangeIS | Format-List
```

```
Name                 : MSExchangeIS
DisplayName          : Microsoft Exchange Information Store
Status               : Running
DependentServices    : {}
ServicesDependedOn   : {NtLmSsp, RPCSS, LanmanWorkstation, LanmanServer, EventLo
                       g}
CanPauseAndContinue  : False
CanShutdown          : True
CanStop              : True
ServiceType          : Win32OwnProcess
```

From this output you can determine the current status for the service (`Status`), any services dependent on this service (`DependentServices`), and services that this service depends on to be running before it can start (`ServicesDependedOn`). Unfortunately, one property administrators find important for managing services is not included in the results of `Get-Service`: the service start type. This information is available only via the Windows Services application or the Registry.

The rest of the services cmdlets are straightforward and almost self-explanatory as shown in the following table.

Cmdlet	Description
Get-Service	Use to list service properties and current status.
Set-Service	Use to set the startup type for a service to one of three values using the StartupType parameter: Automatic, Manual, and Disabled.
Start-Service	Use to start a service that is currently stopped.
Stop-Service	Use to stop a service that is currently running.
Restart-Service	Use to stop and then automatically start a service that is currently running.
Suspend-Service	Use to pause a currently running service.
Resume-Service	Use to resume a service that is currently paused.

Working with Windows Registry

There is probably no such thing as an Exchange administrator who can say he has never had to access the Registry on an Exchange server to confirm or change a Registry setting. The Registry is a hierarchical database used to store configuration information for users, applications, and hardware devices.

Windows has always provided a Registry editing tool such as regedit.exe for just this purpose. Because Windows PowerShell exposes the Registry to the user as a drive, you may find it useful to understand how to access Registry settings and if need be, make changes.

> *Standard boilerplate found on any Microsoft documentation that includes instructions for changing values in the Registry includes a warning that incorrect use of the Registry editor can cause serious problems that may require you to re-install your operating system. Using Windows PowerShell to access and make changes to the Registry is no different from changing the Registry using any other method. If you make a mistake, be prepared. Your efforts may produce unexpected results from which you may be unable to recover.*

The Windows PowerShell Registry provider exposes two Registry hives as Windows PowerShell drives:

❑ The HKEY_LOCAL_MACHINE hive maps to the HKLM: drive. The HKLM: drive exposes configuration information particular to the computer regardless of the currently logged-on user.

❑ The HKEY_CURRENT_USER hive maps to the HKCU: drive. The HKCU: drive exposes configuration information for the user that is currently logged on to the computer.

To access the Registry as a drive, simply change the current location to the appropriate drive using the Set-Location cmdlet or one of its aliases. To view the "contents" of the current location use the Get-ChildItem cmdlet or one of its aliases. For example, to change the current location to the HKCU: drive, and then navigate to the key for the MSExchangeIS service, use the following commands:

```
[PS] C:\>Set-Location HKLM:\SYSTEM\CurrentControlSet\Services\MSExchangeIS
[PS] HKLM:\SYSTEM\CurrentControlSet\Services\MSExchangeIS>Get-ChildItem

    Hive: Microsoft.PowerShell.Core\Registry::HKEY_LOCAL_MACHINE\SYSTEM\CurrentC
ontrolSet\Services\MSExchangeIS

SKC  VC Name                              Property
---  -- ----                              --------
  3   0 Diagnostics                       {}
  4   0 MB001                             {}
  0   7 ParametersNetIf                   {MaxPoolThreads, MaxConcurrency, Thre...
  0   5 ParametersPrivate                 {Background Cleanup, Background Searc...
  0   6 ParametersPublic                  {Background Cleanup, Background Searc...
  1   8 ParametersSystem                  {Working Directory, DB Recovery, DSA ...
  0  13 Performance                       {Close, Collect, Library, Open, PerfI...
  0   1 Security                          {Security}
  0   3 Enum                              {0, Count, NextInstance}

[PS] HKLM:\SYSTEM\CurrentControlSet\Services\MSExchangeIS>
```

Notice that the output here is quite a bit different than what you would see from a regular file system drive. That is because the information held in the Registry is so much different than files and directories. The Registry is made up of keys, which can be thought of as containers. Keys can contain sub-keys and property values that are properties of the key in which they are contained. Sub-keys can contain more sub-keys and property values of their own.

In the output from dir in the previous example, the objects listed under the Name column are sub-keys in the MSExchangeIS key. The SKC (sub-key count) column denotes the number of sub-keys contained in that sub-key. The VC (value count) column contains a count of the number of values in that sub-key. The Property column lists each property value. For example, the Diagnostics sub-key contains three sub-keys of its own, but no property values. The Performance sub-key contains no sub-keys, but has 13 property values.

To work with Registry keys, use Item cmdlets: Get-Item, Set-Item, Rename-Item, Copy-Item, Move-Item, and Remove-Item. To work with Registry property values use ItemProperty cmdlets: Get-ItemProperty, Set-ItemProperty, Rename-ItemProperty, Copy-ItemProperty, Move-ItemProperty, and Remove-ItemProperty.

To create a new Registry key, use the New-Item cmdlet followed by the Path parameter to specify the key in which to create this key as a sub-key, the ItemType parameter to specify the type of item as "key," and the Name parameter to specify the name of the key. For example, to create a sub-key called test under the key MSExchangeIS, use the following command:

```
[PS] C:\>New-Item -Path HKLM:\SYSTEM\CurrentControlSet\Services\MSExchangeIS\
-ItemType key -Name test

    Hive: Microsoft.PowerShell.Core\Registry::HKEY_LOCAL_MACHINE\SYSTEM\CurrentC
ontrolSet\Services\MSExchangeIS

SKC  VC Name                          Property
---  -- ----                          --------
  0   0 test                          {}
```

To remove this key use the Remove-Item cmdlet followed by the Path parameter to specify the full path to the item to be removed:

```
[PS] C:\>remove-Item -Path HKLM:\SYSTEM\CurrentControlSet\Services\MSExchangeIS\
Test
```

Be very careful when using this command because it would be very easy to delete the wrong key from the Registry by entering in an incomplete path. There is no confirmation to prevent you from deleting the wrong value and there is no feedback to report the exact action that was taken.

To see the property values a key contains, use the `Get-ItemProperty` cmdlet followed by the `Path` parameter specifying the path to the key containing the values, and the `Name` parameter to specify the name of the property. If the current location is the key containing the value, use dot sourcing (. \) to specify the current location. By omitting the `Name` parameter, all property values for the key are returned. For example, to see all the property values held in the `MSExchangeIS` key use the following command:

```
[PS]HKLM:\SYSTEM\CurrentControlSet\Services\MSExchangeIS>Get-ItemProperty
-Path .\
```

```
PSPath                   : Microsoft.PowerShell.Core\Registry::HKEY_LOCAL_MACHINE
                           \SYSTEM\CurrentControlSet\Services\MSExchangeIS
PSParentPath             : Microsoft.PowerShell.Core\Registry::HKEY_LOCAL_MACHINE
                           \SYSTEM\CurrentControlSet\Services
PSChildName              : MSExchangeIS
PSDrive                  : HKLM
PSProvider               : Microsoft.PowerShell.Core\Registry
Type                     : 16
Start                    : 2
ErrorControl             : 1
ImagePath                : "C:\Program Files\Microsoft\Exchange Server\bin\store.
                           exe"
DisplayName              : Microsoft Exchange Information Store
DependOnService          : {EventLog, NtLmSsp, RPCSS, LanmanWorkstation, LanmanSe
                           rver}
DependOnGroup            : {}
ObjectName               : LocalSystem
Description              : Manages the Microsoft Exchange Information Store. This
                           includes mailbox stores and public folder stores. If
                           this service is stopped, mailbox stores and public fo
                           lder stores on this computer are unavailable. If this
                           service is disabled, any services that explicitly depe
                           nd on it will fail to start.
DiagnosticsMessageFile : mdbmsg.dll

[PS] HKLM:\SYSTEM\CurrentControlSet\Services\MSExchangeIS>
```

To change a property value use the `Set-ItemProperty` cmdlet with the `Path` parameter to point to the key where the property value is located, the `Name` parameter to specify the name of the property value, and the `Value` parameter to specify the value. In the following example the Start property value is changed to 4, which corresponds to startup type "disabled":

```
[PS] C:\>Set-ItemProperty -Path HKLM:\SYSTEM\CurrentControlSet\Services\MSExchan
geIS -Name startup -Value 4
```

To add a property value, use the `New-ItemProperty` cmdlet with the `Path` parameter to point to the key where the property value is to be located, the `Name` parameter to specify the name of the new property value, the `PropertyType` parameter to specify the type of value to add, and the `Value` parameter to specify the new value. Valid property types are `String`, `ExpandString`, `Binary`, `DWord`, and `MultiString`. In the following example a `DWord` property value called `"OAB Bandwidth Threshold (KBps)"` is being added with a value of `5000` to the `ParameterSystem` sub-key under `MSExchangeIS`:

```
[PS] C:\>New-ItemProperty -path HKLM:\SYSTEM\CurrentControlSet\Services\MSExchan
geIS\ParametersSystem\ -Name "OAB Bandwidth Threshold (KBps)" -PropertyType DWor
d -Value 5000
```

```
PSPath                              : Microsoft.PowerShell.Core\Registry::HKEY_LOCAL
                                      _MACHINE\SYSTEM\CurrentControlSet\Services\MSE
                                      xchangeIS\ParametersSystem\
PSParentPath                        : Microsoft.PowerShell.Core\Registry::HKEY_LOCAL
                                      _MACHINE\SYSTEM\CurrentControlSet\Services\MSE
                                      xchangeIS
PSChildName                         : ParametersSystem
PSDrive                             : HKLM
PSProvider                          : Microsoft.PowerShell.Core\Registry
OAB Bandwidth Threshold (KBps)      : 5000
```

The default behavior when a property value is successfully added is to output the results as shown. Note that the `DWord` value is always shown in decimal, and not in hexadecimal. This avoids the confusion sometimes encountered when entering values from the Registry editor.

To remove a Registry value, use the `Remove-ItemProperty` cmdlet followed by the `Path` parameter to specify the key containing the value to remove, and the `Name` parameter to identify the property value itself. For example, to remove the value added in the preceding example use the following command:

```
[PS] C:\>Remove-ItemProperty -Path HKLM:\SYSTEM\CurrentControlSet\Services\MSExc
hangeIS\ParametersSystem\ -Name "oab bandwidth threshold (kbps)"
```

Be very careful when using this command because it would be very easy to delete the wrong property value from the Registry by entering an incorrect path and/or the wrong property value name. There is no confirmation to prevent you from deleting the wrong value and there is no feedback to report the exact action that was taken.

Working with Event Logs

All good administrators know that the first and best place to check when investigating issues on an Exchange server is the event logs. Many times the nature of an issue is exposed in the events found in one of the relevant event logs.

Exchange Management Shell provides cmdlets for viewing event logs and setting diagnostic logging levels for Exchange components.

Viewing Event Logs

Windows PowerShell uses the `Get-EventLog` cmdlet to provide access to event logs on the local server. Several parameters are included to control how `Get-EventLog` works.

To display a list of all event logs that are available on the server along with their current properties, use the List parameter as shown in this example:

```
[PS] C:\>Get-EventLog -list

  Max(K) Retain OverflowAction        Entries Name
  ------ ------ --------------        ------- ----
  16,384      0 OverwriteAsNeeded       2,512 Application
     512      0 OverwriteAsNeeded         139 Directory Service
     512      7 OverwriteOlder             60 DNS Server
     512      0 OverwriteAsNeeded          14 File Replication Service
     512      7 OverwriteOlder              0 Internet Explorer
 131,072      0 OverwriteAsNeeded      65,785 Security
  16,384      0 OverwriteAsNeeded       1,066 System
  15,360      0 OverwriteAsNeeded         496 Windows PowerShell
```

This list is typical for a server acting as an "all-in-one" box running Windows 2003 Active Directory, DNS, and Exchange Server 2007.

To display the events from a particular event log, use the LogName parameter and the name of the specific event log as shown in the list from the previous example. However, keep in mind that this command lists every event in the log, which is probably not what you really want to do. For a log containing hundreds and maybe even thousands of entries, you would find it next to impossible to use.

Instead, add the Newest parameter followed by an integer value to limit the output to the number specified. For example, to display the five newest events from the Application Event Log, use the following command:

```
[PS] C:\> Get-EventLog -LogName Application -Newest 5

Index Time          Type Source             EventID Message
----- ----          ---- ------             ------- -------
 2513 Aug 04 18:00  Info MSExchange ADAccess    2080 Process MSEXCHANGEADT...
 2512 Aug 04 17:45  Info MSExchange ADAccess    2080 Process MSEXCHANGEADT...
 2511 Aug 04 17:30  Info MSExchange ADAccess    2080 Process MSEXCHANGEADT...
 2510 Aug 04 17:15  Info MSExchange ADAccess    2080 Process MSEXCHANGEADT...
 2509 Aug 04 17:00  Info MSExchange ADAccess    2080 Process MSEXCHANGEADT...
```

In this example the last five events generated are displayed in order from latest to earliest. The output includes the time stamp for when the event was generated, the event type, the event source, the event ID, and the message (truncated). To see the complete event message, pipe the results to Format-Table or Format-List. You may find that using Format-List presents a more comprehensive output than Format-Table does.

What makes more sense is to add a filter clause to filter for events that you may find more interesting. Suppose you would like to check the most recent 2000 events for instances of errors and warnings from source MSExchange ADAccess. The command would use the Where-Object cmdlet described in Chapter 1 to filter for the event type and source as shown in this example:

```
[PS] C:\>Get-EventLog -LogName Application -Newest 2000 | where {($_.entrytype -
eq "Error" -or $_.entrytype -eq "Warning") -and $_.Source -eq "MSExchange ADAcce
ss"}
```

Index	Time		Type	Source	EventID	Message
2191	Jul 22	21:02	Erro	MSExchange ADAccess	2102	Process MAD.EXE (PID=...
863	Jul 14	14:06	Warn	MSExchange ADAccess	2121	Process STORE.EXE (PI...
862	Jul 14	14:06	Erro	MSExchange ADAccess	2104	Process STORE.EXE (PI...
861	Jul 14	14:06	Erro	MSExchange ADAccess	2102	Process MAD.EXE (PID=...

This command uses Get-EventLog to gather the newest 2000 events from the Application event log. This collection of event objects is then passed by pipeline to the where clause for filtering. The first part of the filter checks to see if the event is of type "Error" or of type "Warning". The second part of the filter checks to see if the event is from source "MSExchange ADAccess". If the event is either error or warning and from source MSExchange ADAccess, it is passed to the console for output.

Parsing the event logs using this method can save time when compared to using the Event Viewer Graphical User Interface. Other properties for which you can filter event logs include EventID and Message. You can filter for specific values inside the Message property using the like operator with wildcards to present a string on which to use for filtering. In this way you can filter for events that contain a specific string value such as a user's name or an error code.

Controlling Diagnostic Logging Levels

Exchange Server 2007 has been designed to generate significant events without the need for any additional configuration. These events should alert administrators to the presence of potentially serious problems. However, there may be situations when it becomes necessary to generate additional events based on the level of diagnostic logging that has been set for the corresponding component.

Having the ability to control diagnostic logging levels allows the administrator to "switch on" only the additional logging necessary for troubleshooting the issue at hand. This limits Application Event Log "bloating" and makes it much easier to parse event logs for relevant events. Exchange Management Shell provides two cmdlets for working with diagnostic logging:

❑   Get-EventLogLevel

❑   Set-EventLogLevel

Use the Get-EventLogLevel cmdlet to confirm the current diagnostic logging level, known as the EventLevel setting, for a given Exchange component. Component names are arranged by "category name\component name." There are more than 30 component categories, some of which also have subcategories. To display a list of all categories and their components, enter Get-EventLogLevel without any parameters.

To determine the current EventLevel of a given component, use Get-EventLogLevel followed by the name of the component category, or the name of the specific component. For example, to display the current diagnostic level for the Autodiscover category, use the following command:

```
[PS] C:\>Get-EventLogLevel "msexchange autodiscover"

Identity                                               EventLevel
--------                                               ----------
msexchange autodiscover\Core                           Lowest
msexchange autodiscover\Web                            Lowest
msexchange autodiscover\Provider                       Lowest
```

Notice that the name of the category is encapsulated in quotes because it contains spaces. There are three components under the Autodiscover category: Core, Web, and Provider. To display the EventLevel of an individual component, use the full identity (category name\component name) as input to Get-EventLogLevel.

There are five levels of diagnostic logging set by EventLevel: Lowest, Low, Medium, High, and Expert .Lowest is the default level for all components after installation of Exchange Server 2007. To change the EventLevel setting for a given component, use Set-EventLogLevel followed by the name of the component plus the Level parameter followed by the EventLevel setting.

For example, to set EventLevel on component "msexchange autodiscover\Core" to High, use the following command:

```
[PS] C:\>Set-EventLogLevel "msexchange autodiscover\Core" -Level High
```

Set-EventLogLevel does not take wildcards as input, so it is not possible to change the EventLevel settings for all components in a category by using "category name*" as input. However, Set-EventLogLevel does take pipeline input so it is possible to gather a collection of components with Get-EventLogLevel and pass them to Set-EventLogLevel to change the setting on all the components.

For example, to set EventLevel on all components under "msexchange autodiscover" to Expert, use the following command:

```
[PS] C:\>Get-EventLogLevel "msexchange autodiscover" | Set-EventLogLevel -Level
Expert
```

Setting EventLevel for a given component is recommended only when Microsoft documentation describes diagnostic logging as a way of troubleshooting a specific issue. Turning on diagnostic logging for components not related to an issue can make troubleshooting more difficult due to the number of unrelated events that would be generated in the Application Event Log.

Always remember to set diagnostic logging back to the default level of Lowest once troubleshooting is complete.

Summary

Exchange Management Shell is a vital part of Exchange Server 2007 management and learning how to use it is essential for any Exchange administrator. Many of the operations available in Exchange Management Shell are not included in Exchange Management Console, and many of the operations that are available in the Exchange Management Console are singular and can take action on only one object at a time. Exchange Management Console provides no way for automating even simple operations, whereas scripts run from Exchange Management Shell ensure consistent results and can be used to work out complex administrative tasks.

Each Exchange component has administrative functionality made available via cmdlets. That functionality is always available in the Exchange Management Shell and may be available in the Exchange Management Console. The availability of administrative functionality can be at Parity (available in either interface), Mixed (some available in either interface, some only in the shell), or Exclusive (only in the shell). For some mixed functionality and all exclusive functionality, you have no choice but to use the Exchange Management Shell.

The Exchange Management Console is a well thought out management interface. Understanding the organization of the Exchange Management Console is very helpful for understanding the organization of Exchange Management Shell cmdlets. Its visual arrangement of management elements actually represents the underlying cmdlet organization that cannot be represented in the shell. By learning this structure you learn the basic organization of Exchange cmdlets.

Exchange Management Shell provides more than 500 cmdlets for administering your Exchange organization. Because Exchange Management Shell lacks the hierarchical command interface found in Exchange Management Console, you may find it easier to manage cmdlets by thinking of them as organized into sets that share some commonality.

All action in the Exchange Management Shell starts at the command prompt. To use Exchange Management Shell effectively you must familiarize yourself with some basic concepts for navigation and control. In Windows PowerShell, the concept of file system navigation is expanded to include systems such as the Registry and certificate stores. These other systems can be accessed and navigated from the command line in the same way you would navigate the file system.

Windows PowerShell provides the ability to create and store in memory user-defined command elements. Variables are named objects that can be used to store information that can be used as input to commands. Aliases provide a method for creating shorter or more familiar names for cmdlets. Functions allow administrators to group commands together in a named script block and run them all by entering just the function name. Windows PowerShell profiles allow you to load user-defined Aliases, Variables, and Functions into memory and run additional commands as required each time the shell is opened.

Windows PowerShell provides cmdlets for controlling processes and Windows services. The Windows Registry can be accessed similar to a file system from the command line, allowing the administrator to confirm, add, and remove keys and property values. The Windows event logs are accessible from the command line, and can be parsed using properties such as event ID, source, and event type. Diagnostic logging for Exchange components is also controlled from the command line.

3

Using PowerShell to Deploy Exchange Server 2007

Installing Exchange Server 2007 is different from installing previous generations of Exchange products. New hardware and new server roles are just the tip of the iceberg. There are new clustering and replication engines, more intelligent spam settings, and the ability to encrypt communication between two Exchange Server 2007 organizations. It is indeed a very exciting time to be involved with Exchange.

This chapter discusses installation and deployment of Exchange Server 2007. The installation pieces are broken down into hardware requirements, software requirements, and domain requirements. Each one of these requires some planning because Exchange Server 2007 is 64-bit only. New servers may need to be purchased. You may need to perform compatibility testing of your company's products to ensure that backups, antivirus, and monitoring tools will work, as well as a health check on the AD infrastructure to ensure that the domain is sufficient for Exchange deployment. After the requirements are displayed, the setup switches are explained along with information about what is required to prepare the environment. Though this may seem mundane, it is necessary because there are switches available to ensure compatibility with legacy clients. After the setup switches are discussed, we focus on deployment scenarios. Although we discuss how many servers and what roles should be deployed, it is not an exhaustive list of every deployment scenario. The scenarios are discussed as a prelude to the rest of the book. They are presented to give you a cursory understanding of what the server role provides; the remaining chapters in the book further discuss the individual parameters of their respective roles.

In this chapter you learn:

❑ Exchange Server 2007 requirements

❑ Server installation

❑ Disaster recovery

❑ Deployment scenarios

Deploying Exchange Server 2007

There are many prerequisites for Exchange Server 2007. In order to have a functional and supported configuration, the Exchange administrator needs to understand the requirements and limitations of the requirements.

One of the biggest impacts on the design and deployment of Exchange Server 2007 is how other applications in your environment interact with Exchange. Do you have systems that use forms stored in a public folder, or create items in public folders? Do you have any existing applications that use custom dlls or shims to interact with Exchange? Though these may seem like remote what-if scenarios, in the original release of Exchange Server 2007 not all vendors supported their existing software interacting with Exchange Server 2007. Many companies were left with no choice but to leave a legacy Exchange 2003 server in place to allow the legacy applications to continue to have connectivity to the messaging system. As a result this section discusses the following requirements:

❑   Proper hardware sizing

❑   Software requirements

❑   Domain requirements

❑   Exchange organization requirements

Hardware Requirements

One of the biggest changes that Exchange Server 2007 brought forth is the requirement for a 64-bit processor. Sixty-four-bit processing takes advantage of larger addressable memory, increased number of log files, and improved performance. Thirty-two-bit versions of Exchange Server 2007 are for lab use only and are not supported in a production environment. The 32-bit management tools, however, are supported for production on 32-bit machines. Intel's Extended Memory 64 Technology (EM64T) processor technology and AMD's Opteron line of AMD64 processors are supported 64-bit processors, however Intel's Itanium IA64 processors are not supported.

With Exchange Server 2007, Microsoft committed to reducing the number of disk I/O operations per second (IOPS) that mailbox servers would need by up to 70 percent. One way they were able to accomplish this feat was by using the larger memory space available via 64-bit processing. The Exchange database process which uses the Extensible Storage Engine (ESE) is now able to cache more of the database data in memory, thus it requires less reads from the disk subsystem. Retrieval of data from memory is measured in nanoseconds (10^{-9}), whereas retrieving data from disk is measured in milliseconds (10^{-4}). The difference between 10^{-9} and 10^{-4} of a second would be a similar to comparing a 1 GHz of processing power to 10k kHz of processing power! The suggested memory sizing requirements are to have a minimum of 2GB of memory plus 5MB per mailbox. The Information Store will attempt to use as much memory as possible to cache as many operations as it can. High memory utilization can be expected on the Exchange Server 2007 computers, which is a change from Exchange Server 2003 and is expected behavior.

The page file should be set equal to the amount of physical memory installed on the computer plus an additional 10MB of memory. This is partially for crash dumps, but Exchange will also page out some of its operations to disk. If Exchange is excessively paging, however, it would require adding more physical RAM to the server to improve performance.

The amount of disk storage that is required depends on the role of the server. All servers will need 1.2GB of space for the Exchange install. Microsoft requires an additional 200MB of free space on the system drive for related components. If Unified Messaging is installed on the server, add 500MB for each language pack that will be installed. The Client Access, Hub Transport, Edge Transport, and Unified Messaging roles do not store mailboxes, so disk sizing for these servers will be less than the mailbox servers. However, remember that Hub Transport and Edge Transport servers will need space to queue mail for the duration required to sustain an outage as well as enough space to store message tracking and protocol logs. You will want to take these factors into consideration when finalizing your disk layout for these server roles.

All disk volumes should be formatted as NTFS, the screen resolution needs to be a minimum of 800 × 600, and you will need a DVD-ROM drive to access the installation media. If there isn't a DVD-ROM drive you can make the install bits available on a network drive.

The following list summarizes requirements:

- **Processor:**
  - Intel processor that supports the Intel Extended Memory 64 Technology (Intel EM64T) (The Intel Itanium IA64 processors are not supported)
  - AMD processor that supports the AMD64 platform
- **Memory:**
  - Minimum: 2 gigabytes (GB) of RAM
  - Recommended: 2GB of RAM per server plus 5 megabytes (MB) of RAM per mailbox
- **Page File:**
  - Equal to the amount of RAM in the server plus 10MB
- **Disk Space:**
  - At least 1.2GB on the drive on which you install Exchange
  - An additional 500MB of available disk space for each Unified Messaging (UM) language pack that you plan to install
  - 200MB of available disk space on the system drive
- **Optical Drive:**
  - DVD-ROM drive, local or network accessible (if installing media from a DVD)
- **Screen Resolution:**
  - 800 × 600 or higher
- **File System:**
  - NTFS

Software Requirements

Exchange Server 2007 must be installed on a 64-bit capable server that is running Windows Server 2003, Service Pack 2 x64 Edition. The Exchange installer will verify that Service Pack 2 is installed, and if it isn't the installer will not allow the installation to continue.

Exchange Server 2007 can be installed on the following operating systems:

- ❑ Windows Server 2003 SP2, Standard x64 Edition
- ❑ Windows Server 2003 SP2, Standard x64 Edition, with Multilingual User Interface Pack (MUI)
- ❑ Windows Server 2003 SP2, Enterprise x64 Edition
- ❑ Windows Server 2003 SP2, Enterprise x64 Edition, with MUI
- ❑ Windows Server 2003 R2 with SP2, Standard x64 Edition
- ❑ Windows Server 2003 R2 with SP2, Standard x64 Edition, with MUI
- ❑ Windows Server 2003 R2 with SP2, Enterprise x64 Edition
- ❑ Windows Server 2003 R2 with SP2, Enterprise x64 Edition, with MUI
- ❑ Windows Server 2008 Standard 64-bit Edition
- ❑ Windows Server 2008 Enterprise 64-bit Edition

The Management Tools can be installed on the following operating systems:

- ❑ **64-bit:**
  - ❑ Windows Vista 64-bit
  - ❑ Windows XP Professional x64 Edition
  - ❑ Any operating system that is supported for Exchange Server 2007
- ❑ **32-bit:**
  - ❑ Windows Vista 32-bit
  - ❑ Windows XP SP2 32-bit

The following software components need to be installed. Additional requirements are listed here:

- ❑ **All roles:** .NET 2.0 is required in Windows 2003 and 2008. Installing .NET Framework 3.0 in Windows 2008 is supported.
  - ❑ Windows PowerShell 1.0 is also required if installing the management tools on a non-Exchange machine.
  - ❑ Microsoft Management Console (MMC) 3.0

❑ **Mailbox:** This role provides storage of mail, public folder data, as well as voice mail and fax messages. The following are required:

   ❑ IIS

   ❑ COM+

   ❑ World Wide Web Service

❑ **Client Access Server:** Client Access Server (CAS) provides the front-end functionality for Exchange Server 2007. CAS is used for Outlook Web Access (OWA), Outlook Anywhere (previously RPC/HTTP), Autodiscover and Availability, as well as ActiveSync.

   ❑ IIS

   ❑ COM+

   ❑ World Wide Web Service

   ❑ RPC over HTTP if the CAS server will be providing Outlook Anywhere services

   ❑ ASP.NET 2.0

❑ **Unified Messaging:** Unified Messaging provides voice mail, fax, AutoAttendant, and voice access directly to the user's mailbox. This functionality can further be integrated with Office Communication Server to unleash a full suite of VoIP services for the enterprise.

   ❑ Microsoft Windows Media Encoder

   ❑ Microsoft Windows Media Audio Voice Codec

   ❑ Microsoft Core XML Services 6.0

   ❑ Cannot be installed on a server that has Microsoft Speech Server installed

❑ **Edge:** Edge services provide a non-domain SMTP server capable of message hygiene, antivirus (AV), and antispam (AS) scanning. This role retrieves data through the use of an Active Directory Application Mode (ADAM) instance, so security is further enhanced.

   ❑ ADAM (Active Directory Application Mode)

The following components must **not** be installed on any Exchange server role.

❑ NNTP (Network News Transfer Protocol)

❑ SMTP (Simple Mail Transfer Protocol)

❑ NWLink IPX/SPX/NetBios

Once suitable hardware has been obtained, preparation for the domain can begin.

Domain Requirements

Several requirements for both the domain controllers and for the domain and forest functional levels must be met in order to have a functional and sustainable Exchange organization. Installing Exchange Server 2007 in a new organization will prevent installation of previous versions of Exchange. If there is a need for previous versions of Exchange, install Exchange 2000 or 2003 first and then add Exchange

Server 2007 computers, because there is no way to install these older versions if Exchange Server 2007 was installed prior. The following list outlines domain requirements:

- ❑ **Schema Master:** Requires Windows Server 2003 SP1 or greater
- ❑ **Global Catalog Servers:** Minimum of 1 GC per site must have Windows Server 2003 SP1 or better
- ❑ **Domain Controller:** Windows Server 2003 SP1 or better
    - ❑ Required in each site
    - ❑ Required in each domain parent and child
    - ❑ Required in each domain where /PrepareLegacyExchangePermissions will be run
- ❑ **Non-English Domain Controllers:** Hotfix 919166 or Windows Server 2003 SP2
- ❑ **Active Directory Site:** For every site that has a Mailbox server, a Hub server must also be installed.
    - ❑ For every site that has a Mailbox server, and has the necessity for Outlook 2007 or Outlook Web Access client access, a CAS server must also be installed.
- ❑ **Forest Level Function:** If cross-forest trusts or forest-to-forest delegation is used, the functional level must be Windows Server 2003.
    - ❑ If free/busy information will be available to users in another forest, the functional level must be Windows Server 2003.
    - ❑ If free/busy information is not required, the forest level must be Windows Server 2000 native or better.
- ❑ **Domain Functional Level:** Windows Server 2000 native or better
- ❑ **Exchange Organization:** Native mode
- ❑ **Exchange 5.5 Servers:** Cannot exist in the same Exchange organization as Exchange Server 2007.
    - ❑ Cannot exist in the forest.
- ❑ **Exchange 2000:** Exchange 2000 SP3
    - ❑ Exchange 2000 Post-SP3 rollup kb870540
- ❑ **Exchange 2003:** Exchange 2003 SP2

Once all of the domain requirements have been satisfied, Schema preparation can begin.

Domain Preparation

When a scripted install is invoked for the first Exchange Server 2007 computer in the forest or domain, several preparatory steps must be performed prior to the actual server install. The following list of setup switches will extend the Schema, create new security groups, and confirm the presence of system objects.

Setup /PrepareLegacyExchangePermissions or Setup /pl

If there are Exchange 2000 or 2003 servers in the organization, this command should be run in each domain that contains legacy Exchange servers. If a domain is not specified, setup will attempt to reach all domains in the forest. This step is necessary for the Recipient Update Service (RUS) stamping to work. In previous editions of Exchange, the user's mailbox attributes would be created or set in Active Directory (AD) and then would be read by Exchange servers via the RUS service. For detailed information on permissions set by this switch, see the following topic in the Exchange Server 2007 help file: "Preparing Legacy Exchange Permissions."

Setup /PrepareSchema or Setup /ps

This command connects to the Schema master and applies the Exchange Server 2007 LDIF files to prepare the Schema for Exchange Server 2007 and should only be run in a forest where /PrepareAd will also be run. Manually importing the LDIF files through LDIFDE is not supported. If the /PrepareLegacyExchangePermissions was not run, /PrepareSchema attempts to run it on all domains in the forest.

Setup /PrepareAD or Setup /p

Execution of this command will check the objectVersion value for your organization to verify that the Schema has been updated. An organization name is also required in this step. Specify the org name with the /OrganizationName parameter. Once the Schema check is validated, /PrepareAD then creates the global Exchange objects, the Exchange Universal Security Groups, sets the permissions on the created objects, creates the Exchange Server 2007 Administrative Group, creates the Exchange Server 2007 Routing Group, and then creates the Unified Messaging Voice Originator contact.

The Exchange Administrative Group as well as the Exchange Routing Group cannot be renamed. Also, do not move the Exchange servers out of either of these groups. Doing so creates connectivity issues with legacy versions of Exchange and also creates an unsupportable environment. In the event that /PrepareLegacyExchangePermissions or /PrepareSchema was not run, /PrepareAD runs both of them. It is advisable, however, to run each switch independently.

Setup /PrepareDomain or Setup /pd or Setup /PrepareAllDomains or Setup /pad

When this switch is issued, permissions are set on the domain container for Exchange Servers, Exchange Organization Administrators, Authenticated Users, and Exchange Mailbox Administrators. A new global group called Exchange Install Domain Servers is created and added to the Exchange Servers USG in the root domain. This switch should be run in all domains that will have Exchange Server 2007 installed as well as in domains that contain mail-enabled users.

Once all of the preparatory commands have been issued, installation of the first Exchange Server 2007 computer can begin.

Server Installation

Many different command-line switches are available within `Setup.com`. The individual settings allow for an answer file to be used, however populating all of the data in a text file is inefficient, and does not allow for PowerShell to manipulate the values. The subsequent sections discuss all of the command-line switches used within `Setup.com`. Within each of the explanations, PowerShell is introduced to show how it can enhance the functionality of each switch.

/mode or /m

This parameter specifies how the setup command is used. There are four different setup modes:

❑ **Install:** Used for new installations. If the `/mode` parameter is not specified, setup will default to install mode.

❑ **Upgrade:** Used to upgrade from previous pre-release versions of Exchange Server 2007. In-place upgrades of RTM code are not supported through this option. However, an initial install of Exchange Server 2007 into the Exchange organization can be with SP1. It is not required to install the RTM software and then upgrade to SP1.

❑ **Uninstall:** Used to remove Exchange or a specific role.

❑ **RecoverServer:** Used to perform a disaster recovery of a server. For example, if a server crashes and is rebuilt with the same server name, this option would be invoked to rebuild the server. The server's information is read from Active Directory and Exchange would be reinstalled, and then any other role clean can occur.

To install the UM role on a new server, the command would look like this:

```
Setup /r:UM
```

Because this is an installation, setup defaults to installation mode, therefore `/mode:Install` is unnecessary.

/roles or /r

The `/roles` switch instructs the installer which Exchange roles to install or uninstall on the server. Multiple roles can be installed by using a comma-separated list. The following list provides the roles and their syntax:

❑ Client Access (CA or C)

❑ Edge Transport (ET or E)

❑ Hub (HT or H)

❑ Mailbox (MB or M)

❑ Unified Messaging (UM or U)

To install the Mailbox role on a server the command looks as follows: `Setup.com /role:M`. To remove CAS from a server the command would look like this: `Setup.com /r:c /m:uninstall`.

Windows PowerShell can be used to greatly simplify the installation of Exchange roles. Most organizations have a naming specification based on the role of the server. For example, mailbox servers are usually named MB or MBX, and CAS servers are usually CA or CAS. By using a unified naming structure, PowerShell can read the system hostname and then make a decision on what roles to install based on the server name. The following script presents the decision logic:

```
$server=[system.net.dns]::gethostname()
if ($server -like"*UM*") {"$role=U"} else
{if ($server -like"*ES*") {$role="E"} else
 {if ($server -like"*CA*") {$role="C"} else
  {if ($server -like"*HT*") {$role="H"} else
   {if ($server -like"*MB*") {$role="M"} else
    {if ($server -like"*EX*") {$role="M,H"} else
     {Write-Host "Server name does not match any known naming specification"}
    }
   }
  }
 }
}
```

This script starts by getting the server's hostname using a .NET call to request a DNS lookup on the server. The response is assigned a variable of $server. From there an if else loop is constructed to run using the like operator to search the $server variable for an expression. Based on the pattern that is matched, it will either assign a value to the $role variable or it will write to the console that it was unable to find a suitable match. Using this type of programming logic allows for system integrators, service providers, and other companies to leverage PowerShell to perform an intelligent analysis of the server name variable, and then make a decision as to what role should be installed and assigns the value to $role.

Within the setup executable there are also numerous other command-line switches that allow for a customized installation of Exchange. These switches are not necessary, however they are provided to allow the Exchange administrator to have more control over how the product is installed, how to interoperate with older versions of Exchange, and how to deal with non-default settings.

/OrganizationName or /on

The organization name parameter is used to create the new Exchange organization. This switch is used in conjunction with /PrepareAD. Once the Exchange organization has been set, this parameter is no longer used.

/TargetDir or /t

This switch is used to specify the path the installer will write the files to. If this switch is not used, by default the installer will use the default location of %programfiles%\Microsoft\Exchange Server\.

/SourceDir or /s

The only time this will be used is if the Exchange installation media location has been changed.

/UpdatesDir or /u

Specifying this parameter will instruct the installer to look for Updates.exe or *.msp files in the directory specified.

/DomainController or /dc

This switch is necessary in instances where there are Windows 2000 domain controllers in the organization. Almost all of the install operations that interact with domain controllers must use a Windows 2003 SP1 or better domain controller in order to correctly work. Use this parameter in conjunction with all of the domain preparation commands if there are Windows 2000 domain controllers in the organization. The NetBIOS name or the FQDN are acceptable values.

/AnswerFile or /af

The answer file is used to populate the various parameters within setup. It is the predecessor to using PowerShell to populate data for the installer.

/DoNotStartTransport

When the Exchange installer is complete, by default the transport service will automatically start and begin processing mail. In the event that third-party software needs to be loaded, additional configurations are to be applied, or a final configuration management audit needs to be performed before the server can begin processing mail, set the value for this switch to `true`.

/EnableLegacyOutlook

Although this switch is optional, the purpose it serves is important. Outlook 2000 and Outlook 2003 clients need public folder access. The Offline Address Book and free/busy information reside in the public folder hierarchy and older versions of Outlook require these to be present. If this switch is not used when the Mailbox role is installed, a public folder database will not be created automatically by the Exchange installer. However, a public folder database can be created manually after the installation is complete. This switch is only used for the first mailbox install in the organization. For more information on public folder database creation, see Chapter 5.

/LegacyRoutingServer

This parameter is used to denote connectivity to an Exchange 2000 or 2003 bridgehead server. If interoperability between a legacy Exchange system and Exchange Server 2007 is required, this is used to create the routing group connector.

/EnableErrorReporting

This switch is used to enable error reporting during the installation.

/NoSelfSignedCertificate

Exchange Server 2007 uses certificates for communications between devices. If there are already valid certificates installed, this parameter will bypass self-signed certificate creation. The setting is only available for UM and CAS servers.

/AdamLdapPort

Because Edge servers are not part of the domain, and are on the perimeter network, they will not have access to Active Directory to perform LDAP queries. As a result, Edge servers require an ADAM (Active Directory Application Mode) instance. By default, ADAM uses port 50389. If a different port is required, use this switch to specify another port.

/AdamSslPort

Specifies which port the Edge server should use for SSL connections to the ADAM instance.

/AddUmLanguagePack

When installing Unified Messaging the English language pack will be installed by default. If another language needs to be installed, use this switch to specify the language. Each language takes approximately 500MB of hard disk space. The following table lists the languages available for UM as well as the `.msi` installer filename.

Language	DefaultLanguage Value	Filename
Dutch	nl-NL	Umlang-nl-NL.msi
English (Australia)	en-AU	Umlang-en-AU.msi
English (Great Britain)	en-GB	Umlang-en-GB.msi
English (United States)	en-US	Umlang-en-US.msi
French	fr-FR	Umlang-fr-FR.msi
French (Canadian)	fr-CA	Umlang-fr-CA.msi
German	de-DE	Umlang-de-DE.msi
Italian	it-IT	Umlang-it-IT.msi
Japanese	ja-JP	Umlang-ja-JP.msi
Korean	ko-KR	Umlang-ko-KR.msi
Mandarin (People's Republic of China)	zh-CN	Umlang-zh-CN.msi
Mandarin (Taiwan)	zh-TW	Umlang-zh-TW.msi
Portuguese (Brazil)	pt-BR	Umlang-pt-BR.msi
Spanish	es-ES	Umlang-es-ES.msi
Spanish (Mexico)	es-US	Umlang-es-US.msi
Swedish	sv-SE	Umlang-sv-SE.msi

/RemoveUmLanguagePack

Using this option will remove the specified language pack. The preceding table lists the UM language packs.

Additional Setup Switches Available for Clustered Installs

Clustered installations require more information and as a result more command-line switches. The following command-line switches provide the Exchange administrator the ability to declare the cluster attributes such as the name of the Clustered Mailbox Server (CMS), the CMSIPAddress, and the location of the CMSDataPath. These switches allow the Exchange administrator to further enjoy the benefits of PowerShell scripting and use these switches to provide a base to build cluster scripts against.

- ❑ /NewCms: When creating a new Clustered Mailbox Server, this switch instructs the installer that a new clustered mailbox installation is being performed.

- ❑ /CMSName or /cn: All Clustered Mailbox Servers must have Clustered Mailbox Server names. This switch takes the parameter specified and uses it to create the Clustered Mailbox Server name.

- ❑ /CMSIPAddress or /cip: Every Clustered Mailbox Server must have a unique IP address for clients to connect to. This switch parameter specifies what IP address should be assigned to the CMS.

- ❑ /CMSSharedStorage or /css: Cluster information should be stored on the shared disks. If this switch is selected the installer will interrogate the disks to validate whether the data path is a shared disk resource.

- ❑ /CMSDataPath or /cdp: This switch specifies the location of the shared disk. The location specified has to be an already created folder on the target drive. Exchange Server 2007 will not install directly on the root of a logical drive.

- ❑ /DomainController or /dc: Optional parameter used to specify the domain controller to use during installation.

Disaster Recovery

A full discussion of disaster recovery of Exchange Server 2007 is beyond the scope of this book. However, a relevant discussion of when to properly use the recover server feature, supported uses, and what to expect after a recovery is presented here.

There are several reasons why an Exchange server would need to be rebuilt. For example, the physical hardware of the server could have failed, the operating system could have been corrupted beyond repair, and virus activity or even operator error may require a bare metal restore of the system. Using the recover server feature to migrate certain roles to new hardware, as long as the server name stays the same, is also acceptable.

Do not use the recover server mode as a means to repair a failed installation. The recovery mechanism uses data that is stored in Active Directory to re-create the necessary configuration parameters on the server. If an installation never successfully completes, the data in Active Directory is not complete and a recovery will only further complicate the problem. If the Exchange server that is to be restored has the Edge role installed, using the recover server feature is also not supported. The Edge server's configuration is not stored in Active Directory, so upon recovery there would be no data available to recover! If the server you wish to recover has had its data deleted from Active Directory, recover server will not work. Also do not use the recover server feature to modify cluster configuration settings.

Once the recover server process is complete, there may be instances where additional reconfiguration may be necessary. The following bullet points describe some of the additional configuration options that may be necessary before the server is fully operational:

❑ If any customization has been done to Exchange virtual directories in IIS, the customizations will need to be reapplied.

❑ Any third-party software that is used in conjunction with Exchange will need to be reinstalled.

❑ If a mailbox server contained a public folder database, a new public folder database will need to be created and replication of public folder data will have to take place.

❑ Hub servers may need any queued messages that were saved to be restored.

❑ Hub servers may need their connectors reconfigured.

❑ Dial tone restores require users to create new PINs as well as their greetings. Both of these features are stored in the Exchange database and not in Active Directory.

❑ UM servers need any customized WAV files, prompts, or publishing point restored.

❑ Edge server reconfiguration can be simplified if the Edge server's XML file is available. The Edge server can then run `ImportEdgeConfig.ps1` to import the XML file, and use its settings to reconfigure the role. After the configuration is complete, run `Start-EdgeSynchronization` to force an update of the data in ADAM.

Deployment Scenarios

In order to get the most out of this book, it is important to understand how all the roles tie together and what the environment should look like. With recent advances in virtualization technology, entire environments can be created in a virtual environment. In the past this required an expansive amount of hardware to re-create the network and all of the server components. The scenarios are to be used as a starting point to help assess where the servers should go, how many servers are needed, and what roles are needed within the organization.

Microsoft recommends that server roles be installed in a particular order. Once all of the Schema and domain preparation has been completed, the Exchange roles should be deployed in the following order:

1. Client Access Server role

2. Hub Transport server role

3. Mailbox server role

4. Unified Messaging server role

5. Edge server (this role can be deployed during any step, but will not be functional until after the Hub Transport role has been installed)

Single Server Deployment

For small organizations a single server containing the Client Access, Hub Transport, and Mailbox server roles will be sufficient. The Exchange Server 2007 computer will be new to the existing Exchange organization or could be a brand new deployment of Exchange. If there is an existing Exchange 2003 server, a new Exchange Server 2007 computer will have to be deployed to the organization, and mailboxes and data will have to be migrated to it. A single server will work in a single site Active Directory configuration. It does not provide any level of redundancy or high availability, but is useful in a small office. In the event that the business grows, additional Exchange servers can be deployed, and Exchange roles can be migrated to the new servers. To deploy a single server using this scenario, the following tasks would have to be completed to have a base installation:

- ❏   Setup /PrepareLegacyExchangePermissions
- ❏   Setup /PrepareSchema
- ❏   Setup /PrepareAD
- ❏   Setup /PrepareDomain
- ❏   Setup /r:C,H,M,U

The preceding list includes each of the preparatory steps that are necessary to prepare Active Directory for the first Exchange Server 2007 installation. By specifying the CAS, Hub, Mailbox and Unified Messaging role (C, H, M, U) through the role (/r:) switch, this server will be able to perform all the roles on a single server. This deployment also includes permissions compatible with pre-2007 clients. One of the benefits of using this type of deployment is that it provides a single server that can be used to test the functionality of Exchange Server 2007 against your environment. This type of deployment is also advantageous for smaller companies that do not want to deal with the additional cost of having a dedicated server for each role. By default if the Management Tools are not installed on the server, the installer will also install them.

Standard Deployment

Exchange Server 2003 had a simple configuration wherein a server was basically a front-end or back-end server. Front-end servers were used to provide the entry point of Simple Mail Transport Server (SMTP) messages into the organization, OWA access, ActiveSync connectivity, as well as RPC/HTTP end point termination. Exchange Server 2007 has spilt this into two separate roles to provide better performance and increased security: Edge servers and Client Access Servers. Figure 3-1 shows the topology of a standard deployment. This type of deployment would be for single site. If additional sites are added but are too small to warrant their own Exchange servers, the remote offices would just connect to the CAS and mailbox servers in this site. A single site is advantageous to reduce complexity and hardware costs, but in the event of a network or site outage all messaging services will be impacted.

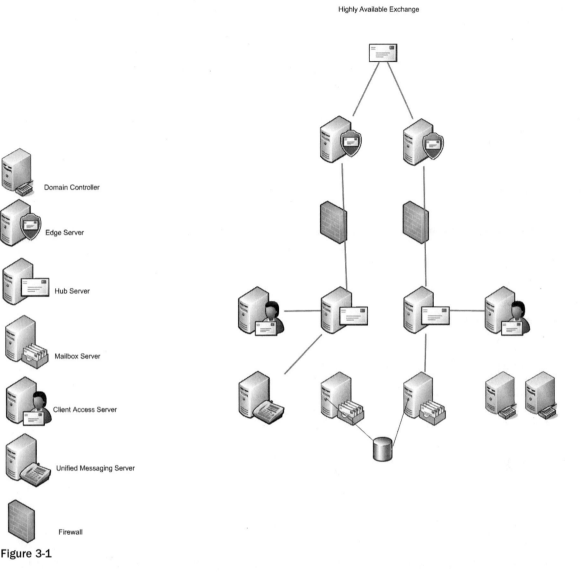

Figure 3-1

In a standard deployment a company would have two Edge servers deployed to provide the SMTP connectivity to the Internet. The Edge servers will perform the message hygiene functions, mail relay, and filtering. A minimum of two servers are required to provide redundant connections for internal and external message flow.

The user-experience pieces — ActiveSync, OWA, and RPC/HTTP — have been rebranded and packaged into the Client Access Server role. The CAS role does not provide any message routing or message management features. It is used to allow users of Outlook Anywhere, ActiveSync, and OWA a point of presence. It also performs the Autodiscover and Availability service. In a standard deployment there would be two CAS servers in the organization. Unlike Edge servers, CAS can be deployed with other roles on the same server.

Whenever a message is sent within an Exchange Server 2007 organization, it must leave the mailbox server and be routed to a Hub Transport server. Because of this, message scanning has been removed from the Information Store to increase stability of the database to the Hub Transport role. As a result of this, the Hub Transport role should also be deployed in a two server minimum configuration. This way in the event of a Hub server maintenance or if the Hub server is unavailable, there is another Hub Transport available. The Hub role can also be installed on any Exchange server that is not an Edge Transport or part of an MSCS cluster server.

Depending on the criticality of users being able to access their mailboxes, several options are available for the Mailbox role. A standard deployment may use only one mailbox server. If a high-availability option is required, Single Copy Cluster (SCC) or Continuous Content Replication (CCR) can be used to deliver a higher level of uptime.

Unified Messaging is a new feature that has been added to Exchange Server 2007. In a standard deployment, your organization may or may not use this feature. It is not required in order for your environment to run, however the increased functionality and integration with Office Communication Server allow for a tighter collaboration of messaging technology. With a standard deployment, one UM server should be deployed to every site. If UM is a key piece of technology within the organization, multiple servers can be deployed and have membership in multiple dial plans. UM can coexist with all other roles except Edge, and cannot be installed on an MSCS cluster.

Complex Deployments

A large deployment can be one that spans multiple physical sites, multiple domains, or even multiple forests. Exchange server placement is highly dependent upon roles and user presence. Edge Transport servers can be geographically dispersed to allow for site redundancy. Hub Transport, Client Access, and mailbox servers can be consolidated to just one data center or geographically dispersed. Server placement depends upon the network infrastructure, the logical boundaries of the domain, and user need. Figure 3-2 shows a multisite, multidomain configuration. The `Exchangeexchange.local` forest has two child domains, US and EU. There are sites two sites within each child domain. Edge servers are deployed outside of the domain at each of the large sites. A failure at one site will not affect the ability to send and receive email from the Internet for the entire company. As required for message routing and for user accessibility, wherever there are mailbox servers there are also CAS and Hub servers. Smaller sites such as sites 2 and 4 require only a global catalog server at the site. These smaller sites connect to the larger office either via Outlook Anywhere, or natively through MAPI. Smaller office deployments may be numerous and each remote office may not be able to justify the cost of having Exchange servers at every site. A deployment of this model results in a hub and spoke topology. When a smaller office grows in capacity to the point where it needs its own Exchange, then new Exchange servers can be configured, and the user mail migrated.

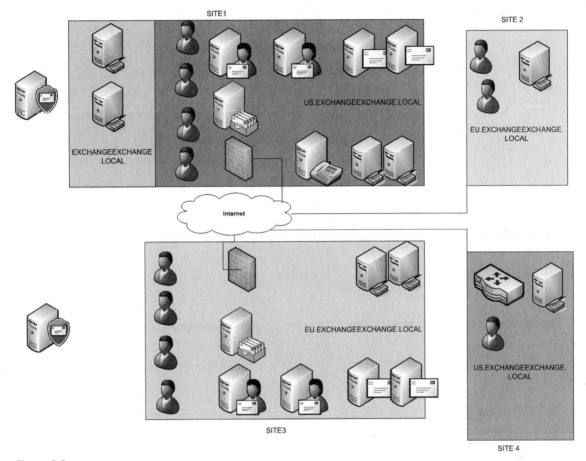

SITE1

SITE 2

US.EXCHANGEEXCHANGE.LOCAL

EU.EXCHANGEEXCHANGE.
LOCAL

EXCHANGEEXCHANGE
.LOCAL

Internet

EU.EXCHANGEEXCHANGE.LOCAL

US.EXCHANGEEXCHANGE.
LOCAL

SITE3

SITE 4

Figure 3-2

Summary

This chapter focused on preparing for and deploying Exchange Server 2007. Exchange Server 2007 is the first Microsoft product to ship that is 64-bit only. The hardware now must be 64-bit capable, just as the software. One of the goals of Exchange Server 2007 was to reduce the overall I/O to the disk subsystem. Taking that goal into consideration along with the 64-bit memory addressing scheme, more objects are now cached into memory on mailbox servers, requiring mailbox servers to have more memory but allowing for less expansive disk systems.

Server roles have evolved from prior editions as well. CAS servers have an increased role over their previous Exchange 2003 front-end counterpart. Just like front-end servers did, CAS handles all of the web-based user connections. However, CAS also handles the new Autodiscover and Availability service. This service is critical because it replaces the free/busy public folder and it also serves as an automatic configuration tool. The hub takes on an increased role due to the fact that all messages, even those sent to users on the same mailbox server, now must pass through the Hub server. If increased security is needed, Edge servers can be deployed to handle the Internet point of presence for SMTP for the organization. Because the servers are not on the domain, in the event of compromise, the attacker does not automatically obtain the ability to have permissions in AD. Though Unified Messaging is not new technology, incorporating it natively into an Exchange product is. This allows for tighter collaboration between Unified Messaging and Office Communication Server.

With the introduction of roles that are installed as a command-line switch, the setup and install has changed considerably from previous editions. However, this considerably reduces the number of extra services installed on a server. Setup includes new switches to allow for backward compatibility of clients as well as to give the administrator the ability to perform a higher degree of customization during install.

Scenarios were provided as a tool to help examine how your organization will look when deploying Exchange Server 2007. Most companies will be performing a migration from a previous edition, and depending on whether it is a 5.5 or 2003 migration, overall planning, scope, and time frame can change considerably.

Working with User and Group Objects

In Exchange Server 2000/2003, Exchange mailbox user objects are created in Active Directory and thereafter can be viewed in Exchange System Manager. The only operations that can be performed on these objects from the Exchange System Manager are to purge, reconnect, or run Exchange tasks. Available tasks performed by the Exchange Tasks Wizard are limited to move mailbox, delete mailbox, and configure Exchange features. No other Recipient type or group can be managed in the Exchange System Manager. Moreover, it is difficult to distinguish Recipient types simply by the object's icon in Active Directory Users and Computers.

In Exchange Server 2007, however, creation and management of Recipient and group objects including their Exchange-related properties have been incorporated into the Exchange Management Console and Exchange Management Shell. The Exchange Management Shell enables you to carry out various operations on Recipient and group objects, some of which are not available in the Management Console. In addition, distinguishing Recipient types is easy in Exchange Server 2007 because explicit Recipient Types properties have been added. Their icon in the Exchange Management Console makes them easy to recognize or you can look at the `RecipientTypeDetails` property for the Recipient in Exchange Management Shell.

At the end of this chapter, you will be able to identify the Recipient and group object types associated with Exchange Server 2007. You will also become familiar with the Exchange Management Shell cmdlets that operate on these objects, differentiate between these object types, and carry out common tasks associated with these objects in the Exchange Management Shell.

This chapter covers:

❑   Recipient scope in the Exchange Management Shell

❑   All available Recipient types in Exchange Server 2007

❑ Creating and modifying Exchange Server 2007 Recipient types including features introduced in Service Pack 1

❑ Bulk management scenarios

Working with Recipients

People and resources are at the core of any messaging system. Ultimately, any server operation is geared toward efficiently delivering a message to a mail Recipient, which could be to an individual, public folder, or designated resource.

Although messages are ultimately delivered to people or resources, the term *Recipients* actually refers to mail-enabled Active Directory Service objects. These objects in themselves do not store messages sent to them, neither are the messages stored in Active Directory; rather, the messages are stored on an Exchange Server mailbox or public folder. Operations performed on these objects by the Microsoft Exchange Management Shell cmdlets affect how messages are sent or received.

You first give attention to the Recipient scope, which can affect results you obtain while working with the Exchange Management Shell.

Recipient Scope in the Exchange Management Shell

While working with user and group objects in the Exchange Management Shell, be sure to keep in mind the Recipient scope of the Exchange Management Shell. The *Recipient scope* refers to the specified portion of the Active Directory Service hierarchy that the Exchange Management Shell uses for Recipient management. When you set the Recipient scope to a specific location within Active Directory, you can view and manage all Recipients stored in that location and all of the containers under it.

You may need to change the scope to view all Exchange Recipients or objects in the forest or Recipients in other domains or organizational units. If you attempt to retrieve or modify objects outside your current Recipient scope, you may receive errors. For example, if the Recipient scope of the Exchange Management Shell is set to a specific OU, `ExchangeExchange.local/ExOU`, say, attempting to create a new user or group in the Users Container that is outside the current Recipient scope would result in the error shown in Figure 4-1. Notice that the Exchange Management Shell scope is set to `ExchangeExchange.local/ExOU`.

Figure 4-1

Subsequently, changing the Recipient scope to the domain using the $AdminSessionADSettings variable enables you to successfully create the group as shown in Figure 4-2. Minimum permissions required are Exchange View-Only Administrator and member of the Local Administrators group on the Exchange Server.

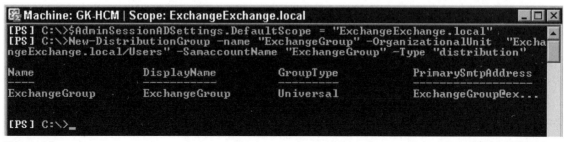

Figure 4-2

When the Recipient scope is changed in the Exchange Management Shell, this variable is retained until the Exchange Management Shell is closed. The default settings are restored the next time the Exchange Management Shell is opened. By default, the Exchange Management Shell starts with the Recipient scope at the domain level. Neither the user account that is being used nor the Exchange servers being managed has bearing on the default value of the Recipient scope. Changing the Recipient scope in the Exchange Management Shell changes the set of Recipients that are returned for the Get- cmdlets of the Recipient.

You can view or modify the Recipient scope by using available fields stored in the $AdminSessionADSettings variable, as shown in the following table:

Field	Description
ViewEntireForest	By default this field is set to $false. Setting it to $True enables you to view and manage all Recipients in the forest using the Exchange Management Shell. To view and manage all Recipients in the forest, set this field to $True by running: $AdminSessionADSettings.ViewEntireForest = $True
DefaultScope	If the ViewEntireForest field is set to $True, the Exchange Management Shell ignores this field. It is set to null. This field stores the Recipient scope for the current session of the Exchange Management Shell in canonical format. For example, if the Recipient scope is set to the ExOU OU in the ExchangeExchange.local domain, the value for DefaultScope will be ExchangeExchange.local/ExOU.

Table continued on following page

Field	Description
PreferredGlobalCatalog	If this field is specified, and if ViewEntireForest is set to $true, the Exchange Management Shell uses the specified global catalog server to query for Recipients. Exchange automatically selects a suitable global catalog server if the PreferredGlobalCatalog is not set.
	You can set a preferred global catalog by running:
	`$AdminSession ADSettings.PreferredDomainControllers = "AD01.ExchangeExchange.local"`
ConfigurationDomainController	This field specifies the domain controller that the Exchange Management Shell uses to read the Exchange configuration information.
PreferredDomainControllers	If this field is specified, and if ViewEntireForest is set to $false, the Exchange Management Shell uses the specified domain controllers to query for Recipients. However, only one domain controller can be specified per domain. If this field is not specified, Exchange automatically selects a suitable domain controller. You can specify multiple domain controllers if the Recipient scope spans more than one domain or ViewEntireForest is set to $true.
	For example, run the following to set the Recipient scope to the entire forest and configure multiple preferred domain controllers as global catalog servers:

	`$AdminSessionADSettings.ViewEntireForest = $True$`
	`AdminSessionADSettings.PreferredGlobalCatalog = "AD01.ExchangeExchange.local"`
	`$AdminSessionADSettings.PreferredGlobalCatalog = "AD02.ExchangeExchange.local"`

Next, you take a closer look at the Recipient and group types available in Exchange Server 2007.

User and Group Object Types

An Exchange Recipient or group object is an Active Directory Services user, contact, or group object that has associated Exchange mail or mailbox properties that enable receipt or delivery of mail. Before reviewing the Exchange Management Shell operations in creating or modifying user and group objects, it would be helpful to identify these object types.

This section covers the following cmdlets for identifying user and group object types available in Exchange Server 2007:

- ❏ `Get-Recipient`
- ❏ `Get-User`
- ❏ `Get-Mailbox`
- ❏ `Get-MailUser`
- ❏ `Get-Contact`
- ❏ `Get-MailContact`
- ❏ `Get-Group`
- ❏ `Get-DistributionGroup`
- ❏ `Get-DynamicDistributionGroup`
- ❏ `Get-OrganizationConfig`
- ❏ `Get-MailPublicFolder`

Get-Recipient

This is perhaps one of the most commonly used cmdlets for returning Recipient objects and their attributes in Active Directory. The list of parameters is shown here. For a detailed list run the following in the Exchange Management Shell: `get-help Get-Recipient -detailed`.

```
Get-Recipient [-Identity <RecipientIdParameter>] [-Credential <PSCredential>]
[-DomainController <Fqdn>] [-OrganizationalUnit <OrganizationalUnitIdParameter>]
[-ReadFromDomainController <SwitchParameter>] [-RecipientType <RecipientType[]>]
[-RecipientTypeDetails <RecipientTypeDetails[]>] [-ResultSize <Unlimited>] [-SortBy
<String>] [<CommonParameters>]
Get-Recipient [-Credential <PSCredential>] [-DomainController <Fqdn>]
[-IgnoreDefaultScope <SwitchParameter>] [-OrganizationalUnit <OrganizationalUnit
IdParameter>] [-ReadFromDomainController <SwitchParameter>] [-RecipientPrev
iewFilter <String>] [-RecipientType <RecipientType[]>] [-RecipientTypeDetails
<RecipientTypeDetails[]>] [-ResultSize <Unlimited>] [-SortBy <String>]
[<CommonParameters>]

Get-Recipient [-Anr <String>] [-Credential <PSCredential>] [-DomainController
<Fqdn>] [-IgnoreDefaultScope <SwitchParameter>] [-OrganizationalUnit
<OrganizationalUnitIdParameter>] [-ReadFromDomainController <SwitchParameter>]
[-RecipientType <RecipientType[]>] [-RecipientTypeDetails <RecipientTypeDetails[]>]
[-ResultSize <Unlimited>] [-SortBy <String>] [<CommonParameters>]
```

This cmdlet does not have any required parameters and running it with no parameters returns a complete list of all Recipients in the organization. It, however, requires the logged-on user to be a member of the Exchange Recipient Administrator Group and belong to the local Administrators group on the computer.

Some key parameters to note include:

❑ RecipientType <RecipientType[]>: Filters to specify the type of Recipient to return. At least eight RecipientTypes can be specified, which are discussed later in the chapter.

❑ RecipientTypeDetails <RecipientTypeDetails[]>: Exchange Server 2007 further distinguishes the Recipient types returned by this parameter. Recipient types are divided into Recipient types and subtypes. For example, the type UserMailbox represents a user account in Active Directory with an associated mailbox. Because there are several mailbox types, each mailbox type is identified by the RecipientTypeDetails parameter. At least 14 RecipientTypeDetails are available to distinguish between Recipient types.

❑ Anr <String>: Specifies a string on which to perform an ambiguous name resolution (ANR) search. By default it searches for CommonName, DisplayName, FirstName, LastName, and Alias.

❑ Credential <PSCredential>: Prompts the user for a password to access Active Directory.

❑ Filter <String>: This is an important parameter. Sometimes you may want to return just a subset of Recipients or Recipients matching a specified criterion. Use the Filter parameter to specify one or more attributes used to restrict the Recipients that are returned by the query. It cannot be used in conjunction with the Anr parameter.

❑ Identity <RecipientIdParameter>: Identifies the Recipient and can use any of the following values: GUID, Domain\Account, UserPrincipalName (UPN), LegacyExchangeDN, SMTP Address, Name, or Alias.

❑ ResultSize <Unlimited>: The ResultSize parameter specifies the maximum number of results to return. If you want to return all Recipients that match the filter, use "unlimited" for the value of this parameter. The default value is 1,000.

Get-Mailbox

This cmdlet is used to view mailbox objects and their attributes on all Exchange Servers in the organization when no parameter is specified. No parameter is required. The list of parameters is shown here. For a detailed list run the following in the Exchange Management Shell: get-help Get-Mailbox -detailed.

```
Get-Mailbox [-Identity <MailboxIdParameter>] [-Credential <PSCredential>]
[-DomainController<Fqdn>] [-OrganizationalUnit <OrganizationalUnitIdParameter>]
[ReadFromDomainController <SwitchParameter>]
[-RecipientTypeDetails<RecipientTypeDetails[]>] [-ResultSize <Unlimited>] [-SortBy
<String>] [<CommonParameters>]
Get-Mailbox [-Credential <PSCredential>] [-DomainController <Fqdn>]
[-IgnoreDefaultScope <SwitchParameter>] [-OrganizationalUnit
<OrganizationalUnitIdParameter>] [-ReadFromDomainController <SwitchParameter>]
[-RecipientTypeDetails <RecipientTypeDetails[]>] [-ResultSize <Unlimited>] [-Server
<ServerIdParameter>] [-SortBy <String>] [<CommonParameters>]

Get-Mailbox [-Credential <PSCredential>] [-Database <DatabaseIdParameter>]
[-DomainController <Fqdn>] [-IgnoreDefaultScope <SwitchParameter>]
[-OrganizationalUnit <OrganizationalUnitIdParameter>] [-ReadFromDomainController
<SwitchParameter>] [-RecipientTypeDetails <RecipientTypeDetails[]>] [-ResultSize
<Unlimited>] [-SortBy <String>] [<CommonParameters>]
```

To accurately evaluate the current storage quota status using the `Get-Mailbox` cmdlet, it is necessary to look at the `UseDatabaseQuotaDefaults` property in addition to the `ProhibitSendQuota`, `ProhibitSendReceiveQuota`, and `IssueWarningQuota` properties. A value of `True` for the `UseDatabaseQuotaDefaults` property means that the per-mailbox settings are ignored and the mailbox database limits are used. If this property is set to `True` and the `ProhibitSendQuota`, `ProhibitSendReceiveQuota`, and `IssueWarningQuota` properties are set to unlimited, the mailbox does not have unlimited size. Instead, you must reference the mailbox database storage limits to see what the limits for the mailbox are. A value of `False` for the `UseDatabaseQuotaDefaults` property means that the per-mailbox settings are used.

Some key parameters to note include:

❑ `RecipientTypeDetails <RecipientTypeDetails[]>`: Exchange Server 2007 further distinguishes the Recipient types returned by this parameter. Recipient types are divided into Recipient types and subtypes. For example, the type `UserMailbox` represents a user account in Active Directory with an associated mailbox. Because there are several mailbox types, each mailbox type is identified by the `RecipientTypeDetails` parameter. There are six `RecipientTypeDetails` that can be specified with this cmdlet.

❑ `Server <ServerIdParameter>`: The `Server` parameter specifies an individual server and is used to limit the results returned. Only mailboxes on the specified server are returned. The CommonName of the server can be used.

❑ `Database <DatabaseIdParameter>`: As with the `Server` parameter, the `Database` parameter specifies the database from which to get the mailbox. The following values can be specified: GUID of the database, Database name, Server name\database name, Server name\storage group\database name.

❑ `Credential <PSCredential>`: If specified the user is prompted for a password to access Active Directory.

❑ `Filter <String>`: This is an important parameter. Sometimes you may want to return just a subset of Recipients or Recipients matching a specified criterion. Use the `Filter` parameter to specify one or more attributes used to restrict the Recipients that are returned by the query. It cannot be used in conjunction with the `Database` parameter.

❑ `Identity <MailboxIdParameter>`: The `Identity` parameter identifies the mailbox and can use any of the following values: GUID, Domain\Account, Distinguished Name (DN), UserPrincipalName (UPN), LegacyExchangeDN, SMTP Address, Name, or Alias.

❑ `SortBy <String>`: The `SortBy` parameter specifies the attribute by which to sort the results. The results will be sorted in ascending order specifying one of the following attributes: Alias, Display name or Name,

Get-MailContact

This cmdlet returns the list of mail contacts and their attributes in Active Directory. The list of parameters is shown here. For a detailed list run the following in the Exchange Management Shell: `get-help Get-MailContact -detailed`.

```
Get-MailContact [-Identity <MailContactIdParameter>] [-Credential <PSCredential>]
[-DomainController <Fqdn>] [-OrganizationalUnit <OrganizationalUnitIdParameter>]
[-ReadFromDomainController <SwitchParameter>] [-RecipientTypeDetails
<RecipientTypeDetails[]>] [-ResultSize <Unlimited>] [-SortBy <String>]
[<CommonParameters>]
Get-MailContact [-Credential <PSCredential>] [-DomainController <Fqdn>] [-Filter
<String>] [-IgnoreDefaultScope <SwitchParameter>] [-OrganizationalUnit
<OrganizationalUnitIdParameter>] [-ReadFromDomainController <SwitchParameter>]
[-RecipientTypeDetails <RecipientTypeDetails[]>] [-ResultSize <Unlimited>] [-SortBy
<String>] [<CommonParameters>]
```

Some key parameters to note include:

❑   `RecipientTypeDetails <RecipientTypeDetails[]>`: Exchange Server 2007 further
distinguishes the Recipient types returned by this parameter. Recipient types are divided into
Recipient types and subtypes. For example, the type `UserMailbox` represents a user account
in Active Directory with an associated mailbox. Because there are several mailbox types,
each mailbox type is identified by the `RecipientTypeDetails` parameter. Only two
`RecipientTypeDetails` are available to distinguish between contact types.

❑   `Credential <PSCredential>`: If specified the user is prompted for a password to access
Active Directory.

❑   `Filter <String>`: This is an important parameter. Sometimes you may want to return just a
subset of Recipients or Recipients matching a specified criterion. Use the `Filter` parameter to
specify one or more attributes used to restrict the Recipients that are returned by the query. It
cannot be used in conjunction with the `Anr` parameter.

❑   `Identity <MailContactIdParameter>`: The `Identity` parameter identifies the contact and
can use any of the following values: ADObjectID, GUID, DistinguishedName, UserPrincipal-
Name (UPN), LegacyDN, E-mail Address, or Alias.

Get-Group

This cmdlet queries for existing groups in Active Directory. The list of parameters is shown here. For a
detailed list run the following in the Exchange Management Shell: `get-help Get-Group -detailed`.

```
Get-Group [-Identity <GroupIdParameter>] [-Credential <PSCredential>]
[-DomainController <Fqdn>] [-OrganizationalUnit <OrganizationalUnitIdParameter>]
[-ReadFromDomainController <SwitchParameter>] [-RecipientTypeDetails
<RecipientTypeDetails[]>] [-ResultSize <Unlimited>] [-SortBy <String>]
[<CommonParameters>]
Get-Group [-Credential <PSCredential>] [-DomainController <Fqdn>] [-Filter
<String>] [-OrganizationalUnit <OrganizationalUnitIdParameter>]
[-ReadFromDomainController <SwitchParameter>] [-RecipientTypeDetails
<RecipientTypeDetails []>] [-ResultSize <Unlimited>] [-SortBy <String>]
[<CommonParameters>]
Get-Group [-Anr <String>] [-Credential <PSCredential>] [-DomainController <Fqdn>]
[-OrganizationalUnit <OrganizationalUnitIdParameter>] [-ReadFromDomainController
<SwitchParameter>] [-RecipientTypeDetails <RecipientTypeDetails[]>]
[-ResultSize <Unlimited>] [-SortBy <String>] [<CommonParameters>]
```

Some key parameters to note include:

❑ `RecipientTypeDetails <RecipientTypeDetails[]>`: Exchange Server 2007 further distinguishes the Recipient types returned by this parameter. Recipient types are divided into Recipient types and subtypes. Five `RecipientTypeDetails` can be specified with this cmdlet. These include `MailEnabledContact`, `MailEnabledForestContact`, `NonuniversalGroup`, `UniversalDistributionGroup`, and `UniversalSecurityGroup`.

❑ `ReadFromDomainController <SwitchParameter>`: The `ReadFromDomainController` parameter specifies that the user information is read from a domain controller in the user's domain. If you set the Recipient scope to include all Recipients in the forest, and if you do not use this parameter, it is possible that the user information is read from a global catalog with outdated information. If you use this parameter, multiple reads might be necessary to get the information. By default, the Recipient scope is set to the domain that hosts your Exchange servers.

❑ `DomainController <fqdn>`: This parameter specifies the `fqdn` of the domain controller you query against to retrieve the data from Active Directory.

❑ `Credential <PSCredential>`: The `Credential` parameter specifies the account to use to read the Active Directory Service. This is especially useful when specifying the global catalog. The password should be requested in a secure manner.

❑ `Identity <MailboxIdParameter>`: The `Identity` parameter identifies the mailbox and can use any of the following values: GUID, Domain\Account, Distinguished Name (DN), UserPrincipalName (UPN), LegacyDN, or Alias.

Get-DistributionGroup

This cmdlet queries for existing Distribution Groups in Active Directory. These groups could be either Distribution Groups used to send mails to multiple Recipients that match a specified filter or Security Groups used to assign permissions to resources for multiple users that match a specified filter. The list of parameters is shown here. For a detailed list run the following in the Exchange Management Shell: `get-help Get-DistributionGroup -detailed`.

```
Get-DistributionGroup [-Identity <DistributionGroupIdParameter>] [-Credential
<PSCredential>] [-DomainController <Fqdn>] [-ManagedBy
<GeneralRecipientIdParameter>] [-OrganizationalUnit
<OrganizationalUnitIdParameter>] [-ReadFromDomainController <SwitchParameter>]
[-RecipientTypeDetails <RecipientTypeDetails[]>] [-ResultSize <Unlimited>] [-SortBy
<String>] [<CommonParameters>]
Get-DistributionGroup [-Credential <PSCredential>] [-DomainController <Fqdn>]
[-Filter <String>] [-ManagedBy <GeneralRecipientIdParameter>] [-OrganizationalUnit
<OrganizationalUnitIdParameter>] [-ReadFromDomainController <SwitchParameter>]
[-RecipientTypeDetails <RecipientTypeDetails[]>] [-ResultSize <Unlimited>] [-SortBy
<String>] [<CommonParameters>]
Get-DistributionGroup [-Anr <String>] [-Credential <PSCredential>]
```

(continued)

(continued)

```
[-DomainController<Fqdn>] [-ManagedBy <GeneralRecipientIdParameter>]
[-OrganizationalUnit <OrganizationalUnitIdParameter>] [-ReadFromDomainController
<SwitchParameter>] [-RecipientTypeDetails <RecipientTypeDetails[]>] [-ResultSize
<Unlimited>] [-SortBy <String>] [<CommonParameters>]
```

Some key parameters to note include:

❑ `RecipientTypeDetails <RecipientTypeDetails[]>`: Exchange Server 2007 further distinguishes the group types returned by this parameter. Three `RecipientTypeDetails` can be specified with this cmdlet. These include: `MailEnabledNonuniversalGroup`, `MailEnabledUniversalDistributionGroup`, and `MailEnabledUniversalSecurityGroup`.

❑ `ReadFromDomainController <SwitchParameter>`: The `ReadFromDomainController` parameter specifies that the user information is read from a domain controller in the user's domain. If you set the Recipient scope to include all Recipients in the forest, and if you do not use this parameter, it is possible that the user information is read from a global catalog with out-dated information. If you use this parameter, multiple reads might be necessary to get the information. By default, the Recipient scope is set to the domain that hosts your Exchange servers.

❑ `DomainController <fqdn>`: This parameter specifies the `fqdn` of the domain controller you query against to retrieve the data from Active Directory.

❑ `Credential <PSCredential>`: The `Credential` parameter specifies the account to use to read the Active Directory Service. This is especially useful when specifying the global catalog. The password should be requested in a secure manner.

❑ `Filter <String>`: The `Filter` parameter indicates the `OPath` filter used to filter Recipients. We discuss `OPath` further later in the chapter.

❑ `Identity <MailboxIdParameter>`: The `Identity` parameter identifies the mailbox and can use any of the following values: GUID, Domain\Account, Distinguished Name (DN), UserPrincipalName (UPN), LegacyDN, or Alias.

Get-DynamicDistributionGroup

This cmdlet queries for existing Dynamic Distribution Groups in Active Directory and retrieves their settings. One key point to note with this cmdlet is that it does not have the `RecipientTypeDetails` parameter. The list of parameters is shown here. For a detailed list run the following in the Exchange Management Shell: `get-help Get-DynamicDistributionGroup -detailed`.

```
Get-DynamicDistributionGroup [-Identity <DynamicGroupIdParameter>] [-Credential
<PSCredential>] [-DomainController <Fqdn>] [-IgnoreDefaultScope <SwitchParameter>]
[-ManagedBy <GeneralRecipientIdParameter>] [-OrganizationalUnit
<OrganizationalUnitIdParameter>] [-ReadFromDomainController <SwitchParameter>]
[-ResultSize <Unlimited>] [-SortBy <String>] [<CommonParameters>]

Get-DynamicDistributionGroup [-Credential <PSCredential>] [-DomainController
<Fqdn>] [-Filter <String>] [-IgnoreDefaultScope <SwitchParameter>] [-ManagedBy
```

```
                  <GeneralRecipientIdParameter>] [-OrganizationalUnit
                  <OrganizationalUnitIdParameter>] [-ReadFromDomainController <SwitchParameter>]
                  [-ResultSize<Unlimited>] [-SortBy <String>] [<CommonParameters>]

                  Get-DynamicDistributionGroup [-Anr <String>] [-Credential <PSCredential>]
                  [-DomainController <Fqdn>] [-IgnoreDefaultScope <SwitchParameter>] [-ManagedBy
                  <GeneralRecipientIdParameter>] [-OrganizationalUnit
                  <OrganizationalUnitIdParameter>] [-ReadFromDomainController <SwitchParameter>]
                  [-ResultSize <Unlimited>] [-SortBy <String>] [<CommonParameters>]
```

Some key parameters to note include:

❑   `ReadFromDomainController <SwitchParameter>`: The `ReadFromDomainController` parameter specifies that the user information is read from a domain controller in the user's domain. If you set the Recipient scope to include all Recipients in the forest, and if you do not use this parameter, it is possible that the user information is read from a global catalog with outdated information. If you use this parameter, multiple reads might be necessary to get the information. By default, the Recipient scope is set to the domain that hosts your Exchange servers.

❑   `DomainController <fqdn>`: This parameter specifies the `fqdn` of the domain controller you query against to retrieve the data from Active Directory.

❑   `-IgnoreDefaultScope <SwitchParameter>`: This parameter instructs the command to ignore the default Recipient scope setting for the Exchange Management Shell and use the entire forest as the scope. This allows the command to access Active Directory objects that are not currently in the default scope. Using the `IgnoreDefaultScope` parameter introduces the following restrictions:

   ❑   You cannot use the `DomainController` parameter. The command uses an appropriate global catalog server automatically.

   ❑   You can only use the DN for the `Identity` parameter. Other forms of identification, such as alias or GUID, are not accepted. You cannot use the `OrganizationalUnit` and `Identity` parameters together. You cannot use the `Credential` parameter.

❑   `Filter <String>`: The `Filter` parameter indicates the `OPath` filter used to filter Recipients. `OPath` is discussed in more detail later in the chapter.

❑   `Identity <MailboxIdParameter>`: The `Identity` parameter identifies the Dynamic Distribution Group and can use any of the following values: GUID, Domain\Account, Distinguished Name (DN), UserPrincipalName (UPN), LegacyDN, Alias, or primary SMTP address.

As mentioned earlier, Exchange Server 2007 incorporates the management of User and Group object types in the Management Console. These objects can be found in the Recipient Configuration node of the Exchange Management Console and fall under one of the following nodes and as shown in Figure 4-3:

❑ Mailbox

❑ Distribution Group

❑ Mail Contact

❑ Disconnected Mailbox

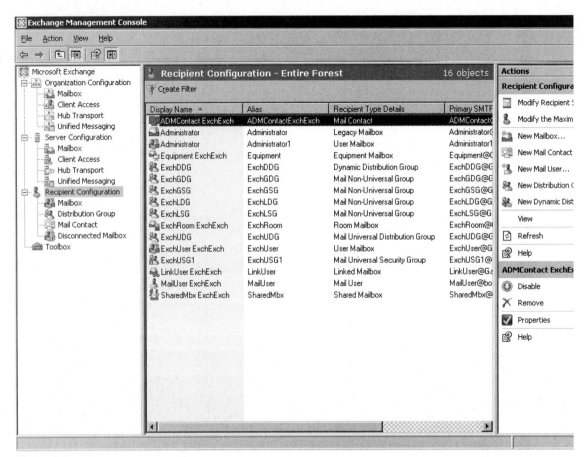

Figure 4-3

The same information is available by running the Exchange Management Shell command. Using the `Get-Recipient` cmdlet in a mixed Exchange Server 2000/2003/2007 environment will display all Recipients including system mailboxes and public folders. In Figure 4-4 the `Format-Table` cmdlet is used to present the output in a viewable friendly format based on the Recipient name, Recipient type, and Recipient type details.

Professional PowerShell For Exchange 2007 | Scope: View Entire Forest

```
[PS] C:\>Get-Recipient | ft name, recipienttype, recipienttypedetails

Name                              RecipientType                RecipientTypeDetails
----                              -------------                --------------------
Administrator                     UserMailbox                  LegacyMailbox
Administrator                     UserMailbox                  UserMailbox
ADMContact ExchExch               MailContact                  MailContact
LinkUser ExchExch                 UserMailbox                  LinkedMailbox
ExchUser ExchExch                 UserMailbox                  UserMailbox
ExchRoom ExchExch                 UserMailbox                  RoomMailbox
Equipment ExchExch                UserMailbox                  EquipmentMailbox
SharedMbx ExchExch                UserMailbox                  SharedMailbox
MailUser ExchExch                 MailUser                     MailUser
ExchDDG                           DynamicDistributionGroup     DynamicDistributionGroup
Default                           PublicFolder                 PublicFolder
exchangeV1                        PublicFolder                 PublicFolder
ExchGDG                           MailNonUniversalGroup        MailNonUniversalGroup
ExchGSG                           MailNonUniversalGroup        MailNonUniversalGroup
ExchLDG                           MailNonUniversalGroup        MailNonUniversalGroup
ExchLSG                           MailNonUniversalGroup        MailNonUniversalGroup
ExchPF                            PublicFolder                 PublicFolder
ExchUDG                       ...UniversalDistributionGroup ...UniversalDistributionGroup
ExchUSG1                          MailUniversalSecurityGroup   MailUniversalSecurityGroup
globalevents                      PublicFolder                 PublicFolder
globalevents 98777413             PublicFolder                 PublicFolder
internal                          PublicFolder                 PublicFolder
internal 73025491                 PublicFolder                 PublicFolder
internal 20111312                 PublicFolder                 PublicFolder
microsoft                         PublicFolder                 PublicFolder
OAB Version 2                     PublicFolder                 PublicFolder
```

Figure 4-4

Using the filter switch and excluding public folders, all Recipient types created in a mixed Exchange environment can be displayed as in Figure 4-5.

Professional PowerShell For Exchange 2007 | Scope: View Entire Forest

```
[PS] C:\>Get-Recipient -filter "-not (RecipientType -eq 'PublicFolder')" | ft name, recipi
enttype, recipienttypedetails

Name                              RecipientType                RecipientTypeDetails
----                              -------------                --------------------
Administrator                     UserMailbox                  LegacyMailbox
Administrator                     UserMailbox                  UserMailbox
ADMContact ExchExch               MailContact                  MailContact
LinkUser ExchExch                 UserMailbox                  LinkedMailbox
ExchUser ExchExch                 UserMailbox                  UserMailbox
ExchRoom ExchExch                 UserMailbox                  RoomMailbox
Equipment ExchExch                UserMailbox                  EquipmentMailbox
SharedMbx ExchExch                UserMailbox                  SharedMailbox
MailUser ExchExch                 MailUser                     MailUser
ExchDDG                           DynamicDistributionGroup     DynamicDistributionGroup
ExchGDG                           MailNonUniversalGroup        MailNonUniversalGroup
ExchGSG                           MailNonUniversalGroup        MailNonUniversalGroup
ExchLDG                           MailNonUniversalGroup        MailNonUniversalGroup
ExchLSG                           MailNonUniversalGroup        MailNonUniversalGroup
ExchUDG                       ...UniversalDistributionGroup ...UniversalDistributionGroup
ExchUSG1                          MailUniversalSecurityGroup   MailUniversalSecurityGroup
```

Figure 4-5

Some Recipient types, though, such as legacy mailbox and mail-enabled nonuniversal groups are unavailable in a native Exchange Server 2007 environment. Figure 4-6 re-runs the same command shown in Figure 4-4, this time in a native Exchange Server 2007 environment. Notice that the RecipientTypeDetails column has no legacy mailbox or mail-enabled nonuniversal group.

Figure 4-6

Exchange Server 2007 Recipient Objects

Exchange Server 2007 contains Recipients that are either mailbox-enabled or mail-enabled.

A user mailbox is a mailbox-enabled Recipient object with an Exchange Server 2007 mailbox. This mailbox houses several types of data such as email messages, contacts, calendar items, tasks, and other documents. This Recipient object is associated with a single Enabled Active Directory Services user object. A user mailbox can be converted to a shared mailbox or resource mailbox and vice versa. Mailbox type conversion can only be accomplished through the Exchange Management Shell. To perform this procedure, the Active Directory User account must be granted the Exchange Recipient Administrator role.

Using the Get-Recipient or Get-Mailbox cmdlets returns user mailboxes in the organization. This object has a Recipient type of UserMailbox.

In Figure 4-7, notice that a shared mailbox, resource mailbox, or even a linked user mailbox all have a Recipient type of UserMailbox.

```
Professional PowerShell For Exchange 2007 | Scope: View Entire Forest
[PS] C:\>Get-Recipient -RecipientType usermailbox

Name                          RecipientType

LinkUser ExchExch             UserMailbox
ExchUser ExchExch             UserMailbox
ExchRoom ExchExch             UserMailbox
Equipment ExchExch            UserMailbox
SharedMbx ExchExch            UserMailbox
Administrator                 UserMailbox


[PS] C:\>get-mailbox

Name                  Alias           ServerName      ProhibitSendQuota

LinkUser ExchExch     LinkUser        ex7b            unlimited
ExchUser ExchExch     ExchUser        ex7b            unlimited
ExchRoom ExchExch     ExchRoom        ex7b            unlimited
Equipment ExchExch    Equipment       ex7b            unlimited
SharedMbx ExchExch    SharedMbx       ex7b            unlimited
Administrator         Administrator   ex3b            unlimited
```

Figure 4-7

Although all the Recipients have a `RecipientType` of `UserMailbox`, only regular mailbox-enabled users created on Exchange Server 2007 and whose Active Directory Services account is enabled will have a `RecipientTypeDetails` property set to `$True` for the Recipient type `UserMailbox`.

Figure 4-8 has the cmdlet run again to display only Recipients with Recipient type of `UserMailbox`, however we define a filter to further distinguish these Recipients with similar Recipient types. Notice that the `recipienttypedetail` property is set to `$True` only for `ExchUser`, which is a regular user mailbox created on Exchange Server 2007.

```
Professional PowerShell For Exchange 2007 | Scope: View Entire Forest          _ □ ×
[PS] C:\>Get-Recipient -Recipienttype usermailbox | ft name, recipienttype, { $_.recipient
typedetails -eq 'usermailbox' }

Name                                         RecipientType $_.recipienttypedetails -eq '
                                                                               usermailbox'
----                                         ------------- ----------------------------
LinkUser ExchExch                            UserMailbox                            False
ExchUser ExchExch                            UserMailbox                             True
ExchRoom ExchExch                            UserMailbox                            False
Equipment ExchExch                           UserMailbox                            False
SharedMbx ExchExch                           UserMailbox                            False
Administrator                                UserMailbox                            False
```

Figure 4-8

A linked mailbox object is also a `UserMailbox` object; however, this mailbox type is accessed by a user in a separate trusted forest. A forest trust must exist before a `LinkedMailbox` can be created. Organizations that deploy Exchange in a dedicated resource forest can allow users in one or more user account trusted forests to access mailboxes on Exchange. Even if a user in a separate forest is used to access the `LinkedMailbox`, a disabled Windows user account in the Exchange resource forest must be associated with the Exchange mailbox. Although the `LinkedMailbox` shows up as a Recipient type of `UserMailbox`, it can be distinguished by the `RecipientTypeDetails` as shown in Figure 4-9.

```
Select Professional PowerShell for Exchange 2007 | Scope: View Entire Forest    _ □ ×
[PS] C:\>Get-Recipient | where { $_.recipienttypedetails -eq 'linkedmailbox' } | ft name,
recipienttype, recipienttypedetails

Name                                 RecipientType              RecipientTypeDetails
----                                 -------------              --------------------
ExchLink ExchExch                    UserMailbox                LinkedMailbox
```

Figure 4-9

To convert a linked mailbox to a user mailbox simply disconnect the `mailbox` object from the `user` object in the external forest by using the `Disable-Mailbox` cmdlet. Next reconnect it to a `user` object existing in the Exchange forest using the `Connect-Mailbox` cmdlet:

```
Disable-Mailbox -Identity ExchLink
Connect-Mailbox -Identity ExchLink -Database "Mailbox Database" -User ExchUser
```

A legacy mailbox is a user mailbox and shares most of the features of user mailboxes however they reside on Exchange 2000 or Exchange 2003 servers. One noticeable feature unavailable with legacy mailboxes is that they cannot be Unified Message (UM) enabled. This mailbox is distinguished from other user mailboxes by its `RecipientTypeDetails` as shown in Figure 4-10.

Figure 4-10

Room mailboxes, also known as conference room mailboxes, are resource mailboxes used for scheduling and assigned to location-specific resources such as meeting rooms, auditoriums, training rooms, and conference rooms. Upon creation, the associated user account is disabled. Its `RecipientType` is `UserMailbox`, however it is distinguished by its `RecipientTypeDetails` property. (See Figure 4-11.)

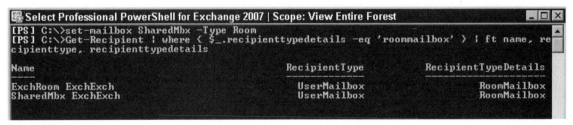

Figure 4-11

The equipment mailbox is also a resource mailbox. It is used for scheduling and assigning non-location-specific resources, which could include printers, projectors, TV, computers, and company cars and trucks. A disabled user account is likewise associated with this mailbox type and it is distinguished by its `RecipientTypeDetails` property of `EquipmentMailbox`. (See Figure 4-12.)

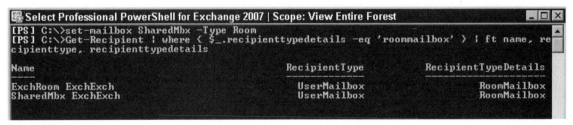

Figure 4-12

As the name implies, shared mailboxes are user mailboxes shared by multiple user accounts. A disabled Active Directory user account must be associated with a shared mailbox. After it is created other Active Directory user accounts can be granted logon rights to the mailbox. In Exchange Server 2000 and Exchange Server 2003, shared mailboxes were used to represent resource mailboxes. When an organization migrates to Exchange Server 2007, these mailboxes will become Exchange Server 2007 shared mailboxes and can be converted to Exchange Server 2007 resource mailboxes. A shared mailbox can also be converted to a user mailbox and vice versa. Although shared mailboxes are available in Exchange Server 2003, use of resource mailboxes is recommended rather than shared mailboxes. Note that a shared mailbox is only visible from the Exchange Management Shell and is not shown in the Exchange Management Console. (See Figure 4-13.)

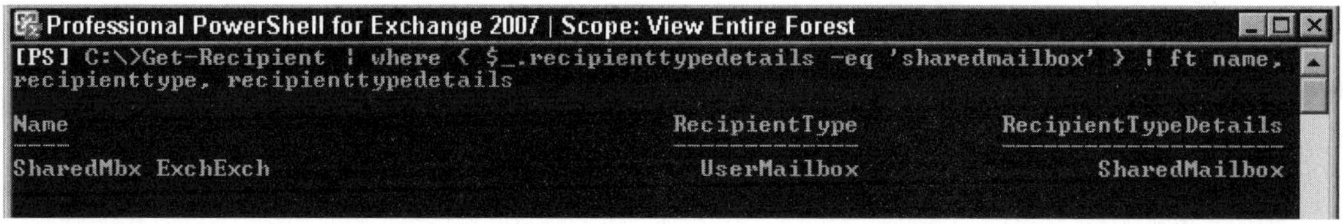

Figure 4-13

You can convert a shared mailbox to a resource mailbox by using the Set-Mailbox cmdlet.

Next use the Get-Recipient cmdlet to view the change. In Figure 4-14 the output is filtered to return only Recipient types of RoomMailbox existing in the organization and SharedMbx, which was previously a shared mailbox but is now a room mailbox.

Figure 4-14

Mail-enabled or non-mailbox-enabled Recipients in Exchange Server 2007 include the mail contact, mail forest user, and mail user.

A mail contact is a non-mailbox-enabled Exchange Server 2007 Recipient. It is an Active Directory Services contact that is used to contain information about people that exist outside of the Exchange organization. Mail contacts can be part of distribution or address lists including the Global Address List (GAL). They are used primarily for mail routing and these contacts do not have access to any internal resources in the Exchange organization. For example, during a migration phase, an Exchange organization may coexist with a Lotus Notes organization and may choose to synchronize all the Lotus Notes users to the Active Directory as mail contacts. After migration, all Lotus Notes users would be converted to mailbox-enabled Active Directory Services users. Although the mail contact has an SMTP address associated with the local Exchange organization, when a message is addressed to the mail contact, the `ExternalEmailAddress` or `PrimarySMTPAddress` properties are used to route and deliver the mail. These properties represent the information about the people existing outside the Exchange organization.

In Figure 4-15, the mail contact will have the `EmailAddresses` property populated with both SMTP proxy addresses of the Exchange organization and external SMTP address of `[smtp:ADMContact@ExchangeExchange.local; ADMContact@bogusdomain.net]`; however, its `PrimarySMTPAddress`, which is used for mail routing, is `ADMContact@bogusdomain.net`.

You can use either the `Get-Recipient` or `Get-MailContact` cmdlets to return a list of mail contacts in the Active Directory forest.

Figure 4-15

The mail forest contact is typically created by Microsoft Identity Integration Server (MIIS) synchronization and represents Recipients existing in an external forest or organization.

The mail user is identical to the mail contact in the sense that it is used to contain information about people outside the Exchange organization and could be part of a Distribution Group or address list. The mail user, however, has logon credentials in the Active Directory forest and can access resources like any other Active Directory user in the forest. You can use either the `Get-Recipient` or `Get-MailUser` cmdlets to return a list of mail users in the organization. (See Figure 4-16.)

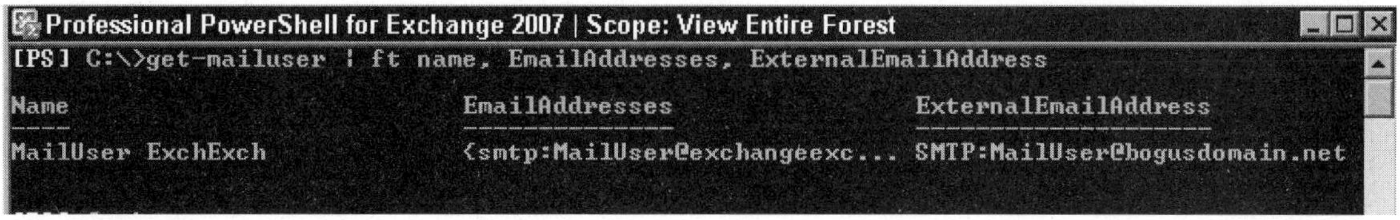

```
Professional PowerShell for Exchange 2007 | Scope: View Entire Forest            _ □ ×
[PS] C:\>get-mailuser | ft name, EmailAddresses, ExternalEmailAddress

Name                         EmailAddresses               ExternalEmailAddress

MailUser ExchExch            {smtp:MailUser@exchangeexc... SMTP:MailUser@bogusdomain.net
```

Figure 4-16

Mail-enabling a public folder extends the basic functionality of allowing users to post messages in a central repository. Users can send or receive email messages to a mail-enabled public folder. The Exchange mail-enabled public folder has an Active Directory object containing Exchange mail properties such as primarysmtpaddress. You can use the Get-MailPublicFolder cmdlet to view mail-enabled public folders. For more information on public folders, see Chapter 5.

This chapter would not be complete without mentioning the Microsoft Exchange Recipient. This is not a mail-enabled or mailbox-enabled Recipient, rather it is a special Recipient used as the sender of system-generated messages. There is only one Microsoft Exchange Recipient in an Exchange forest. In Exchange Server 2003 this was represented by the Post Master mailbox and messages thus generated were from the System Administrator. The Microsoft Exchange Recipient can send the following types of system messages: Delivery Status Notifications (DSNs), Message Journal Reports, Agent-generated Messages, and Quota limit messages. Hence non-deliverable messages, for example, are no longer from the System Administrator but from Microsoft Exchange. This applies only to system-generated messages sent within the Exchange organization. For system-generated messages sent to Recipients outside the Exchange organization, the address specified in the ExternalPostmasterAddress property of the Get-TransportServer cmdlet is used as the "from" address for the Microsoft Exchange Recipient. This address can be configured using the Set-TransportServer cmdlet. Because the Microsoft Exchange Recipient is not your typical Exchange Recipient, the usual Recipient cmdlets cannot be used to view or modify it. You can use the Set-OrganizationConfig cmdlet to configure an additional mail Recipient such as the administrator to receive system-generated messages; to prevent the default email address policy from applying to the Microsoft Exchange Recipient; and to configure email addresses for this Recipient.

The Microsoft Exchange Recipient is exempt from any message limits configured in the Exchange organization. For Exchange organizations in cross-forest topologies, this may present a problem because messages from the Microsoft Exchange Recipient in one forest may not be recognized as coming from the Microsoft Exchange Recipient and thus could be subject to message limit restrictions. Microsoft Exchange Server 2007 will determine that a message is sent by the Microsoft Exchange Recipient by comparing the sender's email address to the list of email addresses specified in the MicrosoftExchangeRecipientEmailAddresses of the Get-OrganizationalConfig cmdlet. To overcome this hurdle, the Microsoft Exchange Recipient of each forest can be configured with an additional email address that matches the primary email address of the Microsoft Exchange Recipient in the other forest. Hence, when a comparison is made of the MicrosoftExchangeRecipientEmailAddresses parameter, a match would be detected thus allowing the system-generated message to bypass message restrictions. This configuration, however, has a drawback if the Microsoft Exchange Recipient in either or both forests is configured with a reply address defined by the MicrosoftExchangeRecipientReplyRecipient parameter. By default this parameter is set to $null.

Exchange Server 2007 Group Objects

As in previous versions of Exchange Server, Distribution Groups are used to enable bulk distribution of email to multiple Recipients both within and outside of an Exchange organization. In Windows Server 2003 and earlier, Active Directory Services Groups could be either Distribution Groups used only for email distribution or Security Groups used for granting permission to resources in the forest. They could be scoped as local, global, or universal groups. In Exchange Server 2007, however, any mail-enabled Active Directory Group object is a Distribution Group regardless of its scope and whether it is a Distribution or Security Group. Distribution Groups available and supported in Exchange Server 2007 include the types discussed in the following sections.

Mail-Enabled Universal Distribution Groups

These are mail-enabled Active Directory Universal Distribution Group objects and are used only for email distribution to multiple Recipients. They cannot be used to grant access to resources in either Exchange or Active Directory. Any Exchange Server 2007 Recipient object mentioned in the preceding section can be a member of these groups. Using the `Get-Recipient`, `Get-Group`, or `Get-DistributionGroup` cmdlets with a `RecipientTypeDetails` of `MailUniversalDistributionGroup` returns all Distribution Groups in the Exchange organization that are mail-enabled Distribution Groups as shown in Figure 4-17.

Figure 4-17

Mail-Enabled Universal Security Groups

These are mail-enabled Active Directory Universal Security Group objects and are used only for email distribution to multiple Recipients and to grant permissions to resources in the Active Directory forest. Any Exchange Server 2007 Recipient object mentioned in the preceding section can be a member of these groups. Using the `Get-Recipient`, `Get-Group`, or `Get-DistributionGroup` cmdlets with a `RecipientTypeDetails` of `MailUniversalSecurityGroup` returns all Security Groups in the Exchange organization that are mail-enabled. (See Figure 4-18.)

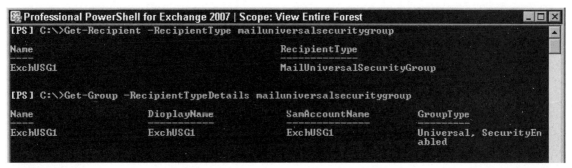

```
Professional PowerShell for Exchange 2007 | Scope: View Entire Forest        _□×

[PS] C:\>Get-Recipient -RecipientType mailuniversalsecuritygroup

Name                                     RecipientType

ExchUSG1                                 MailUniversalSecurityGroup


[PS] C:\>Get-Group -RecipientTypeDetails mailuniversalsecuritygroup

Name               DioplayName         SamAccountName         GroupType

ExchUSG1           ExchUSG1            ExchUSG1               Universal, SecurityEn
                                                             abled
```

Figure 4-18

Mail-Enabled Nonuniversal Groups

These are Active Directory local or global Security or Distribution Group objects. Use of these groups for email distribution is greatly de-emphasized in Exchange Server 2007 because unpredictable group membership expansion could result. Hence, these groups cannot be created from the Exchange Management Console. Organizations migrating to or coexisting with Exchange Server 2007 may have these groups already in Active Directory. Using the Set-Group cmdlet, these groups can be converted to either mail-enabled universal Distribution or Security Groups. In a native Exchange Server 2007 environment, you cannot create a mail-enabled nonuniversal group using the Active Directory Users and Computers as is the case in an Exchange Server 2000/2003 or a mixed Exchange Server 2000/2003/2007 environment. Figure 4-19 shows mail nonuniversal groups in the forest.

```
Professional PowerShell for Exchange 2007 | Scope: View Entire Forest        _□×

[PS] C:\>Get-DistributionGroup -RecipientType MailNonUniversalgroup

Name               DisplayName         GroupType              PrimarySm

ExchGDG            ExchGDG             Global                 ExchGDG@G
ExchGSG            ExchGSG             Global, Security...    ExchGSG@G
ExchLDG            ExchLDG             DomainLocal            ExchLDG@G
ExchLSG            ExchLSG             DomainLocal, Sec...    ExchLSG@G


[PS] C:\>_
```

Figure 4-19

Dynamic Distribution Groups

In Exchange Server 2000/2003, this group type was commonly referred to as Query Based Distribution Groups (QDG). Used to ease the administrator's burden of manually adding Recipients to Distribution Groups, a Dynamic Distribution Group's membership is based upon a preset Recipient filter and calculated each time a message is sent to this group. Group membership can include all

Recipient types including other mail-enabled groups. In Exchange Server 2003, Query Based Distribution Groups accepted emails from all senders. This is, however, different in Exchange Server 2007 because Dynamic Distribution Groups by default accept only emails from authenticated senders. This configuration can be changed by modifying the message delivery restrictions on the Dynamic Distribution Group. You can use the `Get-Recipient` and `Get-DynamicDistributionGroup` cmdlets to display Dynamic Distribution Groups available in the Exchange organization. (See Figure 4-20.)

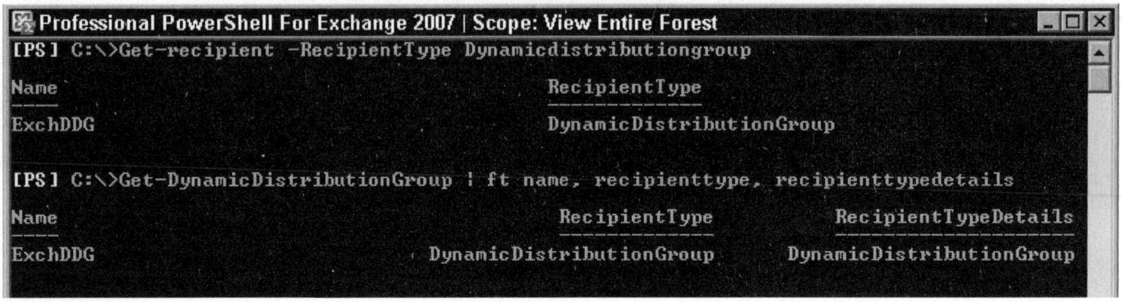

```
Professional PowerShell For Exchange 2007 | Scope: View Entire Forest    _ □ ×
[PS] C:\>Get-recipient -RecipientType Dynamicdistributiongroup

Name                                        RecipientType
____                                        _____
ExchDDG                                     DynamicDistributionGroup

[PS] C:\>Get-DynamicDistributionGroup | ft name, recipienttype, recipienttypedetails

Name                        RecipientType                 RecipientTypeDetails
____                        _____                 _____
ExchDDG                     DynamicDistributionGroup      DynamicDistributionGroup
```

Figure 4-20

You would also notice that when an Exchange Server 2007 Dynamic Distribution Group is created, it stores its `RecipientFilter` in an `OPATH` format, whereas in Exchange Server 2000/2003, the Query Based Distribution Groups filter is stored in an LDAP format. The following blog by Bill Long provides an available PowerShell script to convert LDAP filters to `OPATH` format: `http://msexchangeteam.com/archive/2007/03/12/436983.aspx`.

Finally, Microsoft Exchange Server 2007 contains other group objects that are not mail-enabled, cannot be viewed in the Microsoft Exchange Management Console, and thus cannot be viewed as email Recipients. These are Active Directory Security Groups, discussed in the following list, and are used solely for the administration of Exchange and a new Organizational Unit called Microsoft Exchange Security Groups is created during set up of Exchange to house these Security Groups.

- ❑ **Exchange2003Interop Group:** This is an Active Directory Services Universal Security Group used to grant appropriate permissions when an Exchange Server 2000/2003 organization coexists with an Exchange Server 2007 organization. Group membership must be manually configured. It is created during Exchange setup or after the setup `/PrepareAD` switch is run.

- ❑ **Exchange Servers Group:** This is an Active Directory Services Universal Security Group. It is created during Exchange setup or after the setup `/PrepareAD` switch is run. This group contains all the Exchange Server 2007 computers in the organization and should never be deleted. The Exchange Install Domain Servers Global Group is also a member of this Universal Security Group.

- ❑ **Exchange View-Only Administrators Group:** This is an Active Directory Services Universal Security Group. Users in this group will have permission to read all Exchange configurations and should never be deleted. Users in this group are also added to the Exchange View-Only

Administrators role and have read-only access to the Exchange organization hierarchy in the Configuration container in Active Directory. They also have read access to any domain containers having Exchange Recipients. It is created during Exchange setup or after the setup `/PrepareAD` switch is run.

❑ **Exchange Recipient Administrators Group:** This is an Active Directory Services Universal Security Group. Users in this group can manage Exchange user attributes in Active Directory and perform select mailbox operations. This group should never be deleted. Users added to this group also become members of the Exchange Recipient Administrator role with permissions to modify any Exchange property on a user, contact, group, Dynamic Distribution Group, or Exchange public folder object. They are members of the Exchange view-only administrator group, have read access to all Domain Users Containers and write access to all Exchange attributes in the Domain Users Container in Active Directory. It is created during Exchange setup or after the setup `/PrepareAD` switch is run.

❑ **Exchange Organization Administrators Group:** This is an Active Directory Services Universal Security Group. Users in this group have permission to read and modify all Exchange configurations. This group should never be deleted. Users added to this group also become members of the Exchange Organization Administrator role and as such become owners of the Exchange organization in the Configuration container in Active Directory. They also have read access to all domain user containers and write access to all Exchange-specific attributes in all domain containers in Active Directory. It is created during Exchange setup or after the setup `/PrepareAD` switch is run.

❑ **Exchange Install Domain Servers Group:** This is an Active Directory Services Global Security Group created in the Microsoft Exchange System Objects container. When installing Exchange Server 2007 into domain other than the root domain, the setup `/PrepareDomain` switch is used to prepare the child domain. Upon completion, the Exchange Install Domain Servers global group is created. The creation of this group allows you to avoid installation errors if group memberships have not replicated to the child domain. This global group is a member of the Exchange Servers Universal Security Group.

Creating and Modifying User Objects

After introducing the Recipient objects available in Exchange Server 2007, this section describes how to create and modify these objects. The following list presents cmdlets that can be used to create and modify user objects. We explain some key parameters of some of these cmdlets.

❑ `New-Mailbox`

❑ `Set-Mailbox`

❑ `Connect-Mailbox`

❑ `Move-Mailbox`

❑ `Enable-Mailbox`

❑ `Disable-Mailbox`

❑   `Remove-Mailbox`

❑   `New-Contact`

❑   `New-MailContact`

❑   `Set-CASMailbox`

❑   `Export-Mailbox`

❑   `Import-Mailbox`

New-Mailbox

This cmdlet creates a new user object in Active Directory and mailbox-enables the user. There are several switch parameters associated with this cmdlet as well as required parameters. The list of parameters is shown next. For a detailed list run the following in the Exchange Management Shell: `get-help New-Mailbox -detailed`.

Some key parameters to note include:

❑   `Database <DatabaseIdParameter>`: This is a required parameter and specifies the database to host the new mailbox. It can take several formats such as GUID of database, database name, or server name\database name.

❑   `Equipment <SwitchParameter>`: This switch parameter indicates that a resource mailbox of type `Equipment` is to be created. It is a required parameter if creating an equipment resource mailbox.

❑   `LinkedDomainController <String>`: A required parameter when creating a linked mailbox. It is used to specify the domain controller in the forest where the user account to be granted access to the mailbox resides. It is used in conjunction with the `LinkedMasterAccount` parameter.

❑   `LinkedCredential <PSCredential>`: This parameter specifies the credentials used to access the domain controller referenced in the `LinkedDomainController` parameter.

❑   `LinkedMasterAccount <UserIdParameter>`: This parameter specifies the master account from the external forest, which will be granted mailbox access to the linked mailbox. It is a required parameter when creating linked mailboxes.

❑   `Room <SwitchParameter>`: As with the `Equipment` parameter, this is a switch parameter that indicates that the type of resource mailbox to be created is a room mailbox. It is a required parameter when creating this resource mailbox.

❑   `Shared <SwitchParameter>`: This switch parameter is required when creating a shared mailbox. A detailed description of the shared mailbox is provided earlier in this chapter.

❑   `ManagedFolderMailboxPolicy <MailboxPolicyIdParameter>`: This parameter specifies the managed folder mailbox policy to be applied to the new mailbox. If none is specified, the default `ManagedFolderMailboxPolicy` applies. It is not a required parameter.

❑ `ManagedFolderMailboxPolicyAllowed <SwitchParameter>`: This parameter is used to bypass the warning that messaging records management features are not supported for email clients using versions of Microsoft Outlook earlier than Outlook 2007. It is not a required parameter.

❑ `ActiveSyncMailboxPolicy <MailboxPolicyIdParameter>`: As with the `ManagedFolderMailboxPolicy` parameter, this parameter is used to specify the `ActiveSyncMailboxPolicy` to be applied to the mailbox. If none is specified, the default is used.

❑ `Password <SecureString>`: This parameter specifies the initial password and is required when creating a user mailbox. It is, however, not required when creating a resource mailboxes because the associated accounts are disabled.

Set-Mailbox

This cmdlet is used to modify the settings of an existing mailbox. It can be used for one mailbox at a time. If you want to modify the settings of multiple mailboxes, you can pipeline the output of various `Get` cmdlets to this cmdlet to simultaneously modify their settings. The list of parameters is shown next. For a detailed list run the following in the Exchange Management Shell: `get-help Set-Mailbox -detailed`.

❑ `Type <Regular | Room | Equipment | Shared>`: Can be used to convert from one mailbox type to another. Available options are Regular (User Mailbox), Room, Equipment, and Shared.

❑ `AcceptMessagesOnlyFrom <RecipientIdParameter[]>`: Applies restrictions to the mailbox indicating which Recipients the mailbox will accept messages for.

❑ `AcceptMessagesOnlyFromDLMembers <RecipientIdParameter[]>`: Applies restrictions to the mailbox indicating which distribution list members the mailbox will receive messages for.

❑ `AntispamBypassEnabled <$true | $false>`: Possible values are `True` or `False`. If set to `True`, anti-spam processing is skipped for the mailbox.

❑ `ApplyMandatoryProperties <SwitchParameter>`: If a mailbox is inadvertently created using Exchange 2003 extensions to Active Directory, the mailbox type is tagged `legacymailbox`. This switch parameter modifies the properties of the mailbox removing the `legacymailbox` tag.

❑ `DeliverToMailboxAndForward <$true | $false>`: This parameter specifies whether messages sent to the mailbox can be forwarded to another address.

❑ `ForwardingAddress <RecipientIdParameter>`: If the `DeliverToMailboxAndForward` parameter is set to `$True`, this parameter specifies the forwarding address.

❑ `EmailAddressPolicyEnabled <$true | $false>`: This parameter indicates whether the email address policy for this mailbox is enabled.

❑ `ExternalOofOptions <InternalOnly | External>`: Determines if out-of-office messages can be sent to Recipients outside the Exchange organization.

❑   `LinkedDomainController <String>`: A required parameter when creating a linked mailbox. It is used to specify the domain controller in the forest where the user account to be granted access to the mailbox resides. It is used in conjunction with the `LinkedMasterAccount` parameter.

❑   `LinkedCredential <PSCredential>`: This parameter specifies the credentials used to access the domain controller referenced in the `LinkedDomainController` parameter.

❑   `LinkedMasterAccount <UserIdParameter>`: This parameter specifies the master account from the external forest that will be granted mailbox access to the linked mailbox. It is a required parameter when creating linked mailboxes.

❑   `ManagedFolderMailboxPolicy <MailboxPolicyIdParameter>`: This parameter specifies the managed folder mailbox policy to be applied to the new mailbox. If none is specified, the default `ManagedFolderMailboxPolicy` applies. It is not a required parameter.

❑   `ManagedFolderMailboxPolicyAllowed <SwitchParameter>`: This parameter is used to bypass the warning that messaging records management features are not supported for email clients using versions of Microsoft Outlook earlier than Outlook 2007. It is not a required parameter.

Enable-Mailbox

This cmdlet mailbox enables an existing user or `InetOrgPerson` object in Active Directory Services. When successfully run, it creates additional mail attributes on the object and a mailbox on the Exchange Server database to enable the object to send and receive email messages. Keep in mind that when using this cmdlet, if the `Alias` parameter is not specified, an alias is created for the object using the User Principal Name (UPN) and converts all non-ASCII characters to underscore characters. The list of parameters is shown next. For a detailed list run the following in the Exchange Management Shell: `get-help Enable-Mailbox -detailed`.

Some key parameters to note include:

❑   `Database <DatabaseIdParameter>`: This is a required parameter and specifies the database to host the enabled mailbox. It can take several formats such as GUID of database, database name, or server name\database name.

❑   `Alias <String>`: This parameter modifies the email alias of the mailbox to be enabled.

❑   `Equipment <SwitchParameter>`: This switch parameter indicates that a resource mailbox of type `Equipment` is to be created. It is a required parameter if creating an equipment resource mailbox.

❑   `LinkedDomainController <String>`: A required parameter when creating a linked mailbox. It is used to specify the domain controller in the forest where the user account to be granted access to the mailbox resides. It is used in conjunction with the `LinkedMasterAccount` parameter.

❑   `LinkedCredential <PSCredential>`: This parameter specifies the credentials used to access the domain controller referenced in the `LinkedDomainController` parameter.

- ❑ LinkedMasterAccount <UserIdParameter>: This parameter specifies the master account from the external forest that will be granted mailbox access to the linked mailbox. It is a required parameter when creating linked mailboxes.

- ❑ Room <SwitchParameter>: As with the Equipment parameter, this is a switch parameter that indicates the type of resource mailbox to be created is a room mailbox. It is a required parameter when creating this resource mailbox.

- ❑ Shared <SwitchParameter>: This switch parameter is required when creating a shared mailbox. A detailed description of the shared mailbox is provided earlier in this chapter.

- ❑ ManagedFolderMailboxPolicy <MailboxPolicyIdParameter>: This parameter specifies the managed folder mailbox policy to be applied to the new mailbox. If none is specified, the default ManagedFolderMailboxPolicy applies. It is not a required parameter.

- ❑ ManagedFolderMailboxPolicyAllowed <SwitchParameter>: This parameter is used to bypass the warning that messaging records management features are not supported for email clients using versions of Microsoft Outlook earlier than Outlook 2007. It is not a required parameter.

- ❑ ActiveSyncMailboxPolicy <MailboxPolicyIdParameter>: As with the ManagedFolderMailboxPolicy parameter, this parameter is used to specify the ActiveSyncMailboxPolicy to be applied to the mailbox. If none is specified, the default is used.

Remove-Mailbox

This cmdlet removes the user account associated with a mailbox and processes the deletion of the mailbox based on the parameters specified or the configured mailbox retention policy. A list of parameters is shown next. For a detailed list run the following in the Exchange Management Shell: get-help Remove-Mailbox -detailed.

```
Remove-Mailbox -Identity <MailboxIdParameter> [-DomainController <Fqdn>]
[-Permanent <$true | $false>] [<CommonParameters>]
Remove-Mailbox -Database <DatabaseIdParameter> -StoreMailboxIdentity
<StoreMailboxIdParameter> [-DomainController <Fqdn>] [<CommonParameters>]
```

Notice that the Identity parameter cannot be used in conjunction with the -Database parameter. Also the StoreMailboxIdentity parameter must be used with the Database parameter.

Specifying the Identity parameter alone simply disconnects the mailbox from the user, removes its Active Directory user account, and the mailbox is removed from the Exchange database based on the mailbox retention policy. By default, the mailbox remains disconnected for 30 days and then is purged from the database. Using the Permanent parameter in addition overrides the retention policy and marks the mailbox for deletion immediately.

If there are existing disconnected mailboxes in the Exchange database, perhaps after running the Disable-Mailbox cmdlet, you can use the Database and StoreMailboxIdentity parameters to remove a mailbox object from the Exchange database.

This cmdlet requires the logged-on user to be a member of the Exchange Recipient Administrator Group and belong to the local Administrators group on the computer.

Some key parameters to note include:

❑ Database <DatabaseIdParameter>: The Database parameter specifies the database that contains the mailbox object. It must be used in conjunction with the StoreMailboxIdentity parameter and cannot be used with the Identity parameter. The parameter can be any of the following: GUID, database name, server name\database name, and server name\storage group\database name.

❑ Identity <MailboxIdParameter>: This parameter identifies the mailbox object you want to remove and can be any of the following attributes: ADObjectID, Distinguished Name (DN), UPN, LegacyDN, GUID, email address, or alias. It cannot be used with the Database parameter.

❑ StoreMailboxIdentity <StoreMailboxIdParameter>: The DomainController parameter specifies the domain controller that writes this configuration change to Active Directory. Use the fully qualified domain name (FQDN) of the domain controller that you want to use.

❑ Permanent <$true | $false>: Used in conjunction with the Identity parameter and possible values for this parameter are $true or $false. The default is $false.

Set-CASMailbox

This cmdlet sets client access-related attributes and operates on one mailbox at a time. This cmdlet can be used to configure properties for Microsoft Exchange ActiveSync, Microsoft Office Outlook Web Access, Post Office Protocol version 3 (POP3), and Internet Message Access Protocol version 4rev1 (IMAP4) for a specified user. It can also be used to enable or disable Messaging Application Programming Interface (MAPI) for an Exchange Server 2007 mailbox user. The Identity parameter is a required parameter to use this cmdlet. A list of parameters is shown next. For a detailed list run the following in the Exchange Management Shell: get-help Set-CASMailbox -detailed.

```
Set-CASMailbox -Identity <MailboxIdParameter> [-ActiveSyncAllowedDeviceIDs
<MultiValuedProperty>] [-ActiveSyncEnabled <$true | $false>]
[-ActiveSyncMailboxPolicy <MailboxPolicyIdParameter>] [-ActiveSyncDebugLogging
<Nullable>] [-DisplayName <String>] [-DomainController <Fqdn>] [-EmailAddresses
<ProxyAddressCollection>] [-HasActiveSyncDevicePartnership <$true | $false>]
[-ImapEnabled <$true | $false>] [-ImapMessagesRetrievalMimeFormat <TextOnly |
HtmlOnly | HtmlAndTextAlternative | TextEnrichedOnly |
TextEnrichedAndTextAlternative | BestBodyFormat>] [-ImapUseProtocolDefaults <$true
| $false>] [-MAPIBlockOutlookNonCachedMode <$true | $false>]
[-MAPIBlockOutlookRpcHttp <$true | $false>] [-MAPIBlockOutlookVersions <String>]
[-MAPIEnabled <$true | $false>] [-Name <String>] [-OWAActiveSyncIntegrationEnabled
<Nullable>] [-OWAAllAddressListsEnabled <Nullable>] [-OWACalendarEnabled
<Nullable>] [-OWAChangePasswordEnabled <Nullable>] [-OWAContactsEnabled <Nullable>]
[-OWAEnabled <$true | $false>] [-OWAJournalEnabled <Nullable>]
[-OWAJunkEmailEnabled <Nullable>] [-OWANotesEnabled <Nullable>]
[-OWAPremiumClientEnabled <Nullable>] [-OWARemindersAndNotificationsEnabled
<Nullable>] [-OWASearchFoldersEnabled <Nullable>] [-OWASignaturesEnabled
<Nullable>] [-OWASpellCheckerEnabled <Nullable>] [-OWATasksEnabled <Nullable>]
[-OWAThemeSelectionEnabled <Nullable>] [-OWAUMIntegrationEnabled <Nullable>]
[-OWAUNCAccessOnPrivateComputersEnabled <Nullable>]
[-OWAUNCAccessOnPublicComputersEnabled <Nullable>]
[-OWAWSSAccessOnPrivateComputersEnabled <Nullable>]
[-OWAWSSAccessOnPublicComputersEnabled <Nullable>] [-PopEnabled <$true | $false>]
```

```
[-PopMessagesRetrievalMimeFormat <TextOnly | HtmlOnly | HtmlAndTextAlternative |
TextEnrichedOnly | TextEnrichedAndTextAlternative | BestBodyFormat>]
[-PopUseProtocolDefaults <$true | $false>] [-PrimarySmtpAddress <SmtpAddress>]
[-ProtocolSettings <MultiValuedProperty>] [-SamAccountName <String>]
```

This cmdlet requires the logged-on user to be a member of the Exchange Recipient Administrator Group and belong to the local Administrators group on the computer.

Some key parameters to note include:

❑ `Identity <MailboxIdParameter>`: This is a required parameter. It can be the Active Directory Object ID or a string that represents the GUID, distinguished name, domain or account, user principal name (UPN), legacy Exchange distinguished name, Simple Mail Transfer Protocol (SMTP) address, or alias.

❑ `ActiveSyncAllowedDeviceIDs <MultiValuedProperty>`: This parameter accepts a list of device IDs that are allowed to synchronize with the mailbox.

❑ `ActiveSyncEnabled <Boolean>`: This parameter enables or disables Exchange ActiveSync.

❑ `ImapEnabled <Boolean>`: This parameter specifies whether the IMAP4 protocol is enabled for this mailbox.

❑ `PopEnabled <Boolean>`: This parameter specifies whether the POP3 protocol is enabled for this mailbox.

❑ `MAPIBlockOutlookNonCachedMode <Boolean>`: This parameter specifies whether Outlook can be used in online mode.

❑ `MAPIBlockOutlookRpcHttp <Boolean>`: This parameter specifies whether clients can connect to Outlook by using Outlook Anywhere.

❑ `MAPIEnabled <Boolean>`: This parameter specifies whether the MAPI protocol is enabled for the mailbox.

❑ `OWAChangePasswordEnabled <Nullable>`: This parameter specifies whether users can change their password in Outlook Web Access.

Export-Mailbox

This cmdlet is new in Exchange Server 2007 SP1 and is used to export contents of a mailbox to either a folder or `.pst` file. This is a feature that has been requested by administrators for some time now. You can export data from mailboxes residing on Exchange 2000 SP3, Exchange 2003 SP2, and Exchange Server 2007 servers. There are some considerations to keep in mind while using this cmdlet:

❑ `Export-Mailbox` cannot span multiple Active Directory forests. In other words, the source and target mailboxes must be in the same Active Directory forest.

❑ Although this feature has been requested by many, at this time, you cannot export data to a `.pst` file from a mailbox that is located in a Recovery Storage Group (RSG), nor can you export contents from a public folder database.

❑ You must be running on a 32-bit machine and have Outlook 2003 SP2 or later installed.

Several parameters that provide flexibility with export of mailbox contents are available. For a detailed list run the following in the Exchange Management Shell: get-help export-Mailbox -detailed.

❑ PSTFolderPath <LongPath>: This parameter specifies the path of the .pst file to which data will be exported. If a folder is specified, it must be created first.

❑ TargetFolder <String>: This parameter specifies the top-level mailbox folder that will be created on the mailbox specified by the TargetMailbox parameter. This folder will contain a subfolder called Recovered Data - <source mailbox alias> - <date time stamp>. The subfolder contains the exported data. If the target folder that you specify already exists on the target mailbox, the exported data will be added to the existing folder. If the target folder does not exist, it will be created.

❑ AllContentKeywords <String[]>: This parameter specifies the keywords of the content to include in the move. If the command finds a keyword that you specify in the message body, attachment content, or subject, it will export those messages. This is different from using both the ContentKeywords and SubjectKeywords parameters. If you use both the ContentKeywords and SubjectKeywords parameters, the command will export only those messages that have both the keyword that you specify for the ContentKeywords parameter in the message body or attachment content, and the keyword you specify for the SubjectKeywords parameter in the subject.

❑ TargetMailbox <MailboxIdParameter>: This parameter specifies the mailbox where the target folder will be created. The mailbox that you specify must exist for the command to complete successfully. Possible values are True or False. If set to True, anti-spam processing is skipped for the mailbox.

❑ StartDate <DateTime>: This parameter specifies the start date for filtering content that will be exported from the source mailbox. Only items in the mailbox whose date is later than the start date will be exported. When you enter a specific date, use the short date format that is defined in the Regional Options settings that are configured on the local computer. For example, if your computer is configured to use the short date format mm/dd/yyyy, enter 03/01/2006 to specify March 1, 2006.

❑ ValidateOnly <SwitchParameter>: This parameter provides the option to validate the export without exporting the data. The ValidateOnly parameter validates any prerequisites for the command. If you run the Export-Mailbox command with this parameter, the command will not apply any filters to the messages. It will only check if the source and target mailboxes exist.

❑ AttachmentFilenames <String[]>: This parameter specifies the filter for attachments. You can use wildcard characters in the string. For example, you can use "*.txt" to export items that have a .txt extension.

Import-Mailbox

This cmdlet is also new in Exchange Server 2007 SP1 and it imports mailbox data from a .pst file into a mailbox. As in the case of the Export-Mailbox cmdlet, there are some considerations to keep in mind while using this cmdlet:

❑ You can only import mailbox data to a mailbox residing on Exchange Server 2007. Import to earlier versions of Exchange must use the exmerge utility previously available.

❑ You cannot import data from a `.pst` file to a mailbox that is located in a Recovery Storage Group (RSG), nor can you import data into a public folder database.

❑ You must be running on a 32-bit machine and have Outlook 2003 SP2 or later installed.

Several parameters that provide flexibility with import of mailbox contents are available. For a detailed list run the following in the Exchange Management Shell: `get-help export-Mailbox -detailed`.

❑ `PSTFolderPath <>`: This parameter specifies the path of the `.pst` file from which data will be imported. Can be used to convert from one mailbox type to another.

❑ `AllContentKeywords <>`: The `AllContentKeywords` parameter specifies the keywords of the content to include in the import. If the command finds a keyword that you specify in the message body, attachment content, or subject, it will import those messages. This is different from using both the `ContentKeywords` and `SubjectKeywords` parameters. If you use both the `ContentKeywords` and `SubjectKeywords` parameters, the command will import only those messages that have both the keyword that you specify for the `ContentKeywords` parameter in the message body or attachment content, and the keyword you specify for the `SubjectKeywords` parameter in the subject.

❑ `AttachmentFilenames <>`: This parameter specifies the filter for attachments. You can use wildcard characters in the string. For example, you can use `"*.txt"` to import items that have a `.txt` extension.

❑ `BadItemLimit <>`: This parameter specifies the number of corrupted items in a `.pst` file to skip before the import operation fails.

❑ `MaxThreads <>`: The `MaxThreads` parameter specifies the maximum number of threads to use. The default value is 4.

❑ `SenderKeywords <>`: The `SenderKeywords` parameter specifies the keywords of the content to include in the import. If the command finds a keyword that you specify in the sender, it will import those messages.

❑ `ValidateOnly <>`: This parameter provides the option to validate the import without importing the data. The `ValidateOnly` parameter validates any prerequisites for the command. If you run the `Import-Mailbox` command with this parameter, the command will not apply any filters to the messages. It will only check if the source and target mailboxes exist.

❑ `EndDate <>`: This parameter specifies the end date for filtering content that will be imported to the target mailbox. Only items in the `.pst` file whose date is prior to or the same as the end date will be imported. When you enter a specific date, use the short date format that is defined in the Regional Options settings that are configured on the local computer. For example, if your computer is configured to use the short date format mm/dd/yyyy, enter 03/01/2006 to specify March 1, 2006.

Creating a User Mailbox

The `New-Mailbox` cmdlet is used to create a new user mailbox. This creates a new user account in Active Directory and a new mailbox on a mailbox database on Exchange Server 2007. The mailbox is enabled and ready to send and receive email messages. The `New-Mailbox` cmdlet discussed earlier can also be used to mailbox-enable an existing user account in Active Directory. The account used for setting up the new mailbox must be granted the Exchange Recipient Administrator role and Account Operator role for the Active Directory container the user will be created in. Each Active Directory domain a user mailbox will be created in must be prepared for Exchange Server 2007 using the `setup.com /prepareDomain` switch.

Run the following from the Exchange Management Shell to create a new user mailbox:

```
New-mailbox -UserPrincipalName mstest1@exchangeexchange.local -alias mstest1 -
database "First Storage Group\Mailbox Database" -Name Mstest1Exch -
OrganizationalUnit Users -password $Password -FirstName Mstest1 -LastName Exch -
DisplayName "Mstest1 Exch" -ResetPasswordOnNextLogon $true
```

The previous example creates a user `MSTest1 Exch` in Active Directory and a mailbox for that user. The mailbox is located on the First Storage Group, in mailbox database. The password must be reset at the next logon. Also the Organizational Unit where this user will be created has been specified.

To set the initial value of the password, you can create a variable called `$password` that prompts you to enter an initial password and assigns that password to the variable as a `SecureString` object:

```
$Password = Read-Host "Please Enter your password:" -AsSecureString
```

The `Read-Host` cmdlet reads a line of input from the console. It can be used to prompt for input from a user or to create secure strings. Hence it takes the `prompt` or `AsSecureString` switch parameters. In the previous example, `Read-Host` presents `Please Enter your password:` as a prompt and then each keystroke will be displayed as an asterisk (*). Upon completion the password is stored as a secure string in the variable `$Password`. See Figure 4-21.

Figure 4-21

If the password parameter is not specified during the creation of the user mailbox, Exchange Management Shell prompts for the password before the user is created.

Several other parameters can be specified during the creation of the user such as the `ActiveSyncMailbox` or `ManangedFolderMailbox` policies as well as setting the domain controller against which the user will be created. Also, you can specify the database by "Server name\Database name." This allows you determine the server on which the mailbox will be created. See the detailed list of parameters described earlier in this section.

It is worthwhile to mention a slight change in SP1. In the RTM version of Exchange Server 2007, the Exchange Management Console New Mailbox Wizard presents you with the Server name, Storage group, and Mailbox database fields. (See Figure 4-22.)

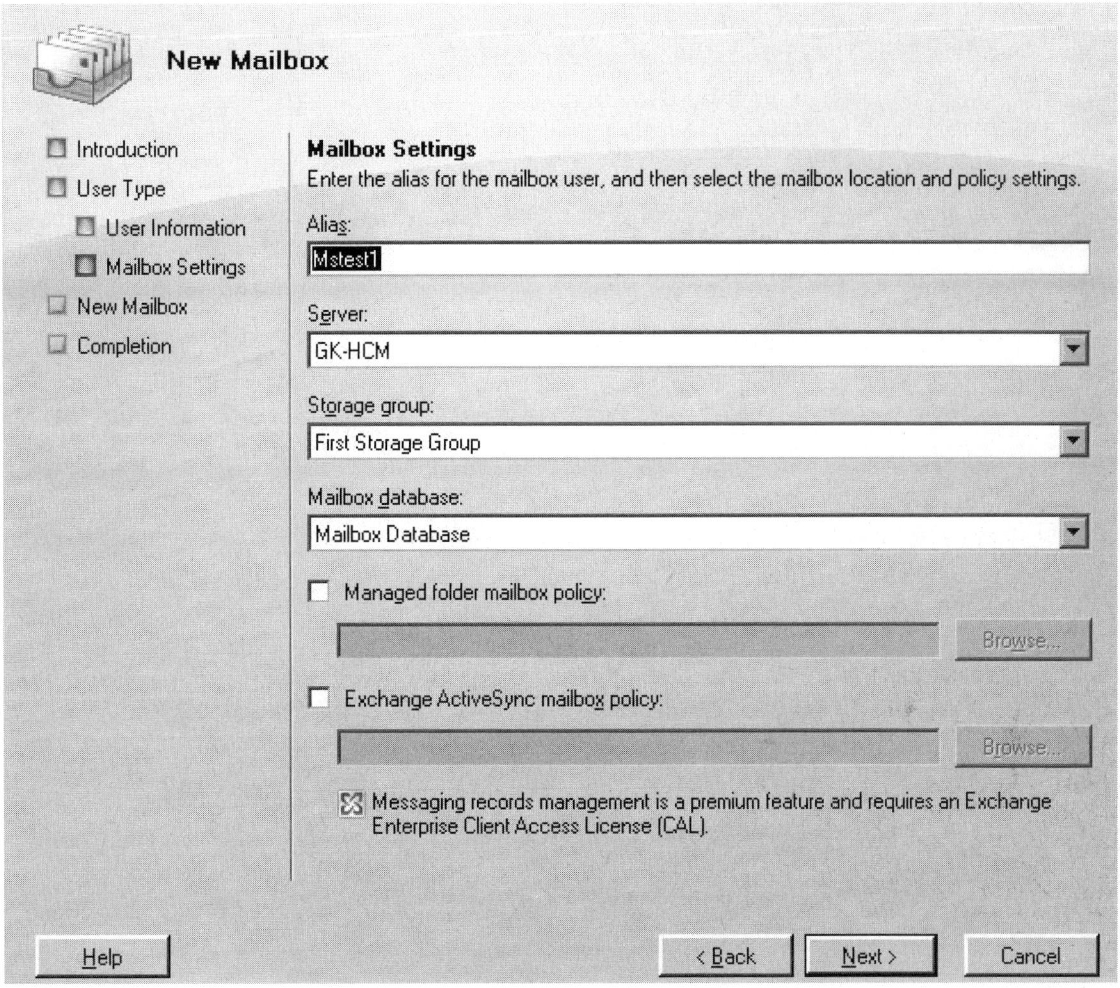

Figure 4-22

In SP1 you simply have the option to select a mailbox database and can browse all the mailbox store databases in the organization depending on the scope of the Management Console (see Figure 4-23). These are simply Management Console changes and do not reflect any changes in the Exchange Management Shell.

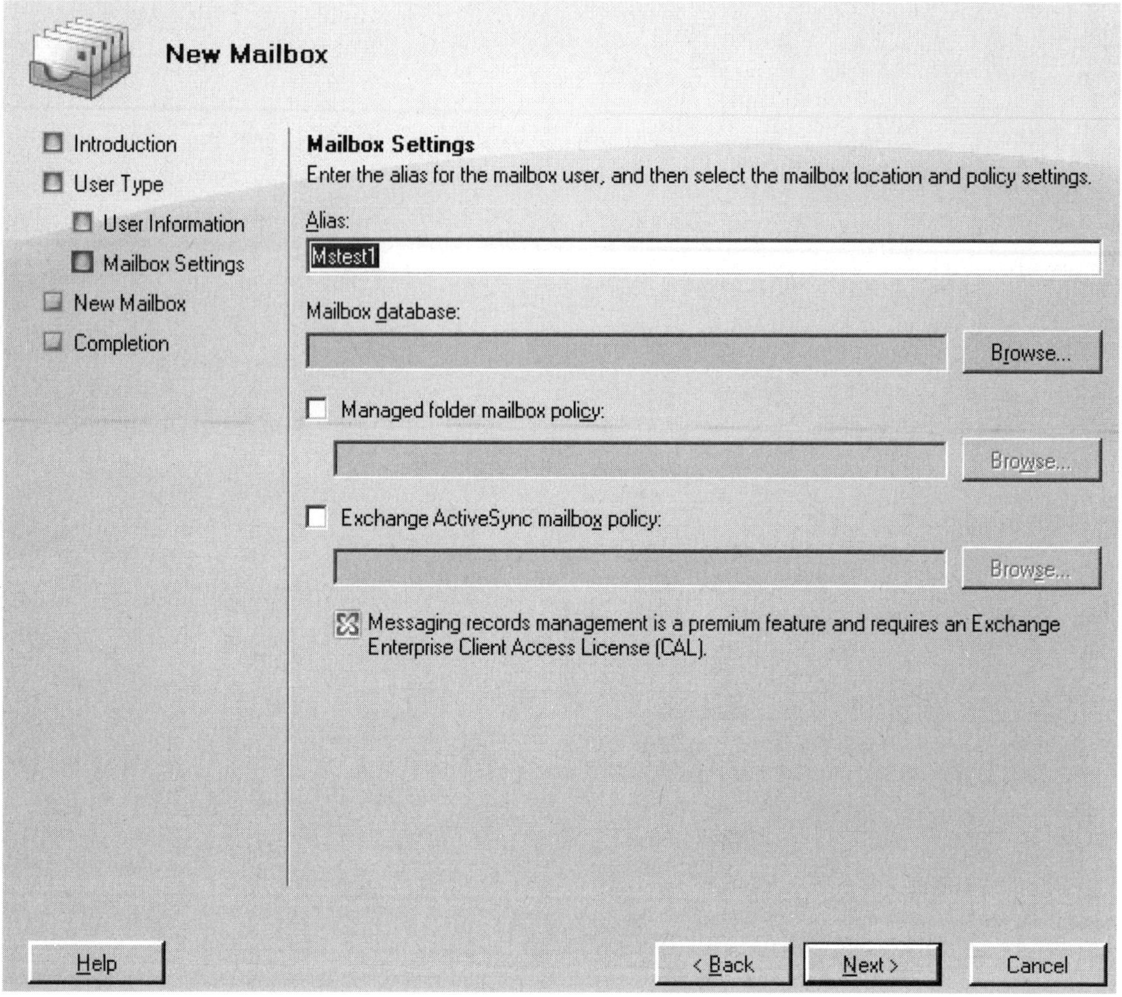

New Mailbox

- Introduction
- User Type
  - User Information
  - Mailbox Settings
- New Mailbox
- Completion

Mailbox Settings
Enter the alias for the mailbox user, and then select the mailbox location and policy settings.

Alias:

Mstest1

Mailbox database:

[   ] Browse...

☐ Managed folder mailbox policy:

[   ] Browse...

☐ Exchange ActiveSync mailbox policy:

[   ] Browse...

Messaging records management is a premium feature and requires an Exchange Enterprise Client Access License (CAL).

[Help]   [< Back]   [Next >]   [Cancel]

Figure 4-23

In the New Mailbox Wizard, when you click the Browse button as shown in Figure 4-23, you are presented with available mailbox databases to select from. (See Figure 4-24.)

For an existing Active Directory user account or interOrgPerson, the Enable-Mailbox cmdlet can be used to create mailbox attributes on the user object. When an email is sent to the user, an Exchange mailbox object is created in the Exchange database. At a minimum, the identity and the database parameters can be specified to enable a mailbox. This cmdlet can be used to enable an existing Active Directory user object as a user mailbox, resource mailbox, linked mailbox, or shared mailbox.

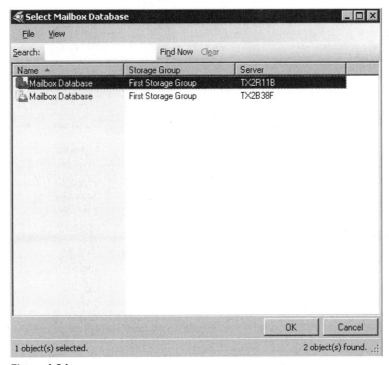

Figure 4-24

A key point to note is that when mailbox-enabling an existing user, if an alias is not specified, the user principal name (UPN) is used and all non-ASCII characters converted to underscore characters. The potential exists for the user account to have a non-ASCII value for the UPN. In this case, when you mailbox-enable the user, the alias will be changed to all underscore characters. To avoid this, confirm that the user account has an ASCII UPN before you create the new mailbox, or make sure you specify a value for the alias. To enable an existing Active Directory object, run the following command:

```
Enable-Mailbox MailUser1@ExchangeExchange.local -Database "Mailbox Database"
```

The New-Mailbox cmdlet is also used to create a new linked mailbox. As you recall, a linked mailbox is a mailbox that is accessed by an external account not in the Exchange forest, although a disabled Windows account in the Exchange forest is associated with it. Hence the following parameters must be specified: LinkedDomainController, LinkedMasterAccount, and LinkedCredential. The example in Figure 4-25 and Figure 4-26 shows how to create a new linked mailbox. This command creates a new linked mailbox called "Mslinked Exch" to be accessed by the user called RemoteAdmin in the Gamisoft Active Directory forest.

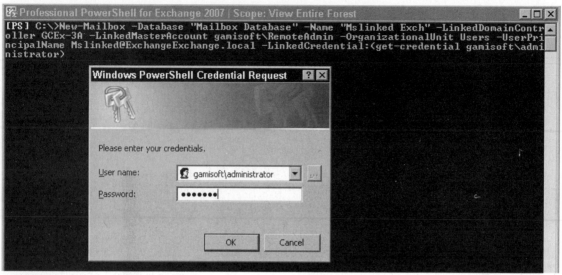

Figure 4-25

First you specify the account to be used to access the linked domain controller in the external forest and you are prompted for its credentials. After supplying the credentials, the linked mailbox is successfully created Using the Get-Recipient cmdlet you verify that the mailbox created is indeed a linked mailbox. (See Figure 4-26.)

```
Professional PowerShell for Exchange 2007 | Scope: View Entire Forest          _ □ X
[PS] C:\>New-Mailbox -Database "Mailbox Database" -Name "Mslinked Exch" -LinkedDomainContr
oller GCEx-3A -LinkedMasterAccount gamisoft\RemoteAdmin -OrganizationalUnit Users -UserPri
ncipalName Mslinked@ExchangeExchange.local -LinkedCredential:(get-credential gamisoft\admi
nistrator)

Name                      Alias                ServerName        ProhibitSendQuota
----                      -----                ----------        -----------------
Mslinked Exch             Mslinked             gk-hcm            unlimited

[PS] C:\>get-recipient mslinked | ft name, recipienttypedetails

Name                                                             RecipientTypeDetails
----                                                             --------------------
Mslinked Exch                                                    ·LinkedMailbox
```

Figure 4-26

As an option, rather than being prompted for the password, you can use the Get-Credential cmdlet to specify the account to be used to access the external forest. This cmdlet creates a credential object for a specified username and password. When a username and password are specified, the cmdlet creates a PSCredential object representing the credentials passed. You can assign it to a variable object and use the variable as an input to cmdlets requesting user authentication.

You can easily convert a linked mailbox to a regular user mailbox. First, however, you must disable the linked mailbox and then reconnect the `Mailbox` object to a `user` object in the same Active Directory forest as the Exchange server:

```
Disable-Mailbox -Identity Mslinked
Connect-Mailbox -Identity Mslinked -Database "Mailbox Database" -User UserLocalAD
```

The New-Mailbox cmdlet is used to create a new shared mailbox. This requires the `shared` switch parameter of the `New-Mailbox` cmdlet. All other parameters remain the same, as shown in Figure 4-27.

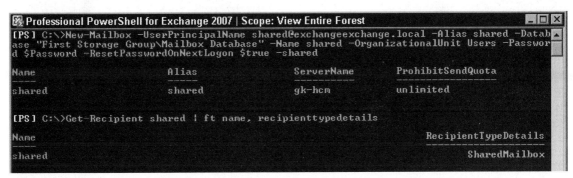

Figure 4-27

Modifying a User Mailbox

After a user mailbox is created, several operations could be performed on the user mailbox ranging from changing one or more attributes to disconnecting and removing the mailbox.

Disabling, Disconnecting, or Removing a User Mailbox

When a user leaves an Exchange organization or due to some administrative reason, it may be necessary to remove the user's mailbox. The `Remove-Mailbox` cmdlet is used to accomplish this, however keep in mind that this cmdlet also removes the Active Directory user object. To disconnect the mailbox for user `Mstest` from `Mstest`'s user account and also delete the user account, run the following command:

```
Remove-Mailbox -Identity ExchangeExchange\Mstest
```

To immediately delete the mailbox and the user account for `Mstest`, run the following command:

```
Remove-Mailbox -Identity ExchangeExchange\Mstest -Permanent $true
```

In both cases, you are prompted to confirm the deletion before proceeding. You can also use the `whatif` parameter to obtain an explanation of what you are about to do.

In some cases you may want to simply disconnect the mailbox from the associated Active Directory user account while retaining the user account. This is similar to removing all Exchange attributes as performed in Exchange Server 2000/2003. In this case, use the `Disable-Mailbox` cmdlet to disconnect the mailbox. The mailbox will be marked for deletion/removal per the mailbox retention policy.

In Figure 4-28 we first obtain a list of disconnected mailboxes on a database on server Ex7B and assign it to a variable. Notice the mailbox `ExTest` is a disconnected mailbox. Next we use the `Remove-Mailbox` cmdlet to purge the mailboxes from the Exchange database. We confirm the mailbox removal by looking at the `MailboxStatistics` again.

```
$Temp = Get-MailboxStatistics -Database "Ex7B\Mailbox Database"  | Where
{$_.DisconnectDate -ne $null}
Remove-Mailbox -Database "Ex7B\Mailbox Database"  -StoreMailboxIdentity
$Temp.MailboxGuid
```

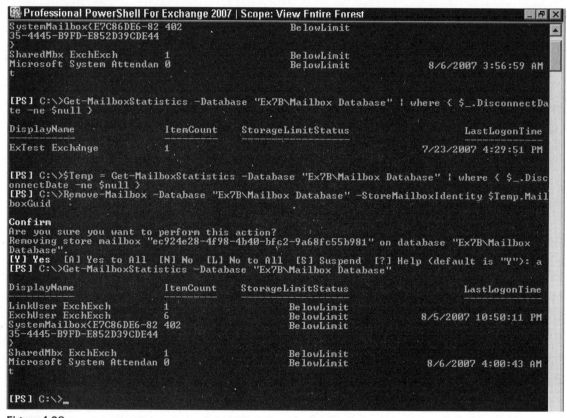

Figure 4-28

Enabling and Disabling Client-Access Related Attributes

Several client-access attributes can be modified for users on Exchange Server 2007. These include Outlook Web Access (OWA), ActiveSync, POP3, and IMAP4 attributes. The `Set-CASMailbox` cmdlet can be used to modify these attributes. For more information on this cmdlet, see the "Set-CASMailbox" section earlier in the chapter. Remember that this cmdlet requires the `identity` property. In addition, you can enable one or multiple features in a single statement. Following are a few examples.

You can enable or disable the ability of clients to use OWA, now known as Outlook Anywhere, in Exchange Server 2007 by setting the `OWAEnabled` parameter to `true` or `false`:

```
Set-CASMailbox -Identity ExchUser@ExchangeExchange.local -OWAEnabled $true
```

You can enable/disable multiple attributes in the same statement. For example, you may want to enable OWA, POP3, IMAP4, and ActiveSync while disabling MAPI access for a user:

```
Set-CASMailbox -Identity ExchUser@ExchangeExchange.local -OWAEnabled: $true -
POPEnabled:$true -ImapEnabled:$true -ActiveSyncEnabled:$true -MAPIEnabled:$false
```

To disable MAPI access for all users, edit the `Disable MAPI Clients` string value in `HKEY_LOCAL_MACHINE\System\CurrentControlSet\Services\MSExchangeIS\ParametersSystem`.

You may need to create this value because it may not exist by default. View the version of the `Emsmdb32.dll` file to determine the MAPI Outlook client version and enter one of the following:

- ❑ To disable a specific MAPI client version, type:`12.1234.01`

- ❑ To disable a range of MAPI client versions, type `11.1234.01-12.1234.01`

- ❑ To disable an open-ended range of MAPI client versions, type `-12.1234.01`

- ❑ To disable multiple sets of MAPI client versions, use either commas or semicolons to separate the sets as follows: `11.1234.01-11.9999.01;12.1234.01-12.5000.01`

Managing Other User Mailbox Properties

You can manage a variety of other properties on the user mailbox such as updating phone or address information, adding email addresses, changing message size limits, configuring storage quota and anti-spam features; the list goes on. Consider a few examples given here.

You can configure message size limits for a user mailbox. This determines the maximum message size a user can send or receive. Although message size limits could be configured at the mailbox level, there are other configurations or settings that can determine conclusively what size a user can send or receive. For example, the message size limit configured on the Hub Transport server, if less than that configured on the user mailbox, may override the size of message the user can send. To set the sending and receiving message sizes for the user mailbox of `ExchUser` to 15 megabytes (MB), run the following command:

```
Set-Mailbox -Identity "ExchUser" -MaxSendSize 15MB -MaxReceiveSize 15MB
```

You can also restrict the number of Recipients a message can have at the mailbox level. Keep in mind that this can also be configured at the Hub Transport, Receive Connector, and Organizational levels. In the following example, you can restrict the number of Recipients per message to 450 for the `ExchUser` mailbox by running the following command:

```
Set-Mailbox -Identity "ExchUser" -RecipientLimits 450
```

Most PowerShell cmdlets allow you to pipe the output of one noun to another noun in order to view or modify related objects. In the following example, you can set the mailbox limit on all mailboxes that reside in a specific mailbox database on a server by running the command:

```
Get-MailboxDatabase "Mailbox Database" | Get-Mailbox | Set-Mailbox -
ProhibitSendQuota 500MB
```

This command retrieves all the mailboxes that reside in the mailbox database and sets their `ProhibitSendQuota` value to 500MB.

You can use the Exchange Management Shell `Move-Mailbox` cmdlet to move a user's mailbox to a different database or server. This can also be accomplished for multiple user mailboxes simultaneously. For example, you can use the `Get-Mailbox` cmdlet to retrieve a list of user mailboxes that match a certain `CustomAttribute` and use the `Move-Mailbox` cmdlet to get them moved:

```
Get-Mailbox -Filter { CustomAttribute3 -eq 'pilots' } | Move-Mailbox -
TargetDatabase "Ex7B\Mailbox Database"
```

Unlike most of the earlier commands, when adding an email address to a user mailbox object it is not possible to accomplish that with a single command. To add an email address to an existing mailbox, you need to store the mailbox configuration in a variable and modify the `EmailAddresses` field of that variable. After storing the `EmailAddresses` field in the variable, use either of the following methods to add two more addresses to the `ExchUser` mailbox:

```
$Temp = Get-Mailbox -Identity
$Temp.EmailAddresses.Add("smtp:ExchUser@2ndEmail.ExchangeExchange.local")
$Temp.EmailAddresses += ("smtp: ExchUser@3rdEmail.ExchangeExchange.local")
Set-Mailbox -Instance $Temp
```

Creating a Resource Mailbox

The `New-Mailbox` cmdlet is also used to create a new resource mailbox. As described earlier in this chapter, in Exchange Server 2007, two resource mailbox types can be created: the room and equipment resource mailboxes. Note that you can also create as shared mailbox, but use of this mailbox type is de-emphasized in Exchange Server 2007. Also mentioned earlier was the fact that the Active Directory user account associated with a resource mailbox is a disabled Windows account. After creating the resource mailbox, re-enabling this account is not recommended. If access is needed to a resource mailbox using a MAPI client or Outlook Web Access, then grant the account full access rights as you would a delegate.

To create a room mailbox, specify the `Room` switch parameter in addition to other parameters as shown here:

```
New-Mailbox -database "EX7B\First Storage Group\Mailbox Database" -Name MediaRoom -
OrganizationalUnit "Conference Rooms" DisplayName "MediaRoom" -UserPrincipalName
MediaRoom@ExchangeExchange.local -Room
```

To create an equipment mailbox, specify the `Equipment` switch parameter:

```
New-Mailbox -database "EX7B\First Storage Group\Mailbox Database" -Name PrinterA -
OrganizationalUnit Equipment -DisplayName "PrinterA" - UserPrincipalName
PrinterA@ExchangeExchange.local -Equipment
```

To create a shared mailbox, specify the `Shared` switch parameter. See Figure 4-28 earlier in this chapter.

To create a resource mailbox using an existing Active Directory user account, use the `Enable-Mailbox` cmdlet. Ensure that the Active Directory account is already disabled and specify the identity of the object and database where the mailbox will be created. Finally, specify the type of resource, either a room or equipment mailbox using the `Room` or `Equipment` switch parameters. If you attempt to use an existing enabled account in the Active Directory, you get the following error:

```
Enable-Mailbox : The user account must be logon-disabled for linked, shared or
resource mailbox.
```

Although the new resource mailbox has been created, it is not completely configured and will not allow for automatic resource scheduling. To enable Auto-Accept use the `Set-MailboxCalendarSettings` cmdlet to allow the resource mailbox to auto-accept meetings for which it is invited. In Figure 4-29, we create a new resource mailbox and enable it to auto-accept meetings to which it is scheduled.

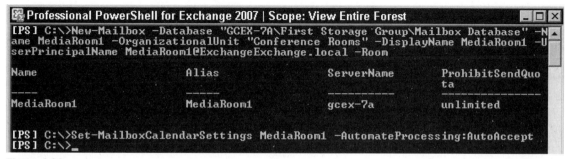

Figure 4-29

Modifying a Resource Mailbox

Once the resource mailbox is created, it can be converted from one type to another. For example, you may wish to convert your existing shared mailbox migrated from Exchange Server 2003 to a conference room or equipment mailbox or even to a user mailbox. In addition, you can disable a resource mailbox or define properties such as the resource capacity, location, and other custom attributes. The `Set-Mailbox` or `Set-ResourceConfig` cmdlets can be used to modify and/or define custom attributes for resource mailboxes.

To convert a shared mailbox to a resource mailbox, use the `Set-Mailbox` cmdlet and specify the identity of the shared mailbox to be converted. Next use the `type` parameter to indicate the type of resource you are converting it to such as room or equipment. As an example, see Figure 4-14 earlier in this chapter.

To disable a resource mailbox, simply use the `Disable-Mailbox` cmdlet. Keep in mind that this operation removes the mailbox's Exchange attributes from Active Directory but the mailbox is not deleted, and can be reconnected to its user at a later date by using the `Connect-Mailbox` cmdlet. On the other hand, using the `Remove-Mailbox` cmdlet will remove the Active Directory user account and mark the mailbox for deletion. To disconnect the resource mailbox, you must specify the identity of the resource mailbox:

```
Disable-Mailbox -Identity "ExchangeExchange.local/Users/Equipment ExchExch"
```

Also keep in mind that if the resource mailbox has been configured to auto-accept meeting requests or any other automated processing of meetings has been configured, these must be disabled first before the resource mailbox can be fully disabled.

To modify the capacity or meeting duration of a conference room mailbox, you use the `Set-Mailbox` and `Set-MailboxCalendarSettings` cmdlets. Figure 4-30 shows the default settings of the MediaRoom1 resource mailbox using the `Get-Mailbox` and `Get-MailboxCalendarSettings` cmdlets; next the capacity and duration of the mailbox is changed using the `Set` cmdlets and the new settings displayed thereafter.

Figure 4-30

Notice the default values set; for example, `MaximumDurationInMinutes` is `1440` and resource capacity is not set. In Figure 4-31, these values are changed. The `ResourceCustom` property, though, is not changed.

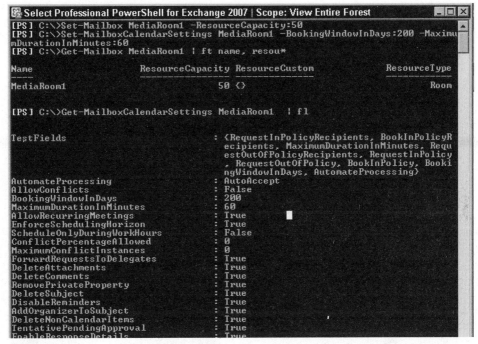

```
Select Professional PowerShell for Exchange 2007 | Scope: View Entire Forest
[PS] C:\>Set-Mailbox MediaRoom1 -ResourceCapacity:50
[PS] C:\>Set-MailboxCalendarSettings MediaRoom1 -BookingWindowInDays:200 -Maximu
mDurationInMinutes:60
[PS] C:\>Get-Mailbox MediaRoom1 | ft name, resou*

Name                      ResourceCapacity ResourceCustom                    ResourceType

MediaRoom1                        50 {}                                       Room


[PS] C:\>Get-MailboxCalendarSettings MediaRoom1 | fl


TestFields                            : {RequestInPolicyRecipients, BookInPolicyR
                                        ecipients, MaximumDurationInMinutes, Requ
                                        estOutOfPolicyRecipients, RequestInPolicy
                                        , RequestOutOfPolicy, BookInPolicy, Booki
                                        ngWindowInDays, AutomateProcessing}
AutomateProcessing                    : AutoAccept
AllowConflicts                        : False
BookingWindowInDays                   : 200
MaximumDurationInMinutes              : 60
AllowRecurringMeetings                : True
EnforceSchedulingHorizon              : True
ScheduleOnlyDuringWorkHours           : False
ConflictPercentageAllowed             : 0
MaximumConflictInstances              : 0
ForwardRequestsToDelegates            : True
DeleteAttachments                     : True
DeleteComments                        : True
RemovePrivateProperty                 : True
DeleteSubject                         : True
DisableReminders                      : True
AddOrganizerToSubject                 : True
DeleteNonCalendarItems                : True
TentativePendingApproval              : True
EnableResponseDetails                 : True
```

Figure 4-31

The `Set-ResourceConfig` cmdlet allows you define custom properties on the resource mailboxes. In Exchange Server 2003, it was difficult to determine what a conference room contained, such as TV, projector, refrigerator, and so on. The only way to determine this was to use the display name to identify the contents of the room (for example, `ConferenceRoom1-Projector-Refrigerator`). In Exchange Server 2007, users can easily locate the type of conference room they desire to use by the additional attributes configured on the conference room or equipment mailbox. This can be accomplished by extending the `ResourcePropertySchema` property of the `ResourceConfig` object. Thereafter you can apply the additional attributes to a desired resource mailbox. This is as shown in Figure 4-32.

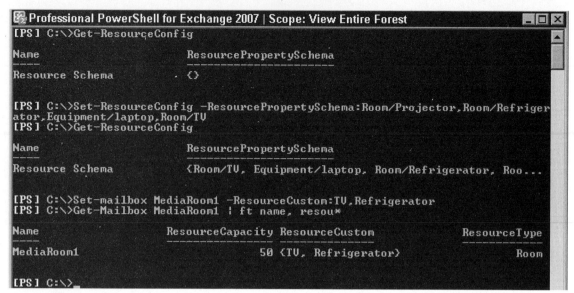

```
Professional PowerShell for Exchange 2007 | Scope: View Entire Forest        _ □ ✕
[PS] C:\>Get-ResourceConfig

Name                           ResourcePropertySchema
----                           ----------------------
Resource Schema                . {}


[PS] C:\>Set-ResourceConfig -ResourcePropertySchema:Room/Projector,Room/Refriger
ator,Equipment/laptop,Room/TV
[PS] C:\>Get-ResourceConfig

Name                           ResourcePropertySchema
----                           ----------------------
Resource Schema                {Room/TV, Equipment/laptop, Room/Refrigerator, Roo...


[PS] C:\>Set-mailbox MediaRoom1 -ResourceCustom:TV,Refrigerator
[PS] C:\>Get-Mailbox MediaRoom1 | ft name, resou*

Name                 ResourceCapacity ResourceCustom              ResourceType
----                 ---------------- --------------              ------------
MediaRoom1                         50 {TV, Refrigerator}                  Room


[PS] C:\>
```

Figure 4-32

Because the `ResourcePropertySchema` property is an array of strings, each time the
`Set-ResourceConfig` cmdlet is used it overwrites rather than appends the existing value. In that
case, to append to any existing value, simply assign a variable to `"Get-ResourceConfig -
ResourcePropertySchema"` and add additional values. Additional values must be added in the format
of `"Room/ "` or `"Equipment/ "`. Then pass the assigned variable to the `Set-ResourceConfig` cmdlet
with the `Instance` parameter.

Creating a Mail User and Mail Contact

Mail contacts and mail users are both mail-enabled Active Directory objects that contain information
about people or organizations not existing in the Exchange organization. However, there is a marked
difference between both. Although the mail contact stores information about a person external to the
Exchange organization, it does not have access to internal resources in the forest. On the other hand, the
mail user has Active Directory logon credentials and has access to local resources to which they are
granted.

To create a new mail contact, use the `New-MailContact` cmdlet. This cmdlet creates a new mail contact
object in Active Directory and mail-enables the object. The `ExternalEmailAddress` parameter specifies
the target address or proxy address of the external person:

```
New-MailContact -Name "John Doe" -ExternalEmailAddress John@Foreigndomain.com -
OrganizationalUnit ForeignDomain
```

You can also enable an existing contact in Active Directory using the `Enable-MailContact` cmdlet and specifying the external email address of the user. This cmdlet also requires that you specify the identity of the existing contact to be mail-enabled:

```
Enable-MailContact -Identity "John Doe" -ExternalEmailAddress John@Foreigndomain.com
```

To create a new mail user, use the `New-MailUser` cmdlet:

```
New-MailUser -Name John -FirstName John -LastName Doe -ExternalEmailAddress
John@ForeignDomain.com -UserPrincipalName John@ExchangeExchange.local -
OrganizationalUnit ForeignDomain -Password
$Password
```

Make sure the password has been assigned a variable `$Password`. In addition, you can also mail-enable an existing Active Directory user object using the `Enable-MailUser` cmdlet.

Modifying a Mail User and Mail Contact

Modifying mail user or mail contact could involve disabling, removing, or simply updating certain attributes of both objects.

To remove an existing mail contact from Active Directory, use the `Remove-MailContact` cmdlet and run the following command:

```
Remove-MailContact -Identity "John Doe" -DomainController ExchangeExchange.Local
```

The `Remove-MailContact` cmdlet has just two parameters: the identity of the object to be removed, which is required, and the FQDN of the domain controller that writes the configuration change to Active Directory. The second parameter is optional. Keep in mind that using this command not only removes the associated Exchange configuration on the contact, but it also removes `MailContact` object itself from Active Directory.

Disabling the mail contact involves removing all the Exchange attributes from the contact. This, however, does not remove the object from Active Directory. To accomplish this, use the `Disable-MailContact` cmdlet. As with the `Remove-MailContact` cmdlet, this cmdlet has two parameters: the identity, which is required, and the FQDN of the domain controller, which writes the change in Active Directory:

```
Disable-MailContact -Identity "John Doe" -DomainController ExchangeExchange.Local
```

The same applies to the mail user. You can remove or disable the mail user using the `Remove-MailUser` and `Disable-MailUser` cmdlets, respectively. For example:

```
Disable-MailUser John@ExchangeExchange.local
```

To change attributes on the mail contact or mail user, use the `Set-User` and `Set-Contact` cmdlets to specify the changes required. The following example shows how the `Set-User` cmdlet is used to configure the phone number and address for an Active Directory user object called John:

```
Set-User -Identity Amy@ExchangeExchange.local -Phone "(972) 660-5005" -
StreetAddress "1098 Huntington  Street" -City "Paris" -StateOrProvince "TX" -
PostalCode "75460"
```

To use the Exchange Management Shell to add a user to an administrator role, run the following command:

```
Add-ExchangeAdministrator -Role OrgAdmin -Identity ExchangeExchange\John
```

Creating and Modifying Group Objects

To facilitate mass distribution of email messages and other information to multiple users in an Exchange organization, Exchange makes use of group objects. Security Group objects are also used to grant multiple Recipients access to a shared resource. Exchange Server 2007 supports four group object types, which are Mail-Enabled Universal Distribution or Security Group, Mail-Enabled Nonuniversal Groups, and Dynamic Distribution Groups. For more information on these group types, see the "Exchange Server 2007 Group Objects" section earlier in this chapter. In this section, we cover the creation and modification or management of these group types. Keep in mind a significant change in the default configuration of group objects in Exchange Server 2007. By default mail-enabled groups created in Exchange Server 2007 will only accept messages from authenticated users. This would prevent external users from sending messages to the group or emailing spam to a large number of users in the organization. In Exchange Server 2000 and 2003, by default, the Distribution Group accepted messages from everyone.

To create a new Mail-Enabled Universal Distribution or Security Group, use the `New-DistributionGroup` cmdlet. This cmdlet requires that the Name, Organizational Unit, SAMAccountName, and Type be specified. The `Type` parameter determines whether the group is a Distribution or Security Group:

```
New-DistributionGroup -Name "ExchUDG" -OrganizationalUnit Users -SAMAccountName
"ExchUDG" -Type "Distribution"
New-DistributionGroup -Name "ExchUSG" -OrganizationalUnit Users -SAMAccountName
"ExchUSG" -Type "Security"
```

To mail-enable an existing Universal group in Active Directory, use the `Enable-DistributionGroup` cmdlet. This cmdlet requires that the identity of the group to be mail-enabled be specified. The identity parameter can be the GUID of the group, Distinguished Name, or `"Domain\Account name"`:

```
Enable-DistributionGroup -Identity "ExchUSG1 Group"
```

As with all other Recipient objects discussed, using the `Remove` cmdlet removes not only the mail-enabled properties but also the object itself from Active Directory. It is the same with Distribution

Groups. Use the `Remove-DistributionGroup` cmdlet to remove a Distribution Group from Active Directory. This cmdlet requires the identity of the group object to be specified.

Group objects have members and any Recipient type including other groups can be members of a Distribution or Security Group. Using the Exchange Management Shell, you can add members to or remove members from a Group object. This can be accomplished using the `Add-DistributionGroupMember` and `Remove-DistributionGroupMember` cmdlets. When removing a member from a group, you are prompted to confirm the removal before the member is removed. Both cmdlets have three parameters, with `Identity` and `Member` being required parameters; `DomainController` is an optional parameter:

```
Add-DistributionGroupMember -Identity "ExchUDG" -Member amy@ExchangeExchange.local

Remove-DistributionGroupMember -Identity "ExchUDG" -Member
amy@ExchangeExchange.local
```

After making changes, use the `Get-DistributionGroupMember` cmdlet to confirm addition or removal of members to the Distribution Group. This cmdlet shows the current members of the Distribution Group.

Exchange Server 2007 allows for the conversion of existing global or local groups to Universal Security or Distribution Group. The `Set-Group` cmdlet is used to accomplish this.

The Dynamic Distribution Group

The Dynamic Distribution Group, previously known as Query Based Distribution Group, differs from other groups supported in Exchange Server 2007. Its membership list is based on a specified precanned or custom filter and this list is calculated each time a message is sent to the Distribution Group. All Recipients that match the filter will receive the message sent to the Distribution Group. Like the other groups supported in Exchange Server 2007, the Dynamic Distribution Group receives messages only from authenticated users.

To create a new Dynamic Distribution Group, use the `New-DynamicDistributionGroup` cmdlet. Required parameters for this cmdlet include the Name, Organizational Unit, `IncludedRecipients`, and `RecipientFilter`. The `RecipientFilter` parameter is used when creating a custom filter for the Distribution Group. In the following example, the `IncludedRecipients` parameter specifies all mailbox users in the organization. The Dynamic Distribution Group is created in the Users Organizational Unit:

```
New-DynamicDistributionGroup -IncludedRecipients MailboxUsers -Name
    "ExchMailboxUsers" -OrganizationalUnit Users
```

A custom filter can also be specified using the `RecipientFilter` parameter. The following filter indicates all user mailboxes residing on server EX7B but excluding the system mailboxes. You must exclude the system mailboxes especially if you are coexisting with Exchange Server 2000/2003:

```
New-DynamicDistributionGroup -Name "EX7BMailboxUsers" -OrganizationalUnit Users -
RecipientFilter {((RecipientType -eq 'UserMailbox' -and ServerName -eq 'EX7B') -and
-not(Name -like 'SystemMailbox{*'))}
```

Unlike the Universal Distribution or Security Groups (`Get-DistributionGroupMembers`), it is not possible to view the Dynamic Distribution Group members with a single cmdlet where a custom filter is used. With the exception of precanned filters, the Exchange Management Console does not provide a means yet of viewing a Dynamic Distribution Group's membership, unlike the preview button that existed with the Query Based Distribution Group.

To view the Dynamic Distribution Group's members, assign a variable to the `Get-DynamicDistributionGroup` cmdlet for the designated group. Each `DynamicDistributionGroup` object has a `RecipientFilter` property, which indicates the group membership criteria. Next use the `Get-Recipient` cmdlet with the `-Filter` string to return the members of the Dynamic Distribution Group:

```
$ExchDDG = Get-DynamicDistributionGroup -Identity "ExchDDG"

Get-Recipient -Filter $ExchDDG.RecipientFilter
```

Bulk Recipient Management

Thus far you have seen how to create and modify various Recipient objects in Exchange Server 2007. Often, however, there is need to create or modify multiple objects at the same time or provide reporting from various objects. In earlier versions of Exchange, most operations of this kind were accomplished using scripts, bat files, or tools specifically for bulk editing such as Admodify. When it comes to working with multiple objects in Exchange Server 2007, most operations are fairly easy to perform from the Exchange Management Shell, sometimes in a single-line shell command. The pipeline can be used effectively to redirect the output of one command into another. For complex bulk management operations, scripts can also be used based on the Exchange Management Shell.

In this section, you explore scenarios where you can use the Exchange Management Shell to perform bulk operations. This is by no means an exhaustive list because we find new ways to accomplish various tasks on a daily basis. Not to be forgotten is the use of templates, which can prove very useful when configuring identical properties on objects. The following cmdlets are discussed in this section:

- ❏ `Import-CSV`
- ❏ `New-Mailbox`
- ❏ `Set-Mailbox`
- ❏ `Enable-Mailbox`
- ❏ `Get-User`
- ❏ `Get-MailboxStatistics`

Bulk Creating Mailboxes

You can create new mailboxes using the New-Mailbox cmdlet as described earlier in this chapter. Sometimes, however, an administrator may be asked to create a large number of user mailboxes based on a comma-separated value spreadsheet. How can you accomplish this with minimal effort? Fortunately, the Import-CSV cmdlet is helpful here. In this case you can easily import the CSV file and use the New-Mailbox cmdlet to quickly create the mailboxes.

So, assume after a job fair that a company's representative passes the following spreadsheet for new hires starting the following Monday. The administrator would have to create their mailboxes and generate their email addresses based on the list in Figure 4-33.

	A	B	C
1	FirstName	LastName	Department
2	Trainee1	User1	Marketing
3	Trainee2	User2	Engineering
4	Trainee3	User3	Engineering
5	Trainee4	User4	Personnel
6	Trainee5	User5	Personnel
7	Trainee6	User6	Marketing
8	Trainee7	User7	Finance
9	Trainee8	User8	Finance
10	Trainee9	User9	Finance
11	Trainee10	User10	Manufacturing
12			

Figure 4-33

The first step is to verify that the CSV file is in a format you can import from. You use the Import-CSV cmdlet and specify the CSV file. You should have an output showing the list of new hires correctly displayed. Next, as discussed earlier in the chapter, you create a temporary password that can be changed by the users at first logon. These steps are shown in Figure 4-34.

```
Professional PowerShell For Exchange 2007 | Scope: ExchangeExchange.local    [_][□][X]
[PS] C:\>Import-Csv NewHire.csv

FirstName                LastName                 Department
_____                _____                 _____
Trainee1                 User1                    Marketing
Trainee2                 User2                    Engineering
Trainee3                 User3                    Engineering
Trainee4                 User4                    Personnel
Trainee5                 User5                    Personnel
Trainee6                 User6                    Marketing
Trainee7                 User7                    Finance
Trainee8                 User8                    Finance
Trainee9                 User9                    Finance
Trainee10                User10                   Manufacturing


[PS] C:\>$Password = Read-Host "Please Enter Your Password" -AsSecureString
Please Enter Your Password: ***********
[PS] C:\>Import-Csv NewHire.csv | ForEach { New-Mailbox -Name $_.FirstName -Alia
s $_.FirstName -FirstName $_.FirstName -LastName $_.LastName -UserPrincipalName
"$_.FirstName@ExchangeExchange.local" -OrganizationalUnit ADUsers -Password $Pas
sword -Database "Mailbox Database" -ResetPasswordOnNextLogon $true }

Name                     Alias                    ServerName     ProhibitSendQuo
                                                                 ta
____                     _____                    _____     _____
Trainee1                 Trainee1                 gk-hcm         unlimited
Trainee2                 Trainee2                 gk-hcm         unlimited
Trainee3                 Trainee3                 gk-hcm         unlimited
Trainee4                 Trainee4                 gk-hcm         unlimited
Trainee5                 Trainee5                 gk-hcm         unlimited
Trainee6                 Trainee6                 gk-hcm         unlimited
Trainee7                 Trainee7                 gk-hcm         unlimited
Trainee8                 Trainee8                 gk-hcm         unlimited
Trainee9                 Trainee9                 gk-hcm         unlimited
Trainee10                Trainee10                gk-hcm         unlimited


[PS] C:\>Get-Mailbox

Name                     Alias                    ServerName     ProhibitSendQuo
                                                                 ta
____                     _____                    _____     _____
Administrator            Administrator            gk-hcm         unlimited
Trainee1                 Trainee1                 gk-hcm         unlimited
Trainee10                Trainee10                gk-hcm         unlimited
Trainee2                 Trainee2                 gk-hcm         unlimited
Trainee3                 Trainee3                 gk-hcm         unlimited
Trainee4                 Trainee4                 gk-hcm         unlimited
Trainee5                 Trainee5                 gk-hcm         unlimited
Trainee6                 Trainee6                 gk-hcm         unlimited
Trainee7                 Trainee7                 gk-hcm         unlimited
Trainee8                 Trainee8                 gk-hcm         unlimited
Trainee9                 Trainee9                 gk-hcm         unlimited


[PS] C:\>_
```

Figure 4-34

Notice that next we passed the output of the Import-CSV cmdlet to the New-Mailbox cmdlet in such a way that it loops through each new hire creating the mailbox with the parameters specified. In doing this the ForEach statement came in handy. Finally, we verified that the mailboxes were created.

Now imagine that these new hires numbered 100 or greater. You now begin to see how much time the Exchange Management Shell can save the administrator.

Working with Templates

Now suppose that these mailboxes were to be created with specific settings; for example, users in the Engineering department were to have a larger email SendQuota than those in the Finance department. Creating mailboxes to these specifications could become overwhelming. Here is where the use of templates comes in handy. The Exchange Management Shell lets you use templates by supporting the `TemplateInstance` parameter on most cmdlets. The administrator can create a template for each department, then create the users based on this template. To accomplish this, first you create a template user for the Engineering department using the `New-Mailbox` cmdlet, and next you use the `Set-Mailbox` cmdlet to customize the user settings as desired. Your next step is to assign a variable to the template user created. These steps are shown in Figure 4-35.

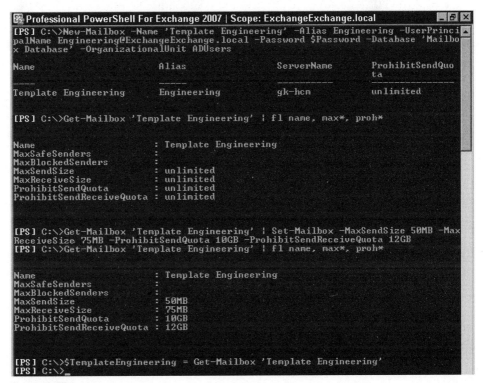

Figure 4-35

Now that you've created your template, you return back to your CSV file. This time it's another set of new hires into various departments provided in the `NewHire1.csv` file shown in Figure 4-36. You need to filter the CSV file to show just the users from the Engineering department. You can do that using either the `Filter` parameter or the `Where-object` cmdlets; here we used the latter:

```
[PS] C:\>Import-Csv newhire1.csv | where {$_.department -eq 'Engineering'}
```

	A	B	C	
1	**FirstName**	**LastName**	**Department**	
2	Trainee11	User11	Marketing	
3	Trainee12	User12	Engineering	
4	Trainee13	User13	Engineering	
5	Trainee14	User14	Development	
6	Trainee15	User15	Personnel	
7	Trainee16	User16	Marketing	
8	Trainee17	User17	Finance	
9	Trainee18	User18	Finance	
10	Trainee19	User19	Engineering	
11	Trainee20	User20	Manufacturing	
12				

Figure 4-36

You can assign this to a variable called $Engineering:

```
[PS] C:\>$Engineering = Import-Csv newhire1.csv | where {$_.department -eq
'Engineering'}
```

Now you can create the users based on the $TemplateEngineering template using the
TemplateInstance parameter. These steps are shown in Figure 4-37.

The users created based on the Engineering template all have the same value for the attributes shown.

Another way to bulk create mailboxes is to specify how many mailboxes to create using dotted notation
and use the ForEach looping expression as an input into the New-Mailbox cmdlet. The following
command quickly creates 2500 mailboxes:

```
[PS] C:\>1..2500 | ForEach { New-Mailbox -name "PSTest$_" -alias "PSTest$_" -
UserPrincipalName PSTest$_@ExchangeExchange.local -password $Password -database
   "Mailbox Database" -OrganizationUnit ADUsers }
```

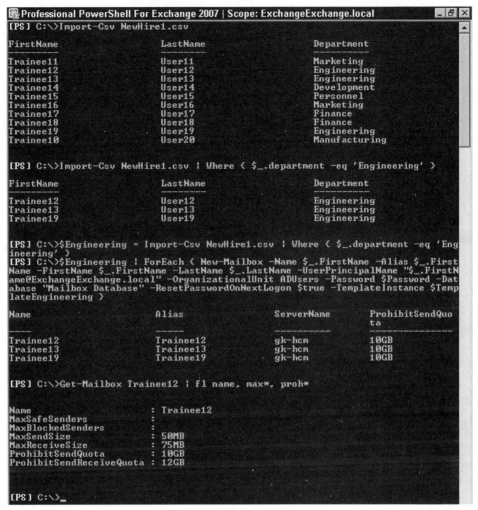

```
Professional PowerShell For Exchange 2007 | Scope: ExchangeExchange.local        _ [] X
[PS] C:\>Import-Csv NewHire1.csv

FirstName                      LastName                       Department
---------                      --------                       ----------
Trainee11                      User11                         Marketing
Trainee12                      User12                         Engineering
Trainee13                      User13                         Engineering
Trainee14                      User14                         Development
Trainee15                      User15                         Personnel
Trainee16                      User16                         Marketing
Trainee17                      User17                         Finance
Trainee18                      User18                         Finance
Trainee19                      User19                         Engineering
Trainee10                      User20                         Manufacturing


[PS] C:\>Import-Csv NewHire1.csv | Where { $_.department -eq 'Engineering' }

FirstName                      LastName                       Department
---------                      --------                       ----------
Trainee12                      User12                         Engineering
Trainee13                      User13                         Engineering
Trainee19                      User19                         Engineering


[PS] C:\>$Engineering = Import-Csv NewHire1.csv | Where { $_.department -eq 'Eng
ineering' }
[PS] C:\>$Engineering | ForEach { New-Mailbox -Name $_.FirstName -Alias $_.First
Name -FirstName $_.FirstName -LastName $_.LastName -UserPrincipalName "$_.FirstN
ame@ExchangeExchange.local" -OrganizationalUnit ADUsers -Password $Password -Dat
abase "Mailbox Database" -ResetPasswordOnNextLogon $true -TemplateInstance $Temp
lateEngineering }

Name                      Alias               ServerName          ProhibitSendQuo
                                                                  ta
----                      -----               ----------          ---------------
Trainee12                 Trainee12           gk-hcm              10GB
Trainee13                 Trainee13           gk-hcm              10GB
Trainee19                 Trainee19           gk-hcm              10GB


[PS] C:\>Get-Mailbox Trainee12 | fl name, max*, proh*


Name                      : Trainee12
MaxSafeSenders            :
MaxBlockedSenders         :
MaxSendSize               : 50MB
MaxReceiveSize            : 75MB
ProhibitSendQuota         : 10GB
ProhibitSendReceiveQuota  : 12GB


[PS] C:\>_
```

Figure 4-37

Bulk-Enabling Existing Users

To bulk-enable existing users, you simply create a filter to get the required users to be bulk-enabled and pass the output of the command to the Enable-Mailbox cmdlet.

To demonstrate this, create a few users in Active Directory. You can take advantage of the Net User command, which has been available in the command prompt. If you need help using this command simply type Net help net user in the Management Shell:

```
[PS] C:\>1..100 | ForEach { Net User "PowerShell$_" Pswd123 /ADD /Domain }
```

Next you can use the `Get-User` cmdlet to list all 100 PowerShell users created. To avoid listing all the users in the shell, you simply assign this output to a variable and pass it to the `Enable-Mailbox` cmdlet. This is shown Figure 4-38. Note that the screen was truncated so as not to show all 100 PowerShell users mailbox-enabled.

Figure 4-38

Remember, you can always create a filter with PowerShell to filter existing users that are not mailbox-enabled and pass that output to the `Enable-Mailbox` cmdlet.

Bulk Modifying Mailbox Attributes

Now back to the new hires. Using that as an example, you can easily modify mailbox settings for the users by using the `Set-Mailbox` cmdlet. In Figure 4-39 we first retrieve all the new hires and set bulk modify their `MaxSendSize` and `ProhibitSendQuota` settings.

Using this technique or pattern you can bulk modify common attributes on Recipient objects in Exchange Server 2007.

Bulk Reconnect Mailboxes

Mailboxes that were disconnected could be reconnected using the following command. The property to search for is `disconnectdate` that will not be `Null`. Using the `Get-MailboxStatistics` cmdlet, loop through each user mailbox checking if its' disconnect date is anything other than null. If it has a time stamp, reconnect the mailbox to the database it was previously associated with:

```
Get-MailboxStatistics -GK-HCM | ForEach { $_.Name | Where { $_.DisconnectDate -
NotLike {} } } | ForEach { Connect-Mailbox -Identity $_.DisplayName -Database
$_.DatabaseName}
```

```
Professional PowerShell For Exchange 2007 | Scope: ExchangeExchange.local
[PS] C:\>get-mailbox Traine* | ft name, MaxSendSize, prohibitSendQuota

Name                           MaxSendSize                    ProhibitSendQuota
----                           -----------                    -----------------
Trainee1                       unlimited                      unlimited
Trainee10                      unlimited                      unlimited
Trainee12                      50MB                           10GB
Trainee13                      50MB                           10GB
Trainee14                      unlimited                      unlimited
Trainee17                      50MB                           10GB
Trainee18                      50MB                           10GB
Trainee19                      50MB                           10GB
Trainee2                       unlimited                      unlimited
Trainee3                       unlimited                      unlimited
Trainee4                       unlimited                      unlimited
Trainee5                       unlimited                      unlimited
Trainee6                       unlimited                      unlimited
Trainee7                       unlimited                      unlimited
Trainee8                       unlimited                      unlimited
Trainee9                       unlimited                      unlimited


[PS] C:\>get-mailbox Traine* | Set-Mailbox -MaxSendSize 5MB -ProhibitSendQuota 5
MB
[PS] C:\>
[PS] C:\>get-mailbox Traine* | ft name, MaxSendSize, prohibitSendQuota

Name                           MaxSendSize                    ProhibitSendQuota
----                           -----------                    -----------------
Trainee1                       5MB                            5MB
Trainee10                      5MB                            5MB
Trainee12                      5MB                            5MB
Trainee13                      5MB                            5MB
Trainee14                      5MB                            5MB
Trainee17                      5MB                            5MB
Trainee18                      5MB                            5MB
Trainee19                      5MB                            5MB
Trainee2                       5MB                            5MB
Trainee3                       5MB                            5MB
Trainee4                       5MB                            5MB
Trainee5                       5MB                            5MB
Trainee6                       5MB                            5MB
Trainee7                       5MB                            5MB
Trainee8                       5MB                            5MB
Trainee9                       5MB                            5MB


[PS] C:\>_
```

Figure 4-39

There are a number of available scripts from Microsoft on Recipient Management. These are for the most part single-line Exchange Management Shell commands to assist with bulk management. See `microsoft.com/technet/scriptcenter/scripts/message/exch2007/default.mspx?mfr=true`.

Summary

Thus far, we have identified the user and group object types available in Exchange Server 2007 and reviewed a key parameter used to distinguish these Recipient types: the `RecipientTypeDetails`. With the many cmdlets available to manipulate Recipient types, the Exchange Management Shell enables you carry out various operations on these Recipients, some of which are not available in the Management Console. The limit to the number of operations on user and group objects with the Management Shell is enormous and you will find yourself discovering new ways to create and modify objects in the Management Shell.

5

Public Folders

Before Exchange 2007 was released there was much discussion about the fate of public folders. Was it finally time to remove public folders from Exchange? Public folders can be an administrator's nightmare because they tend to grow large in size, and can be difficult to manage. Also, Microsoft suggests Microsoft Office SharePoint Server as the path for migration (`http://msdn2.microsoft.com/en-us/library/aa579360.aspx`). On the other hand, public folders still offer features that other solutions do not; one example is data replication.

There are very few changes to the core public-folder architecture in Exchange Server 2007. On the other hand, there is good news for administrators with Exchange Server 2007's release. Exchange Server 2007 removed the hard requirement for new installations to have public folders. Of course, this depends on fully deploying the new Office Outlook 2007 client. As long as there are prior Outlook client versions, public folders are required for system folders (that is, calendar free/busy, offline address book); I will show a method of removing public folders once all clients are upgraded.

Unlike all previous versions of Exchange, prior to Service Pack 1 there was no public folder management in the GUI, so all public folder management must be done through PowerShell.

> *It is also possible to use a free third-party utility called PFDavAdmin for graphical administration.*

This chapter discusses:

- ❏ Database Administration
- ❏ Working with Permissions
- ❏ Folder and Content Administration

Database Administration

The beginning is always a good place to start, and with public folders, that would be creating the data store. Although database administration is similar to working with mailbox databases, public folders have their own set of cmdlets. This section explores how to use the following cmdlets:

- ❏ `Get-PublicFolderDatabase`
- ❏ `New-PublicFolderDatabase`
- ❏ `Remove-PublicFolderDatabase`
- ❏ `Set-PublicFolderDatabase`

Installing Public Folders

In a new installation of Exchange 2007, the setup routine asks whether there are any client computers running Outlook 2003 or earlier. If you select Yes, setup creates a public folder database on the Mailbox server. You can add a public folder database later if it becomes a requirement after the initial installation. Note that in certain continuous cluster configurations it is not possible to install a public folder database on the clustered mailbox server. Chapter 12 explains what the limitations are in this scenario.

To install public folders later, create the database and then configure the Offline Address Book (OAB) for public folder distribution. You set this option in the Exchange Management Console (EMC) under Offline Address Book Properties in the Mailbox Organization Configuration section. Figure 5-1 shows the dialog box in the EMC where this setting is configured.

You must restart the Microsoft Exchange Information Store service before Outlook 2003 and earlier clients will be able to connect to the public folder.

Creating a Public Folder Database

Creating a public folder database with the Exchange Management Console (EMC) is possible, but scripting it is much more fun! Use the cmdlet `New-PublicFolderDatabase` to create a new public folder database:

```
New-PublicFolderDatabase -Name <String> -StorageGroup
<StorageGroupIdParameter> [-CopyEdbFilePath <EdbFilePath>]
[-DomainController <Fqdn>] [-EdbFilePath <EdbFilePath>] [-HasLocalCopy
<$true | $false>] [-TemplateInstance <PSObject>]
```

For example, this cmdlet creates a new public folder database on the test server:

```
New-PublicFolderDatabase -Name "Public folder Database" -StorageGroup "Second
Storage Group" -EdbFilePath "C:\Program Files\Microsoft\Exchange\Mailbox\Second
Storage Group\Public folder
Database.edb"
```

Creating a public folder database is fairly straightforward. The two required parameters are `Name` and `StorageGroup`. The `HasLocalCopy` parameter is used to create a Local Continuous Replication (LCR) copy of the database. You can enable LCR if this is the only public folder database in the organization.

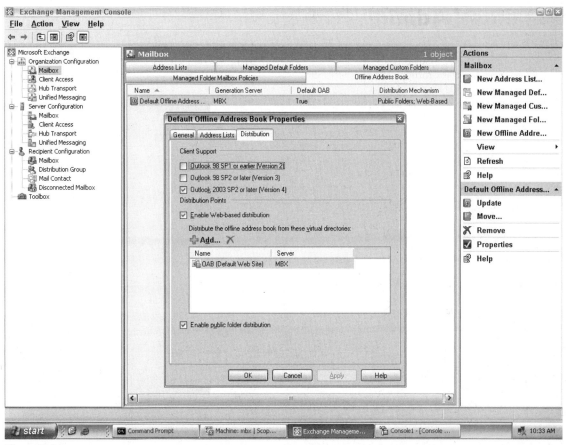

Figure 5-1

It is not possible to create more than one public folder database on a mailbox server. Trying to create additional databases will result in the following error:

```
A Public folder database already exists on the server that you specified. Each
server can contain a maximum of one Public folder database.  Public folder
database: "pub"; Specified server: "MB900".
```

It is also possible to pipe the StorageGroup parameter combining the Get-MailboxDatabase and New-PublicFolderDatabase cmdlets:

```
New-PublicFolderDatabase -Name pub -StorageGroup "MBX\First Storage Group"
Get-MailboxDatabase -server MBX | Set-MailboxDatabase -
PublicFolderDatabase "MBX\First Storage Group\pub"
```

What's going on in this example? The New-PublicFolderDatabase cmdlet takes two parameters. The first is the database name for the new public folder, and the second is the storage group location (consisting of the server name and storage group name).

Next, the script sets all of the mailbox databases' public folder database property to the newly created public folder database.

Get/Set Public Folder Database Information

Now that a public folder database has been created, this section shows how to get and set various parameters on the database. This is accomplished with Get-PublicFolderDatabase and Set-PublicFolderDatabase:

```
Get-PublicFolderDatabase [-Identity <DatabaseIdParameter>] [-DomainController
<Fqdn>] [-IncludePreExchange2007 <SwitchParameter>]
[-Status <SwitchParameter>] [<CommonParameters>]
Get-PublicFolderDatabase -Server <ServerIdParameter> [-DomainController <Fqdn>]
[-IncludePreExchange2007 <SwitchParameter>] [-Status
<SwitchParameter>] [<CommonParameters>]
Get-PublicFolderDatabase -StorageGroup <StorageGroupIdParameter>
[-DomainController <Fqdn>] [-IncludePreExchange2007 <SwitchParameter>]
[-Status <SwitchParameter>] [<CommonParameters>]
```

Running the Get-PublicFolderDatabase without any parameters returns a list of all the servers with public folder stores in the organization. The IncludePreExchange2007 and Status parameters are demonstrated next.

To include pre-Exchange 2007 servers, add the switch IncludePreExchange2007.

Figure 5-2 is an example of the detail returned when run against a specific server.

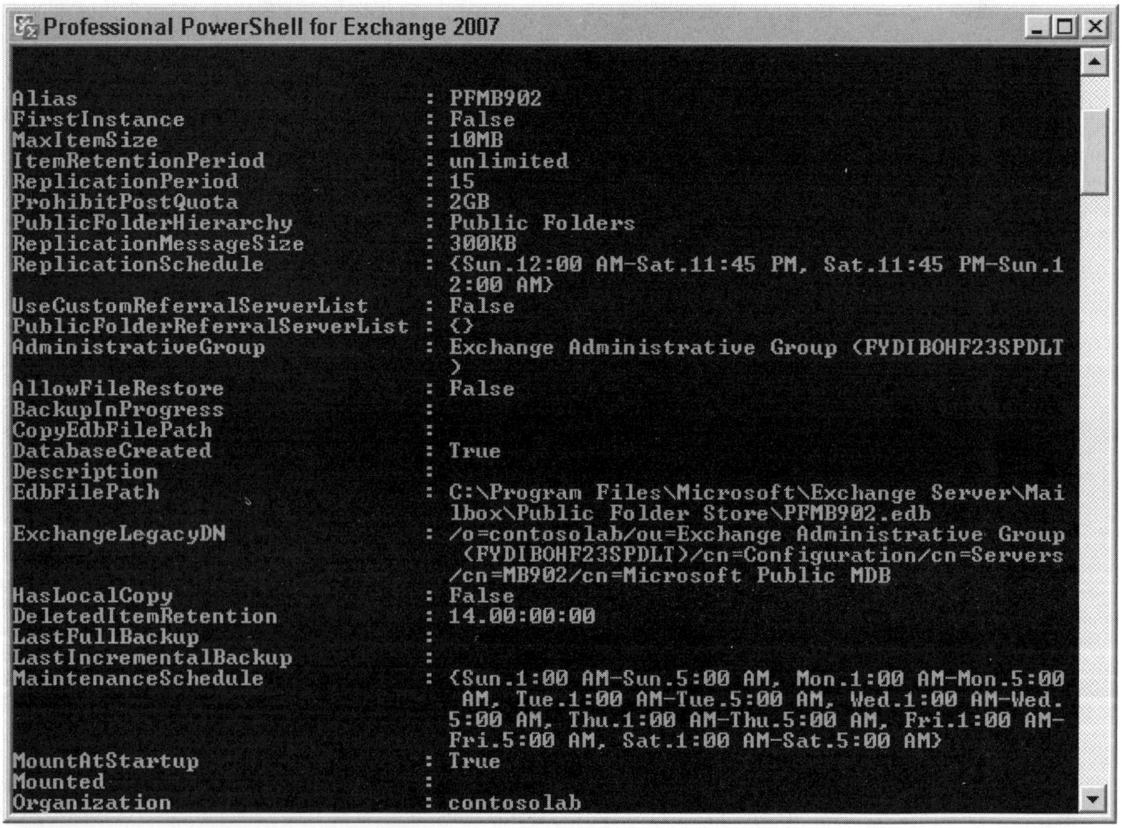

Figure 5-2

Note that the `Mounted` parameter is blank. Supply the `Status` parameter to get information about database state and backup information, as shown in Figure 5-3.

```
Professional PowerShell for Exchange 2007                                    _ □ X
[PS] C:\>Get-PublicFolderDatabase -Server MB902 | fl mounted,*back*


Mounted                       :
BackupInProgress              :
LastFullBackup                :
LastIncrementalBackup         :
RetainDeletedItemsUntilBackup : False


[PS] C:\>Get-PublicFolderDatabase -Server MB902 -Status | fl mounted,*back*


Mounted                       : True
BackupInProgress              : False
LastFullBackup                :
LastIncrementalBackup         :
RetainDeletedItemsUntilBackup : False


[PS] C:\>_
```

Figure 5-3

The `Set-PublicFolderDatabase` cmdlet is used to configure a public folder database. Its syntax is the following:

```
Set-PublicFolderDatabase -Identity <DatabaseIdParameter>
[-AllowFileRestore <$true | $false>] [-Confirm [<SwitchParameter>]]
[-CustomReferralServerList <MultiValuedProperty>] [-DeletedItemRetention
<EnhancedTimeSpan>] [-DomainController <Fqdn>]
[-EventHistoryRetentionPeriod <EnhancedTimeSpan>] [-IssueWarningQuota
<Unlimited>] [-ItemRetentionPeriod <Unlimited>] [-MaintenanceSchedule
<Schedule>] [-MaxItemSize <Unlimited>] [-MountAtStartup <$true | $false>]
[-Name <String>] [-ProhibitPostQuota <Unlimited>]
[-QuotaNotificationSchedule <Schedule>] [-ReplicationMessageSize
<ByteQuantifiedSize>] [-ReplicationPeriod <UInt32>] [-ReplicationSchedule
<Schedule>] [-RetainDeletedItemsUntilBackup <$true | $false>]
[-UseCustomReferralServerList <$true | $false>] [-WhatIf
[<SwitchParameter>]]

Set-PublicFolderDatabase [-AllowFileRestore <$true | $false>] [-Confirm
[<SwitchParameter>]] [-CustomReferralServerList <MultiValuedProperty>]
[-DeletedItemRetention <EnhancedTimeSpan>] [-DomainController <Fqdn>]
[-EventHistoryRetentionPeriod <EnhancedTimeSpan>] [-Instance
<PublicFolderDatabase>] [-IssueWarningQuota <Unlimited>]
[-ItemRetentionPeriod <Unlimited>] [-MaintenanceSchedule <Schedule>]
[-MaxItemSize <Unlimited>] [-MountAtStartup <$true | $false>] [-Name
<String>] [-ProhibitPostQuota <Unlimited>] [-QuotaNotificationSchedule
```

(continued)

(continued)

```
        <Schedule>] [-ReplicationMessageSize <ByteQuantifiedSize>]
        [-ReplicationPeriod <UInt32>] [-ReplicationSchedule <Schedule>]
        [-RetainDeletedItemsUntilBackup <$true | $false>]
        [-UseCustomReferralServerList <$true | $false>] [-WhatIf
        [<SwitchParameter>]]
```

The `Set-PublicFolderDatabase` cmdlet shares many similar options to the private database counterpart. `ProhibitPostQuota`, `IssueWarningQuota`, and `QuotaNotificationSchedule` are parameters related to user quotas for public folders.

The parameters `UseCustomReferralServerList` and `CustomReferralServerList` control how clients locate folders. The `CustomReferralServerList` assigns costs to individual servers with any positive number. Multiple servers can be listed by separating the server names with commas.

For example, to assign a weight of 10 to server PFMB903 and a weight of 5 to server PFMB902 the `CustomReferralServerList` would look like this:

```
    "PFMB902:5","PFMB903:10"
```

Removing a Public Folder Database

The process for removing a public folder database is also a simple command. However, unless all replicas and data have been removed, the deletion fails. In addition, any mailbox databases referencing the public folder must be updated to another public folder server. If this is the last public folder database in the organization, special commands must be used. You examine how to manage public folder replication in the following section. The syntax for `Remove-PublicFolderDatabase` is

```
    Remove-PublicFolderDatabase -Identity <DatabaseIdParameter>
    [-DomainController <Fqdn>] [-RemoveLastAllowed <SwitchParameter>]
```

Using `Remove-PublicFolderDatabase` *does not delete the actual database (*`.edb`*) file and other associated log files; you must manually remove them.*

Working with Permissions

Public folder permissions are separated into Client and Administrator permissions. Client permissions are typically managed with the Outlook client by users. These control who has access to the structure and content of the folder. Administrator permissions, on the other hand, control things like replication and control quotas. The following cmdlets are used to control public folder permissions:

- ❑   `Add-PublicFolderAdministrativePermission`
- ❑   `Get-PublicFolderAdministrativePermission`
- ❑   `Remove-PublicFolderAdministrativePermission`
- ❑   `Add-PublicFolderClientPermission`
- ❑   `Get-PublicFolderClientPermission`
- ❑   `Remove-PublicFolderClientPermission`

Client Folder Permissions

Individual client permissions are combined to form roles. For example, Authors can create items, read items, and see the folder, but they can only edit and delete their own items. You can manage these rights with the Outlook client. Select the public folder and right-click. Select Properties and choose the Permissions tab. The dialog box is shown in Figure 5-4.

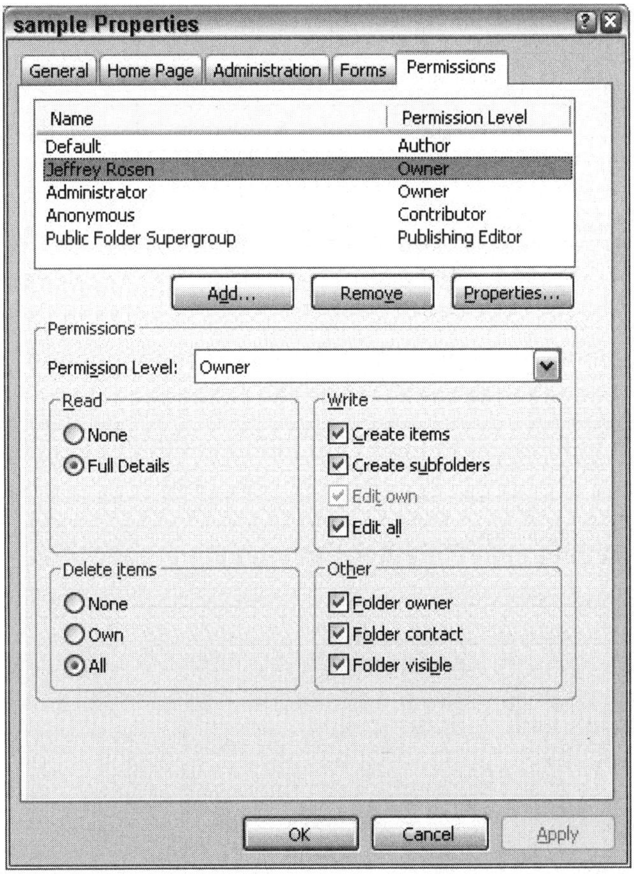

Figure 5-4

That's great for users to use, but administrators can also manage client permissions with PowerShell. One advantage of PowerShell is that an administrator can quickly make bulk changes. A typical example is to grant Active Directory group permissions on every folder:

```
Get-PublicFolder \ -Recurse -ResultSize unlimited | Add-
  PublicFolderClientPermission -User "Public folder Supergroup" -AccessRights
  PublishingEditor
```

This script first gets all the public folder in the `IPM_Subtree` and overrides the default result size of 10,000 folders. The public folder object is then piped to the `Add-PublicFolderClientPermission` cmdlet where it grants the AD mail-enabled security group named "Public Folder Supergroup" the Publishing Editor rights. Publishing Editor grants full rights to the folder, with the exception of setting the group as the folder owner.

Client Folder Permissions Scripts

Four scripts are located in the Scripts directory, by default located in `C:\Program Files\Microsoft\Exchange Server\Scripts`. The scripts are

- ❑ `AddUsersToPFRecursive`: Adds a user to a role in a given public folder and its children. It requires the user, permissions, and the top folder to start from.

- ❑ `ReplaceUserWithUserOnPFRecursive`: Essentially swaps the same permissions from an existing user to a new user for a given folder and its children.

- ❑ `ReplaceUserPermissionOnPFRecursive`: Changes an existing user's permissions with new permissions for a given folder and its children.

- ❑ `RemoveUserFromPFRecursive`: Removes an existing user's permissions from a given folder and its children.

To run the scripts use a `.\` *in front of the script name calling the script from within the folder where the script resides, for example,* `.\AddUsersToPFRecursive.ps1`.

Administrative Folder Permissions

Administrative permissions are needed for setting properties like replication, ACLs, and quotas. By default, Exchange Server administrators have full rights, or the `AllExtendedRights` permission. Following is a list of all of the access rights available for administrative access to public folders:

- ❑ `None`
- ❑ `ModifyPublicFolderACL`
- ❑ `ModifyPublicFolderAdminACL`
- ❑ `ModifyPublicFolderDeletedItemRetention`
- ❑ `ModifyPublicFolderExpiry`
- ❑ `ModifyPublicFolderQuotas`
- ❑ `ModifyPublicFolderReplicaList`
- ❑ `AdministerInformationStore`
- ❑ `ViewInformationStore`
- ❑ `AllExtendedRights`

If you forget the possible Access Rights values, put anything in the `AccessRights` *parameter and the error outputs a list.*

Get, set, and remove administrative folder permissions with these three cmdlets:

- ❏ Get-PublicFolderAdministrativePermission

- ❏ Add-PublicFolderAdministrativePermission

- ❏ Remove-PublicFolderAdministrativePermission

The first, Get-PublicFolderAdministrativePermission, is shown here:

```
Get-PublicFolderAdministrativePermission -Identity <PublicFolderIdParameter>
[-DomainController <Fqdn>] [-Server <ServerIdParameter>] [-User <Security
PrincipalIdParameter>]
[<CommonParameters>]
Get-PublicFolderAdministrativePermission -Identity PublicFolderIdParameter>
[-DomainController <Fqdn>] [-Owner
<SwitchParameter>] [-Server <ServerIdParameter>] [<CommonParameters>]
```

The cmdlet returns the Isinherited *parameter that shows whether the permission comes from a parent object. This is useful in troubleshooting permissions problems.*

Add-PublicFolderAdministrativePermission is shown here:

```
Add-PublicFolderAdministrativePermission -Identity <PublicFolderIdParameter> -
AccessRights <Collection> -User <SecurityPrincipalIdParameter> [-Deny
<SwitchParameter>] [-DomainController <Fqdn>] [-InheritanceType <None | All |
Descendents | SelfAndChildren | Children>] [-Server <ServerIdParameter>]
[<CommonParameters>]

Add-PublicFolderAdministrativePermission -Identity <PublicFolderIdParameter> -
Owner <SecurityPrincipalIdParameter> [-DomainController <Fqdn>] [-Server
<ServerIdParameter>] [<CommonParameters>]
Add-PublicFolderAdministrativePermission [-Identity <PublicFolderIdParameter>] -
Instance PublicFolderAdministrativeAceObject> [-AccessRights <Collection>] [-Deny
<SwitchParameter>] [-DomainController <Fqdn>] [-InheritanceType <None | All |
Descendents | SelfAndChildren | Children>] [-Server <ServerIdParameter>] [-User
<SecurityPrincipalIdParameter>] [<CommonParameters>]
```

AccessRights are rights specific to the Active Directory object itself. ModifyPublicFolderACL, ViewInformationStore, ModifyPublicFolderQuotas, and AllExtendedRights are examples of AccessRights.

InheritanceType controls how children objects have their rights set. Typically rights flow down to all descendents, but this behavior can be overridden by setting this parameter. The valid parameters are:

- ❏ None indicates no inheritance. The security information only applies to the object.

- ❏ All indicates that the security information applies to the object, its children, and its children's descendents.

- ❏ Descendents indicates that the security information applies only to the object's children and their descendents. It does not apply to the object itself.

❑ SelfAndChildren indicates that the security information applies to only the object and its immediate children. It does not include the children's descendents.

❑ Children indicates that the security information applies only to the object's immediate children. It does not apply to the object, or the object's children's descendents.

Here is an example of assigning permissions that grant the user Jeffrey Rosen permissions to modify all properties on the Departments folder:

```
Add-PublicFolderAdministrativePermission -Identity \Departments -User
 "Jeffrey Rosen" -AccessRights AllExtendedRights
```

It is also possible to deny rights by adding the Deny switch parameter. The following cmdlet denies Jeffrey the ability to modify public folder quotas for the Departments folder:

```
Add-PublicFolderAdministrativePermission -Identity \Departments -User
"Jeffrey Rosen" -AccessRights ModifyPublicFolderQuotas -Deny
The third, Remove-PublicFolderAdministrativePermission, is shown here:  Remove-
PublicFolderAdministrativePermission -Identity <PublicFolderIdParameter> -
AccessRights <Collection> -User <SecurityPrincipalIdParameter> [-Deny
<SwitchParameter>] [-DomainController <Fqdn>] [-InheritanceType <None | All |
Descendents | SelfAndChildren | Children>] [-Server <ServerIdParameter>]
[<CommonParameters>]

Remove-PublicFolderAdministrativePermission [-Identity <PublicFolderIdParameter>]
-Instance PublicFolderAdministrativeAceObject> [-AccessRights <Collection>] [-Deny
<SwitchParameter>] [-DomainController <Fqdn>] [-InheritanceType <None | All |
Descendents | SelfAndChildren | Children>] [-Server <ServerIdParameter>] [-User
<SecurityPrincipalIdParameter>] [<CommonParameters>]
```

The parameters for Remove-PublicFolderAdministrativePermission have the same options as the Add-PublicFolderAdministrativePermission cmdlet.

Top-Level Folders

By default, creating or removing top-level public folders, or root folders, is restricted to administrators. There are two approaches to allow users to create folders at the root. One scenario is an administrator can create the root folders and grant permissions to users the ability to create subfolders. This can be done with the Outlook client or with the PowerShell Add-PublicFolderClientPermission cmdlet:

```
Add-PublicFolderClientPermission -Identity <PublicFolderIdParameter> -AccessRights
<Collection> -User <PublicFolderUserIdParameter> [-DomainController <Fqdn>]
[-Server <ServerIdParameter>]
[<CommonParameters>]
```

For example:

```
Add-PublicFolderClientPermission -Identity \SampleFolder -User
jeffreyrosen -AccessRights owner
```

Another approach is to grant users the rights to create top-level folders. This can be done with PowerShell or with an Active Directory editing tool, such as ADSI Edit. The command to grant permissions requires the distinguished name (DN) of the public folder configuration object. The DN can be found in the Configuration partition in Active Directory, and will look similar to the following:

```
CN=Public folderPublic foldersPublic folders,CN=Folder Hierarchies,CN=Exchange
Administrative Group
  (FYDIBOHF23SPDLT),CN=Administrative Groups,CN=<company>,CN=Microsoft
Exchange,CN=Services,CN=Configuration,DC=<company>,DC=com
```

The cmdlet to change top-level permissions is `Add-ADPermission`:

```
Add-ADPermission -Identity <ADRawEntryIdParameter> -User
<SecurityPrincipalIdParameter> [-AccessRights <ActiveDirectoryRights[]>]
[-ChildObjectTypes <ADSchemaObjectIdParameter[]>] [-Deny <SwitchParameter>]
[-DomainController<Fqdn>] [-ExtendedRights <ExtendedRightIdParameter[]>]
[-InheritanceType <None | All | Descendents | SelfAndChildren | Children>]
[-InheritedObjectType <ADSchemaObjectIdParameter>] [-Properties
<ADSchemaObjectIdParameter[]>][<CommonParameters>]
```

For example:

```
Add-ADPermission -id "CN=Public folders,CN=Folder Hierarchies,CN=Exchange
Administrative Group (FYDIBOHF23SPDLT),CN=Administrative Groups,CN=contosolab,
CN=Microsoft Exchange,CN=Services,CN=Configuration,DC=contosolab,DC=com" -User
jeffreyrosen -ExtendedRights ms-exch-create-top-level-public-folder -
AccessRights readproperty,GenericExecute
```

Exchange Server 2007 Service Pack 1 adds a new administrator role, Exchange Public folder Administrators. Users assigned this role have administrative permissions to manage all public folders, they are automatically granted the Create top-level public folder extended right, and they can manage most other public folder settings.

Folder and Content Administration

One of the advantages of public folders in comparison to other solutions is its replication model. The replication is set an administrator and is totally transparent to Outlook clients. The following list presents the cmdlets related to folder and content administration:

- ❏ Get-PublicFolder
- ❏ New-PublicFolder
- ❏ Remove-PublicFolder
- ❏ Set-PublicFolder
- ❏ Update-PublicFolder
- ❏ Update-PublicFolderHierarchy
- ❏ Get-PublicFolderStatistics

❑ `Disable-MailPublicFolder`

❑ `Enable-MailPublicFolder`

❑ `Get-MailPublicFolder`

❑ `Set-MailPublicFolder`

❑ `Suspend-PublicFolderReplication`

❑ `Resume-PublicFolderReplication`

Working with Folders

Exchange Server 2007 supports two different public folder trees: the `IPM_Subtree` and the `Non_IPM_Subtree`. The `IPM_Subtree` is the root that holds folders visible to Outlook clients. The `Non_IPM_Subtree` has the system folders, such as free/busy and offline address book.

```
Get-PublicFolder [-Identity <PublicFolderIdParameter>] [-DomainController
  <Fqdn>] [-Server <ServerIdParameter>]

Get-PublicFolder [-Identity <PublicFolderIdParameter>] -GetChildren
<SwitchParameter> [-DomainController <Fqdn>] [-ResultSize <Unlimited>]
[-Server <ServerIdParameter>]

Get-PublicFolder [-Identity <PublicFolderIdParameter>] -Recurse <SwitchParameter>
[-DomainController <Fqdn>] [-ResultSize <Unlimited>]
[-Server <ServerIdParameter>]
```

The `ResultSize` parameter sets the maximum number of results returned by the cmdlet. It has a maximum value of 10,000. To return all records, set the value to `Unlimited`. This parameter can only be set when used with the `Recurse` or `GetChildren` parameters.

The `Recurse` switch parameter makes the cmdlet return the folder specified in the `Identity` parameter, as well as all of its children.

The `Identity` parameter, by default, shows folders in the `IPM_Subtree`, shown in Figure 5-5.

To work with the system folders, specify `Non_IPM_Subtree` as the identity. (See Figure 5-6.)

Creating and Removing Folders

Most often, creating folders is done with Outlook. But, there are times when folders need to be created administratively. The cmdlet to create folders is `New-PublicFolder`:

```
New-PublicFolder -Name <String> [-DomainController <Fqdn>] [-Path
<PublicFolderIdParameter>] [-Server <ServerIdParameter>]
[<CommonParameters>]
```

Currently, it is only possible to create mail/post type folders using the `New-PublicFolder` cmdlet. Only the Outlook client can create calendar, contact, and other folder types.

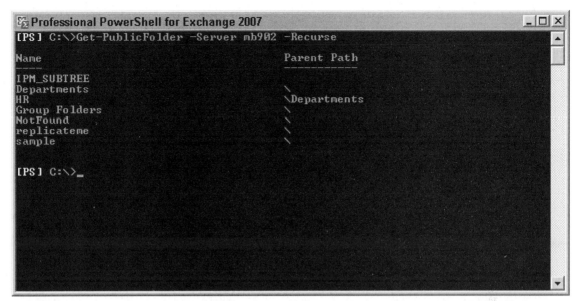

Figure 5-5

Figure 5-6

The following shows how to create a new folder called HR under the departments folder:

```
New-PublicFolder -Name HR -path \departments
```

By default, new folders inherit the settings of their parent.

The cmdlet to remove folders is Remove-PublicFolder:

```
Remove-PublicFolder -Identity <PublicFolderIdParameter> [-DomainController <Fqdn>]
[-Recurse <SwitchParameter>] [-Server <ServerIdParameter>]
[<Common Parameters>]
```

Only Identity is a required parameter. The identity can take the form of GUID, distinguished name (DN), Server\storage group\database name, Server\database name, or Storage groupname\database name. An easier way to get the folder identity is to combine the Get-PublicFolder with Remove-PublicFolder:

```
Get-PublicFolder \sample | Remove-PublicFolder
Similar to the Get-PublicFolder cmdlet, the Recurse parameter makes the cmdlet
operate on the folder specified in the Identity parameter and all of its children.
This example shows how the Recurse parameter removes the folder named sample, as
well as all of its children folders. Remove-PublicFolder -Identity "\sample" -
Recurse
```

Removing Public Folders

Once all of the email clients are upgraded to Office Outlook 2007, it is possible to remove public folders from Exchange. First, move any data in the public folders to another system. One alternative to public folders is Microsoft Office SharePoint Server. There are a number of commercial tools available to facilitate a migration. Also, it is important to consider any organizational forms being used. Microsoft InfoPath is an application that may be used for forms migration. Lastly, reconfigure the OAB to not use public folders for distribution. Remove the public folder stores by removing all of the replicas using the RemoveReplicaFromPFRecursive.ps1 script and allowing time for the information to synchronize. Additionally, to remove all of the folders from the server run the following cmdlets:

```
Get-PublicFolder -Server <Servername> -identity "\" -Recurse -ResultSize:unlimited
-ErrorAction:SilentlyContinue | Remove-PublicFolder
Get-PublicFolder -Server <Servername> -identity "\Non_IPM_Subtree" -Recurse -
ResultSize:unlimited -ErrorAction:SilentlyContinue | Remove-PublicFolder
```

Finally, you have one public folder store remaining. Run the previous cmdlets to remove any last remaining folders. Once all of these steps have been completed, the last public folder store can be removed with PowerShell. It may take some time for the public folder store to complete replication.

After running the final cmdlet Get-PublicFolderDatabase -Server <Server name> | Remove-PublicFolderDatabase, the cmdlet returns a confirmation warning, as shown in Figure 5-7. Understand that once the last folder is removed, only Office Outlook 2007 clients will be able to connect to Exchange. The cmdlet will not remove the database files; they must be manually deleted.

Figure 5-7

Replication

There are two types of public folder replication: hierarchy and data. All of the functionally introduced in Exchange 2003 for public folder administration was carried over in Exchange 2007 cmdlets.

One key thing to remember when working with public folders — patience!

Folder Replication

The ability to create replicas is essential to maintaining high availability for public folder content. Many of the parameters are set at the database level, and can be overridden per folder. This includes settings such as replication schedule, quotas, and retention period. These parameters are set with the `Set-PublicFolder` cmdlet:

```
Set-PublicFolder -Identity <PublicFolderIdParameter> [-AgeLimit <EnhancedTimeSpan>]
[-DomainController <Fqdn>] [-HiddenFromAddressListsEnabled <$true|$false>] [-
MaxItemSize <Unlimited>] [-Name <String>] [-PerUserReadStateEnabled <$true |
$false>] [-PostStorageQuota <Unlimited>] [-Replicas <DatabaseIdParameter[]>] [-
ReplicationSchedule <Schedule>] [-RetainDeletedItemsFor <EnhancedTimeSpan>] [-
Server <ServerIdParameter>] [-StorageQuota <Unlimited>] [-UseDatabaseAgeDefaults
<$true | $false>] [-UseDatabaseQuotaDefaults <$true | $false>] [-
UseDatabaseReplicationSchedule <$true | $false>]
[-UseDatabaseRetentionDefaults <$true | $false>] [<CommonParameters>]

Set-PublicFolder -Identity <PublicFolderIdParameter> [-AgeLimit <EnhancedTimeSpan>]
[-DomainController <Fqdn>] [-HiddenFromAddressListsEnabled <$true|$false>] [-
```

(continued)

(continued)

```
LocalReplicaAgeLimit <EnhancedTimeSpan>] [-MaxItemSize <Unlimited>] [-Name
<String>] [-PerUserReadStateEnabled <$true | $false>] [-PostStorageQuota
<Unlimited>] [-Replicas <DatabaseIdParameter[]>] [-ReplicationSchedule <Schedule>]
[-RetainDeletedItemsFor <EnhancedTimeSpan>] [-Server <ServerIdParameter>] [-
StorageQuota <Unlimited>] [-UseDatabaseAgeDefaults <$true | $false>] [-
UseDatabaseQuotaDefaults <$true | $false>] [-UseDatabaseReplicationSchedule <$true
| $false>] [-
UseDatabaseRetentionDefaults <$true|$false>] [<CommonParameters>]


Set-PublicFolder [-AgeLimit <EnhancedTimeSpan>] [-DomainController <Fqdn>] [-
HiddenFromAddressListsEnabled <$true | $false>] [-Instance <PublicFolder>] [-
MaxItemSize <Unlimited>] [-Name <String>] [-PerUserReadStateEnabled <$true|$false>]
[-PostStorageQuota <Unlimited>] [-Replicas <DatabaseIdParameter[]>] [-
ReplicationSchedule <Schedule>] [-RetainDeletedItemsFor <Enhanced TimeSpan>] [-
Server <ServerIdParameter>] [-StorageQuota <Unlimited>] [-UseDatabaseAgeDefaults
<$true | $false>] [-UseDatabaseQuotaDefaults <$true | $false>] [-
UseDatabaseReplicationSchedule <$true | $false>] [-
UseDatabaseRetentionDefaults <$true | $false>] [<CommonParameters>]
```

One of the most common public folder tasks is to add and remove folder replicas. The parameter `Replicas` is a list of the server name and public folder database name for each server. Use the `Get-PublicFolder` cmdlet to see the current replicas on a folder:

```
Get-PublicFolder \replicateme | fl replicas
```

For example, to add replicas to both of my test servers for the folder `replicateme`, the cmdlet is:

```
Get-PublicFolder \replicateme | Set-PublicFolder -Replicas MBX\PFMB901,
MB902\PFMB902
```

> *It may take some time for the content to begin replication after adding a new replication partner. The section on reporting shows how to retrieve replication state.*

To remove a replication partner, include all the servers in the Replicas list, except for the server to be removed. From the previous example, this cmdlet removes the replica on MB902:

```
Get-PublicFolder \replicateme | Set-PublicFolder -Replicas MBX\PFMB901
```

The replication schedule can be in the form of date/time or always. The `replicationschedule` and the `UsaDatabaseReplicationSchedule` parameters are mutually exclusive.

In Figure 5-8, the public folder `sample` has a blank `replicationschedule` property, and the `UseDatabaseReplicationSchedule` is `True`.

First, the replication schedule is set to Monday through Friday. The `UseDatabaseReplicationSchedule` is automatically set to `False`.

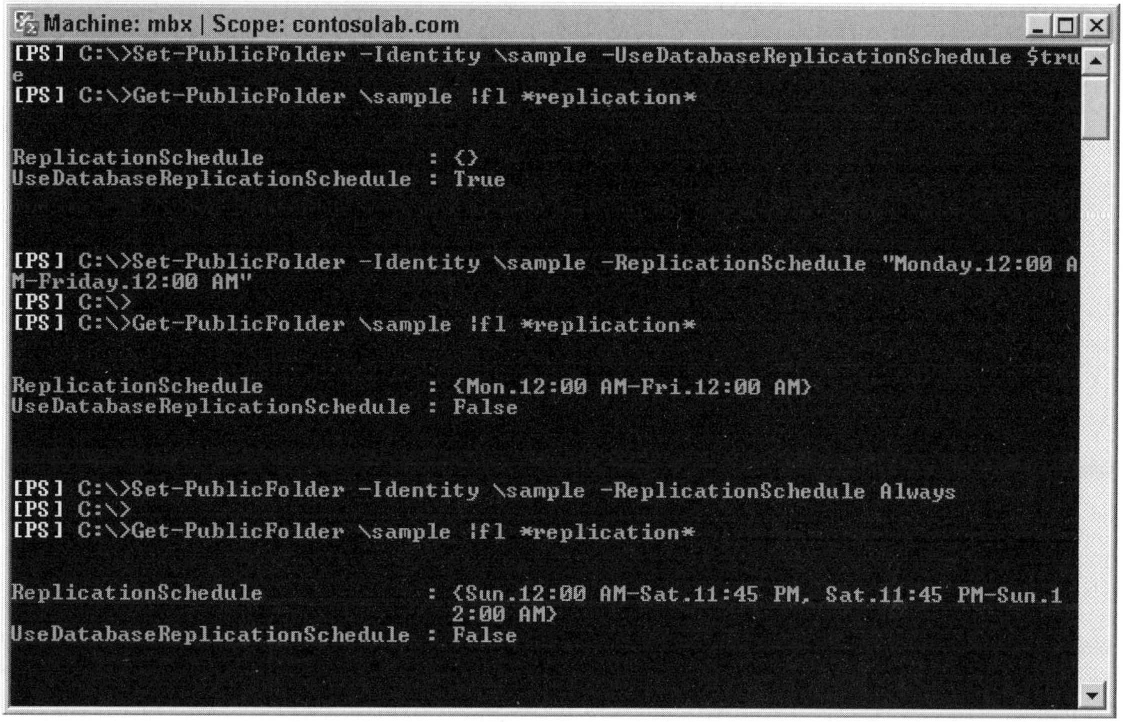

Figure 5-8

Next, the replication schedule is set to `always`. This changes the `ReplicationSchedule` property to the full week.

Setting the schedule to `always` means data replicates every 15 minutes.

Public Folder Hierarchy

The public folder hierarchy contains the structure of every folder in the `IPM_Subtree`. The hierarchy is automatically replicated to every server that contains a public folder store. It is possible for a server's hierarchy to become out of sync. You can force an update with the `Update-PublicFolderHierarchy` cmdlets. The cmdlets require a server specified as the source of replication:

```
Update-PublicFolderHierarchy -Server <ServerIdParameter> [-
DomainController <Fqdn>]
```

An example of updating the hierarchy with the server MB901 as the source would be:

```
Update-PublicFolderHierarchy -Server MB901
```

As noted earlier, view the contents of the hierarchy with the `Get-PublicFolder` cmdlet. By specifying the server, it is easy to compare two server's hierarchies. (See Figure 5-9.)

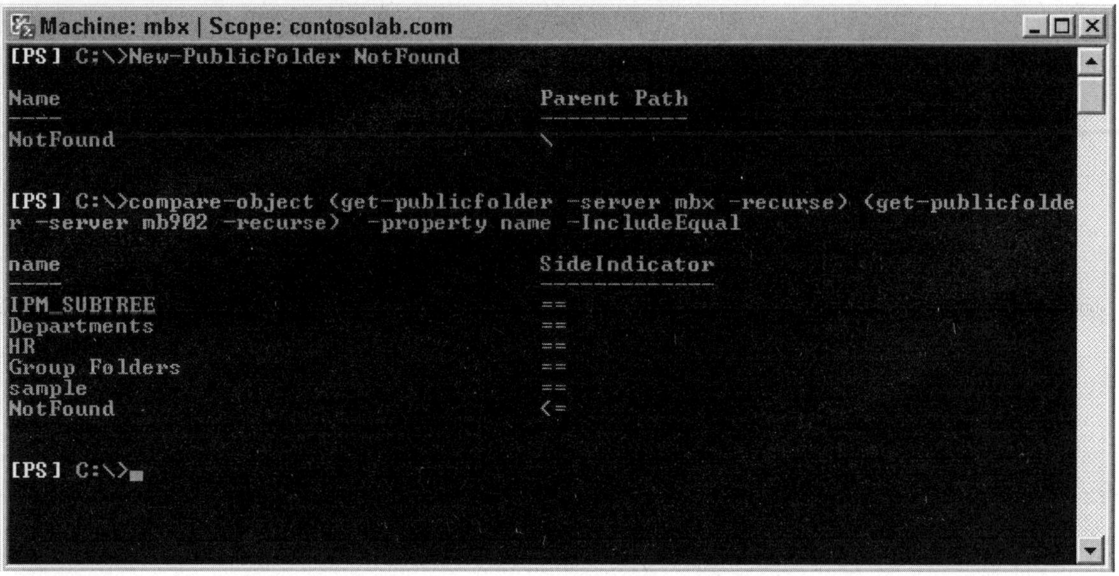

```
Machine: mbx | Scope: contosolab.com                                    _ □ ×
[PS] C:\>New-PublicFolder NotFound

Name                                        Parent Path
----                                        -----------
NotFound                                    \


[PS] C:\>compare-object (get-publicfolder -server mbx -recurse) (get-publicfolde
r -server mb902 -recurse) -property name -IncludeEqual

name                                        SideIndicator
----                                        -------------
IPM_SUBTREE                                     ==
Departments                                     ==
HR                                              ==
Group Folders                                   ==
sample                                          ==
NotFound                                        <=


[PS] C:\>
```

Figure 5-9

How does this work? The `compare-object` cmdlet has a parameter for the reference object and one for the difference object. If the parameter names are not supplied, it assumes the first value is the reference object. The sub-expression is evaluated, and returns the `IPM_Subtree` on a given server. There are other parameters for tweaking the output, such as `includeEqual`, which returns all lines in both files.

Stopping Data Replication

The ability to stop all replication was introduced in Exchange 2003 SP2. If, for example, an administrator accidentally replicated a public folder with a large amount of data it would be possible to stop replication before replication traffic could saturate the network. The administrator could remove the incorrect replication partner and then resume data replication. The `Suspend-PublicFolderReplication` and `Resume-PublicFolderReplication` cmdlets have the following syntax:

```
Suspend-PublicFolderReplication [-DomainController <Fqdn>]
[<CommonParameters>]

Resume-PublicFolderReplication [-DomainController <Fqdn>]
[<CommonParameters>]
```

To check the state of replication, use the following cmdlet:

```
Get-OrganizationConfig | fl heuristics
```

The cmdlet will return Heuristics : SuspendFolderReplication if the replication is suspended.

Public Folder Scripts

In addition to the Exchange cmdlets, there are four scripts included during setup. The scripts for public folders make routine tasks even easier. Also, they provide good examples for building your own scripts. The default location for the following scripts is
C:\Program Files\Microsoft\Exchange Server\Scripts.

- ❏ AddReplicaToPFRecursive.ps1: Adds a server to the replication list
- ❏ RemoveReplicaFromPFRecursive.ps1: Removes a server from the replication list
- ❏ MoveAllFeplicas.ps1: Replaces a server in the replication list
- ❏ ReplaceReplicaOnPfRecursive.ps1: Replaces a server in the replication list with a new server

RemoveReplicaFromPFRecursive removes a server's folder replicas from a given folder, and all of the folder's children:

```
RemoveReplicaFromPFRecursive [ -Server <Server Identity>] -
TopPublicFolder <Folder Path> -ServerToRemove <Server Name>
```

The following example removes all replicas for server MB902 from the \Departments folder and its children. It is operated against the other server that has a public folder store.

```
RemoveReplicaFromPFRecursive -Server MBX -TopPublicFolder \Departments
-ServerToRemove MB902
```

A slight variation is the script ReplaceReplicaOnPfRecursive, which replaces a server with a new server for a given folder, and all of the folder's children:

```
ReplaceReplicaOnPfRecursive [ -Server <Server Identity>]
-TopPublicFolder <Folder Path>
-ServerToRemove <Server Identity> -ServerToAdd <Server Identity>
```

Now, replace the server MBX with MB903 for all folders from the \Departments folder and its children. It is operated against the MBX server.

```
ReplaceReplicaOnPfRecursive -Server MBX -TopPublicFolder \Departments -
ServerToRemove MB902 -ServerToAdd MB903
```

The next script moves all replicas, including system folders, to a new server:

```
MoveAllReplicas -Server <Server Identity> -NewServer <Server Identity>
```

To move all replicas from MBX to MB902, run the following script:

```
MoveAllReplicas -Server MBX -NewServer MB902
```

Finally, `AddReplicaToPFRecursive` adds a server to the replication list for a folder, and all of its children:

```
AddReplicaToPFRecursive [-Server <Server Identity>] -ServerToAdd <Server
  Identity> -TopPublicFolder <Folder Path>
```

The following example adds server MB902 to the `\Departments` folder and its children:

```
AddReplicaToPFRecursive -ServerToAdd MB902 -TopPublicFolder \Departments
```

Mail-Enabling

Just as in prior versions of Exchange, it is possible to enable public folders to receive email messages. The public folder must be created before it can be mail enabled. The cmdlet for enabling public folders is `Enable-MailPublicFolder`:

```
Enable-MailPublicFolder -Identity <PublicFolderIdParameter> [-DomainController
  <Fqdn>] [-HiddenFromAddressListsEnabled <$true | $false>] [-Server
  <ServerIdParameter>] [<CommonParameters>]
```

Hide the folder from the global address list by setting the parameter `HiddenFromAddressListsEnabled` to true.

Reporting

Unlike the hierarchy tree, which is the same across all public folder servers, running the `Get-PublicFolderStatistics` cmdlet generates information only for the folders for which the server has a replica.

```
Get-PublicFolderStatistics [-Identity <PublicFolderIdParameter>]
[-DomainController <Fqdn>] [-Server <ServerIdParameter>] [<CommonParameters>]
```

The following example shows how both of my test servers have different replicas of folders. This command outputs the item count and last access time. (See Figure 5-10.)

```
Get-PublicFolderStatistics -server MB902
Get-PublicFolderStatistics -server MBX
```

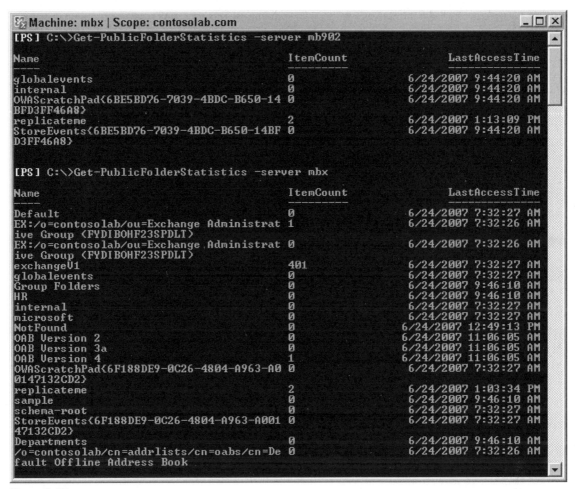

```
Machine: mbx | Scope: contosolab.com                                    _ □ ×
[PS] C:\>Get-PublicFolderStatistics -server mb902

Name                                    ItemCount              LastAccessTime
----                                    ---------              --------------
globalevents                            0                      6/24/2007 9:44:20 AM
internal                                0                      6/24/2007 9:44:20 AM
OWAScratchPad{6BE5BD76-7039-4BDC-B650-14 0                     6/24/2007 9:44:20 AM
BFD3FF46A8}
replicateme                             2                      6/24/2007 1:13:09 PM
StoreEvents{6BE5BD76-7039-4BDC-B650-14BF 0                     6/24/2007 9:44:20 AM
D3FF46A8}


[PS] C:\>Get-PublicFolderStatistics -server mbx

Name                                    ItemCount              LastAccessTime
----                                    ---------              --------------
Default                                 0                      6/24/2007 7:32:27 AM
EX:/o=contosolab/ou=Exchange Administrat 1                     6/24/2007 7:32:26 AM
ive Group {FYDIBOHF23SPDLT}
EX:/o=contosolab/ou=Exchange Administrat 0                     6/24/2007 7:32:26 AM
ive Group {FYDIBOHF23SPDLT}
exchangeV1                              401                    6/24/2007 7:32:27 AM
globalevents                            0                      6/24/2007 7:32:27 AM
Group Folders                           0                      6/24/2007 9:46:10 AM
HR                                      0                      6/24/2007 9:46:10 AM
internal                                0                      6/24/2007 7:32:27 AM
microsoft                               0                      6/24/2007 7:32:27 AM
NotFound                                0                      6/24/2007 12:49:13 PM
OAB Version 2                           0                      6/24/2007 11:06:05 AM
OAB Version 3a                          0                      6/24/2007 11:06:05 AM
OAB Version 4                           1                      6/24/2007 11:06:05 AM
OWAScratchPad{6F188DE9-0C26-4804-A963-A0 0                     6/24/2007 7:32:27 AM
0147132CD2}
replicateme                             2                      6/24/2007 1:03:34 PM
sample                                  0                      6/24/2007 9:46:10 AM
schema-root                             0                      6/24/2007 7:32:27 AM
StoreEvents{6F188DE9-0C26-4804-A963-A001 0                     6/24/2007 7:32:27 AM
47132CD2}
Departments                             0                      6/24/2007 9:46:10 AM
/o=contosolab/cn=addrlists/cn=oabs/cn=De 0                     6/24/2007 7:32:26 AM
fault Offline Address Book
```

Figure 5-10

The only folder replicated across both servers is \replicateme. It is possible to compare the itemcount property to see if they match.

The following provides more detail, such as last modification time, to specify the identity of a folder. (See Figure 5-11.)

```
Get-PublicFolderStatistics -server MB902 -identity \replicateme | fl
```

```
AdminDisplayName          : replicateme
AssociatedItemCount       : 0
ContactCount              : 1
CreationTime              : 6/24/2007 1:03:34 PM
DeletedItemCount          : 0
EntryId                   : 000000001A447390AA6611CD9BC800AA002FC45A0300473F251BD
                            1D56A41B3E6BD1E15F6539000C2634AE64A0000
ExpiryTime                :
FolderPath                : replicateme
IsDeletePending           : False
ItemCount                 : 2
LastAccessTime            : 6/24/2007 1:13:09 PM
LastModificationTime      : 6/24/2007 1:38:48 PM
Name                      : replicateme
OwnerCount                : 1
TotalAssociatedItemSize   : 0B
TotalDeletedItemSize      : 0B
TotalItemSize             : 3506B
ServerName                : MB902
StorageGroupName          : Public Folder Store
DatabaseName              : PFMB902
Identity                  : 000000001A447390AA6611CD9BC800AA002FC45A0300473F251BD
                            1D56A41B3E6BD1E15F6539000C2634AE64A0000
IsValid                   : True
OriginatingServer         : mb902
```

Figure 5-11

Summary

Even though new deployments may be able to run an Exchange environment without public folders, it will be some time before there is complete independence for most organizations. For administrators upgrading from previous versions, managing public folders can prove to be challenging.

This chapter covered all of the tasks an administrator needs to do with public folders. It began creating the public folder database. Once the database was created, the chapter explained security and permissions, as well as how to configure the top-level folders. Next, the chapter covered working with folders and content. This section talked about replication to ensure availability of the folder hierarchy and content. A number of scripts are included on the Exchange install DVD that make it easier to work with folder replicas. Finally, the chapter covered mail-enabling and reporting on folders. Even though Service Pack 1 adds public folder administration in to the GUI management console, this chapter demonstrated the flexibility of working with PowerShell.

Part II

Working with Server Roles

Configuring the Client Access Server Role

The Client Access Server (CAS) plays a similar role to the Exchange Server 2000 or 2003 Front-End computer. It provides client access to Office Outlook Web Access (OWA), Exchange ActiveSync (EAS), Outlook Anywhere, IMAP4, and POP3. The CAS also provides new services—Autodiscover, the Availability Service, and Exchange Web Services. Autodiscover will automatically create Office Outlook 2007 profiles for users by just entering their email address and password. The Availability Service provides calendaring information, such as free/busy for Office Outlook 2007 clients. Exchange Web Services is an interface for building applications integrated with Exchange with the Microsoft .NET platform.

Unlike the Exchange Server 2003 front-end server, the CAS handles more processing to lighten the work done by the Mailbox role. There must be at least one CAS deployed in the organization, and at least one per Active Directory site where there is a Mailbox role. This chapter helps an administrator understand and configure the services provided by the CAS.

This chapter covers the following topics:

- ❏ Working with user settings
- ❏ Configuring POP3 and IMAP4
- ❏ Configuring certificates
- ❏ Working with Autodiscover, proxy, and redirection
- ❏ Working with Outlook Anywhere
- ❏ Working with the Offline Address Book
- ❏ Working with LinkAccess for Outlook Web Access

User Settings

This section explores user settings related to client access. The cmdlets used are:

- ❏ `Set-CASMailbox`
- ❏ `Get-Mailbox`
- ❏ `Get-CASMailbox`

The `Set-CASMailbox` cmdlet has a many parameters to provide granular customization per user. Many of the parameters are used to enable or disable Outlook Web Access features. For example, administrators can turn off the ability to access their calendar or tasks. This can be useful in organizations that provide mail capabilities to a segment of users, but do not want to allow those users calendaring ability. Also, it is a best practice to limit the functionality a mail-enabled service account has. The `Set-CASMailbox` cmdlet has the following syntax:

```
Set-CASMailbox -Identity <MailboxIdParameter> [-ActiveSyncAllowedDeviceIDs
<MultiValuedProperty>] [-ActiveSyncEnabled <$true | $false>]
[-ActiveSyncMailboxPolicy <MailboxPolicyIdParameter>]
[-ActiveSyncDebugLogging <Nullable>] [-DisplayName <String>]
[-DomainController <Fqdn>] [-EmailAddresses <ProxyAddressCollection>]
[-HasActiveSyncDevicePartnership <$true | $false>] [-ImapEnabled <$true |
$false>] [-ImapMessagesRetrievalMimeFormat <TextOnly | HtmlOnly |
HtmlAndTextAlternative | TextEnrichedOnly | TextEnrichedAndTextAlternative
| BestBodyFormat>] [-ImapUseProtocolDefaults <$true | $false>]
[-MAPIBlockOutlookNonCachedMode <$true | $false>]
[-MAPIBlockOutlookRpcHttp <$true | $false>] [-MAPIBlockOutlookVersions
<String>] [-MAPIEnabled <$true | $false>] [-Name <String>]
[-OWAActiveSyncIntegrationEnabled <Nullable>] [-OWAAllAddressListsEnabled
<Nullable>] [-OWACalendarEnabled <Nullable>] [-OWAChangePasswordEnabled
<Nullable>] [-OWAContactsEnabled <Nullable>] [-OWAEnabled <$true |
$false>] [-OWAJournalEnabled <Nullable>] [-OWAJunkEmailEnabled <Nullable>]
[-OWANotesEnabled <Nullable>] [-OWAPremiumClientEnabled <Nullable>]
[-OWARemindersAndNotificationsEnabled <Nullable>] [-OWASearchFoldersEnabled
<Nullable>] [-OWASignaturesEnabled <Nullable>]
[-OWASpellCheckerEnabled <Nullable>] [-OWATasksEnabled <Nullable>]
[-OWAThemeSelectionEnabled <Nullable>] [-OWAUMIntegrationEnabled
<Nullable>] [-OWAUNCAccessOnPrivateComputersEnabled <Nullable>]
[-OWAUNCAccessOnPublicComputersEnabled <Nullable>]
[-OWAWSSAccessOnPrivateComputersEnabled <Nullable>]
[-OWAWSSAccessOnPublicComputersEnabled <Nullable>] [-PopEnabled <$true |
$false>] [-PopMessagesRetrievalMimeFormat <TextOnly | HtmlOnly |
HtmlAndTextAlternative | TextEnrichedOnly | TextEnrichedAndTextAlternative
| BestBodyFormat>] [-PopUseProtocolDefaults <$true | $false>]
[-PrimarySmtpAddress <SmtpAddress>] [-ProtocolSettings
<MultiValuedProperty>] [-SamAccountName <String>]
```

Exchange Server 2007 supports a variety of access methods, including POP3, IMAP4, Exchange ActiveSync, Outlook Anywhere (formerly known as RPC over HTTP), and Outlook Web Access. It is possible to enable and disable access to these features per-mailbox with the Set-CASMailbox cmdlet.

For example, to enable or disable all users the ability to use IMAP4 for email access, set the ImapEnabled parameter. This can be useful to prevent non-MAPI clients, like Outlook Express or Entourage, access for a specific user:

```
Get-Mailbox | Set-CASMailbox -imapenabled:$true
Get-Mailbox | Set-CASMailbox -imapenabled:$false
```

To change a specific user, pass the SMTP address, alias, UPN, DN, or GUID in the Identity parameter:

```
Set-CASMailbox -Identity Jeffrey@exchangeexchange.com -PopEnabled:$false
```

The numerous Set-CASMailbox parameters give granular control to administrators for customizing the user experience.

Disabling Outlook Modes

Exchange Server 2007 provides the ability to lock down the versions and modes that the Outlook client can connect with. This is a great way to provide extra security to the network by preventing access to older or non-patched clients.

In addition, it is now possible to control which modes can be used to connect. For example, you can prevent access of clients using Cached Mode or Outlook Anywhere. This is useful in environments where desktop search applications are installed. Non-Cached Mode clients can generate a significant amount of disk I/O traffic and affect the performance of the server. Forcing all clients to use Cached Mode can prevent performance issues because the desktop applications work against the local machine copy.

```
Get-Mailbox | Set-CASMailbox -MAPIBlockOutlookNonCachedMode $true
```

Behind the scenes the cmdlet is setting the protocolSettings property on the user's Active Directory account. There are a number of tools that can be used to see properties on Active Directory objects. Figure 6-1 shows the protocolSettings property using ADSIEdit. ADSIEdit is included in the Windows Server 2003 support tools, located on the installation CD in the Support\Tools\Suptools .msi. LDP, another directory browsing tool, is also installed with the support tools.

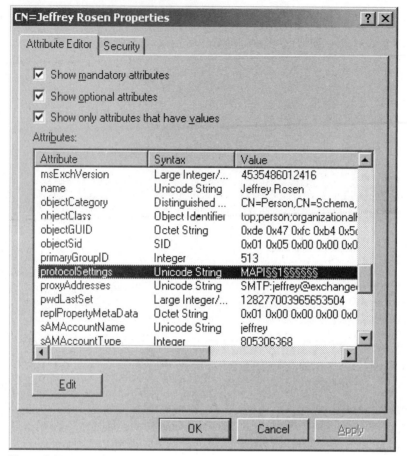

Figure 6-1

Disabling Outlook Versions

In addition to blocking protocols, it is also possible to block specific versions of Outlook. An organization may choose to block versions based on support, features, or security. Restrictions can be a single client version, a range of versions, an open-ended range, or any combination separated by commas. Restrictions are also configured per-user.

Following are some examples of blocking all versions before Outlook 2007, blocking Outlook 2003 RTM through Outlook 2003 Service Pack 2, Outlook 2002 RTM and Outlook 2007 RTM, and finally removing any restrictions:

```
Get-Mailbox | Set-CASMailbox -MAPIBlockOutlookVersions "-12.6024.5000"
Get-Mailbox | Set-CASMailbox -MAPIBlockOutlookVersions "11.5608.5606-11.6568.5658"
Get-Mailbox | Set-CASMailbox -MAPIBlockOutlookVersions "11.5608.5606-11.6568.5658",
"12.4518.1014"
Get-Mailbox | Set-CASMailbox -MAPIBlockOutlookVersions $null
```

The mailbox properties are cached in the information store, and may take several hours before the settings are effective. Microsoft TechNet article http://technet.microsoft.com/en-us/library/bb219050.aspx *provides more detail on this caching.*

To see how a user is configured, pass the mailbox name (alias) to the Get-CASMailbox cmdlet:

```
Get-Mailbox -Identity Jeffrey | fl
```

Figure 6-2 shows the output from this cmdlet.

```
Professional PowerShell for Exchange 2007

[PS] C:\>Get-CASMailbox -Identity jeffrey | fl

EmailAddresses                          : {SMTP:jeffrey@exchangeexchange.local}
LegacyExchangeDN                        : /o=ExchangeExchange/ou=Exchange Adminis
                                          trative Group (FYDIBOHF23SPDLT)/cn=Reci
                                          pients/cn=jeffrey
LinkedMasterAccount                     :
PrimarySmtpAddress                      : jeffrey@exchangeexchange.local
ProtocolSettings                        : {OWA§1, MAPI§§1§§§§§§}
SamAccountName                          : jeffrey
ServerLegacyDN                          : /o=ExchangeExchange/ou=Exchange Adminis
                                          trative Group (FYDIBOHF23SPDLT)/cn=Conf
                                          iguration/cn=Servers/cn=MB100
ServerName                              : mb100
DisplayName                             : Jeffrey Rosen
ActiveSyncAllowedDeviceIDs              : {}
ActiveSyncMailboxPolicy                 :
ActiveSyncDebugLogging                  :
ActiveSyncEnabled                       : True
HasActiveSyncDevicePartnership          : False
OWAEnabled                              : True
OWACalendarEnabled                      : True
OWAContactsEnabled                      : True
OWATasksEnabled                         : False
OWAJournalEnabled                       : False
OWANotesEnabled                         : False
OWARemindersAndNotificationsEnabled     : False
OWAPremiumClientEnabled                 : False
OWASpellCheckerEnabled                  : False
OWASearchFoldersEnabled                 : False
OWASignaturesEnabled                    : False
```

Figure 6-2

Enabling POP3/IMAP4

Out of the box, both POP3 and IMAP4 protocols are disabled. These protocols allow both Windows and non-Windows clients the ability to receive mail from Exchange. Because they provide support for non-Windows clients, they may be required in some organizations. This section shows the following cmdlets:

- ❑ Get-Service
- ❑ Set-PopSettings
- ❑ Set-ImapSettings

To enable either protocol, first the services must be set to Automatic, as shown in Figure 6-3. Next, the service must be started. Figure 6-3 is an example of enabling and starting the IMAP4 service. To enable POP3, replace the references from IMAP4 to POP3.

```
Professional PowerShell for Exchange 2007                                    _ □ ×
[PS] C:\>Set-Service msexchangeimap4 -StartupType automatic
[PS] C:\>Start-Service msexchangeimap4
WARNING: Waiting for service 'Microsoft Exchange IMAP4 (MSExchangeIMAP4)' to
finish starting...
WARNING: Waiting for service 'Microsoft Exchange IMAP4 (MSExchangeIMAP4)' to
finish starting...
WARNING: Waiting for service 'Microsoft Exchange IMAP4 (MSExchangeIMAP4)' to
finish starting...
WARNING: Waiting for service 'Microsoft Exchange IMAP4 (MSExchangeIMAP4)' to
finish starting...
[PS] C:\>
```

Figure 6-3

The following example checks the status of the IMAP4 service, or all the services that start with msexchange:

```
Get-Service msexchangeimap4
Get-Service msexchange*
```

There are a number of options for both protocols that can be fine-tuned. Most of the settings are to change connection and authentication options. Exchange Server 2007 implements higher security out of the box and it is generally unnecessary to change any configuration. However, to change POP3 and IMAP4 settings, use the cmdlets Set-PopSettings and Set-ImapSettings as shown here:

```
Set-PopSettings [-AuthenticatedConnectionTimeout <EnhancedTimeSpan>]
[-Banner <String>] [-CalendarItemRetrievalOption <iCalendar | intranetUrl
 | InternetUrl | Custom>] [-DomainController <Fqdn>] [-Instance
<Pop3AdConfiguration>] [-LoginType <PlainTextLogin |
PlainTextAuthentication | SecureLogin>] [-MaxCommandSize <Int32>]
[-MaxConnectionFromSingleIP <Int32>] [-MaxConnections <Int32>]
[-MaxConnectionsPerUser <Int32>] [-MessageRetrievalMimeFormat <TextOnly |
HtmlOnly | HtmlAndTextAlternative | TextEnrichedOnly |
TextEnrichedAndTextAlternative | BestBodyFormat>]
[-MessageRetrievalSortOrder <Ascending | Descending>] [-OwaServerUrl
<String>] [-PreAuthenticatedConnectionTimeout <EnhancedTimeSpan>]
[-ProxyTargetPort <Int32>] [-Server <ServerIdParameter>] [-SSLBindings
<MultiValuedProperty>] [-UnencryptedOrTLSBindings <MultiValuedProperty>]
[-X509CertificateName <String>]
Set-ImapSettings [-AuthenticatedConnectionTimeout <EnhancedTimeSpan>]
[-Banner <String>] [-CalendarItemRetrievalOption <iCalendar | intranetUrl
 | InternetUrl | Custom>] [-DomainController <Fqdn>] [-Instance
```

```
<Imap4AdConfiguration>] [-LoginType <PlainTextLogin |
PlainTextAuthentication | SecureLogin>] [-MaxCommandSize <Int32>]
[-MaxConnectionFromSingleIP <Int32>] [-MaxConnections <Int32>]
[-MaxConnectionsPerUser <Int32>] [-MessageRetrievalMimeFormat <TextOnly |
HtmlOnly | HtmlAndTextAlternative | TextEnrichedOnly |
TextEnrichedAndTextAlternative | BestBodyFormat>] [-OwaServerUrl <String>]
[-PreAuthenticatedConnectionTimeout <EnhancedTimeSpan>] [-ProxyTargetPort
<Int32>] [-Server <ServerIdParameter>] [-ShowHiddenFoldersEnabled <$true |
$false>] [-SSLBindings <MultiValuedProperty>] [-UnencryptedOrTLSBindings
<MultiValuedProperty>] [-X509CertificateName <String>]
```

One setting that may need to be changed is the logintype. This parameter controls the security around authentication. The security settings are configured with the logintype parameter, which has the following options:

❑   PlainTextLogin requires no encryption (TLS or SSL) over the standard POP3 (110) and IMAP4 (143) ports. Usernames and passwords are in clear text, so this is not practical in a production network. It may be useful for troubleshooting purposes.

❑   PlainTextAuthentication still requires no encryption over the standard ports, but Basic Authentication is permitted only on the secure ports POP3 (995) and IMAP4 (993). Clients can be configured to use Secure Password Authentication (SPA), which is Windows Integrated Authentication, and not use SSL.

❑   SecureLogin is the default logintype. This configuration requires TLS or SSL encryption before authenticating.

This example sets the IMAP4 logintype to plaintext:

```
Set-ImapSettings -logintype plaintextlogin
```

Restarting the POP3 and IMAP4 services is required before configuration changes take effect.

A handy trick to finding out valid parameter values is to pass a made-up value. The error sometimes will contain a list of valid choices, as shown in Figure 6-4.

If the organization will heavily use IMAP4, there are some additional parameters to configure. The MaxConnections parameter sets the maximum number of connections for IMAP4. The default is 2,000 and can be increased up to 25,000. The default for the maximum number of connections from a single IP, MaxConnectionFromSingleIP, defaults to 20. On networks using NAT, this setting can be too low. The value can be increased to a maximum of 1,000. Finally, it is possible to set the maximum number of connections per user. The default is 10 connections, and can be increased to 1,000. It is not recommended to increase the connections per user, unless there is a specific requirement to do so.

This example sets the maximum number of connections to 5,000, and the maximum number of connections from a single IP to 1,000:

```
Set-ImapSettings -Server CA100 -MaxConnections 5000
  -MaxConnectionFromSingleIP 1000
```

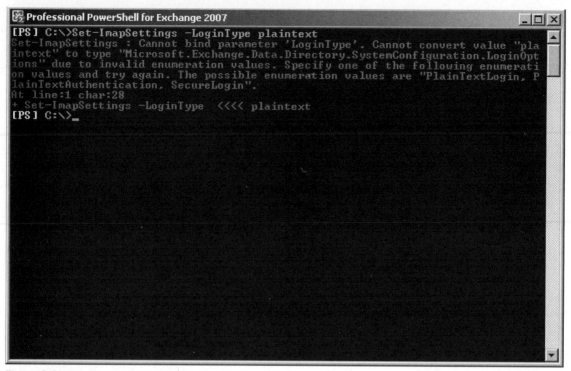

Figure 6-4

Certificates

Perhaps one of the most challenging aspects of configuring the Client Access Server is configuring security. All external communication to a CAS server should be secured using Secure Sockets Layer (SSL) because information like passwords is sent in clear text across un-trusted networks. SSL requires a digital certificate, which acts like a driver's license. To get a driver's license, one must prove that they are who they are to a government issuer, typically with something like a birth certificate. Now, when you present your license to a service, maybe to cash a check, they accept who you are because they trust the government issuer. Clients, like Outlook or Internet Explorer, trust a certification authority that issues the certificate to the web server. Once clients trust that the web server is who it claims to be, because they trust the issuer, the data can be encrypted so it is not readable.

Exchange ActiveSync, Outlook Web Access, Outlook Anywhere, POP3, and IMAP4 are all configurable to be secured with SSL.

This section uses the following cmdlets:

- ❏ New-ExchangeCertificate
- ❏ Import-ExchangeCertificate
- ❏ Enable-ExchangeCertificate

Certificate Types

Out of the box, Exchange uses self-signed certificates to provide secure connections without any administrative configuration. If clients will be accessing the CAS server from external sources, it is necessary to change the default certificate with a new one issued by a trusted certificate authority. Also, self-signed certificates cannot be used with Outlook Anywhere.

Certificates can be obtained from a public (commercial) authority or an internal one—as long as all the clients trust the certificate authority's root certificate. Using a commercial certificate may be less complex because deployment of the internal root certificate means touching every client, including mobile devices.

Because there are multiple services, each with a different possible DNS name, there are three strategies to handle this. First, generate multiple certificates, one for each URL. The second is to use a certificate with Subject Alternate Names (SANs), which allow a list of DNS names. This is also referred to as a Unified Communication certificate. The third is a wildcard certificate, which works for any DNS name in a domain. Not all clients work with SAN or wildcard certificates and may not function correctly. The following table discusses the pros and cons of the different certificate types:

Certificate Type	Benefit	Drawback	Example
Multiple Single Certificates	Very flexible No compatibility issues	May not be cost effective if there are many DNS names. More certificates to manage.	`Webmail.exchangeexchange.com`
Subject Alternate Names	Can use one certificate to cover multiple DNS names	Possible compatibility issues	`Autodiscover .exchangeexchange.com,` `Webmail.exchangeexchange.com`
Wildcard	Can be most cost effective	Likely compatibility issues. In particular, mobile devices may not understand the wildcard certificate.	`*.exchangeexchange.com`

The request process is different than certificate requests for other applications. If the correct process is not followed, the resulting certificate may not be valid. The high-level steps for certificate requests are:

1. Generate the certificate
2. Obtain the certificate from a public certificate authority
3. Import the certificate
4. Enable the certificate
5. Copy the certificate

These steps are discussed in more detail in the following sections.

Generating the Certificate

The first step is to generate the certificate. Certificate requests are generated with the `New-ExchangeCertificate` cmdlet:

```
New-ExchangeCertificate [-DomainController <String>] [-DomainName
<MultiValuedProperty>] [-FriendlyName <String>] [-IncludeAcceptedDomains
<SwitchParameter>] [-IncludeAutoDiscover <SwitchParameter>] [-Instance
<X509Certificate2>] [-KeySize <Int32>] [-PrivateKeyExportable <$true |
$false>] [-Services <None | IMAP | POP | UM | IIS | SMTP>] [-SubjectName
<X500DistinguishedName>]

New-ExchangeCertificate [-BinaryEncoded <SwitchParameter>]
[-DomainController <String>] [-DomainName <MultiValuedProperty>] [-Force
<SwitchParameter>] [-FriendlyName <String>] [-GenerateRequest
<SwitchParameter>][-IncludeAcceptedDomains <SwitchParameter>]
[-IncludeAutoDiscover <SwitchParameter>] [-Instance <X509Certificate2>]
[-KeySize <Int32>][-Path <String>] [-PrivateKeyExportable <$true |
$false>] [-SubjectName <X500DistinguishedName>]
```

One of the key parameters in creating a certificate request is `SubjectName`. The Subject Name is the primary name that matches the certificate to the DNS name in the URL. It is composed of the elements discussed in the following table:

Element	Definition	Example
Common Name (CN)	The fully qualified domain name (FQDN) for the URL / server	`Webmail.ExchangeExchange.com`
Subject Alternative Name (SAN)	Alternate fully qualified domain name (FQDN) for the URL / server	`Autodiscover.ExchangeExchange.Com`
Organization Name (O)	The Full Legal Company Name or Personal Name	`ExchangeExchange`
Organizational Unit (OU)	Typically the branch or group ordering the certificate	`Information Systems`
Domain Component (DC)	Part of a DNS name	`DC=com, DC=ExchangeExchange`
Country (C)	The two-letter country code using the ISO 3166 country names	`US`
State (S)	The state's full name	`Illinois`
Locality (L)	The locality or city full name	`Chicago`

So, putting it all together, a Subject Name may look like this:

```
C=US, S=Illinois, L=Chicago, O=ExchangeExchange, OU=Information Systems,
CN=webmail.exchangeexchange.com
```

For some certificate issuers the company listed in the Organization Name (O) must own the domain name that appears in Common Name. If it does not match, it may fail to issue the certificate.

Running the `New-ExchangeCertificate` cmdlet without any parameters generates a self-signed certificate. The default self-signed certificates have one year before they expire.

As previously discussed, it is possible to request a certificate with multiple names. This is likely to be the most common type of certificate for Exchange Server 2007.

There are a few parameters worth discussing in more detail before generating the certificate for our test domain, `exchangeexchange.com`.

First is the `includeaccepteddomain` parameter. This includes all of the organization's DNS names on the request. For example, the test CAS is joined to the Active Directory domain `ExchangeExchange.local`. Figure 6-5 shows the effects of setting this parameter to `true` on the left and `false` on the right. The request will have both `exchangeexchange.com` and `ExchangeExchange.local`.

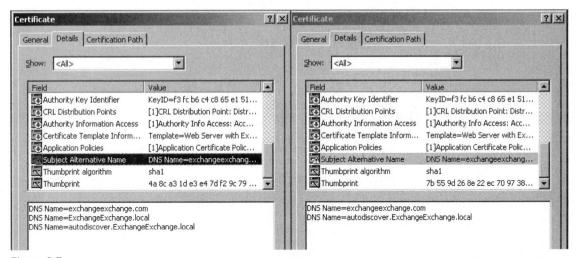

Figure 6-5

Next is the `includeautodiscover` parameter. This will append `autodiscover` to the list of Subject Alternative Names. This is just a convenience, because this can be manually added to the `domainname` parameter. If an Autodiscover domain is already included in the `domainname` parameter, it will not add `autodiscover` twice.

Finally, the `domainname` parameter sets the list of Subject Alternative Names. Figure 6-6 shows the result of setting the `domainname` parameter to `webmail.exchangeexchange.com`, `Autodiscover.exchangeexchange.com`, `pop.exchangeexchange.com`, `imap.exchangeexchange.com`.

This certificate will now be accepted for any of the domains listed. It is not required to have the NetBIOS or fully qualified domain name (FQDN) of the server. However, it may make configuration easier if users will be accessing the CAS from internal networks.

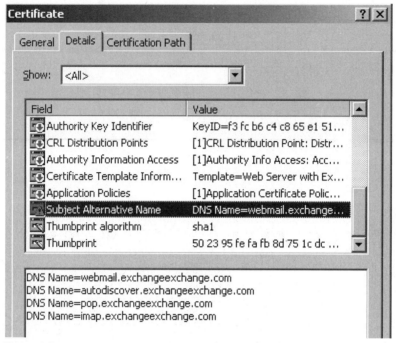

Figure 6-6

Putting all of this together, this is an example for our test domain exchangeexchange.com. The external DNS name is webmail, which is how users access OWA. This request uses a Subject Alternative Name certificate to provide secure access to Autodiscover.exchangeexchange.com for Outlook 2007 clients:

```
New-ExchangeCertificate -GenerateRequest:$true -FriendlyName ExchangeExchangeCert -
PrivateKeyExportable:$true -path c:\temp\certreqSAN.req -subjectname "C=US,
S=Illinois, L=Chicago, O=ExchangeExchange, OU=Information Systems,
CN=webmail.exchangeexchange.com" -DomainName
webmail.exchangeexchange.com,autodiscover.exchangeexchange.com,pop.
exchangeexchange.com,imap.exchangeexchange.com
```

Obtaining the Certificate

The process for obtaining the certificate depends on which certificate authority is used. Most services allow uploading the request file generated in the previous step. Some certificate authorities require pasting the contents of the request file directly. Whichever mechanism is used, once the request is processed, the certificate authority returns a valid digital certificate. This certificate needs to be protected because it contains both the public and the private key.

Importing the Certificate

Once the digital certificate is received, the next step is to import the certificate into the computer's certificate store. This step must be executed on the same machine that made the request. This is because the security on the certificate is unique to the machine that ran the New-ExchangeCertificate cmdlet. If the import is run on a different machine, the resulting imported certificate will not have the private key, and it will not be usable for the next step.

```
Import-ExchangeCertificate -Path <String> [-DomainController <Fqdn>]
[-FriendlyName <String>] [-Password <SecureString>]
```

In the test environment example, the following is the cmdlet used to import the certificate:

```
Import-ExchangeCertificate -Path C:\temp\certreq.req
```

If a mistake is made after a certificate is imported, it can be removed with the Remove-ExchangeCertificate cmdlet. This cmdlet requires confirmation in order to complete the action, as shown in Figure 6-7.

Figure 6-7

Enabling the Certificate

The final step is to enable the certificate. This step ties the certificate to one or more Exchange services, such as POP or Outlook Web Access. Behind the scenes, the cmdlet is updating values in the IIS metabase. The cmdlet `Enable-ExchangeCertificate` is used for this purpose:

```
Enable-ExchangeCertificate -Thumbprint <String> -Services <None | IMAP |
POP | UM | IIS | SMTP> [-DomainController <Fqdn>]
```

The thumbprint is the unique identifier for the certificate, which can be displayed with the `Get-ExchangeCertificate` cmdlet. This cmdlet also shows which certificates are currently enabled for which services.

The `Services` switch specifies which of the services will use the certificate. For example, to enable a certificate for OWA, POP, and IMAP the cmdlet would be:

```
Enable-ExchangeCertificate -thumbprint
   77BADDFAAACB0D3340F60B7D45029968D3F0A75E -Services Pop,Imap,IIS
```

Copy the Certificate

If you have multiple Client Access Servers or ISA servers at the edge, then you may need to copy the certificate to those servers. The easiest way to back up the certificate is with the certificate manager MMC snap-in. After launching the snap-in, a dialog box prompts you to choose which certificate store to manage. Select the Computer Account option and the local computer (this assumes running this on the CAS server). In the Personal store, right-click the certificate and choose Export. This launches the certificate export wizard. Make sure to export the private key, which requires creating a password to protect the certificate. The result is a PFX file that contains both the public and private key pair. It is critical to protect this file, because if it is compromised the certificate must be revoked and a new certificate will need to be generated.

On each target server, use the `Import-ExchangeCertificate` cmdlet as in the previous step. This time, it will be slightly different because the cmdlet requires a credential parameter to finish the import with the private key. To get the password for the parameter, use the sub-expression `Get-Credential` to have the standard username and password dialog box pop up. The username is not important; only the password will be used. Input the password selected during the certificate export. An example of this cmdlet looks like this:

```
Import-ExchangeCertificate -Path c:\temp\CASCert.pfx -Password:
(Get-Credential).password
```

Figure 6-8 shows how the preceding cmdlet prompts the administrator to set the password.

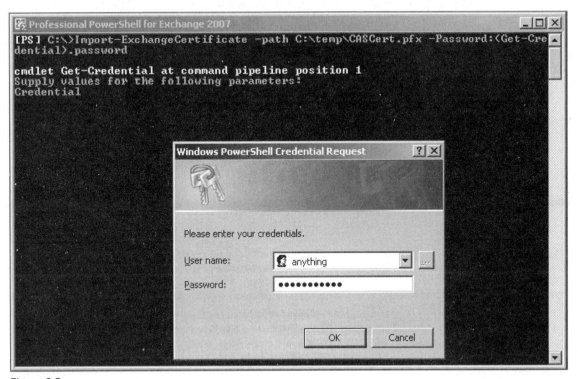

Figure 6-8

Autodiscover

Autodiscover is a new feature in Exchange Server 2007 that works with Outlook 2007 to automatically configure the client's profile. This feature can significantly lower helpdesk calls and directly reduce support costs. It also helps with disaster recovery scenarios because the Outlook 2007 client will update its profile on startup. The user is prompted to enter his email address and password, and if configured correctly, Outlook 2007 receives its configuration and the user can start using email. This even works with Outlook Anywhere from outside the corporate network. The configuration is also periodically checked as long as Outlook is running.

Before discussing how to configure Autodiscover, understanding how it works is helpful. Outlook 2007 processes the Autodiscover process differently depending on whether the client is internal or external. If the client can access Active Directory, it queries for the service connection point (SCP). The SCP holds the location of the Autodiscover URL. The SCP is created during setup, and initially is set to http://<CAS hostname>/Autodiscover/Autodiscover.xml. The SCP object resides in the configuration container with the other Exchange configuration objects.

Figure 6-9 shows the output from a test environment using an LDAP tool called LDP to show the SCP.

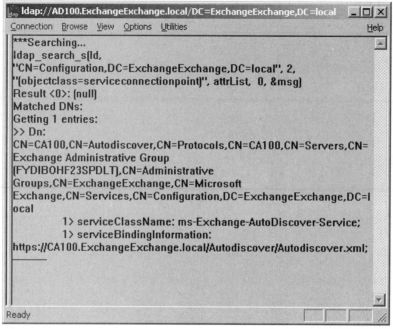

Figure 6-9

It is possible to change the service location by setting the `AutodiscoverServiceInternalURI` parameter in the `Set-ClientAccessServer` cmdlet:

```
Set-ClientAccessServer -identity CA100 -AutodiscoverServiceInternalURI
"https://ca100.exchangeexchange.com"
```

It is not necessary to set the Autodiscover InternalURL and ExternalURL with `Set-AutodiscoverVirtualDirectory`, *because the Outlook client will not use them to locate Autodiscover services.*

Outlook then connects to the Autodiscover URL, which is on the CAS. Finally, the Autodiscover service returns the addresses of the available services. These services include URLs for the Availability Service, Exchange Web Service, Offline Address Book, and Unified Messaging.

In the case where Outlook fails to contact Active Directory, Outlook takes the user's email address and tries some hard-coded locations. The URL will be either `https://<smtp domain address>/Autodiscover/Autodiscover.xml` or `https://autodiscover.<smtp address domain>/Autodiscover/Autodiscover.xml`. The process from this point is the same as the internal scenario.

By default, the CAS is set up with Autodiscover as a virtual directory. To move the Autodiscover virtual directory to another host, for example a web server that already hosts a public website, start by removing the existing virtual directory on the CAS. This is done with the `Remove-AutodiscoverVirtualDirectory` cmdlet:

```
Remove-AutodiscoverVirtualDirectory -Identity <VirtualDirectoryIdParameter>
  [-DomainController <Fqdn>]
```

Once the old virtual directory is removed, create the new one with the
`New-AutodiscoverVirtualDirectory` cmdlet:

```
New-AutodiscoverVirtualDirectory [-ApplicationRoot <String>]
[-AppPoolId <String>] [-BasicAuthentication <$true | $false>] [-Confirm
[<SwitchParameter>]] [-DigestAuthentication <$true | $false>]
[-DomainController <Fqdn>] [-ExternalUrl <Uri>] [-InternalUrl <Uri>]
[-Path <String>] [-TemplateInstance <PSObject>] [-WebSiteName <String>]
[-WhatIf [<SwitchParameter>]] [-WindowsAuthentication <$true | $false>]
```

For example, to create a new Autodiscover virtual directory named `Autodiscover.exchangeexchange`
`.com` that requires Integrated and Digest authentication, run the cmdlet:

```
New-AutodiscoverVirtualDirectory -WebSiteName "Autodiscover.exchangeexchange.com" -
WindowsAuthentication:$true -DigestAuthentication:$true
```

It is possible to test Autodiscover services with Outlook 2007. Once Outlook 2007 is running, hold CRTL
while right-clicking the Outlook icon in the system tray. A Test E-mail AutoConfiguration option is
available, as shown in Figure 6-10.

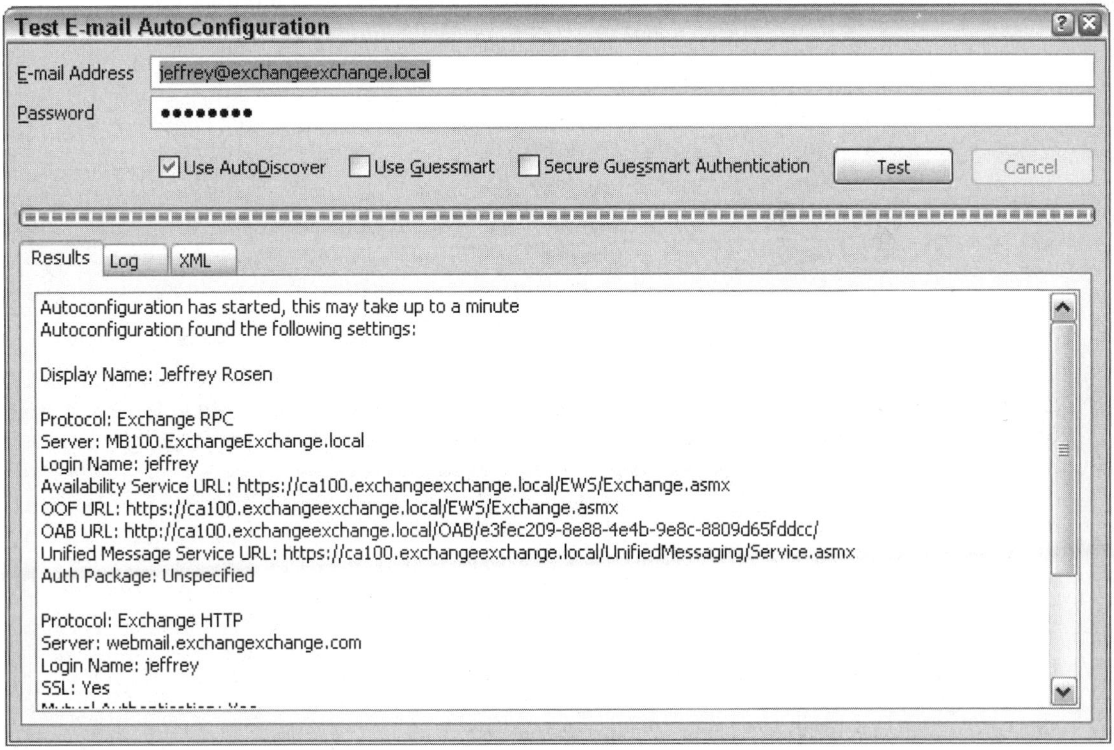

Figure 6-10

Another option is to run the `Test-OwaConnectivity` cmdlet. Before the cmdlet will run, a test user needs to be created. There is a script located in the scripts directory named `New-TestCasConnectivityUser.ps1`. If the script is not run from a mailbox server, one must be piped into the script. Figure 6-11 illustrates creating the connectivity test user with the `new-TestCasConnectivityUser` script.

```
get-mailboxServer | new-TestCasConnectivityUser.ps1 [-UMDialPlan
<dialplanname> -UMExtension <numDigitsInDialplan>]

get-mailboxServer foo | new-TestCasConnectivityUser.ps1 [-UMDialPlan
<dialplanname> -UMExtension <numDigitsInDialplan>]
```

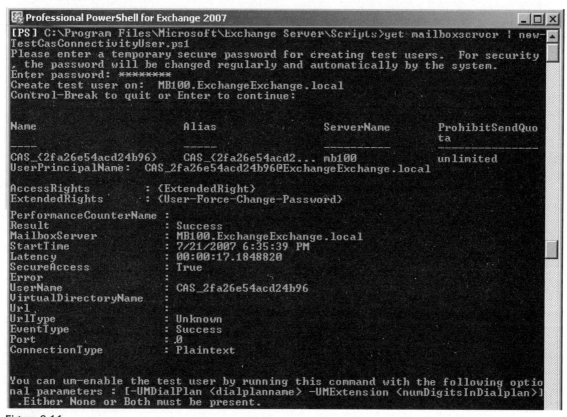

Figure 6-11

Proxy and Redirection

The CAS provides many different types of client access. Each of the services has a namespace associated with it. For example, Outlook Web Access, IMAP, and Exchange ActiveSync clients each require a URL to connect to the service. They do not have to be the same, and in the case of Autodiscover it will likely not be the same. As illustrated previously in the certificates section, features or security needs may require more than a single namespace for a certificate. In addition to security the namespace can have implications on network traffic. In previous versions of Exchange, the front-end server proxy requests to the mailbox server without regard to physical network topology. Exchange Server 2007 tries to provide the "best" service by using a CAS located closest to the user's mailbox server.

There are architectural decisions on where to place a Client Access Server, and how to create a namespace for external access. These design points are beyond the scope of this book, but understanding the impact and how to configure the CAS to handle these configurations is not. This discussion focuses on Outlook Web Access, but proxy and redirection affects the other CAS services too. Check with the Exchange Server 2007 online help to learn in detail how the other services use proxy and redirection.

Only one Client Access Server must be Internet facing. Exchange will proxy OWA requests to the Client Access Server in other sites if configured correctly. There must be at least one Client Access Server in each AD site to use these services. For Exchange to proxy correctly, the Internet-facing CAS has the ExternalURL property set and the other CAS has only the InternalURL set. (See Figure 6-12.)

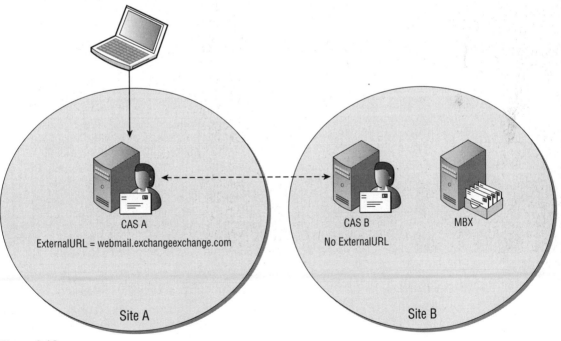

Figure 6-12

If the second CAS has the `ExternalURL` set, the Internet CAS redirects the connection to the URL specified. This is often used when there are multiple geographies or costly WAN links. Exchange always tries to use the CAS closest to the user's mailbox. (See Figure 6-13.)

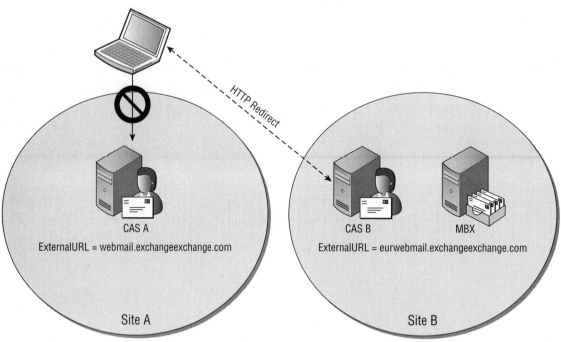

Figure 6-13

It is possible to override the redirection behavior so a CAS will proxy the connection even when the `ExternalURL` is set. In this scenario, the user attempts to connect to `webmail.exchangeexchange.com`, which is CAS A. CAS A sees that the `ExternalURL` parameter is configured on CAS B, so it tries to redirect the client. If the Internet connection to CAS B is unavailable for any reason, the user's attempt to use OWA (CAS B) fails. By temporarily setting the `RedirectToOptimalServer` to false, CAS A will proxy, even though CAS B has the `ExternalURL` set. Of course this requires that Site A and Site B can still communicate with each other. (See Figure 6-14.)

The cmdlet to the override redirection would look like this:

```
Set-OwaVirtualDirectory -Identity "owa (default web site)" -
RedirectToOptimalOWAServer:$false
```

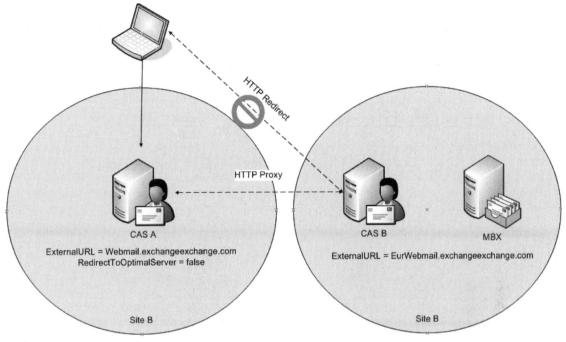

Figure 6-14

Outlook Anywhere

Outlook Anywhere was formerly known in previous versions of Exchange as RPC over HTTP. This feature allows the full Outlook client to access Exchange securely through the Internet. It also works seamlessly through firewalls.

The cmdlet used for Outlook Anywhere configuration is:

❑   Enable-OutlookAnywhere

The `Enable-OutlookAnywhere` cmdlet is used to enable or disable this feature. It has the following syntax:

```
Enable-OutlookAnywhere -ExternalAuthenticationMethod <Basic | Digest |
```

```
Ntlm | Fba | WindowsIntegrated | Misconfigured> -ExternalHostname
<Hostname> -SSLOffloading <$true | $false> [-DomainController <Fqdn>]
[-Server <ServerIdParameter>] [-TemplateInstance <PSObject>]
[<CommonParameters>]
```

There is not a lot of configuration needed to enable Outlook Anywhere. There are four parameters to configure: the external name, the authentication type, the servers enabled for Outlook Anywhere, and whether or not an SSL will be offloaded. All the prerequisites for enabling RPC over HTTP must be configured before running `Enable-OutlookAnywhere`.

This example shows how to enable Outlook Anywhere on the test CAS server:

```
Enable-OutlookAnywhere -Server CA100 -ExternalHostNname
"webmail.exchangeexchange.com" -ExternalAuthenticationMethod NTLM
-SSLOffloading:$false
```

Working with the Offline Address Book

The Offline Address Book is a copy of an address book that an Outlook client can download and use while disconnected. Previous versions of Exchange stored Offline Address Book (OAB) files in a system Public folder. New to Exchange Server 2007 is the option to distribute the OAB through IIS over HTTPS and the Background Intelligent Transfer Service (BITS). Only Outlook 2007 clients can use this new method.

Offline Address Book related cmdlets are:

❑   Set-OabVirtualDirectory

❑   Set-OfflineAddressBook

Creating the Offline Address Book

When the Client Access Server role is installed, a virtual directory named OAB is created on the default IIS website. The OAB is not accessible from outside the corporate network until the ExternalURL parameter is set with the Set-OabVirtualDirectory cmdlet:

```
Set-OabVirtualDirectory -Identity <VirtualDirectoryIdParameter>
[-DomainController <Fqdn>] [-ExternalUrl <Uri>] [-InternalUrl <Uri>]
[-PollInterval <Int32>] [-RequireSSL <$true | $false>][<CommonParameters>]

Set-OabVirtualDirectory [-DomainController <Fqdn>] [-ExternalUrl <Uri>]
[-Instance <ADOabVirtualDirectory>] [-InternalUrl <Uri>] [-PollInterval
<Int32>] [-RequireSSL <$true | $false>] [<CommonParameters>]
```

For example:

```
Set-OabVirtualDirectory -;Identity "CA100\OAB (Default Web Site)" -ExternalURL
"https://OAB.exchangeexchange.com/OAB"
```

The IIS virtual directory does not require SSL security by default. This can be enforced either through IIS Manager or with PowerShell. To require SSL, the cmdlet would be:

```
Set-OABVirtualDirectory -Identity "OAB (Default Web Site) -RequireSSL $true
```

For clients to be able to retrieve the OAB, distribution points need to be configured. Only Outlook 2007 can take advantage of the web-based distribution. All legacy clients require a Public folder installed and configured as a distribution point.

To configure the Offline Address Book properties, use the Set-OfflineAddressBook cmdlet. The specifics on how distribution works and how it is configured follows this section.

```
Set-OfflineAddressBook -Identity <OfflineAddressBookIdParameter>
[-AddressLists <AddressBookBaseIdParameter[]>] [-DiffRetentionPeriod
<Nullable>] [-DomainController <Fqdn>] [-IsDefault <$true | $false>]
[-Name <String>] [-PublicFolderDistributionEnabled <$true | $false>]
[-Schedule <Schedule>] [-Versions <Collection>] [-VirtualDirectories
<VirtualDirectoryIdParameter[]>] [<CommonParameters>]
Set-OfflineAddressBook [-AddressLists <AddressBookBaseIdParameter[]>]
[-DiffRetentionPeriod <Nullable>] [-DomainController <Fqdn>] [-Instance
<OfflineAddressBook>] [-IsDefault <$true | $false>] [-Name <String>]
 [-PublicFolderDistributionEnabled <$true | $false>] [-Schedule <Schedule>]
[-Versions <Collection>] [-VirtualDirectories
<VirtualDirectoryIdParameter[]>] [<CommonParameters>]
```

To set the test CAS as a web distribution point, the cmdlet would be:

```
Set-OfflineAddressBook -Identity "\Default Offline Address Book"
-VirtualDirectories "CA100\OAB (Default Web Site)"
```

Running this cmdlet results in the settings shown in Figure 6-15 in the GUI.

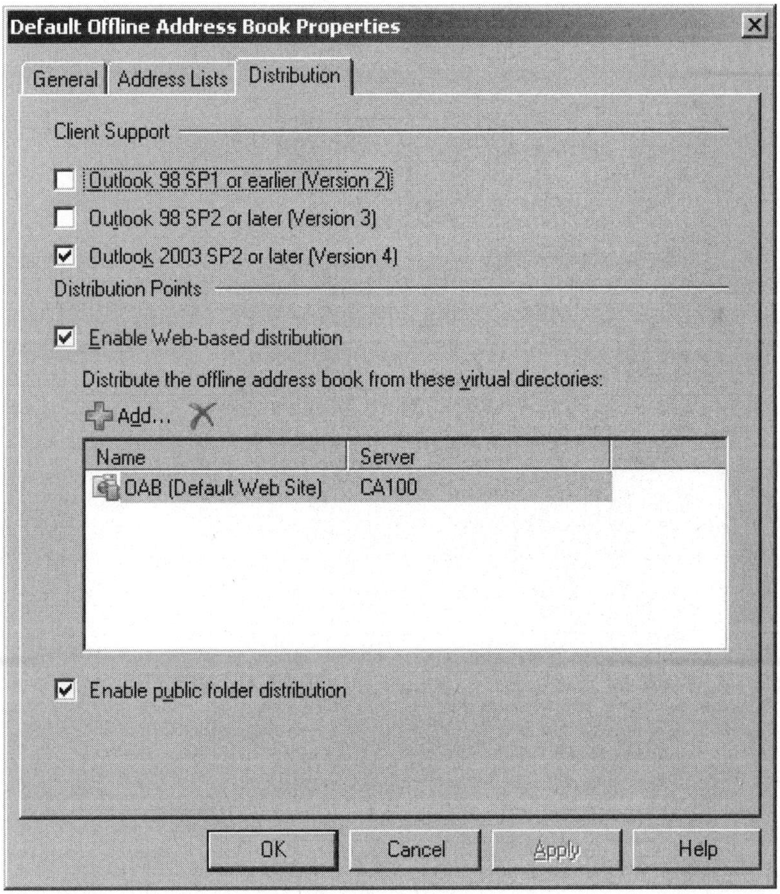

Figure 6-15

Address Book Generation

The Offline Address Book (OAB) is generated once per day by default. If Public folder distribution is enabled, it places a copy in a system Public folder. It uses the Public folder server that is set as the default Public folder store for the generation server. It is up to an administrator to make sure there are replicas on other Public folder servers. The chapter on Public folders explains how to add replicas to Public folders.

Web-based distribution is actually done by the Client Access Server. The Exchange File Distribution Service runs on the CAS and it is responsible for copying the updated files from the OAB file share on the OAB generation server. By default, this polls every 8 hours from the time the service starts. This means it can be at most 32 hours before a change is propagated throughout the system. Restarting the Exchange File Distribution Service forces it to check if updates need to be copied.

> *The default location where the System Attendant service publishes the Offline Address Book files is* `%installdir%\ExchangeOAB`. *This is configurable in Service Pack 1.*

For example, if the generation process is daily at 5:00AM, and a user is added after the process finishes, say 6:00AM, the next time the user will be in the Offline Address Book is 24 hours later. If a Client Access Server polls before the generation is complete, it will be another 8 hours until the CAS picks it up for web distribution. This can be configured to generate more frequently if needed using the `Set-OfflineAddressBook` cmdlet.

This example changes the generation frequency to twice daily at 5am and 5pm. Check the online help for detailed information on formatting the schedule parameter.

```
Set-OfflineAddressBook -Identity "\Default Offline Address Book" -Schedule
Sun.5:00 AM-Sun.5:15 AM, Sun.5:00 PM-Sun.5:15 PM, Mon.5:00 AM-Mon.5
:15 AM, Mon.5:00 PM-Mon.5:15 PM, Tue.5:00 AM-Tue.5:15 AM, Tue.5:00
PM-Tue.5:15 PM, Wed.5:00 AM-Wed.5:15 AM, Wed.5:00 PM-Wed.5:15 PM,
Thu.5:00 AM-Thu.5:15 AM, Thu.5:00 PM-Thu.5:15 PM, Fri.5:00 AM-Fri.5:15
AM, Fri.5:00 PM-Fri.5:15 PM, Sat.5:00 AM-Sat.5:15 AM, Sat.5:00 PM-Sa
t.5:15 PM
```

LinkAccess

LinkAccess is a new feature that provides read-only Outlook Web Access (OWA) integration with Microsoft Office SharePoint Services and file shares. For example, users can access documents from a home directory connecting through OWA on a home computer. LinkAccess is fairly wide open out of the box. Users have access to all file shares and SharePoint libraries from public or private computers.

Link access–related cmdlets are:

❑   `Set-OWAVirtualDirectory`

❑   `Set-CasMailbox`

Another feature that compliments LinkAccess is a feature called WebReady Document viewing. WebReady converts documents to HTML on the fly and displays them in a browser. This is extremely useful when a user may not have the target application installed. For example, a user is traveling and is sent an important Microsoft Word document, but he does not have Microsoft Office installed. With WebReady enabled, the CAS displays the Word document as HTML in a browser. Settings can be configured separately whether the user selects the public or private computer option when logging in to OWA, as shown in Figure 6-16. It is possible to block LinkAccess functionality while still providing WebReady Document viewing.

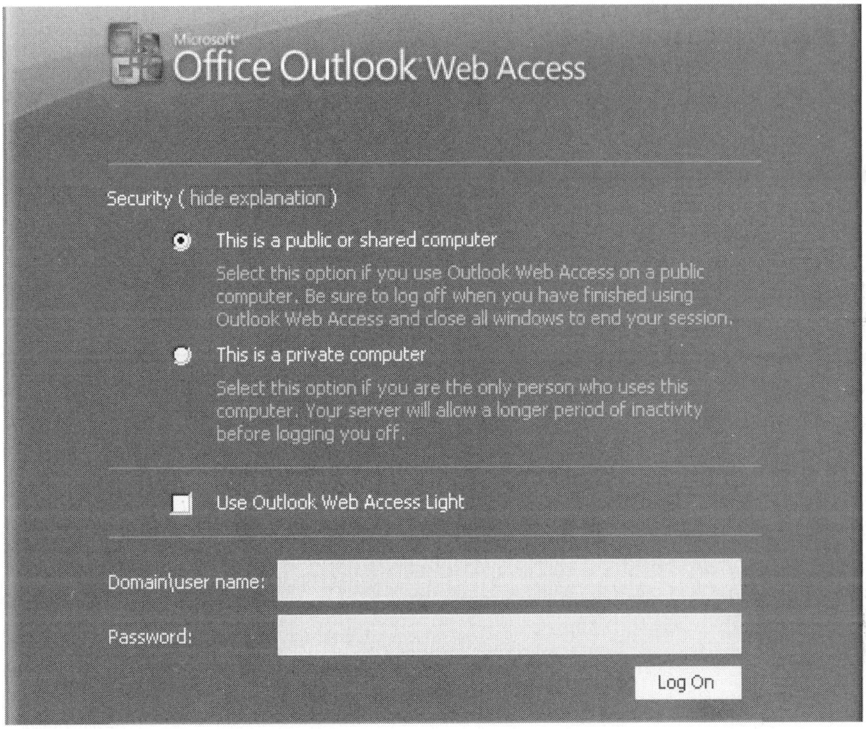

Figure 6-16

Support for the latest Office 2007 format will be added in Exchange Server 2007 Service Pack 1.

This option is user-selected, so there is nothing to stop a user from picking This Is A Private Computer on a public machine. This may force administrators to configure the settings the same way for both public and private. These settings are configurable under Server Configuration, Client Access. Select the Client Access Server and select the properties on the OWA virtual directory. But, because this is a book about PowerShell, here is how to configure it with the `Set-OwaVirtualDirectory` cmdlet.

The `Set-OwaVirtualDirectory` cmdlet has more than 60 parameters, but only a few will be covered here.

There are four properties that control whether or not the LinkAccess is available.
`UNCAccessOnPrivateComputer` and `WSSAccessOnPrivateComputer` control file-share and
SharePoint access for the login option "This is a private computer" by setting it to either `true` or `false`
. `UNCAccessOnPublicComputer` and `WSSAccessOnPublicComputer` control file-share and SharePoint
access for the login option "This is a public computer."

This example shows disabling the LinkAccess for SharePoint and file shares when using public
computers:

```
Set-OWAVirtualDirectory -Identity "owa (default web site)"
-WSSAccessOnPublicComputersEnabled:$false
-UNCAccessOnPublicComputersEnabled:$false
```

After setting these two parameters, the next time the user logs in his menu bar in OWA there will no
longer be a Documents tab. In this scenario, users still can use WebReady for attachments to view them
in HTML. (See Figure 6-17.)

Figure 6-17

It is also possible to set these features on a per-user basis. For example:

```
Set-CASMailbox -Identity Jeffrey
-OWAWSSAccessOnPublicComputersEnabled:$false
-OWAUNCAccessOnPublicComputersEnabled:$false
```

Another important setting is configuring access to remote file servers. There are separate settings to
allow specific servers and deny specific servers. A decision must be made on the default security access
for unknown remote servers. It can be configured to either allow or block servers not specifically listed.
For tighter security, blocking access to remote file servers that are not in the block and allow list is
recommended.

Similar to LinkAccess there are parameters to control public and private computers. `WebReadyDocumentViewingOnPublicComputersEnabled` and `WebReadyDocumentViewingOnPrivateComputersEnabled` control this feature.

```
Set-OWAVirtualDirectory -Identity "owa (default web site)"
-WebReadyDocumentViewingOnPublicComputersEnabled:$false
```

There is a default list of file attachment types that can be allowed or blocked. By default, users are forced to save files with unknown file types. Additional file types can be added or existing ones removed from the default list. The list is "global" to all users using that OWA virtual directory and cannot be configured per person. Editing the lists is a little more complicated because they are multi-valued properties. So if the following cmdlet was executed, it would erase all the existing file types and replace them with the new list:

```
Set-OWAVirtualDirectory -Identity "owa (default web site)" -AllowedFileTypes ".jef"
```

Because this is not likely to be what you intended, another method is to work with the virtual directory as an object. Save the virtual directory to a variable and then add or remove file types. Finally, save the changes back to the "real" virtual directory. This example adds a new file type and removes and existing one from the `AllowedFileTypes` parameter:

```
$owaVdir = Get-OwaVirtualDirectory -Identity "owa (default web site)"
$owaVdir.AllowedFileTypes.Add(".jef")
$owaVdir.AllowedFileTypes.Remove(".txt")
$owaVdir | set-OwaVirtualDirectory
```

Summary

The Client Access Server plays a larger role than the legacy Front-End server. New features such as WebReady and LinkAccess provide significant productivity benefits to users. Exchange Server 2007 gives administrators tools to make sure all of the services are up and running. As shown in this chapter, there are a lot of configuration tasks, so careful planning and testing are needed to ensure a successful implementation.

7

Configuring the Hub
Transport Role

Exchange Server 2000/2003 used the concept of bridgehead servers and connectors. A bridgehead server referred to an Exchange server that served as a connection point for delivering email from one routing group to another and to remote or external email systems. Bridgehead servers used connectors to make information flow between routing groups and remote or external systems possible. Several types of connectors were available: SMTP, Routing Group, and X.400.

Exchange Server 2007 introduces the concept of the Hub Transport role. Computers running Exchange Server 2007 with the Hub Transport role are called Hub Transport servers and are identical to bridgehead servers in Exchange 2000/2003; however, they differ greatly in core transport functionality. The Hub Transport server role is installed in any Active Directory site that contains the Mailbox server role and is responsible for mail delivery within the Active Directory site. It can be installed on separate hardware as the only server role or on the same server hardware in conjunction with other non-clustered Exchange Server 2007 roles. The Hub Transport server receives messages from and sends messages to servers running the Mailbox server role. Every message sent and received by an Exchange mailbox must pass through the Hub Transport server, hence transport rules and journal policies are not skipped for any message. In a multi-site organization, messages destined for a user in a different site are transferred to a Hub Transport server in that site for delivery. Messages destined for the Internet or other messaging systems are sent to the Edge Transport server for delivery. We discuss the Edge Transport role further in Chapter 9. The Hub Transport server role uses *Send* Connectors and *Receive* Connectors for email routing and delivery.

This chapter covers:

- ❑   Understanding the core transport architecture implemented by the Hub Transport and Edge Transport servers.
- ❑   Using and configuring the Hub Transport server
- ❑   Configuring various types of connectors in Exchange Server 2007
- ❑   Using email address policies and accepted domains

The Transport Server Architecture

The core transport architecture was rewritten in Exchange Server 2007 and is very different from previous versions of Exchange. Those familiar with Exchange Server 2000/2003 might quickly notice that transport is no longer dependent on Internet Information Server (IIS). In fact, it is required that you uninstall the SMTP and NNTP services prior to installing Exchange Server 2007 unlike Exchange Server 2000/2003, which required both services to be installed. Additionally, all core components required for message categorization, routing, and delivery are included in Exchange Transport Service with no components dependent on IIS. This section briefly reviews the core transport architecture from the perspective of the Management Shell.

The following Hub Transport–related cmdlets are discussed:

- ❏   Get-Queue
- ❏   Set-Queue
- ❏   Suspend-Queue
- ❏   Resume-Queue
- ❏   Retry-Queue
- ❏   Get-TransportPipeline
- ❏   Get-TransportServer
- ❏   Set-TransportServer
- ❏   Get-TransportConfig
- ❏   Set-TransportConfig
- ❏   Get-NetworkConnectionInfo

A number of components make up the core transport architecture implemented by both the Hub Transport server and Edge Transport server roles. These components as well as other processes and queues constitute the *transport pipeline* in Exchange Server 2007. Think of it as a series of processes that make message delivery or relay possible. Every message sent or received must go through the transport pipeline. The transport pipeline consists of the following:

- ❏   **SMTP Receive:** This component accepts connections on port 25 inbound to the Hub Transport or Edge Transport servers. This component is controlled by the SMTP Receive Connector, which is similar to the SMTP virtual server in Exchange Server 2000/2003. It is at this stage of the transport pipeline that anti-virus and anti-spam agents are implemented to filter incoming connections, message content, determine the sender, and apply any compliance or transport rules configured. Actual message hygiene or transport rules performed vary slightly depending on which server role is installed, either the Hub Transport role or Edge Transport role. A series of events are triggered as the message is received and agents are executed against the message.

❑ **Submission Queue:** After a message is accepted into the organization either from SMTP Receive or Pickup/Replay directory, it is placed into the Submission queue by the Submission process. Submission can also occur when the store driver retrieves outbound messages from users' outboxes and places them in the Submission queue. (See Figure 7-1.) This queue is essentially an ESE database similar to the server mailbox store database. This differs markedly from Exchange Server 2000/2003 where incoming SMTP messages or messages from the pickup queue were placed in the Queue folder, a physical NTFS partition.

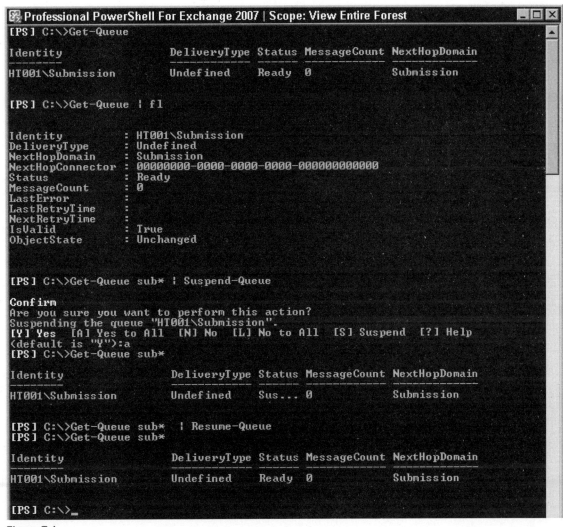

Figure 7-1

As shown in Figure 7-1, when there are no messages sent or delivered by the Hub Transport the `Get-Queue` cmdlet returns only the Submission queue. Notice that the `DeliveryType` is undefined and `NextHopConnector` is all zeros. The next hop is the Categorizer. Like any other message queue in Exchange Server 2007, it can be suspended and resumed. When this is done, the Hub Transport server no longer processes new incoming messages; rather, the message count continually increases by the number of new messages received. When the queue is resumed, the Submission queue is de-queued and messages are picked up once again by the Categorizer. The `Suspend-Queue` and `Resume-Queue` cmdlets are used to pause and resume message queues as shown in Figure 7-1. Notice the change in queue status when the queue is suspended and when resumed. With the exception of the Submission queue, for other message queues, the `Retry-Queue` cmdlet can be used to retry messages in the queue after a transient failure.

❑ **Categorizer:** The Categorizer collects and processes messages placed in the Submission queue. This key component of the transport pipeline is responsible for several functions depending on whether the transport server is the Hub or Edge server role. On the Edge server, categorization simply involves routing the submitted message to a delivery queue based on the recipient domain. On the Hub Transport server, categorization involves recipient resolution, distribution list expansion, message content conversion, routing, and application of any rules defined. Thereafter message delivery is either MAPI Delivery or Remote Delivery to another Hub server or Edge Transport server. On the Edge Transport server, unlike the Hub Transport server, after categorization, message delivery will always be via Send Connectors to the target destination. Figure 7-4 shows the transport pipeline exposing two events of the Categorizer: the `OnSubmittedMessage` and `OnRoutedMessage` events.

❑ **Local (MAPI) Delivery:** This stage of the transport pipeline delivers messages from a Hub Transport server to a mailbox on a mailbox server in the Active Directory site. After a message has been categorized and its next hop identified as a mailbox store within the Active Directory site, the message is moved to the MAPI Delivery queue. The store driver component involved at this stage connects to the Recipients mailbox store and writes the message to the inbox, after which the message is deleted from the MAPI Delivery queue. There can be multiple MAPI Delivery queues depending on the number of mailbox servers in the local site for which messages are destined. Figure 7-2 shows local delivery queues to multiple mailbox servers when the `Get-Queue` cmdlet is run.

❑ **SMTP Send/Remote Delivery:** After categorization, messages destined for users not in the local Active Directory site or for remote SMTP servers or domains are placed in the Remote Delivery queue. This component is controlled by the SMTP Send Connector, which is similar to the SMTP Connector in Exchange Server 2000/2003. There can be several Remote Delivery queues and you may see a separate queue for each remote domain that messages are to be delivered to. If an Edge Transport server exists, remote delivery for all Internet domains will be through the Send Connector to the Edge Transport server. If coexisting with an earlier version of Exchange, messages destined for these servers will be relayed to the routing group where these servers reside. Figure 7-3 shows two Remote Delivery queues, one with a `deliverytype` of `SmtpRelayToRemoteAdSite` to a Hub server in a different Active Directory site and another with `Deliverytype` called `SmtpRelayToTiRg` with the next hop being an Exchange 2003 server in the "First Routing" group. The `MapiDelivery` queue shown is discussed shortly.

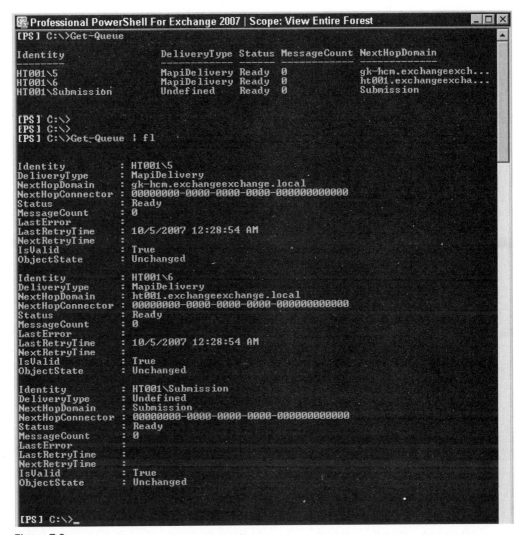

Figure 7-2

Figure 7-3

Finally, after successful delivery, the message is removed from the transport pipeline.

Please note that there are some Unified Messaging and Client Access instances that do not interact directly with the transport pipeline. When a sent message is finally put in the outbox on behalf of the sender, processing occurs by the same process as the submission process described previously.

To view the Hub Transport pipeline, use the `Get-TransportPipeline` cmdlet as shown in Figure 7-4. The `TransportPipeline` cmdlet also exposes two transport agents installed by default on the Hub Transport server: the Journaling Agent and the Transport Rule Agent. Agents are reviewed in Chapter 9.

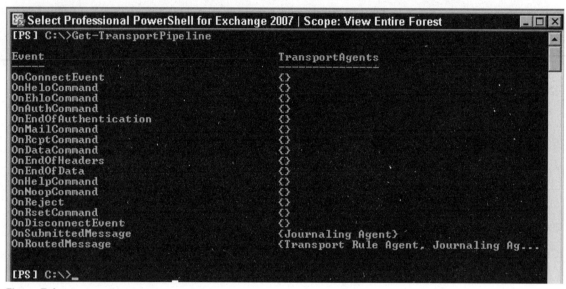

```
Select Professional PowerShell for Exchange 2007 | Scope: View Entire Forest          _ □ ×
[PS] C:\>Get-TransportPipeline

Event                                    TransportAgents
-----                                    ---------------
OnConnectEvent                           {}
OnHeloCommand                            {}
OnEhloCommand                            {}
OnAuthCommand                            {}
OnEndOfAuthentication                    {}
OnMailCommand                            {}
OnRcptCommand                            {}
OnDataCommand                            {}
OnEndOfHeaders                           {}
OnEndOfData                              {}
OnHelpCommand                            {}
OnNoopCommand                            {}
OnReject                                 {}
OnRsetCommand                            {}
OnDisconnectEvent                        {}
OnSubmittedMessage                       {Journaling Agent}
OnRoutedMessage                          {Transport Rule Agent, Journaling Ag...

[PS] C:\>_
```

Figure 7-4

Messages can enter the transport pipeline through any of four methods:

❑   Through an SMTP Receive Connector communicating on port 25.

❑   Through message files dropped into the Pickup or Replay directories.

❑   Through placement of messages in the Submission queue by the store driver.

❑   Through message submission via an agent.

In a nutshell, when a message is received by transport either through SMTP communication with another mail host or dropped into the Pickup or Replay directories, it is placed in the Submission queue to be picked up and processed by the Categorizer. The message recipients are resolved by the Categorizer, the message is bifurcated, and it goes through content conversion, after which its route is determined. If the message is bound for a mailbox on a Mailbox server in the local Active Directory site, it is routed via the MAPI Delivery and placed in the user's inbox by the store driver component. If the message is to be routed to a user outside the local Active Directory site or organization, message delivery is SMTP-based and would be routed via the Remote Delivery queue to a Hub Transport server in another Active Directory site, or to an Edge Transport server for Internet delivery. The message can also be routed directly from the Hub Transport server if no Edge Transport server is configured.

Configuring the Hub Transport Server

The Hub Transport server implements the core transport functionality and is responsible for all message flow within an Exchange organization. As mentioned earlier, it must be deployed into any Active Directory site that contains the Mailbox server role. All configuration information for the Hub Transport server is stored in Active Directory and changes made take effect on all Hub Transport servers in the organization. By default, the Hub Transport server configures and enables two transport policy and compliance agents, the Transport Rule Agent and the Journaling Agent. Unified Messaging messages such as voice and fax messages could bypass transport rules; however, in Exchange Server 2007 SP1 transport rules now act on Unified Messaging messages.

The `Get-TransportServer` and `Set-TransportServer` cmdlets enable you to view and change the property configuration on the Hub Transport server. Changing the configuration alters how the server processes messages. These changes are not organization wide, but affect only the specified server. This differs from the `Get-TransportConfig` and `Set-TransportConfig` cmdlets, which enable you to view and modify transport configuration for the whole Microsoft Exchange Server 2007 organization.

The `Get-TransportServer` cmdlet displays transport information for computers running the Hub Transport or Edge Transport role in the Exchange organization. It has two parameters: `Identity` for specifying the Hub Transport server to retrieve its information and `DomainController`, the fully qualified domain name of the domain controller used to retrieve the Hub Transport's server information. These parameters do not apply to the Edge Transport server. The `Identity` parameter always returns the local Edge Transport server and the domain controller parameter is not supported on the Edge Transport server because it is installed in a perimeter network with no access to Active Directory on a domain controller. Figures 7-5 and 7-6 display all the transport server settings available on the Hub Transport server.

The following section takes a quick look at a couple of the settings.

DNS Configuration

By default if `InternalDNSAdapterEnabled` is set to `True`, the Hub Transport server will always use the DNS servers configured on the internal network adapter. This is also the case even if `ExternalDNSAdapterEnabled` is `True`. If `InternalDNSAdapterEnabled` is set to `False` and DNS servers are manually specified, then the servers listed in the `InternalDNSServers` parameter will always be used. The Hub Transport only uses DNS servers specified with the `ExternalDNSServers` parameter or the external network adapter when a Send Connector is configured to use it.

In Figure 7-5, notice that both `InternalDNSAdapterEnabled` and `ExternalDNSAdapterEnabled` parameters are set to `True` on the transport server. This is the case even if the server is configured with a single network card. The DNS server(s) specified on the network card is used. Also, both `InternalDNSAdapterGuid` and `ExternalDNSAdapterGuid` are all zeros, indicating that DNS lookups will be performed using any available adapter on the server. To use a list of DNS servers other than those on the adapter, first disable `InternalDNSAdapterEnabled` and `ExternalDNSAdapterEnabled` by setting them to `false` using the `Set-TransportServer` cmdlet, then specify the DNS servers using the `ExternalDNSServers` or `InternalDNSServers` parameter. If multiple adapters exist and you

```
Professional PowerShell For Exchange 2007 | Scope: View Entire Forest          _ □ X
[PS] C:\>Get-TransportServer HT001 | fl

Name                                    : HT001
AntispamAgentsEnabled                   : False
ConnectivityLogEnabled                  : False
ConnectivityLogMaxAge                   : 30.00:00:00
ConnectivityLogMaxDirectorySize         : 250MB
ConnectivityLogMaxFileSize              : 10MB
ConnectivityLogPath                     : C:\Program Files\Microsoft\Exchange S
                                          erver\TransportRoles\Logs\Connectivit
                                          y
DelayNotificationTimeout                : 04:00:00
ExternalDelayDsnEnabled                 : True
ExternalDNSAdapterEnabled               : True
ExternalDNSAdapterGuid                  : 00000000-0000-0000-0000-000000000000
ExternalDNSProtocolOption               : Any
ExternalDNSServers                      : {}
ExternalIPAddress                       :
ExternalDsnDefaultLanguage              : en-US
ExternalDsnLanguageDetectionEnabled     : True
ExternalDsnMaxMessageAttachSize         : 10MB
ExternalDsnReportingAuthority           : ExchangeExchange.local
ExternalDsnSendHtml                     : True
ExternalPostmasterAddress               :
InternalDelayDsnEnabled                 : True
InternalDNSAdapterEnabled               : True
InternalDNSAdapterGuid                  : 00000000-0000-0000-0000-000000000000
InternalDNSProtocolOption               : Any
InternalDNSServers                      : {}
InternalDsnDefaultLanguage              : en-US
InternalDsnLanguageDetectionEnabled     : True
InternalDsnMaxMessageAttachSize         : 10MB
InternalDsnReportingAuthority           : HT001.ExchangeExchange.local
InternalDsnSendHtml                     : True
MaxConcurrentMailboxDeliveries          : 7
MaxConcurrentMailboxSubmissions         : 20
MaxConnectionRatePerMinute              : 1200
MaxOutboundConnections                  : 1000
MaxPerDomainOutboundConnections         : 20
MessageExpirationTimeout                : 2.00:00:00
MessageRetryInterval                    : 00:01:00
MessageTrackingLogEnabled               : True
MessageTrackingLogMaxAge                : 30.00:00:00
MessageTrackingLogMaxDirectorySize      : 250MB
MessageTrackingLogMaxFileSize           : 10MB
MessageTrackingLogPath                  : C:\Program Files\Microsoft\Exchange S
                                          erver\TransportRoles\Logs\MessageTrac
                                          king
MessageTrackingLogSubjectLoggingEnabled : True
OutboundConnectionFailureRetryInterval  : 00:10:00
IntraOrgConnectorProtocolLoggingLevel   : None
PickupDirectoryMaxHeaderSize            : 64KB
PickupDirectoryMaxMessagesPerMinute     : 100
PickupDirectoryMaxRecipientsPerMessage  : 100
PickupDirectoryPath                     : C:\Program Files\Microsoft\Exchange S
                                          erver\TransportRoles\Pickup
PipelineTracingEnabled                  : False
ContentConversionTracingEnabled         : False
PipelineTracingPath                     : C:\Program Files\Microsoft\Exchange S
                                          erver\TransportRoles\Logs\PipelineTra
                                          cing
PipelineTracingSenderAddress            :
PoisonMessageDetectionEnabled           : True
```

Figure 7-5

```
PoisonThreshold                      : 2
QueueMaxIdleTime                     : 00:03:00
ReceiveProtocolLogMaxAge             : 30.00:00:00
ReceiveProtocolLogMaxDirectorySize   : 250MB
ReceiveProtocolLogMaxFileSize        : 10MB
ReceiveProtocolLogPath               : C:\Program Files\Microsoft\Exchange S
                                       erver\TransportRoles\Logs\ProtocolLog
                                       \SmtpReceive

RecipientValidationCacheEnabled      : False
ReplayDirectoryPath                  : C:\Program Files\Microsoft\Exchange S
                                       erver\TransportRoles\Replay

RootDropDirectoryPath                :
RoutingTableLogMaxAge                : 7.00:00:00
RoutingTableLogMaxDirectorySize      : 50MB
RoutingTableLogPath                  : C:\Program Files\Microsoft\Exchange S
                                       erver\TransportRoles\Logs\Routing

SendProtocolLogMaxAge                : 30.00:00:00
SendProtocolLogMaxDirectorySize      : 250MB
SendProtocolLogMaxFileSize           : 10MB
SendProtocolLogPath                  : C:\Program Files\Microsoft\Exchange S
                                       erver\TransportRoles\Logs\ProtocolLog
                                       \SmtpSend

TransientFailureRetryCount           : 6
TransientFailureRetryInterval        : 00:05:00
AntispamUpdatesEnabled               : False
IsValid                              : True
OriginatingServer                    : GK-GC.ExchangeExchange.local
ExchangeVersion                      : 0.1 (8.0.535.0)
DistinguishedName                    : CN=HT001,CN=Servers,CN=Exchange Admin
                                       istrative Group (FYDIBOHF23SPDLT),CN=
                                       Administrative Groups,CN=ExchangeExch
                                       ange,CN=Microsoft Exchange,CN=Service
                                       s,CN=Configuration,DC=ExchangeExchang
                                       e,DC=local

Identity                             : HT001
Guid                                 : 09d9f0a8-e928-4caf-82eb-5fc0875d3afe
ObjectCategory                       : ExchangeExchange.local/Configuration/
                                       Schema/ms-Exch-Exchange-Server
ObjectClass                          : {top, server, msExchExchangeServer}
WhenChanged                          : 7/2/2007 9:55:36 PM
WhenCreated                          : 7/2/2007 9:43:28 PM


[PS] C:\>
```

Figure 7-6

intend to use a specific adapter, specify the adapter by its GUID. The GUID can be obtained using the `Get-NetworkConnectionInfo` cmdlet.

Figure 7-7 shows how to configure the transport server to use a specific adapter for internal and external lookup by specifying its GUID and view changes made.

Back Pressure

Hub Transport and Edge Transport servers monitor important system resources using the back pressure feature. System resources monitored include available disk space and memory. This feature enables transport servers to reject new connections and messages when a configured resource threshold is reached. In the RTM release of Exchange Server 2007, the disk resource limit was 4GB, hence if a Hub Transport server has less than 4GB of drive space all new mail processing stops. However, this has been changed to 500MB in Exchange Server 2007 SP1. The configuration options for back pressure can be modified in the `EdgeTransport.exe.config` application configuration file.

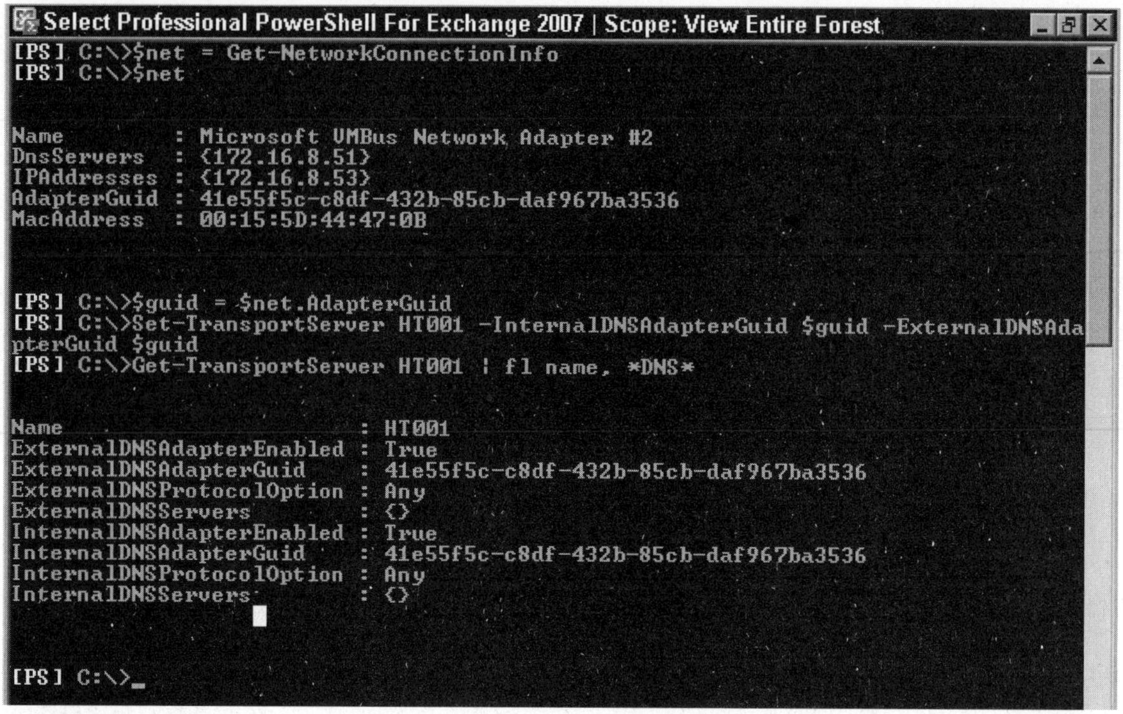

```
Select Professional PowerShell For Exchange 2007 | Scope: View Entire Forest.    _ ☐ ✕
[PS] C:\>$net = Get-NetworkConnectionInfo
[PS] C:\>$net


Name         : Microsoft VMBus Network Adapter #2
DnsServers   : {172.16.8.51}
IPAddresses  : {172.16.8.53}
AdapterGuid  : 41e55f5c-c8df-432b-85cb-daf967ba3536
MacAddress   : 00:15:5D:44:47:0B



[PS] C:\>$guid = $net.AdapterGuid
[PS] C:\>Set-TransportServer HT001 -InternalDNSAdapterGuid $guid -ExternalDNSAda
pterGuid $guid
[PS] C:\>Get-TransportServer HT001 | fl name, *DNS*


Name                        : HT001
ExternalDNSAdapterEnabled   : True
ExternalDNSAdapterGuid      : 41e55f5c-c8df-432b-85cb-daf967ba3536
ExternalDNSProtocolOption   : Any
ExternalDNSServers          : {}
InternalDNSAdapterEnabled   : True
InternalDNSAdapterGuid      : 41e55f5c-c8df-432b-85cb-daf967ba3536
InternalDNSProtocolOption   : Any
InternalDNSServers          : {}



[PS] C:\>_
```

Figure 7-7

Priority Queuing

Priority queuing is new to Exchange Server 2007 SP1 and allows Hub Transport servers to process messages based on the priority defined by the sender (Low, Normal, High). As discussed earlier in this chapter, after a message is categorized, it is placed in a delivery queue, either local (MAPI) or remote delivery. With the Priority Queuing feature enabled, all messages placed in a specific delivery queue are processed to their destination based on the message priority stored in the X-Priority header field. As with the back pressure feature, the configuration options priority queuing can be modified in the EdgeTransport.exe.config application configuration file. However, the settings configured override the limits set by the Set-TransportServer cmdlet (discussed in the following section). Figure 7-8 shows timeout values configured on the Hub server.

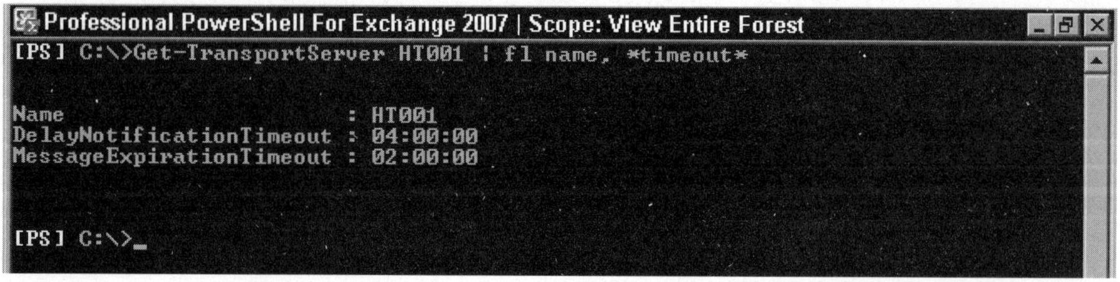

```
Professional PowerShell For Exchange 2007 | Scope: View Entire Forest    _ ☐ ✕
[PS] C:\>Get-TransportServer HT001 | fl name, *timeout*


Name                      : HT001
DelayNotificationTimeout  : 04:00:00
MessageExpirationTimeout  : 02:00:00



[PS] C:\>_
```

Figure 7-8

Transport Server Limits

Several limits that apply to message and connection retry attempts, message expiration, connection limits, and restrictions can be set on the Hub server. Using the `Set-TransportServer` cmdlet you can modify these settings. For example, when a message delivery fails due to a transient failure, it continually retries and expires after two days. You can change the `MessageExpirationTimeout` value within the range of 1 and 90 days. The same applies to the transport log settings for the message tracking, connectivity, and Protocol logs. Figure 7-9 shows how to modify message expiration timeout settings.

```
Select Professional PowerShell For Exchange 2007 | Scope: View Entire Forest      _ 8 X
[PS] C:\>Set-TransportServer HT001 -MessageExpirationTimeout 10:00:00
[PS] C:\>Get-TransportServer HT001 | fl


Name                                  : HT001
AntispamAgentsEnabled                 : False
ConnectivityLogEnabled                : False
ConnectivityLogMaxAge                 : 30.00:00:00
ConnectivityLogMaxDirectorySize       : 250MB
ConnectivityLogMaxFileSize            : 10MB
ConnectivityLogPath                   : C:\Program Files\Microsoft\Exchange S
                                        erver\TransportRoles\Logs\Connectivit
                                        y
DelayNotificationTimeout              : 04:00:00
ExternalDelayDsnEnabled               : True
ExternalDNSAdapterEnabled             : True
ExternalDNSAdapterGuid                : 41e55f5c-c8df-432b-85cb-daf967ba3536
ExternalDNSProtocolOption             : Any
ExternalDNSServers                    : {}
ExternalIPAddress                     :
ExternalDsnDefaultLanguage            : en-US
ExternalDsnLanguageDetectionEnabled   : True
ExternalDsnMaxMessageAttachSize       : 10MB
ExternalDsnReportingAuthority         : ExchangeExchange.local
ExternalDsnSendHtml                   : True
ExternalPostmasterAddress             :
InternalDelayDsnEnabled               : True
InternalDNSAdapterEnabled             : True
InternalDNSAdapterGuid                : 41e55f5c-c8df-432b-85cb-daf967ba3536
InternalDNSProtocolOption             : Any
InternalDNSServers                    : {}
InternalDsnDefaultLanguage            : en-US
InternalDsnLanguageDetectionEnabled   : True
InternalDsnMaxMessageAttachSize       : 10MB
InternalDsnReportingAuthority         : HT001.ExchangeExchange.local
InternalDsnSendHtml                   : True
MaxConcurrentMailboxDeliveries        : 7
MaxConcurrentMailboxSubmissions       : 20
MaxConnectionRatePerMinute            : 1200
MaxOutboundConnections                : 1000
MaxPerDomainOutboundConnections       : 20
MessageExpirationTimeout              : 10:00:00
MessageRetryInterval                  : 00:01:00
```

Figure 7-9

Creating and Modifying Connectors

Connectors determine the path a message takes when routed between servers within an organization, to and from the Internet, and between messaging organizations. They provide single direction or one-way connections between a source server and a destination server. In Exchange Server 2007, at least four types of connectors can be explicitly created and configured. These include the Send Connector, Receive Connector, Routing Group Connector, and Foreign Connector. There also exists implicitly created Send or Receive Connectors created on Hub Transport server's internal mail flow within the Active Directory site and across Active Directory sites in an Exchange Server 2007 forest. This enables Hub Transport servers to communicate with each other. Hence, you do not have to configure any connectors between Hub Transport servers within the Active Directory forest. If an Edge Transport server exists in the organization, the Edge Subscription process is recommended to automatically create and configure connectors between the Edge Transport server and a Hub Transport server in a designated Active Directory site. The following cmdlets are covered in this section; some are discussed later in more detail.

- ❏ `Get-SendConnector`
- ❏ `Set-SendConnector`
- ❏ `New-SendConnector`
- ❏ `Remove-SendConnector`
- ❏ `Get-ReceiveConnector`
- ❏ `Set-ReceiveConnector`
- ❏ `New-ReceiveConnector`
- ❏ `Remove-SendConnector`
- ❏ `Format-List`
- ❏ `Get-TransportConfig`
- ❏ `Set-TransportConfig`
- ❏ `Get-ADPermission`

New-ReceiveConnector

The New-ReceiveConnector cmdlet creates a new Receive Connector. The Name, Bindings, and, RemoteIPRanges are required parameters. The following switch parameters are important to note: `Custom`, `Client`, `Partner`, `Internal`, and `Internet`. These indicate the types of Receive Connectors that can be created. They can be specified separately or using the `Usage` parameter but cannot be used in conjunction with this parameter. If no usage type is specified, the default usage type of custom will be used.

- ❏ `Custom <SwitchParameter>`: This parameter can be used to specify the custom usage type. The usage type specifies the default permission groups and authentication methods that are assigned to this connector. The Custom Receive Connector is a customized connector used to connect systems that are not Exchange servers.

- ❏ `Client <SwitchParameter>`: This parameter can be used to specify the client usage type. The usage type specifies the default permission groups and authentication methods that are assigned to this connector. The Client Receive Connector is used to receive email from users of Microsoft Exchange. It is configured to accept client submissions only from authenticated Microsoft Exchange users.

- ❏ `Internal <SwitchParameter>`: This parameter can be used to specify the internal usage type. The usage type specifies the default permission groups and authentication methods that are assigned to the Receive Connector. The Internal Receive Connector is used to receive email from servers within the Exchange organization. It is configured to accept connections only from Exchange Servers.

❑ `Internet <SwitchParameter>`: This parameter can be used to specify the Internet usage type. The usage type specifies the default permission groups and authentication methods that are assigned to this connector. The Internet Receive Connector is used to receive email from Internet servers. It is configured to accept connections from anonymous users.

❑ `Partner <SwitchParameter>`: This parameter can be used to specify the partner usage type. The usage type specifies the default permission groups and authentication methods that are assigned to this connector. The Partner Receive Connector is used to receive email from partner domains. This connector is configured to accept connections from servers that authenticate with Transport Layer Security (TLS) certificates for SMTP domains that are included in the list of domain-secured domains. You can use the `TLSReceiveDomainSecureList` parameter of the `Set-TransportConfig` cmdlet to add domains to this list.

New-SendConnector

The `New-SendConnector` cmdlet is used to create new Send Connectors in Exchange Server 2007. Required parameters include `AddressSpaces` and `name`. The following switch parameters, `Custom`, `Partner`, `Internal`, and `Internet`, indicate the four types of Send Connectors that can be created in Exchange Server 2007. They can be specified separately or using the `Usage` parameter but cannot be used in conjunction with this parameter. If no usage type is specified, the default usage type of custom will be used to create the Send Connector. These switch parameters are discussed further in the following list:

❑ `Custom <SwitchParameter>`: This parameter can be used to specify the custom usage type. The usage type specifies no default permissions and no authentication methods to the Send Connector. This connector will be used to connect with systems that are not Exchange Servers.

❑ `Internal <SwitchParameter>`: This parameter can be used to specify the internal usage type. The usage type specifies the default permission groups and authentication methods that are assigned to the Send Connector. The Internal Send Connector is used to send email from servers within the Exchange organization. It is configured to route email to internal Exchange Servers as smart hosts.

❑ `Internet <SwitchParameter>`: This parameter can be used to specify the Internet usage type. The usage type specifies the default permissions and authentication methods that are assigned to this connector. This Send Connector is used to send emails to the Internet and configured to use DNS MX records to route messages.

❑ `Partner <SwitchParameter>`: This parameter can be used to specify the partner usage type. The usage type specifies the default permissions and authentication methods that are assigned to this connector. The Partner Send Connector is used to send email to partner domains. This connector is configured to only allow connections to servers that authenticate with Transport Layer Security (TLS) certificates for SMTP domains that are included in the list of domain-secured domains. You can use the `TLSReceiveDomainSecureList` parameter of the `Set-TransportConfig` cmdlet to add domains to this list.

Configuring Receive Connectors

The Receive Connector is identical in some ways to the SMTP virtual server in Exchange Server 2003. It listens for incoming SMTP connections and accepts or rejects them based on its configuration. The Receive Connector is configured with an IP address, a listening port, and the range of IP addresses that can submit messages to it. In reality, though, it is the MSExchangetransport.exe service, otherwise known as the Process Manager, that actively listens for incoming requests. Requests are acted upon by an existing or new transport worker (Edgetransport.exe) process spurned by the Process Manager. Edgetransport.exe accepts the incoming SMTP connection, evaluates the connection criteria (IP address, port, remote IP range) and applies the session to a matching Receive Connector. Communication is always SMTP-based and each Receive Connector must have a unique combination of local IP address, port, and remote IP range configurations throughout the organization. In Exchange Server 2003, you could create multiple SMTP virtual servers but they had to be unique to either a port or IP address. In Exchange Server 2007, you can create multiple Receive Connectors with the same IP address and port; however, the remote IP range must be unique.

On a Hub Transport server, two Receive Connectors are created by default as shown in Figure 7-10. The bindings indicate that the Receive Connectors are configured to listen on all IP addresses on available network adapters on the server and on the designated ports. The Default Receive Connector is configured to listen on port 25 while the Client Receive Connector listens on port 587. The Client Receive Connector accepts SMTP connections from all non-MAPI clients, such as POP and IMAP. To view all the properties on both Receive Connectors, use the Format-List cmdlet in addition to the Get-ReceiveConnector cmdlet. A basic difference between both connectors besides the bindings is the permissiongroups attribute also shown in Figure 7-10. This makes sense because only non-MAPI clients connect to the Client Receive Connector.

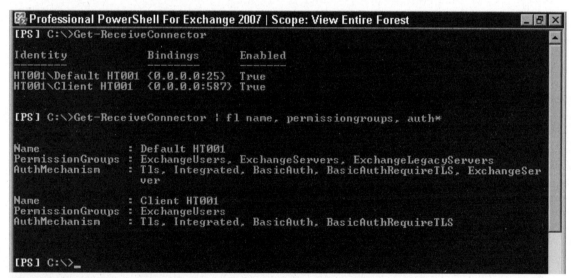

Figure 7-10

As mentioned earlier, to create a new Receive Connector, use the New-ReceiveConnector cmdlet. The Name, Bindings, and RemoteIPRanges are required parameters. You can create a Receive Connector based on its intended use. The following switch parameters, Custom, Client, Partner, Internal, and Internet, indicate the types of Receive Connectors that can be created in Exchange Server 2007. They can be specified separately or using the Usage parameter but cannot be used in conjunction with this parameter. If no usage type is specified, the default usage type of custom will be set; and a Receive Connector identical in attributes to the Default Receive Connector with the exception of the specified parameters is created.

Note that in Exchange Server 2007 SP1, you must specify a usage type when using the
`New-ReceiveConnector` cmdlet. Also note that Exchange Server 2007 SP1 supports the Internet
Protocol Version 6 (IPv6) addresses and when deployed on Windows Server 2008, you can specify both
IPv4 and IPv6 addresses for the RemoteIPRange parameter. Figure 7-11 shows how to create a new
Receive Connector, and then display the connectors created with differences in authentication methods
and permission groups. Some connectors have been created in advance.

Figure 7-11

Next, you use the `Remove-ReceiveConnector` cmdlet to bulk remove the connectors created, as shown in Figure 7-12.

```
Professional PowerShell For Exchange 2007 | Scope: View Entire Forest        _ ⊟ ×
[PS] C:\>Get-ReceiveConnector | where {$_.name -like "RC*" } | Remove-ReceiveCon
nector

Confirm
Are you sure you want to perform this action?
Removing Receive connector "HT001\RC Client".
[Y] Yes  [A] Yes to All  [N] No  [L] No to All  [S] Suspend  [?] Help
(default is "Y"):a
[PS] C:\>Get-ReceiveConnector

Identity            Bindings          Enabled
--------            --------          -------
HT001\Default HT001 {0.0.0.0:25}      True
HT001\Client HT001  {0.0.0.0:587}     True


[PS] C:\>_
```

Figure 7-12

Setting Relay Restrictions and Submit Permissions

After creating the Receive Connector, you can control how messages flow through the connector. In Exchange Server 2000/2003, you could configure relay restrictions to determine if messages could be relayed to users not in the Exchange organization. You could also configure permissions to determine who could submit a message to the SMTP virtual server. The same can be accomplished in Exchange Server 2007 when you specify permission groups for the connector. In Figure 7-11 you saw the permission groups assigned to each type of Receive Connector created. There are specific permissions associated with these permission groups. For example, the `ms-Exch-SMTP-Accept-Any-Recipient` permission allows the session to relay messages through the connector. To view the permissions, use the `Get-ADPermission` cmdlet in conjunction with the `Get-ReceiveConnector` cmdlet, as shown in Figure 7-13. Such granular changes can be made directly to Active Directory or by using the `Add/Remove-ADPermission` cmdlet. On the other hand, the `Set-ReceiveConnector` cmdlet can be used to add/remove permission groups.

For example, you may have created a Receive Connector with a Partner domain. By default the permission group associated with that connector allows for the partner server account to submit (`ms-Exch-SMTP-Submit`) messages and retain all the receive headers (`ms-Exch-Accept-Headers-Routing`) over a secure TLS session. If due to acquisition or some other valid reason you later choose to allow the partner server account to relay messages through the connector, then simply grant the granular permission `Ms-Exch-SMTP-Accept-Any-Recipient` or add the ExchangeUsers permission group to the Receive Connector, as shown in Figure 7-14.

Notice that when using the `Set-ReceiveConnector` cmdlet with permission groups, you have to write all the permissions over again and not simply the permission you want to add, or else the existing permissions are overwritten.

```
Professional PowerShell For Exchange 2007 | Scope: View Entire Forest          _ 8 X
[PS] C:\>Get-ReceiveConnector 'HT001\Default HT001' | Get-ADPermission | ft user
, Extendedrights

User                                         ExtendedRights
----                                         --------------
EXCHEXCH\ExchangeLegacyInterop               {ms-Exch-Accept-Headers-Forest}
EXCHEXCH\ExchangeLegacyInterop               {ms-Exch-Accept-Headers-Organization}
NT AUTHORITY\Authenticated Users             {ms-Exch-SMTP-Submit}
NT AUTHORITY\Authenticated Users             {ms-Exch-Bypass-Anti-Spam}
NT AUTHORITY\Authenticated Users             {ms-Exch-Accept-Headers-Routing}
NT AUTHORITY\Authenticated Users             {ms-Exch-SMTP-Accept-Any-Recipient}
EXCHEXCH\Exchange Servers                    {ms-Exch-SMTP-Accept-Any-Sender}
EXCHEXCH\Exchange Servers                    {ms-Exch-SMTP-Accept-Exch50}
EXCHEXCH\Exchange Servers                    {ms-Exch-SMTP-Accept-Authoritative-D...
EXCHEXCH\Exchange Servers                    {ms-Exch-SMTP-Submit}
EXCHEXCH\Exchange Servers                    {ms-Exch-Accept-Headers-Organization}
EXCHEXCH\Exchange Servers                    {ms-Exch-Bypass-Message-Size-Limit}
EXCHEXCH\Exchange Servers                    {ms-Exch-SMTP-Accept-Any-Recipient}
EXCHEXCH\Exchange Servers                    {ms-Exch-Accept-Headers-Routing}
EXCHEXCH\Exchange Servers                    {ms-Exch-Bypass-Anti-Spam}
EXCHEXCH\Exchange Servers                    {ms-Exch-SMTP-Accept-Authentication-...
EXCHEXCH\Exchange Servers                    {ms-Exch-Accept-Headers-Forest}
EXCHEXCH\ExchangeLegacyInterop               {ms-Exch-SMTP-Accept-Any-Recipient}
EXCHEXCH\ExchangeLegacyInterop               {ms-Exch-Accept-Headers-Routing}
EXCHEXCH\ExchangeLegacyInterop               {ms-Exch-SMTP-Accept-Exch50}
EXCHEXCH\ExchangeLegacyInterop               {ms-Exch-SMTP-Accept-Any-Sender}
EXCHEXCH\ExchangeLegacyInterop               {ms-Exch-SMTP-Submit}
EXCHEXCH\ExchangeLegacyInterop               {ms-Exch-SMTP-Accept-Authoritative-D...
EXCHEXCH\ExchangeLegacyInterop               {ms-Exch-Bypass-Anti-Spam}
EXCHEXCH\ExchangeLegacyInterop               {ms-Exch-Bypass-Message-Size-Limit}
EXCHEXCH\ExchangeLegacyInterop               {ms-Exch-SMTP-Accept-Authentication-...
MS Exchange\Hub Transport Servers            {ms-Exch-SMTP-Accept-Authoritative-D...
MS Exchange\Hub Transport Servers            {ms-Exch-SMTP-Accept-Authentication-...
MS Exchange\Hub Transport Servers            {ms-Exch-Accept-Headers-Forest}
MS Exchange\Hub Transport Servers            {ms-Exch-Accept-Headers-Routing}
MS Exchange\Hub Transport Servers            {ms-Exch-SMTP-Accept-Any-Sender}
MS Exchange\Hub Transport Servers            {ms-Exch-Accept-Headers-Organization}
MS Exchange\Hub Transport Servers            {ms-Exch-Bypass-Anti-Spam}
MS Exchange\Hub Transport Servers            {ms-Exch-SMTP-Submit}
MS Exchange\Hub Transport Servers            {ms-Exch-SMTP-Accept-Exch50}
MS Exchange\Hub Transport Servers            {ms-Exch-SMTP-Accept-Any-Recipient}
MS Exchange\Hub Transport Servers            {ms-Exch-Bypass-Message-Size-Limit}
MS Exchange\Edge Transport Servers           {ms-Exch-SMTP-Accept-Authentication-...
MS Exchange\Edge Transport Servers           {ms-Exch-Bypass-Message-Size-Limit}
MS Exchange\Edge Transport Servers           {ms-Exch-Bypass-Anti-Spam}
MS Exchange\Edge Transport Servers           {ms-Exch-Accept-Headers-Forest}
MS Exchange\Edge Transport Servers           {ms-Exch-SMTP-Accept-Any-Recipient}
MS Exchange\Edge Transport Servers           {ms-Exch-Accept-Headers-Organization}
MS Exchange\Edge Transport Servers           {ms-Exch-SMTP-Accept-Exch50}
MS Exchange\Edge Transport Servers           {ms-Exch-Accept-Headers-Routing}
MS Exchange\Edge Transport Servers           {ms-Exch-SMTP-Accept-Any-Sender}
MS Exchange\Edge Transport Servers           {ms-Exch-SMTP-Submit}
MS Exchange\Edge Transport Servers           {ms-Exch-SMTP-Accept-Authoritative-D...
```

Figure 7-13

Several other configurable attributes exist on each Receive Connector and can be modified using the
Set-ReceiveConnector cmdlet. These include changing the response *banner* for the server,
MaxMessageSize limit, MessageRateLimit, and so forth. For a detailed list of attributes that can be
configured, run get-help set-receiveconnector -detailed in the Exchange Management Shell.

```
Professional PowerShell For Exchange 2007 | Scope: View Entire Forest         _ [] X
[PS] C:\>Get-ReceiveConnector 'RC Partner' | fl name, permiss*, auth*


Name              : RC Partner
PermissionGroups  : Partners
AuthMechanism     : Tls


[PS] C:\>Set-ReceiveConnector 'RC Partner' -PermissionGroups Partners, Exchangeu
sers
[PS] C:\>Get-ReceiveConnector 'RC Partner' | fl name, permiss*, auth*


Name              : RC Partner
PermissionGroups  : ExchangeUsers, Partners
AuthMechanism     : Tls


[PS] C:\>_
```

Figure 7-14

Configuring Send Connectors

Send Connectors provide one-way outbound connections to a next hop or final destination for message delivery. They are functionally the same as SMTP connectors in Exchange Server 2000/2003 and can be configured to use DNS to route mail or forward to a smart host. They can be configured to send mail to other SMTP servers on the Internet, an Edge Transport server, or an Exchange 2000/2003 server in the same organization.

Unlike the Receive Connectors, by default when a Hub Transport or Edge Transport server is installed no explicit Send Connectors are created. However, to enable Hub Transport servers within an Exchange organization to communicate, implicit or invisible Send Connectors are automatically created. The Send Connectors are computed based on the Active Directory site topology and the site where the Hub server is installed. These implicit connectors are, however, not visible via the Exchange Management Console or Exchange Management Shell.

To create a Send Connector, use the New-SendConnector cmdlet. Required parameters include AddressSpaces and name. Three parts make up address spaces: the address space type, the address itself, and the cost of delivery to that address. It takes the following format: SMTP:ExchangeExchange .local;10 representing the type, address, and cost, respectively. The Send Connector can accommodate address space types other than SMTP, such as NOTES, FAX, and so forth. Send Connectors configured with address spaces that are non-SMTP must be configured to route to a smart host and not use DNS for resolution and delivery. You can also specify multiple address spaces but they must be enclosed in double quotation marks and separated by commas.

In configuring a Send Connector, you can also specify its scope. The IsScopedConnector parameter set to $True indicates that the Send Connector is scoped to the local Active Directory site. What this means is that this connector will only be visible by Hub Transport servers that are in the same local Active Directory site as the Source servers configured on the Send Connector. It is not available to Hub servers in other Active Directory sites. The default value is $False. This parameter is new in Exchange Server 2007 SP1.

In Figure 7-15, two new connectors with different usage types are created. However, for the second connector the `IsScopedConnector` parameter limits its visibility to only Hub Transport servers in the local Active Directory site.

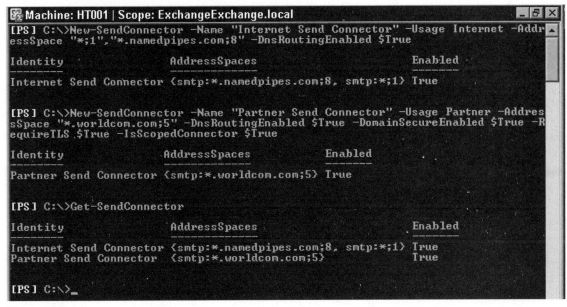

Figure 7-15

Next in Figure 7-16, using the `Format-List` cmdlet provides both Send Connectors, noting the difference in scope for both connectors.

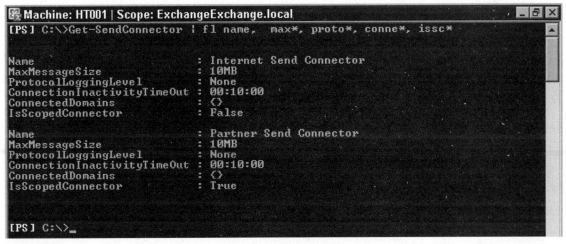

Figure 7-16

Setting Send Connector Permissions and Authentication

Like the Receive Connector, the Send Connector is associated with certain permissions based on the type of Send Connector configured. The custom type has no default permissions. The internal connector is configured for Exchange Server Authentication and has the following permission settings: `ms-Exch-Send-Headers-Organization`, `ms-Exch-SMTP-Send-Exch50`, `ms-Exch-SMTP-Send-Exch50`, and `ms-Exch-Send-Headers-Routing`. The Internet-type Send Connector has `ms-Exch-Send-Headers-Routing` granted to the Anonymous user with no host authentication mechanism. Send Connectors connecting to Partner domains grant the Partner servers the `ms-Exch-Send-Headers-Routing` permission and can negotiate transport security.

You can modify various parameters on the Send Connector as well as remove the Send Connectors using the `Set-SendConnector` and `Remove-SendConnector` cmdlets. Figure 7-17 shows how to increase the `MaxMessageSize` of the Send Connectors, increase logging level, and modify the scope of the Partner Send Connector to be visible throughout the Exchange organization. Finally, you remove all configured connectors.

```
Machine: HT001 | Scope: ExchangeExchange.local
[PS] C:\>Get-SendConnector | Set-SendConnector -MaxMessageSize 50MB -ProtocolLog
gingLevel verbose -ConnectionInactivityTimeOut 00:20:00
[PS] C:\>Set-SendConnector "Partner Send Connector" -IsScopedConnector $False
[PS] C:\>Get-SendConnector | fl name, max*, proto*, conne*, issc*


Name                          : Internet Send Connector
MaxMessageSize                : 50MB
ProtocolLoggingLevel          : Verbose
ConnectionInactivityTimeOut   : 00:20:00
ConnectedDomains              : {}
IsScopedConnector             : False

Name                          : Partner Send Connector
MaxMessageSize                : 50MB
ProtocolLoggingLevel          : Verbose
ConnectionInactivityTimeOut   : 00:20:00
ConnectedDomains              : {}
IsScopedConnector             : False



[PS] C:\>Get-SendConnector | Remove-SendConnector

Confirm
Are you sure you want to perform this action?
Removing Send connector "Internet Send Connector".
[Y] Yes  [A] Yes to All  [N] No  [L] No to All  [S] Suspend  [?] Help
(default is "Y"):a
[PS] C:\>Get-SendConnector
[PS] C:\>_
```

Figure 7-17

Linking Connectors

Under certain circumstances, Send and Receive Connectors could be linked in such a way that messages received via a specific Receive Connector are always sent out via a designated Send Connector. Some organizations contract out their spam filtering solution to a vendor that checks these messages for spam or email compliance and then pushes them back into the organization for delivery. In such cases Linked Connectors could be used to direct the mail flow regardless of recipient address.

Figure 7-18 shows creating the Receive Connector and corresponding Send Connector, then linking both connectors. Note that you would have to specify a smart host to ensure that mail gets delivered as required.

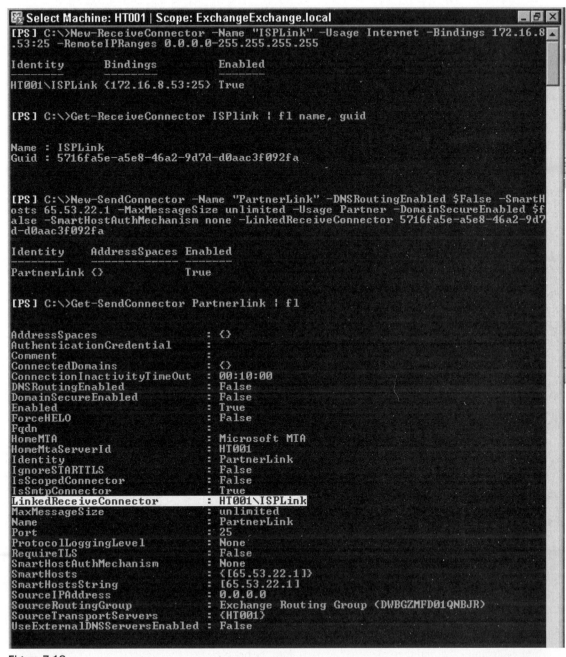

```
Select Machine: HT001 | Scope: ExchangeExchange.local                           _ □ X
[PS] C:\>New-ReceiveConnector -Name "ISPLink" -Usage Internet -Bindings 172.16.8
.53:25 -RemoteIPRanges 0.0.0.0-255.255.255.255

Identity        Bindings            Enabled
--------        --------            -------
HT001\ISPLink   {172.16.8.53:25}    True


[PS] C:\>Get-ReceiveConnector ISPlink | fl name, guid


Name : ISPLink
Guid : 5716fa5e-a5e8-46a2-9d7d-d0aac3f092fa


[PS] C:\>New-SendConnector -Name "PartnerLink" -DNSRoutingEnabled $False -SmartH
osts 65.53.22.1 -MaxMessageSize unlimited -Usage Partner -DomainSecureEnabled $f
alse -SmartHostAuthMechanism none -LinkedReceiveConnector 5716fa5e-a5e8-46a2-9d7
d-d0aac3f092fa

Identity        AddressSpaces Enabled
--------        ------------- -------
PartnerLink {}               True


[PS] C:\>Get-SendConnector Partnerlink | fl


AddressSpaces                   : {}
AuthenticationCredential        :
Comment                         :
ConnectedDomains                : {}
ConnectionInactivityTimeOut     : 00:10:00
DNSRoutingEnabled               : False
DomainSecureEnabled             : False
Enabled                         : True
ForceHELO                       : False
Fqdn                            :
HomeMTA                         : Microsoft MTA
HomeMtaServerId                 : HT001
Identity                        : PartnerLink
IgnoreSTARTTLS                  : False
IsScopedConnector               : False
IsSmtpConnector                 : True
LinkedReceiveConnector          : HT001\ISPLink
MaxMessageSize                  : unlimited
Name                            : PartnerLink
Port                            : 25
ProtocolLoggingLevel            : None
RequireTLS                      : False
SmartHostAuthMechanism          : None
SmartHosts                      : {[65.53.22.1]}
SmartHostsString                : [65.53.22.1]
SourceIPAddress                 : 0.0.0.0
SourceRoutingGroup              : Exchange Routing Group (DWBGZMFD01QNBJR)
SourceTransportServers          : {HT001}
UseExternalDNSServersEnabled    : False
```

Figure 7-18

Configuring a Routing Group Connector

When migrating to Exchange Server 2007 from an Existing Exchange 2000/2003 environment, there may be a period of coexistence whereby Exchange Server 2007 computers must communicate with Exchange Server 2000/2003. A Routing Group Connector is required for this communication to take place. When the first Exchange Server 2007 computer is installed into the organization, a Routing Group Connector is automatically created. To manually create this connector to another routing group, use the following command. This also enables public folder referral.

```
New-RoutingGroupConnector -Name "Coexist RGC" -SourceTransportServers
"HT001.ExchangeExchange.local" -TargetTransportServers "ExB.ExchangeExchange.local"
-Cost 100 -Bidirectional $true -PublicFolderReferralsEnabled $true
```

Service Pack 1 for Exchange Server 2007 introduced support for configuring a limit on the Routing Group Connector, hence the MaxMessageSize parameter. This parameter existed on other connectors but not the Routing Group Connector. To set the MaxMessageSize for an existing connector, simply pass the Set-RoutingGroupConnector to the output of the Get-RoutingGroupConnector as shown here:

```
Get-RoutingGroupConnector | Set-RoutingGroupConnector -MaxMessageSize 50MB
```

Configuring Foreign Connectors

Foreign Connectors enable third-party vendors using non-SMTP gateways to route messages to foreign mail systems via Exchange Server 2007. This could include but is not limited to FAX systems. Exchange Server 2007 provides Foreign Connectors, which enables these messages to be placed in a drop directory to be picked up by the third-party mail system.

In the queue viewer the next hop type for these messages is identified by NonSmtpGatewayDelivery queue with the actual hop being the GUID of the Foreign Connector.

While the New-ForeignConnector cmdlet is used to create a new Foreign Connector, the Get/Set/Remove-ForeignConnector cmdlets can be used to view and modify the connector. Among other things that can be modified is the drop directory where messages are deposited to be picked up by the third-party's mail system. You use the following command to create a new Foreign Connector:

```
New-ForeignConnector -Name "FAX Foreign Connector" -AddressSpaces
"FAX:*.contoso.com;5" -SourceTransportServers "HT001"
```

Active Directory IP Site Links

Thus far, you've seen the various connectors that can be configured in Exchange Server 2007. Although connectors control the direction a message will take, Exchange Server 2007 takes advantage of the Active Directory topology and routes messages based on available Active Directory sites. In Exchange Server 2000/2003, routing was based on logical groupings of servers into routing groups. We discuss this further in Chapter 11.

Most Exchange Administrators do not have permissions to administer the Active Directory Sites and may not have control over the path that an email could traverse in a large Active Directory site. Two things can be done in this situation. An administrator may choose to specify a Hub site using the Set-ADSite cmdlet. This forces all mail flow in that path through the Hub Transport servers in the designated Hub site before they are routed to their final destination. Something else available to an Exchange administrator is the ability to introduce an Exchange-aware attribute to existing Active Directory site links, which Exchange Server 2007 servers will consider while routing between sites. This is a cost value assigned to each IP site link evaluated by Exchange Server 2007. Messages will then be routed based on lower-cost IP site links overriding existing Active Directory site link costs. This change is made using the `Set-ADSiteLink` cmdlet.

As with the Routing Group Connector, Exchange Server 2007 SP1 now enables you to configure a `MaxMessageSize` parameter for the `ADSiteLink`. A Non Delivery Report (NDR) is generated if a message is over the specified limit.

To designate an Active Directory site as a Hub site, use the following cmdlet:

```
Set-AdSite -Identity "Site A" -HubSiteEnabled $true
```

To set the `MaxMessageSize` to the `ADSiteLink` use the following cmdlet:

```
Set-AdSiteLink -Identity DEFAULTIPSITELINK -ExchangeCost 25 -MaxMessageSize 50MB
```

Understanding Accepted Domains and Email Address Policies

Before concluding this chapter, a few words on email address policies and accepted domains is required, because these play a huge role in email address resolution and mail routing. The following cmdlets can be used to view and change accepted domains:

- ❑ Get-AcceptedDomain
- ❑ Set-AcceptedDomain
- ❑ New-AcceptedDomain
- ❑ Remove-AcceptedDomain
- ❑ Get-RemoteDomain
- ❑ Set-RemoteDomain
- ❑ New-RemoteDomain
- ❑ Remove-RemoteDomain
- ❑ Get-EmailAddressPolicy
- ❑ Set-EmailAddressPolicy
- ❑ New-EmailAddressPolicy
- ❑ Remove-EmailAddressPolicy
- ❑ Update-EmailAddressPolicy

Accepted Domains

Accepted domains are used to identify which domains the Exchange Server organization is authoritative for and thus can accept mails, and which domains it is not authoritative for and perhaps can relay mail for or return to sender. Hence, an Exchange organization will send and receive mail for an accepted domain. In Exchange Server 2007 non-authoritative domains are further segmented into internal relay domains and external relay domains. Authoritative and internal relay domains are considered to be inside the Exchange organization. Exchange accepts messages for internal relay domains and attempts to route them to a connector that can deliver the message. Both authoritative and internal relay domains can impact Email address policies and transport rules.

Exchange, on the other hand, can be configured with an external relay domain. They are identical in functionality with the internal relay domains; however, with external domains, the messages are received and processed by the Edge server, and then relayed to the destination email system. External relay domains cannot be used for email address policies.

Use the `Get-AcceptedDomain` and `Set/New/Remove-AcceptedDomain` cmdlets to view and modify the Accepted domains.

Email Address Policies

Email address policies dictate the formatting of addresses on mail-enabled objects in the Exchange organization. Email policies formally known as Recipient Policies in Exchange 2000/2003 determine what proxy addresses are stamped on mail-enabled objects in Active Directory. Exchange Server 2007 only supports two address types: SMTP and Custom. Email address policies generate the primary and secondary email addresses for recipient objects to enable them to receive and send email.

Exchange Server 2007 has an email address policy for each user that is mail-enabled. By default, the recipient alias is used as the local part of the recipient's email address and the default accepted domain is appended after the "@" sign. Hence, a mail-enabled user will have an address such as `alias@accepteddomain.com` (`Trainee9@ExchangeExchange.local`). However, you can change how your recipients' email addresses will display. For example, you can specify that your recipients' email addresses display as `firstname.lastname@ExchangeExchange.local`.

Email addresses are applied to user and other mail-enabled objects when created. To force the email address policies to re-evaluate the mail-enabled objects, use the `Update-EmailAddressPolicy` cmdlet.

Summary

Thus far, you have seen how much Exchange Server 2007 differs from earlier versions of Exchange in its transport functionality. The core transport architecture was re-written and transport improvements made in Exchange Server 2007 SP1 also make for reliable mail flow across an Exchange organization. The changes in core transport architecture changed the way messages are delivered in an Exchange organization. Without the presence of at least one Hub Transport server in an Active Directory site, there can be no mail flow. The Hub Transport server, as you have seen, implements the core transport functionality and serves to ensure intra-organizational email communication and compliance.

Additionally, this chapter showed the various connectors that can be created in Exchange Server 2007. Send Connectors and Receive Connectors are generally used to control message flow, however other connectors also can be configured such as Linked Connectors, Routing Group Connectors, and Foreign Connectors. With the creation of Send Connectors and Receive Connectors, several usage types are possible, which specify the authentication mechanism and permission groups to be associated with that connector. As you will recall, by default two explicit Receive Connectors are created with the installation of the Hub Transport server role and no explicit Send Connectors are installed; however, an implicit Send Connector exists to enable Hub Transport servers in the same Active Directory site exchange email messages. Hence no explicit Send Connectors are required to configure mail flow between Hub Transport servers in the same Active Directory site. Finally, we briefly reviewed the concept of accepted domains and email address policies.

## 8

Configuring the Mailbox Server Role

The Mailbox role is at the heart of the server roles. Mailbox and public folder data is stored on the Mailbox role. Other processes, such as managed folders and address book generation run on the Mailbox role. Unlike previous versions, the mailbox server does not send or receive mail without going through a hub transport.

The Mailbox role can be configured for high availability using traditional clustering or a few new options. High-availability options are discussed in Chapter 12.

This chapter covers:

- ❏ Creating a mailbox store and database
- ❏ Configuring a mailbox store and database
- ❏ Recovering mailbox data with Recovery Storage Groups

Storage Groups

Exchange groups mailboxes into logical units called databases. Exchange groups databases together to share a set of transaction log files and this database group is called a storage group. New to Exchange Server 2007 is the ability to have up to 50 databases distributed in up to 50 storage groups. However, there is still a maximum of five databases in one storage group. It is a best practice to have one database per storage group. Another change from previous versions is that the streaming database has been removed.

Some of the cmdlets that are used in working with storage groups are:

❑ New-StorageGroup

❑ Move-StorageGroupPath

❑ Remove-StorageGroup

Creating Storage Groups

After installation of the Mailbox role an initial storage group will be created. Most of the mailbox management can be done with the Exchange Management Console (EMC). One nice feature of the console is that it will show the PowerShell command after executing the operation. The New-StorageGroup cmdlet is used to create new storage groups:

```
New-StorageGroup -Name <String> -Server <ServerIdParameter>
[-CircularLoggingEnabled <$true | $false>] [-CopyLogFolderPath
<NonRootLocalLongFullPath>] [-CopySystemFolderPath
<NonRootLocalLongFullPath>] [-DomainController <Fqdn>] [-HasLocalCopy
<$true | $false>] [-LogFolderPath <NonRootLocalLongFullPath>]
[-SystemFolderPath <NonRootLocalLongFullPath>] [-TemplateInstance
<PSObject>] [-ZeroDatabasePages <$true | $false>]

New-StorageGroup [-Name <String>] -Recovery <SwitchParameter> -Server
<ServerIdParameter> [-DomainController <Fqdn>] [-LogFolderPath
<NonRootLocalLongFullPath>] [-SystemFolderPath <NonRootLocalLongFullPath>]
[-TemplateInstance <PSObject>]
```

The LogFolderPath and SystemFolderPath parameters set the location of the log and system files for the storage group. The parameters are used to set the location and properties associated with the log files. The parameter CircularLoggingEnabled is used to enable circular logging. By default, the parameter is set to false, meaning circular logging is not enabled. The recovery storage group parameter is to set up the new storage group for recovery. Recovery Storage Groups (RSG) are covered later in this chapter.

The following example creates a new storage group on the server MB001, and sets the location of the log and system folders:

```
New-StorageGroup -Name "Storage Group 2" -Server MB001
-LogFolderPath "D:\Logs\Second Storage Group"
-SystemFolderPath "D:\Logs\Second Storage Group"
```

Moving Storage Groups

One administrative task for storage groups is to move their location. During the move, all databases in the storage group will be dismounted and unavailable for clients. The Move-StorageGroupPath cmdlet must be run locally on the mailbox server. Also note that the path cannot be at the root of the drive. This cmdlet has most of the same parameters as the New-StorageGroup cmdlet:

```
Move-StorageGroupPath -Identity <StorageGroupIdParameter>
[-ConfigurationOnly <SwitchParameter>] [-CopyLogFolderPath
<NonRootLocalLongFullPath>] [-CopySystemFolderPath
<NonRootLocalLongFullPath>] [-DomainController <Fqdn>] [-Force
```

```
<SwitchParameter>] [-LogFolderPath <NonRootLocalLongFullPath>]
[-SystemFolderPath <NonRootLocalLongFullPath>]

Move-StorageGroupPath -Identity "First Storage Group" -LogFolderPath "C:\SG\SG1"
-SystemFolderPath "C:\SG\SG1"
```

Removing Storage Groups

Another task is to remove storage groups. Before removing a storage group, all databases must be removed. After running the `Remove-StorageGroup` cmdlet, the log files must be manually removed with Windows Explorer or the `del` cmdlet. The syntax for `Remove-StorageGroup` is:

```
Remove-StorageGroup -Identity <StorageGroupIdParameter> [-DomainController <Fqdn>]
```

Removing the storage group from the previous example would look like this:

```
Get-MailboxDatabase -StorageGroup "mb001\Storage Group 2" | Remove-MailboxDatabase
Remove-StorageGroup -Identity "MB001\Storage Group 2"
```

Mailbox Stores

Mailbox stores, or databases, are where all of the user and public folder data is stored. Each storage group can contain up to five databases. Each database can be mounted or un-mounted independently.

Cmdlets used for managing mailbox stores are:

- ❏ New-MailboxDatabase
- ❏ Set-MailboxDatabase
- ❏ Get-MailboxDatabase
- ❏ Remove-MailboxDatabase

Creating Databases

The `New-MailboxDatabase` cmdlet creates the database object. The location of the database file (`.edb`) is mandatory, as is the identity of the storage group where the database will exist:

```
New-MailboxDatabase -Name <String> -StorageGroup <StorageGroupIdParameter>
  [-CopyEdbFilePath <EdbFilePath>] [-DomainController <Fqdn>] [-EdbFilePath
  <EdbFilePath>] [-HasLocalCopy <$true | $false>] [-OfflineAddressBook
  <OfflineAddressBookIdParameter>] [-PublicFolderDatabase
<DatabaseIdParameter>] [-TemplateInstance <PSObject>]

New-MailboxDatabase [-Name <String>] -MailboxDatabaseToRecover
  <DatabaseIdParameter> -StorageGroup <StorageGroupIdParameter> [-DomainController
```

(continued)

(continued)

```
<Fqdn>] [-EdbFilePath <EdbFilePath>] [-TemplateInstance
<PSObject>]

New-MailboxDatabase -StorageGroup "mb100\Storage Group 2" -Name "Mailbox Database
2" -EdbFilePath "C:\SG2\Database\DB2.edb"
```

Configuring Databases

One common task is to set the quota level for users. Quotas can be either set at the database level or per-user. It is common to set the default levels at the mailbox database, and override as needed at the user object. Quotas and other parameters are set with the Set-MailboxDatabase cmdlet.

There are three available quota settings:

❑   IssueWarningQuota: When the user reaches this threshold, the system will generate an email warning him about his quota.

❑   ProhibitSendQuota: When the user reaches this threshold the system will prohibit the user from sending new mail. This setting must be equal or greater than the IssueWarningQuota value.

❑   ProhibitSendReceiveQuota: When the user reaches this threshold the system will prohibit the user from sending mail, and will not deliver new mail to the user's mailbox. This setting must be equal or greater than the IssueWarningQuota and ProhibitSendQuota values.

```
Set-MailboxDatabase -Identity <DatabaseIdParameter> [-AllowFileRestore
<$true | $false>] [-DeletedItemRetention <EnhancedTimeSpan>]
[-DomainController <Fqdn>] [-EventHistoryRetentionPeriod
<EnhancedTimeSpan>] [-IndexEnabled <$true | $false>] [-IssueWarningQuota
<Unlimited>] [-JournalRecipient <RecipientIdParameter>] [-MailboxRetention
<EnhancedTimeSpan>] [-MaintenanceSchedule <Schedule>] [-MountAtStartup
<$true | $false>] [-Name <String>] [-OfflineAddressBook
<OfflineAddressBookIdParameter>] [-ProhibitSendQuota <Unlimited>]
[-ProhibitSendReceiveQuota <Unlimited>] [-PublicFolderDatabase
<DatabaseIdParameter>] [-QuotaNotificationSchedule <Schedule>]
[-RetainDeletedItemsUntilBackup <$true | $false>]

Set-MailboxDatabase [-AllowFileRestore <$true | $false>]
[-DeletedItemRetention <EnhancedTimeSpan>] [-DomainController <Fqdn>]
[-EventHistoryRetentionPeriod <EnhancedTimeSpan>] [-IndexEnabled <$true |
$false>] [-Instance <MailboxDatabase>] [-IssueWarningQuota <Unlimited>]
[-JournalRecipient <RecipientIdParameter>] [-MailboxRetention
<EnhancedTimeSpan>] [-MaintenanceSchedule <Schedule>] [-MountAtStartup
<$true | $false>] [-Name <String>] [-OfflineAddressBook
<OfflineAddressBookIdParameter>] [-ProhibitSendQuota <Unlimited>]
[-ProhibitSendReceiveQuota <Unlimited>] [-PublicFolderDatabase
<DatabaseIdParameter>] [-QuotaNotificationSchedule <Schedule>]
[-RetainDeletedItemsUntilBackup <$true | $false>]
```

This example sets the quotas for the database. One cool feature of PowerShell is the ability to specify the units, so it is not necessary to convert between megabytes and gigabytes.

```
Set-MailboxDatabase -Identity "mb100\mailbox database" -IssueWarningQuota 512MB -
ProhibitSendReceiveQuota 1GB
```

This cmdlet when viewed with the management console looks like Figure 8-1.

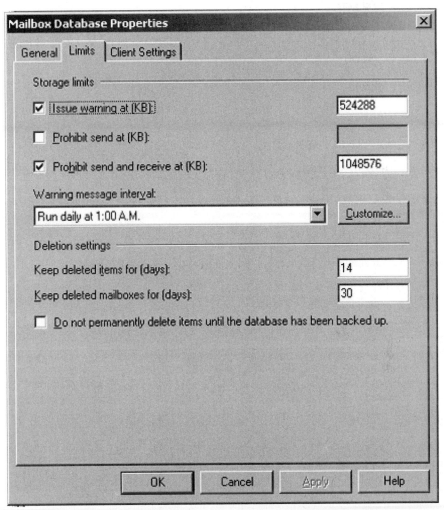

Figure 8-1

Two settings related to recovery are `MailboxRetention` and `DeletedItemRetention`. `MailboxRetention` specifies the length of time to keep deleted mailboxes. The default in Exchange Server 2007 is 30 days, and can be configured to a maximum of 24,855 days. The section on managing mailboxes explains deleted mailboxes and how to reconnect them.

`DeletedItemRetention` specifies the length of time to keep deleted items that have been emptied from the deleted items folder or hard-deleted using SHIFT + Delete. The default in Exchange 2007 is 14 days, and can be configured to a maximum of 24,855 days. Deleted items are recoverable with the Outlook client or with Outlook Web Access in Exchange Server 2007 Service Pack 1. This setting will apply to all users in the database unless the users have their own retention time set.

To view the current settings on existing mailbox databases, use the `Get-MailboxDatabase` cmdlet:

```
Get-MailboxDatabase [-Identity <DatabaseIdParameter>] [-DomainController
<Fqdn>] [-IncludePreExchange2007 <SwitchParameter>] [-Status
<SwitchParameter>]

Get-MailboxDatabase -Server <ServerIdParameter> [-DomainController <Fqdn>]
[-IncludePreExchange2007 <SwitchParameter>] [-Status <SwitchParameter>]

Get-MailboxDatabase -StorageGroup <StorageGroupIdParameter>
[-DomainController <Fqdn>] [-IncludePreExchange2007 <SwitchParameter>]
[-Status <SwitchParameter>]
```

The `IncludePreExchange2007` parameter returns information about pre-Exchange 2007 databases. The `Status` switch retrieves extra information about the databases. By default the cmdlet does not show information about the `Mounted` status, `BackupInProgress`, and `OnlineMaintenanceInProgress`. Including the `Status` switch takes extra processing, so scoping the storage group may speed up the results.

This example retrieves the `Mounted` status for every database in the organization:

```
Get-MailboxDatabase -Status | ft Name, StorageGroup, Mounted
```

Removing Databases

The `Remove-MailboxDatabase` cmdlet removes the database object, but does not remove the actual files. Before the cmdlet can be called, all users must be moved to another database or deleted.

```
Remove-MailboxDatabase -Identity <DatabaseIdParameter>
[-DomainController <Fqdn>] [<CommonParameters>]
An example follows:Remove-MailboxDatabase -Identity "mb100\First Storage
Group\mailbox database"
```

Managing Mailboxes

While most mailbox management is done with the Exchange Management Console, the ability to perform bulk operations or make scripts to automate mailbox activities is easy with PowerShell.

Cmdlets discussed in this section are:

- ❏ `Remove-Mailbox`
- ❏ `Disable-Mailbox`
- ❏ `Get-MailboxStatistics`

- ❏ `Set-MailboxDatabase`
- ❏ `Clean-MailboxDatabase`
- ❏ `Connect-Mailbox`

One common surprise for first time administrators using the management console is discovering that the AD user object is deleted when they try to just remove the Exchange mailbox. This is because the Remove action deletes both the mailbox and the AD object. To correctly remove an Exchange mailbox, use the Disable action. Figure 8-2 shows this with PowerShell.

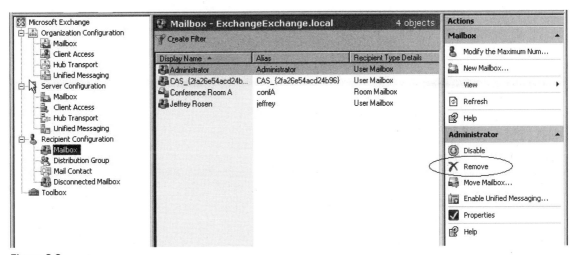

Figure 8-2

To remove both the AD account and the Exchange account, use the `Remove-Mailbox` cmdlet:

```
Remove-Mailbox -Identity <MailboxIdParameter> [-DomainController <Fqdn>]
[-Permanent <$true | $false>] [<CommonParameters>]

Remove-Mailbox -Database <DatabaseIdParameter> -StoreMailboxIdentity
<Store MailboxIdParameter> [-DomainController <Fqdn>] [<CommonParameters>]
```

To remove just the Exchange mailbox and not delete the AD account, use the `Disable-Mailbox` cmdlet:

```
Disable-Mailbox -Identity <MailboxIdParameter> [-DomainController <Fqdn>]
[<CommonParameters>]
```

When a mailbox is deleted, it is not really gone; it becomes tombstoned, creating a disconnected mailbox. This allows for recovery from accidental deletions without having to restore from backup. The default setting for the mailbox recovery tombstone period is 30 days. However, if the `Permanent` parameter is set to `true` in the `Remove-Mailbox` cmdlet, the mailbox will not tombstone and will not be recoverable without going to backup media.

To find all disconnected mailboxes, type the following expression:

```
Get-MailboxStatistics [-Database <DatabaseIDParameter>] | where {$_.DisconnectDate
-ne $null}
```

The next example retrieves all of the disconnected mailboxes from the mailbox database. Just omit the database parameter to see all disconnected mailboxes in the organization.

```
Get-MailboxStatistics -Database "mb100\mailbox database" | where {$_.DisconnectDate
-ne $null}
```

To change the default 30-day tombstone period, use the `Set-MailboxDatabase` cmdlet to set the `MailboxRetention` parameter. Changing this value may impact mailbox storage requirements. The value of `MailboxRetention` is the number of days, hours, minutes, and seconds the mailboxes will be tombstoned.

The following cmdlet sets the test environment to tombstone for 15 days:

```
Set-MailboxDatabase -Identity "mb100\mailbox database" -MailboxRetention
15.00:00:00
```

Under most circumstances it is not necessary to *run* `Clean-MailboxDatabase`. Typically, when a mailbox is removed or disabled, it is marked as disconnected. If a mailbox was removed while the database was offline, it may not show up as disconnected right away. It is possible to force this process with the `Clean-MailboxDatabase` cmdlet. This is the same process as the Clean-up Agent in Exchange 2003.

```
Clean-MailboxDatabase -Identity <DatabaseIdParameter> [-DomainController
<Fqdn>]
Following is an example:Clean-MailboxDatabase -Identity "mb100\mailbox database"
```

Another option for a disconnected mailbox is to connect it to a new Active Directory user object. An administrator may need to do this if she accidentally deletes a mailbox, or a manager needs access to a former employee's mailbox. Once connected, the target user account has full access and rights to the mailbox. The `Connect-Mailbox` cmdlet has a number of combinations depending on which parameters are used:

```
Connect-Mailbox -Identity <StoreMailboxIdParameter> -Database
<DatabaseIdParameter> [-ActiveSyncMailboxPolicy
<MailboxPolicyIdParameter>] [-Alias <String>] [-DomainController <Fqdn>]
[-ManagedFolderMailboxPolicy <MailboxPolicyIdParameter>]
[-ManagedFolderMailboxPolicyAllowed <SwitchParameter>] [-User
<UserIdParameter>]

Connect-Mailbox -Identity <StoreMailboxIdParameter> -Database
<DatabaseIdParameter> -ValidateOnly <SwitchParameter> [-DomainController
<Fqdn>]

Connect-Mailbox -Identity <StoreMailboxIdParameter> -Database
<DatabaseIdParameter> -Shared <SwitchParameter> [-ActiveSyncMailboxPolicy
<MailboxPolicyIdParameter>] [-Alias <String>] [-DomainController <Fqdn>]
```

```
            [-ManagedFolderMailboxPolicy <MailboxPolicyIdParameter>]
            [-ManagedFolderMailboxPolicyAllowed <SwitchParameter>] [-User
            <UserIdParameter>]

            Connect-Mailbox -Identity <StoreMailboxIdParameter> -Database
            <DatabaseIdParameter> -Equipment <SwitchParameter>
            [-ActiveSyncMailboxPolicy <MailboxPolicyIdParameter>] [-Alias <String>]
            [-DomainController <Fqdn>] [-ManagedFolderMailboxPolicy
            <MailboxPolicyIdParameter>] [-ManagedFolderMailboxPolicyAllowed
            <SwitchParameter>] [-User <UserIdParameter>]

            Connect-Mailbox -Identity <StoreMailboxIdParameter> -Database
            <DatabaseIdParameter> -LinkedDomainController <Fqdn> -LinkedMasterAccount
            <UserIdParameter> [-ActiveSyncMailboxPolicy <MailboxPolicyIdParameter>]
            [-Alias <String>] [-DomainController <Fqdn>] [-LinkedCredential
            <PSCredential>] [-ManagedFolderMailboxPolicy <MailboxPolicyIdParameter>]
            [-ManagedFolderMailboxPolicyAllowed <SwitchParameter>] [-User
            <UserIdParameter>]

            Connect-Mailbox -Identity <StoreMailboxIdParameter> -Database
            <DatabaseIdParameter> -Room <SwitchParameter> [-ActiveSyncMailboxPolicy
            <MailboxPolicyIdParameter>] [-Alias <String>] [-DomainController <Fqdn>]
            [-ManagedFolderMailboxPolicy <MailboxPolicyIdParameter>]
            [-ManagedFolderMailboxPolicyAllowed <SwitchParameter>] [-User
            <UserIdParameter>]

            Connect-Mailbox -Identity <StoreMailboxIdParameter> -Database
            <DatabaseIdParameter> [-DomainController <Fqdn>]
```

If no User parameter is supplied, the cmdlet tries to match off of the legacyExchangeDN and the DisplayName. The ValidateOnly switch parameter simulates the mailbox connection only. Using ValidateOnly is a good way to see which account will be associated without committing the action.

Recovery Storage Groups

The recovery storage group (RSG) is a feature used for recovering mailbox data from a special database. The RSG differs from user and public folder storage groups. It is not possible to use any clients, such as Outlook or Outlook Web Access, to access the mounted database. RSGs can be used to recover mailbox data, or as part of recovery from a dial-tone recovery strategy. To use the Exchange Management Console to create an RSG, select the Database Recovery Management tool in the toolbox.

Creating an RSG can be broken down into the following steps:

1. Create an RSG storage group.
2. Create a recovery database linked to an existing database.
3. Set the recovery database to allow overwrite.
4. Restore the database.
5. Mount the database.
6. Restore mailbox data.

The following are cmdlets discussed in this section:

- ❏ New-StorageGroup

- ❏ Get-StorageGroup

- ❏ New-MailboxDatabase

- ❏ Set-MailboxDatabase

- ❏ Mount-Database

- ❏ Restore-Mailbox

- ❏ Get-MailboxStatistics

- ❏ Remove-Database

Create the RSG

The first step is to create the RSG. This task is similar to creating the regular storage group from earlier in this chapter. The inclusion of the recovery parameter is what makes it different from a regular storage group.

```
New-StorageGroup -Server mb100 -LogFolderPath c:\rsg -name RSG -SystemFolderPath
c:\rsg -Recovery
```

The Get-StorageGroup shows how the newly created storage group is marked for recovery. (See Figure 8-3.)

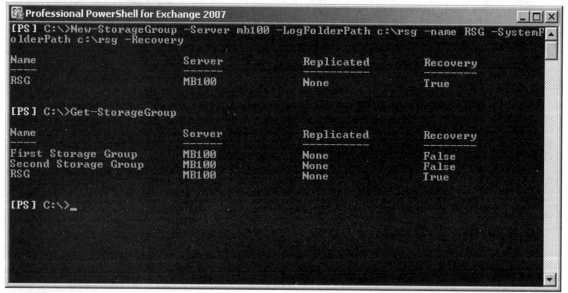

Figure 8-3

Create the RSG Database

Next, create the recovery database with `New-MailboxDatabase`. The `MailboxDatabaseToRecover` parameter is what links the RSG to the target database. Figure 8-4 shows the results of the following cmdlet that creates a new RSG:

```
New-MailboxDatabase -MailboxDatabaseToRecover "Mailbox Database" -StorageGroup
mb100\rsg -EdbFilePath c:\rsg\rsg.edb
```

<rsg new db.tif>

Figure 8-4

If needed, mark the mailbox database to allow overwrites. Setting this value to `true` allows a database that does not match the information in Active Directory to mount. Forcing administrators to explicitly set the database overwrite flag prevents accidentally mounting an incorrect database.

```
Set-MailboxDatabase -Identity "mb100\RSG\mailbox database" -AllowFileRestore:$true
```

Restore the Database

Restore the database file from tape or disk. Selecting the Last Restore Set checkbox means that after the file restore, Exchange will perform a hard recovery. Figure 8-5 illustrates the database restore options when using the System Backup utility. Exchange automatically redirects any restores to the RSG instead of the original location.

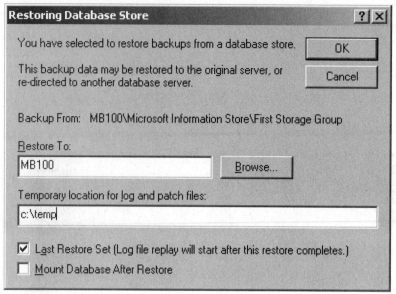

Figure 8-5

Mount the Database

The last step before being able to export mail is to mount the database:

```
Mount-Database -Identity "mb100\RSG\mailbox database"
```

Restore Mail

There are several methods to restore mail to users with the restore-Mailbox cmdlet:

```
Restore-Mailbox -Identity <MailboxIdParameter> -RSGDatabase
<DatabaseIdParameter> [-AllContentKeywords <String[]>]
[-AttachmentFilenames <String[]>] [-BadItemLimit <Int32>]
[-ContentKeywords <String[]>] [-EndDate <DateTime>] [-ExcludeFolders
<MapiFolderPath[]>] [-GlobalCatalog <Fqdn>] [-IncludeFolders
<MapiFolderPath[]>] [-Locale <CultureInfo>] [-MaxThreads <Int32>]
[-ReportFile <LocalLongFullPath>] [-StartDate <DateTime>]
[-SubjectKeywords <String[]>] [-ValidateOnly <SwitchParameter>]

Restore-Mailbox -Identity <MailboxIdParameter> -RSGDatabase
<DatabaseIdParameter> -RSGMailbox <StoreMailboxIdParameter> -TargetFolder
<String> [-AllContentKeywords <String[]>] [-AttachmentFilenames
<String[]>] [-BadItemLimit <Int32>] [-ContentKeywords <String[]>]
[-EndDate <DateTime>] [-ExcludeFolders <MapiFolderPath[]>] [-GlobalCatalog
<Fqdn>] [-IncludeFolders <MapiFolderPath[]>] [-Locale <CultureInfo>]
[-MaxThreads <Int32>] [-ReportFile <LocalLongFullPath>] [-StartDate
<DateTime>] [-SubjectKeywords <String[]>] [-ValidateOnly
<SwitchParameter>]
```

To recover a single mailbox and restore mail to the original location, specify the identity of a user mailbox as the target. The restore matches the target mailbox's GUID to the mailbox in the recovery storage group. For example, to restore Jeffrey's mailbox, enter the following:

```
Restore-Mailbox -Identity Jeffrey -RSGDatabase "MB100\rsg\mailbox database"
```

The output from the `Restore-Mailbox` cmdlet will look like Figure 8-6.

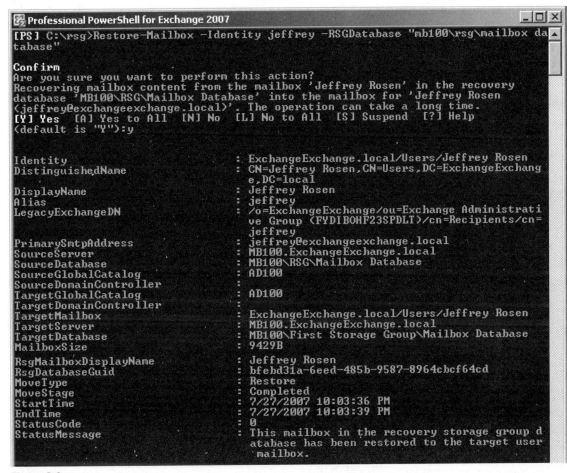

Figure 8-6

The following recovers all mailboxes in the RSG to the live database:

```
Get-MailboxStatistics -Database "RSG\mailbox database" | Restore-Maibox -
RSGDatabase "RSG\mailbox database"
```

It is possible to restore the contents of one mailbox into another user's folders. In Exchange Server 2007 RTM (Release to Manufacturing, or the initial release), it is only possible to export to an Exchange mailbox. However Service Pack 1 adds the ability to be able to export mailbox data to an Outlook data file (PST file),

This example shows restoring Jeffrey's mailbox into the administrator's mailbox. `TargetFolder` needs to be supplied and it will automatically append `\Recovered Data - mailbox name` as a subfolder.

```
Restore-Mailbox -RSGMailbox "jeffrey rosen" -RSGDatabase "RSG\mailbox database" -
Identity "Administrator" -TargetFolder "restores"
```

Figure 8-7 shows the output from running the `Restore-Mailbox` cmdlet. The cmdlet outputs a lot of information letting the administrator see exactly what parameters were used during the restore.

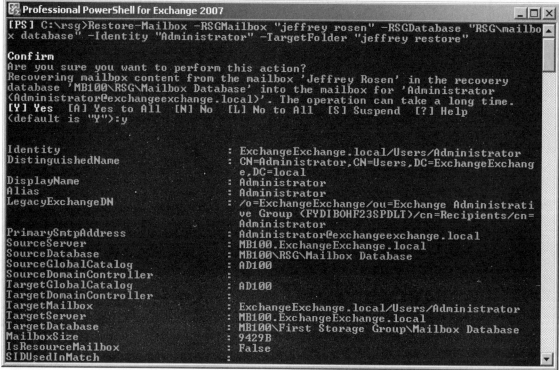

Figure 8-7

There are a number of parameters for filtering content. Examples are keywords, date ranges, and specific folders. The next example shows exporting only Microsoft Word documents from Jeffrey's mailbox between March 3rd and July 1st:

```
Restore-Mailbox -Identity Jeffrey - RSGDatabase "mb100\rsg\mailbox database"
-StartDate '03/03/07' -EndDate '07/01/07'-AttachmentFilenames "*.docx"
```

After all the data has been restored the following procedure removes the RSG:

```
Remove-Database -Identity "mb100\rsg\mailbox database"
Remove-StorageGroup -Identity "mb100\rsg"
```

The cmdlet warns that any files, such as the database (.edb) and log files, must be manually removed, as shown in Figure 8-8.

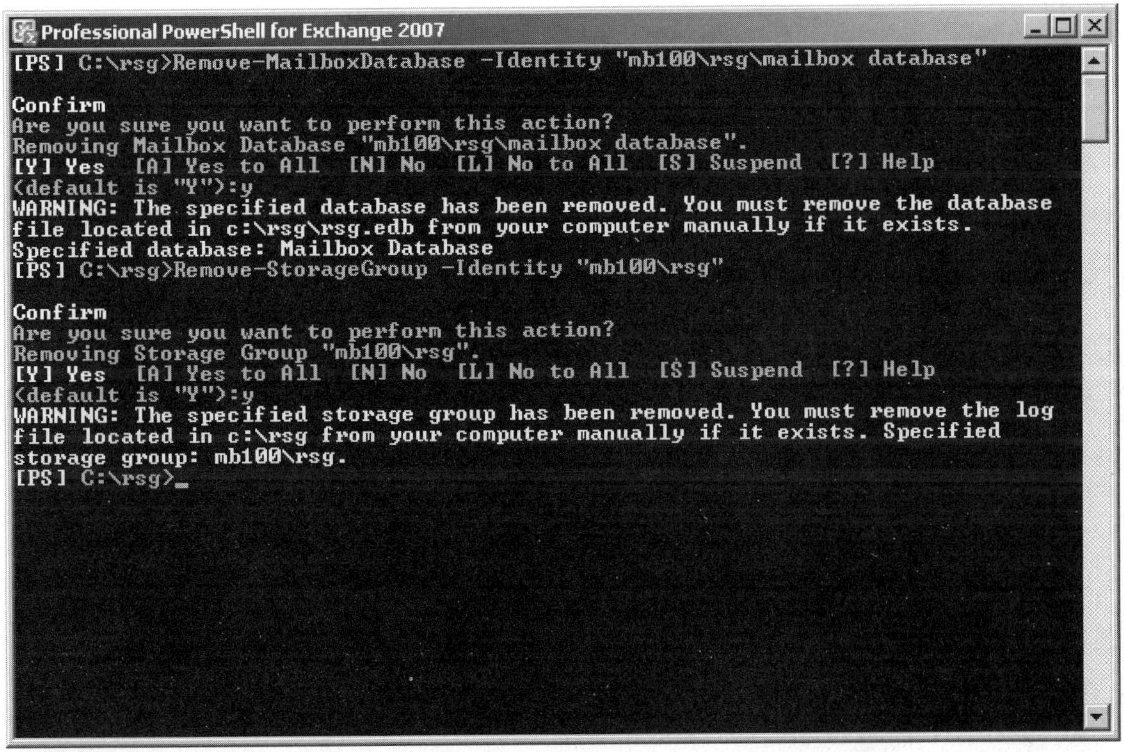

Figure 8-8

Public Folders

Public folders are special databases where users can share information. Also, various system folders store information in public folders. Public folders are explained in more detail in Chapter 5, so this section only briefly touches upon the subject.

The cmdlet used in this section is:

❑   New-PublicFolderDatabase

A mailbox server can have multiple storage groups and databases, but only one Public folder store per mailbox server. Instead of using the New-MailboxDatabase cmdlet, to create a Public folder database use the New-PublicFolderDatabase cmdlet:

```
New-PublicFolderDatabase -Name <String> -StorageGroup
<StorageGroupIdParameter> [-CopyEdbFilePath <EdbFilePath>]
[-DomainController <Fqdn>] [-EdbFilePath <EdbFilePath>] [-HasLocalCopy
<$true | $false>] [-TemplateInstance <PSObject>] [<CommonParameters>]
```

Following is an example:

```
New-PublicFolderDatabase -Name "Public Folder DB" -StorageGroup "mb100\Public
Folder Storage Group"
```

The output in Figure 8-9 shows the error if creating multiple Public folder stores on a server is attempted.

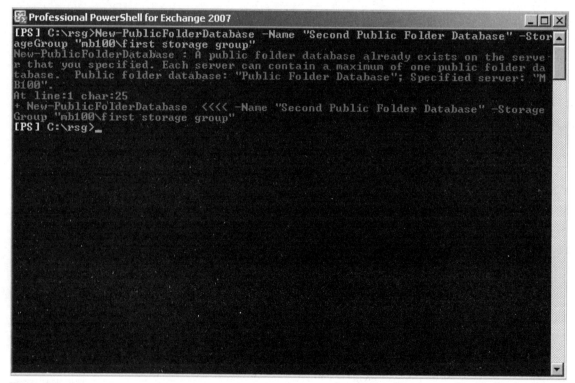

Figure 8-9

Summary

The mailbox server is the heart of Exchange. User and mailbox management is probably where administrators will spend most of their time. This chapter covered storage group and database installation and configuration. The next topic covered in detail was user quotas. This demonstrated PowerShell's built-in conversion capabilities. Another point to remember is the status parameter, which gives extra information about a mailbox database. Without it, key information such as if a database is mounted would be left out. A very common mistake is the first time administrators use the GUI console to delete a mailbox and they end up deleting the Active Directory account. The same confusion can happen in PowerShell if the administrator uses `Remove-Mailbox` instead of `Disable-Mailbox`.

Next, the chapter showed how to configure various mailbox availability features, such as deleted item retention, mailbox recover, and Recovery Storage Groups. Recovery Storage Groups is a powerful feature that is used for a number of reasons. It is used as part of a dial-tone recovery strategy, a way to do "compliance" searches across mailboxes, or simply a way to recover lost data.

Lastly, the chapter showed how to create a new public folders database. Working with public folders is explained thoroughly in Chapter 5.

9

Configuring the Edge Transport Server Role

Chapter 7 discussed the transport architecture in Exchange Server 2007 and Hub Transport server role. This chapter discusses the Edge Transport server role, which is identical to the Hub server role in many respects and implements the core transport architecture. Although both roles share identical features, they differ in default configuration and functionality. Whereas the focus of the Hub Transport server role is intra-organizational email communication and compliance, the focus of the Edge Transport server is for inter-organizational email communication, message hygiene, and security. This implementation of the Edge Transport server new to the Exchange line of messaging products arose as a result of increasing Unsolicited Commercial E-mail (UCE) volume and the risk of denial of service attacks perpetrated via email. It reduces the attack surface of such threats by providing a means for organizations to segment such email traffic even before it enters the Exchange organization, while preventing access to internal resources. Some of the features of the Edge Transport server have been implemented in earlier versions of Exchange, however this role segmentation was never possible in any other version of Exchange. Message filtering functionality such as sender, Recipient, connection filtering, and so forth, which existed in Exchange Server 2003, have been improved and implemented on the Edge Transport server role.

By the end of this chapter, you'll have an overview of the components of the Edge Transport server and be able to configure the Edge Transport server for email message flow into and out of an Exchange organization, using the Exchange Management Shell. You will also gain an idea of how agents work in message hygiene.

This chapter covers the following:

- ❑ A brief overview of the Edge Transport server role and its architecture
- ❑ The Active Directory Application Mode (ADAM) service requirement for the Edge Transport server role
- ❑ Configuration of the Edge Transport server
- ❑ Message hygiene and transport agents

The following is a list of Edge-related cmdlets that could be used to view and configure the Edge Transport server role in Exchange Server 2007. Some are discussed later in more detail.

- ❏ Get-EdgeSubscription
- ❏ New-EdgeSubscription
- ❏ Remove-EdgeSubscription
- ❏ Start-EdgeSynchronization
- ❏ Test-EdgeSynchronization
- ❏ Get-AcceptedDomain
- ❏ Set-AcceptedDomain
- ❏ New-AcceptedDomain
- ❏ Remove-AcceptedDomain
- ❏ Get-RemoteDomain
- ❏ Set-RemoteDomain
- ❏ New-RemoteDomain
- ❏ Remove-RemoteDomain
- ❏ Get-AdSite
- ❏ Get-SendConnector
- ❏ Set-SendConnector
- ❏ New-SendConnector
- ❏ Remove-SendConnector
- ❏ Get-ReceiveConnector
- ❏ Set-ReceiveConnector
- ❏ New-ReceiveConnector
- ❏ Remove-ReceiveConnector
- ❏ Disable-TransportAgent
- ❏ Enable-TransportAgent
- ❏ Get-TransportAgent
- ❏ Set-TransportAgent
- ❏ Uninstall-TransportAgent

Overview of the Edge Transport Server Role

The actual focus of this role is relaying inbound and outbound messages to and from an Exchange organization while providing message hygiene and security. It is essentially an SMTP relay server. Unlike the Hub Transport server role, the Edge Transport server role does not require direct access to Active Directory. It is installed in a perimeter network on either a Windows member server or workstation with no domain membership. Information required by the Edge Transport server to perform its functions is provided in the Active Directory Application Mode (ADAM) directory service. It is important to note that this is a one-way replication of information and not all data in Active Directory is synchronized with the ADAM directory. Only Recipient, configuration, and topology information required by the Edge server to perform its functions of message relay, message hygiene, anti-spam, and the application of transport rules are replicated to ADAM. How, then, is this information kept up to date? The MSExchangeEdgeSync service, which runs only on the Hub Transport server, pushes updates and changes from Active Directory to ADAM on a scheduled basis.

For communication with Hub Transport servers within the Exchange organization and synchronization of updates, it is recommended that the Edge Transport server be subscribed to an Active Directory site in the Exchange Server organization. Edge subscription provides secure replication of information from Active Directory to ADAM and simplifies the configuration of the Edge Transport server to relay messages into and out of the Exchange organization. It also simplifies the configuration made on the Hub Transport servers such that they know to route outbound Internet mail to the Edge Transport server for Internet delivery. The edge subscription process also enables Recipient lookups and anti-spam features.

The Edge Transport server accepts incoming mail from the Internet and routes outbound mail to the Internet based on DNS resolution of Mail Exchanger (MX) records of Internet domains or it can be configured to forward mails to another smart host, such as an ISP or a message compliance system. Send and Receive Connectors are also configured on the Edge Transport server to control how a message is routed. The Edge Transport server also provides a message address rewrite agent. When companies merge and want to present a single email address for all outgoing emails irrespective of the internal company, address rewrite becomes invaluable.

Message hygiene is achieved by providing different layers of spam filtering and implementation of anti-spam and anti-virus agents, thus blocking viruses and spam at the network perimeter. In addition, transport rules act on messages that meet certain configured criteria, spam confidence level (SCL) ratings, or have certain message contents and reject or quarantine these messages as configured.

The Edge Transport server's architecture is identical to that of the Hub Transport server. Both implement the core transport components mentioned in Chapter 7. The key differences are in message categorization and implementation of transport agents. By default the number of agents configured on the Edge Transport server is more than those configured on the Hub Transport server. Agents are discussed later in this chapter.

Message Categorization

As noted in Chapter 7, the Categorizer on the Hub Transport server is notified about messages in the Submission queue and begins message categorization. It resolves Recipients, expands distribution lists, applies any Recipient restriction configured, and performs routing based on the Recipients. On the Edge Transport server, however, no Recipient resolution or distribution list expansion occurs. The domain portion of the message Recipient is used to determine how the message is routed. There are only two routing options or next hops for each message. Either a message is routed based on DNS resolution of the Recipient domain or the message is forwarded to a smart host. In addition, content conversion of the message is bypassed on the Edge Transport server.

Active Directory Application Mode

Active Directory Application Mode (ADAM) is a stand-alone directory service that provides Lightweight Directory Access Protocol (LDAP) connectivity to a directory database and can be used by directory-enabled applications. It is stand-alone in the sense that it does not depend on the existence of an Active Directory domain or forest to provide its service. It is a repository for application-related information, which it replicates with the Active Directory. ADAM provides an LDAP service and an Extensible Storage Engine (ESE) database for accessing and storing configuration, Recipient, and topology information required by the Edge Transport server role.

The ADAM database is an ESE database called `adamntds.dit` stored in the `\Exchange Server\ TransportRoles\data\Adam` directory.

You are required to install ADAM prior to installing the Edge Transport server role. When the Edge Transport server role is installed, an ADAM instance called MSexchangeAdam is started. When the service starts it opens ports for LDAP and Secure LDAP connections. These ports are set to 50389 and 50636, respectively. The ADAM service implemented by the Edge Transport server role is `ADAM_MSExchange`, its process name is `Dsamain`, and it has the service dependencies shown in Figure 9-1.

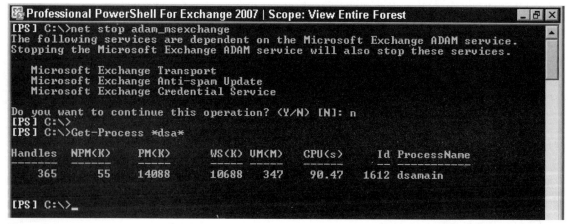

Figure 9-1

Edge Subscription and Synchronization

As noted earlier, the Edge Transport server resides in a perimeter network and uses the ADAM directory service. However, to function optimally, this directory must be updated with certain information from Active Directory within the Exchange organization. Hence, edge subscriptions are used to securely populate a subset of data from Active Directory into ADAM. Edge synchronization, which is initiated by the EdgeSync service that runs on the Hub Transport server, ensures that changes are replicated to ADAM at configured intervals.

An Edge Transport server is subscribed to an Active Directory site; this enables the Edge Transport server to receive updates to ADAM from Active Directory. A partnership is created based on exchanged credentials between the Edge Transport server and all the Hub Transport servers in the Active Directory site. An implicit Send Connector is created, which enables Hub Transport servers in the Exchange organization to relay messages to the Edge Transport server for delivery to the Internet without you having to configure explicit Send Connectors.

The process of edge subscription starts when you run the `New-EdgeSubscription` cmdlet on the Edge Transport server. This creates a public-private key pair as well as ADAM bootstrap credentials that are used for communication between the Edge Transport server and Hub Transport server to synchronize data. Next you run the same cmdlet on a Hub Transport server in the Active Directory site and specify the site the Edge Transport server will be subscribed to. After subscription on both servers, the EdgeSync process running on the Hub Transport server generates a new set of credentials for the Hub Transport servers and replicates this information to the Edge Transport server, discarding the bootstrap credential. Thereafter EdgeSync continues to run periodically, pushing changes made in Active Directory to ADAM.

The type of data replicated includes Send Connector configuration, accepted domains, remote domains, message classifications, safe senders lists, Recipients, Transport Layer Security (TLS) send and receive domain secure lists, an internal SMTP servers list, and the list of Hub Transport servers subscribed to the Active Directory site. Most of the data replicated, such as the Recipient information, is translated, hence if the Edge Transport server and ADAM are compromised, no Recipient information is exposed. Various types of data are replicated at different intervals. Configuration data is replicated every hour, Recipient data is replicated every 4 hours, and topology information is replicated every 5 minutes.

If edge subscription and EdgeSync are not configured, you cannot use the Recipient lookup feature or safelist aggregation.

After the edge subscription process completes, all the Hub Transport servers that are installed in that Active Directory site at that time can participate in the EdgeSync process. What happens if one of these Hub Transport servers is removed or if a new Hub Transport server is added to the site? If a Hub Transport server is removed, all the other Hub Transport servers continue to participate in the EdgeSync process. If a new server is added, it isn't automatically able to participate in the EdgeSync process. The edge subscription must be removed from the Edge Transport server or servers and the associated Active Directory site. It must then be re-subscribed to enable new Hub Transport server to participate in the EdgeSync process.

Features Introduced in Exchange Server 2007 SP1

Exchange Server 2007 Service Pack 1 (SP1) supports deployment of server roles on a Windows Server 2008 computer. If the Edge Transport server is installed on Windows Server 2008, ADAM is replaced by Active Directory Lightweight Directory Services (AD LDS).

Exchange Server 2007 Service Pack 1 (SP1) introduces a new parameter for the Test-EdgeSynchronization cmdlet called VerifyRecipient. This cmdlet and parameter can be run only on a Hub Transport server to verify the EdgeSync synchronization status for a single Recipient to determine whether the Recipient is synchronized. It returns results as shown in Figure 9-2.

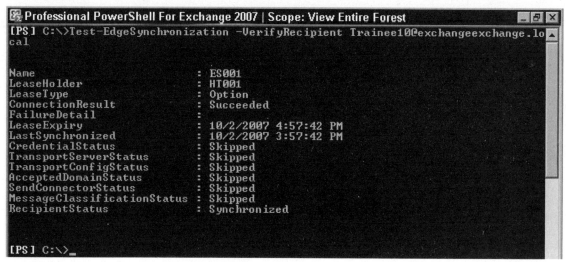

Figure 9-2

Exchange Server 2007 introduced cloned configuration for the Edge Transport server to enable administrators installing multiple Edge Transport servers to deploy a consistent configuration across their servers. In addition, they could restore the Edge Transport servers from a cloned configuration if needed due to a server failure. In the Release To Manufacturing (RTM) version, however, the cloned configuration did not include the TransportConfig object. Hence, after cloning a target Edge Transport server, the transport configuration attributes on the target server are different than those on the original Edge Transport server. In Exchange Server 2007 SP1, the information that is cloned now includes the TransportConfig object. The TransportConfig object controls server-wide settings for the Edge Transport server role. This information is written to the intermediate XML file. This way, the transport configuration setting is identical on the target Edge Transport server. The following cmdlets include some new parameters:

- ❏ `Start-EdgeSynchronization`: This cmdlet now has a new `server` parameter. This allows an administrator to start edge synchronization from a remote computer by simply specifying the Hub Transport server edge synchronization will be run against.

- ❏ `Update-SafeList`: This cmdlet also now has a new `includeddomains` parameter. One of the responsibilities of EdgeSync is to replicate safelist aggregation data to the Edge Transport server role. This safelist is based upon data stored on Outlook user or Outlook Web Access user mailboxes. This safelist causes the Content Filter agent (discussed later in this chapter) to bypass content filtering for users specified in the safelist. In Exchange Server 2007 SP1, you can now use the `includeddomains` parameter to add domains to the safelist. This parameter should be used with caution because adding a domain may inadvertently provide addresses that could be used to spoof emails by spammers.

Edge Transport Server Configuration

Several steps are required to ensure that the Edge Transport server works efficiently to provide message hygiene and route mail into and out of an Exchange organization. As mentioned earlier, the Edge Transport server cannot be installed if the ADAM service is not installed. You will be prompted to install ADAM during the prerequisite checks.

This section covers the following list of Edge-related cmdlets:

- ❏ `Get-EdgeSubscription`
- ❏ `New-EdgeSubscription`
- ❏ `Remove-EdgeSubscription`
- ❏ `Start-EdgeSynchronization`
- ❏ `Test-EdgeSynchronization`
- ❏ `Get-AcceptedDomain`
- ❏ `Set-AcceptedDomain`
- ❏ `New-AcceptedDomain`
- ❏ `Remove-AcceptedDomain`
- ❏ `Get-RemoteDomain`
- ❏ `Set-RemoteDomain`
- ❏ `New-RemoteDomain`
- ❏ `Remove-RemoteDomain`

- ❑   `Get-AdSite`
- ❑   `Get-SendConnector`
- ❑   `Set-SendConnector`
- ❑   `New-SendConnector`
- ❑   `Remove-SendConnector`
- ❑   `Get-ReceiveConnector`
- ❑   `Set-ReceiveConnector`
- ❑   `New-ReceiveConnector`

New-EdgeSubscription

This cmdlet is used to export an edge subscription file from an Edge Transport server and to import the edge subscription file to a Hub Transport server in an Active Directory site.

For a detailed list run the following in the Exchange Management Shell: `Get-Help New-EdgeSubscription -detailed`. The syntax for this cmdlet has the following parameters:

```
New-EdgeSubscription -FileName <LongPath> [-Confirm [<SwitchParameter>]]
[-CreateInboundSendConnector <$true | $false>] [-CreateInternetSendConnector <$true |
$false>] [-DomainController <Fqdn>] [-Force <SwitchParameter>] [-Site
<AdSiteIdParameter>] [-WhatIf [<SwitchParameter>]] [<CommonParameters>]
```

Some key parameters to note include:

- ❑   `FileName <LongPath>`: This is the only required parameter when exporting the subscription file from the Edge Transport server. You must specify the full path to the file as well as the extension.

- ❑   `CreateInboundSendConnector <$true | $false>`: This parameter when set to `$false` will not create the Send Connector from the Edge Transport server to the Hub Transport servers. The default value is `$True`. The Send Connector address space will be set to `--`, the smart hosts will be set to `--`, the Edge Transport server will be set as the source server, and Domain Name System (DNS) routing will be disabled. This parameter is only used when you run the command on the Hub Transport server.

- ❑   `CreateInternetSendConnector <$true | $false>`: This parameter is only used when run on the Hub Transport server. When set to false it will not create the Send Connector to the Internet. The default value is `$true`. The Send Connector address space will be set to all domains (`*`), the Edge Transport server will be set as the source server, and DNS routing will be enabled.

- ❑   `DomainController <Fqdn>`: Use the `DomainController` parameter to specify the host name or fully qualified domain name (FQDN) of the domain controller that will process this command. This parameter is used only when you run the command on a Hub Transport server.

❑ `Force <SwitchParameter>`: Use the `Force` parameter to bypass the confirmation prompt when you run the `New-EdgeSubscription` command on an Edge Transport server. This parameter also causes the command to overwrite an existing edge subscription file with the same name as the file you are creating. This parameter is useful when you script the Edge Subscription command and when you re-subscribe an Edge Transport server.

❑ `Site <AdSiteIdParameter>`: This parameter is used to specify the name of the Active Directory site that contains the Hub Transport servers with which the Edge Transport servers will be associated. Only used when run on a Hub Transport server and it is a required parameter when the command is run on a Hub Transport server.

Remove-EdgeSubscription

This cmdlet is used to export an edge subscription file from an Edge Transport server and to import the edge subscription file to a Hub Transport server in an Active Directory site.

For a detailed list run the following in the Exchange Management Shell: `Get-Help Remove-EdgeSubscription -detailed`. The syntax for this cmdlet has the following parameters:

```
Remove-EdgeSubscription -Identity <TransportServerIdParameter> [-Confirm
[<SwitchParameter>]]
[-DomainController <Fqdn>] [-WhatIf [<SwitchParameter>]]
```

❑ `Identity<TransportServerIdParameter>`: This parameter specifies the identity of the Edge Transport server for which you want to remove the edge subscription. The identity is expressed as the host name of the Edge Transport server.

❑ `Confirm <SwitchParameter>`: The `Confirm` parameter causes the command to pause processing and requires the administrator to acknowledge what the command will do before processing continues. The default value is `$true`.

❑ `DomainController <Fqdn>`: Use the `DomainController` parameter to specify the host name or fully qualified domain name (FQDN) of the domain controller that will write this change to Active Directory. This parameter is used only when the procedure is run on the Hub Transport server.

Start-EdgeSynchronization

This cmdlet is used to start the synchronization of configuration data to the Edge Transport server after it is subscribed to the Exchange organization.

For a detailed list run the following in the Exchange Management Shell: `Get-Help Start-EdgeSynchronization -detailed`. The syntax for this cmdlet has the following parameters:

```
Start-EdgeSynchronization [-Confirm [<SwitchParameter>]] [-Server
<ServerIdParameter>] [-WhatIf
[<SwitchParameter>]]
```

Test-EdgeSynchronization

This cmdlet is used to determine the status of subscribed Edge Transport servers. It includes a new parameter `VerifyRecipient`, which was introduced in Exchange Server 2007 SP1, used to test the synchronization status of a specific Recipient.

For a detailed list run the following in the Exchange Management Shell: `Get-Help Test-EdgeSynchronization -detailed`. The syntax for this cmdlet has the following parameters:

```
Test-EdgeSynchronization [-Confirm [<SwitchParameter>]] [-DomainController <Fqdn>]
[-ExcludeRecipientTest <SwitchParameter>] [-MaxReportSize <Unlimited>]
[-MonitoringContext <$true | $false>] [-WhatIf [<SwitchParameter>]]

Test-EdgeSynchronization -VerifyRecipient <ProxyAddress> [-Confirm
[<SwitchParameter>]] [-DomainController <Fqdn>] [-WhatIf [<SwitchParameter>]]
```

❑ `ExcludeRecipientTest <SwitchParameter>`: This parameter excludes validation of Recipient data synchronization. When specified only the synchronization of configuration objects will be validated.

❑ `VerifyRecipient`: This parameter is used to verify the synchronization status of a single Recipient. You identify the Recipient by specifying a proxy address that is assigned to the Recipient. The proxy address is the Recipient's email address. The Recipient verification test is mutually exclusive of the test that verifies synchronization of configuration data.

❑ `MaxReportSize<Unlimited>`: This parameter when used specifies the total number of objects and properties that will be listed in the results. Results include both objects in-sync and out-of-sync.

❑ `MonitoringContext <$true | $false>`: This parameter is used only when MOM is being used for server monitoring. When set to `$true`, it populates the monitoring context with events and performance counters used by MOM. By default this parameter is set to `$false`.

Although the discussion in this section covers the configuration of the Edge Transport server in an Exchange Server 2007 environment, it is worth mentioning that the Edge Transport server can also be deployed in the perimeter network of an existing Exchange Server 2000/2003 environment. It does not require the upgrade of Exchange Server 2000/2003 servers or Active Directory forest or domain preparation to deploy the Edge Transport server in this environment because the Edge Transport server is dependent on ADAM. With appropriate configuration of Send and Receive Connectors, DNS configuration, accepted domains, and SMTP Connectors, the Edge Transport server can be used as a smart host for the Exchange 2000/2003 messaging environment. However, to take advantage of all the anti-spam and anti-virus features of the Edge Transport server, the Edge Transport server should be subscribed to the Exchange organization. To achieve this in an existing Exchange 2000/2003 environment, at least one Exchange Server 2007 Hub Transport server role should deployed into the existing Exchange organization to complete the edge subscription process.

The Edge Transport servers in the perimeter network and the Hub Transport servers in the Exchange organization must be able to locate each other by using host name resolution. You must specify the appropriate DNS suffix for the Edge Transport server prior to its installation.

Preparing the Edge Transport Server

After you install the Microsoft Exchange Server 2007 Edge Transport server role, if you do not use edge subscription and EdgeSync to automate your configuration, then you must configure the Send and Receive Connectors. For complete mail flow, the Edge Transport server must have connectors that support mail flow to and from the Internet, and to and from the organization. The actual steps to prepare the Edge Transport server will vary depending on whether edge subscription and EdgeSync will be performed. It is highly recommended that you use edge subscription and EdgeSync to subscribe the Edge Transport server to an Active Directory site in the Exchange organization because this automates and simplifies the configuration on the Edge Transport servers.

In this section, you examine both scenarios for configuring the Edge Transport server to function with an Exchange Server 2007 organization: first, where no edge subscription and EdgeSync is implemented and second, where edge subscription and EdgeSync is performed. The tasks that must be completed on the Edge Transport server based on these scenarios are discussed.

The first scenario is where edge subscription and EdgeSync will not be performed. In this scenario, to prepare the Edge Transport server, the following tasks are performed:

1. **Ports:** Verify that the perimeter network firewall that separates the Edge Transport server from the Exchange organization is configured to enable SMTP communications on port 25. This is required for the both the Edge Transport and Hub Transport servers to send and receive emails.

2. **DNS:** The Edge Transport servers in the perimeter network and the Hub Transport servers in the Exchange organization must be able to locate each other by using host name resolution. You must specify the appropriate DNS suffix for the Edge Transport server prior to its installation. On the DNS servers that both the Edge Transport and Hub Transport servers are configured to point to, configure host records in the appropriate forward lookup zones to resolve each server. Alternatively, you can create host file entries on both the Edge Transport and Hub Transport servers to resolve each other.

3. **Send Connector to Internet:** Create and configure a Send Connector to route outbound Internet messages. The address space to be configured on this connector is *, which means it can route messages to all Internet domains. It is typically configured to use DNS but can also be configured to forward to a smart host such as an ISP or other third-party vendor. The usage type for this connector is Internet. Figure 9-3 shows the creation of a new Send Connector for this purpose. The source bridgehead will be the Edge Transport server; however, you do not have to specify this in the New-SendConnector cmdlet. Whenever Send Connectors are created on an Edge Transport server, the SourceTransportServers parameter should be empty because the local Edge Transport server is always assumed as the Source bridgehead server.

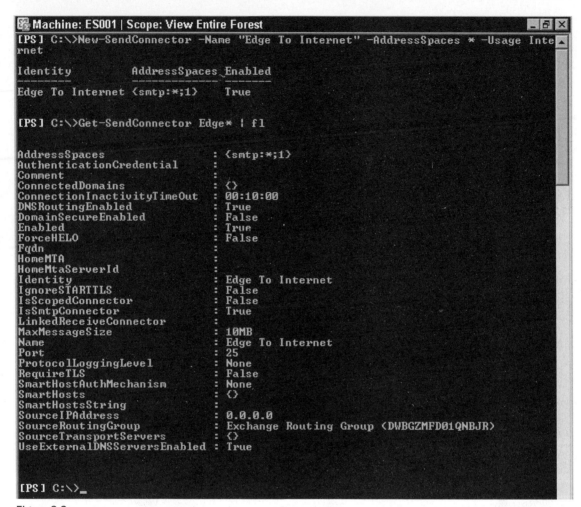

```
Machine: ES001 | Scope: View Entire Forest                           _ ☐ ✕
[PS] C:\>New-SendConnector -Name "Edge To Internet" -AddressSpaces * -Usage Inte
rnet

Identity              AddressSpaces Enabled
--------              ------------- -------
Edge To Internet      {smtp:*;1}    True


[PS] C:\>Get-SendConnector Edge* | fl

AddressSpaces                  : {smtp:*;1}
AuthenticationCredential       :
Comment                        :
ConnectedDomains               : {}
ConnectionInactivityTimeOut    : 00:10:00
DNSRoutingEnabled              : True
DomainSecureEnabled            : False
Enabled                        : True
ForceHELO                      : False
Fqdn                           :
HomeMTA                        :
HomeMtaServerId                :
Identity                       : Edge To Internet
IgnoreSTARTTLS                 : False
IsScopedConnector              : False
IsSmtpConnector                : True
LinkedReceiveConnector         :
MaxMessageSize                 : 10MB
Name                           : Edge To Internet
Port                           : 25
ProtocolLoggingLevel           : None
RequireTLS                     : False
SmartHostAuthMechanism         : None
SmartHosts                     : {}
SmartHostsString               :
SourceIPAddress                : 0.0.0.0
SourceRoutingGroup             : Exchange Routing Group {DWBGZMFD01QNBJR}
SourceTransportServers         : {}
UseExternalDNSServersEnabled   : True


[PS] C:\>_
```

Figure 9-3

The Edge Transport server will automatically be used as the source bridge head server for this connector.

4. **Receive Connector from Internet:** Next, you create a Receive Connector that will accept messages from the Internet. The configuration on this connector should be such that it will listen on all IP address ranges and will allow anonymous connections. This connector will also be configured on the external network interface of Edge Transport server. This is shown in Figure 9-4.

```
Professional PowerShell For Exchange 2007 | Scope: View Entire Forest          _ 8 X
[PS] C:\>New-ReceiveConnector -Name "Edge Receive From Internet" -Bindings 172.1
6.8.54:25 -Fqdn ES001.ExchangeExchange.com -Usage Internet

Identity                          Bindings               Enabled
--------                          --------               -------
ES001\Edge Receive From Internet  {172.16.8.54:25}       True


[PS] C:\>Get-ReceiveConnector Edge* | fl

AuthMechanism                             : Tls
Banner                                    :
BinaryMimeEnabled                         : True
Bindings                                  : {172.16.8.54:25}
ChunkingEnabled                           : True
DefaultDomain                             :
DeliveryStatusNotificationEnabled         : True
EightBitMimeEnabled                       : True
DomainSecureEnabled                       : False
EnhancedStatusCodesEnabled                : True
LongAddressesEnabled                      : False
OrarEnabled                               : False
Fqdn                                      : ES001.ExchangeExchange.com
Comment                                   :
Enabled                                   : True
ConnectionTimeout                         : 00:05:00
ConnectionInactivityTimeout               : 00:01:00
MessageRateLimit                          : 600
MaxInboundConnection                      : 5000
MaxInboundConnectionPerSource             : 20
MaxInboundConnectionPercentagePerSource   : 2
MaxHeaderSize                             : 64KB
MaxHopCount                               : 30
MaxLocalHopCount                          : 8
MaxLogonFailures                          : 3
MaxMessageSize                            : 10MB
MaxProtocolErrors                         : 5
MaxRecipientsPerMessage                   : 200
PermissionGroups                          : AnonymousUsers
PipeliningEnabled                         : True
ProtocolLoggingLevel                      : None
RemoteIPRanges                            : {0.0.0.0-255.255.255.255}
RequireEHLODomain                         : False
RequireTLS                                : False
EnableAuthGSSAPI                          : False
Server                                    : ES001
SizeEnabled                               : Enabled
TarpitInterval                            : 00:00:05
AdminDisplayName                          :
ExchangeVersion                           : 0.1 (8.0.535.0)
Name                                      : Edge Receive From Internet
```

Figure 9-4

Notice the RemoteIPRange and PermissionGroups settings to allow all inbound Internet traffic on port 25. The Receive Connector is bound to the external NIC on the server.

Thus far you have a Send Connector to send mail to the Internet and a Receive Connector to receive mail from the Internet. Two more connectors are required based on this scenario.

5. **Send Connector to Hub Server(s):** Another Send Connector needs to be created and configured to send messages inbound from the Internet to the Hub Transport servers inside the Exchange organization. The usage type for this connector is internal. This connector's address space will

be configured based on the accepted domains configured for the organization. An easy way to configure the address space for this connector is to specify "- -" (2 dashes) for the address space. This essentially means that this connector will route mail for any authoritative domain or internal relay domain configured for the organization. The smart host configured for this Send Connector will be one or more Hub Transport servers in the Exchange organization. The source bridgehead as usual will be the Edge Transport server but it is not specified. This is shown in Figure 9-5.

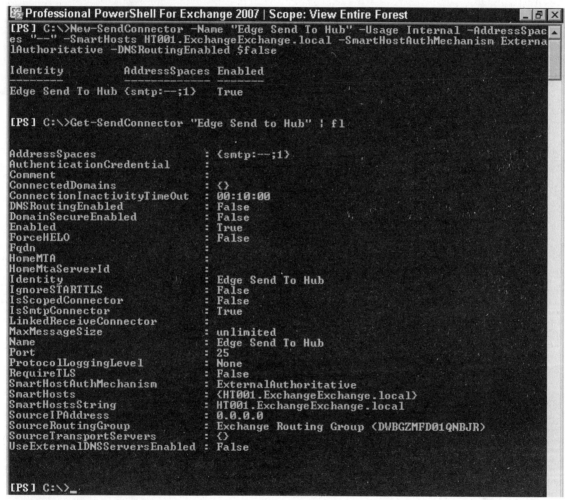

Figure 9-5

6. **Receive Connector from Hub Server(s):** Finally, because this scenario does not use edge subscription and EdgeSync, it is recommended that you create another Receive Connector on the Edge Transport server other than the default. The default Receive Connector has a usage

type of Internet, which means it can accept anonymous connections. If edge subscription was used, the EdgeSync process would be able to negotiate the authentication seamlessly. However, because this is a manual configuration, you would need to create a Receive Connector of usage type internal. It must be bound to the internal network adapter of the Edge Transport server. This connector is shown in Figure 9-6.

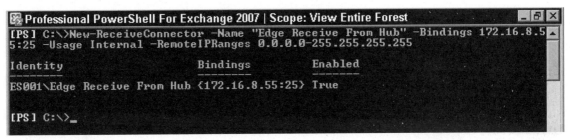

Figure 9-6

The Receive Connector is bound to the internal adapter with an IP address of 172.16.8.55 and allows all Hub Transport servers in the remote IP range to connect to the Edge Transport server.

Hence, after completing a manual configuration, you should have the connectors configured on the Edge Transport server shown in Figure 9-7. Note that the only connector created automatically was the Default Internal Receive Connector.

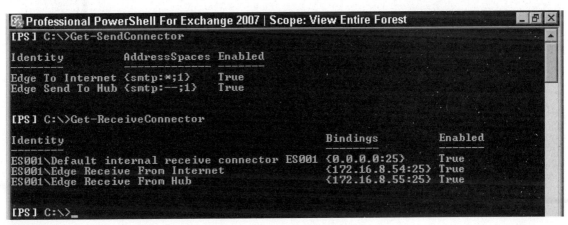

Figure 9-7

The second scenario, which is the one that is *recommended*, is where edge subscription and EdgeSync will be performed. The following tasks are performed to fully integrate and associate the Edge Transport server with the Exchange organization. This process ensures that the organization takes full advantage of the message hygiene and anti-virus protection built into the Edge Transport server role. It also requires the least administrative effort:

1. **Ports:** Verify that the perimeter network firewall that separates the Edge Transport server from the Exchange organization is configured to enable communications on ports 25 and 50636. Because EdgeSync replicates data between Active Directory and ADAM, secure LDAP port 50636 for TCP communication must be opened on the firewall to enable directory synchronization from the Hub Transport to ADAM on the Edge Transport server. Recall that synchronization is single directional, hence the port can be opened one-way from the Hub to the perimeter network. Also verify that on the Edge Transport server, you can connect locally to the LDAP port 50389. This is the port to access the ADAM instance. An easy way to test this is to use the ldp.exe utility found in the `C:\WINDOWS\ADAM` directory. Connect using the NetBIOS name of the Edge Transport server and if no credentials are specified, it binds with the credentials of the locally logged-on user. Finally, ensure that SMTP port 25 is open on the firewall for both the Edge Transport and Hub Transport servers to send and receive emails.

2. **DNS:** The Edge Transport servers in the perimeter network and the Hub Transport servers in the Exchange organization must be able to locate each other by using host name resolution. You must specify the appropriate DNS suffix for the Edge Transport server prior to its installation. On the DNS servers that both the Edge Transport and Hub Transport servers are configured to point to, configure host records in the appropriate forward lookup zones to resolve each server. Alternatively, you can create host file entries on both the Edge Transport and Hub Transport servers to resolve each other.

3. **License Edge Transport Server:** You should license the server prior to running edge subscription so that the subscribed Edge Transport server will appear as a licensed server. If performed after the edge subscription, this information does not get updated for the organization without re-subscribing the Edge Transport server.

4. **Configure Accepted and Remote Domains:** This step must be performed on the Hub Transport server and prepares the information to be propagated to the Edge Transport server. This step is discussed further in the section "Preparing the Hub Transport Server" later in this chapter.

5. **Export Edge Subscription:** This step is performed on an Edge Transport server and generates a subscription file. This subscription file contains a public-private key pair as well as ADAM bootstrap credentials that will be used to set up the initial synchronization between the Edge Transport and Hub Transport servers. This file must be manually copied over to the Hub Transport server and imported. The `New-EdgeSubscription` cmdlet is used to perform these tasks. The syntax used for this cmdlet is `New-EdgeSubscription -FileName "c:\EdgeSubscription01.xml"`.

    Any filename can be specified but it must have an `.xml` extension. Figure 9-8 shows what you will see when this cmdlet is run.

The process of generating this subscription file also creates an ExchangeSync Replication Account (ESRA) in the ADAM database, which will be used for the initial synchronization. Figure 9-9 shows this account.

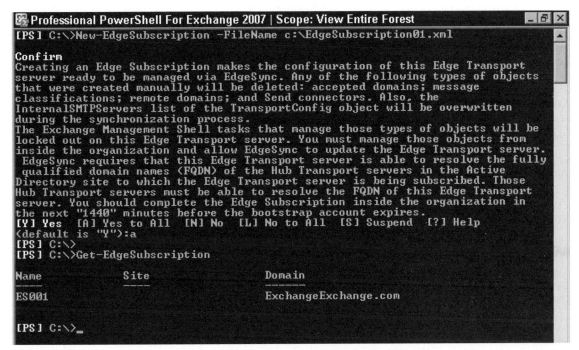

Figure 9-8

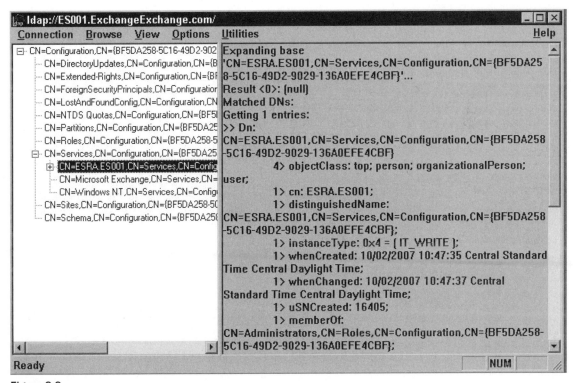

Figure 9-9

6. **Import Edge Subscription:** This step is completed on the Hub Transport server. You manually copy the `EdgeSubscription01.xml` file to the Hub Transport server and import it. This file must be imported within 24 hours of its creation on the Edge Transport server. This step is required on the Hub Transport server to complete the process of subscribing the Edge Transport server to the Exchange organization. The `New-EdgeSubscription` cmdlet is used to specify the file imported from the Edge Transport server as well as the Active Directory site the Edge Transport server will be subscribed to. Figure 9-10 shows how this step is accomplished.

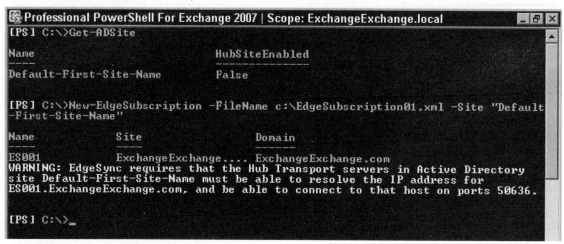

Figure 9-10

So in Figure 9-10 the `Get-ADSite` cmdlet first obtains the Active Directory site name. Then the `EdgeSubscription01.xml` file is imported and finally the `Start-EdgeSychronization` cmdlet initiates synchronization.

At the end of this scenario, the connectors shown in Figure 9-11 are created automatically by the edge subscription process: a Send Connector from the Edge Transport server to the Internet and a Send Connector from the Edge Transport server to the Hub Transport servers in the Active Directory site to which the Edge Transport server is subscribed. The Receive Connector already exists by default when the Edge Transport role is installed.

```
Professional PowerShell For Exchange 2007 | Scope: View Entire Forest           _ 🗗 ✕
[PS] C:\>Get-SendConnector

Identity                                      AddressSpaces  Enabled
--------                                      -------------  -------
edgesync - default-first-site-name to internet {smtp:*;100}  True
edgesync - inbound to default-first-site-name  {smtp:--;100}  True


[PS] C:\>Get-ReceiveConnector

Identity                                      Bindings       Enabled
--------                                      --------       -------
ES001\Default internal receive connector ES001 {0.0.0.0:25}  True


[PS] C:\>_
```

Figure 9-11

See Figure 9-15 in the next section for connectors created on the Hub Transport server after edge subscription is imported. Keep in mind that an implicit Send Connector from the Hub Transport servers that are in the same forest as the Edge Transport server is also created so all the Hub servers know how to route outbound Internet mail to the Edge Transport server.

Preparing the Hub Transport Server

The actual steps required to prepare the Hub Transport server vary depending on whether edge subscription and EdgeSync will be performed. It is highly recommended that you use edge subscription and EdgeSync to subscribe the Edge Transport server to an Active Directory site in the Exchange organization because this automates and simplifies the configuration on both the Edge and Hub Transport servers.

First consider the scenario where edge subscription and EdgeSync will not be performed. In this case, to prepare the Hub Transport server, you should perform the following tasks:

1. **Ports:** Verify that the perimeter network firewall that separates the Edge Transport server from the Exchange organization is configured to enable SMTP communications on port 25. This is required for both the Edge Transport and Hub Transport servers to send and receive emails.

2. **DNS:** The Edge Transport servers in the perimeter network and the Hub Transport servers in the Exchange organization must be able to locate each other by using host name resolution. You must specify the appropriate DNS suffix for the Edge Transport server prior to its installation. On the DNS servers that both the Edge Transport and Hub Transport servers are configured to point to, configure host records in the appropriate forward lookup zones to resolve each server. Alternatively, you can create host file entries on both the Edge Transport and Hub Transport servers to resolve each other.

3. **Send Connector to Edge Server:** Configure a Send Connector to forward all outbound Internet mail to the Edge Transport server for onward relay to the Internet. The address space for this connector is typically "*" indicating that this connector will forward mails for all Internet domains. The usage type will be internal and the authentication mechanism will be either basic or Externally Secured. The source bridgehead server will be one or more Hub Transport servers in the Active Directory site. In Figure 9-12 a Send Connector is configured to route outbound mail to the Edge Transport server and its authentication mechanism is set to `ExternalAuthoritative`.

4. The default Receive Connector automatically created during the installation of the Hub Transport role suffices to receive mail from the Edge Transport server. No further configuration is required.

   Hence, at the end of a manual configuration of the Hub Transport server, you should have the connectors shown in Figure 9-13.

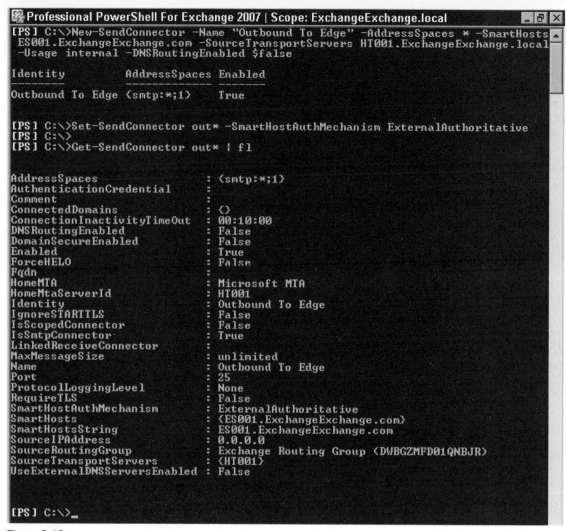

```
Professional PowerShell For Exchange 2007 | Scope: ExchangeExchange.local        _ |F|X

[PS] C:\>New-SendConnector -Name "Outbound To Edge" -AddressSpaces * -SmartHosts
 ES001.ExchangeExchange.com -SourceTransportServers HT001.ExchangeExchange.local
 -Usage internal -DNSRoutingEnabled $false

Identity           AddressSpaces Enabled
--------           ------------- -------
Outbound To Edge  {smtp:*;1}    True


[PS] C:\>Set-SendConnector out* -SmartHostAuthMechanism ExternalAuthoritative
[PS] C:\>
[PS] C:\>Get-SendConnector out* | fl


AddressSpaces                : {smtp:*;1}
AuthenticationCredential     :
Comment                      :
ConnectedDomains             : {}
ConnectionInactivityTimeOut  : 00:10:00
DNSRoutingEnabled            : False
DomainSecureEnabled          : False
Enabled                      : True
ForceHELO                    : False
Fqdn                         :
HomeMTA                      : Microsoft MTA
HomeMtaServerId              : HT001
Identity                     : Outbound To Edge
IgnoreSTARTTLS               : False
IsScopedConnector            : False
IsSmtpConnector              : True
LinkedReceiveConnector       :
MaxMessageSize               : unlimited
Name                         : Outbound To Edge
Port                         : 25
ProtocolLoggingLevel         : None
RequireTLS                   : False
SmartHostAuthMechanism       : ExternalAuthoritative
SmartHosts                   : {ES001.ExchangeExchange.com}
SmartHostsString             : ES001.ExchangeExchange.com
SourceIPAddress              : 0.0.0.0
SourceRoutingGroup           : Exchange Routing Group (DWBGZMFD01QNBJR)
SourceTransportServers       : {HT001}
UseExternalDNSServersEnabled : False


[PS] C:\>
```

Figure 9-12

```
Professional PowerShell For Exchange 2007 | Scope: ExchangeExchange.local        _ |F|X

[PS] C:\>Get-ReceiveConnector

Identity           Bindings         Enabled
--------           --------         -------
HT001\Default HT001 {0.0.0.0:25}    True
HT001\Client HT001  {0.0.0.0:587}   True


[PS] C:\>Get-SendConnector

Identity           AddressSpaces Enabled
--------           ------------- -------
Outbound To Edge  {smtp:*;1}    True


[PS] C:\>
```

Figure 9-13

The *second* scenario, which is the one recommended for the Hub Transport server, occurs when edge subscription and EdgeSync are performed. In this scenario, to prepare the Hub Transport server, you should perform the following tasks. The edge subscription process is discussed in greater detail later in this chapter.

1. **Ports:** Verify that the perimeter network firewall that separates the Edge Transport server from the Exchange organization is configured to enable communications on the following specified ports. Because EdgeSync replicates data between Active Directory and ADAM, secure LDAP port 50636 for TCP communication must be opened on the firewall to enable directory synchronization from the Hub Transport to ADAM on the Edge Transport server. Recall that synchronization is single directional, hence the port can be opened one-way from the Hub to the perimeter network. As in the previous scenario, also ensure that SMTP port 25 is open on the firewall for both the Edge Transport and Hub Transport servers to send and receive emails.

2. **DNS:** The Edge Transport servers in the perimeter network and the Hub Transport servers in the Exchange organization must be able to locate each other by using host name resolution. You must specify the appropriate DNS suffix for the Edge Transport server prior to its installation. On the DNS servers that both the Edge Transport and Hub Transport servers are configured to point to, configure host records in the appropriate forward lookup zones to resolve each server. Alternatively, you can create host file entries on both the Edge Transport and Hub Transport servers to resolve each other.

3. **Configure Accepted and Remote Domains:** This step must be performed on the Hub Transport server and prepares the information to be propagated to the Edge Transport server. Accepted domains are any Simple Mail Transfer Protocol (SMTP) namespace for which an Exchange organization will send or receive email, including domains for which the Exchange organization is authoritative, which means the Exchange organization will handle email delivery for Recipients of that domain. By default one accepted domain is created and configured as authoritative during Exchange installation. Accepted domains may also include domains for which the Exchange organization will receive emails and then relay them to another email server outside the organization for delivery to the intended Recipient. Such domains could be configured as internal relay or external relay domains.

   Remote domains define settings for message delivery to external domains outside the Active Directory forest. They override default delivery settings for all outbound messages.

   Hence, determine what domains will be authoritative and what domains will be relay, then create corresponding accepted domains. Similarly, if you have need to control the types of messages that are sent to a specific domain, create a remote domain entry.

   Figure 9-14 shows using the `Get-AcceptedDomain` cmdlet to view the configured accepted domain `ExchangeExchange.local`. By default the domain name is configured as an authoritative accepted domain. Now because this Exchange organization is authoritative for `ExchangeExchange.com`, add it as an accepted domain with a DomainType of Authoritative. Next, assume you acquired a subsidiary called Namedpipes.net and must relay for this domain. Create a new accepted domain with a `DomainType` of `InternalRelay` to their email server. Finally, assume you send regularly to a remote domain called Mailtask.com and they only accept messages in plain text. Then create and configure a remote domain called `Mailtask.com` using the `New-RemoteDomain` cmdlet.

```
Professional PowerShell For Exchange 2007 | Scope: ExchangeExchange.local      _ □ X

[PS] C:\>Get-AcceptedDomain

Name                             DomainName                        DomainTy Default
                                                                   pe
----                             ----------                        -------- -------
ExchangeExchange.local           ExchangeExchange.local            Autho... True


[PS] C:\>New-AcceptedDomain -Name Exchange -DomainName ExchangeExchange.com -Dom
ainType Authoritative

Name                             DomainName                        DomainTy Default
                                                                   pe
----                             ----------                        -------- -------
Exchange                         ExchangeExchange.com              Autho... False


[PS] C:\>Set-AcceptedDomain -MakeDefault $True

cmdlet Set-AcceptedDomain at command pipeline position 1
Supply values for the following parameters:
Identity: Exchange
[PS] C:\>New-AcceptedDomain -Name NamePipe -DomainName Namedpipes.net -DomainTyp
e InternalRelay

Name                             DomainName                        DomainTy Default
                                                                   pe
----                             ----------                        -------- -------
NamePipe                         Namedpipes.net                    Inter... False


[PS] C:\>Get-AcceptedDomain

Name                             DomainName                        DomainTy Default
                                                                   pe
----                             ----------                        -------- -------
ExchangeExchange.local           ExchangeExchange.local            Autho... False
Exchange                         ExchangeExchange.com              Autho... True
NamePipe                         Namedpipes.net                    Inter... False


[PS] C:\>New-RemoteDomain -Name MailTask -DomainName MailTask.com

Name                             DomainName                        AllowedOOFType
----                             ----------                        --------------
MailTask                         MailTask.com                      External


[PS] C:\>Get-RemoteDomain

Name                             DomainName                        AllowedOOFType
----                             ----------                        --------------
Default                          *                                 External
MailTask                         MailTask.com                      External


[PS] C:\>Set-RemoteDomain Mailtask -ContentType MimeText
```

Figure 9-14

Additionally, you may configure internal SMTP servers on the Hub Transport server. The `InternalSMTPServers` attribute specifies a list of internal Simple Mail Transfer Protocol (SMTP) server IP addresses or IP address ranges that should be ignored by Sender ID and connection filtering. This list of internal servers must be specified using the `Set-TransportConfig` cmdlet prior to configuring EdgeSync. This setting will be propagated to the Edge Transport server after EdgeSync is configured.

4. **Import Edge Subscription:** Finally, you import the edge subscription file created on the Edge Transport server. This file must be imported at least 24 hours after it is created on the Edge Transport server. This step is required on the Hub Transport server to complete the process of subscribing the Edge Transport server to the Exchange organization. The `New-EdgeSubscription` cmdlet is used to specify the file imported from the Edge Transport server as well as the Active Directory site the Edge Transport server will be subscribed to. This step was shown earlier in this chapter in the section on "Preparing the Edge Transport Server."

At the end of this scenario, the Send Connectors shown in Figure 9-15 are created automatically on the Hub Transport server by the edge subscription process. No other Receive Connector is created other than the defaults.

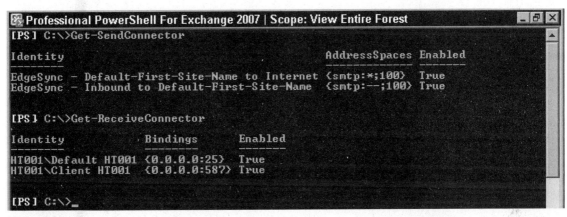

Figure 9-15

Verifying Configuration

There are a couple of things to observe after the edge subscription and edge synchronization process completes. You can use the `Start-EdgeSynchronization` cmdlet to ensure that the synchronization is kicked off and the `Test-EdgeSynchronization` cmdlet to view the synchronization status. The `Start-EdgeSynchronization` cmdlet is shown in Figure 9-16.

Some key items to always check here after running the `Start-EdgeSynchronization` cmdlet are the result, type, and failure details as well as items scanned or deleted. These provide an insight into whether changes made are getting updated on the Edge Transport server. For example, if you create a new user, you can determine by the items scanned in the Recipients type to see if it was incremented.

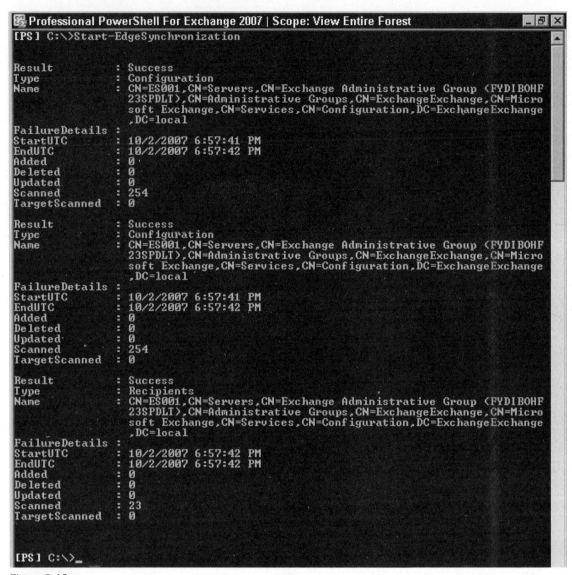

```
Professional PowerShell For Exchange 2007 | Scope: View Entire Forest     _ 5 X
[PS] C:\>Start-EdgeSynchronization

Result          : Success
Type            : Configuration
Name            : CN=ES001,CN=Servers,CN=Exchange Administrative Group (FYDIBOHF
                  23SPDLT),CN=Administrative Groups,CN=ExchangeExchange,CN=Micro
                  soft Exchange,CN=Services,CN=Configuration,DC=ExchangeExchange
                  ,DC=local
FailureDetails  :
StartUTC        : 10/2/2007 6:57:41 PM
EndUTC          : 10/2/2007 6:57:42 PM
Added           : 0
Deleted         : 0
Updated         : 0
Scanned         : 254
TargetScanned   : 0

Result          : Success
Type            : Configuration
Name            : CN=ES001,CN=Servers,CN=Exchange Administrative Group (FYDIBOHF
                  23SPDLT),CN=Administrative Groups,CN=ExchangeExchange,CN=Micro
                  soft Exchange,CN=Services,CN=Configuration,DC=ExchangeExchange
                  ,DC=local
FailureDetails  :
StartUTC        : 10/2/2007 6:57:41 PM
EndUTC          : 10/2/2007 6:57:42 PM
Added           : 0
Deleted         : 0
Updated         : 0
Scanned         : 254
TargetScanned   : 0

Result          : Success
Type            : Recipients
Name            : CN=ES001,CN=Servers,CN=Exchange Administrative Group (FYDIBOHF
                  23SPDLT),CN=Administrative Groups,CN=ExchangeExchange,CN=Micro
                  soft Exchange,CN=Services,CN=Configuration,DC=ExchangeExchange
                  ,DC=local
FailureDetails  :
StartUTC        : 10/2/2007 6:57:42 PM
EndUTC          : 10/2/2007 6:57:42 PM
Added           : 0
Deleted         : 0
Updated         : 0
Scanned         : 23
TargetScanned   : 0

[PS] C:\>_
```

Figure 9-16

Another way to verify if a user created was replicated to the ADAM database is to use the Test-EdgeSynchronization cmdlet. This is shown in Figure 9-17.

When this cmdlet is run, it displays some important information. The name specified is always that of the Edge Transport server and the LeaseHolder is the Hub Transport server. The ConnectionResult determines whether the test run was successful. If it is not, the FailureDetail property is populated with the status of the failure.

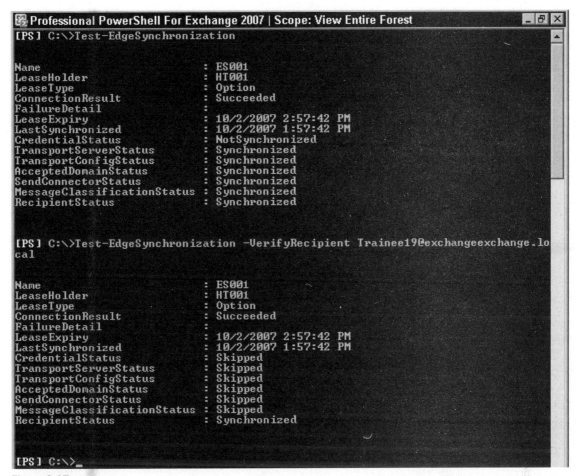

```
Professional PowerShell For Exchange 2007 | Scope: View Entire Forest       _ 8 X
[PS] C:\>Test-EdgeSynchronization

Name                           : ES001
LeaseHolder                    : HT001
LeaseType                      : Option
ConnectionResult               : Succeeded
FailureDetail                  :
LeaseExpiry                    : 10/2/2007 2:57:42 PM
LastSynchronized               : 10/2/2007 1:57:42 PM
CredentialStatus               : NotSynchronized
TransportServerStatus          : Synchronized
TransportConfigStatus          : Synchronized
AcceptedDomainStatus           : Synchronized
SendConnectorStatus            : Synchronized
MessageClassificationStatus    : Synchronized
RecipientStatus                : Synchronized


[PS] C:\>Test-EdgeSynchronization -VerifyRecipient Trainee19@exchangeexchange.lo
cal

Name                           : ES001
LeaseHolder                    : HT001
LeaseType                      : Option
ConnectionResult               : Succeeded
FailureDetail                  :
LeaseExpiry                    : 10/2/2007 2:57:42 PM
LastSynchronized               : 10/2/2007 1:57:42 PM
CredentialStatus               : Skipped
TransportServerStatus          : Skipped
TransportConfigStatus          : Skipped
AcceptedDomainStatus           : Skipped
SendConnectorStatus            : Skipped
MessageClassificationStatus    : Skipped
RecipientStatus                : Synchronized


[PS] C:\>
```

Figure 9-17

Also in Figure 9-17, we used the VerifyRecipient parameter of the Test-EdgeSynchronization cmdlet to verify whether Trainee19 has been replicated to the Edge Transport server. The status Synchronized for the RecipientStatus tells us that it has.

Another way to verify that the initial edge synchronization completed is to notice the OU= OU=MSExchangeGateway, CN=Recipients hierarchy on the ADAM database populated as shown in Figure 9-18.

Sometimes due to a non delivery report or Recipient failure event logged on the Edge Transport server, it may be necessary to determine which Recipient a specific CN points to. In the example in Figure 9-19, in ADAM we select a CN for a Recipient 6ff45354-9502-4771-b178-7c97a864cdef.

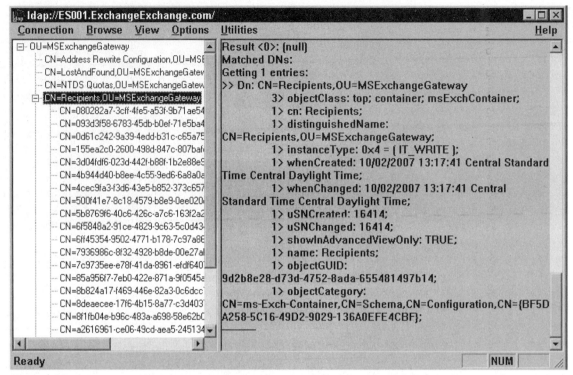

Figure 9-18

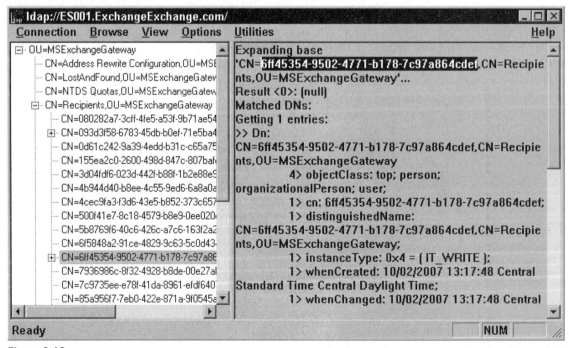

Figure 9-19

You can simply take this information to a domain controller in the Active Directory site and enter the search filter shown in Figure 9-20.

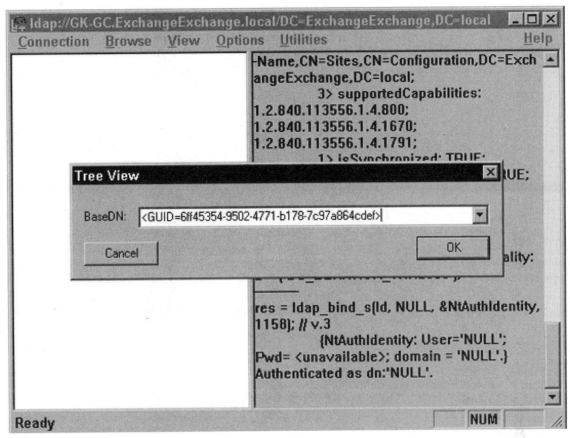

Figure 9-20

Notice that this points to `CN=Trainee5,OU=ADUsers,DC=ExchangeExchange,DC=local` as shown in Figure 9-21.

Failures to deliver to a Recipient could result if the user's primary SMTP address, for example, is modified and EdgeSync did not synchronize the change to ADAM for some reason. Ensure that the EdgeSync service is running and use the `VerifyRecipient` parameter to test that the user is synchronized.

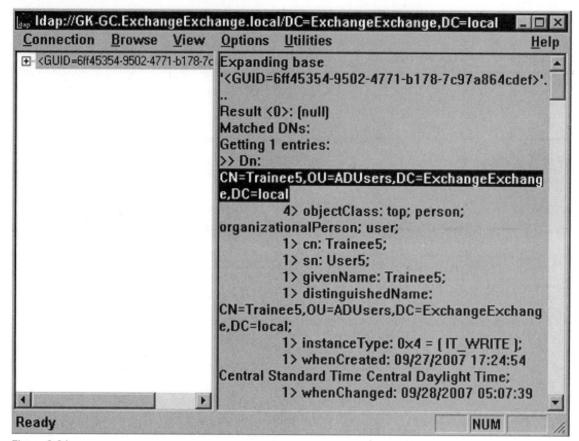

Figure 9-21

For message flow inbound to the Exchange organization via the Edge Transport server, the queues will show a DeliveryType of Smart host with the Hub Transport server as the next hop. (See Figure 9-22.)

```
Professional PowerShell For Exchange 2007 | Scope: View Entire Forest
[PS] C:\>Get-Queue

Identity              DeliveryType  Status  MessageCount  NextHopDomain
--------              ------------  ------  ------------  -------------
ES001\4               SmartHost...  Ready   0             ht001
ES001\Submission      Undefined     Ready   0             Submission

[PS] C:\>_
```

Figure 9-22

Edge Cloning

Organizations are not limited to a single Edge Transport server install. You can install and configure multiple Edge Transport servers in your perimeter network. This is advantageous because it provides redundancy and enables load balancing if your DNS is configured with multiple Mail Exchanger (MX) records pointing to one of each Edge Transport server with the same priority.

However, to make sure all the Edge Transport servers deployed in the perimeter network are of identical configuration, cloned configuration scripts are provided in the Exchange Management Shell to copy the configuration of one Edge Transport server and duplicate it on as many target Edge Transport servers as needed. These scripts are located in the `C:\Program Files\Microsoft\Exchange Server\Scripts` directory if you chose the default path for installation.

The clone configuration process involves exporting the source Edge Transport server configuration using the `ExportEdgeConfig.ps1` script to an intermediate XML file. Next you validate whether the settings exported are valid for the target server by running the `ImportEdgeConfig.ps1` script, which checks the intermediate XML file and creates an answer file. Finally, you clone the target Edge Transport server by importing the configuration using a combination of the `ImportEdgeConfig.ps1` script, the intermediate XML file, and the answer file.

As mentioned earlier, in Exchange Server 2007 SPI, the information that is cloned now includes the `TransportConfig` object.

Transport Agents

In previous versions of Exchange, you could use event sinks to customize some functionality not available by default in the product, such as adding disclaimers to messages or acting on messages depending on where the message is located in transport, for example `OnMessagePostCategorize`, `OnMessagePreCategorize`, `OnArrival`, and so forth. In Exchange Server 2007, transport event sinks have been replaced by transport agents. These agents or rules allow you to create customized software solutions that act on messages as they pass through the transport pipeline on a Hub Transport server or Edge Transport server.

The following is list of transport agent cmdlets used to view and configure transport agents in Exchange Server 2007:

- ❏ `Disable-TransportAgent`
- ❏ `Enable-TransportAgent`
- ❏ `Get-TransportAgent`
- ❏ `Set-TransportAgent`
- ❏ `Uninstall-TransportAgent`

Get-TransportAgent

This cmdlet allows you view the configuration of a transport agent. It has only two parameters, the `Identity` and `DomainController` parameters. The syntax for this cmdlet is:

```
Get-TransporAgent[-Identity <String>] [-DomainController <Fqdn>]
```

For a detailed list run the following in the Exchange Management Shell: `get-help` `Get-TransportAgent -detailed`.

Set-TransportAgent

This cmdlet allows you modify the configuration of a transport agent. For a detailed list run the following in the Exchange Management Shell: `Get-Help Set-TransportAgent -detailed`. The syntax for this cmdlet and parameters are shown here:

```
Set-TransportAgent -Identity <String> [-Confirm [<SwitchParameter>]]
[-DomainController <Fqdn>] [-Priority <Nullable>] [-WhatIf
[<SwitchParameter>]]
```

A key parameter to note is `Priority <Nullable>`. This parameter is used to specify the priority of an agent that controls the order in which the agent processes email messages. The maximum value set should not exceed the number of agents installed. The minimum value is 0. Transport agents with a priority closer to 0 process emails first.

Enable-TransportAgent

This cmdlet allows you to enable a configured transport agent. For a detailed list run the following in the Exchange Management Shell: `Get-Help Enable-TransportAgent -detailed`. The syntax for this cmdlet and parameters are shown here:

```
Enable-TransportAgent -Identity <String> [-Confirm [<SwitchParameter>]]
[-DomainController <Fqdn>] [-WhatIf
[<SwitchParameter>]]
```

Some transport agents are installed by default on both the Edge Transport and Hub Transport server but the number of agents installed differs. Whereas the Hub Transport server has two transport agents by default — the Transport Rule agent and Journaling agent — the Edge Transport server has the agents shown in Figure 9-23 installed by default. The agents existing by default on the Hub Transport server do not exist on the Edge Transport server.

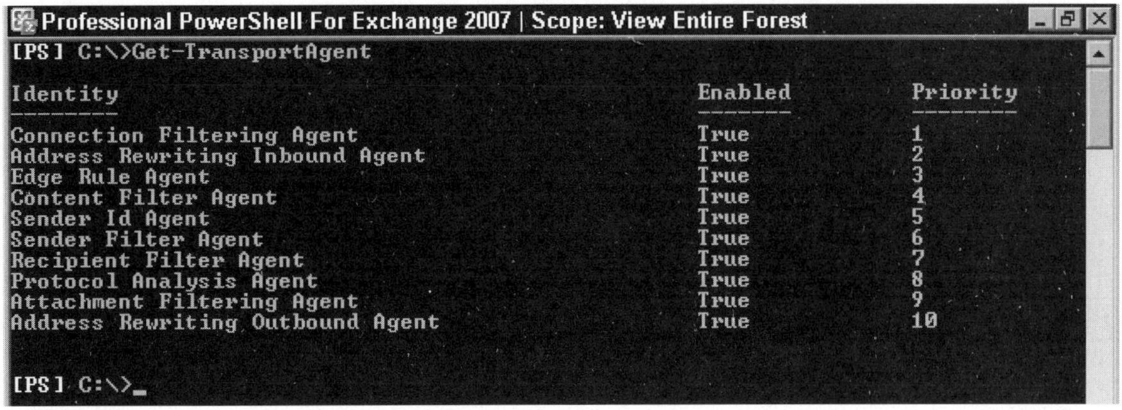

```
Professional PowerShell For Exchange 2007 | Scope: View Entire Forest        _ □ X
[PS] C:\>Get-TransportAgent

Identity                                        Enabled         Priority

Connection Filtering Agent                      True            1
Address Rewriting Inbound Agent                 True            2
Edge Rule Agent                                 True            3
Content Filter Agent                            True            4
Sender Id Agent                                 True            5
Sender Filter Agent                             True            6
Recipient Filter Agent                          True            7
Protocol Analysis Agent                         True            8
Attachment Filtering Agent                      True            9
Address Rewriting Outbound Agent                True            10


[PS] C:\>_
```

Figure 9-23

These transport agents, written to take advantage of SMTP events, can be triggered at various stages of the `TransportPipeline` as shown in Figure 9-24.

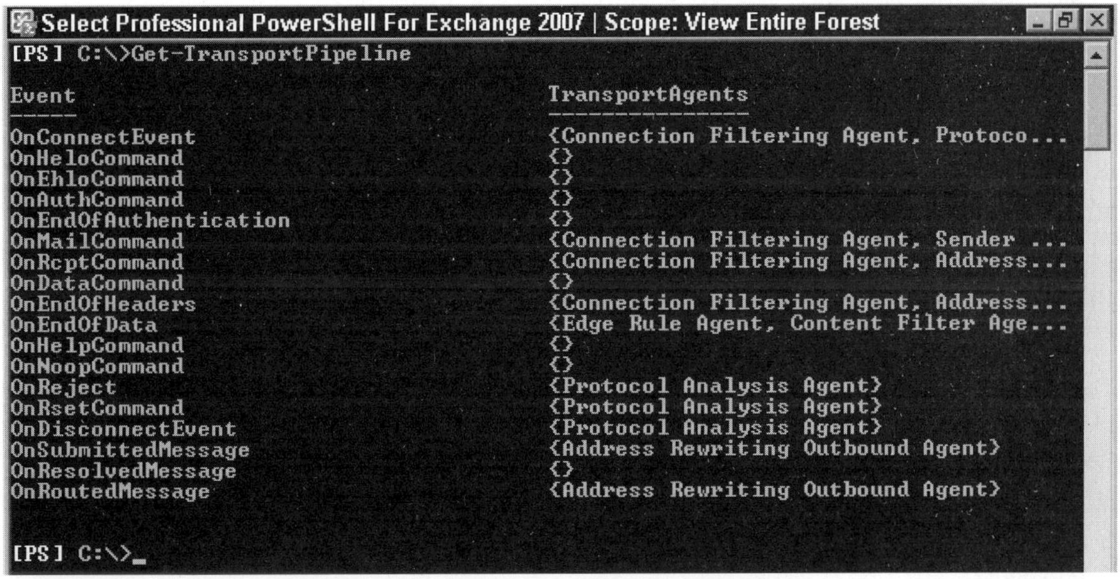

```
Select Professional PowerShell For Exchange 2007 | Scope: View Entire Forest    _ □ X
[PS] C:\>Get-TransportPipeline

Event                          TransportAgents

OnConnectEvent                 {Connection Filtering Agent, Protoco...
OnHeloCommand                  {}
OnEhloCommand                  {}
OnAuthCommand                  {}
OnEndOfAuthentication          {}
OnMailCommand                  {Connection Filtering Agent, Sender ...
OnRcptCommand                  {Connection Filtering Agent, Address...
OnDataCommand                  {}
OnEndOfHeaders                 {Connection Filtering Agent, Address...
OnEndOfData                    {Edge Rule Agent, Content Filter Age...
OnHelpCommand                  {}
OnNoopCommand                  {}
OnReject                       {Protocol Analysis Agent}
OnRsetCommand                  {Protocol Analysis Agent}
OnDisconnectEvent              {Protocol Analysis Agent}
OnSubmittedMessage             {Address Rewriting Outbound Agent}
OnResolvedMessage              {}
OnRoutedMessage                {Address Rewriting Outbound Agent}


[PS] C:\>_
```

Figure 9-24

It is worth noting that although message hygiene and other Edge Transport agents are not installed on a Hub Transport server by default, they can still be installed manually if the Hub Transport server is Internet facing. A few of the agents installed on the Edge Transport server are discussed next.

Address Rewrite Agent

The Edge Transport server provides message address rewrite functionality. When companies merge and want to present a single email address for all outgoing emails irrespective of the internal company, address rewrite becomes invaluable. Address rewriting agents function by rewriting the SMTP headers on email messages that are sent and received by an Edge Transport server. It consists of the Outbound Address Rewrite agent and the Inbound Address Rewrite agent. The following cmdlets are used to configure this agent:

❑ `Get-AddressRewriteEntry`

❑ `New-AddressRewriteEntry`

❑ `Set-AddressRewriteEntry`

❑ `Remove-AddressRewriteEntry`

Edge Rules Agent

This agent is identical to the Transport Rules agent implemented by default on the Hub Transport server. By use of transport rules, this agent limits the number of unwanted messages entering the organization. By acting on messages on the perimeter network before entering the messaging organization, unwanted messages, denial of service attacks, and risks due to virus are mitigated. Each computer running the Edge Transport server role contains its own transport rule configuration stored locally in ADAM.

Journaling Rule Agent

This agent runs only on the Hub Transport server and is mainly for email compliance. It is installed and enabled by default on the Hub Transport server. When configured it enforces email retention policies on messages sent or received by Recipients within the Exchange organization or to and from Internet Recipients or both. The following cmdlets can be used to configure this agent on the Hub Transport server:

❑ `Disable-JournalRule`

❑ `Enable-JournalRule`

❑ `Get-JournalRule`

❑ `New-JournalRule`

❑ `Remove-JournalRule`

❑ `Set-JournalRule`

Anti-Spam Agents

The Edge Transport server role guarantees message hygiene using anti-spam agents by evaluating the following things about every email message: the message sender, the sending server, IP address and domain, the destination Recipient, and the contents of the message. Based on these, anti-spam agents are implemented by the Edge Transport server. A spam confidence level (SCL) is stamped on each message evaluated and messages can be accepted or rejected based on the organization's configuration. Anti-spam filtering installed by default includes the following:

- ❑ IP Allow List
- ❑ IP Allow List Provider
- ❑ IP Block List
- ❑ IP Block List Provider
- ❑ Content Filtering
- ❑ Sender Filtering
- ❑ SenderID Sender Reputation
- ❑ Recipient Filtering
- ❑ Recipient Filtering

These are discussed in the following sections.

IP Allow List

This feature indicates the IP addresses that are always allowed to connect to and transmit email messages to this server. You can configure the feature to accept connections from individual IP addresses or from ranges of IP addresses. IP addresses found in this list will bypass most anti-spam agents except sender and Recipient filtering. The following cmdlets are used to view and configure the IP Allow List:

- ❑ Get-IPAllowListConfig
- ❑ Set-IPAllowListConfig
- ❑ Add-IPAllowListEntry
- ❑ Get-IPAllowListEntry
- ❑ Remove-IPAllowListEntry

IP Allow List Provider

IP Allow List Providers maintain lists of email sending domains that can be relied on to not send junk email. The following cmdlets are used to view and configure the IP Allow List Provider:

- ❑ Get-IPAllowListProvider
- ❑ Add-IPAllowListProvider
- ❑ Remove-IPAllowListProvider
- ❑ Set-IPAllowListProvider
- ❑ Test-IPAllowListProvider
- ❑ Get-IPAllowListProvidersConfig
- ❑ Set-IPAllowListProvidersConfig

IP Block List

This list contains IP addresses that are never allowed to connect to the Edge Transport or Hub Transport server if configured on it. You can specify individual or a range of IP addresses. The following cmdlets can be used to view and modify the IP Block List:

- ❏ Get-IPBlockListConfig
- ❏ Set-IPBlockListConfig
- ❏ Get-IPBlockListEntry
- ❏ Add-IPBlockListEntry
- ❏ Remove-IPBlockListEntry

IP Block List Provider

This feature allows real-time block list provider services to track servers on the Internet suspected of sending UCE mails. While you specify providers to use, you can also specify domains that would bypass this real-time block list. The following cmdlets can be used to view and configure this feature:

- ❏ Get-IPBlockListProvider
- ❏ Set-IPBlockListProvider
- ❏ Add-IPBlockListProvider
- ❏ Remove-IPBlockListProvider
- ❏ Test-IPBlockListProvider
- ❏ Get-IPBlockListProvidersConfig
- ❏ Set-IPBlockListProvidersConfig

If you have previously configured the anti-spam connection filtering in your Exchange 2003 environment and you are migrating to Exchange Server 2007, you can take advantage of a new tool now available from Microsoft that migrates your list of allow/deny addresses, block list providers, blocked senders, and domains. You can download the tool from the following link: microsoft.com/downloads/details.aspx?FamilyId=805EAF35-EBB3-43D4-83E4-A4CCC7D88C10&displaylang=en.

Content Filtering

This feature filters junk email by a method that learns what is and what is not spam. This agent filters all messages that come through all Receive Connectors on the server. It is not a best practice, however, to filter messages from trusted partners or from inside the Exchange organization to reduce the chance of false positives. The contents of the message are constantly scanned for specific words or phrases and over time what constitutes spam can be easily determined. You can set the message filtering threshold, how content is analyzed, and what action to take when the filter detects junk email. The underlying technology used is the Intelligent Message Filter (IMF), which existed in Exchange Server 2003 but is now greatly improved. Microsoft Anti-spam Update Service provides updates regularly to ensure that the most up-to-date information is always included when the Intelligent Message Filter runs.

The Content Filter agent assigns a spam confidence level (SCL) rating to each message. The SCL rating ranges from 0 to 9 with a higher rating indicating that a message is more likely to be spam. If a message is detected to be spam, the Content Filter agent can be configured to delete the message, reject the message, or quarantine the message. Some organizations may configure the Content Filter agent to delete messages that have an SCL rating of 8 or higher, reject messages with an SCL rating of 7, and quarantine messages with an SCL rating of 5.

To accommodate false positives, in which case a valid message is incorrectly tagged as spam, the spam quarantine feature is available in the Content Filter agent to provide a temporary storage location for messages that are identified as spam and that should not be delivered to a user mailbox inside the organization. After a configured period of time, the messages can be deleted.

Another protection available in the Content Filter agent is the ability to act on a safelist aggregation. This feature collects safelists that Outlook or Outlook Web Access clients configure for users that can always send to them regardless of the SCL rating of the message. The Content Filter agent takes this information and makes it available on the Edge Transport server. The following cmdlets can be used to configure the Content Filter agent:

- ❏ Get-ContentFilterConfig
- ❏ Set-ContentFilterConfig
- ❏ Add-ContentFilterPhrase
- ❏ Get-ContentFilterPhrase
- ❏ Remove-ContentFilterPhrase
- ❏ Update-SafeList

To configure the Content Filter agent, several steps are required:

1. First the Content Filter agent must be enabled on the Edge Transport server. Where multiple Edge Transport servers exist, it must be configured separately on each. To enable the Content Filter agent, run following:

```
Set-ContentFilterConfig -Enabled $True
```

2. By default, though, the Content Filter agent is enabled on the Edge Transport server for external messages. It can, however, be enabled for internal messages also. This cannot be performed via the Exchange Management Console. To enable content filtering for internal messages, run the following:

```
Set-ContentFilterConfig -InternalMailEnabled $True
```

3. Next, if you are going to configure a quarantine SCL threshold, a spam quarantine mailbox must be specified. This will enable all messages at or greater than the quarantine threshold to be sent to a configured email address. To achieve this, it is recommended that a separate Exchange Server database be large enough to hold quarantined messages. Then create an Active Directory user account with an Exchange mailbox and create a profile for it.

4. Next, configure the Content Filter agent with the email address of the spam quarantine mailbox configured earlier. You can do that by running the following command:

```
Set-ContentFilterConfig -QuarantineMailbox spam@ExchangeExchange.local
```

5. Finally, configure the SCL threshold for messages and continually monitor the spam quarantine mailbox. In here you can use the Send Again option in Outlook to release legitimate messages by resending the original message. You can also monitor the agent log for false positives and adjust the SCL threshold accordingly. To diagnose why a message is flagged as spam, you can review the anti-spam stamp and anti-spam report on the message by looking at the Internet headers in Outlook 2007. Here is an example of an anti-spam report:

```
X-MS-Exchange-Organization-Antispam-Report: SenderOnRecipientSafeList
X-MS-Exchange-Organization-SCL: -1
```

X-MS-Exchange-Organization-SenderIdResult: PASSJunk E-Mail Filter

Because anti-spam is a two-prong approach, on the client side, the Outlook Junk E-Mail filter evaluates whether a message should be treated as a junk email based on factors such as time, time message was sent, message content, and other data collected by the Exchange Server anti-spam filters. When a message is flagged by this filter, it is delivered to the junk email folder rather than the inbox. The Recipient can manually move the message to the inbox and add the sender into its safelist if it's a legitimate sender.

Sender Filtering

You use this feature to specify a list of email senders that you want to block receipt of email from. You can configure the feature to block individuals, single domains, or entire domain hierarchies. You can also specify how Exchange Gateway Services will respond when the blocked sender transmits a message to this server. The following cmdlets can be used to view and configure SenderID filtering:

❑ Get-SenderFilterConfig

❑ Set-SenderFilterConfig

SenderID

This feature, currently a proposed standard, was established to counter email domain spoofing and to provide greater protection against phishing. You can use this feature to check the sender's Purported Responsible Address (PRA) when the Edge Transport server receives an email. You can also specify how Edge Transport server should handle messages from senders lacking an acceptable PRA. The following cmdlets allow you to configure SenderID:

❑ Get-SenderIdConfig

❑ Set-SenderIdConfig

❑ Test-SenderId

Sender Reputation

The Sender Reputation feature collects information about recent email messages received from specific IP addresses. As it evaluates each message, if a sender IP address appears to be the source of junk or spam email, the source is added to the list of blocked IP addresses. Other parameters can be configured such as the length of time the sender will be blocked. The following cmdlets will be covered in this section:

❑   `Get-SenderReputationConfig`

❑   `Set-SenderReputationConfig`

Recipient Filtering

This agent's feature specifies email Recipients from which the server will not accept emails. It can be configured to block individuals, domains, or even messages to users not included in the Recipient directory. You can configure exceptions as well as how the Edge Transport server will respond when a message is blocked. The following cmdlets are used to view and configure this agent:

❑   `Get-RecipientFilterConfig`

❑   `Set-RecipientFilterConfig`

Summary

This chapter discussed the new Exchange server role introduced in Exchange Server 2007 — the Edge Transport server role. This role is unique among other server roles because it is not directly dependent on Active Directory and is installed in a perimeter network. The focus of the Edge Transport server is for inter-organizational email communication, message hygiene, and security. It tackles Unsolicited Commercial E-mail (UCE) and risk of denial of service attacks perpetrated via email.

You also saw how the edge subscription and edge synchronization processes enable the Edge Transport server obtain information from Active Directory via its replication to the ADAM directory service. Although you can manually configure Send and Receive Connectors after installing the Edge Transport server, it is highly recommended that you use the edge subscription and synchronization processes to associate the Edge Transport server to an Active Directory site in your Exchange organization. Only when this is done can you use the Recipient lookup feature or safelist aggregation. You also saw the features introduced in Exchange Server 2007 SP1 to enhance the functionality of the Edge Transport server.

You looked at the two scenarios for integrating the Edge Transport server into an organization: when it is manually configured and when edge subscription and EdgeSync are used.

Finally, this chapter looked at Edge Transport server cloning and message hygiene using transport agents.

10

Unified Messaging

When Microsoft released Exchange Server 2007, one of the coolest features included was Unified Messaging. For those who are not familiar with this, Unified Messaging, or UM (pronounced either as the two letters individually or as the interjection that speech coaches despise), is a role within Exchange that allows users to receive voicemail and faxes directly to their mailboxes! It will even let you dial a number and then play your messages, read your email, and dictate your schedule to you. This role also integrates with Microsoft Office Communicator Server to create one of the feature-rich IP voice systems to date. UM fills a very important niche because it allows IT departments to reduce the complexity of the infrastructure and enables them to retire aging voice mail platforms. For more information on UM please see `microsoft.com/technet/prodtechnol/exchange/2007/evaluate/overview/default.mspx`.

To get the most out of this chapter, you must have the UM role installed on a server (see Chapter 3 for installation information). It is also advantageous, though not required, to have a cursory understanding of how phone systems, PBXs, and audio encoding work.

In Chapter 3 you learned how to install the UM role. Now you are going to build from there and configure UM with the minimum amount of options to make it work. From there you add onto these cmdlets, introduce new cmdlets, configure the UM Virtual Directory, and finish up the chapter with a list of the UM cmdlets. For an authoritative definition of every cmdlets option, refer to the Microsoft Exchange Server 2007 help file (also knows as the CHM file).

This chapter covers the following topics:

- ❏ Creating UMDialPlan, UMIPGateway, UMMailboxPolicy, and UM Server
- ❏ Using the `Get-UM` cmdlets to retrieve data
- ❏ UM user management
- ❏ AutoAttendant management
- ❏ Removing and disabling UM features

Figure 10-1 shows the architecture and components used in a Unified Messaging environment.

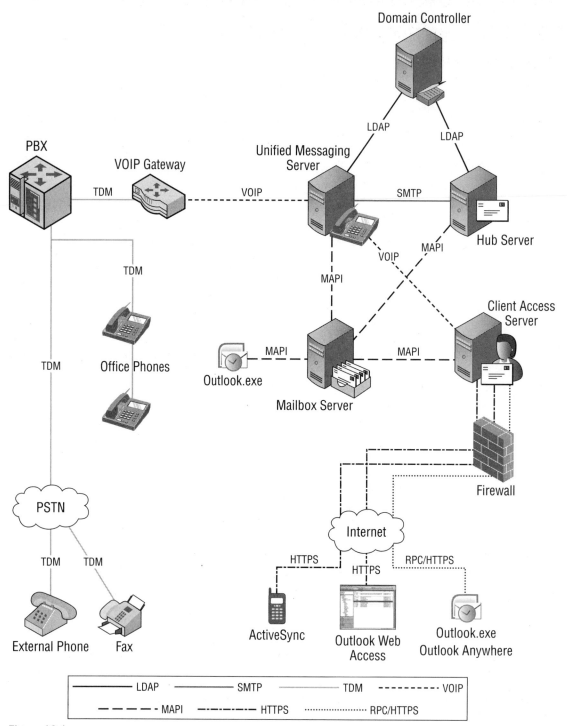

Figure 10-1

Creating UMDialPlan, UMIPGateway, and UMMailboxPolicy, and Setting up the UM Server

This section covers the following cmdlets:

- ❑ New-UMDialPlan
- ❑ New-UMIPGateway
- ❑ New-UMMailboxPolicy
- ❑ Set-UMServer
- ❑ Enable-UMMailbox
- ❑ Set-UMDialPlan
- ❑ Set-UMIPGateway

To get UM up and running you must first run a few cmdlets in order to have a working configuration. The first cmdlet is the New-UMDialPlan. There are two required parameters: the dial plan name and the number of digits in the extension. The Name refers to the name of the UM dial plan; in this instance it is test. The number of digits in extension refers to the number of digits in the end user's telephone number. For most organizations it is the last four in the phone number. The URI type is not necessary, but can be added if your system is not using TelExtn and is using E164 or SipName to receive information from the PBX. If you do not know how Exchange will communicate with the PBX, it would be wise to ask your PBX admin to find out what options your PBX has for interfacing with the UM server. For a list of supported connections, see microsoft.com/technet/prodtechnol/exchange/telephony-advisor.mspx. The last required option is to generate the UM mailbox policy. If you were to use the wizard in the EMC it would automatically create one. The syntax for the New-UMDialPlan is as follows:

```
New-UMDialPlan -Name <String> -NumberOfDigitsInExtension <Int32> [-
AccessTelephoneNumbers <MultiValuedProperty>] [-Confirm [<SwitchParameter>]] [-
DomainController <Fqdn>] [-FaxEnabled <$true | $false>] [-GenerateUMMailboxPolicy
<$true | $false>] [-NDREnabled <$true | $false>] [-TemplateInstance <PSObject>] [-
URIType <TelExtn | E164 | SipName>] [-VoIPSecurity <SIPSecured |Unsecured |
Secured>] [-WhatIf [<SwitchParameter>]] [<CommonParameters>]
```

In the following example, the UM mailbox policy is blank so you can learn what goes into a UM mailbox policy:

```
New-UMDialPlan -name test -NumberOfDigitsInExtension 4 -URIType TelExtn -
GenerateUMMailboxPolicy $false
```

The second component required in a working UM configuration is to configure the UM IP gateway. For the New-UMIPGateway cmdlet there are also three required parameters: name, IP address, and UM dial plan. The name is how the UM IP gateway will be referred to. The IP address of this device is what will originate the SIP conversation. The IP address can refer to a standalone device that acts as a bridge between PBX and the IP world via SIP, or it can be a card within the PBX that handles the SIP initiation.

Lastly, the UM dial plan will be the name of the dial plan created earlier. The New-UMIPGateway cmdlet has the following syntax:

```
New-UMIPGateway -Name <String> -Address <UMSmartHost> [-Confirm
[<SwitchParameter>]] [-DomainController <Fqdn>] [-TemplateInstance <PSObject>] [-
UMDialPlan <UMDialPlanIdParameter>] [-WhatIf [<SwitchParameter>]]
[<CommonParameters>]
```

In our case, we are able to use the NewUMIPGateway cmdlet to create a dial plan named test using the following command:

```
New-UMIPGateway -Name test -Address 2.4.191.254 -UMDialPlan test.
```

By specifying a dial plan, a default hunt group is automatically created and assigned to the UMIPGateway. If no dial plan is specified, the UMHuntgroup will have to be created and associated manually via the New-UMHuntGroup cmdlet. Creating the UM hunt group manually requires the setting the associated dial plan, the IP gateway of the SIP appliance, and a descriptive name.

The next step is to create the UM mailbox policy using the New-UMMailboxPolicy cmdlet. The UMMailboxPolicy cmdlet has the following syntax:

```
New-UMMailboxPolicy -Name <String> -UMDialPlan <UMDialPlanIdParameter> [-Confirm
[<SwitchParameter>]] [-DomainController <Fqdn>] [-TemplateInstance <PSObject>] [-
WhatIf [<SwitchParameter>]] [<CommonParameters>]
```

There are two required parameters for this cmdlet. The first is the name of the UM mailbox policy and the second is the associated dial plan:

```
New-UMMailboxPolicy -name UMpolicy1 -UMDialPlan test.
```

The final component that needs to be configured in order to have a working configuration is that the UM dial plan needs to be associated to the UM server. Using the Set-UMServer cmdlet with the -DialPlan parameter finishes the basic configuration:

```
Set-UMServer -Identity Server -DialPlan test
```

Now that the server-side components have been created, all that is left to do is enable users. To accomplish this, you use the Enable-UMMailbox cmdlet. This cmdlet has only two required parameters: the identity of the user that will be activated and the UMMailboxPolicy. The Enable-UMMailbox cmdlet has the following syntax:

```
Enable-UMMailbox -Identity <MailboxIdParameter> -UMMailboxPolicy
<MailboxPolicyIdParameter> [-AutomaticSpeechRecognitionEnabled <$true | $false>] [-
Confirm [<SwitchParameter>]] [-DomainController <Fqdn>] [-Extensions
<MultiValuedProperty>] [-IgnoreDefaultScope <SwitchParameter>] [-NotifyEmail
<String>] [-PilotNumber <String>] [-Pin <String>] [-PinExpired <$true | $false>] [-
SIPResourceIdentifier <String>] [-ValidateOnly <SwitchParameter>] [-WhatIf
[<SwitchParameter>]] [<CommonParameters>]
```

For the sake of this writing, it is best practice to include the `Extensions` parameter. For the identity of the user, any of the following are accepted for the `Identity` parameter:

❑ **ADObjectID:** `exchangeexchange.com\sales\john doe` The syntax of the AD object is `domain\OU\name`.

❑ **GUID Ex:** (43CBD6FF-AC3B-4A8F-8906-F14EB33A0B31) A GUID is a globally unique identifier. Think of it as a serial number or a MAC address. Two GUIDs cannot be the same in an Active Directory forest.

❑ **DN:** The distinguished name can be the full name.

The distinguished name is the LDAP listing of the user. It contains the user's full name the organizational unit (OU) that they reside in as well as the domain name. The following is an example of a user whose full name is John Doe, resides in the Sales OU, and is in the domain `exchangeexchange.com`: `CN=John Doe,OU=Sales,DC=exchangeexchange,DC=com`.

❑ **Domain\Account – User account, and so on:** Typically this is the user's logon name that is used when the user logs in to the domain. Following a naming convention of the first initial of the first name and the complete last name, John Doe from sales would have the following logon name: `jdoe`.

❑ **UPN:** The UPN, or user principal name, is default the user's logon name @ domain. So for John Doe, it would be `jdoe@exchangeexchange.com`. The UPN, like the domain name and the GUID, must be unique to the domain.

❑ **LegacyExchangeDN:** Legacy DN is included for backward compatibility for previous versions of Exchange. `/o=ExchangeExchange/ou=Exchange Administrative Group (FYDIBOHF23SPDLT)/cn=Configuration/cn=Servers/cn=MB902`

❑ **SmtpAddress:** This is the address that the user uses to send/receive mail. For example: `John.Doe@exchangeexchange.com`.

❑ **Alias:** This is usually the short name of a user.

In the following example, the `-Extensions`, `-PIN`, `-PINExpired`, and `-UMMailboxPolicy` have been set to allow for a more functional UM user once you enable the UM mailbox:

```
Enable-UMMailbox -Identity john.doe@exchangeexchange.com -Extensions 4242 -PIN
458236 -PINExpired $false -UMMailboxPolicy UMpolicy1
```

If everything on the PBX and network has been configured correctly, you have a basic working configuration that allows the UM server to receive voice mail, and for UM-enabled users to call in and have the voice mails, email, and calendars read to them. However, if you were to leave the UM cmdlets here and go to the next chapter you would be doing a great disservice to all the really cool features that make the users forget their antiquated, feature-lacking voice mail systems.

Now that you've run a couple of UM cmdlets, you're going to review the configurations that you have made. In order to do this you use the cmdlets that start with "Get-UM". The `Get-UMDialPlan` will show the dial plan that was just created, the name of the server that it has been applied to, and the current status (enabled).

`Get-UMIPGateway` shows the configured UM IP gateway. Remember if you want to see more detailed information on any of the `Get-*` cmdlets, pipe the output to a `Format-List` (`| fl`) to see more information.

Use `Get-UMMailboxPolicy | fl` to see the output of what you created with the `New-UMMailboxPolicy` and to see all the additional parameters that can be configured for a more feature-rich deployment of UM!

The `Get-UMServer` shows the configuration applied to the UM server. If no additional parameters are specified with the cmdlet, it displays the server name, the dial plan, languages installed for the UM role, and the status.

To verify which users have Unified Messaging enabled, the `Get-UMMailbox` cmdlet returns all active UM users. This cmdlet also shows users who have been disabled in Active Directory, but are still UM enabled.

A quick review shows that you have created the UMDialPlan, UMIPGateway, and the UMMailboxPolicy. From there you applied these to the UM server and enabled a test UM user. From there you used some of the `Get-UM*` cmdlets to verify your configurations. Now you build on some of these cmdlets to enable and set more of the features Unified Messaging has to offer.

Setting UM Features using the Set-UM Cmdlets

Once the initial UM components have been created using the New-UM cmdlets, additional functionality can be added or removed through the use of the Set-UM cmdlets. This section deals with the following cmdlets:

❑   `Set-UMDialPlan`

❑   `Set-UMIPGateway`

❑   `Set-UMMailboxPolicy`

Setting the UM Dial Plan

One of the first things to change after the system has been configured is the options that are available under the `Set-UMDialPlan`. The Set-UMDialPlan cmdlet has a dizzying array of options to allow for customizing dial plans. Some features that are configurable within the dial plan deal with changes to the fax status, audio encoding, country codes, default languages, announcements, security, recordings, greetings, and the operator extension. None of these are required parameters, but if you are replacing an aging voice mail system, it is important to provide the same level of features, if not more features, than the old system. Unified Messaging has native support for faxing capabilities. If your PBX can pass a T.38 tone or is fax over IP (FoIP) capable, the UM server can be configured to receive faxes. To enable the UM server to receive faxes use the `Set-UMDialPlan -Identity "dial plan name" -FaxEnabled`

$true. If at a later time you do not want to use faxing, or decide to use a different dial plan, it can be disabled using the same cmdlet with the $false option. During our initial implementation of Unified Messaging a lot of testing was done with different audio codecs. UM has three options available: G711, WMA, and GSM. Each codec has a different sampling rate and will result in a different size of the voice mail file attachment. By default this is set to WMA, but you may need to change it to compensate for poor voice quality or latency issues. To change the audio codec, you pass one of the three options, G711, WMA, or GSM, to the AudioCodec parameter. If you want to change the list of users that someone can choose from when they call in and try to dial by name, you use the ContactScope parameter. This parameter has five options to choose from: DialPlan, GlobalAddressList, Extension, AutoAttendantLink, and AddressList. By default the mailbox users that are included in the dial plan.

UM administrators will want to configure the country or region code (CountryOrRegionCode) as well as the international access code (InternationalAccessCode) to allow for international dialing or dialing outside of your area. This does not need to be configured for area codes in the United States. Also set the outside line access code if users typically have to dial 9+number (OutsideLineAccessCode).

The next set of options pertains to user settings within the call. To keep the number of available lines open for users to call in, it may be necessary to adjust the number of times an incorrect logon can be entered before the call is disconnected. This is accomplished with the LogonFailuresBeforeDisconnect parameter. The default value is 3. During the pilot phase of UM, it would be prudent to set this value higher, because it may take users some time to acclimate to this new voice mail system. Once the user has successfully entered a PIN and is navigating through the call tree, two parameters may need to be modified to compensate for user error and latency. Input failures (InputFailuresBeforeDisconnect) refers to the number of times a user can incorrectly enter input into the system, either verbally or via DTMF, before the call is disconnected. By default this value is set to 3. The other parameter is the input timeout (InputTimeout). The value for this parameter is measured in seconds and is 5 by default. In this case pilot phase of UM a lot of effort was concentrated on simulating different kinds of user behaviors. We tested users who would enter each digit very slowly, all the way up to users who had the call tree memorized and would dial four of five digits in rapid succession. These two parameters help compensate for both ends of the spectrum. For your users to successfully use the voice mail functions, it is important to understand the user base and adjust the timeout value and the retry options. Two other useful functions are the DialByNamePrimary and DialByNameSecondary functions. Dial by name is set by default to search by last name when the user utilizes the dialing features within UM. This parameter has three values that allow the user to search by first name, last name, or SMTP address. The dial by name secondary allows the UM admin to create a secondary look key based off one of the three mentioned values.

Users can receive informational announcements when they dial into UM. This can be useful for disseminating information to users about office hours, weather conditions, or other reminders. These files need to be in .wav file format. To enable this feature two parameters need to be passed to the Set-UMDialPlan cmdlet. The first enables the informational announcements and the second is the location of the file that is to be set as the announcement. So to enable a WAV file called Summer Hours.wav, located in D:\announcements, the command would look as follows: Set-UMDialPlan -InfoAnnouncementEnabled true -InfoAnnouncementFilename D:\announcements\SummerHours.wav. The true could also be replaced with $Uninterruptible if you do not want users to escape out of the message.

To complement informational announcements, the UM administrator can also modify the welcome greeting or completely turn it off. The informational announcement plays when a user calls into the UM system and it can be modified to include corporate branding with the VM system. Implementation and the requirements are similar to the informational announcements. Two parameters are passed to the dial plan: one to enable the greeting and the other to specify the location of the greeting WAV file. The following replaces the default greeting with the corporate greeting. The WAV file is located in `D:\greetings`. `Set-UMDialPlan -WelcomeGreetingEnabled $true -WelcomeGreetingFilename "D:\Greetings\Corporate Greeting.wav"`. Remember to quote any input that has spaces in it or the command will fail.

At least once, everyone has enjoyed a voice mail from someone who accidentally called and left a voice mail while walking around in the mall or with their phone in their pocket. To keep these errant calls from going on forever, or until the server runs out of space to record the voice mail, UM has included a `MaxRecordingDuration`. By default it is quite generous at 20 minutes; however this can be set to a more conservative value if needed. In the event that someone were to accidentally dial a UM-enabled extension and attempt to leave a voice mail with no audio, the UM server sends a disconnect command after 5 seconds of no audio input. This is advantageous and helps reduce the number of calls leaving accidental voice mail. If for some reason the UM administrator wanted to change the idle timeout value, he would use the `-RecordingIdleTimeout` parameter with a value that better suited his needs. There is one other option that is applicable to durations. Maximum call duration sets the amount of time in minutes that a UM user can have an active session before being disconnected. This setting is for all activity in a single call. Using UM to read all the email that you missed while taking the summer off to go backpacking across Europe may require multiple calls because this feature terminates a call once it has reached the maximum call time. By default this is set to 30 minutes, which should be enough time for all but the most aggressive UM users to have their email, voice mail, and calendaring notices read to them. However, if the need arises to modify the timeout value, the `MaxCallDuration` can be invoked. A word of caution: modifying this value affects port availability on the IP gateway appliance. If users stay connected longer, there may be times where there are not enough lines available to accept new requests. Changing this value should be done only after analyzing the impact this will have to availability.

In all phone systems, whether public or private, there has been one ambiguous person who handles all manual intervention of call screening, forwarding, and transferring of calls: the operator. This chapter would be incomplete and users everywhere would be remiss if Unified Messaging did not include operator support. Alas, there is an option within the `Set-UMDialPlan` that sets the operator extension, so you do not lose your connection to the master of call transferring. By using `Set-UMDialPlan OperatorExtension`, the operator will still be available as an option with the call tree. This option is also necessary in order to allow transferring to the operator.

For UM administrators who will be dealing with Unified Messaging deployments that span across multiple languages, Unified Messaging can be configured with language packs that allow users to interact with the system in their native language. At the time of this writing, Microsoft Exchange 2007 Unified Messaging supports the following languages:

Language	-DefaultLanguage Value
Dutch	nl-NL
English (Australia)	en-AU
English (Great Britain)	en-GB
English (United States)	en-US
French	fr-FR
French (Canadian)	fr-CA
German	de-DE
Italian	it-IT
Japanese	ja-JP
Korean	ko-KR
Mandarin (People's Republic of China)	zh-CN
Mandarin (Taiwan)	zh-TW
Portuguese (Brazil)	pt-BR
Spanish	es-ES
Spanish (Mexico)	es-US
Swedish	sv-SE

If the language pack is not installed, DefaultLanguage *causes an error.*

For an updated list, refer to the following Microsoft TechNet site: http://technet.microsoft.com/en-us/exchange/bb330845.aspx.

After exploring some of the additional features that the UM dial plan contains, some examples of a Set-UMDialPlan may look like this:

```
Get-UMDialPlan | Set-UMDialPlan -FaxEnabled $true -MaxRecordingDuration 5 -
ContactScope GlobalAddressList -InternationalAccessCode 011 -OutsideLineAccessCode 9
Set-UMDialPlan -Identity UM901 -InfoAnnouncementEnabled $true -
InfoAnnouncementFilename "D:\Info files\Company news.wav" -Language en-GB
```

Setting the UM IP Gateway

When we created a new UM IP Gateway earlier using the New-UMIPGateway cmdlet, it was a minimal configuration. A few additional parameters within the Set-UMIPGateway allow for increased functionality as well as a simulation mode to assist in UM testing. We briefly discuss the options within the Set-UMIPGateway here.

In the course of piloting a UM rollout, there may be instances where there is a split voice mail system within the infrastructure. This may include the legacy voice mail systems as well as the pilot rollout of Unified Messaging. To accomplish a pilot integration or a full system cut over, there may be one or more SIP gateways deployed. Each gateway appliance is defined by a unique name that in subsequent terms is referred to as the identity, as well as the IP address of the appliance. There also may be times when the IP address of the gateway changes and the UM server needs to be updated to show the new IP of the appliance. To accomplish this, use the `Set-UMIPGateway` cmdlet. Remember that the `identity` parameter is required in all of these set commands. When the UM IP gateway is created, an IP address is required for the SIP conversation to take place. If the IP address of the appliance changes, you use the `address` parameter to define the new IP address of the IP gateway.

Another feature is the use of outbound calls from the IP gateway. These are typically IP to PBX calls. This can be used for a Unified Messaging and OCS VoIP deployment, or to utilize the "play on phone" feature that is available for voice mails from within Outlook 2007. If this setting is disabled, the play on feature doesn't work, which eliminates the "play on phone" feature from within Outlook 2007, but still allows for call transfers from within UM. To enable or disable this feature, use the `OutCallsAllowed` and set the Boolean value to `$true` or `$false`.

By default the port that SIP conversations originate from on the IP gateway is 5060. If there is a need to run this on an off-number port, the IP gateway can be modified via use of the `Port` parameter. This parameter takes any port in the IP stack. Remember that using an off-numbered port in hopes that it will trick a hacker is not a good security practice. Security by obscurity will not defeat a dedicated hacker. If increased security is the end result, deploy an encrypted solution and configure the UM dial plan to use `VOIPSecurity $true`. The `status` parameter allows the UM admin to set the operation of the IP gateway to one of three values: `Enabled`, `Disabled`, or `NoNewCalls`. Setting this parameter to a nonenabled status can be useful when maintenance is necessary on the IP gateway.

The last feature for setting the IP gateway pertains to a simulation mode. This mode is either set to `Simulator $true` or `Simulator $false` and is used to test connectivity and functionality to the UM server. An IP gateway is not necessary if a pilot user is using the Unified Messaging test phone. The test phone is an application that can be installed on a PC and configured to connect to the UM server to test the unified messaging components without the use of an IP gateway. This may be of particular benefit for test labs, or Exchange administrators looking to provide a proof of concept on the increased functionality of Exchange Server 2007.

Setting the UM Mailbox Policy

When the original UM mailbox policy was created, only the two required parameters (the name of the policy and the associated dial plan) were provided. Because that example was simplistic in nature, we will build off of it and describe some of the other parameters that you can use to provide customization to UM users.

Any configuration changes that are issued with the `Set-UMMailboxPolicy` cmdlet require that the `Identity` parameter be specified. Although the `Identity` parameter is positional and providing the value is sufficient, while getting used to PowerShell it is recommended to include it.

The first modifiable option is to allow common patterns (`AllowCommonPatterns`) within the PIN. This parameter allows for a tradeoff between ease of use for the end user and a best practice for the security of passwords. When modifying this parameter a thorough analysis of your company's security policies should be performed to keep the users' PINs acceptable within your security policy. Remember, the PIN is a password to the voice mail of a user. If someone guesses a trivial PIN for a member of executive management or another employee with access to sensitive information, he would be able to read and respond to that user's email, voice mail, and calendar. Consider the ramifications of this setting before actually setting it.

Access to dialing another user's extension or to dial outside the country can be controlled on a user-by-user basis also. The two parameters that control this are `AllowDialPlanSubscribers` and `AllowExtensions`. Allowing the dial plan subscribers lets users dial an extension within the same dial plan without any of the prefixing. This would typically be used for interoffice communication and is set to `$true` by default. Setting `AllowExtensions` provides the ability for users to dial the number of digits in the extension that was set in the `New-UMDialPlan` cmdlet.

Unified Messaging sends emails that fall into the following categories: missed calls, voice mails, fax text, UM enabling, and for PIN resets. The following paragraphs describe how to modify the appearance of the text that is contained within the body of the emails.

When a UM-enabled user misses a call, an email will be sent to that user. By default the text specifies that you missed a call and then displays the inbound number. Depending on how the PBX is configured that the IP gateway is connected to, there may be times where the inbound number is just a single digit or a two-digit code. This is not an error in the UM logic, rather in the way the PBX is passing call data to the UM server. There are two ways to change this behavior from the UM server's perspective. The first is to create an entry in the GAL that maps the two-digit number to an identity. For example, if you receive missed calls or emails from 42, you can create a contact that maps 42 to Exchange Unified Messaging Missed Call Assistant. It is more aesthetically pleasing than a missed call by 42. The second option is to turn off missed call notifications. Not many phone systems provide this functionality now, so the loss of functionality may be transparent to the end user. To accomplish this use the `AllowMissedCallNotifications` and set the value to `$false`.

Changing the fax text produces the same result and has the same limitation as the missed call notification. The text is limited to 512 bytes. To change the text use the `FaxMessageText` and enclose the information that you want displayed in the email in quotes. The voice mail text is similar to the previous two parameters and can be changed with the `VoiceMailText` parameter.

When users have their account UM enabled or re-enabled, an email is sent from Microsoft Exchange to the user. The email body will contain the basic "Welcome to Exchange Unified Messaging" with the extension and the PIN. There is an opportunity to add value especially in this email by directing users how to log in to the UM system via their phone and change their PIN. This will assist in leveraging the automation of the UM-generated email and help reduce service desk calls. At this point it may also be advantageous to put into the email how users can reset their PIN. There are three correct ways for end users to change their PIN. Users can use the UM system to change their PIN if they remember their old PIN. If the users have access to Microsoft Office Outlook 2007 they can change their PIN from within the Tools ⇨ Options ⇨ Voice Mail menu. The last way to perform a PIN reset request is to log in to OWA, click Options, and then click Voice Mail. Within the page there is a link to reset the PIN.

The last type of email that users will get from UM is the PIN reset email. Content from this email will contain the user's new PIN. To modify the text use the `ResetPINText` and add in any additional information that may be needed for the end users in order assist them in logging in with their new PIN.

Five PIN functions are contained within the `Set-UMMailboxPolicy` cmdlet. The reset PIN text has already been discussed, which leaves PIN length, PIN history, PIN lifetime, and logon failures before PIN reset. PIN length refers to the number of digits the users will have to enter into the phone system when they attempt to use UM. The range for the `MinPINLength` is from 4 to 24 with 6 being the default value. `PINHistoryCount` sets the value for the number of previous PINs to retain before the PIN can be used again. The default value is 5 but can range from 1 to 20. Think of this setting as being similar to the enforce password history value within password policies on the domain. The `PINLifetime` parameter is how long the issued PIN is good for. By default the value is 60, but can be set from 1 to 999. To prevent a user's password from ever expiring, pass the `PINLifetime` parameter with the `unlimited` value. During the pilot phase of a UM implementation, there may be times when correctly entering the PIN sounds like an easy task, but in all reality it is not. Timing issues between the user input and the timeout value, latency between the IP gateway and the UM server, or DTMF issues can prevent a user from successfully logging in to the UM system. For users to be able to gain access to the UM system, a reset PIN after too many failures can be configured. By default this value is set to 5 and can be set to 999 to disable automatic reset of users' PINs. To configure this setting, use the `LogonFailuresBeforePINReset` to set a value between 0 to 999.

One other feature that can be set in the UM mailbox policy pertains to the security of the user. After too many unsuccessful logon attempts, the UM portion of a user's account can be locked out. By default, this is set to 15, which will allow users to have multiple chances to access their account. If the default value is too relaxed, you can modify it with the `MaxLogonAttempts`. The value range for this is 1 to 999. If you are planning on using the PIN reset email, set the maximum logon attempts to a value higher than that of the PIN reset email, otherwise the account will become locked out before the reset is generated.

The last feature to set on the mailbox policy is the maximum greeting duration. By default it is set to 5 minutes, but can range from 1 to 10. A 5-minute greeting for a user's mailbox may be excessive, and can be corrected with the `MaxGreetingDuration` parameter.

To take some of the new parameters and put them into action, the following are applied to the mailbox policy:

```
Get-UMMailboxPolicy | Set-UMMailboxPolicy -AllowCommonPatterns $true -
FaxMessageText "Unified Messaging has a fax for you." -LogonFailuresBeforePINReset
5 -MaxGreetingDuration 1 -MinPINLength 4 -PINHistoryCount 12 -PINLifetime 30
Get-UMMailboxPolicy | Set-UMMailboxPolicy -AllowCommonPatterns $false -
AllowMissedCallNotifications $false -LogonFailuresBeforePINReset 1-AllowExtensions
$false
```

Retrieving UM Information Using the Get-UM Cmdlets

Thus far, we have been using PowerShell to set properties and values. It therefore would be necessary to see, or retrieve, the data that has been set. In order to do this, Exchange Server 2007 has shipped with a series of `Get-UM*` cmdlets. These wonderful cmdlets allow for the retrieval of data as well as using the data as pipelined input into other cmdlets. This section deals with the following cmdlets:

❑   `Get-UMAutoAttendant`
❑   `Get-UMDialPlan`

- ❑ `Get-UMHuntGroup`
- ❑ `Get-UMIPGateway`
- ❑ `Get-UMServer`
- ❑ `Get-UMVirtualDirectory`
- ❑ `Get-UMMailbox`
- ❑ `Get-UMMailboxPIN`
- ❑ `Get-UMMailboxPolicy`

When looking at the `Get-UM` cmdlets, they can be broken down into two categories, SIP/Server facing and user facing. The Sip/Server-facing cmdlets allow for the retrieval of the UMIPGateway, or a UMDialPlan name. The user-facing cmdlets deal with `UMMailboxPolicies` or a `UMMailboxPIN` number. First we discuss the SIP-facing `Get-UM` cmdlets.

During day-to-day operations, the UM administrator may want to see what the current call volume looks like on a particular server, dial plan, or gateway. `Get-UMActiveCalls` allows that. The syntax for `Get-UMActive` calls is as follows:

```
Get-UMActiveCalls [-DomainController <Fqdn>] [-Server <ServerIdParameter>]
[<CommonParameters>]
Get-UMActiveCalls -InstanceServer <UMServer> [-DomainController <Fqdn>]
[<CommonParameters>]
Get-UMActiveCalls -DialPlan <UMDialPlanIdParameter> [-DomainController <Fqdn>]
[<CommonParameters>]
Get-UMActiveCalls -IPGateway <UMIPGatewayIdParameter> [-DomainController <Fqdn>]
[<CommonParameters>]
```

If the cmdlet is run without any parameters, it will return statistics for the local server. However, it does allow for scoping down to the dial plan level using the `DialPlan` parameter, or the IP gateway using the `IPGateway` parameter. To pull statistics for a remote UM server, the `InstanceServer` parameter would be invoked along with the name of the remote UM server.

To retrieve settings for `UMAutoAttendants`, use `Get-UMAutoAttendant`. If the `Identity` parameter is not used it will display all `UMAutoAttendants` in Active Directory. Remember to see all information returned from a `Get-` cmdlet, use `|fl`.

`Get-UMDialPlan` has already been used to confirm some of the settings that were created earlier in the chapter. It has one optional parameter, `Identity`. If the `Identity` parameter is not specified, it will display information for all `UMDialPlans` in Active Directory.

`Get-UMHuntGroup` is used to display any hunt group that has been created. Earlier in the chapter, during the `New-UMIPGateway` creation, the hunt group used for this scenario was automatically created. To see the settings of a particular `UMHuntGroup`, include the `Identity` parameter.

`Get-UMIPGateway` is used to retrieve any `UMIPGateways` in Active Directory. This cmdlet also includes the option of displaying any `UMIPGateways` that were created to operate in a simulator mode. To view simulated UMPgateways, use the `IncludeSimulator` parameter.

Get-UMServer is used to retrieve information about UMServers. If the Identity parameter is not used, it will display all UMServers. This cmdlet will also show what UMDialPlans the UMServer is associated with.

Get-UMVirtualDirectory displays the current configuration of the UM virtual directory on all CAS servers, unless the Server parameter is invoked. Expanding the information using |fl will allow you to see the internal URL, external URL, as well as the authentication methods set. For more information about UMVirtualDirectory, see Chapter 6.

The next three cmdlets are user-facing. They deal with retrieving information that is user-specific.

Get-UMMailbox by default will list all users and whether or not they are UM enabled. This is a very flexible cmdlet that can be manipulated to display a number of different values. By default every user is listed. In larger environments that is painful. To look for a specific user, specify the Identity parameter. As input it will accept the ADObjectID, GUID, DN, domain\account, UPN, LegacyExchangeDN, SMTP address, or the alias. Using the Identity parameter will narrow down the search to a specific user. To change the scope of the search and to see just one OU, the OrganizationalUnit parameter can be used. It accepts the canonical name for the OU. To see just the UM-enabled users, run the following cmdlet:

```
Get-UMMailbox | where {$_.UMEnabled -eq $true}
```

Get-UMMailboxPIN is useful when working with users to see if they have locked out the UM portion of their account. If the Identity parameter is not used, it will display the PIN properties, not the actual PIN, of all UM users. If a user is specified, her lockout status as well as her PIN is shown. As input it will accept the ADObjectID, GUID, DN, domain\account, UPN, LegacyExchangeDN, SMTP address, or the alias.

The last user-facing UM cmdlet is Get-UMMailboxPolicy. This cmdlet will show all UM mailbox policies present. To look at a specific policy, use the Identity parameter. To see all of the values in the policy append | fl to the end of the cmdlet.

UM User Management

In the day-to-day support and administration of a UM environment, there will be the need to field requests from users to unlock accounts, reset PINs, and to disable and enable UM accounts. To perform these actions, there are a few additional UM cmdlets that can increase the efficiency of performing these actions. This section deals with the following cmdlets:

❑   Set-UMMailboxPIN

❑   Disable-UMMailbox

❑   Enable-UMMailbox

When a user incorrectly logs in too many times his account will become locked out. To date, there is no automatic unlocking interval and manual administrator intervention is required. The two ways to unlock the UM portion of the account are to use the GUI or the Set-UMMailboxPIN cmdlet. Using the cmdlet offers a greater degree of usability because it can be collaborated into a suite of cmdlets that could have a console application or a web-based front end created for them and allows service-desk personnel to perform user management functions. The other bonus to using cmdlets is that they can be used in addition to other personal information to create an employee self-service portal. To unlock the account the `Set-UMMailboxPIN` must have the `Identity` parameter. This parameter takes any of the following:

- ❑ **ADObjectID:** The syntax of the AD object is `domain\OU\name`. So for example, you might have this: `exchangeexchange.com\sales\john doe`

- ❑ **GUID Ex: (43cbd6ff-ac3b-4a8f-8906-f14eb33a0b31)**—A GUID is a globally unique identifier. Think of it as a serial number or a MAC address. Two GUIDs cannot be the same in an Active Directory forest.

- ❑ **DN:** The distinguished name can be the full name. The distinguished name is the LDAP listing of the user. It contains the user's full name, the organizational unit (OU) that he resides in, as well as the domain name. The following is an example of a user whose full name is John Doe, resides in the Sales OU, and is in the domain `exchangeexchange.com`: `CN=John Doe,OU=Sales,DC=exchangeexchange,DC=com`.

- ❑ **Domain\Account – User account:** Typically this is the user's logon name that is used when the user logs in to the domain. Following a naming convention of the first initial of the first name and the complete last name, John Doe from sales would have the following logon name: `jdoe`.

- ❑ **UPN:** The UPN, or user principal name, is default the user's logon name @ domain. So for John Doe, it would be `jdoe@exchangeexchange.com`. The UPN, like the domain name and the GUID, must be unique to the domain.

- ❑ **LegacyExchangeDN:** Legacy DN is included for backward compatibility for previous versions of Exchange. `/o=ExchangeExchange/ou=Exchange Administrative Group (FYDIBOHF23SPDLT)/cn=Configuration/cn=Servers/cn=MB902`

- ❑ **SmtpAddress:** This is the address that the user uses to send/receive mail. For example: `John.Doe@exchangeexchange.com`.

- ❑ **Alias:** This is usually the short name of a user.

If the PIN (`PIN`) is not specified, a new PIN will be automatically created and emailed to the user. The PIN Expired (`PINExpired`) is also not required and will assume that the PIN should be treated as an expired PIN and request the user to change it upon first successful login. When a PIN reset is performed with the `Set-UMMailboxPIN`, unless explicitly specified with the `LockedOut $true` parameter, the account will automatically become unlocked.

When a user is disabled in UM he will no longer be able to access any of the UM features and UM will no longer accept voice mail or faxes for the user. To disable a UM user, use the `Disable-UMMailbox` with the `Identity` parameter. There is one other parameter worth noting for this cmdlet. If you want to keep the user's configuration, extension, mailbox policy, and so on, then also add `KeepProperties $true` when disabling the user. This retains the user settings and when the user is enabled again via the `Enable-UMMailbox` cmdlet, the user information will not need to be re-entered.

If all UM-enabled users in sales needed to have their UM settings disabled, the following will disable all users in sales and retain their properties for activation at a later date:

```
Get-UMMailbox | where {$_.identity -match "Sales"} | Disable-UMMailbox -
KeepProperties $true -Confirm:$false
```

When introducing UM into an existing environment, there will already be an established user base. These users will not be able to automatically start using UM. Their accounts must first be configured and enabled for UM. In order to do that, the `Enable-UMMailbox` is used. This cmdlet has only two required parameters: the identity of the user that will be activated and the `UMMailboxPolicy`. However, for the sake of this writing, it is best practice to include the `Extensions` parameter. For the identity of the user, it will accept the ADObjectID, GUID, DN, domain\account, UPN, LegacyExchangeDN, SMTP address, or the alias.

The `Extensions`, `PIN`, `PINExpired`, and `UMMailboxPolicy` have been set to allow users to immediately access their UM mailboxes:

```
Enable-UMMailbox -Identity john.doe@exchangeexchange.com -Extensions 4242 -PIN
458236-PINExpired $false -UMMailboxPolicy UMpolicy1
```

AutoAttendants

Unified Messaging allows for the creation of AutoAttendants (AA). The creation of an AA can allow for internal or external users to dial a single number and be directed to various departments, and allow for different greetings based on business hours and other factors. The following paragraphs focus on creating a new UM AutoAttendant and adding features to the newly created AutoAttendant. This section deals with the following UM AutoAttendant cmdlets:

- ❑ `New-UMAutoAttendant`
- ❑ `Enable-UMAutoAttendant`
- ❑ `Set-UMAutoAttendant`

To create a new AutoAttendant, the `New-UMAutoAttendant` cmdlet is used. The New-UMAutoAttendany has the following syntax:

```
New-UMAutoAttendant -Name <String> -UMDialPlan <UMDialPlanIdParameter> [-Confirm
[<SwitchParameter>]] [-DomainController <Fqdn>] [-DTMFFallbackAutoAttendant
<UMAutoAttendantIdParameter>] [-PilotIdentifierList <MultiValuedProperty>] [-
SpeechEnabled <$true | $false>] [-Status <Enabled | Disabled>] [-TemplateInstance
<PSObject>] [-WhatIf [<SwitchParameter>]] [<CommonParameters>]
```

This cmdlet requires that a unique name for the AutoAttendant from within the forest be used, which is set by the `Name` parameter. The AA must be associated with a dial plan too. These are the only two required parameters to create an AutoAttendant:

```
New-UMAutoAttendant -Name PilotAA -UMDialPlan test.
```

Now this newly created dial plan will not work until it is enabled. It can either be set during the New-UMAutoAttendant creation by setting Status to enabled or enabled by using the Enable-UMAutoAttendant:

```
Enable-UMAutoAttendant -Identity PilotAA
```

The AutoAttendant has these main feature groups: business hours parameters, after hour parameters, and dial plan related parameters. The first two have all new parameters, and the dial plan has several features that are also listed in the UM dial plan.

Within the business hours parameters, the options available can be broken down further into four categories: custom prompts, key mapping, hours, and operator. If custom prompts are needed they will have to be in .wav file format. This is a requirement for all audio files within UM. Two parameters are necessary to enable custom prompts: BusinessHoursMainMenuCustomPromptEnabled and BusinessHoursMainMenuCustomPromptFilename. The first parameter expects a Boolean value. The second parameter is the location on the server where the .wav file resides. Once these two parameters are used with the Set-UMAutoAttendant cmdlet, during business hours, users will hear the new prompts that were just deployed.

To set the business hours key mapping, the map must first be created with the BusinessHoursKeyMapping parameter and then enabled with the BusinessHoursKeyMappingEnabled parameter. The business hours key mapping parameter is a multi-valued property that has three different ways to use it:

- ❏ "<key>,<name>,<extension>,,[promptFileName],[asrPhrase]"
- ❏ "<key>,<name>,,<autoAttendantName>,[promptFileName],[asrPhrase]"
- ❏ "<key>,<name>,,,<promptFileName>,[asrPhrase]"

The key value is a 1–9 number. This value is what the user presses when presented with this option. Zero is not used because it is reserved for the operator. Name is used for the logical grouping of the key. For example: "For sales press 1." The extension is the actual number for the user or the hunt group that will be dialed when the user presses the key. Prompt filename is the recorded .wav file for this key/name/extension set, and is optional in the first two, but required in the third. An ASR phrase is the automated speech recognition that a user can speak in lieu of pressing they corresponding key. To use the speech recognition feature, SpeechEnabled needs to be set to $true. Now that the key mapping has been generated, it must be enabled. To accomplish this, add the BusinessHoursKeyMappingEnabled $true to the Set-UMAutoAttendant cmdlet.

Now that some custom prompts have been added, and a key map has been generated, the next step is to determine the business hours functions. In this section you set the business hours, set the filename for the business greeting, and enable the greeting for this AutoAttendant. The business hours operator function is also covered.

The business hours schedule determines the day and time that all of the functions that have been set thus far will be used. The format of the values for BusinessHoursSchedule can be one of the following: "day.timeopen AM/PM-day.timeclose AM/PM" or "day.open-close". This parameter also accepts the time in "military time" and can span across days. To have 24x7 business hours, the parameter and value would look like this: `-BusinessHoursSchedule "mon.12:00 AM-sun.11:59 PM"` or `"mon.00:00-sun.23:59"`. If your office is open during the week from 9 AM to 5 PM, the parameter and value would be as follows: `Set-AutoAttendnat -Identity PilotAA -BusinessHoursSchedule -mon.0900-mon.1700, tue.0900-tue.1700, wed.0900-1700,thu.9:00 AM-7:00 PM,fri.09:00 AM-05:00 PM"`. Mixing AM/PM and 24-hour time within the same day will not work and will result in an error. For ease of management and to be aesthetically pleasing, simplify the business hours to use one format.

Like all greetings and prompts for UM, the business hours greeting can be modified to play a custom WAV file. There are two parameters needed to use the business hours greeting. The first sets the WAV file location, `BusinessHoursWelcomeGreetingFilename`, and the second enables/disables it, `BusinessHoursWelcomeGreetingEnabled`. The latter is a true/false Boolean value.

The last order of business for business hours is to decide whether to allow call transfer to the operator for service. By default this value is set to false. To enable this feature use `BusinessHoursTransferToOperatorEnabled` to set the value to `$true`. Some AutoAttendants may not want users to escape the call to the operator and keep them confined to the key mapping that was previously created. This setting only applies to the AutoAttendant, and not to the UM mailbox policy.

The after hours section uses the same of parameters that `Set-UMAutoAttendant` uses, but instead of all the parameters being prefaced with `BusinessHours`, they are replaced with `AfterHours`. The exact parameters are listed here:

- ❑ `AfterHoursKeyMapping`
- ❑ `AfterHoursKeyMappingEnabled`
- ❑ `AfterHoursMainMenuCustomPromptEnabled`
- ❑ `AfterHoursTransferToOperatorEnabled`
- ❑ `AfterHoursWelcomeGreetingEnabled`
- ❑ `AfterHoursWelcomeGreetingFilename`

Many of the features that are in the dial plan are also available for the AutoAttendant. Domestic and international groups are allowed. AutoAttendant users can be configured to call extensions, dial by name, and have informational and welcome greetings. There is one other parameter that is of particular interest. A holiday schedule can be set that will use a custom WAV file for each individual set holiday. `HolidaySchedule` has three values that are required and one optional value. To enable a special holiday for the 4th of July, the command would look like this:

```
Set-UMAutoAttendant -Identity -HolidaySchedule "name of holiday, wav file, start
day, [end day]"
Set-UMAutoAttendant -Identity PilotAA -HolidaySchedule "4th of July, 4th.wav,
7/4/2007"
```

Removing and Disabling UM Features

When a server or a UM component is no longer needed, a simple removal of the UM role from the UM server is not enough. The data is still present in Active Directory and can be assigned. The Exchange team has provided a series of disable and remove cmdlets that allow the Exchange administrator to disable functions or to remove them completely. This section of the chapter deals with clean and removal of the AutoAttendant, IP gateway, dial plans, hunt groups, UM-specific mailbox policies, and even the UM server itself. This section discusses the following cmdlets that are used to disable or remove UM properties:

- ❏   `Disable-UMServer`
- ❏   `Copy-UMCustomPrompt`
- ❏   `Disable-UMAutoAttendant`
- ❏   `Disable-UMIPGateway`
- ❏   `Enable-UMIPGateway`
- ❏   `Remove-UMAutoAttendant`
- ❏   `Remove-UMDialPlan`
- ❏   `Remove-UMHuntGroup`
- ❏   `Remove-UMIPGateway`
- ❏   `Remove-UMMailboxPolicy`
- ❏   `Remove-UMVirtualDirectory`

Disabling a UM resource does not remove the object from Active Directory; it prevents assignment of properties to the UM object and further processing of calls. This functionality is useful for temporarily suspending access to a feature. During the technology life cycle, a server will reach a period where it will be retired and replaced with a newer model. During that transitional period, one of the systems may need to be online but not necessarily taking production traffic. As the new UM server comes online, via the `Enable-UMServer` cmdlet, the old server will be disabled via the `Disable-UMServer` cmdlet. The `Disable-UMServer` only requires the name of the server to disable. Because the `Identity` parameter is positional, the `Identity` itself is not required, just the value. If a confirmation before disable is required, the `Confirm` parameter can be used. However, if an immediate termination of all calls is necessary, using the `Immediate` parameter set to `$true` will drop all calls.

The first UM server contains a share that contains all of the custom WAV files that are created for custom prompts. Before the first UM server in the organization is retired, the custom prompts will need to be moved to a different UM server and then have their publishing point updated. Using the `Copy-UMCustomPrompt` will copy the files to a new location and update the publishing point. `Copy-UMCustomPrompt` requires either a source path location, specified by the `Path` parameter, or the `TargetPath` designates which WAV file to copy from a publishing point and `UMAutoAttendant`, or the `UMDialPlan`. At the next UM update interval, the UM servers will copy the file locally.

Disabling an AutoAttendant prevents further use of the attendant, but keeps the setting stored in Active Directory. Being able to do this is useful when testing attendant features. To disable an AutoAttendant, all that is needed is the AA's identity. The cmdlet is `Disable-UMAutoAttendant -Identity Test`.

During the life cycle of any product, there are times where devices will need to have firmware or software patches applied. UM IP gateways are no exception. It may become necessary to temporarily remove the device from service to perform maintenance activities. The cmdlet to disable the UM IP gateway is `Disable-UMIPGateway`. The identity of the UM IP gateway is required. One other parameter for this command is the `Immediate` parameter. If this parameter is set to true, the UM server will drop all conversations immediately with the affected UM IP gateway. The UM IP gateway that was created earlier in the chapter was given the name `test`. To immediately end all calls to test the cmdlet would look like this:

```
Disable-UMIPGateway test -Immediate $true
```

When maintenance is complete on these devices they can be returned to service using the `Enable` set of cmdlets. Enabling the UM server is easy. All that is required is the name of the UM server. The cmdlet is `Enable-UMServer`. Once the server is enabled it will begin processing any available calls that it has in the associated UM dial plan. The UM IP gateway that was disabled to have some patches applied can now start taking calls again. The `Enable-UMIPGateway` is similar to its disable counterpart. All that is required is the identity of UM IP gateway. To enable our test gateway the cmdlet would look like this:

```
Enable-UMIPGateway -Identity test
```

When devices are no longer used or functionality no longer needed, they can be removed via the `Remove-*` set of cmdlets. These cmdlets will remove the associated data from Active Directory. At this time there is no undo function for a remove cmdlet. As a result, care should be taken when removing any UM object. With enable and disable the UM administrator had the ability to set the status of the UM server. It would seem logical that the UM server, then, would be able to be disabled using a similar cmdlet. This is not the case. Using `step.com /m:uninstall /r:u` is the only supported way to remove the UM server from the Exchange topology.

There are six `Remove` cmdlets. All require the `Identity` value as the only required value. Though this may seem simplistic in nature, there is a certain amount of preprocessing that must occur. The `UMDialPlan` cannot be removed if there are any `UMIPGateway` or `UMMailbox` policies associated with it. Any `UMMailboxPolicy` that the UM administrator wants to delete must have no users associated with the `UMMailboxPolicy`. So though these cmdlets may seem easy to use, the successful implementation of them depends largely on how well the pre-cleanup and disassociation of previous objects was performed. The six cmdlets to remove UM functions are as follows:

❑ `Remove-UMAutoAttendant`: Deletes the AA. No new calls to the configured extension will be processed.

❑ `Remove-UMDialPlan`: Removes the AA only if there is no associated `UMIPGateway` or `UMMailboxPolicy`.

❑ `Remove-UMHuntGroup`: Removes the `UMHuntGroup`. If all `UMHuntGroups` are removed from the associated `UMIPGateway`, no call processing will be performed.

❑ `Remove-UMIPGateway`: Removes the `UMIPGateway`. No further SIP conversations will be performed with this device.

❑   Remove-UMMailboxPolicy: Removes the UMMailboxPolicy, only if there are no UM user mailboxes using the UMMailboxPolicy.

❑   Remove-UMVirtualDirectory: Removes the specified virtual directory. This cmdlet is specific to CAS servers, not UM servers.

Summary

In this chapter the basic configuration of Unified Messaging through the use of PowerShell was explained. Dial plans, mailbox policies, IP gateways, and AutoAttendants were created using the New-UM* cmdlets. Once a base configuration was deployed, additional functionality was added through the use of the Set-UM* cmdlets. All UM settings can be verified through the use of the Get-UM* cmdlets.

Several important items have been discussed in this chapter. One of the most important items is to have an understanding of, or the ability to work with, the telco team and their terms. As with most new undertakings, a solid plan that lists goals, purpose, timeline, and a division of responsibility is crucial for the success of a new product deployment.

Part III

Working with PowerShell in a Production Environment

11

Exchange Server 2007 Routing

Routing determines how a message gets from a source server to its destination server. Routing decides on the best and least-expensive path a message takes when transferred between Exchange servers within an organization and to servers in other organizations. In Exchange Server 2000/2003, several components were involved in routing, including Link State, Routing Groups, Connectors, and Routing Group Masters. Routing Groups were logical groupings of Exchange servers determined by the administrator. In Exchange Server 2007, because the transport core functionality has changed as noted in Chapter 7, message routing has also been changed. Rather than using the Routing Engine found in Exchange 2000/2003, the Categorizer (see "The Transport Server Architecture" in Chapter 7) now has a routing stage that determines the ultimate destination for a message, selects a route to that destination, and selects and resolves the next hop for that destination to a server(s) and IP addresses.

Link state was one of the components of routing in Exchange 2000/2003 many Exchange administrators were happy to see go away. Although link state had some benefits, managing it in some cases required a significant overhead. In some large Exchange Server environments, the orgInfo packet, which holds the routing information for the organization, became quite large and caused significant network bandwidth utilization during data transfer among servers. Also, transient network and Active Directory replication problems caused connector oscillations. Rather than use a logical groups of servers, Exchange Server 2007 takes advantage of Active Directory site topology in routing messages within and outside an Exchange organization.

By the end of this chapter, you will be familiar with message routing and its components in Exchange Server 2007 as well as the few Exchange Management Shell cmdlets that can be used to manage message routing. This chapter covers the following topics:

❑   Routing changes in Exchange

❑   Basics of Exchange Server 2007 routing

❑ Routing troubleshooting

❑ How Active Directory sites affect message routing

❑ Coexistence with Exchange 2003 and link state considerations

The following cmdlets are covered in this chapter; some of these were also covered in earlier chapters.

❑ `Get-AdSite`

❑ `Get-AdSiteLink`

❑ `Get-TransportServer`

❑ `Get-SendConnector`

❑ `Get-RoutingGroupConnector`

❑ `Get-ExchangeServer`

❑ `Set-AdSite`

❑ `Set-AdSiteLink`

❑ `Set-TransportServer`

❑ `Set-SendConnector`

❑ `Set-RoutingGroupConnector`

❑ `New-SendConnector`

❑ `New-RoutingGroupConnector`

❑ `Remove-SendConnector`

❑ `Remove-RoutingGroupConnector`

Routing Changes in Exchange

Exchange Server 2007 introduces routing changes that take advantage of the existing Active Directory Service site topology and the underlying network to provide an efficient, deterministic routing topology. When Exchange Server 2007 coexists with Exchange 2003 or Exchange 2000, you must perform additional configuration tasks to support message routing between the server versions. The following table summarizes the changes in message routing between versions of Exchange Server.

Exchange Server 2007	Exchange 2000 Server and Exchange Server 2003
Exchange uses Active Directory sites to determine an intra-organizational routing topology. All Exchange Server 2007 computers are associated with a single routing group for the purposes of routing to earlier versions of Exchange Server.	Exchange uses routing groups to determine an intra-organizational routing topology.
Exchange determines the least cost route between Hub Transport servers by using Active Directory Service IP site link costs.	Exchange determines the least cost route between bridgehead servers by using Routing Group Connector costs.
Exchange uses direct relay to deliver messages between Hub Transport servers.	Exchange relays through bridgehead servers in each routing group in the routing path.
When Exchange can't connect, it uses the least cost routing path information to back off from the destination until a connection can be made to a Hub Transport server. Messages queue at the reachable site that is closest to the destination. This behavior is known as *queue at point of failure.*	When Exchange can't connect to the next hop in a routing path, it tries to reroute the message over an alternative path.
When a message is being sent to multiple recipients, Exchange delays message splitting until a fork in the routing path is reached. This behavior is known as *delayed fan-out.*	When a message is being sent to multiple recipients, message splitting occurs immediately after recipient resolution.
Each Hub Transport server queries Active Directory separately to retrieve the routing configuration used to calculate a routing table and to receive configuration updates.	Exchange uses a link state table to store a routing table and advertises configuration changes by using link state updates. The routing group master retrieves updates from Active Directory and coordinates the propagation of link state changes that are learned by servers in its routing group.

Basics of Exchange Server 2007 Routing

One of the most important changes in Exchange Server 2007 is the way basic mail routing is handled. Unlike in previous versions of Exchange, all mail now must flow through a Hub Transport server role. For example, in Exchange 2003, two users mailing each other on the same mailbox servers would never route through a bridgehead. This is an important change because now Exchange can guarantee that every message can have transport rules applied. One of the most requested features in Exchange is to apply a disclaimer message to emails. The new transport architecture makes this an easy thing to do.

Because of this new routing design, every Active Directory site that has a Mailbox server role must also have a least one Hub Transport server role. It does not mean *all* Active Directory sites must have a Hub Transport server role, only sites with Exchange servers in them.

Active Directory Site-Based Routing

The removal of routing and administrative groups in Exchange Server 2007 brings tighter integration with Active Directory. This change can be a source of frustration in organizations where the Exchange administrators have little interaction with the Directory administrators. Exchange administrators may feel that the new routing architecture removes a large part of what they controlled in the past. As this chapter shows, this is not entirely true. Even with Active Directory–based routing, it is possible to manipulate mail flow if needed. This chapter shows various solutions that enable these scenarios.

However, most organizations do not require custom routing and Active Directory has established an effective routing topology for its replication. This provides better return on investment on the company's investment in Active Directory.

Active Directory Sites

An *Active Directory site* is defined as a collection of well-connected TCP/IP subnets. Well-connected means reliable and fast connections, generally LAN-type connections. Active Directory sites typically closely reflect the physical network layout. Sites are the boundaries for Active Directory replication and they localize directory authentication.

Active Directory sites are connected by site links. Administrators can configure link cost, availability, and other properties. Active Directory automatically builds the replication topology based on the site configuration. Building the replication topology is the responsibility of the Knowledge Consistency Checker (KCC). The KCC runs on all domain controllers and on 15-minute intervals. Specifically, the Inter-Site Topology Generator (ISTG) on one domain controller evaluates the costs and checks on new or retired domain controllers. It passes this information to the KCC, which adds or removes connection objects to create the most efficient replication.

On an Exchange server, it is the Microsoft Exchange Active Directory Topology service that checks the site membership of the server against stored configuration information. If the site has changed, the service updates the server object in Active Directory with the new information. This process occurs when the service starts, and is verified every 15 minutes. The Topology service receives its information from the Net Logon service. Because the Net Logon service polls every 5 minutes, there can be up to a 20-minute latency between the time the site membership changes and the update to the server object.

The details of configuring Active Directory integration are coming up in the section called "Working with Active Directory Sites."

In addition to routing, Exchange uses Active Directory site membership in the following ways:

❑   The mailbox server to determine which Hub Transport servers are located in the same site.

❑   To prioritize the list of servers used for public folder referrals.

- ❑ The Unified Messaging server to determine which Hub Transport servers are located in the same site.

- ❑ The Client Access Server determines the site of the user's mailbox server and performs redirection if needed.

Route Selection Process

This section examines how Exchange chooses mail routes. Because of the tight Active Directory integration and changes in functionality for Exchange Server 2007, this results in many benefits to message routing including the following:

- ❑ **Implicit Connectors:** Explicitly creating connectors to route mail between Hub Transport servers is no longer required.

- ❑ **Deterministic Routing:** Routing is no longer determined by link state. Because of this, it is easier for an administrator to understand and predict the path a message takes.

- ❑ **Direct Connections:** Exchange attempts a direct connection to the destination server. It is no longer necessary to route the message through a series of hops.

Exactly how does transport select the route a message will take? Exchange Server 2007 follows some simple rules:

- ❑ The route is selected based on lowest cost only.

- ❑ Bifurcation, the process of breaking the message into copies for multiple recipients with different destinations, is delayed as long as possible.

- ❑ It attempts direct delivery unless message flow is controlled by other means, such as a Hub site.

- ❑ It relies on IP networks to provide redundancy at the network layer.

Note that in coexistence with legacy Exchange, there are additional considerations about connector restrictions. Exchange Server 2007 ignores most restrictions on Routing Group Connectors. These restrictions are discussed later in this chapter in the section on coexistence with Exchange 2003.

The process starts when the user clicks Send; the Microsoft Exchange Mail Submission service notifies an available Hub Transport server in the same Active Directory site. If the Hub Transport role is co-located on the mailbox server it will always be chosen. If the Hub Transport role is not co-located, the service uses a round-robin process to distribute the load. The Hub Transport server that is notified retrieves the message and begins transport processing.

The next step is to determine the ultimate destination, which is the end-to-end route. After it is selected, the route is not recalculated unless there are routing configuration changes. The route selection is calculated from a set of routing tables that are generated when the Microsoft Exchange Transport service starts. The information in the routing tables is logged. By default are they are located in C:\Program Files\ Microsoft\Exchange Server\TransportRoles\Logs\Routing.

Route selection uses an algorithm to match valid connectors against all connectors in the organization except Routing Connectors, until a single path is left. If no paths are left after running through the process, recipients are marked as unreachable or a non-delivery report (NDR) is generated. The algorithm is based on the following:

- ❑ Connector scope

- ❑ Target address space

- ❑ Connector restrictions

- ❑ The path with the lowest cost from source to destination, with the preference to stay within the Exchange Server 2007 routing group as long as possible

- ❑ The path with the least number of hops

- ❑ The first site alphanumerically sorted

The destination address is a combination of delivery type and domain. For example, sending a mail to `Jeffrey.Rosen@chicago.exchangeexchange.com` has a delivery type of SMTP, and a destination domain `exchangeexchange.com`. Exchange routing always tries to find the best match, which is defined by the number of characters that match to the address space configured on the connector. This concept is shown in the following table. The best match is `Chicago.exchangeexchange.com`.

Address Space	Count
`*.exchangeexchange.com`	21
`Chicago.exchangeexchange.com`	28
`Exchangeexchange.com`	-

During processing, the Hub Transport decides on the message routing. By default, the site link cost associated with Active Directory replication is used. This can be overridden by setting explicit Exchange routing costs. The section "Working with Active Directory Sites" explains the cmdlets used for this process.

After the route is selected, the message is relayed from the source to the next hop.

Next Hop Selection Process

The next hop selection process is responsible for getting the message as close to the ultimate destination as possible. There are different scenarios in which direct delivery may not be possible. For example, an administrator can force all mail delivery through a particular Active Directory site.

Part of the next hop selection process is to determine where the message will queue for delivery. There are five main types of delivery methods. Visually, an administrator can see this in the queue viewer, as shown in Figure 11-1.

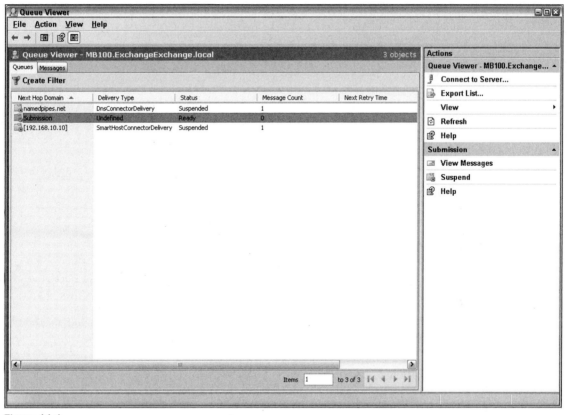

Figure 11-1

These destination types are defined as:

❑ **SmartHost Delivery:** This type of delivery is used when the recipients have external addresses. It routes to a server with a Send Connector that matches the recipient's domain address space. The message is delivered to the destination SmartHost.

❑ **DNS Delivery:** This type of delivery is used when the recipients have external addresses. The message routes to a server with a Send Connector that matches the recipient's domain address space. The message is delivered to the destination with a connector that uses DNS delivery.

❑ **Non-SMTP Gateway Delivery:** This delivery is used when the recipient's domain address space matches the address space of a Foreign Connector. The message is routed to the server that has the Foreign Connector on it.

❑ **SMTP relay:** This delivery is used when the delivery is to an Exchange user or system object and they are not in the local Active Directory site. The route is takes depends on the destination server. The possible types are:

  ❑ **SMTPRelayWithAdSite:** Messages are routed for delivery to a Hub Transport in the local Active Directory site.

  ❑ **SMTPRelayWithinAdSiteToEdge:** Messages are routed for an external recipient by using a connector on an Edge Transport server in the local Active Directory site.

- ❑ **SMTPRelayToRemoteADSite:** Messages are routed for delivery to a Hub Transport server in a remote Active Directory site. The next hop domain is the AD site. Enhanced DNS resolves the AD site to a list of remote Hub servers.

- ❑ **SMTPRelayToTiRG:** Messages are routed for delivery to an Exchange 2003 Routing Group Connector. Enhanced DNS is also used to resolve a routing group into a list of target bridgehead servers.

- ❑ **MAPI Delivery:** This delivery is used when the recipient is an Exchange user or system object and they are located in the same Active Directory site. The message is routed to the mailbox server for local delivery.

There are two additional types: Undefined and Unreachable. Undefined means the message are in the Submission queue, and the next hop destination has not been resolved. Unreachable means no route to the recipient was calculated.

Hub Sites

An example of how a Hub site can be necessary is shown in Figure 11-2. Suppose a user in Site A sends a message to a user in Site C. The Hub Transport in Site A tries to send the message directly to the Hub Transport in Site C, but there is a firewall preventing SMTP traffic. Site B, however, can pass SMTP traffic to either site. In this case, Site B should be designated as a Hub site to allow message traffic to be routed successfully.

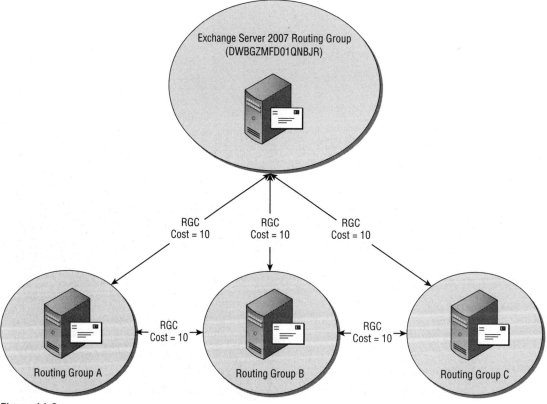

Figure 11-2

Hub sites must exist along the least cost route between the two Hub servers in order for mail to be routed there. In other words, just designating a site as a Hub site does not guarantee all mail will route through it. It must already be a possible hop along the calculated path. Creating Hub sites is discussed later in this chapter in the "Working with Active Directory Sites" section.

Backoff

If direct relay fails to all the Hub servers in the destination site, Exchange performs a backoff routine. The backoff routine tries to determine a new delivery point as close to the point of failure as possible. Remember, link state information is not stored, so it retries connection attempts to the unavailable site. The message queue is automatically put into a retry state and attempts redelivery based on message retry interval settings. If there are more than four hops to the destination, a slightly different process called binary backoff is used. Binary backoff selects a connection halfway between the source and destination.

Figure 11-3 shows an example of backoff. The Hub Transport server in Site A tries to deliver a message to the Hub Transport servers in Site C. The Hub Transport servers in Site C are unavailable, so the Hub Transport server in Site A attempts to deliver the message to the Hub Transport server in Site B, where it is put in a queue.

The current retry settings are retrieved with the Get-TransportServer cmdlet. The syntax for Get-TransportServer is:

```
Get-TransportServer [-Identity <TransportServerIdParameter>]
[-DomainController <Fqdn>]
```

Figure 11-3 shows the output when the Get-TransportServer cmdlet is run against a Hub Transport server. This example shows just the configuration settings related to message retry with the following cmdlet:

```
Get-TransportServer | fl *retry*, *expiration*
```

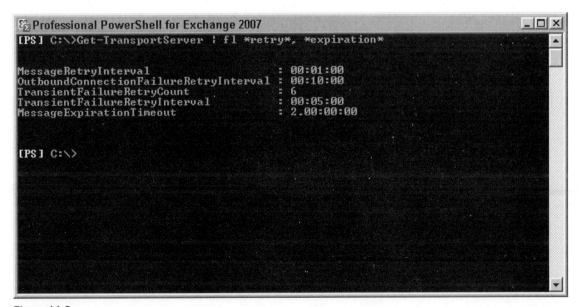

Figure 11-3

The `Set-TransportServer` cmdlet is used to reconfigure the retry settings. The syntax for `Set-TransportServer` is:

```
Set-TransportServer -Identity <ServerIdParameter> [-AntispamAgentsEnabled
<$true | $false>] [-Confirm [<SwitchParameter>]] [-ConnectivityLogEnabled
<$true | $false>] [-ConnectivityLogMaxAge <EnhancedTimeSpan>]
[-ConnectivityLogMaxDirectorySize <Unlimited>]
[-ConnectivityLogMaxFileSize <Unlimited>] [-ConnectivityLogPath
<LocalLongFullPath>] [-ContentConversionTracingEnabled <$true | $false>]
[-DelayNotificationTimeout <EnhancedTimeSpan>] [-DomainController <Fqdn>]
[-ExternalDelayDsnEnabled <$true | $false>] [-ExternalDNSAdapterEnabled
<$true | $false>] [-ExternalDNSAdapterGuid <Guid>]
[-ExternalDNSProtocolOption <Any | UseUdpOnly | UseTcpOnly>]
[-ExternalDNSServers <MultiValuedProperty>] [-ExternalDsnDefaultLanguage
<CultureInfo>] [-ExternalDsnLanguageDetectionEnabled <$true | $false>]
[-ExternalDsnMaxMessageAttachSize <ByteQuantifiedSize>]
[-ExternalDsnReportingAuthority <SmtpDomain>] [-ExternalDsnSendHtml <$true
| $false>] [-ExternalIPAddress <IPAddress>] [-ExternalPostmasterAddress
<Nullable>] [-InternalDelayDsnEnabled <$true | $false>]
[-InternalDNSAdapterEnabled <$true | $false>] [-InternalDNSAdapterGuid
<Guid>] [-InternalDNSProtocolOption <Any | UseUdpOnly | UseTcpOnly>]
[-InternalDNSServers <MultiValuedProperty>] [-InternalDsnDefaultLanguage
<CultureInfo>] [-InternalDsnLanguageDetectionEnabled <$true | $false>]
[-InternalDsnMaxMessageAttachSize <ByteQuantifiedSize>]
[-InternalDsnReportingAuthority <SmtpDomain>] [-InternalDsnSendHtml <$true
| $false>] [-IntraOrgConnectorProtocolLoggingLevel <None | Verbose>]
[-MaxConcurrentMailboxDeliveries <Int32>]
[-MaxConcurrentMailboxSubmissions <Int32>] [-MaxConnectionRatePerMinute
<Int32>] [-MaxOutboundConnections <Unlimited>]
[-MaxPerDomainOutboundConnections <Unlimited>] [-MessageExpirationTimeout
<EnhancedTimeSpan>] [-MessageRetryInterval <EnhancedTimeSpan>]
[-MessageTrackingLogEnabled <$true | $false>] [-MessageTrackingLogMaxAge
<EnhancedTimeSpan>] [-MessageTrackingLogMaxDirectorySize <Unlimited>]
[-MessageTrackingLogMaxFileSize <Unlimited>] [-MessageTrackingLogPath
<LocalLongFullPath>] [-MessageTrackingLogSubjectLoggingEnabled <$true |
$false>] [-OutboundConnectionFailureRetryInterval <EnhancedTimeSpan>]
[-PickupDirectoryMaxHeaderSize <ByteQuantifiedSize>]
[-PickupDirectoryMaxMessagesPerMinute <Int32>]
[-PickupDirectoryMaxRecipientsPerMessage <Int32>] [-PickupDirectoryPath
<LocalLongFullPath>] [-PipelineTracingEnabled <$true | $false>]
[-PipelineTracingPath <LocalLongFullPath>] [-PipelineTracingSenderAddress
<Nullable>] [-PoisonMessageDetectionEnabled <$true | $false>]
[-PoisonThreshold <Int32>] [-QueueMaxIdleTime <EnhancedTimeSpan>]
[-ReceiveProtocolLogMaxAge <EnhancedTimeSpan>]
[-ReceiveProtocolLogMaxDirectorySize <Unlimited>]
[-ReceiveProtocolLogMaxFileSize <Unlimited>] [-ReceiveProtocolLogPath
<LocalLongFullPath>] [-RecipientValidationCacheEnabled <$true | $false>]
[-ReplayDirectoryPath <LocalLongFullPath>] [-RootDropDirectoryPath
 <String>] [-RoutingTableLogMaxAge <EnhancedTimeSpan>]
[-RoutingTableLogMaxDirectorySize <Unlimited>] [-RoutingTableLogPath
```

```
<LocalLongFullPath>] [-SendProtocolLogMaxAge <EnhancedTimeSpan>]
[-SendProtocolLogMaxDirectorySize <Unlimited>]
[-SendProtocolLogMaxFileSize <Unlimited>] [-SendProtocolLogPath
<LocalLongFullPath>] [-TransientFailureRetryCount <Int32>]
[-TransientFailureRetryInterval <EnhancedTimeSpan>] [-WhatIf
[<SwitchParameter>]]
```

There are quite a few configurable parameters for this cmdlet. The parameters related to message retry are:

❑ OutboundConnectionFailureRetryInterval: This parameter sets the interval for subsequent connection attempts to a remote server. The default value for Hub Transport servers is 10 minutes, and 30 minutes on an Edge Transport server. The value is a type time span, which has the syntax hh:mm:ss. The hours are hh, the minutes are mm, and the seconds are ss. The valid range is 00:00:01 to 20:00:00.

❑ TransientFailureRetryCount: This parameter defines the maximum number of immediate connection retries when the Hub Transport first has a connection failure. The default value is six attempts, and is configurable from 0 to 15. After the TransientFailureRetryCount limit is reached, the next connection attempt is determined by the OutboundConnectionFailure-RetryInterval parameter.

❑ TransientFailureRetryInterval: This parameter defines the time interval for subsequent attempts during the TransientFailureRetryCount period. The default is 5 minutes on a Hub Transport server, and 10 minutes on an Edge server. The value is a type time span, which has the syntax hh:mm:ss. The hours are hh, the minutes are mm, and the seconds are ss. The valid range for TransientFailureRetryInterval is 00:00:01 to 12:00:00.

❑ MessageExpirationTimeout: This parameter specifies the maximum time a message can be queued. After the timeout period, the message is returned to the sender as a failure. The default value is two days, and is also a time span value, but has the syntax dd.hh:mm:ss. Days are dd, hours are hh, minutes are mm, and seconds are ss. The valid range for MessageExpiration-Timeout is 00.00:00:05 to 90.00:00:00.

It is possible to configure the wait time period before the sender receives a delivery status notification (DSN) by setting the parameter DelayNotificationTimeout. A DSN lets the sender know that a message has not yet been successfully delivered, but the system will continue to retry sending the message. The default is 4 hours, and is a time span value. The syntax is dd.hh:mm:ss. Days are dd, hours are hh, minutes are mm, and seconds are ss. The valid range for DelayNotificationTimeout is 00.00:00:01 to 30.00:00:00. The value should always be greater than the setting in the TransientFailureRetryCount multiplied by the TransientFailureRetryInterval parameter.

Delayed Fan-out

When a message has multiple recipients with different destinations, Exchange must bifurcate (make copies) of the message for each distinct destination. Depending on where the bifurcation happens, there may be considerable bandwidth consumed. For example, a message with 10 different recipients is bifurcated on the source server. This means up to 10 separate copies of the message must be routed to the next hop. Now, if it is possible to bifurcate the message further down the route, it is easy to see how much bandwidth could be saved.

Exchange Server 2007 tries to bifurcate, or fan-out, as late in the routing as possible to save network traffic. If two or more recipients have different destinations, but the least cost paths share some hops, the message fans out on the hop before the paths diverge. It is not possible to configure or alter delayed fan-out settings.

Figure 11-4 shows an example of delayed fan-out. A user in Site A, sends a message to three recipients. Christine is in Site D, and Isabel and Madison are in Site E. A single copy of the message is sent to Site B, where it is split for delivery. From Site B, a direct delivery is made to Christine in Site D, and Isabel and Madison in Site E.

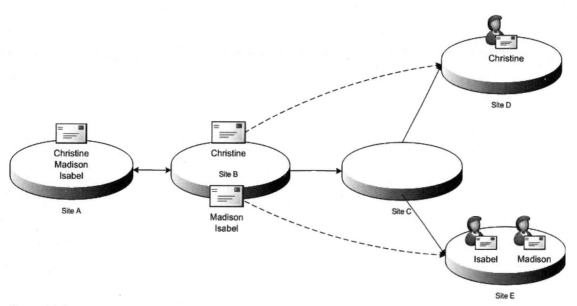

Figure 11-4

Routing Troubleshooting

As explained at the beginning of this chapter, there must be at least one functioning Hub Transport server in each Active Directory site where there is a mailbox server. A few key events are logged when there are issues with a Hub server.

Common Errors

The following table lists common errors related to routing that are logged to the Windows Application log.

Event ID	Description
Event 1010	There is no local server object for the Hub Transport server in Active Directory.
Event 1009	There is a local Hub Transport server, but it is not active. There are several reasons it may not be active: ❑ The Microsoft Exchange Transport Service is not running ❑ MAPI RPC is blocked between the mailbox and the Hub ❑ The Hub Transport server has exhausted its submission threads. For example, the mailbox server submits more traffic than the Hub Transport can handle.
Event 1008	The Mail Submission Service cannot locate any Hub Transport servers in the local Active Directory site. This can be caused by: ❑ The Hub Transport server is not working ❑ There are network or connectivity issues to the Hub Transport server ❑ No server in the local site is running the Hub Transport role

Routing Log Viewer

Service Pack 1 introduces a new tool for viewing routing information. Previous versions of Exchange had a utility called WinRoute. WinRoute could connect to the Routing Engine service and retrieve the current routing information as seen by that server. Exchange Server 2007 routing information is logged, and the Routing Log Viewer provides similar functionality for Exchange Server 2007 that WinRoute had in previous versions. The Log Viewer provides information on Active Directory sites, Exchange servers, connectors, and address spaces. Another nice feature is the ability to compare two log files and see what changes occurred between the logs. The tool is part of the mail flow tools within the Exchange Management Console Toolbox.

Figure 11-5 shows an example of the Routing Log Viewer's compare log feature. This example shows that a new Send Connector was added between the time the first log was created and the second log was created. This can be extremely useful when trying to figure out what changed when a message takes an unexpected route.

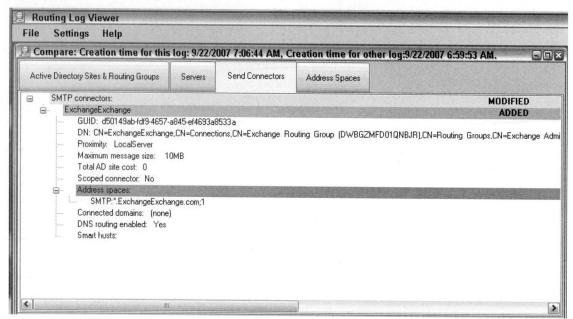

Figure 11-5

Message Tracking

Exchange uses message tracking to log activity as a message is routed throughout the system. Messages are tracked on the Mailbox, Hub, and Edge Transport server roles. Message tracking is another useful tool when troubleshooting message delivery. It logs each message event separately, allowing an administrator to follow the path a message used. At each step, there are a number of fields logged with information about the message transfer state, the recipients, and the server names. However, no message content is stored in the tracking logs.

To configure message tracking, use the Set-TransportServer cmdlet for configuring the Hub or Edge servers. Set-TransportServer was discussed earlier in this chapter during the discussion of the back-off routine and configuring message retry parameters. To configure message tracking on the mailbox server, use the Set-MailboxServer cmdlet. The following table shows message tracking related parameters and their defaults.

Of course, there is message tracking in the Exchange Management Console, but it can also be searched with PowerShell. The Get-MessageTrackingLog cmdlet is used for this purpose. Its syntax is:

```
Get-MessageTrackingLog [-DomainController <Fqdn>] [-End <DateTime>]
[-EventId <String>] [-InternalMessageId <String>] [-MessageId <String>]
[-MessageSubject <String>] [-Recipients <String[]>] [-Reference <String>]
[-ResultSize <Unlimited>] [-Sender <String>] [-Server <ServerIdParameter>]
[-Start <DateTime>]
```

Parameter	Description	Default
MessageTrackingLogEnabled	Enables or disables message tracking	Enabled
MessageTrackingLogPath	The location of the message tracking logs	C:\Program Files\ Microsoft\Exchange Server TransportRoles\ Logs\MessageTracking
MessageTrackingLogMax-FileSize	The maximum size of an individual tracking log	10MB
MessageTrackingLogMax-DirectorySize	The maximum size of the tracking log directory. When the maximum is reached, the oldest log is deleted. Only log files are counted in the calculation.	250MB
MessageTrackingLogMaxAge	The maximum file age of a log. Logs older than this date are deleted.	30 Days
MessageTrackingLogSubject-LoggingEnabled	Enables or disables including the subject in the logs	Enabled

The common fields used in searching are listed next.

The EventID parameter is the event-id field in the tracking logs. This value is the event classification for the message. Possible values are:

- ❑ Badmail
- ❑ Defer
- ❑ Deliver
- ❑ DSN
- ❑ Expand
- ❑ Fail
- ❑ PoisonMessage
- ❑ Receive
- ❑ Redirect
- ❑ Resolve
- ❑ Submit
- ❑ Transfer

311

The Subject parameter corresponds to the message-subject field in the tracking logs. This supports using partial values.

The MessageID parameter corresponds to the message-id field in the tracking logs. This value never changes for the lifetime of the message.

The Start and End parameters correspond to the date-time field in the tracking logs. Either parameter used by itself retrieves all entries before or after the specified date. If both are used, the messages fall within the range between the Start and End. The date-time field is stored in Coordinated Universal Time (UTC). When including a Start or End time, enter the regional date-time of the computer used to perform the search. The cmdlet and tracking tool convert the search and the results to and from UTC.

The ResultSize parameter can limit the number of items returned from the search. The default is 1,000 records, but using the value Unlimited returns all records.

All parameters are optional to filter the results. If no parameters are used, the cmdlet returns the last 1,000 records from the tracking logs. Edge servers require the Get-MessageTrackingLog cmdlet to be executed locally on the Edge server.

A new script, GetMessageTrackingE2LogWithTime.ps1, is included in Service Pack 1. It makes searching across all Hub and mailbox servers easier. The script has the following parameters:

- MessageID: This is required if the MessageSubject parameter is not used. This parameter searches the tracking logs for the specified message-id.

- MessageSubject: This is required if the MessageID parameter is not used. This parameter searches the tracking logs for the specified message-subject.

- End: This optional parameter contains the end date and time to search up to (not including).

- Sender: This optional parameter contains the sender's SMTP email address.

- Servers: This optional parameter is a comma-separated list of Hub or mailbox servers to limit the tracking log search to.

- Start: This optional parameter contains the beginning date and time to search from (not including).

Some examples of message tracking searches are shown next.

To search all messages from 9/01/2007 6:00 AM to 9/15/2007 6:00 PM from jrosen@exchangeexchange.com on a Hub server, run the following cmdlet:

```
Get-MessageTrackingLog -ResultSize Unlimited -Start "9/01/2007 6:00AM" -End
"9/15/2007 6:00PM" -Sender "jrosen@exchangeexchange.com"
```

To search all mailbox and Hub servers for messages containing "Hello World" from the sender jrosen@exchangeexchange.com, run the following script:

```
GetMessageTrackingE2LogWithTime.ps1 -MessageSubject "Hello World" -Sender
"jrosen@exchangeexchange.com"
```

Working with Active Directory Sites

How Active Directory sites are used in routing was shown earlier in this chapter. This section gives the details on how to configure sites to control routing. The following is a list of cmdlets discussed in this section:

- ❏   Get-ADSiteLink
- ❏   Set-ADSiteLink
- ❏   Get-ADSite
- ❏   Set-ADSite

Determining Site Membership

The server's IP address defines the AD site the server belongs to. Active Directory administrators configure site information with the Active Directory Sites and Services MMC. Figure 11-6 is an example of a simple site configuration. This example shows one subnet, 192.168.1.0/24, and two sites, Default-First-Site-Name and Chicago.

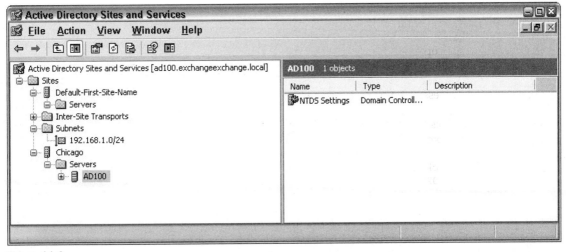

Figure 11-6

The subnet is associated with the Chicago site as shown in Figure 11-6. This dialog box is reached by selecting the Chicago site, and right-clicking to select Properties. Any servers that fall within the 192.168.1.0-192.168.1.255 are automatically part of the Chicago Active Directory site. Overlapping subnets should not be associated with different sites because the server will not be able to correctly determine its site membership and this causes errors.

The process Exchange uses to determine site membership was described earlier in this chapter. The Microsoft Exchange Active Directory Topology service is responsible for checking and maintaining site information in Active Directory for the server object.

One easy way to determine the Active Directory site a server thinks it belongs to is to use the support utility called Nltest. Nltest is installed from the Windows Server installation disc, in the support directory in the supptools.msi package. After installation you can run the following command at a command prompt:

```
Nltest /dsgetsite
```

The output in this example for a server AD100 is:

```
C:\Program Files\Support Tools>nltest /dsgetsite
Chicago
The command completed successfully
```

Dedicated Exchange Sites

It was a common practice in Exchange 2000 and Exchange 2003 to create a dedicated Active Directory site for large organizations. Creating a dedicated site for Exchange was done mainly to keep domain controllers from being used by other services and applications. Because Exchange Server 2007 maps routing directly to Active Directory sites, this practice no longer is recommended in most circumstances.

One way to mitigate the impact of competing resources is to upgrade domain controllers to the 64-bit Windows platform. According to the Exchange team's guidance, a 32-bit domain controller can co-exist with other applications and support up to 10,000 Exchange users. The 64-bit platform increases this to 20,000 Exchange users, effectively double the load.

It is possible to create an effect similar to a dedicated site by using DNS to alter record priority and weights. The TechNet article "Creating an Active Directory Site for Exchange Server" found at microsoft.com/technet/itsolutions/msit/operations/adforexchangenote.mspx details the steps for this design in the section on "How to Isolate Client Authentication Traffic from Exchange Facing Domain Controllers."

It is also still possible to specify a static set of domain controllers for each Exchange server, but this is not recommended. This solution requires a lot of manual work to maintain and can easily lead to problems.

Site Links

Site link costs help Active Directory determine the least cost route for replication and domain controller site coverage. The lower the site link cost, the faster the link. Higher costs are slower or more expensive. Because the site link should map closely to the physical network, the costs should also reflect the speed or expense. If for some reason the site link costs do not create optimal mail routing, it is possible to set an Exchange cost on the site link. This cost will not affect Active Directory replication or site coverage calculations. To see the current configuration of a site link, use the Get-ADSiteLink cmdlet. The syntax for Get-ADSiteLink is:

```
Get-ADSiteLink [-Identity <AdSiteLinkIdParameter>] [-DomainController <Fqdn>]
```

Figure 11-7 shows the sample output from the Get-ADSiteLink cmdlet:

```
Get-ADSiteLink | fl
```

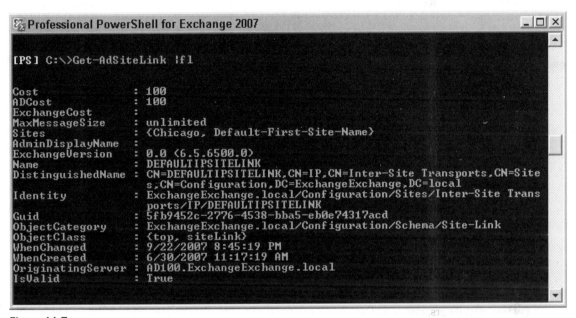

```
[PS] C:\>Get-AdSiteLink |fl


Cost                : 100
ADCost              : 100
ExchangeCost        :
MaxMessageSize      : unlimited
Sites               : {Chicago, Default-First-Site-Name}
AdminDisplayName    :
ExchangeVersion     : 0.0 (6.5.6500.0)
Name                : DEFAULTIPSITELINK
DistinguishedName   : CN=DEFAULTIPSITELINK,CN=IP,CN=Inter-Site Transports,CN=Site
                      s,CN=Configuration,DC=ExchangeExchange,DC=local
Identity            : ExchangeExchange.local/Configuration/Sites/Inter-Site Trans
                      ports/IP/DEFAULTIPSITELINK
Guid                : 5fb9452c-2776-4538-bba5-eb0e74317acd
ObjectCategory      : ExchangeExchange.local/Configuration/Schema/Site-Link
ObjectClass         : {top, siteLink}
WhenChanged         : 9/22/2007 8:45:19 PM
WhenCreated         : 6/30/2007 11:17:19 AM
OriginatingServer   : AD100.ExchangeExchange.local
IsValid             : True
```

Figure 11-7

Notice the ExchangeCost is null by default. To set the ExchangeCost parameter's value, use the Set-ADSiteLink cmdlet. Its syntax is:

```
Set-AdSiteLink -Identity <AdSiteLinkIdParameter> [-Confirm
[<SwitchParameter>]] [-DomainController <Fqdn>] [-ExchangeCost <Nullable>]
[-MaxMessageSize <Unlimited>] [-Name <String>] [-WhatIf
[<SwitchParameter>]]

Set-AdSiteLink [-Confirm [<SwitchParameter>]] [-DomainController <Fqdn>]
[-ExchangeCost <Nullable>] [-Instance <ADSiteLink>] [-MaxMessageSize
<Unlimited>] [-Name <String>] [-WhatIf [<SwitchParameter>]]
```

Figure 11-8 shows an example of setting the `ExchangeCost` parameter to 150.

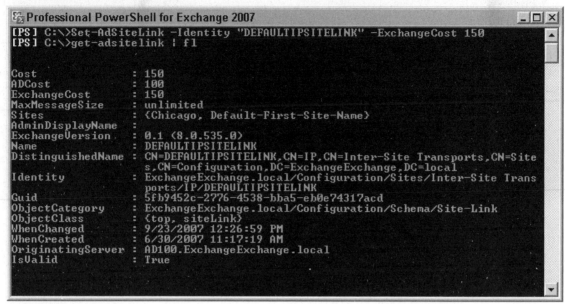

Figure 11-8

To remove any existing values, set the `ExchangeCost` parameter to `$null`.

A new feature in Service Pack 1 is the `MaxMessageSize` parameter. This parameter allows an administrator to set message size limits on an IP site link. This is particularly useful for preventing large messages from going over an expensive or slow link.

Working with Hub Sites

Hub sites are used to alter the least cost route to force routing through a specific Active Directory site. This could be for political or technical reasons, such as network connectivity. To see if an Active Directory site is enabled as a Hub site, use the `Get-ADSite` cmdlet. Its syntax is:

```
Get-ADSite [-Identity <AdSiteIdParameter>] [-DomainController <Fqdn>]
```

Figure 11-9 shows the output from `Get-ADSite`. There are two sites; neither is enabled as Hub sites.

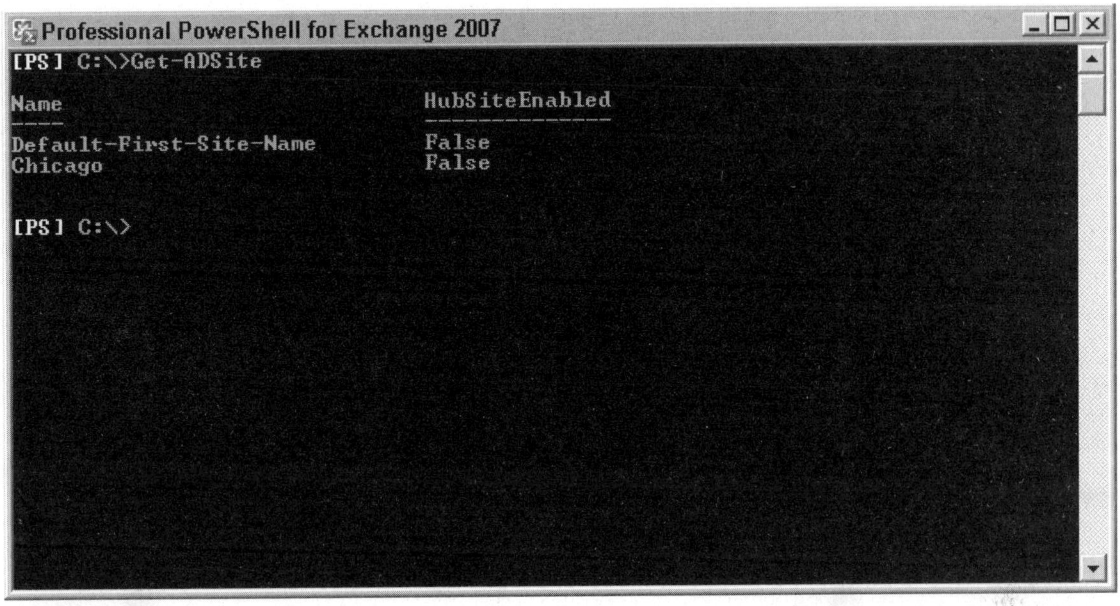

```
Professional PowerShell for Exchange 2007                          _ |□| X|
[PS] C:\>Get-ADSite

Name                              HubSiteEnabled
----                              --------------
Default-First-Site-Name           False
Chicago                           False


[PS] C:\>
```

Figure 11-9

Before enabling a site as a Hub site, check the routing log to see the least cost routing path from the current Active Directory site to any remote Active Directory site. Hub sites are used only if they are part of the least cost route. To enable an Active Directory site as a Hub site, use the Set-ADSite cmdlet. The syntax for Set-ADSite is:

```
Set-AdSite -Identity <AdSiteIdParameter> [-Confirm [<SwitchParameter>]]
[-DomainController <Fqdn>] [-HubSiteEnabled <$true | $false>] [-Name
<String>] [-WhatIf [<SwitchParameter>]]

Set-AdSite [-Confirm [<SwitchParameter>]] [-DomainController <Fqdn>]
[-HubSiteEnabled <$true | $false>] [-Instance <ADSite>] [-Name <String>]
[-WhatIf [<SwitchParameter>]]
```

This example sets the Chicago site as a Hub site:

```
Set-ADSite -Identity "Chicago" -HubSiteEnabled:$true
```

Coexistence with Exchange 2003

How does message routing occur when Microsoft Exchange Server 2007 coexists in the same Exchange organization with Exchange Server 2003 or Exchange 2000 Server computers? When a large organization is transitioning from Exchange 2003 to Exchange Server 2007, a period of coexistence between the versions is likely. All of the information for Exchange 2003 applies to Exchange 2000.

Exchange Server 2007 does not support coexistence with Exchange 5.5. A new Exchange Server 2007 organization does not support installation of previous versions into the organization.

Before Exchange Server 2007 can be installed into an Exchange 2003 organization, it must meet the following criteria:

❑ No servers can be running Exchange 5.5 in the organization

❑ The Site Replication Service (SRS) must be decommissioned

❑ All Active Directory connectors must be removed

❑ The organization must be running Exchange 2003 native mode

During the first Exchange Server 2007 Hub Transport server installation, the administrator must select an initial legacy routing group to create connectors to. The Exchange Server 2007 computers are all part of a single routing group — DWBGZMFD01QNBJR — and a single administrative group — FYDIBOHF-23SPDLT. It is important that these routing and administrative groups are not renamed or any Exchange Server 2007 computers removed from them.

The name for the Exchange Server 2007 routing and administrative groups come from a simple Caesar cipher. Shifting all the letters one space reveals EXCHANGE12ROCKS.

After installation, it is a best practice to add additional source and target servers for load balancing and fault tolerance. The default cost for the routing group connector is 1.

Another potential problem with coexistence is the use of restrictions on Exchange 2003 connectors. The restrictions can be content related, such as allowing system and non-system messages. There are other restrictions such as user permissions and scheduling. Exchange Server 2007 does not support these restrictions with the exception of size and public folder referrals. They can cause a message to pass from Exchange Server 2007 to Exchange 2003 over a connector that will not route the message due to restrictions. It is a best practice, therefore, to remove any restrictions from Exchange 2003 connectors prior to Exchange Server 2007's installation.

Link State Considerations

To understand the impact that link state has on routing, this section first takes a look at how Exchange 2003 uses link state information. Exchange 2003 uses link state to make routing decisions that avoid routes that have connection problems. Exchange actually breaks down link state changes by major, minor, and user versions.

❑ **Major version number:** These are physical changes in routing topology. Examples include the addition of a new connector to the routing group and changes to a connector's configuration.

- ❑ **Minor version number:** These are changes to the state of existing connectors. Connectors are reported as STATE UP or STATE DOWN. Minor changes are delayed by 10 minutes to prevent oscillating connectors.

- ❑ **User version number:** These are changes such as services starting or stopped. Also, they occur when the routing group master changes or when another server is added to the routing group.

The major changes have the highest priority, the minor changes are next, and the user version changes are last.

It may be necessary with the introduction of Exchange Server 2007 to suppress minor state changes. Without minor state changes, Exchange 2003 doesn't mark connectors as down. This ensures Exchange 2003 always uses least cost routing, and doesn't try to calculate an alternative route. It is recommended to suppress link state if:

- ❑ The organization has more than one Exchange 2003 routing group

- ❑ There will be more than one Routing Group Connector between Exchange 2003 and Exchange Server 2007

The minor link state must be suppressed on every Exchange 2003 server in the organization. The process for suppressing minor link state is:

1. Launch the Registry Editor.

2. Open `HKEY_LOCAL_MACHINE\System\CurrentControlSet\Services\RESvc\Parameters`.

3. Right-click Parameters and select New ➪ DWORD value. Set the name to `SuppressStateChanges`.

4. In the value field enter **1**.

5. Close the Registry Editor and restart the Simple Mail Transfer Protocol (SMTP) service, the Microsoft Exchange Routing Engine, and the Microsoft Exchange MTA Stacks service.

Link State Islands

Exchange 2003 servers share link state information between servers in different routing groups through the SMTP verb `X-Link2State`. Exchange Server 2007 does not understand the `X-Link2State` verb, thus it will not propagate link state information to Exchange 2003. Even though minor link state is suppressed, Exchange 2003 still needs to receive major updates, which are changes in the routing topology. During migration, Exchange 2003 routing groups can become isolated. In this case, the routing group won't be able to submit routing changes, or receive routing changes from other routing groups. To ensure link state islands do not develop, leave Routing Group Connectors between Exchange 2003 routing groups. When routing is not desirable, set the Routing Group Connector cost to 100. This prevents normal traffic, but allows link state information to continue to propagate.

Here is an example on how link state islands can occur. Figure 11-10 shows an Exchange Server 2007 routing group and three Exchange 2003 routing groups — A, B, and C. Routing Group B is a hub for Exchange 2003 routing.

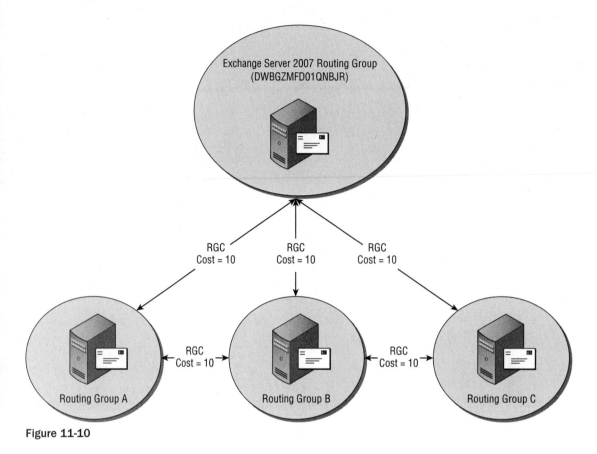

Figure 11-10

Now, Routing Group B is fully migrated to Exchange Server 2007 and the administrator decommissions and removes the routing group and its connectors as illustrated in Figure 11-11.

Figure 11-11

Figure 11-12 shows clearly how now Routing Groups A and C are link state islands. Because the only connectivity is through the Exchange Server 2007 routing group, there is no way for link state information to flow between the Exchange 2003 routing groups.

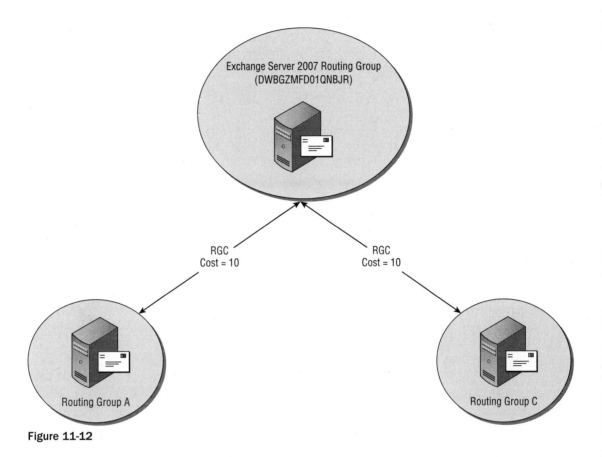

Figure 11-12

One way to prevent or correct this problem is to add Routing Group Connectors between Routing Group A and Routing Group C. Setting the cost to 100 prevents mail flow, but allows the sites to exchange link state information. See Figure 11-13.

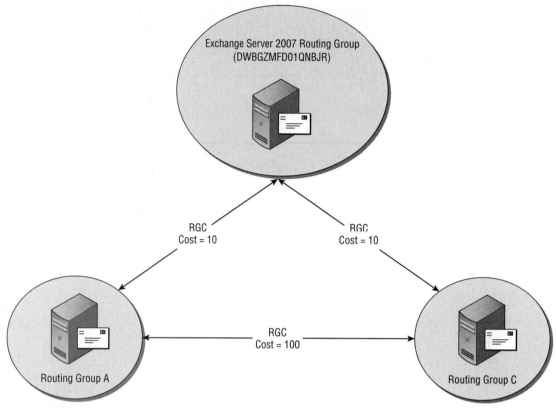

Figure 11-13

Coexistence Routing

Earlier in the chapter, the least cost routing algorithm was explored. This section looks at the impact of Exchange 2003 coexistence on routing. The connector cost is comprised of the destination address space as well as the site or connector cost. The cost can be thought of as the Exchange 2003 "legacy" Routing Group Connector cost and the Exchange Server 2007 Active Directory site cost. The best route is the route with the best legacy cost followed by the Active Directory site cost. Because of this design, routes can stay within the Exchange Server 2007 routing group and go across site connectors with higher costs.

Consider the example in Figure 11-14. A user in Site 1 on Exchange Server 2007 sends a mail to an external recipient at exchangeexchange.com.

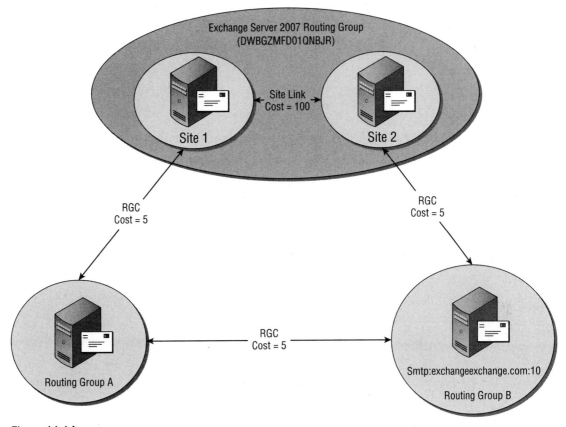

Figure 11-14

There are two routes the message could take in Figure 11-14, shown in the following table.

Option	Path	Cost (Legacy, Site)
1	Site 1 to Routing Group A; Routing Group A to Routing Group B	20, 0
2	Site 1 to Site 2; Site 2 to Routing Group B	15, 100

Even though the lowest cost route appears to be option 1, with a total cost of 20 is the path from Site 1 to Routing Group A, then to Routing Group B. The other path has the lowest legacy cost, 15, and option 2 will be used.

Building on that example, if a third Active Directory site is added to the picture, and Send Connectors are added to the Hub Transport servers in Site 2 and Site 3, the routing now looks like Figure 11-15.

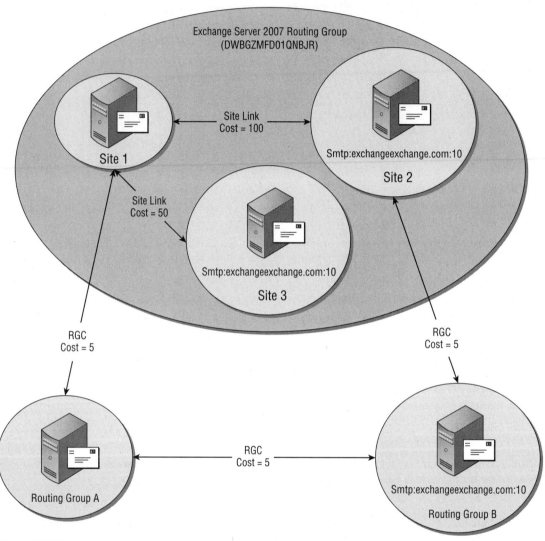

Figure 11-15

The costs are summarized in the following table.

Option	Path	Cost (Legacy, Site)
1	Site 1 to RG A; RG A to RG B	20, 0
2	Site 1 to Site 2; Site 2 to RG B	15, 70
3	Site 1 to Site 2	0, 80
4	Site 1 to Site 3	0, 60

The resulting route would be option 4, from Site 1 to Site3. This is because it has the lowest legacy cost, followed by the lowest site cost.

Summary

This chapter started by showing the differences between Exchange 2003 and Exchange Server 2007. The routing has gone through significant modifications, including integration with Active Directory sites, deterministic routing, and separation of transport from the mailbox server. This chapter showed how these changes enable more efficient routing based on Active Directory replication and network topology. It also enables transport rules enforcement, which guarantees every message routes through a Hub Transport server, even when users are located on the same server, or even the same database.

This chapter explained the route selection process and how Exchange builds a least cost route. Another major change is that messages are directly routed when possible. Once the route is selected, the server must decide which queue and connector to submit the message to. It is possible to alter the route with Hub sites. It is important to understand that if a Hub site is along a least cost path, all messages must route through it. This enables specific scenarios, such as a firewall preventing end-to-end network connectivity. Next, this chapter showed how Exchange Server 2007 performs its backoff process when the destination server is unavailable. This is also where the message retry settings where explained.

Another new concept to Exchange Server 2007 is delayed fan-out. To help conserve network bandwidth, Exchange tries to split the message destined for multiple recipients as close as possible to the remote sites.

An examination of troubleshooting showed common errors, the new Routing Log Viewer, and how to configure and use message tracking. All of these methods are valuable to an administrator trying to understand what happened to a message when a customer wants verification that a message was delivered.

The next section showed the detail on how to configure link costs and Hub sites. It addressed the common design in Exchange 2003 of the dedicated Exchange Active Directory site. Finally, the chapter looked at the intricacies of coexistence with legacy Exchange implementations. There are a number of link state considerations and impact to routing when there are Exchange 2003 servers in the organization.

12

Working with Continuous Replication

Many companies have grown to recognize email as a business-critical application. Also, messaging platforms have integrated into areas such as Unified Messaging and workflow processes. New ways to access mail and documents through mobile phones and VPNs make user access 24x7x365. Because of this reliance on these services, companies need to make Exchange available without interruption. It is no longer acceptable to take a service offline — even for maintenance. In response to customer needs, Microsoft designed Exchange to work in a Windows cluster. In this configuration, Exchange is fault tolerant to hardware failure by sharing a single copy of the database and log files. This solution also provides the benefit for administrators to minimize downtime due to regular server maintenance, such as applying security updates.

However, in recent years, catastrophic events like Hurricane Katrina and the World Trade Center bombing in 1993 and terrorist attacks on 9/11 forced companies to think about site resiliency. In Exchange 2003 and earlier, organizations that wanted geographical fault tolerance needed to turn to third parties to provide data replication. A typical scenario in Exchange 2003 was an Exchange cluster attached to a SAN for hardware/software replication of Exchange data to a second SAN. This solution could be costly and some solutions had no support from Microsoft. Clustering in general is more complicated and requires well-defined processes. For example, the hardware selection and software installation differs significantly compared to a non-clustered server. Unfortunately, many administrators were not trained adequately, and outages could actually become longer or more severe due to administration mistakes.

In response to the growing demand for a supported, less costly, and easier to administer cluster design, Exchange Server 2007 introduces three forms of continuous replication — Local Continuous Replication (LCR), Clustered Continuous Replication (CCR), and new in Service Pack 1 — Standby Continuous Replication (SCR). In addition, Exchange still offers traditional Single Copy Clusters (SCCs).

In this chapter you learn about:

- ❑ Installing different types of continuous replication
- ❑ Seeding replications
- ❑ Monitoring system health
- ❑ Failover and fallback

Understanding Continuous Replication

Continuous replication is the new cluster model in Exchange Server 2007. Before learning what continuous replication is, you need to understand what clustering was like in previous versions. Exchange clustering is built on top of Windows Server 2003 Server Clustering (WSSC). WSSC clusters allow for multiple nodes, or servers, to share a set of resources. In Exchange, the database and log files are examples of shared resources. Also, Exchange creates a virtual Exchange server, called the Clustered Mailbox Server (CMS). The CMS is what mail clients use as their mailbox server. The clustering service is able to detect a fault in the network, node, or storage and tries to move the resources to the operational node. Exchange supports up to eight nodes in a Single Copy Cluster, where at least one node is a passive node. A passive node is a server node in the cluster that is simply waiting for a failure on an active node so that it can take ownership of the resources and restore service. Mail clients have no idea that the CMS is not a "real" server and will simply reconnect when the resources are brought online on the passive node.

Another piece of the WSSC cluster is that the nodes need to make sure only one server has ownership of the resources at a time. This is achieved through the use of a quorum resource, which is shared disk. The quorum resource is also shared across all the nodes and contains cluster state and configuration information. Whichever node has ownership of the quorum is the active node. If the quorum resource fails, all nodes will go offline, because the nodes will not be able to know which is the active node.

Although this design provides high availability, it has some shortcomings. The challenges behind a Single Copy Cluster are complexity, cost, and there are still single points of failure. To address these issues, Microsoft added a continuous replication model. Other Microsoft technologies, such as Microsoft SQL Server, already offer a similar form of clustering. In the continuous replication model, the cluster nodes do not share disk resources. This solution addresses one of the single points of failure in SCC, which is that a single copy of the data exists across all nodes. Now in continuous replication, each node maintains its own copy of the data. How is this accomplished? To keep the nodes in sync, Exchange uses asynchronous replication, also called log shipping. The first step in forming the cluster is to copy the Exchange database to the passive node. This process is called seeding. Once the passive node has a full copy of the database, it pulls closed log files from the active node. After the copy process completes and the log file is checked for integrity, the passive node replays the log into its copy of the database. In a Clustered Continuous Replication (CCR) cluster, the replay happens immediately after validation. In a Local Continuous Replication (LCR) cluster, it is batched on 10 logs or 60 seconds, whichever comes first. This is changed in Service Pack 1, and LCR no longer batches replay. Because the passive node must wait for the active log file to be closed, there is a delay in the passive node's ability to stay completely in sync.

Continuous replication is used in three different high-availability solutions in Exchange Server 2007 with Service Pack 1. The next few sections explain the differences between the models, and will help an administrator decide which models are appropriate to meet the organization's service level agreements.

Clustered Continuous Replication

Now that continuous replication has been explained, the first solution to consider is Clustered Continuous Replication (CCR). CCR is a high-availability solution that is built on top of WSSC, similar to SCC described earlier. Figure 12-1 shows all of the pieces that make up a CCR.

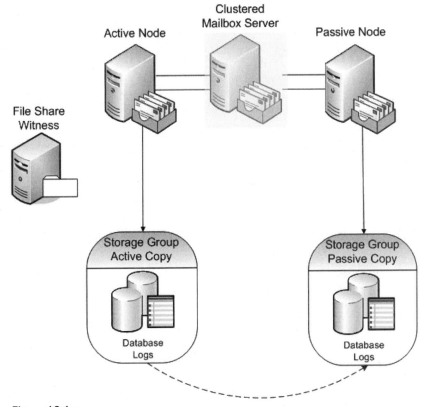

Figure 12-1

First, CCR is limited to two nodes, one active and one passive. The virtual "floating" Exchange instance is called the Clustered Mailbox Server. As shown in the figure, each node has its own separate storage. This is very different from the SCC model. As a result of no shared storage, a new solution had to be created for the quorum resource. A new quorum model was added to Windows Server 2003 called Majority Node Set (MNS) quorum with file share witness. The feature is available as a hotfix to Windows Server 2003, or it's included in Windows Server 2003 Service Pack 2.

The file share witness (FSW) is a file share that resides on a server outside of the cluster. Typically, the FSW is created on a Hub server. The MNS cluster requires two of the three cluster resources available for the cluster to stay online. For example, the FSW can go offline and not affect the cluster, because both nodes can still communicate with each other. The nodes use a heartbeat, or periodic check, to ensure the resource is available. Similarly, one node can lose communication and the cluster will stay online as long as the FSW is available. If two resources cannot communicate, the entire cluster will shut down. This is because without the heartbeat and connectivity to the FSW, the node cannot determine if it's the active node. If both nodes think they are the active node, this condition is called split brain syndrome. Unlike in SCC, split brain cannot occur in a CCR cluster because if there is no majority, the nodes will not come online.

What are the other differences between SCC and CCR?

❏ Both data and server resilience. SCC provides only server resilience unless additional third-party SAN replication is used.

❏ No special hardware. Not required to use Windows Hardware Compatibility List (WHCL) certified hardware and each node can run different hardware.

❏ No shared storage. It is possible to use a variety of storage solutions.

❏ No split brain syndrome.

On the surface it would appear CCR requires double the storage needed compared to an SCC cluster, because each node has a copy of the database and logs. However, many organizations use third-party solutions to provide data resiliency in an SCC SAN solution. So, in fact it is common for SCC and CCR to use the same amount of storage.

The third bullet, no shared storage, allows a company to use either SAN technologies or direct attached storage (DAS). DAS has come a long way since Exchange 5.5, and is a low-cost alternative to using a SAN. Most of the features offered by a SAN are from the software that runs the disk array. The actual hard drives do not differ between the storage solutions. Because Exchange provides data replication out of the box, there is no need to turn to third-party offerings, which are often costly. For companies that have an existing SAN strategy, it is perfectly fine to use it for CCR. However, to provide true redundancy, the nodes should not be connected to the same SAN.

You might choose CCR for your deployment because:

❏ High availability is required for both hardware and Exchange data.

❏ Eliminate all single points of failure without third-party software

❏ Ability to use low-cost DAS storage

❏ Ability to use a variety of hardware — not restricted to WHCL certification

Next is Local Continuous Replication, which is another continuous replication architecture.

Local Continuous Replication

Local Continuous Replication (LCR) is similar to CCR, except it requires only one server. This provides data protection only; because there is only one server, clustering LCR is not supported. Figure 12-2 illustrates a single LCR server design.

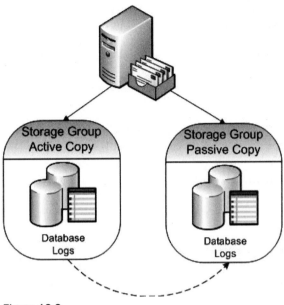

Figure 12-2

LCR provides a great way to provide quick recovery for one or more storage groups, with the only costs being additional disk and processor power. LCR takes approximately 20 percent more CPU processing to handle the log file verification and log file replay. It is also suggested to use an additional 1 gigabyte of RAM in this configuration.

The storage group configuration is the same as CCR, one database per storage group. Unlike CCR, it is possible to enable LCR on per storage group basis. This gives organizations the flexibility of redundancy for users that may have a higher SLA, without incurring the cost of doubling the disk for the entire server. The passive copy should use its own dedicated set of disks to prevent performance problems. Using iSCSI storage for the passive storage is not recommended because iSCSI connects over a local or wide area network and may not provide enough bandwidth or low latency. It is critical to maintaining high availability that log shipping stay up to date, and this configuration makes it difficult to predict bandwidth usage impact from other applications.

Another best practice is to use volume mount points for database and log LUNs. A *LUN* is a disk volume, typically made from multiple physical disks configured in an array. Most administrators are familiar with volumes as drive letters. Instead of using drive letters for disk volumes, mount points allow LUNs to be mounted into a folder on a different physical disk. Instead of mounting each storage group LUN with drive letters, first create a small root directory with a drive letter and a folder; for example, a small 1-gigabyte volume assigned a drive letter K: and a root folder Storage Groups. Then mount the storage group LUN to the K:\Storage Groups folder. In this example, the LUN for storage group one would be K:\Storage Groups\SG1. To applications like Exchange, this grafting is completely transparent — it appears as one volume. Using mount points has several advantages. One is that there is a 26 drive OS limitation. On a fully loaded Exchange Server 2007 computer with 50 storage groups, there would not be enough drive letters to have each disk volume assigned a drive letter. Mount points reduce the number of drive letters needed because of the reasons discussed earlier. Another benefit to using mount points is that it gives a lot of flexibility during a recovery scenario because it is possible to replace the failed disk volume by grafting the LCR copy disk volume in its place.

Do not enable LCR for the storage group that contains the public folder database if more than one public folder server exists in the organization. Public folders are always replicating content and hierarchy information. If there is a failover, an item originated on the failed node would exist on the other public folder servers. To prevent this situation, if there is an unscheduled failover the public folder server will not mount until the original database is brought back online. If a log was lost, the database will not mount to prevent data integrity issues.

You might choose LCR because:

❑ High availability is required for just Exchange and not the hardware

❑ High availability is required for specific sets of users, not everyone

❑ Ability to use low-cost DAS storage

❑ Ability to use a variety of hardware — not restricted to WHCL certification

Standby Continuous Replication

Standby Continuous Replication is a new option for site resiliency introduced in Service Pack 1. SCR uses the same continuous replication as CCR and LCR, but it has some key differences:

❑ There can be multiple CCR targets per storage group

❑ The replication can be delayed allowing for network bandwidth control and prevention of logical data corruption

❑ It is not possible to back up an SCR copy

The SCR source can be a stand-alone mailbox server, an LCR-enabled mailbox server, a Single Copy Cluster, or a CCR cluster. The SCR target can be a stand-alone mailbox server, or a clustered server that does not have a Clustered Mailbox Server configured. Some of these options are shown in Figure 12-3.

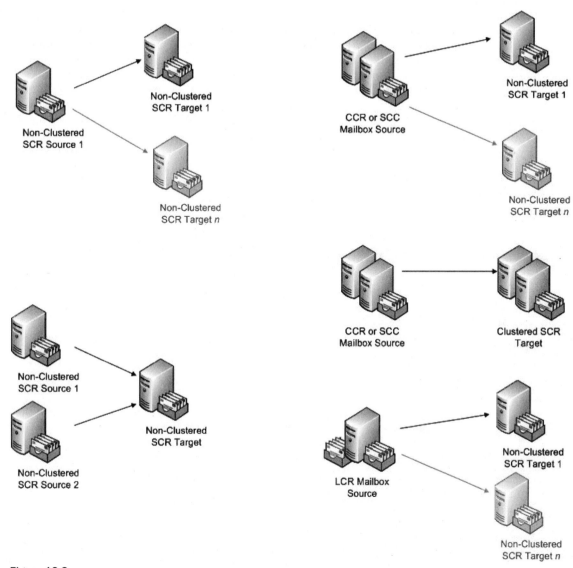

Figure 12-3

As mentioned previously, it is possible to create multiple SCR targets for a single SCR source. For example, a company may have a main datacenter and use CCR to provide local high availability, and configure two SCR targets — each in different physical locations. It is recommended that a source have four or fewer targets. It is also possible to have multiple SCR sources replicate to a single SCR target, as long as the total number of storage groups on the target does not exceed the 50 storage group limit.

You might choose SCR because:

❑ Site resiliency is required

❑ High availability is required for specific sets of users

❑ Ability to use low-cost DAS storage

❑ Ability to use a variety of hardware — not restricted to WHCL certification

This chapter discusses installing, seeding, monitoring, failover, and failback of LCR, CCR, and SCR clusters.

Installing LCR, CCR, SCR

This section examines the installation process for CCR, LCR, and SCR. LCR and SCR can be added on after installation, whereas CCR must be configured during the server install. The following cmdlets are used during installation:

❑ New-MailboxDatabase

❑ Enable-DatabaseCopy

❑ New-PublicFolderDatabase

❑ Enable-StorageGroupCopy

❑ Get-MailboxDatabase

❑ New-StorageGroup

Installing Local Continuous Replication (LCR)

LCR can be enabled to an existing database, or enabled when creating a new database.

Overall the steps for enabling LCR are:

1. Ensure 1-1 storage group to database design
2. Enable LCR on the database
3. Enable LCR on the storage group

Enabling the Database

The first step in enabling LCR on an existing mailbox server is to ensure there are not multiple databases per storage group: It may be necessary to create additional storage groups and databases and move users. Once the storage group is ready, enable LCR with the Enable-DatabaseCopy cmdlet:

```
Enable-DatabaseCopy -Identity <DatabaseIdParameter> [-CopyEdbFilePath
<EdbFilePath>] [-DomainController <Fqdn>]
```

The `Identity` parameter is the database source that will be LCR enabled. This database cannot be a recovery storage group database.

The parameter `CopyEdbFilePath` is the location of the backup database (`.edb`) file. This path cannot be the same as the source location. Also, the LCR database filename must be identical to the source database filename.

The following example enables LCR on the first storage group on the server MB100:

```
Enable-DatabaseCopy -Identity "MB100\First StorageGroup\Mailbox Database"
-CopyEdbFilePath "E:\LCRbackup\storagegroups\sg1db\mailbox database.edb"
```

To check the status of the LCR on a database, check the `HasLocalCopy` parameter from the `Get-MailboxDatabase` cmdlet. If `HasLocalCopy` is `true`, LCR is enabled for that database, and it is `false` otherwise. The following example outputs the LCR status of all mailbox databases in the organization:

```
Get-MailboxDatabase | fl Identity, HasLocalCopy
```

Enabling the Storage Group

Before LCR is enabled, the storage group must also be configured with the `Enable-StorageGroupCopy` cmdlet:

```
Enable-StorageGroupCopy -Identity <StorageGroupIdParameter> [-Confirm
[<SwitchParameter>]] [-CopyLogFolderPath <NonRootLocalLongFullPath>]
[-CopySystemFolderPath <NonRootLocalLongFullPath>] [-DomainController
<Fqdn>] [-ReplayLagTime <Nullable>] [-SeedingPostponed
<SwitchParameter>] [-StandbyMachine <String>] [-TruncationLagTime
<Nullable>] [-WhatIf [<SwitchParameter>]]
```

The `CopyLogFolderPath` and `CopySystemFolderPath` parameters must contain a different path than the source storage group. No other storage groups can share the same path.

The `SeedingPostponed` switch parameter takes no value and prevents the newly enabled storage group copy from automatic seeding. Seeding is discussed in the next section.

This cmdlet continues the previous example, and LCR enables the first storage group on the server MB100 without an initial seeding:

```
Enable-StorageGroupCopy -Identity "mb100\first storage group"
-CopyLogFolderPath "E:\LCRBackup\Logs\SG1Logs" -CopySystemFolderPath
"E:\LCRBackup\Logs\SG1Logs" -SeedingPostponed
```

Installing Clustering Continuous Replication (CCR)

Unlike LCR, CCR can be enabled only when installing the mailbox server. The cluster must be configured before installing the Clustered Mailbox Server (CMS). The CMS is analogous to the Exchange Virtual Server (EVS) in Exchange 2003.

The steps to installing a CCR cluster are:

1. Create the cluster service account
2. Install Windows 2003 R2 SP2 and requirements
3. Create the cluster
4. Create and assign the file share witness
5. Configure the cluster heartbeat
6. Configure the network interfaces
7. Create the Clustered Mailbox Server Active Directory Object
8. Install the Mailbox server role on the primary node
9. Install the Mailbox server role on the secondary node

> *You can find complete non-scripting based instructions for installing Clustering Continuous Replication at* http://technet.microsoft.com/en-us/library/aa997144.aspx *or in the Exchange Server 2007 help file.*

Creating the Cluster Service Account

The service account for the cluster service needs to be a member of the domain. If the installation of the cluster is done by an administrator that is not the service account, the service account will be added to the local administrators group on each node during the installation process. Using this PowerShell script creates a new Organizational Unit (OU) in the Exchangeexchange domain, and creates a new user within that OU and sets his or her password to neverexpire. The final portion also sets the user password:

```
$DC1="exchangeexchange"
$DC2="local"
$DC3=$DC1+"."+$DC2+":389"
$Service_Account_OU="SVC_Accounts"
$User="svc-mb001"
$Password="P@55w0rd"
$objDomain = [ADSI]"LDAP://$DC3/dc=$DC1,dc=$DC2"
$objOU = $objDomain.Create("organizationalUnit", "ou=$Service_Account_OU")
$objOU.SetInfo()
$objOU = [ADSI]"LDAP://$DC3/ou=$Service_Account_OU,dc=$DC1,dc=$DC2"
$objUser = $objOU.Create("user", "cn=$User")
$objUser.Put("sAMAccountName", "$User")
$objUser.SetInfo()
$objUser.SetPassword("$Password")
$objUser.SetInfo()
$objUser.Put("UserAccountControl", "66048")
$objUser.SetInfo()
```

Installing Windows 2003 R2 SP2

Install Windows Server R2 Service Pack 2 on both nodes. Exchange Server 2007 Service Pack 1 requires Service Pack 2 for Windows 2003. The Mailbox server role requires the following components be installed:

- ❏ WWW Service
- ❏ IIS Manager
- ❏ IIS Common Files
- ❏ COM+ Network Access

It is possible to script adding these Windows components with the command-line utility Sysocmgr.exe:

```
Sysocmgr /i:<master_oc_inf> /u:<unattend_spec></q></w></r>
```

- ❏ The /i parameter is the full path to the master OC file. The default location is C:\windows\ inf\sysoc.inf.
- ❏ The /u parameter is the full path to the unattend file that has the components to be installed.
- ❏ The /q switch runs the unattended install without a user interface. The /u switch must be specified to use the /q switch.
- ❏ The /w switch prompts before a reboot. The /u switch must be specified to use the /w switch.
- ❏ The /r switch suppresses a reboot.

For example, first create the Answerfile.inf file with the following lines:

```
[components]
complusnetwork=on
iss_commmon=on
iis_www=on
iis_inetmer=on
```

Next, use Syscomgr.exe to install the components:

```
sysocmgr /i:C:\windows\inf\sysoc.inf /u:c:\answerfile.inf
```

After the installation is complete, it is possible to check the installation with the Add/Remove Programs control panel applet.

Creating the Cluster

Now that Windows and the prerequisites are installed, the Windows cluster can be created. The Windows cluster service manages the shared resources, ensures only one node is active, and performs failover when necessary. The cluster command-line utility, cluster.exe, will install and configure the two-node cluster:

1. To use cluster.exe to create a new cluster, the following parameters are required:

   ❑ Cluster name

   ❑ Cluster IP address

   ❑ User account that will run the cluster service

   ❑ Password for the cluster service user account

   ❑ Hostname of the node that the cluster will be installed on

   Instead of statically defining all of the required parameters, you can use PowerShell as shown here to set all of the parameters as variables, and then you could run the cluster install the script:

```
$Cluster_Name="MB100MSCS"
$Cluster_IP="192.168.1.90"
$Cluster_Subnet="255.255.255.0"
$Interface1_New="Public"
$User (reused from user configuration)
$Password (reused from user configuration)
$Node1_Hostname="MB001A"
$Logfile="c:\mscs_install.txt"
cluster /cluster:$Cluster_Name /create
/IPAddr:$Cluster_IP,$Cluster_Subnet,$Interface1_New
/USER:$User /pass:$Password /node:$Node1_Hostname /verbose > $Logfile
```

2. The command creates a new cluster, but it is not the correct quorum type. There is no way to set the cluster to the type Majority Node Set (MNS) during the initial creation. This will be configured in Steps 3 and 4.

```
Cluster /cluster:$Cluster_Name /create /IPAddr:$Cluster_IP /USER:$User
/password:$Password /node:$Node1_Hostname /verbose > $logfile
```

3. The next command creates the Majority Node Set resource in the cluster group:

```
Cluster resource "Majority Node Set" /create -group:"cluster group"
-type:"Majority Node Set" /online /wait
```

4. Now, change the cluster from a local quorum to Majority Node Set:

```
Cluster -quorum:"Majority Node Set"
```

5.   The last step is to remove the Local Quorum resource that was created in the initial install:

```
Cluster res "Local Quorum" -offline -delete
```

6.   Once the install is complete, the second node can be added by using the following script:

```
$Cluster_Name (reused from the initial configuration above)
$Node2_Hostname="MB101"
$Password (reused from user configuration)
Cluster /cluster:$Cluster_Name /add:$Node2_Hostname /password:$Password /verbose
```

Creating and Assigning the File Share Witness

The file share witness (FSW) feature is an update for MNS clusters. It was released as a post-Windows 2003 SP1 download in kb921181. It is included in Service Pack 2 for Windows 2003. The FSW quorum allows the cluster nodes to share a file share outside of the cluster to add an additional vote for cluster status. As long as any two resources are available, the cluster nodes know which node is active. If two resources go offline, the entire cluster shuts down because it is not possible for a node to know if it is active or passive.

The recommended location for the FSW is on a CAS or Hub server. Another recommendation is to use a DNS CName record for the server name hosting the FSW. This makes changing the server that has the replacement FSW easier because the cluster configuration does not have to change, only the DNS record needs to be updated. If the DNS alias is not used, an administrator would have to go through the steps in this section again to create the new FSW. This process is more time consuming than a simple record update.

1.   First set the parameters needed for the FSW creation:

❑   User is the cluster service account

❑   Cluster_Name is the name of the cluster

❑   User_Perm is the full permission for the cluster service account

❑   Share_Path is the full path for the file share

❑   DirPath is the full path the shared directory

❑   CMS_Name is the name of the Clustered Mailbox Server

```
$Cluster_Name (reused from the initial configuration above)
$User_Perm=$User+":F"
$Share_Path="\\MBFSW\MNS_FSW_MBCCR"
$Share_Name="MNS_FSW_MBCCR"
$Dir_Path="C:\FSWMB100CCR"
$CMS_Name="MB100CCR"
$Share_DNS_Name="MBFSW"
$FSW_Server_Name="CA100.exchangeexchange.local"
$FSW_Share_Full_Path="Mbfsw.exchangeexchange.local\MNS_FSW_MBCCR"
```

2.   From the root of the C drive on the Client Access Server, create the FSW path:

```
Mkdir $Dir_Path
```

3. Next, assign the full permission for the cluster service account to the share:

```
Cacls $Dir_Path /G BUILTIN\Adminsitrators:F $User_Perm
```

4. Create the file share and grant the cluster service account full control:

```
Net share $Share_Name=$Dir_Path /GRANT:"$User,FULL"
```

5. Create the DNS entry for the FSW CName:

```
Dnscmd $DNS_Server /recordadd $DNS_Zone $Share_DNS_NAME CNAME $FSW_Server_Name
```

In order for the CAS to respond to requests with a different hostname, follow `http://support` *.microsoft.com/kb/281308 to implement security workarounds if the connection returns an error when making a connection.*

6. Next, configure the MNS quorum to use the new FSW. This command should be run on the active node:

```
Cluster $Cluster_Name res "Majority Node Set" /priv
MNSFileShare=$FSW_Share_Full_Path
```

7. If the command is successful it will output a warning stating that the changes just made will not take immediate effect. Open the FSW file share and see that it created a new directory. This is where the cluster will store its quorum files.

```
System warning 5024 (0x000013a0).
The properties were stored but not all changes will take effect until the next time
the resource is brought online.
```

8. To force the changes to take effect, fail the cluster group to the passive node:

```
Cluster $Cluster_Name group "Cluster Group" /move
Moving resource group 'Cluster Group'...

Group                Node              Status
-------------------- ----------------  ------
Cluster Group        MB100             Online
```

9. Repeat this again to fail back to the original active node. Finally, check the status of the FSW resource with the following command:

```
Cluster $Cluster_Name res "Majority Node Set" /priv
```

The output from the test server is:

```
T  Resource             Name                             Value
-- -------------------- -------------------------------- -----------------------
S  Majority Node Set    MNSFileShare
\\Mbfsw.exchangeexchange.
local\MNS_FSW_MBCCR
D  Majority Node Set    MNSFileShareCheckInterval        240 (0xf0)
D  Majority Node Set    MNSFileShareDelay                4 (0x4)
```

Configuring the Cluster Heartbeat

Four additional parameters can be changed to control failover behavior:

- ❑ MNSFileShareCheckInterval

- ❑ MNSFileShareDelay

- ❑ HeartBeatLostInterfaceTicks

- ❑ HeartBeatLostNodeTicks

The first two parameters, MNSFileShareCheckInterval and MNSFileShareDelay, control the file share witness health checks. In general, these two settings do not need to be changed.

MNSFileShareCheckInterval is the time interval the cluster uses to verify the health of the file share witness. The default value is 4 minutes (240 seconds), and can be set from 4 seconds to 268,435,455 seconds.

MNSFileShareDelay is the delay in seconds that the cluster node (which does not currently own the file share witness) will wait until it tries to get the vote from the witness. This allows the current owner of the file share witness resource to be preferred when trying to win the vote.

The other two parameters configure the heartbeat. The cluster heartbeat is periodic communications sent between the nodes to confirm the node's network interface is still active. The goal is to minimize unnecessary failovers if a few packets get delayed or dropped. The default configuration sends a heartbeat message every 1.2 seconds from each node. It is not possible to change the timing of the heartbeat message; rather it is possible to configure the number of heartbeats needed to report interface or node failure with the parameters HeartBeatLostInterfaceTicks and HeartBeatLostNodeTicks.

HeartBeatLostInterfaceTicks is 3 missed heartbeats by default and can be configured from 2 to 20. The default for HeartBeatLostNodeTicks is 6 and can be anywhere from 2 to 20.

> http://support.microsoft.com/kb/921181 *goes into great depth explaining the algorithms used to determine heartbeat failures.*

This example sets the heartbeat for the interface to four missed heartbeats, which is about 5 seconds. The node heartbeat is set to 8, which is about 9.6 seconds.

1. First, make sure all the cluster nodes are up with the following command:

```
Cluster $cluster_name node
```

The output should look something like this:

```
Listing status for all available nodes:
Node            Node ID Status
--------------  ------- --------------------
MB101              2       Up
MB100              1       Up
```

2. Next, configure the heartbeat parameters. The `HeartBeatLostInterfaceTicks` should be set to one number higher than the desired missed heartbeats due to the way the algorithm works.

```
Cluster $Cluster_Name /priv HeartBeatLostInterfaceTicks=5:DWORD
Cluster $Cluster_Name /priv HeartBeatLostNodeTicks=8:DWORD
```

3. Finally, restart the cluster service on both nodes:

```
Net stop clussvc
Net start clussvc
```

Configuring the Network Interfaces

One last configuration is to change the private network for cluster use. By default the private adapter is set for all communications. Because the private interfaces are connected via cross-over cables or a non-routed network, the interface should be set to handle only internal cluster communication.

1. The following command changes the private network interface from mixed mode to internal cluster communications only:

```
Cluster network Private /prop Role=1
```

2. The network order must also be set to the public interface first, and then the private interface next. To check the current binding order, run the following command:

```
Cluster $Cluster_Name /listnetpri
```

The output from the test environment is:

```
Listing the priority order of internal networks:

    Network Name
    ---------------
  1 Private
  2 Public
```

3. Because this is the incorrect order, the next step is to set the public interface first. Run the following command:

```
cluster $Cluster_Name /SetnetPri:"public,private"
```

Now the output shows the correct order:

```
Listing the priority order of internal networks:

    Network Name
    ---------------
  1 Public
  2 Private
```

Creating the Clustered Mailbox Server Active Directory Object

In order to be able to create a cluster, a service account must be created in Active Directory. The process consists of the following two steps:

1. This step creates the AD object for the CMS. Because the CMS is not a physical server, it will not be created automatically. First, create a connection to the ExchangeServers OU and save it in a variable. Then set some of the variables that will be used later. Next, create a new computer object and set the common name and sAMaccountName properties. The setInfo() command commits the in-memory computer object and creates a disabled computer object in AD. To enable the account, the UserAccountControl property is set to 4096. Finally, the DNSHostName property is set to the DNS name of the host.

```
$objOU=[ADSI] "LDAP://$dc3/ou=ExchangeServers,dc=$dc1,dc=$dc2"
$CMS_Name="MB100CCR"
$CMS_SAM_Name="MB100CR$"
$objCMS = $objOU.Create("Computer","cn=$CMS_Name")
$objCMS.put("sAMAccountName", "$CMS_SAM_Name")
$objCMS.setinfo()
$objCMS.put("UserAccountControl","4096")
$objCMS.setinfo()
$objCMS.put("DNSHostName",$CMS_Name+"."+$dc1+"."+$dc2)
$objCMS.setinfo()
```

2. Next, assign rights for the cluster service account to the new CMS AD object:

```
#Read Permissions
Add-ADPermission -Identity
"cn=$CMS_Name,ou=exchangeservers,dc=exchangeexchange,dc=local" -User exchexch\svc-
mb001 -AccessRights readcontrol -InheritanceType none

#List Contents
Add-ADPermission -Identity
"cn=$CMS_Name,ou=exchangeservers,dc=exchangeexchange,dc=local" -User exchexch\svc-
mb001 -AccessRights listchildren -InheritanceType none

#Read Property
Add-ADPermission -Identity
"cn=$CMS_Name,ou=exchangeservers,dc=exchangeexchange,dc=local" -User exchexch\svc-
mb001 -AccessRights ReadProperty -InheritanceType none

#List Object
Add-ADPermission -Identity
"cn=$CMS_Name,ou=exchangeservers,dc=exchangeexchange,dc=local" -User exchexch\svc-
mb001 -AccessRights ListObject -InheritanceType none

#Control Access
Add-ADPermission -Identity
"cn=$CMS_Name,ou=exchangeservers,dc=exchangeexchange,dc=local" -User exchexch\svc-
mb001 -AccessRights ExtendedRight -InheritanceType none
```

(continued)

(continued)

```
#Write Property - Logon Information
Add-ADPermission -Identity
"cn=$CMS_Name,ou=exchangeservers,dc=exchangeexchange,dc=local" -User exchexch\svc-
mb001 -AccessRights WriteProperty -Properties User-Logon -InheritanceType none

#Write Property - Description
Add-ADPermission -Identity
"cn=$CMS_Name,ou=exchangeservers,dc=exchangeexchange,dc=local" -User exchexch\svc-
mb001 -AccessRights WriteProperty -Properties description -InheritanceType none

#Write Property - sAMAccountName
Add-ADPermission -Identity
"cn=$CMS_Name,ou=exchangeservers,dc=exchangeexchange,dc=local" -User exchexch\svc-
mb001 -AccessRights WriteProperty -Properties sAMAccountName -InheritanceType none

#Write Property - Account Restrictions
Add-ADPermission -Identity
"cn=$CMS_Name,ou=exchangeservers,dc=exchangeexchange,dc=local" -User exchexch\svc-
mb001 -AccessRights WriteProperty -Properties User-Account-Restrictions -
InheritanceType none

#Validated write to DNS host name
Add-ADPermission -Identity
"cn=$CMS_Name,ou=exchangeservers,dc=exchangeexchange,dc=local" -User exchexch\svc-
mb001 -accessrights self -Properties DNS-Host-Name -InheritanceType none

#Validated write to service principal name
Add-ADPermission -Identity
"cn=$CMS_Name,ou=exchangeservers,dc=exchangeexchange,dc=local" -User exchexch\svc-
mb001 -accessrights self -Properties Service-Principal-Name -InheritanceType none
```

Installing the Mailbox Server Role on the Primary Node

At this point the cluster is finished, but Exchange has not yet been installed. Now that all the prerequisites are complete it is time to install the Clustered Mailbox Server. Again, the CMS is the "floating" Exchange server that can move between nodes. This is what mail clients, such as Outlook, connect to. Unattended installs are run from setup.com on the Exchange DVD. There are many arguments for setup, but only a few are related to installing the CCR cluster.

The mode parameter can be Install, Uninstall, and RecoverServer. If it is not specified, Install is assumed.

The role parameter indicates which server role is installed. Possible values are MB or M for the Mailbox role.

The switch /newcms denotes the mailbox install with be a clustered install:

```
./setup.com /mode:install /role:mb /newcms /cmsname:$CMS_Name
/cmsIPAddress:$CMS_IPADDRESS
```

Note the ./ before setup.com. *This is a security mechanism in PowerShell to prevent malicious code or an administrator from inadvertently running an executable.*

Installing the Mailbox Server Role on the Secondary Node

To install the passive node, simply run the setup on the second node:

```
./setup.com /mode:install /role:mb
```

Once the passive node install is complete, the next step is to create storage groups and other configurations. Creating storage groups and other mailbox-configuration tasks is covered in Chapter 8.

Installing Standby Continuous Replication (SCR)

There are a number of requirements to enable an SCR target. An SCR target is a mailbox server that is not part of a cluster, and it receives a copy of a storage group from another mailbox server. This design is described at the beginning of this chapter.

- ❑ SCR targets must be in the same Active Directory domain.

- ❑ SCR targets have a maximum of 50 replicated storage groups. It is a good idea to keep an SCR source to SCR target at a 1:1 ratio, rather than configuring multiple SCR sources to the same SCR target.

- ❑ The database and transaction log paths must match on the SCR source and SCR target. This includes the drive letters as well.

- ❑ An SCR target cannot enable LCR on the replicated storage group.

- ❑ An SCR target configured with CCR or SCC must not have a Clustered Mailbox Server installed.

There are a few ways to create SCR targets for storage groups. One way is with the New-StorageGroup cmdlet. This cmdlet is covered in detail in Chapter 8, but it has been updated to include the ability to create a storage group enabled for SCR.

```
New-StorageGroup -Name <String> [-CircularLoggingEnabled <$true | $false>]
[-Confirm [<SwitchParameter>]] [-CopyLogFolderPath <NonRootLocalLongFullPath>]
[-CopySystemFolderPath <NonRootLocalLongFullPath>] [-DomainController <Fqdn>]
[-HasLocalCopy <$true | $false>] [-LogFolderPath <NonRootLocalLongFullPath>]
[-ReplayLagTime <Nullable>] [-Server <ServerIdParameter>] [-StandbyMachine
<String>] [-SystemFolderPath <NonRootLocalLongFullPath>] [-TemplateInstance
<PSObject>] [-TruncationLagTime <Nullable>] [-WhatIf [<SwitchParameter>]]
[-ZeroDatabasePages <$true | $false>]
New-StorageGroup [-Name <String>] -Recovery <SwitchParameter> [-Confirm
[<SwitchParameter>]] [-DomainController <Fqdn>] [-LogFolderPath
<NonRootLocalLongFullPath>] [-Server <ServerIdParameter>] [-SystemFolderPath
<NonRootLocalLongFullPath>] [-TemplateInstance <PSObject>] [-WhatIf
[<SwitchParameter>]]
```

Enabling existing storage groups is similar to the process for enabling LCR clustering. Both LCR and SCR use the `Enable-StorageGroupCopy` cmdlet. The Service Pack 1 versions for these cmdlets contain three new parameters for SCR:

- ❏   `StandbyMachine`

- ❏   `ReplayLagTime`

- ❏   `TruncationLagTime`

The `StandbyMachine` string parameter specifies the name of the mailbox server that will be the SCR target.

The `ReplayLagTime` parameter sets the amount of time the SCR target will wait before replaying log files from the source. The syntax is `Days.Hours:Minutes.Seconds`, and has a default setting of 24 hours. The minimum value is 0, however there is an overall minimum of 50 log files that cannot be changed. Having a lag of 50 log files reduces the chance for the need to reseed the SCR target if the SCR source experiences a lossy failover.

The SCR target does not create its database until it receives the first 50 logs.

The `TruncationLagTime` parameter sets the amount of time the SCR target waits before truncating log files that have been replayed into the SCR target's database copy. The syntax is `Days.Hours:Minutes.Seconds` and can be set from 0 to 7 days.

To change `ReplayLagTime` or `TruncationLagTime`, SCR must be disabled and re-enabled with the new values.

For this example, the Mailbox server role was added to the CA100, the test Client Access Server. Next, SCR was enabled for the "First Storage Group" storage group on the CCR cluster MB100CCR:

```
Enable-StorageGroupCopy -Identity "MB100CCR\First Storage Group"
-StandbyServer CA100
```

Seeding

After continuous replication has been enabled, the next step is to seed the passive node. *Seeding* is the process of making a complete copy of the source database file. Once the database file has been copied, the asynchronous log file shipping can start. The database can either be manually copied, or copied with the `Update-StorageGroupCopy` cmdlet.

The following cmdlets are necessary for seeding:

- ❏   `Suspend-StorageGroupCopy`

- ❏   `Update-StorageGroupCopy`

- ❏   `Resume-StorageGroupCopy`

- ❏   `Get-StorageGroupCopyStatus`

- ❏   `Get-StorageGroup`

Seeding can also be required under the following conditions:

- ❑ Initial seed
- ❑ Offline defragmentation was run against the source database
- ❑ Database divergence as a result of failover
- ❑ The LCR or CCR copy is corrupt
- ❑ Server loss

The process for seeding is the same for LCR, CCR, and SCR. First, `Suspend-StorageGroupCopy` stops any current log replication. This step may not be necessary for a first-time seed.

```
Suspend-StorageGroupCopy -Identity <StorageGroupIdParameter>
[-DomainController <Fqdn>] [-SuspendComment <String>] [-WhatIf <Boolean>]
[-Confirm <Boolean>]
```

The `SuspendComment` is an optional string used for commenting on why the storage group was suspended. Even though this is an optional parameter, it is a good idea to use it. For example, after a disaster recovery the suspend comment in the event log can help pinpoint when tasks were done.

This example suspends all of the storage groups on server MB100:

```
Get-StorageGroup -Server mb100 | Suspend-StorageGroupCopy
```

To check the status, run `Get-StorageGroupCopyStatus`:

```
Get-StorageGroupCopyStatus [-Identity <StorageGroupIdParameter>]
[-DomainController <Fqdn>] [-DumpsterStatistics <SwitchParameter>]
[-StandbyMachine <String>]
Get-StorageGroupCopyStatus -Server <ServerIdParameter> [-DomainController <Fqdn>]
[-DumpsterStatistics <SwitchParameter>] [-StandbyMachine <String>]
```

The `Identity` and `Server` parameters allow the results to be scoped to a particular server or storage group. This cmdlet is detailed in the next section on monitoring continuous replication.

This example shows the status of the storage group on the mailbox server mb100 that was suspended in the previous example:

```
[PS] C:\>Get-StorageGroupCopyStatus

Name                 SummaryCopySt CopyQueueLeng ReplayQueueL LastInspecte
                     atus          th            ength        dLogTime
----                 ------------- ------------- ------------ ------------
First Storage Group  Suspended     0             0            8/17/2007...
```

Once replication has been suspended, the `Update-StorageGroupCopy` cmdlet does the seeding:

```
Update-StorageGroupCopy -Identity <StorageGroupIdParameter> [-Confirm
[<SwitchParameter>]] [-DataHostNames <String[]>] [-DeleteExistingFiles
<SwitchParameter>] [-DomainController <Fqdn>] [-Force <SwitchParameter>]
[-ManualResume <SwitchParameter>] [-StandbyMachine <String>] [-TargetPath
<LocalLongFullPath>] [-WhatIf [<SwitchParameter>]]
```

The new string parameter `StandbyMachine` is used to seed an SCR target.

The `Update-StorageGroupCopy` must be run on the node that will be seeded.

The switch `DeleteExistingFiles` tells the cmdlet to delete any existing database and log files after it successfully copies the files from the source node:

```
Get-StorageGroup | Update-StorageGroupcopy -DeleteExistingFiles
```

As the reseed copies the files, a progress bar appears. Figure 12-4 shows the storage group updating.

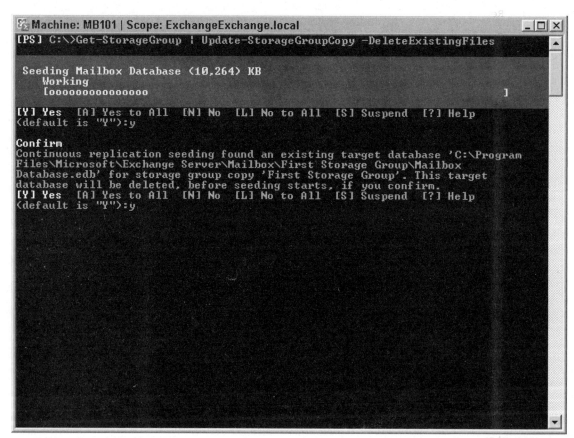

Figure 12-4

After successfully running the update command on the passive node, replication is automatically resumed unless the `ManualResume` switch was included. Running the `Get-StorageGroupCopyStatus` after the reseed shows the copy as healthy:

```
Get-StorageGroupCopyStatus
Name                  SummaryCopySt CopyQueueLeng ReplayQueueL LastInspecte
                      atus          th            ength        dLogTime
----                  ------------- ------------- ------------ -----------
First Storage Group   Healthy       5             0            8/17/2007...
```

Monitoring

Let's dig a little deeper into learning how to assess the health of a cluster. A number of cmdlets are used to discover the health of the server and clustering related services:

- ❏   Get-StorageGroupCopyStatus
- ❏   Get-ClusteredMailboxServerStatus
- ❏   Resume-StorageGroupCopy
- ❏   Get-StorageGroupCopyStatus
- ❏   Get-StorageGroup
- ❏   Stop-ClusteredMailboxServer

Cluster Status

The first place to look for server health is the Clustered Mailbox Server (CMS) state. This returns the state of the cluster and resource ownership:

```
Get-ClusteredMailboxServerStatus [-Identity <ServerIdParameter>]
[-DomainController <Fqdn>] [<CommonParameters>]
```

The result of `Get-ClusteredMailboxServerStatus` in the test environment shows that MB100 is the active node and also has the quorum resource:

```
Identity                    : mb100ccr
ClusteredMailboxServerName  : MB100CCR.ExchangeExchange.local
State                       : Online
OperationalMachines         : {MB100 <Active, Quorum Owner>, MB101}
FailedResources             : {}
IsValid                     : True
ObjectState                 : Unchanged
```

To show how the cluster would look offline, use the `Stop-ClusteredMailboxServer` cmdlet to shut down the cluster. It is important to use PowerShell cmdlets, not the Cluster Administrator utility to perform these actions. The Cluster Administrator utility is not Exchange aware. The PowerShell cmdlets perform additional checks to ensure the passive node is up to date. Cluster Administrator does not perform any of these checks and could cause problems. Also, the cmdlets allow an administrator to comment on the failover reason.

```
Stop-ClusteredMailboxServer -Identity <MailboxServerIdParameter>
-StopReason <String> [-DomainController <Fqdn>] [<CommonParameters>]
```

The `StopReason` string parameter is required, and should provide an explanation as to why the administrator is taking the cluster offline. By default, the cmdlet also requires confirmation to continue.

After running the `Stop-ClusteredMailboxServer` cmdlet, the status shows the state is `Offline` and in a `Valid` state:

```
[PS] C:\>Stop-ClusteredMailboxServer -StopReason "Server Maintenance"
-Identity MB100CCR

Confirm
Are you sure you want to perform this action?
Clustered mailbox server "MB100CCR" is stopping with stop reason "Server
Maintenance".
[Y] Yes  [A] Yes to All  [N] No  [L] No to All  [S] Suspend  [?] Help
(default is "Y"):y

FailedToOffline :
Identity        : mb100ccr
State           : Offline
IsValid         : True
ObjectState     : Changed
```

Replication Status

Another area for measuring cluster health is looking at the replication status. The `Get-StorageGroupCopyStatus` cmdlet was covered briefly in the section on seeding. As shown before, the cmdlet returns a brief snapshot of the current replication state:

```
Get-StorageGroupCopyStatus
Name                      SummaryCopySt CopyQueueLeng ReplayQueueL LastInspecte
                          atus          th            ength        dLogTime
----                      ------------- ------------- ------------ -----------
First Storage Group       Healthy       5             0            8/17/2007...
```

Piping the cmdlet to `format-list` (`fl`) gives more detail about the cluster server health. The key fields are `SummaryCopyStatus`, `CopyQueueLength`, `ReplayQueueLength`, and `LastInspectedLogTime`. Looking at the last log parameters shows the log shipping is current by comparing the log number. If the `CopyQueueLength` is more than 5 generations behind or the `ReplayQueueLength` is more than 20 logs behind, the reason should be investigated and corrected. In addition, the `LastInspectedLogTime` should be recent.

New in Service Pack 1 is the `DumpsterStatistics` switch parameter. This returns additional information about the transport dumpster. For example, in the test environment, running the following cmdlet:

```
Get-ClusteredMailboxServerStatus -DumpsterStatistics | fl
```

generates the following output:

```
Identity                          : mb100ccr\First Storage Group
StorageGroupName                  : First Storage Group
SummaryCopyStatus                 : Healthy
NotSupported                      : False
NotConfigured                     : False
Disabled                          : False
ServiceDown                       : False
Failed                            : False
Initializing                      : False
Resynchronizing                   : False
Seeding                           : False
Suspend                           : False
CCRTargetNode                     : MB101
FailedMessage                     :
SuspendComment                    :
CopyQueueLength                   : 0
ReplayQueueLength                 : 0
LatestAvailableLogTime            : 8/25/2007 2:51:19 PM
LastCopyNotificationedLogTime     : 8/25/2007 2:51:19 PM
LastCopiedLogTime                 : 8/25/2007 2:51:19 PM
LastInspectedLogTime              : 8/25/2007 2:51:19 PM
LastReplayedLogTime               : 8/25/2007 2:51:19 PM
LastLogGenerated                  : 113
LastLogCopyNotified               : 113
LastLogCopied                     : 113
LastLogInspected                  : 113
LastLogReplayed                   : 113
LatestFullBackupTime              : 8/25/2007 9:34:28 AM
LatestIncrementalBackupTime       :
SnapshotBackup                    : False
IsValid                           : True
ObjectState                       : Unchanged
DumpsterServersNotAvailable       : {}
DumpsterStatistics                : {CA100(8/18/2007 8:38:06 PM;1;2450MB)}
```

To obtain information about an SCR target, the StandbyMachine string parameter must be included with the name of the SCR target.

Service Pack 1 introduces the Test-ReplicationHealth cmdlet. The Test-ReplicationHealth cmdlet incorporates tests for all parts of the replication process.

```
Test-ReplicationHealth [-ActiveDirectoryTimeout <Int32>] [-Confirm
[<SwitchParameter>]] [-DomainController <Fqdn>] [-MonitoringContext
<$true | $false>] [-TransientEventSuppressionWindow <UInt32>] [-WhatIf
[<SwitchParameter>]]
```

When set to $true, the MonitoringContext parameter includes extra information in the cmdlet's output.

In the following example the cmdlet is run from the active node on the test mailbox cluster:

```
Test-ReplicationHealth -MonitoringContext:$true
```

to produce the following:

```
Server          Check                   Result      Error
------          -----                   ------      -----
MB100           PassiveNodeUp           Passed
MB100           ClusterNetwork          Passed
MB100           QuorumGroup             Passed
MB100           FileShareQuorum         Passed
MB100           CmsGroup                Passed
MB100           NodePaused              Passed
MB100           DnsRegistrationStatus   Passed
MB100           ReplayService           Passed
MB100           DBMountedFailover       Passed

Events                  : {Source: MSExchange Monitoring ReplicationHealth
                          Id: 10000
                          Type: Success
                          Message: No monitoring errors occurred. All Exchange
                          replication health checks passed.}
PerformanceCounters : {}
```

Performance Monitor

Another way to monitor the system is through Performance Monitor. The following example shows the script pattern that can be used to retrieve any counter. The first thing to do is the counter, object, instance, and server parameters. The script sets the variables to get the CopyQueueLength on the passive node. To get information about replication, the server must be set to the passive node. This example also shows how to make the output overwrite itself, instead of continually scrolling.

```
$Current = $host.UI.RawUI.Get_CursorPosition()
$Object="MSExchange Replication"
$Counter="CopyQueueLength"
$Instance="First Storage Group"
$Passive_Node="MB101"

$perf = New-Object System.diagnostics.performancecounter( $Object, $Counter,
$Instance, $Passive_Node)

While (1)
{
 $perf.RawValue
 Start-Sleep -seconds 1
 $host.UI.RawUI.Set_CursorPosition($Current)
}
```

Failover Types

There are two types of failover in Exchange Server 2007: planned and unplanned. The various methods of continuous replication have different recovery strategies. This section examines the difference between the two, and how to control failover features. The following cmdlets are used:

- ❏ `Move-ClusteredMailboxServer`
- ❏ `Set-MailboxServer`
- ❏ `Restore-StorageGroupCopy`
- ❏ `Mount-Database`
- ❏ `Dismount-Database`

The continuous replication model uses asynchronous log shipping to keep the passive node up to date. The Microsoft Exchange Replication Service on the passive node is responsible for copying the 1MB logs as they are created on the active node. Because the passive node is always at least one log file behind (the active log) Exchange implemented Lost Log Resiliency (LLR). LLR delays the active node from committing the log files as they are closed. This allows an administrator to mount the passive node without all of the log files, and not cause divergence. Divergence is when the active and passive nodes have different copies of a database. Once the nodes have diverged, the only remedy is to reseed the database. When a failover occurs and one or more log files are missing, this is called a lossy failover. If all the logs are able to be copied to the passive node, this is called a lossless failover.

During a planned (administrative) failover, all of the logs are copied to the passive node. This means that a planned failover is always lossless.

The transport dumpster feature helps minimize loss of mail during a lossy failover. The transport dumpster holds on to a limited amount of mail. After a lossy failover, the mailbox server then requests redelivery of messages to minimize any data loss from the missing log files. The mail server just deletes any messages that it already has committed. Keep in mind, this only covers items that flow through the Hub transport servers. Other items, such as updating personal contacts, tasks, and appointments, or flagging a message will not be redelivered and are lost. The transport dumpster feature was only available to CCR clusters in the release version of Exchange Server 2007. Service Pack 1 extends the feature for LCR clusters as well.

Failover in Local Cluster Replication

LCR provides a quick recovery method when there is trouble with the active database and log files. It is a manual process to bring the database back online. The actual recovery steps may differ depending on what the cause of the failure is and what state the production database and log files are in.

The actual steps may change based upon the cause of the failure, and the condition of the active database and log files. The general recovery process starts with dismounting the active database. The dismount is performed using the `Dismount-Database` cmdlet. For example:

```
Dismount-Database -Identity "MB100ccr\first storage group\mailbox database"
```

Once the database has dismounted, the LCR passive copy needs to be activated, and the LCR copy stopped. The `Restore-StorageGroupCopy` cmdlet does both, and leaves the storage group and database paths unchanged. Leaving the paths unchanged is preferred to minimize confusion as to where the active copy should be. In this scenario, it is necessary to move the files, or mount the passive node LUNs to replace the failed active ones.

```
Restore-StorageGroupCopy -Identity "MB100ccr\first storage group\mailbox database"
```

If it is not possible to recover by moving the files or swapping LUNs, then the `Restore-StorageGroupCopy` cmdlet should include the `ReplaceLocations` option to alter the database and system paths:

```
Restore-StorageGroupCopy -Identity "MB100ccr\first storage group\mailbox
database" - ReplaceLocations:$true
```

Finally, the database can be mounted with the `Mount-Database` cmdlet:

```
Mount-Database -Identity "MB100ccr\first storage group\mailbox database"
```

It is easy to see how the addition of LCR can greatly reduce the downtime due to disk failure or corruption. LCR can be used to alter the standard backup process because the first level of recovery is online disk. A company may choose to have short SLAs for database recovery, but use longer SLAs for server failures.

Failover in Continuous Cluster Replication

Unlike LCR, CCR has a fully automated unplanned failover process. There are administrative settings that tune the failover process. Because an unplanned failover may have data loss, it is possible to set the rules under which the passive node will mount databases. This logic is tuned with the `AutoDatabaseMountDial` parameter. There are three possible settings:

- ❑ Lossless
- ❑ GoodAvailability
- ❑ BestAvailability

The `Lossless` setting prevents the passive node from mounting if any logs are missing. In most circumstances the system will need to wait until the failed node is back online and the missing logs can be copied to the passive node. This setting allows for an administrator to explicitly decide when to bring a failed system online.

`GoodAvailability` sets the copy queue to three logs and `BestAvailability` is six logs.

The next tuning parameter is `ForceDatabaseMountAfter`. The `ForceDatabaseMountAfter` setting forces the database to mount after a specified period of time. For example, if `ForceDatabaseMountAfter` is set to one hour, if the passive node fails to copy all required logs the database will mount with some data loss.

Both of these parameters are configured with the `Set-MailboxServer` cmdlet:

```
Set-MailboxServer -Identity <MailboxServerIdParameter> [-AutoDatabaseMountDial
<Lossless | GoodAvailability | BestAvailability>] [-ClusteredStorageType
<Disabled | NonShared | Shared>] [-Confirm [<SwitchParameter>]]
[-DomainController <Fqdn>] [-FolderLogForManagedFoldersEnabled <$true |
$false>] [-ForcedDatabaseMountAfter <Unlimited>]
[-JournalingLogForManagedFoldersEnabled <$true | $false>] [-Locale
<MultiValuedProperty>] [-LogDirectorySizeLimitForManagedFolders <Unlimited>]
[-LogFileAgeLimitForManagedFolders <EnhancedTimeSpan>]
[-LogFileSizeLimitForManagedFolders <Unlimited>] [-LogPathForManagedFolders
<LocalLongFullPath>] [-ManagedFolderAssistantSchedule <ScheduleInterval[]>]
[-MAPIEncryptionRequired <$true | $false>] [-MessageTrackingLogEnabled <$true
| $false>] [-MessageTrackingLogMaxAge <EnhancedTimeSpan>]
[-MessageTrackingLogMaxDirectorySize <Unlimited>]
[-MessageTrackingLogMaxFileSize <Unlimited>] [-MessageTrackingLogPath
<LocalLongFullPath>] [-MessageTrackingLogSubjectLoggingEnabled <$true |
$false>] [-RedundantMachines <MultiValuedProperty>] [-ReplicationNetworks
<PrivateOnly | PrivateThenMixed | AllNetworks>]
[-RetentionLogForManagedFoldersEnabled <$true | $false>]
[-SubjectLogForManagedFoldersEnabled <$true | $false>]
[-SubmissionServerOverrideList <MultiValuedProperty>] [-WhatIf
[<SwitchParameter>]]
Set-MailboxServer [-AutoDatabaseMountDial <Lossless | GoodAvailability |
BestAvailability>] [-ClusteredStorageType <Disabled | NonShared | Shared>]
[-Confirm [<SwitchParameter>]] [-DomainController <Fqdn>]
[-FolderLogForManagedFoldersEnabled <$true | $false>]
[-ForcedDatabaseMountAfter <Unlimited>] [-Instance <MailboxServer>]
[-JournalingLogForManagedFoldersEnabled <$true | $false>] [-Locale
<MultiValuedProperty>] [-LogDirectorySizeLimitForManagedFolders <Unlimited>]
[-LogFileAgeLimitForManagedFolders <EnhancedTimeSpan>]
[-LogFileSizeLimitForManagedFolders <Unlimited>] [-LogPathForManagedFolders
<LocalLongFullPath>] [-ManagedFolderAssistantSchedule <ScheduleInterval[]>]
[-MAPIEncryptionRequired <$true | $false>] [-MessageTrackingLogEnabled <$true
| $false>] [-MessageTrackingLogMaxAge <EnhancedTimeSpan>]
[-MessageTrackingLogMaxDirectorySize <Unlimited>]
[-MessageTrackingLogMaxFileSize <Unlimited>] [-MessageTrackingLogPath
<LocalLongFullPath>] [-MessageTrackingLogSubjectLoggingEnabled <$true |
$false>] [-RedundantMachines <MultiValuedProperty>] [-ReplicationNetworks
<PrivateOnly | PrivateThenMixed | AllNetworks>]
[-RetentionLogForManagedFoldersEnabled <$true | $false>]
[-SubjectLogForManagedFoldersEnabled <$true | $false>]
[-SubmissionServerOverrideList <MultiValuedProperty>] [-WhatIf
[<SwitchParameter>]]
```

Some interesting parameters related to continuous clustering include:

❑   `AutoDatabaseMountDial`

❑   `ForcedDatabaseAfterMount`

❑   `ReplaceLocations`

❑   `ReplicationNetworks`

There are a number of scenarios when an administrator must take manual actions to bring the passive node online with the `Restore-StorageGroupCopy` cmdlet.

Some examples are:

- ❑ In a CCR cluster the `AutoDatabaseMountDial` setting is lossless
- ❑ In a CCR cluster the database fails to automatically mount
- ❑ To bring the passive copy online in an LCR cluster
- ❑ To bring the SCR target online in an SCR cluster

The syntax of the `Restore-StorageGroupCopy` cmdlet is:

```
Restore-StorageGroupCopy -Identity <StorageGroupIdParameter> [-Confirm
[<SwitchParameter>]] [-DomainController <Fqdn>] [-Force <SwitchParameter>]
[-ReplaceLocations <SwitchParameter>] [-StandbyMachine <String>] [-WhatIf
[<SwitchParameter>]]
```

The `ReplaceLocations` switch is used in an LCR configuration only. This switch stops replication and changes the storage group and database paths to the LCR copy.

New in Service Pack 1 is the `StandbyMachine` string parameter. This parameter specifies the name of the SCR host to activate.

The `Force` switch defaults to `$true` if not specified. The `Force` switch must be present to activate an SCR target when the SCR source is not available.

After the `Restore-StorageGroupCopy` cmdlet completes, the administrator can mount the database with the `Mount-Database` cmdlet.

The syntax for `Mount-Database` is:

```
Mount-Database -Identity <DatabaseIdParameter> [-AcceptDataLoss
<SwitchParameter>] [-Confirm [<SwitchParameter>]] [-DomainController
<Fqdn>] [-Force <SwitchParameter>] [-WhatIf [<SwitchParameter>]]
```

New in Service Pack 1 is the `AcceptDataLoss` switch. This switch causes the cmdlet to accept data loss caused by missing committed log files.

Putting the steps together, this is an example of making the passive node viable for mounting with the `Restore-StorageGroupCopy` cmdlet. To make the passive node active, the database is then mounted with `Mount-Database`. If there is data loss or the SCR source is unavailable, the `Force` parameter is required to override the warnings.

```
Restore-StorageGroupCopy -Identity "First Storage Group"
Mount-Database -Identity "MB101\First Storage Group\Mailbox Database"
```

One shortcut is the addition of a new script located by default at `C:\program files\Microsoft\Exchange Server\Scripts`. The script's name is `GetSCRSources.ps1`. Given an SCR target, the script will output all of the SCR sources it is a target for. For example, instead of running multiple `Restore-StorageGroupCopy` cmdlets:

```
Restore-StorageGroupCopy -Identity "mb100CCR\First Storage Group"
-StandbyMachine ca100 -force

Restore-StorageGroupCopy -Identity "mb100CCR\Second □Storage Group"
-StandbyMachine ca100 -force

Restore-StorageGroupCopy -Identity "mb100CCR\Third Storage Group"
-StandbyMachine ca100 -force
```

you can use the following:

```
GetSCRSources | Restore-StorageGroupCopy -StandbyMachine $env:ComputerName
-Force
```

The steps are the same for a single target SCR or a clustered target SCR. The failback steps are different, and are covered in the next section.

Another key new feature introduced in Service Pack 1 is the ability to replicate transaction log files over different networks. In the RTM version, only the public interface was used during normal replication. This setting is controlled with the `ReplicationNetworks` parameter. The parameter can be set to `PrivateOnly`, `PrivateThenMixed`, or `AllNetworks`:

```
Set-MailboxServer -Identity mb100ccr -ReplicationNetworks PrivateThenMixed
```

If the mailbox servers are connected with a cross-over cable, this can save significant traffic from the public network.

Failover in Standby Continuous Replication

Like LCR, Standby Continuous Replication is not an automated failover. SCR is meant for significant failures, not routine maintenance or other smaller outages. The steps are very similar to LCR, except the recovery is to a standby server using the database portability feature of Exchange Server 2007. Because the server name changes, it impacts all Outlook clients. Office Outlook 2007 clients will automatically reconfigure their profiles with Autodiscover, but older clients may need to be manually updated. The process is different if failing to a single server or a CCR cluster. First are the steps used to activate the passive node on a single SCR target.

The high-level steps are:

1. Dismount the source database

2. Validate the passive node database and log files

3. Run the `Restore-StorageGroupCopy` cmdlet to allow the target to mount the database

4. Run the `Move-StorageGroupCopyPath` cmdlet to update the storage group path

5. Run the `Move-DatabasePath` cmdlet to update the database path

6. Mark the database for `AllowFileRestore` with the `Set-MailboxDatabase` cmdlet

7. Mount the database on the SCR target

8. Move the users' mailbox configuration with the `Move-Mailbox` cmdlet

9. On clustered SCR sources, clear the local CMS configuration with `Setup.com`

The SCR target should be configured with an empty storage group and database, with paths that will not conflict with the SCR target paths. These will be the storage group and database used for the portability recovery.

In this example scenario, the CMS will failover to the standby server ca100:

1. The first step in activating the SCR target is to dismount the SCR source database on mb100ccr:

```
Dismount-Database -Identity "mb100ccr\first storage group\mailbox database"
```

2. Next, run the `Restore-StorageGroupCopy` cmdlet to allow the SCR target's database copy to be mounted. This step will try to copy any remaining log files, and also report on the data loss if applicable. If the storage group prefix is different between the SCR source and SCR target, run `Eseutil` in recovery mode. The prefix, in this case E00, represents the first storage group. The second storage group will be E01, and so forth. Because the SCR target may have different servers as SCR sources, the storage group numbers (and prefixes) will not match. In this example the log prefix is E00:

```
Eseutil /r E00

Restore-StorageGroupCopy -Identity "mb100ccr\first storage group"
-StandbyMachine ca100
```

3. Now the database and system paths must be updated in Active Directory with the new location on the SCR target server. This is accomplished with the `Move-StorageGroupPath` and `Move-DatabasePath` cmdlets:

```
Move-StorageGroupPath -Identity ca100\SG1Temp -SystemFolderPath
"C:\Program files\Microsoft\Exchange\mailbox\First Storage Group"
-LogFolderPath "C:\Program files\Microsoft\Exchange\mailbox\First Storage
Group" -ConfigurationOnly

Move-DatabasePath -Identity "ca100\SG1Temp\Mailbox Database" -EdbFilePath
"C:\Program files\Microsoft\Exchange\mailbox\First Storage Group" -
ConfigurationOnly
```

4. Before the database can be mounted, it must be enabled with the "`This database can be overwritten by a restore`" property on the database. The following cmdlet sets this on the SCR target database:

```
Set-MailboxDatabase -Identity "ca100\SG1Temp\Mailbox Database"
-AllowFileRestore:$true
```

5. Finally, mount the database:

```
Mount-Database -Identity "ca100\SG1Temp\Mailbox Database"
```

6. Before clients can access the database, they must be re-homed to the SCR target. The following example moves all of the mailboxes from the SCR source to the SCR target. Note the example prevents system accounts from being included.

```
Get-MailboxStatistics -Database mb100ccr\first storage group\mailbox database
|where {$_.ObjectClass -NotMatch '(SystemAttendantMailbox | ExOleDbSystemMailbox)'}
| Move-Mailbox -ConfigurationOnly -TargetDatabase
"ca100\Sg1Temp\Mailbox Database"
```

For scenarios with the SCR source as an SCC or CCR cluster, a few additional steps need to be run in order to prevent any conflicts when the failed source is brought online.

In this example the CCR cluster, mb100ccr, is made of an active node (mb100) and the passive node (mb101). Bring up mb100 first, then mb101. The Clustered Mailbox Server will remain offline to prevent duplicate names on the network.

1. On the node that owns the resource group for the Clustered Mailbox Server, run setup to clear the CMS and its resources. The following command is run on mb100:

```
Setup.com /ClearLocalCMS /CMSName:mb100ccr
```

2. Verify with Cluster Administrator that all cluster server resources have been removed. These are all of the steps needed; however, all of the configuration information must replicate through Active Directory before all clients can access the SCR target.

Failback

Failback is the process of returning servers to their original state after a failure. It is equally important to understand and practice as failing over. Each type of replication has its own methods of failback. This section introduces the following cmdlets that relate to failback:

❑ Move-ClusteredMailboxServer

❑ Set-MailboxServer

❑ Restore-StorageGroupCopy

❑ Mount-Database

❑ Dismount-Database

Failback in Local Continuous Replication

The method you use to return to the original configuration for LCR depends on how the LCR failover was performed. In the scenario where the original paths were kept and the underlying storage was switched, recovery consists of fixing passive storage and re-enabling LCR.

If the paths were reconfigured during passive node activation, then the same process can be used to revert back to the original storage. The original storage is brought back online and is LCR enabled. From this point, the process is the same as in the original failover.

The steps previously discussed are:

1. Run `Dismount-Database` on the active database
2. Run `Restore-StorageGroupCopy` to allow the passive node to mount the database
3. Mount the database on the passive copy

Failback in Cluster Continuous Replication

Failing back from a failure in a CCR is simply performing an administrative failover. Before the failover, the passive node may need to be reseeded to bring the node to current state.

In the event that a server needs to be rebuilt, there are some additional steps to follow. On the new server, install the mailbox server role on. Next run `setup.com` in recovery mode:

```
Setup.com /recoverCMS /CMSName mb100ccr /CMSIPaddress:192.168.1.80
```

For CCR, reseed the node to bring the node to current state. Once replication is healthy, an administrative failover will return the original node back as it was before failure.

Failback in Standby Continuous Replication

Once the SCR source is brought back online, the Clustered Mailbox Server can return to the original cluster. At this point, the two original nodes are clustered without a CMS, and they have the mailbox role installed.

1. The first step is to dismount the database on the SCR target cluster:

```
Dismount-Database -Identity "ca100\SG1Temp\Mailbox Database"
```

2. Next, use `Restore-StorageGroupCopy` to prepare the storage group for mounting on the SCR source cluster. The `force` parameter is not used because the SCR source is available.

```
Restore-StorageGroupCopy -Identity ca100\SG1Temp -StandbyMachine mb100
```

3. The CMS on ca100 should be stopped using `Stop-ClusteredMailboxServer`:

```
Stop-ClusteredMailboxServer -Identity mb100ccr -StopReason "Server Failback"
```

4. Once the CMS has stopped, start recovery on mb100 with the setup command:

```
Setup.com /RecoverCMS /CMSName:mb100ccr /CMSIPAddress:192.168.1.80
```

5. For CCR clusters storage group replication is suspended at this point. If the passive node does not contain a good copy of the database and logs, then reseed with `Update-StorageGroupCopy` from the passive node (mb101).

```
Update-StorageGroupCopy -Identity "mb100ccr\First Storage Group"
-DeleteExistingFiles
```

6. Reconfigure the backup site to reestablish ca100 as the SCR target. The cluster configuration information needs to be removed from ca100.

```
Setup.com /ClearLocalCMS /CMSName mb100ccr
```

7. Verify the cluster information was removed successfully using Cluster Administrator. Re-enable ca100 as the SCR target.

```
Enable-StorageGroupCopy -Identity "mb100ccr\First Storage Group"
-StandbyMachine ca100
```

At this point the original cluster is running and SCR is available for site resiliency.

Summary

This chapter detailed how to add high availability by using new features in Exchange Server 2007. It is important to understand that high availability is much more than adding CCR, LCR, or SCR. High availability is only achieved by process, people, and technology. In fact, because of the complexity of these high-availability solutions, companies without good processes and people may actually find less availability after implementing clusters.

Microsoft has made continual updates to Exchange to make it easier to manage and configure. Service Pack 1 addressed a large number of customer concerns with major feature improvements to the GUI as well as PowerShell. They have also addressed the changing demands of companies that made email grow from a little-used application to a business-critical application while making high availability more affordable.

## 13

Single Copy Clusters

Single Copy Clusters (SCCs) are Microsoft Exchange Server 2007's traditional approach to active/ passive clustering of mailboxes. In this release of Exchange only active/passive configurations are supported. The active/active role is no longer supported; one passive node is always required in a cluster. Also, the Mailbox role is the only role supported for deployment in a Microsoft Cluster Service (MSCS) configuration. Clustering mailboxes, through SCC, provides a higher level of uptime and availability to end users. If there is a hardware failure on one of the nodes in the cluster, any resources that were on that node are relocated to another node in the cluster. Individual nodes can be taken down for patching without disrupting the overall application uptime to the client. This does not provide a 100 percent uptime guarantee, but will provide a higher level of service over a standalone mailbox server. Clients will still incur a slight pause in service while the resources are moved to another node, but to most users this will be nearly transparent.

One of the primary goals of this chapter is to demonstrate how to use PowerShell to interact with native operating system commands to accomplish automated tasks with the use of PowerShell variables.

SCCs reside as clustered resources within a traditional Microsoft Cluster Server (MSCS) environment. To guarantee a successful SCC deployment within MSCS, there are several prerequisite steps that must be followed. This first half of this chapter focuses on using PowerShell to install the various components of an MSCS cluster and then to perform the actual Exchange SCC install.

The second half of this chapter focuses on Exchange-specific resource management within an SCC environment. The Exchange administrator will learn how to use PowerShell to move and manage resources, as well as how to check the health of an SCC cluster.

In this chapter the following topics are discussed:

❏   Automating a Single Copy Cluster (SCC) install

❏   Resource management

Automating an MSCS Install

Installation of an MSCS cluster is possible through the use of PowerShell and some of the various Microsoft command-line programs. The following sections discuss how you can use PowerShell with these programs to create scripts to aid in the deployment of MSCS clusters, one of the prerequisites of an SCC cluster. The following topics are covered:

❑ Hardware requirements

❑ Software requirements

❑ Microsoft Server Cluster installation

❑ Primary node installation

❑ Secondary node installation

Hardware Requirements

To deploy any cluster successfully, all of your equipment must be on the hardware compatibility list. To verify your hardware configuration visit `windowsservercatalog.com`. For testing purposes, this chapter focuses on deploying a two-node active/passive configuration. In addition to the standard requirements for Microsoft Exchange Server 2007, the following additional hardware is required:

❑ One additional network adapter on each server to act as the heartbeat.

❑ Shared disks accessible by both nodes. This can be either fibre channel or iSCSI. Each logical disk should reside on a LUN or physical spindles. This is necessary for disk I/O and for fault tolerance.

❑ Both servers should be the same model, chip set, and have the same components.

Software Requirements

Before installing MSCS there are several additional items that the Exchange administrator needs to take into consideration, such as specific software versions, additional network requirements, and logical placement within Active Directory. Figure 13-1 shows an example of an SCC configuration of a two-node network. The following list describes the software requirements for a two-node MSCS deployment:

❑ Because the SCC cluster uses Microsoft Server Clustering Service (MSCS), it is necessary to use Microsoft Windows 2003 Server, or R2, Enterprise edition or Data Center edition. Clustering is not available on the Web or Standard editions.

❑ SCC clusters can be in different data centers, but must reside within the same AD site.

❑ Microsoft Exchange Server 2007 Enterprise is required for SCC clusters. If you are deploying standard, then Local Continuous Clustering (LCR) is the only available clustering option.

❑ Four IP addresses on the production network. One for each server, one for the MSCS cluster name, and one address for the Clustered Mailbox Server.

❑ Two IP addresses for heartbeat, or private network, communication: one for each node of the cluster.

❑ IIS must be installed on both nodes.

In addition you must verify that both nodes are running the same firmware on all hardware components and are at the same patch level and service pack.

Running other versions of Exchange (2000 or 2003), Microsoft SQL Server, or non-Mailbox roles is not supported. Also, clustering on a domain controller is not supported.

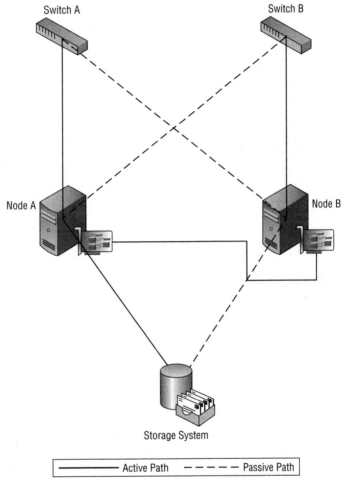

Figure 13-1

Microsoft Server Cluster Installation

When installing the MSCS cluster services, there are a lot of steps to implementing the cluster. These steps can be broken down into the following:

1. Create the cluster service account

2. Create the cluster DNS record

3. Configure the network

4. Prepare the shared disks

5. Install the cluster software

Chapter 4 discussed using PowerShell to create users. The service account for the cluster service needs to be a member of the domain. If the installation of the cluster is done by an administrator that is not the service account, the service account will be added to the local administrators group on each node during the installation process. Using this PowerShell script creates a new Organizational Unit (OU) in the Exchangeexchange domain, creates a new user within that OU, and sets her password to never. The final portion also sets the user password:

```
$DC1="exchangeexchange"
$DC2="local"
$DC3=$DC1+"."+$DC2+":389"
$Service_Account_OU="SVC_Accounts"
$User="svc-mb002"
$Password="P@55w0rd"
$objDomain = [ADSI]"LDAP://$DC3/dc=$DC1,dc=$DC2"
$objOU = $objDomain.Create("organizationalUnit", "ou=$Service_Account_OU")
$objOU.SetInfo()
$objOU = [ADSI]"LDAP://$DC3/ou=$Service_Account_OU,dc=$DC1,dc=$DC2"
$objUser = $objOU.Create("user", "cn=$User")
$objUser.Put("sAMAccountName", "$User")
$objUser.SetInfo()
$objUser.SetPassword("$Password")
$objUser.SetInfo()
$objUser.Put("UserAccountControl", "66048")
$objUser.SetInfo()
```

Using PowerShell, the script connects to the LDAP service on the domain controller via ADSI and creates a variable ($objDomain) for the domain name. $DC1 is the domain name. $DC2 is the domain suffix. $DC3 is the complete name of the domain taken from $DC1 and $DC2 where the user will be created.

Next the script creates a new variable for the OU ($objOU), creates the new OU called SVC_Accounts, and then sets the info.

Setting the OU creates the new object in Active Directory.

From there the script creates a new variable ($objUser), takes the existing variable of the OU ($objOU), and creates a user named svc-mb002, taken from the ($User) variable, in the new OU.

The $objUser.SetInfo() creates the object in AD.

The next step sets the user's password with the $objUser.SetPassword. The password is set from the ($Password) variable. This password is used later in the cluster installation.

The user's password is set to never expire by setting the UserAccountControl to 66048.

For more information on User Account Control settings see support.microsoft.com/kb/305144.

Verify that the user account exists using Active Directory Users and Computers (dsa.msc) or through dsquery, as shown in Figure 13-2.

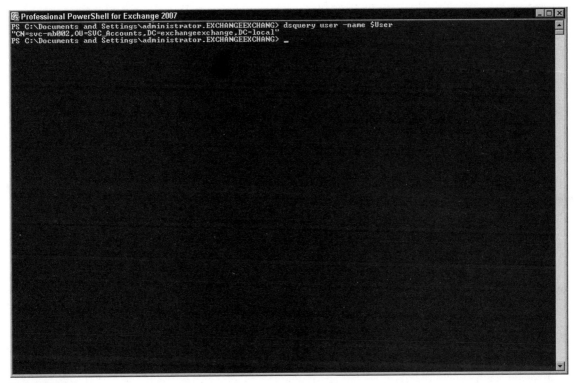

```
Professional PowerShell for Exchange 2007
PS C:\Documents and Settings\administrator.EXCHANGEEXCHANG> dsquery user -name $User
"CN=svc-mb002,OU=SUC_Accounts,DC=exchangeexchange,DC=local"
PS C:\Documents and Settings\administrator.EXCHANGEEXCHANG> _
```

Figure 13-2

Now that the service account has been created, the next step is to create the DNS record for the MSCS cluster. Also if your DNS infrastructure does not allow for the dynamic updates of 'A' records, then you also use this script to create the DNS record for the Clustered Mailbox Server.

To use DNS scripting, the Windows support tools need to be installed on the server that will run the script. The support tools are located in the \Support\Tools directory on the install CD. The following script will connect to the DNS server, contact the DNS zone specified, and create the new 'A' record. This is necessary because one of the required resources in an MSCS cluster is the cluster name, which is dependent upon the also required cluster IP address.

```
$DNS_Server="exchangeexchange.local"
$DNS_Zone="exchangeexchange.local"
$Cluster_Name="MB002MSCS"
$Cluster_IP="2.4.191.90"
dnscmd $DNS_Server /recordadd $DNS_Zone $Cluster_Name a $Cluster_IP
```

This script can be divided into three pieces. The first is the command (dnscmd). This is the executable that will perform the work based upon the given parameters, shown in Figure 13-3.

```
Professional PowerShell for Exchange 2007
PS C:\Documents and Settings\administrator.EXCHANGEEXCHANG> dnscmd

Usage: DnsCmd <ServerName> <Command> [<Command Parameters>]

<ServerName>:
    IP address or host name      -- remote or local DNS server
    .                            -- DNS server on local machine
<Command>:
    /Info                        -- Get server information
    /Config                      -- Reset server or zone configuration
    /EnumZones                   -- Enumerate zones
    /Statistics                  -- Query/clear server statistics data
    /ClearCache                  -- Clear DNS server cache
    /WriteBackFiles              -- Write back all zone or root-hint datafile(s)
    /StartScavenging             -- Initiates server scavenging
    /ResetListenAddresses        -- Set server IP address(es) to serve DNS requests
    /ResetForwarders             -- Set DNS servers to forward recursive queries to
    /ZoneInfo                    -- View zone information
    /ZoneAdd                     -- Create a new zone on the DNS server
    /ZoneDelete                  -- Delete a zone from DNS server or DS
    /ZonePause                   -- Pause a zone
    /ZoneResume                  -- Resume a zone
    /ZoneReload                  -- Reload zone from its database (file or DS)
    /ZoneWriteBack               -- Write back zone to file
    /ZoneRefresh                 -- Force refresh of secondary zone from master
    /ZoneUpdateFromDs            -- Update a DS integrated zone by data from DS
    /ZonePrint                   -- Display all records in the zone
    /ZoneResetType               -- Change zone type
    /ZoneResetSecondaries        -- Reset secondary\notify information for a zone
    /ZoneResetScavengeServers    -- Reset scavenging servers for a zone
    /ZoneResetMasters            -- Reset secondary zone's master servers
    /ZoneExport                  -- Export a zone to file
    /ZoneChangeDirectoryPartition -- Move a zone to another directory partition
    /EnumRecords                 -- Enumerate records at a name
    /RecordAdd                   -- Create a record in zone or RootHints
    /RecordDelete                -- Delete a record from zone, RootHints or cache
    /NodeDelete                  -- Delete all records at a name
    /AgeAllRecords               -- Force aging on node(s) in zone
    /EnumDirectoryPartitions     -- Enumerate directory partitions
    /DirectoryPartitionInfo      -- Get info on a directory partition
    /CreateDirectoryPartition    -- Create a directory partition
    /DeleteDirectoryPartition    -- Delete a directory partition
    /EnlistDirectoryPartition    -- Add DNS server to partition replication scope
    /UnenlistDirectoryPartition  -- Remove DNS server from replication scope
    /CreateBuiltinDirectoryPartitions -- Create built-in partitions

<Command Parameters>:
    DnsCmd <CommandName> /? -- For help info on specific Command
PS C:\Documents and Settings\administrator.EXCHANGEEXCHANG> _
```

Figure 13-3

The second section, as shown next, is for the location of the DNS server ($DNS_Server) and the zone ($DNS_Zone) that the record will be added to:

```
Insert dns server /recordadd dns zone here
```

The last section includes the name ($Cluster_Name) and the IP address ($Cluster_IP) of the 'A' record that will be created. (See Figure 13-4.) At this point, you may be wondering why the DNS record and the user have been created from the command line and not through the GUI. At the end of this chapter we bring all of these separate scripts together to show how using PowerShell to automate common tasks saves time and reduces errors in the deployment of Single Copy Clusters.

Verify the 'A' record was created by using nslookup, as shown in Figure 13-5.

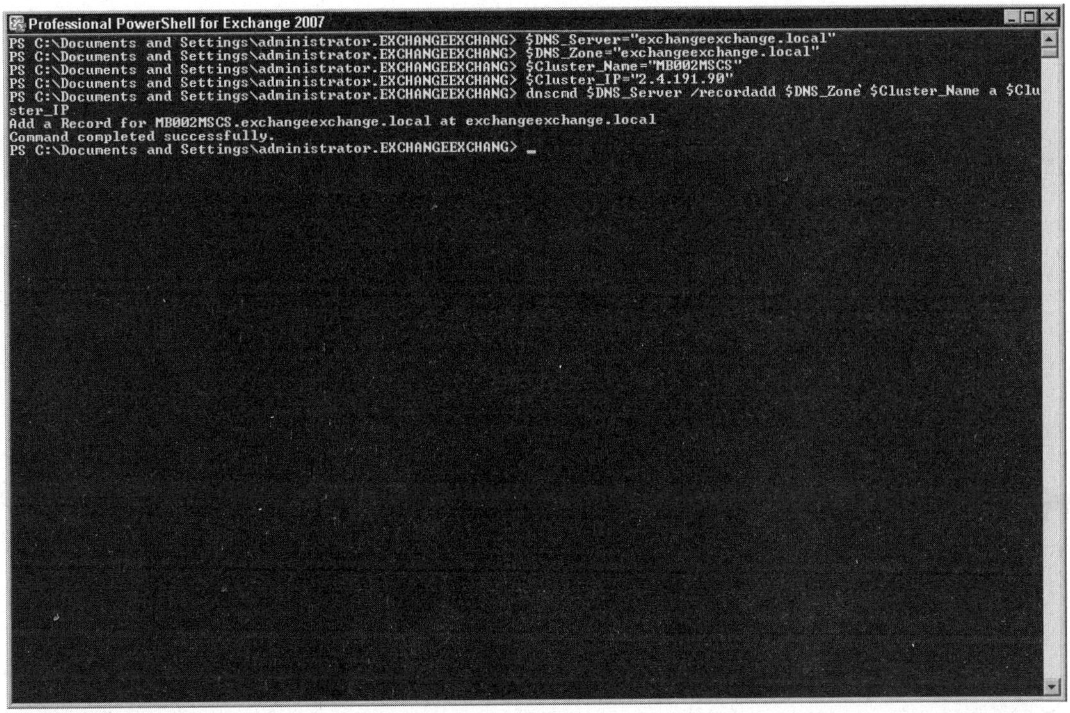

Figure 13-4

Figure 13-5

The next step is to configure the network interfaces on both servers. By default the first network connection on any server is always named "Local Area Connection". Each additional network connection appends a numeral to the connection name. Though simplistic in its nature, this naming convention of network interfaces is not very intuitive. A better way to name the NICs is to differentiate between the production interface and the private interface. Figure 13-6 shows the standard NIC configuration.

Figure 13-6

As shown here, using netsh from within PowerShell allows for variables to be used within the command:

```
$Interface1="Local Area Connection"
$Interface1_New="Public"
$Interface2="Local Area Connection 2"
$Interface2_New="Private"
$IP="10.10.10.1"
$Subnet="255.255.255.0"
```

```
netsh interface set interface name = "$Interface1" newname = "$Interface1_New"
netsh interface set interface name = "$Interface2" newname = "$Interface2_New"
netsh interface ip set address name="$Interface2_New" source=static "$IP" "$Subnet"
netsh interface ip set dns name="$Interface2_New" static none none
netsh interface set interface "$Interface2_New" enable
```

This script configures the first interface's name ($Interface1) and renames the interface ($Interface1_New). The second interface is the heartbeat connection between both servers. Typically this connection would not be actively used in a regular server and would be disabled. The script takes the old interface name ($Interface2) and renames it ($Interface2_New). From there the NIC receives an IP address ($IP) and subnet mask ($Subnet). The next step sets the DNS server to null, and removes the checkbox to automatically register this connection in DNS. Once all of the configuration parameters are set, the last line of the script enables the new interface. (See Figure 13-7.)

Figure 13-7

Preparing the Shared Disk

Before any disk can be presented to the OS, a partition must be created, followed by a disk letter, file system type, and a volume name. Mount points can be used in place of disk letters. For more information on how to configure mount points in a Microsoft Cluster, see Microsoft kb article 280297. The following snippet shows how you can use PowerShell to create variables to automate the work of creating and formatting disks:

```
$Disk="C:\disk.txt"
$Disk1="1"
$Disk1_Letter="Q"
$Disk2="2"
$Disk2_Letter="S"
$Disk3="3"
$Disk3_Letter="T"
Set-Content -path $Disk -encoding ascii -value "select disk $Disk1 `r
create partition primary align=32 `r
select partition 1 `r
assign letter=$Disk1_Letter `r
select disk $Disk2 `r
create partition primary align=32 `r
select partition 1 `r
assign letter=$Disk2_Letter `r
select disk $Disk3 `r
create partition primary align=32 `r
select partition 1 `r
assign letter=$Disk3_Letter"
```

This script contains variables for each disk in the array and uses the set-content cmdlet to create the text file. The path parameter is required because Set-Content needs to know the location and the name of the file to create. Using the encoding Ascii parameter allows for the formatting of the data. This particular configuration has three disks with three variables for each disk. The disk number ($Disk#) can be attained through diskpart or through diskmgmt.msc. The second value is the drive letter ($Disk#_Letter) and is used to assign the drive letter to the newly created logical drive. When each partition is created, the partition is automatically sector aligned to the disk, via align=32.

When DISKPART.EXE is run programmatically, the /s switch is required as well as the location of the file. In the following example, diskpart uses all of the commands that were placed into the disk.txt file, via the Set-Content cmdlet, and executes them using the disk variable listed previously:

```
Diskpart.exe /s $Disk
del $Disk
```

Once the disk creation is complete, the diskpart.txt file is deleted. Successful completion of the task can be verified through disk manager (diskmgmt.msc). See Figure 13-8.

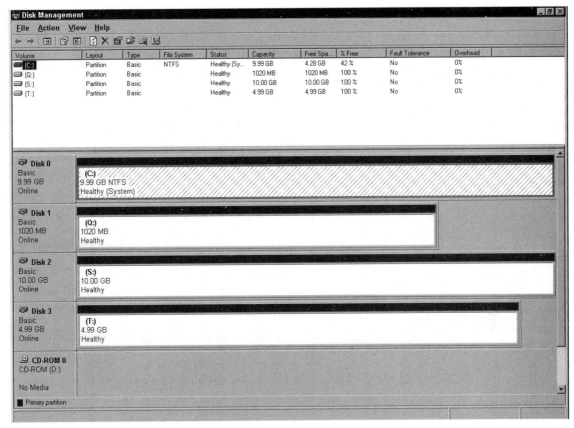

Figure 13-8

The next component is to format the newly created disks. When you assign drive letters to the ($Disk#_Letter) variables, those variables are then appended with a colon (:) and formatted using the portion of the following script. The last two commands set variables that are used in the cluster management section.

```
$Disk1_Volume="Quorum"
$Disk2_Volume="Data"
$Disk3_Volume="Logs"
format $Disk1_Letter.Insert(1,":") /FS:NTFS /V:$Disk1_Volume /y
format $Disk2_Letter.Insert(1,":") /FS:NTFS /V:$Disk2_Volume /y
format $Disk3_Letter.Insert(1,":") /FS:NTFS /V:$Disk3_Volume /y

$Disk2_Drive=$Disk2_Letter.Insert(1,":")
$Disk3_Drive=$Disk3_Letter.Insert(1,":")
```

Figure 13-9 shows the script formatting each of the disk drives that were created in Figure 13-8.

```
Professional PowerShell for Exchange 2007                                                    _ □ ×
PS C:\Documents and Settings\administrator.EXCHANGEEXCHANG> $Disk1_Volume="Quorum"
PS C:\Documents and Settings\administrator.EXCHANGEEXCHANG> $Disk2_Volume="Data"
PS C:\Documents and Settings\administrator.EXCHANGEEXCHANG> $Disk3_Volume="Logs"
PS C:\Documents and Settings\administrator.EXCHANGEEXCHANG> format $Disk1_Letter.Insert(1,":") /FS:NTFS /V:$Disk1_Volume
/y
The type of the file system is RAW.
The new file system is NTFS.
Verifying 1019M
Creating file system structures.
Format complete.
    1044192 KB total disk space.
    1036582 KB are available.
PS C:\Documents and Settings\administrator.EXCHANGEEXCHANG> format $Disk2_Letter.Insert(1,":") /FS:NTFS /V:$Disk2_Volume
/y
The type of the file system is RAW.
The new file system is NTFS.
Verifying 10236M
Creating file system structures.
Format complete.
    10482380 KB total disk space.
    10427388 KB are available.
PS C:\Documents and Settings\administrator.EXCHANGEEXCHANG> format $Disk3_Letter.Insert(1,":") /FS:NTFS /V:$Disk3_Volume
/y
The type of the file system is RAW.
The new file system is NTFS.
Verifying 5114M
Creating file system structures.
Format complete.
    5237156 KB total disk space.
    5208548 KB are available.
PS C:\Documents and Settings\administrator.EXCHANGEEXCHANG> $Disk2_Drive=$Disk2_Letter.Insert(1,":")
PS C:\Documents and Settings\administrator.EXCHANGEEXCHANG> $Disk3_Drive=$Disk3_Letter.Insert(1,":")
PS C:\Documents and Settings\administrator.EXCHANGEEXCHANG> _
```

Figure 13-9

Once again, verify the formatting using disk manager, as shown in Figure 13-10.

By using PowerShell to interact with common command-line executables, you have configured the service account user and OU for the cluster, configured the network settings on both servers, and prepared the shared disks for the cluster installation.

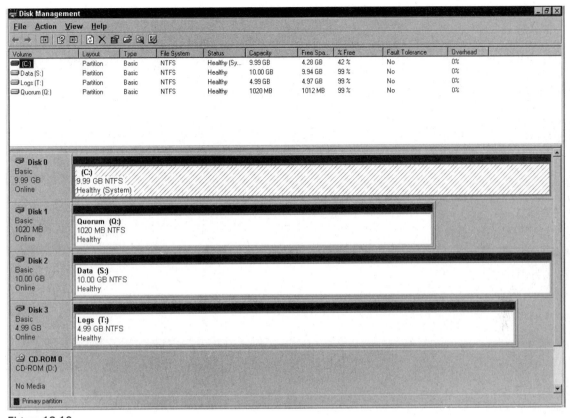

Figure 13-10

Cluster Installation

Thus far all of the preparatory work in this chapter has been to properly deploy a two-node cluster using PowerShell. The cluster install continues to build off of the previous work and uses `cluster.exe`, the cluster utility command-line tool, to install and configure the cluster. (See Figure 13-11.)

To use `cluster.exe` to create a new cluster the following parameters are required:

❑ Cluster name

❑ Cluster IP address

❑ User account that will run the cluster service

❑ Password for the cluster service user account

❑ Hostname of the node that the cluster will be installed on

Figure 13-11

Instead of statically defining all of the required parameters, you can use PowerShell as shown here to set all of the parameters as variables, and then run the cluster install script:

```
$Cluster_Name="MB002MSCS"
$Cluster_IP="2.4.191.91"
$User (reused from user configuration)
$Password (reused from user configuration)
$Node1_Hostname="MB002A"
$Logfile="c:\mscs_install.txt"
cluster /cluster:$Cluster_Name /create /IPAddr:$Cluster_IP,$Cluster_Subnet
/USER:$User /pass:$Password
  /node:$Node1_Hostname /verbose > $Logfile
```

Performing scripted installs like this guarantees that any cluster deployed in this manner produces a repeatable, consistent set of results. This type of deployment is particularly advantageous for hosted

Exchange providers or large Exchange organizations. The preceding script performs a verbose logging of the cluster install, which can be reviewed to assist in troubleshooting a failed cluster install or to provide a summary of a successful install. Once the install is complete, the second node can be added by using the following script:

```
$Cluster_Name (reused from the initial configuration above)
$Node2_Hostname="MB002B"
$Password (reused from user configuration)
cluster /cluster:$Cluster_Name /add:$Node2_Hostname /password:$Password /verbose
```

When complete, the cluster will look like the one shown in Figure 13-12.

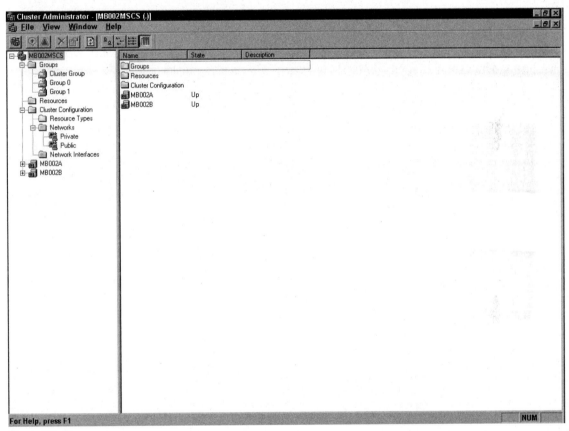

Figure 13-12

And via the command line, it looks like Figure 13-13.

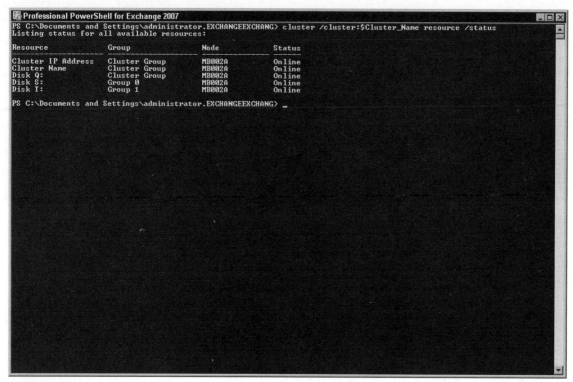

```
Professional PowerShell for Exchange 2007
PS C:\Documents and Settings\administrator.EXCHANGEEXCHANG> cluster /cluster:$Cluster_Name resource /status
Listing status for all available resources:

Resource              Group              Node       Status
--------------------  -----------------  ---------  --------
Cluster IP Address    Cluster Group      MB002A     Online
Cluster Name          Cluster Group      MB002A     Online
Disk Q:               Cluster Group      MB002A     Online
Disk S:               Group 0            MB002A     Online
Disk T:               Group 1            MB002A     Online

PS C:\Documents and Settings\administrator.EXCHANGEEXCHANG> _
```

Figure 13-13

There are two final post-installation tasks. One is required for correct performance, and the other is for ease of management once Exchange is installed. The required configuration change is to set the `Private` interface's communication mode. Because this interface is either directly connected to the other node by a cross-over cable or is connected to a non-routable VLAN on a switch, it cannot take public traffic and needs to be configured for internal cluster communications only (private network). The following single cluster command fixes this:

```
$Interface2_New (reused from the network configuration section)
cluster network $Interface2_New /prop Role=1
```

The next two commands consolidate the non quorum disks into a single group and delete the empty group:

```
$Disk3_Drive (reused from the disk format section)
$Cluster_Name (reused from the MSCS install section)
cluster resource "Disk $Disk3_Drive" /move: "Group 0"
cluster /cluster:$Cluster_Name group "group 1" /delete
```

Figure 13-14 shows verification of the cluster configuration through `cluadmin`.

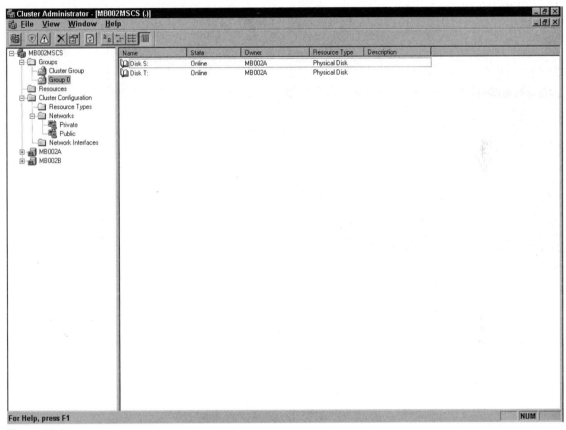

Figure 13-14

And through the command line as shown in Figure 13-15.

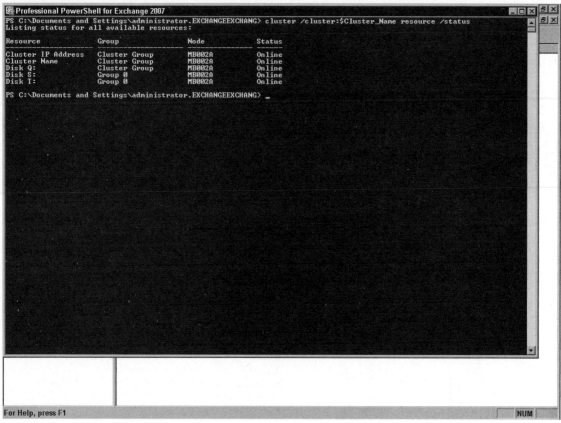

Figure 13-15

The MSCS cluster has been installed and configured and is ready for the Exchange install.

Installing Exchange on an SCC Cluster

When installing Exchange on the SCC cluster, the installation must be performed once on the active node and once on the standby node. The configuration on the first node will set up the new CMS name, CMS IP address, and the CMS data path. By providing these details, the installer will deploy the Mailbox role, as well as the clustered mailbox role. All of the install parameters that were discussed in Chapter 3 pertain to an SCC cluster install.

In the most basic deployment, SCC cluster installation via PowerShell requires a CMS name (which also becomes the group name in Cluster Administrator), an IP address for the CMS name, and the CMS data path. Using variables for each of these parameters results in the basic installation script listed here:

```
$Install_Directory="S:\Bits"
$Cluster_MBX_Name="MB002"
$Cluster_MBX_IP="2.4.191.91"
$Cluster_MBX_Path="S:\MDB"
Cd $Install_Directory
Mkdir $Cluster_MBX_Path
./Setup.com /role:m /NewCMS /CMSName:$Cluster_MBX_Name
 /CmsIpAddress:$Cluster_MBX_IP /CmsSharedStorage /CMSDataPath:$Cluster_MBX_Path
```

This script installs Exchange on the first node of the cluster as a Clustered Mailbox Server. The mailbox server name is defined by ($Cluster_MBX_Name), the IP address is set by the ($Cluster_MBX_IP) variable, and the ($Cluster_MBX_Path) tells the installer where to put the database and log files. If the folder is not created on the drive where the database and logs are going, the installer will error out.

Once the installation is complete, open the Exchange Management Shell and use Get-ClusteredMailboxServerStatus to show the newly created cluster. Notice there is only one node present. To install the clustered mailbox onto the passive node, the setup command does not need to specify any of the CMS install information, and the resources can stay on the first node. All that is required for installation in the passive node is the role switch with the mailbox parameter. If any other parameters such as the install directory or the ADAM port were defined, they also need to be used here. For more information about install switches, please see Chapter 3.

```
$Install_Directory="C:\EX2007"
Cd $install_Directory
./Setup.com /role:m
```

The installer checks for cluster membership. If the server is the member of a cluster that contains the clustered mailbox role, the installer will automatically add the passive node into the cluster. When complete the cluster will look like Figure 13-16.

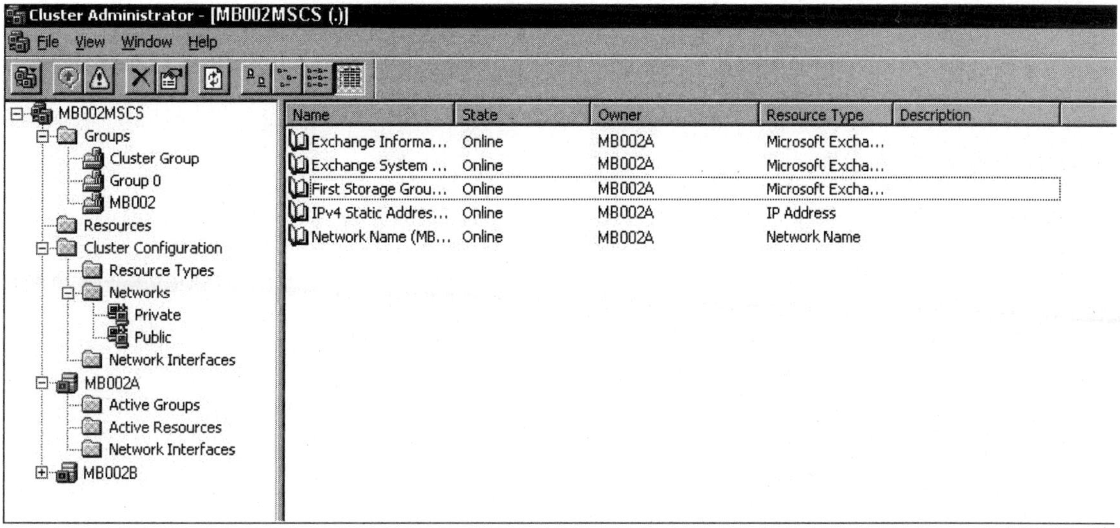

Figure 13-16

SCC cluster resources have undergone resource model dependency changes that require a manual dependency be created and assigned. The physical disk resources are now dependencies of the mailbox database. These dependencies are not automatically created when the mailbox cluster is installed. Within our current configuration, it would be best practice to move the physical disk resources out of Group 0, place them into MB002, and then delete Group 0. This can be accomplished with the following script:

```
$Cluster_MBX_Name (reused from Exchange install)
cluster resource "Disk S:" /move:$Cluster_MBX_Name
cluster resource "Disk T:" /move:$Cluster_MBX_Name
cluster group "Group 0" /delete
```

Once the physical disk resources are in the same group as the Exchange resources, the dependency can be created. Note: having the physical disk resource in the same resource group is not required, but is a best practice for managing Exchange cluster resources. The mailbox database needs to be offline for the next step. Creating the dependencies can be done by using PowerShell to set the Microsoft Exchange Database Instance dependent upon the disks like this:

```
$Cluster_MBX_Name (reused from Exchange install)
cluster resource "First Storage Group/Mailbox Database ($Cluster_MBX_Name)"
/offline
cluster resource "First Storage Group/Mailbox Database ($Cluster_MBX_Name)"
/adddep: "Disk $Disk2_Drive" /adddep: "Disk $Disk3_Drive"
cluster resource "First Storage Group/Mailbox Database ($Cluster_MBX_Name)" /online
```

In this example the $Cluster_MBX_Name is reused from the install steps, and $Disk2_Drive and $Disk3_Drive are variables that are created during the drive formatting steps. This script should be run for every physical disk resource that Exchange is using. For more information about resource dependencies for Exchange Server 2007, please see the Microsoft 2007 help file (.chm).

One last component needs to be configured for this cluster. You may have noticed that the data and logs reside on the same logical drive. The Move-StorageGroupPath from within the Exchange Management Shell can correct this. By specifying the -LogFolderPath as the T:\logs path, the EMS will check the path, create the folder if it does not exist, and prompt you to verify the movement of the log files. This action will take the database offline, and will have to be brought online manually. Hence another cmdlet to move the log files to the correct location. This script adds in an additional feature; it requires the use of the Exchange Management Shell. It is perfectly acceptable to run this from within the EMS, however if you want to try this script with all of the previous scripts to create a deployment script, you must add in the Exchange Management PowerShell.

```
$Disk3_Drive (reused from disk section)
Add-PSSnapin Microsoft.Exchange.Management.PowerShell.Admin
Move-StorageGroupPath "First Storage Group" -LogFolderPath
$Disk3_Drive.Insert($Disk3_Drive.Length,"\Logs"
```

This script may seem a little excessive at first, but it takes PowerShell, calls the Exchange snap-in for PowerShell, calls an Exchange cmdlet, and then uses part of the native .NET functionality to manipulate the variable into something useful!

Thus far this chapter has shown how to use PowerShell to create, format, and present disks to the servers and to create the necessary connections. From there an automated installation and configuration of the MSCS cluster was performed, which then allowed for a scripted install of the Mailbox role in a clustered mailbox configuration. After the Mailbox role was installed, further PowerShelling provided the rest of the Exchange resource configuration. A manual deployment of a two-node cluster can take several hours and is prone to error if the administrator is not diligent in making sure that both systems are configured properly. However, by using PowerShell the deployment time is cut considerably, system configuration is reduced in complexity, and the scripts can be reused for future deployments or for disaster testing.

Resource Management

Exchange Server 2007 allows Exchange administrators the ability to control cluster resources, natively, from PowerShell. The cluster cmdlets perform the same essential functions as the `cluster.exe` command, but are simpler to use, have a streamlined appearance, and have documented help on how to perform Exchange-specific tasks. The following cmdlets are discussed:

- ❏   `Get-ClusteredMailboxServerStatus`
- ❏   `Stop-ClusteredMailboxServer`
- ❏   `Start-ClusteredMailboxServer`
- ❏   `Move-ClusteredMailboxServer`

This section discusses how to move clustered resources between nodes, how to stop and start the cluster, and how to check the cluster's health. Open the Exchange Management Shell using the `Get-ClusteredMailboxServerStatus`. The output of this shows the Clustered Mailbox Server name, the operational state, the nodes present in the cluster, and a list of any failed resources. From there, you can take the clustered mailbox offline to perform maintenance by using `Stop-ClusteredMailboxServer`. The cmdlet only requires two parameters: the name of the clustered mailbox (`Identity`) and the reason that it is being taken offline (`StopReason`). To take your scc2mbx cluster offline you would issue the following:

```
Stop-ClusteredMailboxServer -Identity MB002 -StopReason "Firmware patching on SAN"
```

Figure 13-17 shows stopping the clustered resource for maintenance on the SAN.

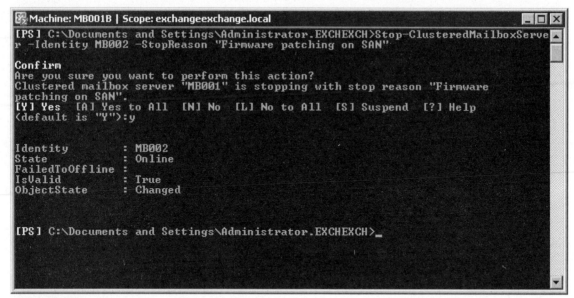

Figure 13-17

This cmdlet takes all of the resources in the MB002 resource group offline. When the Clustered Mailbox Server is ready to come online, Start-ClusteredMailboxServer would be issued, as shown in Figure 13-18.

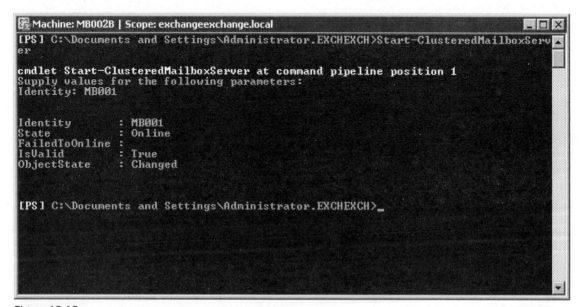

Figure 13-18

If a manual failover of resources needs to occur, this too can be accomplished through the Exchange Management Shell by using the `Move-ClusteredMailboxServer` cmdlet. This cmdlet has three necessary parameters: the name of the Clustered Mailbox Server (`Identity`), the node that will receive the Exchange resources (`TargetMachine`), and the reason for the resource movement (`MoveComment`). The command to move the MB002 mailbox resources from MB002A to MB002B for server maintenance would look like this:

```
Move-ClusteredMailboxServer MB002 -TargetMachine MB002A -MoveComment "Moving
resource to perform maintenance on MB002B."
```

The `Get-ClusteredMailboxServerStatus` cmdlet verifies that the resource move was correctly processed. Additional verification can be performed using the cluster administrator. The CMS can only be moved to a node that does not have another CMS already running on it, must be a member of the same MSCS cluster, and will maintain the operational state (online or offline) on the new node it had on the old node. Figure 13-19 shows the cluster status.

```
Machine: MB002B | Scope: exchangeexchange.local
[PS] C:\Documents and Settings\Administrator.EXCHEXCH>Get-ClusteredMailboxServer
Status

Identity                          : MB002
ClusteredMailboxServerName        : MB002.exchangeexchange.local
State                             : Online
OperationalMachines               : {MB002B (Active), MB002A (Quorum Owner)}
FailedResources                   : {}
OperationalReplicationHostNames    : {mb002b, mb002a}
FailedReplicationHostNames         : {}
InUseReplicationHostNames          : {mb002b, mb002a}
IsValid                           : True
ObjectState                       : Unchanged


[PS] C:\Documents and Settings\Administrator.EXCHEXCH>_
```

Figure 13-19

Putting It All Together

Throughout the chapter, individual components of an SCC install have been presented to show that there are numerous tasks that are required to make the cluster functional. By using PowerShell, these individual components have scripted to allow for reusable variables, faster deployment, and a documented repeatable process. The methodology of showing each individual script and how it automates a subcomponent was designed to lead the Exchange administrator to the point of putting all of the scripts together to have a fully automated deployment of SCC. The following script does that. It is a collective install and will take a base system that has all of the required hardware installed, and move it through network configuration, disk configuration, MSCS install, the Exchange installer, and ultimately to configuring the resources to pass an ExBPA audit.

```
NodeA
$DC1="exchangeexchange"
$DC2="local"
$DC3=$DC1+"."+$DC2+":389"
$Service_Account_OU="SVC_Accounts"
$User="svc-mb002"
$Password="P@55w0rd"
$DNS_Server="exchangeexchange.local"
$DNS_Zone="exchangeexchange.local"
$Interface1="Local Area Connection"
$Interface1_New="Public"
$Interface2="Local Area Connection 2"
$Interface2_New="Private"
$IP="10.10.10.1"
$Subnet="255.255.255.0"
$Disk ="C:\disk.txt"
$Disk1="1"
$Disk1_Letter="Q"
$Disk2="2"
$Disk2_Letter="S"
$Disk3="3"
$Disk3_Letter="T"
$Disk1_Volume="Quorum"
$Disk2_Volume="Data"
$Disk3_Volume="Logs"
$Cluster_Name="MB002MSCS"
$Cluster_IP="2.4.191.90"
$Node1_Hostname="MB002A"
$Logfile="c:\mscs_install.txt"
$Node2_Hostname="MB002B"
$Cluster_MBX_Name="MB002"
$Cluster_MBX_IP="2.4.191.91"
$Cluster_MBX_Path="S:\MDB"
$Install_Directory="S:\Bits"

$objDomain = [ADSI]"LDAP://$DC3/dc=$DC1,dc=$DC2"
$objOU = $objDomain.Create("organizationalUnit", "ou=$Service_Account_OU")
$objOU.SetInfo()
$objOU = [ADSI]"LDAP://$DC3/ou=$Service_Account_OU,dc=$DC1,dc=$DC2"
$objUser = $objOU.Create("user", "cn=$User")
$objUser.Put("sAMAccountName", "$User")
$objUser.SetInfo()
$objUser.SetPassword("$Password")
$objUser.SetInfo()
$objUser.Put("UserAccountControl", "66048")
$objUser.SetInfo()


dnscmd $DNS_Server /recordadd $DNS_Zone $Cluster_Name a $Cluster_IP
netsh interface set interface name = "$Interface1" newname = "$Interface1_New"
netsh interface set interface name = "$Interface2" newname = "$Interface2_New"
```

```
netsh interface ip set address name="$Interface2_New" source=static "$IP" "$Subnet"
netsh interface ip set dns name="$Interface2_New" static none none
netsh interface set interface "$Interface2_New" enable
Set-Content -path $Disk -encoding ascii -value "select disk $Disk1 `r
create partition primary align=32 `r
select partition 1 `r
assign letter=$Disk1_Letter `r
select disk $Disk2 `r
create partition primary align=32 `r
select partition 1 `r
assign letter=$Disk2_Letter `r
select disk $Disk3 `r
create partition primary align=32 `r
select partition 1 `r
assign letter=$Disk3_Letter"
diskpart /s $Disk
del $Diskformat $Disk1_Letter.Insert(1,":") /FS:NTFS /V:$Disk1_Volume /y
format $Disk2_Letter.Insert(1,":") /FS:NTFS /V:$Disk2_Volume /y
format $Disk3_Letter.Insert(1,":") /FS:NTFS /V:$Disk3_Volume /y
$Disk2_Drive=$Disk2_Letter.Insert(1,":")
$Disk3_Drive=$Disk3_Letter.Insert(1,":")
cluster /cluster:$Cluster_Name /create /IPAddr:$Cluster_IP /USER:$User
/pass:$Password /node:$Node1_Hostname /verbose > $Logfile
cluster /cluster:$Cluster_Name /add:$Node2_Hostname /password:$Password /verbose
cluster network $Interface2_New /prop Role=1
cluster resource "Disk $Disk2_Drive" /move:"Group 0"
cluster /cluster:$Cluster_Name group "group 1" /delete
cd $Install_Directory
./Setup.com /role:m /NewCMS /CMSName:$Cluster_MBX_Name
/CmsIpAddress:$Cluster_MBX_IP /CmsSharedStorage /CMSDataPath:$Cluster_MBX_Path
cluster resource "$Disk2_Drive" /move:$Cluster_MBX_Name
cluster resource "$Disk3_Drive" /move:$Cluster_MBX_Name
cluster group "Group 0" /delete
cluster resource "First Storage Group/Mailbox Database ($Cluster_MBX_Name)"
/offline
cluster resource "First Storage Group/Mailbox Database ($Cluster_MBX_Name)"
/adddep: "Disk $Disk2_Drive" /adddep: "Disk $Disk3_Drive"
cluster resource "First Storage Group/Mailbox Database ($Cluster_MBX_Name)" /online
Add-PSSnapin Microsoft.Exchange.Management.PowerShell.Admin
Move-StorageGroupPath "First Storage Group" -LogFolderPath
$Disk3_Drive.Insert($Disk3_Drive.Length,"\Logs")
cluster resource "First Storage Group/Mailbox Database ($Cluster_MBX_Name)" /online

NodeB
(The network interfaces should be configured before MSCS is installed on the first
node).
$Interface1="Local Area Connection"
$Interface1_New="Public"
$Interface2="Local Area Connection 2"
$Interface2_New="Private"
$IP="10.10.10.2"
$Subnet="255.255.255.0"
```

(continued)

(continued)

```
netsh interface set interface name = "$Interface1" newname = "$Interface1_New"
netsh interface set interface name = "$Interface2" newname = "$Interface2_New"
netsh interface ip set address name="$Interface2_New" source=static "$IP" "$Subnet"
netsh interface ip set dns name="$Interface2_New" static none none
netsh interface set interface "$Interface2_New" enable

$Install_Directory="C:\EX2007"
Cd $Install_Directory
./Setup.com /role:m
```

Summary

This chapter described the implementation and management of a two-node SCC cluster. The first half of the chapter described the individual components and how through PowerShell these install steps are automated. Before PowerShell, performing an automated install would have required knowledge of batch scripts, Visual Basic, and a hodgepodge of unattended files and still would not have provided the same result as using PowerShell. Using PowerShell in conjunction with system and application commands provides for an easier, more efficient use of scripts to perform common administrative tasks. The power of having .NET functionality built in allows for manipulation of variables, objects, and data that is more robust and has a better framework.

14

Troubleshooting Exchange Issues

This chapter deals with troubleshooting Microsoft Exchange Server 2007 through the use of cmdlets. Microsoft has created several test cmdlets that allow the system administrator to programmatically test various Exchange roles and services. These cmdlets are built into Exchange. No longer do you need to write cumbersome multilanguage test scripts! This chapter covers the following:

- ❑ Determining server health
- ❑ Determining Exchange system health
- ❑ Testing anti-spam functions
- ❑ Troubleshooting Client Access Server Role functions
- ❑ Testing Web Services
- ❑ Troubleshooting MAPI connectivity
- ❑ Testing Mailflow
- ❑ Testing the Exchange Search service
- ❑ Troubleshooting edge synchronization
- ❑ Troubleshooting Unified Messaging connectivity
- ❑ Using `Get-EventLog`
- ❑ Using `Get-Message`
- ❑ Tracking messages
- ❑ Working with event log levels

To receive the greatest benefit from these cmdlets, a fully configured Exchange environment is required. CAS, Hub, and Mailbox roles are required for tests in this chapter. Also, Internet connectivity is recommended so the test cmdlets can retrieve updates from Microsoft.

Determining Server Health

This section covers the following cmdlets:

- ❑   `Test-ServiceHealth`
- ❑   `Get-ExchangeServer`

The `Test-ServiceHealth` cmdlet queries the targeted Exchange server's roles and then checks to make sure that the required services are running. The account that runs this cmdlet must be a member of the Exchange Server Administrators Group as well as a local administrator on that computer. By using the `Server` parameter, a remote server can be queried. If the `Server` parameter is not used, the cmdlet runs the health check locally. The domain controller to query can be set via the `DomainController` parameter, as well as the AD timeout value `ActiveDirectoryTimeout`, 15 seconds by default. This cmdlet can be run in a monitoring mode by setting the `MonitoringContext` to `$true`. This allows the cmdlet to pull events and performance counters. When `Test-ServiceHealth` is run against the local machine, the output by default will look like Figure 14-1.

```
Professional PowerShell for Exchange 2007                              _ □ X
[PS] C:\Documents and Settings\Administrator.EXCHEXCH>Test-ServiceHealth

Role              RequiredServicesRunning  ServicesRunning          ServicesNotRunning
----              -----------------------  ---------------          ------------------
Mailbox           True                     IISAdmin
                                           MSExchangeADTopology
                                           MSExchangeIS
                                           MSExchangeMailboxAssis
                                           tants
                                           MSExchangeMailSubmissi
                                           on
                                           MSExchangeRepl
                                           MSExchangeSA
                                           MSExchangeSearch
                                           MSExchangeServiceHost
                                           MSExchangeTransportLog
                                           Search
                                           MSFTESQL-Exchange
                                           W3Svc
Client Access     True                     IISAdmin
                                           MSExchangeADTopology
                                           MSExchangeFDS
                                           MSExchangeServiceHost
                                           W3Svc
Hub Transport     True                     MSExchangeADTopology
                                           MSExchangeEdgeSync
                                           MSExchangeTransport
                                           MSExchangeTransportLog
                                           Search
```

Figure 14-1

W3Svc is stopped. This is particularly bad for a server with the CAS role installed. Start-Service w3svc fixes this problem. To check on an individual service, issue `Get-Service service name`.

This cmdlet can have its usefulness expanded by using it in a pipeline with other cmdlets. Thus far it has been used only on a single server. If you wanted to check the health of all of your Exchange servers within your organization, you could issue `Get-ExchangeServer | Test-ServiceHealth`. The output is displayed in Figure 14-2.

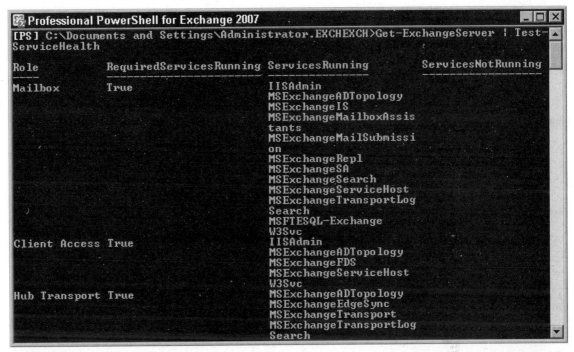

Figure 14-2

Though this is informative, in its current state it is not very useful. All the services for each server are listed, but none of the server names are present. When troubleshooting this can be frustrating, and needs a little more PowerShell to be functional:

```
$a=Get-ExchangeServer
foreach ($z in $a) {echo $z.name (Test-ServiceHealth $z)}
```

The variable $a contains the value of the output of `Get-ExchangeServer`. Next a `foreach` loop is constructed to test each value in the array. Once the `foreach` loops has its value it needs to execute the parameters that are contained within the { }. This script echoes the name of the server ($z.name) and then runs through `Test-ServiceHealth` using $z as the server name. The output in Figure 14-3 shows the server name associated with each set of service health checks.

```
Professional PowerShell for Exchange 2007                              [_][□][X]
[PS] C:\Documents and Settings\Administrator.EXCHEXCH>foreach ($z in $a) {echo $
z.name (Test-ServiceHealth $z)}
MB002

Role                 RequiredServicesRunning  ServicesRunning          ServicesNotRunning
----                 -----------------------  ---------------          ------------------
Mailbox              True                     IISAdmin
                                              MSExchangeADTopology
                                              MSExchangeIS
                                              MSExchangeMailboxAssis
                                              tants
                                              MSExchangeMailSubmissi
                                              on
                                              MSExchangeRepl
                                              MSExchangeSA
                                              MSExchangeSearch
                                              MSExchangeServiceHost
                                              MSExchangeTransportLog
                                              Search
                                              MSFTESQL-Exchange
                                              W3Svc
Client Access        True                     IISAdmin
                                              MSExchangeADTopology
                                              MSExchangeFDS
                                              MSExchangeServiceHost
                                              W3Svc
Hub Transport        True                     MSExchangeADTopology
                                              MSExchangeEdgeSync
                                              MSExchangeTransport
                                              MSExchangeTransportLog
                                              Search
MB001
Mailbox              True                     IISAdmin
                                              MSExchangeADTopology
                                              MSExchangeIS
                                              MSExchangeMailboxAssis
                                              tants
                                              MSExchangeMailSubmissi
                                              on
                                              MSExchangeRepl
                                              MSExchangeSA
                                              MSExchangeSearch
                                              MSExchangeServiceHost
                                              MSExchangeTransportLog
                                              Search
                                              MSFTESQL-Exchange
                                              W3Svc
```

Figure 14-3

To perform a health check on servers that contain a particular role, modify the Get-ExchangeServer to include the role that you will query. Get-ExchangeServer | where {$_.IsMemberOfCluster -eq"Yes"} or Get-ExchangeServer | where {$_.IsMailboxServer -eq"True"}. This performs the health check only on clusters within the organization. If you wanted to check on a specific site, after, say, a power outage, you could change the scope to include the site with the Get-ExchangeServer. In Exchange 2007 sites are now defined by the AD site boundary. Therefore all site names come from the AD sites and Services naming. To check on all Exchange servers in New York, with a site name of NY, the Get-ExchangeServer portion would be changed to Get-ExchangeServer | where {$_.Site -eq "exchangeexchange.local/Configuration/Sites/NY"}. The flexibility of Test-ServiceHealth is not in the cmdlet itself, but in the pipelined input passed to it.

Determining Exchange System Health

This section covers the following cmdlet:

❏   `Test-SystemHealth`

This PowerShell version of ExBPA is possibly one of the coolest cmdlets Microsoft has created. The `Test-SystemHealth` cmdlet runs against the local server unless you specify the `ServerList` parameter. When this cmdlet is initiated, it attempts to run an Internet update to retrieve the latest BPA, and then performs the BPA test. Errors and critical warnings appear on the screen in red; warnings appear in yellow.

This cmdlet has several parameters, which are described in the following list:

❏   `ADCredentials`: This parameter is used if alternative credentials are used to query AD. By default the current user is used.

❏   `Analyze`: Used to perform the analysis on gathered data. This is enabled by default. The values for this parameter are `$true` or `$false`.

❏   `Collect`: Enabled by default, this parameter enables the data collector.

❏   `ConfigurationFileLocation`: If the BPA files are located in a directory other than `%path%\ Microsoft\Exchange Server\Bin\%language%`, use this parameter to specify the location of the BPA files. If the Exchange server that the cmdlet is being run from does not have web access, and your desktop or another device has the ExBPA files, `ConfigurationFileLocation` can also use an SMB connection and read the XML files from the remote device.

❏   `Description`: This parameter designates a friendly name for the scan being performed.

❏   `DomainController`: Specifies the domain controller to use to query AD. If this parameter is used, use the FQDN for the domain controller.

❏   `DownloadConfigurationUpdates`: By default this parameter is set to `true`, and is responsible for downloading the latest version of the BPA conf files. If the server that is running the `Test-SystemHealth` does not have web access, set this to `false`.

❏   `ExchangeCredentials`: If the user running this cmdlet does not have the necessary permissions, this parameter can be used to specify an alternate user's credentials.

❏   `Export`: By default this is set to `false`. This parameter is used in conjunction with `OutFileLocation` and removes "sensitive" data — any data that the Exchange administrator would need in order to use the BPA report — from the report.

❏   `GenerateEvents`: This parameter, which is reserved for internal use, lists events after the test is complete. It displays errors, warnings, and informational alerts if it is set to `true`. If you use this parameter in an interactive session, use an output modifier such as a format list.

❏   `GenerateSQMData`: This parameter is reserved for internal use. Use it to create Service Quality Monitoring files to upload to Microsoft. By default this is set to `true`.

❏   `MaxThreads`: This parameter is reserved for internal use. Setting this parameter tells the cmdlet the number of threads available for execution of this task. By default this is set to 25 threads.

❑ OutFileLocation: Setting this parameter tells the cmdlet to output to details of the test to the given location. This parameter requires the full path in the output. For example, OutFileLocation server1 will fail. -OutFileLocation.\server1 will also fail. The only output destinations that work are a full path, D:\logs\server1 or \\servername\share\server1. If you save the files as XML, you can further manipulate them and make inserting them into a configuration database easier.

❑ Roles: This parameter is reserved for internal use. It specifies the role to check, however passing any acceptable parameter to it will cause the test to run. So if you have a Mailbox server and specify the UnifiedMessaging option, it still runs and returns any discrepancies found.

❑ ScanType: This parameter is reserved for internal use; it specifies the type of test to run. The following scan types are valid:

   ❑ Health: Checks for misconfigurations, problems, outdated drivers, missing patches, the last time db backups were performed, message size settings, cluster configurations, and so on. This is the catch-all task and will find most of the problems in the environment.

   ❑ Perf: Runs for two hours and looks for performance problems.

   ❑ Permissions: Checks for missing or misconfigured permissions within AD sites, AD domains, the Exchange configuration, and checks the permission structure.

   ❑ ConnectivityTask: Checks for basic network connectivity problems, queries AD for site membership and for Exchange group membership.

   ❑ BaselineTask: Used to compare configurations and allows for file version checking.

   ❑ Ex2007Readiness: Performs a basic check against the server and the domain for feasibility of installing Exchange 2007 in the forest.

   ❑ PrecheckInstall: This is the pre-deployment check. If this is run against a server that already has Exchange 2007 installed, it will error out.

   ❑ PrecheckUninstall: Similar to the install, but checks all the requirements before the uninstall.

   ❑ PrecheckUpgrade: Requirement check before upgrading from a prior version.

   ❑ PrecheckDR: Checks requirements before recovering the server.

   ❑ Postcheck: Checks deployment after installation.

❑ ServerList: Specifies the server to run the test against. This parameter can be a single server, or a list of servers. If this parameter is not specified, the test will run against the local machine.

❑ Timeout: Period of time before the cmdlet will error out. By default it is set to 300 seconds, but can go up to 9,999,999.

Figure 14-4 shows the output of the Test-SystemHealth cmdlet. As you can see, this cmdlet can be quite informational. This particular figure shows that the network drivers may need to be updated as well as an immediate need to conduct a backup of the Exchange databases!

When the Test-SystemHealth cmdlet completes, any information that it finds will be displayed on the console. If OutFileLocation is used, you can take the file, rename the extension as .xml if you did not save it as such, and use ExBPA to read it. By using ExBPA it will perform all of the formatting and give the results a more graphically appealing look.

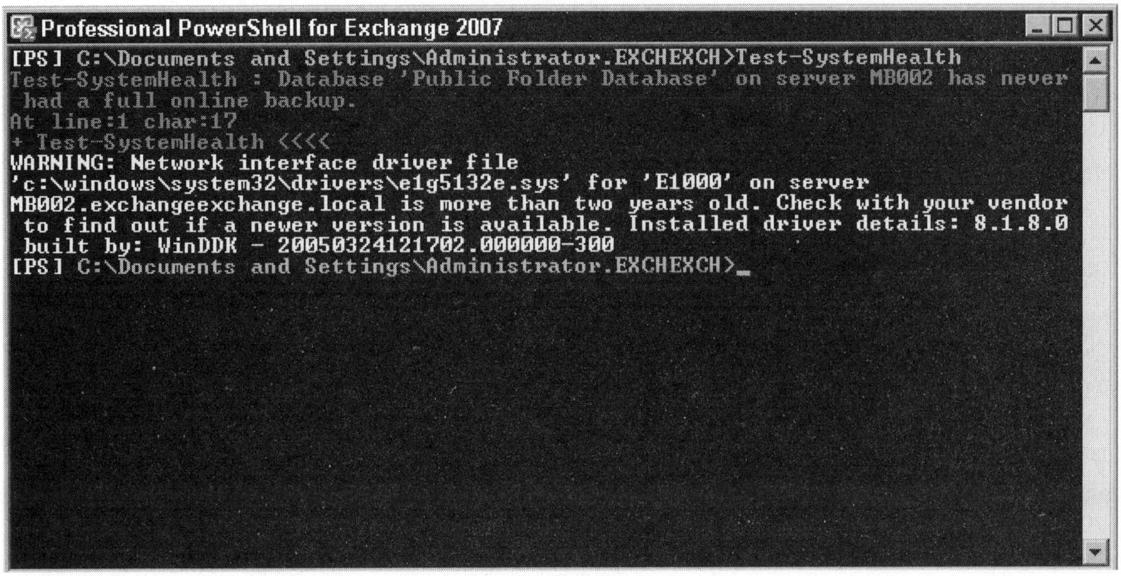

```
Professional PowerShell for Exchange 2007                                    _ □ X
[PS] C:\Documents and Settings\Administrator.EXCHEXCH>Test-SystemHealth
Test-SystemHealth : Database 'Public Folder Database' on server MB002 has never
  had a full online backup.
At line:1 char:17
+ Test-SystemHealth <<<<
WARNING: Network interface driver file
'c:\windows\system32\drivers\e1g5132e.sys' for 'E1000' on server
MB002.exchangeexchange.local is more than two years old. Check with your vendor
  to find out if a newer version is available. Installed driver details: 8.1.8.0
  built by: WinDDK - 20050324121702.000000-300
[PS] C:\Documents and Settings\Administrator.EXCHEXCH>_
```

Figure 14-4

Testing the Anti-Spam Functions

We are now going to review the following cmdlets that will assist in troubleshooting issues with the anti-spam features of Exchange Server 2007. The following cmdlets are covered in this section:

❑ Test-IPAllowListProvider

❑ Test-IPBlockListProvider

❑ Test-SenderId

Test-IPAllowListProvider

The first cmdlet is Test-IPAllowListProvider and is used to test an IP address to determine if it is listed on a configured service provider that performs email safe lists.

The following parameters are available for this cmdlet:

❑ Identity: This is the IPAllowListProviderId name that was specified when the IPAllowListProvider was created.

❑ IPAddress: The IP address of the remote device you want the safe list server to check.

❑ DomainController: Sets the DC to query.

❑ Server: Specifies what server to run the test on.

The cmdlet may seem a little confusing at first; however after a couple of IP address lookups it will seem more intuitive. Basically the cmdlet tests the validity of the remote IP address as a possible source of unsavory email. The allow list provider either confirms or denies that they are a reputable source from the provider's aggregation of spam and junk emails. If the IP address is deemed good, it will return a value of true on the cmdlet.

Figure 14-5 shows using Get-IPAllowListProvider and using the value returned as pipelined input for the Test-IPAllowListProvider.

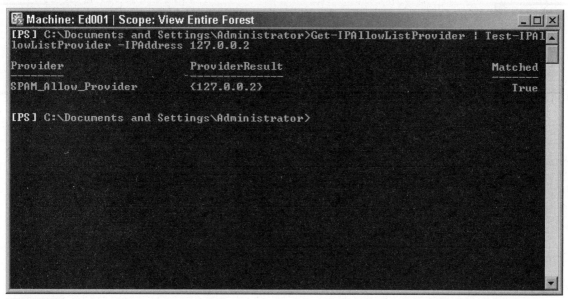

Figure 14-5

Test-IPBlockListProvider

The next cmdlet is the Test-IPBlockListProvider, which provides lookup for real-time block lists. This test cmdlet is very similar to Test-IPAllowListProvider, except it performs lookups for IP addresses that are on a block list and are considered spammers' IP addresses.

The following parameters are available for this cmdlet:

❏ Identity: This is the IPAllowListProviderId name that was specified when the IPBlockListProvider was created.

❏ IPAddress: The IP address of the remote device you want the safe list server to check.

❏ DomainController: Sets the DC to query.

❏ Server: Specifies what server to run the test on.

Figure 14-6 shows using two RBL providers to check the validity of an IP address.

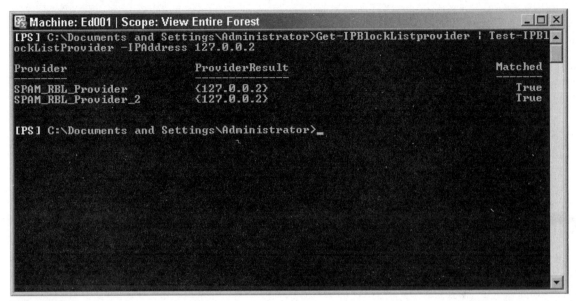

Figure 14-6

Test-SenderID

Using the Test-SenderId cmdlet tests the Sender ID functionality of a target domain's address or your own. For information about what Sender ID is, consult the Exchange help file or www.microsoft.com/ mscorp/safety/technologies/senderid/default.mspx. This cmdlet must be run on a server that has the Hub or Edge role installed. There are two required parameters for this cmdlet:

❏   IPAddress: The value for this parameter is the IP address of the server that you want to check the credentials of. For example, if you wanted to check Microsoft's SPF record to make sure its Sender ID was up to par, you would use the IP address of Microsoft's mail server. In this instance one of them is 131.107.115.212.

❏   PurportedResponsibleDomain: This is the domain name of the remote domain you are querying. In our example this would be Microsoft.com. The cmdlet would look like this: Test-SenderId -Address 131.107.115.212 -PurportedResponsibleDomain Microsoft.com. As you can see in Figure 14-7, the IP address and domain name for Microsoft are configured correctly.

The other parameters for this cmdlet are as follows:

❏   IPAddress: The IP address of the server you are querying.

❏   PurportedResponsibleDomain: Domain name that you are attempting to verify.

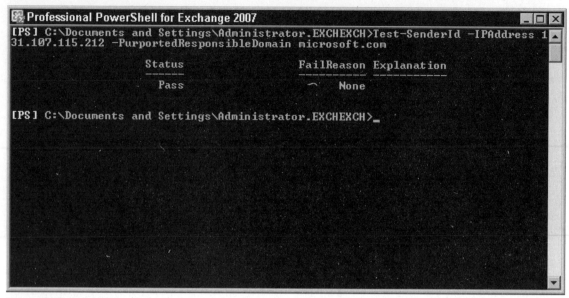

Figure 14-7

❏ `DomainController`: Sets the DC to query. For Hub servers this is the FQDN of the domain controller. In Edge installations this parameter refers to the local ADAM instance. This parameter is not required.

❏ `HelloDomain`: The HELO or EHLO SMTP commands that are issued from the sender.

❏ `Server`: The server name that the cmdlet will execute this script against. If the server name is not provided, this cmdlet will run against the local machine.

Understanding Sender ID

Sender ID was a joint development effort between Microsoft and other industry companies in an effort to combat spam. It is a cost-free authentication solution that uses the Sender Policy Framework (SPF). How this is accomplished is the administrator creates an SPF record that contains the IP address of all external-facing email servers and the MX record of your email server. How does this work?

1. Email is sent to your domain.

2. Your mail relay accepts the message and performs an SPF record lookup in DNS.

3. If the sending mail server's name and IP address are correct it is sent on. If they fail verification, this message may be deleted, blocked, or sent to the junk folder. This works in part with the Anti-Spam stamping.

Troubleshooting the Client Access Server Role Functions

Now you are going to look at the following key cmdlets that can be used to troubleshoot the Client Access Server (CAS) role.

- ❏ `Test-OutlookWebServices`
- ❏ `Test-ActiveSyncConnectivity`
- ❏ `Test-OwaConnectivity`
- ❏ `Test-WebServicesConnectivity`

Test-OutlookWebServices

The `Test-OutlookWebServices` cmdlet runs a series of tests against the Autodiscover service on a server that has the Client Access Server role installed. The Autodiscover service is extremely important to organizations; Autodiscover is responsible for the Availability server, Outlook Anywhere, Offline Address Book publishing, free busy, and Unified Messaging retrieval. During initial deployments of Exchange Server 2007, the Autodiscover service was one of the most widely misconfigured components and it remains so to this day. The value this script provides is to allow the Exchange administrator to have a proactive means of testing service availability of all the components with the Autodiscover service, and not rely on the end user as an accurate measure of usability.

The following parameters listed for `Test-OutlookWebServices` are all optional. The cmdlet executes without any command-line input.

- ❏ `ClientAccessServer`: Specifies the CAS server that the cmdlet will test against.
- ❏ `Identity`: This parameter can use any valid email address in the forest. Alternate input can include domain\user name or the user's GUID. The cmdlet will query AD and translate the input into the user's email address and then perform the test.
- ❏ `MonitoringContext`: This true/false value sets whether to include the monitoring events and performance data. It also passes the data onto MOM if the MOM agent is installed.
- ❏ `TargetAddress`: Specifying this parameter will test that the recipient can retrieve the data that the `Test-OutlookWebServices` is requesting. This would be a valid SMTP address in your domain.

Figure 14-8 shows the output of a test against the `OutlookWebServices`.

The following are the steps that the `Test-OutlookWebServices` cmdlet uses:

1. Tests Autodiscover with the email address specified in the `Identity` parameter or if none is specified, uses the current user.

2. Contacts the Autodiscover site `http://mb002.exchangeexchange.local/Autodiscover/Autodiscover.xml`.

```
Professional PowerShell for Exchange 2007                              _ □ X
[PS] C:\Documents and Settings\Administrator.EXCHEXCH>Test-OutlookWebServices

               Id                    Type Message
               --                    ---- -------
              1003             Information About to test AutoDisc...
              1007             Information Testing server MB002.e...
              1019             Information Found a valid AutoDisc...
              1006             Information Contacted AutoDiscover...
              1016                 Success [EXCH]-Successfully co...
              1015                 Success [EXCH]-Successfully co...
              1014                 Success [EXCH]-Successfully co...
              1006                 Success Successfully tested Au...


[PS] C:\Documents and Settings\Administrator.EXCHEXCH>_
```

Figure 14-8

3. Contacts the AS also known as the Availability Service (Free/Busy) `http://mb002/exchangeexchange.local/EWS.Exchange.asmx`.

4. Contacts the OAB (Offline Address Book) service `http://mb002.exchangeexchange.local/EWS/Exchange.asmx`.

5. Contacts the UM (Unified Messaging) service `http://mb002.exchangeexchange.local/UnifiedMessaging/Service.asmx`.

6. Tests any external URLs that have been set.

7. If RPC/HTTP is used it attempts to contact the service `http://exchangexchange.com/Rpc`. Each of these steps will report results to the screen allowing the administrator to review and react to any of the errors that are generated.

Test-ActiveSyncConnectivity

The `Test-ActiveSyncConnectivity` cmdlet tests a full synchronization of a mailbox using Microsoft ActiveSync. Though ActiveSync configuration is not a complicated task, for some unknown reason it still generates a lot of calls to help desks and Exchange administrators. Using this cmdlet, the Exchange admin can test synchronization and configuration against any user. By default all users are ActiveSync enabled. If no user is specified, the cmdlet uses the monitoring mailbox, which is the CAS user.

The following parameters are available for this cmdlet:

❑ `AllowUnsecureAccess`: Necessary if you are not using SSL.

❑ `ClientAccessServer`: Specifies a particular CAS server to synchronize against.

- ❑ `DomainController`: Sets the DC to query.

- ❑ `MailboxCredential`: User that the cmdlet should attempt to synchronize against. If no user is specified the CAS user is used. Using `MailboxCredential:(Get-Credential test@ exchangeexchange.local)` prompts for the password of the user `'test'`. Once the password is entered, the test cmdlet runs.

- ❑ `MailboxServer`: Mailbox server that contains the mailbox to test. If no server is specified, connectivity to all mailbox servers will be tested.

- ❑ `MonitoringContext`: This true/false value sets whether to include the monitoring events and performance data. This also passes the data onto MOM if the MOM agent is installed.

- ❑ `MonitoringInstance`: Used in conjunction with `MonitoringContext`. This parameter is a true/false value and determines whether to run the cmdlet as the current user.

- ❑ `ResetTestAccountCredentials`: Resets the test account password. This may become necessary if the cmdlet errors out due to password issues.

- ❑ `TrustAnySSLCertificate`: Accepts any SSL certificate that is sent during the ActiveSync test.

- ❑ `URL`: Used to specify the URL used for ActiveSync.

- ❑ `UseAutodiscoverForClientAccessServer`: Boolean value to determine if the cmdlet should query Autodiscover to find a CAS server.

The following are the steps of a `Test-ActiveSyncConnectivity` connection:

1. Connect to the CAS server and issue HTTP OPTIONS to retrieve Exchange ActiveSync, EAS, protocol version.

2. Perform a `FolderSync` command and get the folder hierarchy.

3. Issue a `First Sync` command to initialize the partnership to the test folder.

4. Issue a `GetItemEstimate` command and retrieve the number of items to sync.

5. Perform synchronization against the test folder.

6. Execute the `Ping` command to test `DirectPush`. A test item is created in the test folder to instantiate the Ping.

7. Sync the newly created test item.

To check multiple CAS servers you can use `Get-ExchangeServer` to find all servers with the CAS role installed, and then construct a `foreach` loop to test the connectivity of each CAS server to the mailbox server. The script is similar to the `Test-ServiceHealth` script described earlier in the chapter:

```
$b=Get-ExchangeServer | where {$_.IsClientAccessServer -eq"true"}
foreach ($z in $b) {test-ActiveSyncConnectivity -ClientAccessServer $z}
```

Figure 14-9 shows a successful test of connectivity from the CAS role on MB002 to the Mailbox role on MB002 and MB001.

An easier way to do this is to use `Get-ClientAccessServer | Test-ActiveSyncConnectivity`.

```
Professional PowerShell for Exchange 2007                              _ □ ×
[PS] C:\Documents and Settings\Administrator.EXCHEXCH>$b=Get-ExchangeServer | wh
ere ($_.IsClientAccessServer -eq"True")
[PS] C:\Documents and Settings\Administrator.EXCHEXCH>foreach ($z in $b) {Test-A
ctiveSyncconnectivity -ClientAccessServer $z}

CasServer   MailboxServer Scenario         Result     Latency(MS) Error
---------   ------------- --------         ------     ----------- -----
mb002       MB002         Options          Success       2562.5
mb002       MB002         FolderSync       Success       3453.12
mb002       MB002         First Sync       Success        656.25
mb002       MB002         GetItemEstimate  Success        343.75
mb002       MB002         Sync Data        Success         93.75
mb002       MB002         Ping             Success       1578.12
mb002       MB002         Sync Test Item   Success        578.12
mb002       MB001         Options          Success         46.88
mb002       MB001         FolderSync       Success        109.38
mb002       MB001         First Sync       Success         78.12
mb002       MB001         GetItemEstimate  Success         31.25
mb002       MB001         Sync Data        Success         46.88
mb002       MB001         Ping             Success       1156.25
mb002       MB001         Sync Test Item   Success         46.88


[PS] C:\Documents and Settings\Administrator.EXCHEXCH>_
```

Figure 14-9

Test-OwaConnectivity

OWA connectivity is very important for the mobile workforce or for remote users who do not need all the features of Outlook. In Exchange 2007 OWA has undergone a major facelift in order to close the gap between the online web application and Outlook. As the OWA development team continues to work on closing the feature gap, OWA will continue to gain favor in the user base.

This cmdlet, by default, tests all the virtual directories on a CAS server. No input parameters are necessary to conduct a basic test.

The following is a list of parameters available for this cmdlet:

❑   AllowUnsecureAccess: Boolean values that if set runs the cmdlet against virtual directories that do not use SSL.

❑   ClientAccessServer: Designates which CAS server to perform the test against. This parameter cannot be used in conjunction with the URL parameter. If this parameter is specified, it tests only Exchange 2007 virtual directories. Exchange 2000 and 2003 virtual directories as well as non 2007 mailboxes will not be tested.

❑   DomainController: Sets the DC to query.

❑   MailboxCredential: User that the cmdlet should attempt to synchronize against. If no user is specified, the CAS user is used. If this parameter is used, use the UPN of the user. Using MailboxCredential:(Get-Credential test@exchangeexchange.local) prompts for the password of the user 'test'. Once the password is entered, the test cmdlet will run.

❑   MailboxServer: Mailbox server that contains the mailbox to test. If no server is specified, connectivity to all mailbox servers will be tested.

❑ `MonitoringContext`: This true/false value sets whether to include the monitoring events and performance data. This also passes the data onto MOM if the MOM agent is installed.

❑ `ResetTestAccountCredentials`: Resets the test account password. This may become necessary if the cmdlet errors out due to password issues.

❑ `TestType`: Used to set whether to test the internal or external URL. The cmdlet retrieves the internal and external URL from OwaVirtualDirectory's `InternalUrl` and `ExternalUrl`. If you use this parameter and the cmdlet's result is skipped, this is most likely because that URL was not set. See Chapter 6 for information on how to use the `Get` and `Set-OwaVirtualDirectory` cmdlets. `TestType` cannot be used in conjunction with `URL`.

❑ `TrustAnySSLCertificate`: Accept any SSL certificate that is sent during the connectivity test.

❑ `URL`: This parameter specifies the OWA URL to test. If used, the cmdlet tests only this URL. This parameter cannot be used in conjunction with `ClientAccessServer` or `TestType`.

❑ `VirtualDirectoryName`: Specifies the virtual directory name to test. If this parameter is not used, the cmdlet tests all Exchange 2007 virtual directories. Exchange 2000 and 2003 virtual directories and mailboxes will not be tested.

The connection steps for this cmdlet are short. All testing is performed by connecting to the website, logging in, and verifying the webpage. Figure 14-10 shows an OWA connectivity test using the administrator account. The authentication method returned from the Client Access Server is forms based authentication, FBA, against the Client Access Server MB002.exchangeexchange.local. The result of the logon scenario was successful and was performed of a secure link, defined under SecureAccess. Additional information returned shows whether the access was to the internal or external URL as well as the exact URL that was used. All of this is useful when attempting to troubleshoot CAS logon failures or to isolate failure to a specific server.

Figure 14-10

Testing the Web Services with Test-WebServicesConnectivity

This cmdlet's name is a bit of a misnomer because there are several other test cmdlets that test web service connectivity. The cmdlets test the functionality of Outlook Anywhere. Exchange 2003 used the term RPC instead of HTTP; however in 2007 it has been renamed to something a little more marketing friendly.

The following is a list of parameters available for this cmdlet:

❑ `AllowUnsecureAccess`: Necessary if you are not using SSL.

❑ `ClientAccessServer`: Specify the CAS server that the cmdlet will test against.

❑ `MailboxCredential`: User that the cmdlet should attempt to synchronize against. If no user is specified the CAS user is used. Using `MailboxCredential:(Get-Credential test@ exchangeexchange.local)` will prompt for the password of the user `'test'`. Once the password is entered, the test cmdlet runs.

❑ `MailboxServer Mailbox`: Server that contains the mailbox to test. If no server is specified, connectivity to the local mailbox server will be tested.

❑ `MonitoringContext`: This true/false value sets whether to include the monitoring events and performance data. This also passes the data onto MOM if the MOM agent is installed.

❑ `ResetTestAccountCredentials`: Resets the test account password. This may become necessary if the cmdlet errors out due to password issues.

❑ `TrustAnySSLCertificate`: Accept any SSL certificate that is sent during the `WebServicesConnectivity` test.

❑ `UseAutodiscoverForClientAccessServer`: Boolean value to determine whether the cmdlet should query Autodiscover to find a CAS server.

This cmdlet works well with pipeline input. It will display the CAS server as well as the Mailbox server name.

```
Get-ClientAccessServer | Test-WebServicesConnectivity
```

The following are the steps that the `Test-WebServicesConnectivity` cmdlet uses:

1. Issues a `GetFolder` call to retrieve the folder.

2. Issues a `SyncFolderItems` to synchronize the folder's items.

3. Creates an item in the folder.

4. Issues a `SyncFolderItems` to resynchronize the folder's items.

5. Issues a `DeleteItem` to remove an item from the folder.

6. Issues a `SyncFolderItems` to resynchronize the folder's items.

The cmdlet tests the latency in getting items, creating, deleting, and then synchronizing after each step. Read, Write, Delete, and Synchronize are the basic functions that Outlook Anywhere users will perform.

Troubleshooting the Mailbox Server Role Functions

The following cmdlets are discussed for testing MAPI connectivity:

- ❑ `Test-MapiConnectivity`
- ❑ `Test-Mailflow`
- ❑ `Test-ExchangeSearch`

Troubleshooting MAPI Connectivity

The `Test-MapiConnectivity` cmdlet checks connectivity to the mailbox layer. Mailbox availability is a very important statistic because some service level agreements (SLA) are written to the uptime of the mailbox. The cmdlet tests two very important features. The first is the Active Directory (AD) health, which is tested through AD queries via DSAccess. The second test is the MAPI connectivity to the mailbox, which tests access to the information store, storage group, the mailbox database, and down to the mailbox. Like the other test cmdlets, this cmdlet requires no options in order to run.

The following is a list of parameters available for this cmdlet:

- ❑ `Database`: Specifies which database to test connectivity to. If no parameter is specified, the cmdlet tests all databases on the server.
- ❑ `Identity`: Specifies which user mailbox to test. The following values are accepted for the `Identity` parameter:
  - ❑ GUID
  - ❑ Distinguished name (DN)
  - ❑ Domain\account
  - ❑ User principal name (UPN)
  - ❑ Legacy DN
  - ❑ Simple Mail Transfer Protocol Address (SMTP)
  - ❑ Alias
- ❑ If the `Identity` parameter is not used, the cmdlet will use the `SystemMailbox` on each database.
- ❑ `ActiveDirectoryTimeout`: By default this value is set to 15 seconds. This setting determines how long to wait on AD to return results before timing out.
- ❑ `AllConnectionsTimeout`: Specifies the total connection time for all transactions to complete before timing out. This timer begins once all pertinent information is received from AD.
- ❑ `DomainController`: Sets the DC to query.
- ❑ `MonitoringContext`: Boolean value that specifies whether to include events and performance objects of the MAPI transaction.

❑ `PerConnectionTimeout`: By default this parameter is set to 10 seconds. This parameter is for each transaction.

❑ `Server`: Specifies which server to test MAPI connectivity against. When the `Server` parameter is used, the cmdlet tests connectivity to the system mailbox within each database on the specified server.

To test all mailbox servers in the organization, use `Get-MailboxServer | Test-MapiConnectivity`, as shown in Figure 14-11.

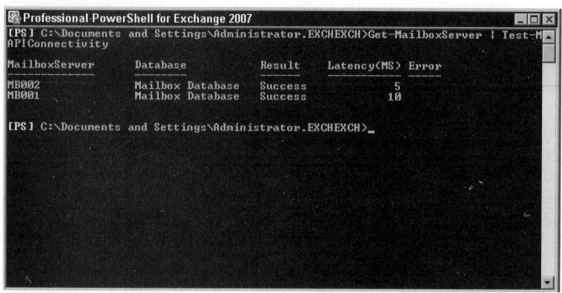

Figure 14-11

Testing Mailflow

Using the `Test-Mailflow` cmdlet allows the Exchange administrator to test mail connectivity to the local mailbox server, between servers in the forest, or even to an external email address. If no parameters are specified, the cmdlet sends and receives mail to the local machine.

The following is a list of parameters available for this cmdlet:

❑ `AutoDiscoverTargetMailboxServer`: Uses the Autodiscover service to request a list of all mailbox servers from AD and then sends a test email to each mailbox server that was returned from the Autodiscover service.

❑ `TargetEmailAddress`: Used to specify the SMTP address of a remote mailbox. An email will be sent to the remote user's mailbox. This is useful for testing connectivity through the Internet.

❑ `TargetMailboxServer`: Tells the cmdlet which mailbox servers to send test messages to.

❑ `ActiveDirectoryTimeout`: By default this value is set to 15 seconds. This setting determines how long to wait on AD to return results before timing out.

❑ `DomainController`: Sets the DC to query.

❑ `ErrorLatency`: Used by MOM to determine if there is excessive latency. The response times for a local test are 15 seconds by default and 180 seconds for mail submitted to a remote server.

❑ `ExecutionTimeout`: Specifies how long to the cmdlet will run and wait for a response before the task times out. By default an interactive session will wait 240 seconds (4 minutes) before issuing a failure. When used in conjunction with the `MonitoringContext`, the default is set to 15 seconds.

❑ `Identity`: The mailbox server or a valid SMTP address. If no parameter is set, the cmdlet will use the local mailbox server.

❑ `MonitoringContext`: This true/false value sets whether to include the monitoring events and performance data. This also passes the data onto MOM if the MOM agent is installed.

❑ `TargetEmailAddressDisplayName`: Sets the display name of the mailbox where the test email is delivered.

Figure 14-12 shows a `Test-Mailflow` to the local server.

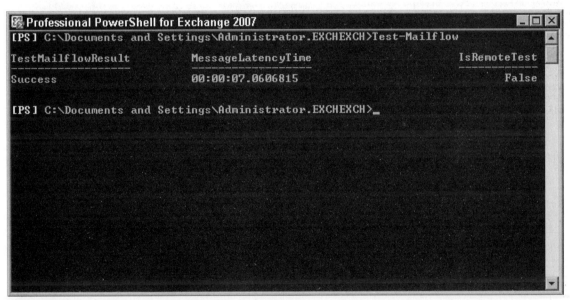

Figure 14-12

Testing the Exchange Search Service

In previous editions of Exchange, the database index was created within a schedule. Therefore, the index was no longer current and as new mail arrived, it would not be introduced into the index until the next indexing cycle. Exchange 2007 updates the index every time a new message is received into the database. Windows Mobile 6, OWA, and Outlook users all query against the database index, so it is more important that the index always be up to date. This is where the `Test-ExchangeSearch` cmdlet comes in; it will insert an email into the mailbox, wait for the index to be updated, and then search the index for the test message. If the content of the message is not found, or the index timeout is exceeded, the cmdlet will issue a failure. If no mailbox is specified, the cmdlet will use the system mailbox.

The following is a list of parameters available for this cmdlet:

❑　`DomainController`: Sets the DC to query.

❑　`Identity`: Specifies which user mailbox to test. The following values are accepted for the `Identity` parameter:

❑　GUID

❑　Distinguished name (DN)

❑　Domain\account

❑　User principal name (UPN)

❑　Legacy DN

❑　Simple Mail Transfer Protocol Address (SMTP)

❑　Alias

❑　`IndexingTimeout`: The timer for this parameter starts once the message is inserted into the mailbox. Timeout value specifies the amount of time to wait for the transaction to complete. By default this is set to 2 minutes.

❑　`MonitoringContext`: This true/false value sets whether to include the monitoring events and performance data. This will also pass the data onto MOM if the MOM agent is installed.

❑　`Server`: Specifies the mailbox server to test.

The cmdlet can be executed from pipelined input, but in doing so it will not display the mailbox server's name. In an organization with more than one mailbox server, this would be problematic. So using a `foreach` loop to print the mailbox server's name with the output from the `Test-ExchangeSearch` will work:

```
$mbx=Get-MailboxServer
Foreach ($mbxname in $mbx) {echo $mbxname.name (test-exchangesearch -server
$mbxname) | fl}
```

Figure 14-13 shows the results for the `foreach` script. If the `$mbxname.name` is omitted, the test results will not map an index search response time to a server, and this can become messy in larger environments.

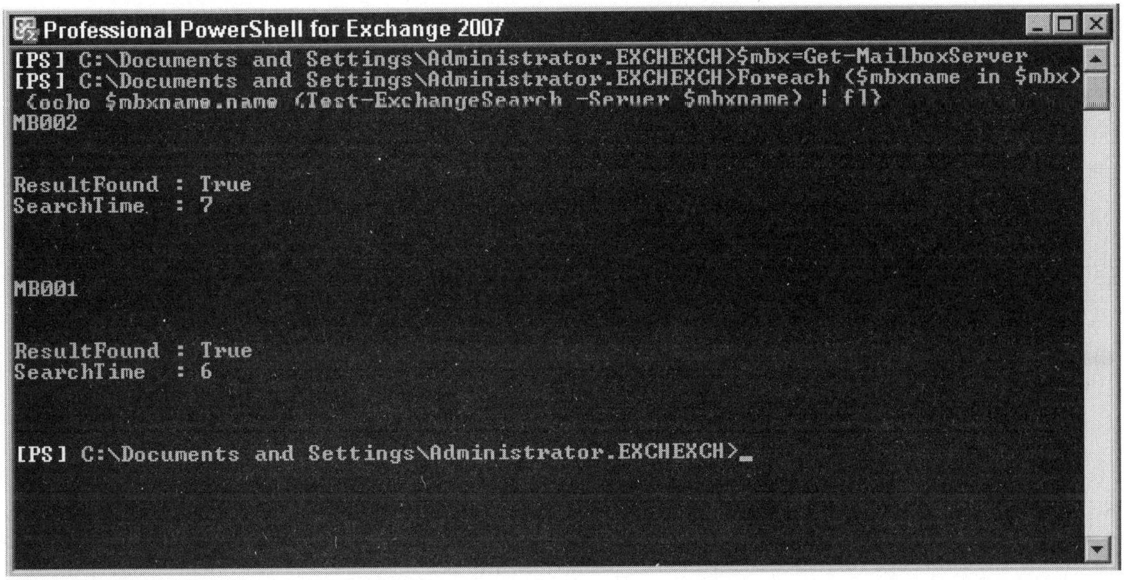
Professional PowerShell for Exchange 2007
[PS] C:\Documents and Settings\Administrator.EXCHEXCH>$mbx=Get-MailboxServer
[PS] C:\Documents and Settings\Administrator.EXCHEXCH>Foreach ($mbxname in $mbx)
{echo $mbxname.name (Test-ExchangeSearch -Server $mbxname) | fl}
MB002
ResultFound : True
SearchTime : 7
MB001
ResultFound : True
SearchTime : 6
[PS] C:\Documents and Settings\Administrator.EXCHEXCH>_

Figure 14-13

Troubleshooting Edge Synchronization

This section discusses the single Edge test cmdlet:

- `Test-EdgeSynchronization`

The `Test-EdgeSynchronization` cmdlet tests synchronization of Edge servers. Edge servers use an ADAM (Active Directory Application Mode) instance instead of connecting to AD directly. Edge servers are not in the domain, so any information that is needed for messaging or recipients, connectors, and anti-spam is stored in ADAM. The ADAM instance periodically updates its cache against AD to prevent stale data and to improve response time. This cmdlet needs to be run against a server that has the Hub role installed.

The following is a list of parameters available for this cmdlet:

- `DomainController`: Sets the DC to query.
- `ExcludeRecipientTest`: Boolean value that if set to `true` ignores the recipient objects and queries only the configuration objects for validity.

❑   MaxReportSize: Specifies how many results will be included on the report. The report includes all objects and properties in the ADAM instance and AD that are out of sync. By default the -MaxReportSize is 1,000 entries.

❑   MonitoringContext: This true/false value sets whether to include the monitoring events and performance data. This will also pass the data onto MOM if the MOM agent is installed.

Troubleshooting Unified Messaging Connectivity

This section discusses using the Unified Messaging test cmdlet to determine UM Health:

❑   Test-UMConnectivity

The Test-UMConnectivity cmdlet tests the UM (Unified Messaging) component of Exchange 2007. Because Unified Messaging and telephony may be new to some Exchange administrators, this cmdlet should provide some comfort in troubleshooting the new component. The cmdlet has two different test patterns. The first test pattern tests only the UM role. The second test, which is more comprehensive, is instantiated via the -IPGateway parameter, and tests connectivity across the entire UM infrastructure. The UM server, IP Gateway, and the PBX will be tested in the second test.

The following is a list of parameters available for this cmdlet:

❑   Phone: The extension that is used when the test call is redirected. This extension should be configured to forward calls to the UM hunt group.

❑   PIN: This parameter specifies the PIN for the UM-enabled mailbox.

❑   TUILogon: Boolean value that if set to true notifies the cmdlet to log in to the UM-enabled mailboxes. Any mailboxes in the test must be in the same dial plan as the UM server. By default this parameter is set to false. If this parameter is used, UMDialPlan, Phone, and PIN must also be specified.

❑   TUILogonALL: Similar to TUILogon but attempts to log on to every UM-enabled mailbox in the AD site. By default this parameter is set to false.

❑   UMIPGateway: The IP address of the IP gateway to test. If this value is set, the phone parameter must also be used.

❑   UMDialPlan: The UM dial plan that is to be tested. If this parameter is used, Phone, PIN, and TUILogon must also be specified.

❑   DomainController: Sets the DC to query.

❑   Fax: Boolean value to set the cmdlet to run the test as a fax instead of a voice call. This is true by default.

❑   ListenPort: By default the listening port is set to 9,000. If a different port is needed, set it here.

❑   MonitoringContext: This true/false value sets whether to include the monitoring events and performance data. This also passes the data onto MOM if the MOM agent is installed.

❑   Secured: Boolean value that sets the cmdlet to run in an encrypted mode. If your IP gateway is not set to take encrypted communications, setting this value causes the cmdlet to error out.

❑   Timeout: Period of time for the cmdlet to run. By default this parameter is set to 180 seconds.

❑   ResetPIN: Boolean value to reset the PIN for any of the specified mailboxes.

Figure 14-14 shows testing UM connectivity.

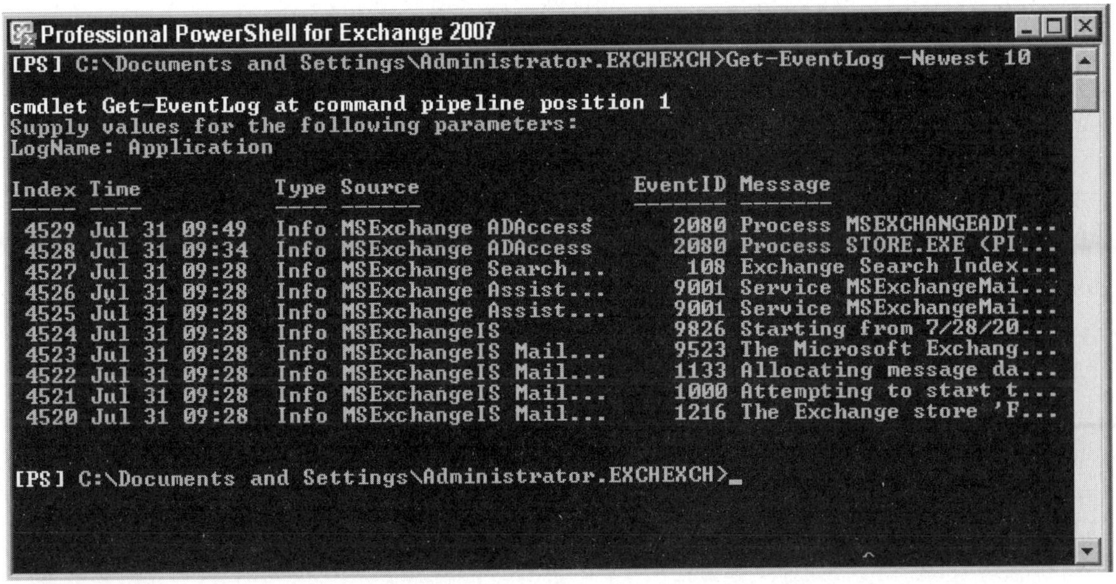

Figure 14-14

Using Get and Set Cmdlets to Gather System and Application Data

This section discusses using the following cmdlets to retrieve system and application data:

❑   Get-Eventlog

❑   Get-Message

❑   Get-MessageTrackingLog

❑   Get-EventLogLevel

❑   Set-EventLogLevel

Using Get-Eventlog

The `Get-Eventlog` cmdlet reads any of the event logs stored on the local computer. It is a very powerful and flexible cmdlet that can be used to parse event logs without complex scripting. If you have created a custom event log source, this cmdlet can parse them. Do you need to look for a particular word inside an event? This script will find it. Do you want all the logs from a particular day conveniently exported to a CSV file for further analysis? This is your cmdlet.

The following is a list of parameters available for this cmdlet:

❑ `logName`: This is a required parameter. It indicates which log file the cmdlet is to run against.

❑ `list`: Shows all of the event logs on the system, their current size, retention setting, their overflow action, and the number of entries in each log.

❑ `asString`: Creates the output as a string as opposed to a series of objects.

❑ `newest`: Tells the cmdlet to retrieve a specified number of events.

Figure 14-15 shows the output of `Get-Eventlog Newest 10`. It is running against the Application log.

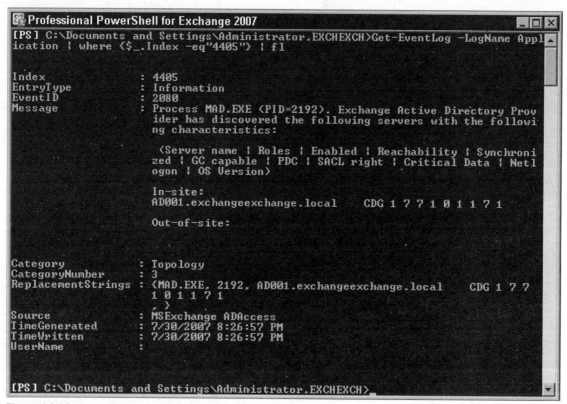

Figure 14-15

Let's take one event and explore all of the fields that are available for manipulation. To do this you select one event by setting the `Index` value equal to `4405` and the use `| fl` to expand the output. The command looks as follows:

```
Get-EventLog -LogName Application | where {$_.Index -eq"4405"} | fl
```

The results of the cmdlet are displayed in Figure 14-16.

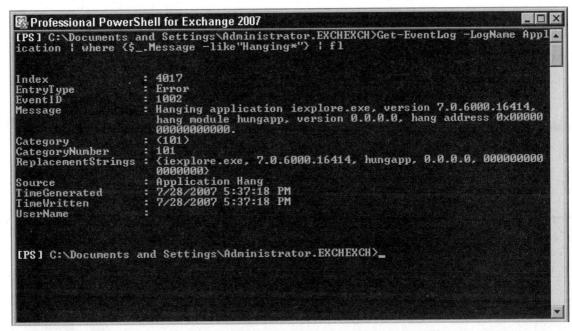

Figure 14-16

The following fields can be queried by the cmdlet:

- ❑ Index
- ❑ Message
- ❑ ReplacementStrings
- ❑ TimeWritten
- ❑ EntryType
- ❑ Category
- ❑ Source
- ❑ EventID
- ❑ CategoryNumber
- ❑ TimeGenerated

If you had an application hang, but could not find it because you forgot the event id, you could query the Application log to search all events and retrieve any event that had "Hanging" in the message. You may be tempted to use the `Contains` parameter but in doing so you must match the exact message. `Contains` is similar to `Equals`. If you do not have the exact message you are searching for, place wildcards in front of and behind the keywords you are searching for. The following query performs this action and you can see Internet Explorer hang in the results of Figure 14-17:

```
Get-EventLog -LogName Application | Where {$_.Message -like"Hanging*"} | fl
```

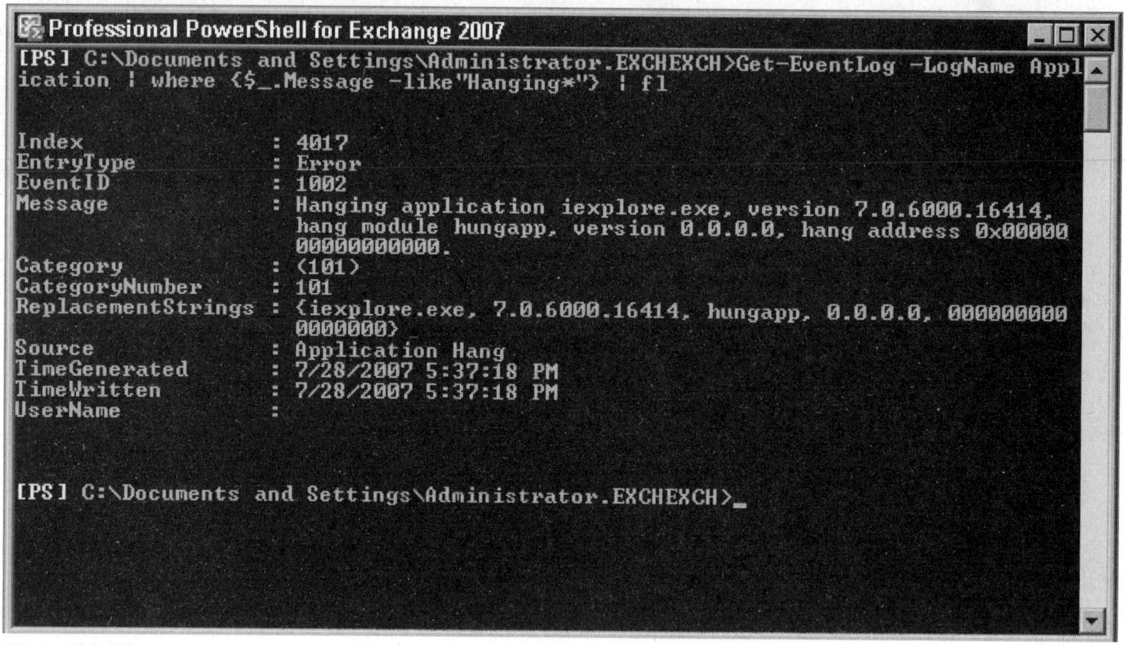

Figure 14-17

To retrieve all errors from the system log for a particular day, the cmdlet used in Figure 14-17 can be modified to use `TimeGenerated` and `EntryType` to specify the new search parameters. The `LogName` value has also been switched from `Application` to `System`. (See Figure 14-18.)

Lastly, to export data from this cmdlet or from any cmdlet, pipeline the cmdlet to `export-csv` and specify the `.csv` filename. The output is redirected to the `.csv` file and will not display on the screen. From there, the `.csv` file can be loaded into Excel or programmatically inserted in SQL through a DTS package or via Service Broker.

Using Get-Message

The `Get-Message` cmdlet provides the ability for the Exchange administrator to view the message queue through PowerShell. Imagine this as your scriptable queue viewer across the enterprise. The cmdlet runs against a Hub or Edge server and can be used to look at the queue of a remote server. If no parameters are specified, the cmdlet attempts to run against the local machine. Also by default the result size is limited to 1,000 entries.

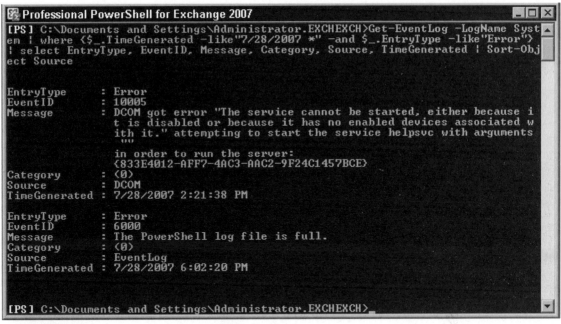

Figure 14-18

The following is a list of parameters available for this cmdlet:

❑ BookmarkIndex: Used to specify a position from within the result set that the displayed results are sent to the output device. This parameter cannot be used in conjunction with the BookmarkObject parameter.

❑ BookmarkObject: Similar to BookmarkIndex but is used to specify an object in lieu of a position.

❑ Filter: This parameter is used to specify what parameter is used to filter the query. Filter is used in conjunction with a comparison operator. The filter parameters are listed below:

    ❑ DateReceived: Date the message was received.

    ❑ ExpirationTime: Time the message expires.

    ❑ FromAddress: SMTP address of the sender.

    ❑ Identity: Message option, server handler, and queue identifier.

    ❑ InternetMessageId: Value from the Message-ID of the email header.

    ❑ LastError: Last error present for the message.

    ❑ MessageSourceName: Name that is used for the component that submits the message to the queue. If the cmdlet is run locally, the MessageSourceName will be 'FromLocal'.

    ❑ Queue: Name of the queue that contains the messages. Formatted in the server\destination format.

- ❏ RetryCount: Number of times delivery was attempted.

- ❏ SCL: Spam confidence level. Valid values are –1 to 9.

- ❏ Size: Represented in bytes.

- ❏ SourceIP: IP address of the originating server.

- ❏ Status: Current status. The following are acceptable values: Active, Retry, Suspended, PendingSuspend, and PendingRemove.

- ❏ Subject: Text present in the subject of the email.

- ❏ Identity: Can be one of the following:

  - ❏ Server\QueueIdentity\MessageIdentity

  - ❏ QueueIdentity\MessageIdentity

  - ❏ Server*\MessageIdentity

  - ❏ MessageIdentity

- ❏ IncludeBookmark: Boolean value used to specify if the bookmark object is included in the result set. This parameter can be used with BookmarkObject or BookmarkIndex parameters.

- ❏ IncludeRecipientInfo: If this value is used, the values from the recipients filed in the email will be displayed. The following are valid recipient values:

  - ❏ Address: SMTP address of the recipient.

  - ❏ Type: Recipient type. Either External, Mailbox, or a Distribution List (DL).

  - ❏ FinalDestination: Distinguished name (DN) that is used to route the message. This can be a connector mailbox server or an expansion server.

  - ❏ Status: Can be one of the following: Complete, Ready, or Retry.

  - ❏ LastError: SMTP response from the last attempted delivery.

- ❏ Queue: Queue name of the queue that contains the messages. Formatted in the server\destination format.

- ❏ ResultSize: By default this value is set to 1,000 but can go up to 250,000.

- ❏ ReturnPageInfo: Boolean value that is a hidden parameter. It can be used to gather the current number of results.

- ❏ SearchForward: This parameter is used to specify whether to search forward or backward within a result set. By default it will search forward. It calculates the value based on forward or backward search and then from the start of the result set or from the bookmark location if used.

- ❏ Server: The FQDN of the remote server that you are attempting to query. If this parameter is not used, the cmdlet executes against localhost.

- ❏ SortOrder: Allows for manipulation of the result set. By setting a + or – in front of a property, the property's values are sorted by ascending or descending order. If multiple properties are to be sorted, separate each property with a comma.

In Figure 14-19, the `Get-Message` is run against a remote server.

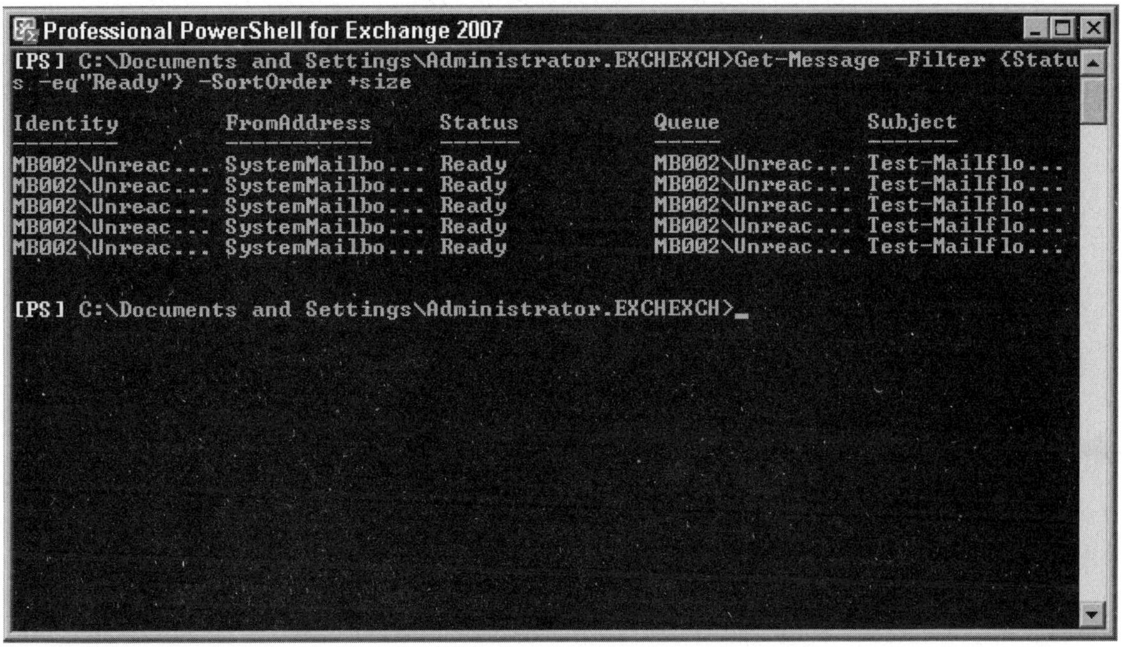

Figure 14-19

The filtering section may be a bit confusing at first, but it is similar to any other cmdlet that uses a comparison to qualify the search and produce specific results. This script shows all messages on the local server that are in a ready status and sorts them by size. The results are shown in Figure 14-20. If you execute the same script again and use `format-list (|fl)` you can see what the last error was and help troubleshoot why these messages are still in queue.

Figure 14-21 shows using `Format-List` in more detail.

Tracking Messages

Every message that is routed through Exchange Server 2007 has the route it takes through the system stored in a message tracking log. Tracking logs exist of Hub, Edge, and mailbox server. As a message traverses the Exchange organization, each hop that it takes through a transport server is updated in a message tracking log. The tracking log is a good place to start when there are reported mail delivery problems or as a proactive measure to test mail flow through the organization.

The following is a list of parameters available for the `Get-MessagesTrackingLog` cmdlet:

❑ `DomainController`: Sets the DC to query.

❑ `End`: Setting this parameter notifies the cmdlet to send log items up to, but not including, the end date.

❑ `EventId`: Scrapes the tracking log of specified event categories. The following are valid search terms: `BadMail`, `Defer Deliver`, `DSN`, `Expand`, `Fail`, `PoisonMessage`, `Receive`, `Redirect`, `Resolve`, `Send`, `Submit`, and `Transfer`.

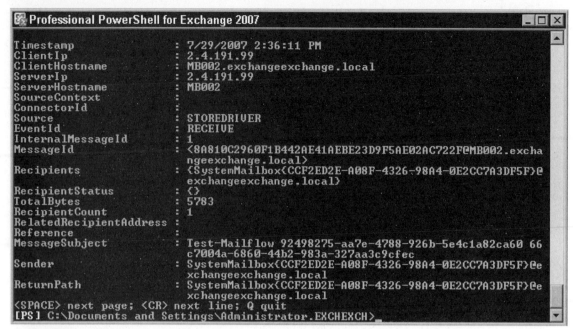

```
Professional PowerShell for Exchange 2007
Timestamp                : 7/29/2007 2:36:11 PM
ClientIp                 : 2.4.191.99
ClientHostname           : MB002.exchangeexchange.local
ServerIp                 : 2.4.191.99
ServerHostname           : MB002
SourceContext            :
ConnectorId              :
Source                   : STOREDRIVER
EventId                  : RECEIVE
InternalMessageId        : 1
MessageId                : <8A810C2960F1B442AE41AEBE23D9F5AE02AC722F@MB002.excha
                           ngeexchange.local>
Recipients               : {SystemMailbox{CCF2ED2E-A08F-4326-98A4-0E2CC7A3DF5F}@
                           exchangeexchange.local}
RecipientStatus          : {}
TotalBytes               : 5783
RecipientCount           : 1
RelatedRecipientAddress  :
Reference                :
MessageSubject           : Test-Mailflow 92498275-aa7e-4788-926b-5e4c1a82ca60 66
                           c7004a-6860-44b2-983a-327aa3c9cfec
Sender                   : SystemMailbox{CCF2ED2E-A08F-4326-98A4-0E2CC7A3DF5F}@e
                           xchangeexchange.local
ReturnPath               : SystemMailbox{CCF2ED2E-A08F-4326-98A4-0E2CC7A3DF5F}@e
                           xchangeexchange.local
<SPACE> next page; <CR> next line; Q quit
[PS] C:\Documents and Settings\Administrator.EXCHEXCH>_
```

Figure 14-20

```
Professional PowerShell for Exchange 2007
[PS] C:\Documents and Settings\Administrator.EXCHEXCH>Get-MessageTrackingLog

EventId   Source    Sender              Recipients              MessageSubject
-------   ------    ------              ----------              --------------
RECEIVE   STORE...  SystemMailbox{CCF... {SystemMailbox{CC...   Test-Mailflow 92...
DELIVER   STORE...  SystemMailbox{CCF... {SystemMailbox{CC...   Test-Mailflow 92...
DSN       DSN       MicrosoftExchange... {SystemMailbox{CC...   Delivered: Test-...
DELIVER   STORE...  MicrosoftExchange... {SystemMailbox{CC...   Delivered: Test-...
RECEIVE   STORE...  SystemMailbox{CCF... {brendan_p_keane@...   Test-Mailflow 7e...
TRANSFER  ROUTING   SystemMailbox{CCF... {brendan_p_keane@...   Test-Mailflow 7e...
RECEIVE   STORE...  SystemMailbox{070... {brendan_p_keane@...   Test-Mailflow 1b...
TRANSFER  ROUTING   SystemMailbox{070... {brendan_p_keane@...   Test-Mailflow 1b...
RECEIVE   STORE...  SystemMailbox{CCF... {brendan_p_keane@...   Test-Mailflow 3b...
TRANSFER  ROUTING   SystemMailbox{CCF... {brendan_p_keane@...   Test-Mailflow 3b...
RECEIVE   STORE...  SystemMailbox{CCF... {brendan_p_keane@...   Test-Mailflow 10...
TRANSFER  ROUTING   SystemMailbox{CCF... {brendan_p_keane@...   Test-Mailflow 10...
RECEIVE   STORE...  SystemMailbox{070... {brendan_p_keane@...   Test-Mailflow 26...
TRANSFER  ROUTING   SystemMailbox{070... {brendan_p_keane@...   Test-Mailflow 26...
RECEIVE   STORE...  SystemMailbox{CCF... {SystemMailbox{CC...   Test-Mailflow 81...
DELIVER   STORE...  SystemMailbox{CCF... {SystemMailbox{CC...   Test-Mailflow 81...
DSN       DSN       MicrosoftExchange... {SystemMailbox{CC...   Delivered: Test-...
DELIVER   STORE...  MicrosoftExchange... {SystemMailbox{CC...   Delivered: Test-...
SUBMIT    STORE...  SystemMailbox{CCF... {}                     Test-Mailflow 92...
SUBMIT    STORE...  SystemMailbox{CCF... {}                     Test-Mailflow 7e...
SUBMIT    STORE...  SystemMailbox{CCF... {}                     Test-Mailflow 3b...
SUBMIT    STORE...  SystemMailbox{CCF... {}                     Test-Mailflow 10...
SUBMIT    STORE...  SystemMailbox{CCF... {}                     Test-Mailflow 81...
RECEIVE   STORE...  SystemMailbox{CCF... {SystemMailbox{CC...   Test-Mailflow 9e...
DELIVER   STORE...  SystemMailbox{CCF... {SystemMailbox{CC...   Test-Mailflow 9e...
DSN       DSN       MicrosoftExchange... {SystemMailbox{CC...   Delivered: Test-...
```

Figure 14-21

- ❏ `InternalMessageId`: Returns all message tracking log entries that meet the pattern specified. `InternalMessageId` is unique across each server.

- ❏ `MessageId`: Returns all message tracking log entries that contain the specified Message-ID field from within the message header.

- ❏ `MessageSubject`: Returns all message tracking log entries that contain the specified Subject from with the message header.

- ❏ `Recipients`: Returns all message tracking log entries that contain the specified recipient's SMTP address. To specify multiple recipients separate the values with a comma.

- ❏ `Reference`: Returns all message tracking log entries that contain the specified value in the reference field. The following are valid search items: `Send`, `Transfer`, and `DSN`.

- ❏ `ResultSize`: Sets the number of results to display. By default 1,000 entries will be displayed. If you need to see all results for a particular query, set the `ResultSize` to unlimited.

- ❏ `Sender`: Returns all message tracking log entries that contain the specified sender's SMTP address.

- ❏ `Server`: Specifies the server to request tracking logs from. This value can be the server name, FQDN, DN, Legacy DN, or the GUID of the server. If this parameter is not specified, the cmdlet executes against the local machine.

- ❏ `Start`: Specifies the date and time that the results will start from.

Figure 14-22 shows the base output of `Get-MessageTrackingLog`.

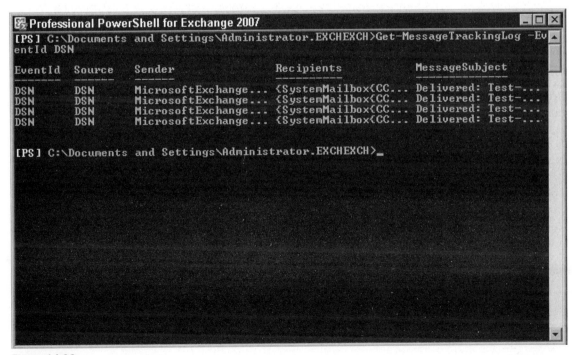

Figure 14-22

Figure 14-23 shows how to use the EventId to retrieve all the DSN notifications from the message tracking logs from the local server.

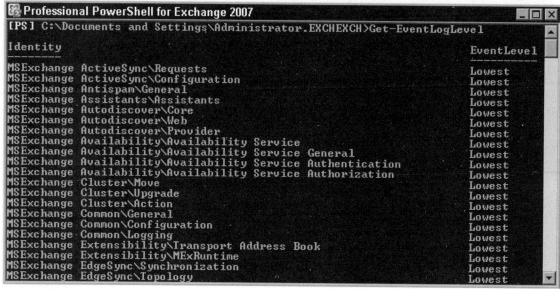

Figure 14-23

Working with Event Logging Levels

When you are troubleshooting a problem it is important to log the correct data to the event log. To determine what level of logging is taking place use the Get-EventLogLevel cmdlet. There are two parameters that can be specified but cannot be used together:

❑   Server: Specifies the server to retrieve event log categories for.

❑   Identity: Specifies the ECIdParameter. The ECIdParameter is the identity of the individual Exchange component. Figure 14-24 shows some of the ECId parameters and their current logging levels.

The Set-EventLogLevel cmdlet sets the diagnostic logging levels of the individual Exchange components. Use of this command will manipulate the verbosity of the logging of events in the Application log. This is useful for when troubleshooting Exchange issues. OALGen even writes an event to the Application log if there were errors created during generation, and specifies to turn up the logging for that particular parameter! After you have set the logging level on any of the parameters, you can then use Get-EventLog to gather the new information from the Application log.

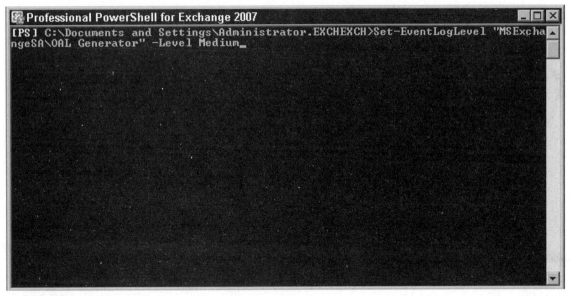

```
Professional PowerShell for Exchange 2007                                      _ □ X
[PS] C:\Documents and Settings\Administrator.EXCHEXCH>Set-EventLogLevel "MSExcha
ngeSA\OAL Generator" -Level Medium_
```

Figure 14-24

There are two parameters for this cmdlet:

❑   Identity: Specifies the ECIdParameter. The ECIdParameter is the identity of the individual Exchange component. To get a list of all the ECId parameters, run the Get-EventLogLevel cmdlet.

❑   Level: Sets the logging level for the identity. There are five levels of logging, starting with the least logging:

   ❑   Lowest

   ❑   Low

   ❑   Medium

   ❑   High

   ❑   Expert

Figure 14-25 shows setting the Event log leveling to medium on the MSExchangeSA\OAL Generator.

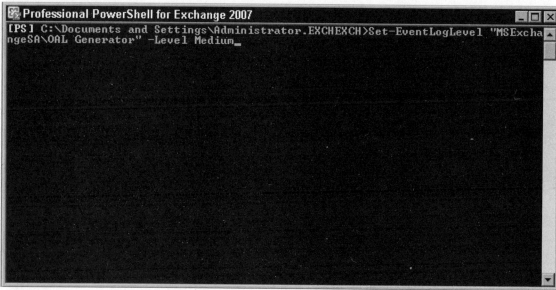

```
Professional PowerShell for Exchange 2007                              _ □ ×
[PS] C:\Documents and Settings\Administrator.EXCHEXCH>Set-EventLogLevel "MSExcha
ngeSA\OAL Generator" -Level Medium_
```

Figure 14-25

Summary

The `Test-*` cmdlets explained in this chapter provide a wealth of troubleshooting cmdlets to assist in troubleshooting and configuration management. Providing the Exchange administrator a resource to test connectivity and response times for individual components, across server roles, and for external connectivity in an automated fashion is something that has only been available in higher-end monitoring systems. The scriptability of these cmdlets allows for their flexible framework to be manipulated for whatever test the Exchange administrator can think of. Plus, with the openness of such cmdlets as `Get-EventLog` or `Get-MessageTrackingLog` the flexibility to perform complex analysis with only a few lines of code is very cool indeed. The Exchange team was the first at Microsoft to ship a product that uses PowerShell as the basis for its administration. The standard has been set, the reviews are in, and people love it. Now they will have to see how quickly they can integrate it into all their products.

Part IV

Automating Administration

## 15

User, Group, and Public Folder Administration

All good administrators know scripts are used to automate everyday tasks and ensure consistent results with a minimum of effort. The built-in scripting capabilities of Windows PowerShell, and by extension Exchange Management Shell, offer a level of control previously unavailable when using administrative tools supplied in earlier versions of Exchange Server.

This chapter examines these scripting capabilities via a thorough examination of sample administrative scripts, starting at a basic level and expanding to scripts that accomplish more complex tasks.

This chapter explores scripts that complete these tasks:

- ❏ Mailbox-enable users
- ❏ Assign group membership based on user attributes
- ❏ Load-balance mailbox creation across databases based on user names
- ❏ Create a public folder for a user

Sample Scripts for Creating New Mailbox-Enabled Users

One of the best examples of an administrative task easily automated via scripting is the creation of new mailbox-enabled user accounts.

This section covers four sample scripts for automating the creation of new mailbox-enabled accounts. The first script is very simple and covers the basics you need to know when creating a script that uses Exchange Management Shell commands. A second script expands on the first to add error control and advanced techniques for developing a more comprehensive solution. A third script extends the second by adding automated group membership based on department and office attributes. A fourth script takes things a step further and automates database selection based on the last name of the new user.

The scripts in this section use these cmdlets:

- ❏ Read-Host
- ❏ New-Mailbox
- ❏ Import-Csv
- ❏ Write-Host
- ❏ Out-File
- ❏ Test-Path
- ❏ Write-Progress
- ❏ Set-User
- ❏ Add-DistributionGroupMember
- ❏ Get-DistributionGroup

The Simple Script

The sample script simplebulk-newmailbox.ps1 creates mailbox-enabled user accounts based on the contents of a comma-separated value (CSV) file created by the administrator. The script is run by entering its name followed by the path to the CSV file used as input. The administrator is prompted once to enter a secure temporary password that is set on each account as it is created. The results are displayed at the command line as the default output from the underlying Exchange Management Shell command used in the script to create the mailboxes.

The following code shows the contents of script file simplebulk-newmailbox.ps1:

```
# simplebulk-newmailbox.ps1

# Input parameter
param([string]$CSVUpath)

# Prompt for the master password to set on the new mailbox enabled accounts
$password = (Read-Host -AsSecureString "Enter Password")

# Read input from the CSV file
$users = (Import-Csv $CSVUpath)

# Create the mailbox enabled accounts
foreach ($user in $users)
    {
        New-Mailbox -Name:$user.name -Database:$user.Database
-OrganizationalUnit:$user.OrganizationalUnit
-UserPrincipalName:$user.UserPrincipalName -Password:$password
-ResetPasswordOnNextLogon:$true
    }
```

For analysis, this script is broken down into four segments, each marked with a comment line (using the # character) to describe what the segment does. The following paragraphs explain how each segment works and are followed by the specific segment of code they describe.

The first code segment uses the param keyword to specify the input parameter value to set on variable $CSVUpath. This variable holds the path of the CSV file containing the information to be used for creating the mailbox-enabled user accounts. The $CSVUpath variable is cast as a string data type by the use of the [string] prefix. The user must enter the full CSV file path value following the script name when running the script.

```
# Input Parameter
param([string]$CSVUpath)
```

The next code segment creates a variable to store a master secure password value to set on each Active Directory account created by New-Mailbox. A value with data type of System.Security .SecureString is required by New-Mailbox. The Read-Host cmdlet provides the AsSecureString parameter to allow the creation of a SecureString object. The execution of this command displays Enter Password: as a prompt on the command line and then pauses for input.

As the administrator types a password value, each key press results in the display of an asterisk (*) character to obfuscate the value. Pressing Enter stores the password value as a SecureString object in the $password variable. Note that the password entered must meet the password complexity requirements enforced by the Active Directory group policy applied to the domain where the accounts are to be created or the script will fail.

```
# Prompt for the master password to set on the new mailbox enabled accounts
$password = (Read-Host -AsSecureString "Enter Password")
```

This next code segment creates a variable to store objects based on values read from the CSV file specified in variable $CSVUpath. The Import-Csv cmdlet reads the file and stores each line as an object in the variable $users. The property names are determined by the header structure of the CSV file, which is covered in more detail later in this section. If the content structure of the CSV file does not match what is expected by Import-Csv or if the file is not found, the command fails.

```
# Read input from the CSV file
$users = (Import-Csv $CSVUpath)
```

The last code segment is where the bulk of the work is actually done and the mailbox-enabled accounts are created using the cmdlet New-Mailbox. This segment uses the foreach loop command to iterate (step through) a collection of items, in this case the objects stored previously in the $users variable. The syntax of foreach is as follows:

```
foreach ($<item> in $<collection>) {command_block}.
```

The command executes the contents of the script block on each object in the collection one at a time. Simply stated, the foreach command in the sample script does this: for each individual object ($user) in a collection of objects ($users), execute the script block (New-Mailbox...).

The $user variable represents the current object being acted upon. Inside the script block, dot notation is used to de-reference each object property value for that object. For example, $user.name is the name perty value for the current object, $user.database is the database property value, and so on. The property names are determined by the header values used in the CSV file.

The Password property value is provided by the $password variable created earlier in the script. The script uses the minimum parameters required by New-Mailbox to successfully create a mailbox-enabled user account, plus the ResetPasswordOnNextLogon parameter to force the new users to set their own passwords the first time they log in to the domain. This is a good administrative practice.

```
# Create the mailbox enabled accounts
foreach ($user in $users)
    {
        New-Mailbox -Name:$user.name -Database:$user.Database `
        -OrganizationalUnit:$user.OrganizationalUnit `
        -UserPrincipalName:$user.UserPrincipalName -Password:$password `
        -ResetPasswordOnNextLogon:$true
    }
```

Note the use of the grave accent character (`) at the end of each line following the New-Mailbox cmdlet. When this escape character is used at the end of a command line with no other character immediately following, it instructs Windows PowerShell to continue reading the command line from the beginning of the next line. This is a simple way to wrap long commands so they are more readable.

More on Parameter Values

When used in a script, parameter values for the New-Mailbox cmdlet can be supplied as part of a CSV file, as prompted input from the command line when the script is run, or as a static value inside the script. Some parameter values such as the ones used in the simplebulk-newmailbox.ps1 script are always required by New-Mailbox and cannot be omitted. Some are optional and can be used according to their need. There are certain parameters that are exclusive and cannot be used in conjunction with some others.

The following table describes in detail the parameters for New-Mailbox as they relate to being used in a script.

Parameter	Description
Required: these parameters must always be used and supplied in the CSV file unless otherwise noted.	
Name	Must be unique.
Database	Must already exist.
Password	Must comply with length and complexity requirements. Not required when creating a disabled account (linked, shared, room, and equipment mailboxes).
OrganizationalUnit	Must already exist.
UserPrincipalName	Should use valid UPN suffix (no validation).
Recommended: you should use these parameters as best practice.	
FirstName	Is null on the new account unless supplied in CSV file.
LastName	Is null on the new account unless supplied in CSV file.

Parameter	Description
ResetPasswordOnNextLogon	Use when creating enabled accounts. Allows new users to set their own passwords the first time they log on.
Optional: these parameters are not required and can only be used in certain combinations.	
Alias	Is based on prefix of UserPrincipalName if not supplied in CSV file.
ActiveSyncMailboxPolicy	Must already exist. Supply in CSV file.
DisplayName	Is based on Name if not supplied. Supply in CSV file.
DomainController	Use when you want to create the new accounts on a specific Domain Controller. Prompt the user or use as a static script element.
Equipment	Creates disabled account and equipment mailbox. Cannot be used in conjunction with Room or Shared parameters. Use as a script element.
Initials	Maximum length six characters. Supply in CSV file.
LinkedDomainController	Required when creating a linked mailbox. Prompt the user or use as a static script element.
LinkedMasterAccount	Creates disabled account and linked mailbox. Supply in CSV file.
LinkedCredential	Required to access the Domain Controller specified by LinkedDomainController. Prompt the user.
ManagedFolderMailboxPolicy	Must already exist. Supply in CSV file.
ManagedFolderMailboxPolicyAllowed	Use when specifying ManagedFolderMailboxPolicy. Use as a script element.
Room	Creates disabled account and room mailbox. Cannot be used in conjunction with Equipment or Shared parameters. Use as a script element.
SamAccountName	Is based on prefix of UserPrincipalName if not supplied in CSV file.
Shared	Creates disabled account and shared mailbox. Cannot be used in conjunction with Room or Equipment parameters. Use as a script element.
TemplateInstance	Use to create a new mailbox with configuration settings based on an existing mailbox object. Use as a script element.

..e is a data file made up of text stored in columns/fields separated by commas, and
.ecords separated by newlines (CR+LF). Spreadsheet applications are ideal for creating CSV files.
.allow administrators to populate information in a structured row/column format before saving
.results as a CSV file.

The Import-Csv cmdlet requires the first row in a CSV file to contain the names for each column of
information. This first row is often referred to as the "header." The names used in the header determine
the property names for the objects created when the CSV file is read by Import-Csv. Property names are
completely arbitrary but must not contain any spaces. For consistency, you should use names that
correspond to the cmdlet parameter names for which the property values are to be used as input.

The following example shows the first few lines of a CSV file that could be used as input for the
simplebulk-newmailbox.ps1 script. The header row contains the names of each individual property
required as input by New-Mailbox. Each line that follows the header represents an individual user
account that is to be created based on the given property values. Note that in this example the lines are
wrapped to fit the format of this page.

```
Name,Database,OrganizationalUnit,UserPrincipalName
User One,MB001\First Storage Group\Mailbox Database,exchangeexchange.local/
Users,user1@exchangeexchange.com
User Two,MB001\First Storage Group\Mailbox Database,exchangeexchange.local/
Legal,user2@exchangeexchange.com
User Three,MB001\First Storage Group\Mailbox Database,exchangeexchange.local/
Users,user3@exchangeexchange.com
```

Running the Script

To exhibit the behavior of the simplebulk-newmailbox.ps1 script, a CSV file has been constructed to
supply property values to create eight new mailbox-enabled user accounts, named User One through
User Eight. Certain values have been used in the CSV file to ensure some failures to demonstrate the
shortcomings of a script that offers no error handling.

The script file was placed in the Exchange scripts folder (by default C:\Program Files\Microsoft\
Exchange Server\scripts\) so it can be run from the current location of C:\ without the need to
provide the full path to the script. This is also a best practice for keeping track of your scripts by always
storing them in the same location on the server.

Execution starts by entering the name of the script file followed by the path name of the CSV file. The
administrator is prompted to enter a password, after which the main script execution takes place. Each
time the New-Mailbox command embedded in the foreach loop is executed the results are displayed
on the console screen using the default output of the New-Mailbox cmdlet, as shown in the following
example output. This continues until all the objects in the $users variable have been processed.

```
[PS] C:\>simplebulk-newmailbox.ps1 c:\users.csv
Enter Password: *********

Name                      Alias             ServerName      ProhibitSendQuo
                                                            ta

----                      -----             ----------      ---------------
User One                  user1             mb001           unlimited
Organizational unit "exchangeexchange.local/Legal" was not found. Please make sure
you have typed it correctly.
At C:\Program Files\Microsoft\Exchange Server\Scripts\simplebulk-newmailbox.ps1
:17 char:9
+        N <<<< ew-Mailbox -Name:$user.name -Database:$user.Database -Organiza
tionalUnit:$user.OrganizationalUnit -UserPrincipalName:$user.UserPrincipalName
-FirstName:$user.FirstName -LastName:$user.LastName -Password:$password -ResetP
asswordOnNextLogon:$true
User Three                user3             mb001           unlimited
User Four                 user4             mb001           unlimited
User Five                 user5             mb001           unlimited
Database "MB001\Second Storage Group\Mailbox Database" was not found. Please ma
ke sure you have typed it correctly.
At C:\Program Files\Microsoft\Exchange Server\Scripts\simplebulk-newmailbox.ps1
:17 char:9
+        N <<<< ew-Mailbox -Name:$user.name -Database:$user.Database -Organiza
tionalUnit:$user.OrganizationalUnit -UserPrincipalName:$user.UserPrincipalName
-FirstName:$user.FirstName -LastName:$user.LastName -Password:$password -ResetP
asswordOnNextLogon:$true
User Seven                user7             mb001           unlimited
User Eight                user8             mb001           unlimited
```

As you can see in the first line of output, User One has been created without issue as indicated by the default output from New-Mailbox. However, creation of the next user has failed as per the error message shown. In this case the error indicates the OrganizationalUnit property value passed to New-Mailbox did not exist in Active Directory. Creation of another user failed in a similar fashion because the Database property value specified does not exist.

The way these errors appear in the default output demonstrates one of the biggest weaknesses of this simple version of a user creation script: error handling. You can probably recognize from this output that User Two and User Six have failed creation by the position of the error messages among the other lines of output.

Now imagine that a CSV file contains hundreds of entries, with real names instead of sequentially numbered test accounts. Notice that the error messages contain no information about the object being processed when failures occur. That means an administrator would have to search through the contents of a CSV file to discover the users that have failed creation.

The script also does a poor job of giving the administrator feedback when other errors occur. For example, when an invalid CSV file path is specified, the standard error message for the underlying command is displayed. In most cases this feedback is more cryptic than necessary and does not always imply a corrective action to take.

The next section explores an improved version of the `simplebulk-newmailbox.ps1` script that incorporates some advanced techniques to address the shortcomings of the simple script and provide a more complete solution.

The Improved Script

The script `bulk-newmailbox.v1.ps1` includes several improvements that make it a more robust solution for creating new mailbox-enabled user accounts:

❑ Comments have been added to the header of the script to include Synopsis, Usage, and Example information. This is always good practice, especially when sharing scripts with other administrators.

❑ Error checking has been added to validate the path and format of the CSV file. The user is prompted to take specific corrective action if there is not an existing file in the path given, or if the file is not a properly formatted CSV file.

❑ The `FirstName` and `LastName` properties have been included as input from the CSV file. If these values are not provided at the time of account creation, they remain blank. In most cases this does not cause an issue. However, if you specify an email address policy that uses the first and last name attributes to form an address (`%g.%s@exchangeexchange.com`), you would not be able to stamp that address on these user accounts. As a good practice when creating mailbox-enabled user accounts you should always include first and last names when possible.

❑ The default output of `New-Mailbox` is suppressed. Instead, all output including errors are redirected to a log file that can be used afterwards for diagnostic purposes. The information written to the log identifies the objects being processed and any specific errors encountered.

❑ A progress bar is displayed during execution to indicate the current user being processed and the percentage of users that have been processed overall.

At first glance you may think that these improvements are going to be difficult to implement, but actually you'll be able to take advantage of functionality already provided by built-in commands. Once you break the script down into its component pieces and look at them individually they are quite easy to understand.

The following code shows the contents of the script file `bulk-newmailbox.v1.ps1`:

```
# bulk-newmailbox.v1.ps1
#
# Synopsis: This script creates one or more mailbox enabled user accounts based on
#           input values read from a comma separated value (CSV) file. This script
#           has to be run by an administrator who is a member of the Exchange
#           Recipient Administrators group.
#
#           The CSV file must contain these header values on the first line:
#
#           Name,Database,OrganizationalUnit,UserPrincipalName,FirstName,LastName
#
#           This script writes the results to log file bulk-newmailbox.log in the
#           home directory of the current user. New entries are appended to an
#           existing log file.
```

```
#
# Usage: bulk-newmailbox.v1.ps1 <full path to CSV file>
#
# Example: bulk-newmailbox.v1.ps1 c:\users.csv

param([string]$CSVUPath)

# Turn off error reporting to the display
$ErrorActionPreference = "SilentlyContinue"

# This function validates the path to the CSV input file
function ValidatePath
{
    $notValidPath = $false

    if ($CSVUPath -eq "")
    {
        $notValidPath = $true
        Write-Host -fore yellow "`nYou must enter the full path to a CSV file to
use as input to this script.`n"
        return $notValidPath
    }

    if (!(Test-Path -PathType:leaf $CSVUPath))
    {
        $notValidPath = $true
        Write-Host -fore yellow "`nThe file path entered is invalid. Please check
the file path and try again.`n"
        return $notValidPath
    }

    return $notValidPath
}

# Validate the path to the input CSV file, if it fails validation, exit
if (validatePath) { exit }

# Read input from the CSV file, if there is a failure reading the file, exit
$Users = (Import-Csv $CSVUPath)

if (!$users)
{
    Write-Host -fore yellow "`nFailed to read the input file. It is either invalid
or improperly formatted.`n"
    exit
}

# Prompt for the master password to set on the new mailbox enabled accounts
Write-Host -Fore green "`nPlease enter a temporary secure password for the new user
accounts`n"
```

(continued)

(continued)

```
$password = (Read-Host -AsSecureString "Enter Password")

# Initialize log file
$datetime = Get-Date

$logHeader = "
***********************************************************************
Run time = $dateTime using input file $CSVUPath
***********************************************************************"

$logFile = "$home\My Documents\bulk-newmailbox.log"

Out-File $logFile -InputObject $logHeader -Append

# Set variables used to write to the log file
$err = $null
$blankLine = "-----------------------------------------------------------"
$total = 0
$errorTotal = 0

# Create the mailbox enabled accounts
foreach ($user in $users)
    {
        New-Mailbox -Name:$user.name -Database:$user.Database `
        -OrganizationalUnit:$user.OrganizationalUnit `
        -UserPrincipalName:$user.UserPrincipalName `
        -FirstName:$user.FirstName -LastName:$user.LastName `
        -Password:$password -ResetPasswordOnNextLogon:$true `
        -ErrorVariable err | out-null

        If ($err -ne $null)
        {
            $errorString = "[ERROR]: Processing user $($user.name) failed with the
following error:"
            Out-File $logfile -Append -Inputobject $blankLine, `
            $errorString, $err[0], $blankLine
            $errorTotal += 1
        }
        else
        {
            $outString = "[SUCCESS]: New mailbox created for $($user.name) on
database: $($user.database)"
            Out-File $logFile -Inputobject $outString -append
        }

    $total += 1

    write-progress -Activity "Processed User: $($user.name)" -Status "Progress:" `
    -PercentComplete ($total/$users.count*100)
    }

# output the summary
Write-Host -Fore yellow "`nProcessing complete. $total users were processed with
$errorTotal errors. Please refer to $logfile for more details.`n"
```

Examining the Improved Script

For analysis, this script is broken down into individual segments, each marked with a comment line to describe what the segment does. The following paragraphs explain how each segment works and are followed by the specific segment of code they describe.

First, you should notice the comments at the beginning of the script. Think of this section as the script's documentation. You should always put any information you feel is important for those interested in using your script. As a good practice you should consider placing revision notes in this section if you make changes to a script over its lifetime. At minimum your comments should include the script name, script usage, and an example:

```
# bulk-newmailbox.v1.ps1
#
# Synopsis: This script creates one or more mailbox enabled user accounts based on
#           input values read from a comma separated value (CSV) file. This script
#           has to be run by an administrator who is a member of the Exchange
#           Recipient Administrators group.
#
#           The CSV file must contain these header values on the first line:
#
#           Name,Database,OrganizationalUnit,UserPrincipalName,FirstName,LastName
#
#           This script writes the results to log file bulk-newmailbox.log in the
#           home directory of the current user. New entries are appended to an
#           existing log file.
#
# Usage: bulk-newmailbox.v1.ps1 <full path to CSV file>
#
# Example: bulk-newmailbox.v1.ps1 c:\users.csv
```

The first segment of code is identical to that found in the simple script and uses the `param` keyword to specify the input parameter value to set on variable `$CSVUpath`.

```
param([string]$CSVUpath)
```

The second code segment "turns off" errors normally displayed at the console by setting the automatic variable `$ErrorActionPreference` to the value of `SilentlyContinue`. This setting affects error reporting only in the scope of the script; the way errors are displayed returns to normal after the script completes. Any errors encountered during script execution are interpreted by the script. If the user needs to take action, a user-friendly message is displayed. All other errors are recorded to the log file:

```
# Turn off error reporting to the display
$ErrorActionPreference = "SilentlyContinue"
```

The third code segment defines a function block called `ValidatePath` that is used to validate the path to the CSV file by testing the input value and whether or not it resolves to an existing file. It is standard practice to define functions up front in a script because they have to be stored in memory before they can be processed later in the script.

First, the $notValidPath variable is created to store the results of the tests. It is set to $false before the tests are run and changes to $true if one of the tests fails. The value of $notValidPath is returned to the command that calls this function, and will be used to determine if script processing is halted or continues:

```
# This function validates the path to the CSV input file
function ValidatePath
{
    $notValidPath = $false
```

Next the value of the $CSVUpath variable is tested to see if a value was entered at the command line when the script was run, and if so whether that value resolves to an existing file. To make these tests, if statements are used. The syntax of an if statement is quite simple:

```
if (<conditional test>) {<code block>}
```

Basically, an if statement works like this: If the <conditional test> evaluates true, execute the contents of the <code block>. If the <conditional test> evaluates false, skip the <code block> and go to the next command.

The first if statement tests the value stored in $CSVUpath to see if it is equal to null, which would mean the user forgot to supply an input value when the script was run. If that is so, the conditional test evaluates to true, and the code block is executed.

If the script block runs, the $notValidPath variable is set to $true. The Write-Host cmdlet is used to display a text message advising the user to enter the full path to a CSV file. The fore parameter is used to change the text color to yellow so it stands out as a warning. The text string value includes a special character combination of the grave accent escape character and the letter n (`n) that causes the shell to display the text that follows at the start of a new line. This ensures that the message is displayed on a line by itself for maximum readability.

The return command is used to return the value stored in $notValidPath to the command that called the ValidatePath function. At this point all processing of the function is complete.

```
    if ($CSVUPath -eq "")
    {
        $notValidPath = $true
        Write-Host -fore yellow "`nYou must enter the full path to a CSV file to
use as input to this script.`n"
        return $notValidPath
    }
```

If the first conditional test evaluates to false, then at least some value was passed at the command line. But is that value a valid path to a file? To find out, the next command is an if statement that uses the Test-Path cmdlet to test the path stored in $CSVUpath to see if it resolves to an existing file. The PathType parameter specifies a leaf object, which corresponds to a file type as opposed to a container object, which is a directory type. That prevents the user from entering only a path to a directory and not the full path to a file.

The result of running `Test-Path` is `True` if the file is found and `False` if the file is not found. Because an `if` statement only executes the contents of the code block when the conditional test is `True`, the result of the `Test-Path` command must be changed to `True` if the file was not found. To accomplish this, the conditional test has been wrapped by parentheses and the `NOT` operator (`!`) is used to change the result of the test to the opposite value; true becomes false and false becomes true.

If the conditional test evaluates to true (the file was not found), the code block is executed. The `$notValidPath` variable is set to `$true` and the `Write-Host` cmdlet is used to display a text message advising the user to check the file path entered and try again. The value stored in `$notValidPath` is then returned to the command that called the `ValidatePath` function and processing of the function is complete.

```
if (!(Test-Path -PathType:leaf $CSVUPath))
{
    $notValidPath = $true
    Write-Host -fore yellow "`nThe file path entered is invalid. Please check
the file path and try again.`n"
    return $notValidPath
}
```

The last command in the function executes only when both `if` statements have evaluated `false`. The initial value stored in `$notValidPath` would not have been changed because neither `if` statement executed, so the value returned to the command that called the function would be `$false`.

```
return $notValidPath
```

The next code segment uses an `if` statement to evaluate the result of calling the `ValidatePath` function. If the result is true, which would be the case if one of the tests in `ValidatePath` failed, then the code block is executed. The only command in the code block is `exit`, which causes Windows PowerShell to stop processing and exit the script immediately.

If the result of calling the `ValidatePath` function is false, which would be the case if both of the tests in `ValidatePath` passed, then the code block is skipped and the script continues to execute.

```
# Validate the path to the input CSV file, if it fails validation, exit
if (validatePath) { exit }
```

Now that the input file path for the CSV has been confirmed, the next code segment handles loading the file. This code segment is very similar to that used for the same purpose in the simple version of the script, but adds error checking for importing the contents of a CSV file.

```
# Read input from the CSV file, if there is a failure reading the file, exit
$Users = (Import-Csv $CSVUPath)
```

When running this script it is possible to enter the path of a file that is not a CSV file. When the `Import-Csv` cmdlet attempts to read this file, it can report an error if it finds the file is either improperly formatted or the file cannot be opened for one reason or another. Because the result of `Import-Csv` is stored in the `$users` variable, it can be tested with another `if` statement to see if the result is true (importing the file succeeded) or false (importing the file failed).

If $users is false, NOT changes the result of the conditional test to true and the code block executes. The Write-Host cmdlet displays a warning message telling the user the file specified is either invalid or is not a properly formatted CSV file. After that the script exits. If $users is true, NOT changes the result of the conditional test to false and the code block is skipped.

```
if (!$users)
{
    Write-Host -fore yellow "`nFailed to read the input file. It is either invalid
or improperly formatted.`n"
    exit
}
```

The next code segment prompts the user for a secure password and again is very similar to the code used for the same purpose in the simple version of the script. A better user message has been added to inform the user about the purpose of the secure password prompt.

```
# Prompt for the master password to set on the new mailbox enabled accounts
Write-Host -Fore green "`nPlease enter a temporary secure password for the new user
accounts`n"

$password = (Read-Host -AsSecureString "Enter Password")
```

The next code segment initializes the log file. It starts by storing the current date and time in a variable called $datetime. This provides a date stamp that is added to the log header information each time the script is run. The next variable, $logheader, is used to store strings that form the header section of the log. The strings are stored in the variable formatted in the same way they appear in the script: three separate lines of text. Where the $datetime and $CSVUpath variables are used in the second line of text, their values are stored in the variable $logheader in those positions.

The $logfile variable is used to store the full path to the bulk-newmailbox.log file. The default location is the My Documents folder of the currently logged on user. The Out-File cmdlet is used to write to the file specified by $logfile, using the strings stored in $logheader as specified by the InputObject parameter. The log file is created if it does not already exist. The Append parameter forces Out-File to add to the end of an existing log file instead of overwriting it.

```
# Initialize log file
$datetime = Get-Date

$logHeader = "
*****************************************************************
Run time = $dateTime using input file $CSVUPath
*****************************************************************"

$logFile = "$home\My Documents\bulk-newmailbox.log"

Out-File $logFile -InputObject $logHeader -Append
```

This code segment sets several variables that are used during mailbox creation to track processing and write information to the log file. The $err variable is used by the New-Mailbox cmdlet to store any errors it encounters. The $blankLine variable is used to store a string value that is simply a series of dashes. This string is used later in the script when error messages are written to the log file, to make them more readable. The lines of dashes are used above and below the error message to make it easier to distinguish an individual instance when multiple instances appear in sequence in the log.

The $total variable is used to keep a running total of the number of users processed. The $errorTotal variable is used to keep a running total of the number of errors generated during the user creation process.

```
# Set variables used to write to the log file
$err = $null
$blankLine = "------------------------------------------------------------"
$total = 0
$errorTotal = 0
```

The next code segment handles the creation of mailbox-enabled user accounts using New-Mailbox in a foreach loop. This is similar to that used for the same purpose in the first version of the script, but incorporates error control and logging features as well as the addition of some important parameters.

The FirstName and LastName parameters are used to specify the first and last name attributes of the new user accounts. The ErrorVariable parameter is used to specify a variable to which all errors encountered by New-Mailbox are to be written. The $err variable is specified, but note that the $ character is not used when naming the variable.

The output from New-Mailbox normally goes to the console screen for display. Because logging is being implemented, there is no need to see the default output. Therefore it is directed to the Out-Null cmdlet via pipeline. All default output from New-Mailbox is basically "thrown away."

```
# Create the mailbox enabled accounts
foreach ($user in $users)
    {
        New-Mailbox -Name:$user.name -Database:$user.Database `
        -OrganizationalUnit:$user.OrganizationalUnit `
        -UserPrincipalName:$user.UserPrincipalName `
        -FirstName:$user.FirstName -LastName:$user.LastName `
        -Password:$password -ResetPasswordOnNextLogon:$true `
        -ErrorVariable err | out-null
```

After each execution of New-Mailbox, an if statement is used to test if $err is holding a value not equal to null. If New-Mailbox encountered no errors during execution, the value of $err should still be set to null. If there was an error during execution, $err holds an error message corresponding to the error that was encountered. If an error was encountered the conditional test evaluates as true and the code block is executed.

The $errorString variable is used to store a text message string that includes the name of the user ($user.name) that was being processed when the error occurred. The string includes the keyword [ERROR] to make it easier to search the log file when looking for errors. Note that this is an arbitrary word and not a specific Windows PowerShell keyword.

The Out-File cmdlet is used to append the bulk-newmailbox.log file with the contents of a combination of variables that comprise the error message to be added to the log. These variables are specified by the InputObject parameter followed by the variables' names, separated by commas.

The $blankline variable defined earlier in the script adds a line of dashes to identify the beginning of an error message in the log. The $errorString variable adds the error string identifying the user. The $err[0] variable adds the specific error message generated by New-Mailbox. Note that $err is an array, therefore to extract the error message it contains you must specify the first element in the array by enclosing the index number (the first element is always 0) in square brackets. Finally, another $blankline variable is used to add a line of dashes to mark the end of the error message.

After the error message is output to the log file, the $errorTotal variable is incremented by 1. This is accomplished using the addition assignment operator (+=), which instructs Windows PowerShell to assign a new value that is the current value plus 1.

```
If ($err -ne $null)
    {
        $errorString = "[ERROR]: Processing user $($user.name) failed with the
following error:"
        Out-File $logfile -Append -Inputobject $blankLine, `
        $errorString, $err[0], $blankLine
        $errorTotal += 1
    }
```

The if statement is followed by an else statement. An else statement is used as a way of executing an alternate command when the conditional test of an if statement evaluates false. The else statement has no conditional test of its own and instead relies on the result of the preceding if statement. Therefore the else statement code block only executes when New-Mailbox successfully creates a mailbox-enabled user account.

The $outstring variable is used to store a text message string that includes the name of the user that was successfully processed by New-Mailbox. This variable is used by Out-File to append the message to the bulk-newmailbox.log file.

```
    else
    {
        $outString = "[SUCCESS]: New mailbox created for $($user.name) on
database: $($user.database)"
        Out-File $logFile -Inputobject $outString -append
    }
```

To track the total number of users processed, the $total variable is incremented by 1 each time the foreach loop executes. This value will be used later in the summary display to report the total number of users processed.

```
    $total += 1
```

The last command in the foreach loop is the Write-Progress cmdlet, which is used to generate a progress bar display on the console screen as the foreach loop executes. The progress bar is made up of three visible elements: the activity label, the status label, and the progress indicator.

The activity label is specified by the `Activity` parameter and is set to display `"Processed User: <current user>"`. The current user value changes dynamically as users are processed. The status label is specified by the `-Status` parameter and is set to `"Progress:"`. This value is static and does not change.

The progress indicator is simply a series of characters (lowercase o) that increase in number left to right to indicate the percentage of users that have been processed, as shown in this example that includes all three elements as they appear at the top of the console screen:

```
Processed User: John Doe
    Progress:
    [oooooooooooooooooooooooooooooooooooooooooooooooooooooooooooooo                    ]
```

The `PercentageComplete` parameter is used to specify an equation that calculates the percentage of users that have been processed through the current iteration of the `foreach` loop. In this equation the current total of users processed (`$total`) is divided by the total number of users to be processed overall (`$users.count`). That result is then multiplied by 100 to produce a percentage.

For example, if 4 users out of 10 have been processed, the percentage processed at that point would be 40% of the total (4/10*100). The resulting progress indicator display would then show approximately 28 "o" characters out of 70 total to represent 40%.

```
    write-progress -Activity "Processed User: $($user.name)" -Status "Progress:" `
    -PercentComplete ($total/$users.count*100)
    }
```

Once the `foreach` loop has finished processing all users, the last code segment of the script uses `Write-Host` to display a final summary message to the console screen. This message includes the total number of users processed (`$total`), the total number of errors encountered during processing (`$errorTotal`), and the path to the `bulk-newmailbox.log` file (`$logfile`).

```
# output the summary
Write-Host -Fore yellow "`nProcessing complete. $total users were processed with
$errorTotal errors. Please refer to $logfile for more details.`n"
```

Running the Improved Script

The improved script has better error handling than the simple script. It does a better job of providing error feedback to the user and suggests corrective action to take when needed. The user receives current status information via the progress indicator as the script executes. All actions are recorded in a log file for examination after the script completes.

The error handling incorporated into the improved script first becomes obvious when attempting to run the script with invalid input information. The following examples demonstrate what happens when input data fails preliminary testing before any main script processing is attempted.

When no CSV file is specified as input, this error message is generated:

```
[PS] C:\>bulk-newmailbox.v1.ps1
```

```
You must enter the full path to a CSV file to use as input to this script.
```

When an invalid file path is specified (in this example `bogus.csv` does not exist) this error message is generated:

```
[PS] C:\>bulk-newmailbox.ps1 c:\bogus.csv

The file path entered is invalid. Please check the file path and try again.
```

When a valid path is specified, but the file is either not a CSV file or is not properly formatted (in this example `invalid.csv` is a plain text file) this error message is generated:

```
[PS] C:\>bulk-newmailbox.ps1 c:\invalid.csv

Failed to read the input file. It is either invalid or improperly formatted.
```

The user is only prompted for a secure master password after a valid input file is specified and all the preliminary checks complete without failure. As the user types in the password, the keystrokes are echoed to the screen as asterisks. Once the user presses Enter, the script continues to execute.

Note that the master secure password must satisfy the password length and complexity requirements for the domain where the users will be created. If not, all accounts fail creation and the resulting errors generated are recorded in the log file.

```
[PS] C:\>bulk-newmailbox.ps1 c:\users.csv

Please enter a temporary secure password for the new user accounts

Enter Password: ********

Processing complete. 8 users were processed with 2 errors. Please refer to C:\
Documents and Settings\Administrator\My Documents\bulk-newmailbox.log for more
details.
```

The progress indicator appears at the top of the console screen and remains in place while the accounts are being created. As the progress indicator updates, it displays the name of the last user that was processed. Note that even if user creation fails, the name still appears in the progress indicator.

Once the last user is processed, the progress indicator disappears and the summary message is displayed. The summary message includes a total count of all users processed and the number of errors encountered. The full path for the `bulk-newmailbox.log` file is given so the user knows where to find the log file.

The following example shows the log file generated from the instance that generated the screen output in the last example. The log file header includes the date and time the script was run and the file used as input. Error messages are clearly marked so they can be quickly distinguished from success messages.

```
*********************************************************************
Run time = 07/07/2007 09:23:07 using input file users.csv
*********************************************************************
[SUCCESS]: New mailbox created for User One on database: MB001\First Storage Group\
Mailbox Database
----------------------------------------------------------
[ERROR]: Processing user User Two failed with the following error:
Organizational unit "exchangeexchange.local/Legal" was not found. Please make
sure you have typed it correctly.
----------------------------------------------------------
[SUCCESS]: New mailbox created for User Three on database: MB001\First Storage
Group\Mailbox Database
[SUCCESS]: New mailbox created for User Four on database: MB001\First Storage
Group\Mailbox Database
[SUCCESS]: New mailbox created for User Five on database: MB001\First Storage
Group\Mailbox Database
----------------------------------------------------------
[ERROR]: Processing user User Six failed with the following error:
Database "MB001\Second Storage Group\Mailbox Database" was not found. Please
make sure you have typed it correctly.
----------------------------------------------------------
[SUCCESS]: New mailbox created for User Seven on database: MB001\First Storage
Group\Mailbox Database
[SUCCESS]: New mailbox created for User Eight on database: MB001\First Storage
Group\Mailbox Database
```

Adding Group Assignments for the New Users

The improved script creates mailbox-enabled user accounts that are ready to use without any additional actions. Administrative tasks that follow the creation of a new mailbox-enabled user account typically include adding the account to one or more Distribution Groups. With a few lines of additional code this functionality can be incorporated into the bulk-newmailbox.v1.ps1 script.

Active Directory user accounts include several named attributes such as City, Title, Department, Office, and Manager, to name a few. User attributes offer a convenient method for determining Distribution Group membership. For example, a user's Department attribute can be used to determine membership in a Distribution Group for that department.

To demonstrate this concept, the script bulk-newmailbox.v2.ps1 extends the first version to add automatic Distribution Group membership based on the Department and Office attributes. These attribute values must be included in the CSV file used as input to the script.

The additional code that adds this functionality is limited to the foreach loop that creates the mailbox-enabled accounts, therefore that is the only section of code from bulk-newmailbox.v2.ps1 that needs to be examined.

```
# Create the mailbox enabled accounts
foreach ($user in $users)
    {
        New-Mailbox -Name:$user.name -Database:$user.Database `
        -OrganizationalUnit:$user.OrganizationalUnit `
        -UserPrincipalName:$user.UserPrincipalName `
        -FirstName:$user.FirstName -LastName:$user.LastName `
        -Password:$password -ResetPasswordOnNextLogon:$true `
        -ErrorVariable err | Out-Null

        If ($err -ne $null)
        {
            $errorString = "[ERROR]: Processing user $($user.name) failed with the
following error:"
            Out-File $logfile -Append -Inputobject $blankline, `
            $errorString, $err[0], $blankline
            $errorTotal += 1
        }
        else
        {
            $errorString = "[ERROR]: Creation of mailbox enabled account for user
$($user.name) succeeded, but "

            Set-User -Identity:$user.name -Department:$user.department `
            -Office:$user.office -ErrorVariable err

            If ($err -ne $null)
            {
                $errorString += "property assignment failed with error:"
                Out-File $logFile -Append -Inputobject $blankLine, $errorString, `
                $err[0], $blankLine
                $errorTotal += 1
            }
            else
            {
                $noErrors = $true

                if ($dgdept = (Get-DistributionGroup | where {$_.name -like `
                "*$($user.department)*"}))
                {
                    Add-DistributionGroupMember -Identity:$dgdept `
                    -Member:$user.name -ErrorVariable err

                    If ($err -ne $null)
                    {
                        $thiserror = $errorString + "addition to Distribution Group
$($dgdept.name) failed with error:"
                        out-file $logfile -append -inputobject $blankline, `
                        $thiserror, $err[0], $blankline
                        $noErrors = $false
                        $errorTotal += 1
                    }
                }
```

```
            else
            {
                    $thiserror = $errorString + "Distribution Group based on
Department `'$($user.department)`' could not be found"
                    out-file $logfile -append -inputobject $blankline, `
                    $thiserror, $blankline
                    $noErrors = $false
                    $errorTotal += 1
            }

            if ($dgoff = (Get-DistributionGroup | where {$_.name -like `
            "*$($user.office)*"}))
            {
                    Add-DistributionGroupMember -Identity:$dgoff `
                    -Member:$user.name -ErrorVariable err

                    If ($err -ne $null)
                    {
                            $thiserror = $errorString + "addition to Distribution Group
$($dgoff.name) failed with error:"
                            out-file $logfile -append -inputobject $blankline, `
                            $thiserror, $err[0], $blankline
                            $noErrors = $false
                            $errorTotal += 1
                    }
            }
            else
            {
                    $thiserror = $errorString + "Distribution group based on Office
`'$($user.office)`' could not be found"
                    out-file $logfile -append -inputobject $blankline, `
                    $thiserror, $blankline
                    $noErrors = $false
                    $errorTotal += 1
            }

            if ($noErrors)
            {
                    $outstring = "[SUCCESS]: Creation of mailbox enabled account
for user $($user.name) succeeded, with mailbox on database: $($user.database)"
                    out-file $logfile -inputobject $outstring -append
            }
        }
    }

    $total = $total + 1

    write-progress -activity "Processed User: $($user.name)" -status "Progress:" `
    -percentcomplete ($total/$users.count*100)
    }
```

Examining the bulk-newmailbox.v2.ps1 Script

The first few lines of this `foreach` block are identical to those used in `v1` of the script. The `New-Mailbox` cmdlet creates each mailbox-enabled user account, and an `if` statement is used to test if the account was successfully created. It is after this point that the new lines of code are introduced.

In short, the new code starts by setting the Department and Office attribute values on the new user account. If there is a failure when setting the attributes, an error message is written to the log and processing for that user is complete, else processing continues. If there is a Distribution Group with a name that matches the Department attribute value, the current user is added to that group, else an error message is written to the log and processing continues.

This operation is repeated for a Distribution Group with a name that matches the Office attribute value. If there is an error adding the user to either group, an error message is written to the log accordingly. If the user is successfully added to both Distribution Groups, a success message is written to the log and processing for that user is complete.

The following paragraphs examine in detail the code segments used to accomplish this functionality followed by the specific segment of code they describe.

All of the new code is encapsulated in an `else` statement that executes only if the `New-Mailbox` operation is successful. The `$errorString` variable is used to store a string value that will be used as the basis for all error messages written to the log file. When an error is generated, additional text will be concatenated to the end of `$errorString` to complete the error message.

```
else
{
        $errorString = "[ERROR]: Creation of mailbox enabled account for user
$($user.name) succeeded, but "
```

Because the `New-Mailbox` cmdlet does not provide for setting non-mail-related attributes when creating a user account, the `Set-User` cmdlet is used in a separate command to set the `Department` and `Office` properties. The values used are taken from the data read from the same CSV file that supplied the values used to create the account with `New-Mailbox`.

```
Set-User -Identity:$user.name -Department:$user.department `
-Office:$user.Office -ErrorVariable err
```

The `if` block following `Set-User` checks to see if there were any errors when setting the attribute values. Neither attribute is validated when they are set, so it is not likely that setting these values would cause an error. However, should there be an error generated by `Set-User`, there should be no attempt to add the user account to a Distribution Group because the attributes that determine group membership are compromised.

The error is captured in the `$err` variable and is used along with the text stored in the `$errorString` variable plus the text string shown to construct the error message written to the log file. At this point all processing for the current user is complete and control passes back to the `foreach` loop to process the next user.

```
If ($err -ne $null)
{
        $errorString += "property assignment failed with error:"
        Out-File $logFile -Append -Inputobject $blankLine, $errorString, `
        $err[0], $blankLine
        $errorTotal += 1
}
```

If user attributes are successfully set, the `if` statement is skipped and the `else` block that follows it executes instead. It is in this `else` block that the user attributes are evaluated and the account is added to the corresponding Distribution Groups. There are two separate Distribution Group add operations in this block. Each operation has a chance to fail so there is a potential to log two separate error messages. The `$noErrors` variable is used to keep track of these individual failures. An overall success message is written to the log only when `$noErrors` is still true when all processing for the current user is complete.

```
else
{
        $noErrors = $true
```

The next `if` statement is used to add the user to a Distribution Group based on Department. The condition block for this `if` statement serves two purposes. First, the `$dgdept` variable is set with the object returned by `Get-DistributionGroup` where the name is similar to the user's `Department` attribute value. This also results in a true condition if a Distribution Group is found, and a false condition if not found. Therefore the `if` statement only executes when a Distribution Group is found.

```
if ($dgdept = (Get-DistributionGroup | where {$_.name -like `
"*$($user.department)*"}))
{
```

The `Add-DistributionGroupMember` cmdlet is used to add the user specified by `Member` to the Distribution Group stored in the variable `$dgdept`.

```
Add-DistributionGroupMember -Identity:$dgdept `
-Member:$user.name -ErrorVariable err
```

The `if` statement that follows the `Add-DistributionGroupMember` command checks to see if the operation was successful by testing if `$err` is not equal to null. If true, the error captured in `$err` is used along with the text stored in the `$errorString` variable plus the text string shown to construct the error message written to the log file. Also `$noErrors` is set to `$false` and `$errorTotal` is incremented by 1.

```
If ($err -ne $null)
{
        $thiserror = $errorString + "addition to Distribution Group
$($dgdept.name) failed with error:"
        out-file $logfile -append -inputobject $blankline, `
        $thiserror, $err[0], $blankline
        $noErrors = $false
        $errorTotal += 1
}
```

If a Distribution Group is not found, the `if` statement is skipped and the `else` statement that follows it executes instead. The `$thisError` variable is used to store the contents of `$errorString` plus the text string shown to form the error message written to the log file. Also `$noErrors` is set to `$false` and `$errorTotal` is incremented by 1.

```
            else
            {
                $thiserror = $errorString + "Distribution Group based on
    Department `'$($user.department)`' could not be found"
                out-file $logfile -append -inputobject $blankline, `
                $thiserror, $blankline
                $noErrors = $false
                $errorTotal += 1
            }
```

At this point all operations related to adding the current user to a Distribution Group based on the Department attribute value are complete.

The next segment of code adds the user to a Distribution Group based on the Office attribute value and is identical in form to the code described in the last few paragraphs so an in-depth examination is not required. Instead we can skip ahead to the last segment of new code.

A final `if` statement is used to check the state of the variable `$noErrors`. If it is still `$true`, then there have been no errors and the success message for the current user is written to the log file. If `$noErrors` is `$false`, then an error message for the current user has already been written to the log file and the `if` statement is skipped. At this point all processing for the current user is complete.

```
            if ($noErrors)
            {
                $outstring = "[SUCCESS]: Creation of mailbox enabled account
    for user $($user.name) succeeded, with mailbox on database: $($user.database)"
                out-file $logfile -inputobject $outstring -append
            }
```

The final lines of code left in the `foreach` loop are identical to that used in the first script version. The `$total` variable is incremented by 1, and the progress indicator is updated to show the user that was processed and the percent of users processed overall.

Running the bulk-newmailbox.v2.ps1 Script

The requirements for running `bulk-newmailbox.v2.ps1` are identical to those for running `bulk-newmailbox.v1.ps1`, except for the CSV input file, which must also include the values for the Department and Office attributes.

To demonstrate the errors that might be logged when creating new users with `bulk-newmailbox.v2`
`.ps1`, a CSV file with values that were sure to cause failures was used to produce the following log file:

```
**************************************************************
Run time = 07/18/2007 13:01:27 using input file users2.csv
**************************************************************
[SUCCESS]: Creation of mailbox enabled account for user User One succeeded, with
mailbox on database: MB001\First Storage Group\Mailbox Database
-----------------------------------------------------------
[ERROR]: Creation of mailbox enabled account for user User Two succeeded, but
addition to Distribution Group Manufacturing failed with error:
Add-DistributionGroupMember : Active Directory operation failed on MB001.exchan
geexchange.local. This error is not retriable. Additional information: Insuffic
ient access rights to perform the operation.
Active directory response: 00002098: SecErr: DSID-03150A45, problem 4003 (INSUF
F_ACCESS_RIGHTS), data 0

At C:\Program Files\Microsoft\Exchange Server\Scripts\bulk-newmailbox.v2a.ps1:1
29 char:48
+                      Add-DistributionGroupMember  <<<< -Identity:$dgdept `
-----------------------------------------------------------
-----------------------------------------------------------
[ERROR]: Creation of mailbox enabled account for user User Two succeeded, but
Distribution group based on Office 'Boston' could not be found
-----------------------------------------------------------
[SUCCESS]: Creation of mailbox enabled account for user User Three succeeded, with
mailbox on database: MB001\First Storage Group\Mailbox Database
[SUCCESS]: Creation of mailbox enabled account for user User Four succeeded, with
mailbox on database: MB001\First Storage Group\Mailbox Database
[SUCCESS]: Creation of mailbox enabled account for user User Five succeeded, with
mailbox on database: MB001\First Storage Group\Mailbox Database
-----------------------------------------------------------
[ERROR]: Creation of mailbox enabled account for user User Six succeeded, but
Distribution Group based on Department 'Legal' could not be found
-----------------------------------------------------------
[SUCCESS]: Creation of mailbox enabled account for user User Seven succeeded, with
mailbox on database: MB001\First Storage Group\Mailbox Database
[SUCCESS]: Creation of mailbox enabled account for user User Eight succeeded, with
mailbox on database: MB001\First Storage Group\Mailbox Database
```

As you can see adding User Two to Distribution Group "Manufacturing" failed with a permission error,
and adding User Two to Distribution Group "Boston" failed because no such Distribution Group could
be found. The script is able to handle two separate errors for the same user and record both in the log
successfully.

Load Balancing User Creation Across Mailbox Servers

The previous two example scripts used hard values read from a CSV file to determine the mailbox
database where the mailboxes would be created. Administrators may find working out these database
assignment values a tedious and time-consuming task. Because scripting is all about automating tasks,
wouldn't it be nice to let the script work out where the mailboxes will be created?

There are several schemes administrators may choose to use when balancing users across mailbox databases. One of the simplest methods is to use the first initial of the user's last name to categorize the user into a group that covers a set range of initials, for example the last name "Adams" would correspond to the group "A" through "F". The group would then correspond to a mailbox database where that group's mailboxes are to be created.

The administrator could then disperse all new mailboxes based on a pattern that guarantees an even distribution, as long as the groups of initials correspond to the even distribution of users across the organization. For the example script bulk-newmailbox.v3.ps1 this section explores, the following ranges of initials are being used: "A" through "F", "G" through "K", "L" through "P", "Q" through "T", and "U" through "Z".

Examining the bulk-newmailbox.v3.ps1 Script

The code that enables this functionality is spread across what is an updated version of the bulk-newmailbox.v2.ps1 script, so the following paragraphs describe the code changes where they appear followed by the code they describe. Note that much of the code is simply a modification of the original code, whereas some of the code is completely new.

The first line of code adds a second parameter input value $CSVDBPath that is used to store the values from a CSV file containing a list of databases where the new mailboxes are to be created. This makes the script more dynamic in that the database names are not hardcoded and can be changed each time the script is run.

```
param([string]$CSVUPath, [string]$CSVDBPath)
```

The next segment of code is a reworked version of the ValidatePath function. Because two CSV files are being read as input, the function is updated to validate both files. To accomplish this, an -or comparison operator is used in each if statement conditional test to check both input parameters. When using an -or operator in a conditional test, if either test result is true, the entire conditional test is true. Note that the display messages have been changed from those used in earlier versions of the script to handle the ambiguity of multiple input files.

```
function ValidatePath
{
    $validPath = $true

    if (($CSVUPath -eq "") -or ($CSVDBPath -eq ""))
    {
        $validPath = $false
        Write-Host -fore yellow "`nYou must enter the full path to the CSV files
used as input to this script.`n"
        return $validPath
    }

    if (!(test-path -pathType:leaf $CSVUPath) -or
        !(test-path -pathType:leaf $CSVDBPath))
```

```
    {
        $validPath = $false
        Write-Host -fore yellow "`nA file path entered is invalid. Please check
file paths and try again.`n"
        return $validPath
    }

    return $validPath
}
```

A new function called GetDatabase is used to determine the database where the current user's mailbox is created. The function starts with a parameter definition to assign the user's last name to the variable $lastname. Next, the string variable $firstchar is assigned the value of the first character of the string stored in the variable $lastname. This is accomplished using the built-in ToCharArray method available for manipulating string values. Because the method converts the string value to an array, the first element in the array (the first element is always zero) that holds the first character is de-referenced using square brackets ([0]).

Now that the first character is stored in $firstchar, the value can be used to test a series of character arrays to determine to which group the user belongs. The character arrays are created later in the script, but must be referenced in the function when it is defined. To test the arrays, an if and a series of elseif statements are used to test whether the given character array contains the character stored in $firstchar.

Before the tests begin, the variable $targetDB is used to store a null value that can be returned to the command that called the function in case all the tests fail. The first test is made by an if statement that checks whether the character array variable $a2f contains the value stored in $firstchar. If the result of this test is true, then $targetDB is set to the databasename property of the first mailbox database object stored in array variable $mailboxdatabases. The array $mailboxdatabases is set later in the script by reading the CSV file that contains the list of mailbox databases.

If the first test in the if statement is false, then the next test is made using an elseif statement. An elseif statement is used as an alternative statement that is processed when an if statement evaluates false. A series of elseif statements can be used for different tests, one after the other following an if statement. The first elseif statement that evaluates true is processed, else control passes to the next elseif statement. It is in this way that the remaining character arrays are tested for the value stored in $firstchar.

The first elseif statement tests the character array variable $g2k, which if true sets $targetDB to the databasename of the second mailbox database stored in $mailboxdatabases. The second elseif statement tests the character array variable $l2p, the third elseif statement tests $q2t, and the last elseif statement tests $u2z. If all the tests evaluate false, then the else statement at the end of the line returns the current value stored in $targetDB, which was set to null before entering the if-elseif statements.

When the if statement or one of the elseif statements evaluates true, the value of $targetDB is set accordingly and the statement is exited. Control passes to the first command past the else statement, which returns the value of $targetDB to the command that called the function.

```
# This function determines the target database
function GetDatabase
{
    param([string]$lastname)

    # Get the first character of the last name value
    [string]$firstchar = $lastname.ToCharArray()[0]

    # Test the first character against the array values to find the target database
    $targetDB = $null

    if ($a2f -contains $firstchar)
    {
        $targetDB = $mailboxdatabases[0].databasename
    }
    elseif ($g2k -contains $firstchar)
    {
        $targetDB = $mailboxdatabases[1].databasename
    }
    elseif ($l2p -contains $firstchar)
    {
        $targetDB = $mailboxdatabases[2].databasename
    }
    elseif ($q2t -contains $firstchar)
    {
        $targetDB = $mailboxdatabases[3].databasename
    }
    elseif ($u2z -contains $firstchar)
    {
        $targetDB = $mailboxdatabases[4].databasename
    }
    else
    {
        return $targetdb
    }

    return $targetdb
}
```

The next section of new code reads the CSV file stored in the input parameter $CSVDBPath using Import-CSV and stores the objects in the variable $mailboxdatabases. The if statement that immediately follows checks if $mailboxdatabases was successfully set. If not, an error message is passed to the display and the script is exited.

```
# Read from the database CSV file, if there is a failure reading the file, exit
$mailboxdatabases = (Import-Csv $CSVDBPath)

if (!$mailboxdatabases)
{
    Write-Host -fore yellow "`nFailed to read the database input file. It is either invalid or improperly formatted.`n"
    exit
}
```

The `$logheader` variable is updated to include the name of the CSV file used as input for the mailbox database list.

```
$logheader = "
****************************************************************
Run time - $datetime using input files $CSVUPath & $CSVDBPath
****************************************************************"
```

Finally, the character variable arrays used to determine the group to which the current user should be matched are defined. The variables are set as arrays by using the @ character before a set of parentheses holding each individual string character value separated by commas.

```
# Create arrays to collate user based on first character of last name
$a2f = @("a", "b", "c", "d", "e", "f")
$g2k = @("g", "h", "i", "j", "k")
$l2p = @("l", "m", "n", "o", "p")
$q2t = @("q", "r", "s", "t")
$u2z = @("u", "v", "w", "x", "y", "z")
```

The `New-Mailbox` command in the `foreach` loop has to be modified as well because the mailbox database values are not taken from the user CSV file. To set the mailbox database value stored in the variable `$database`, the `getdatabase` function is called using the current user's last name as an input value. Once the value is set, it is used to specify the `Database` parameter value for `New-Mailbox`.

```
# Create the mailbox enabled accounts
foreach ($user in $users)
    {
        $database = (getdatabase $user.LastName)

        New-Mailbox -Name:$user.name -Database:$database `
        -OrganizationalUnit:$user.OrganizationalUnit `
        -UserPrincipalName:$user.UserPrincipalName `
        -FirstName:$user.FirstName -LastName:$user.LastName `
        -Password:$password -ResetPasswordOnNextLogon:$true `
        -ErrorVariable err | Out-Null
```

Finally, the success output message written to the log file has been updated to use the value stored in `$database` to report where the mailbox was created.

```
        elseif ($errorlocal -eq 0)
        {
            $outstring = "[SUCCESS]: Creation of mailbox enabled account
for user $($user.name) succeeded, with mailbox on database: $database"
            out-file $logfile -inputobject $outstring -append
        }
```

Running the bulk-newmailbox.v3.ps1 Script

Running `bulk-newmailbox.v3.ps1` requires the input of two CSV files, the first for user information and the second for mailbox database information. The mailbox database CSV file needs only one name in the header to represent the database name property, and the values should be presented in <server name>\<storage group name>\<database name> format. For example, the following would be sufficient content to use as input:

```
DatabaseName
MB001\Storage Group a-f\a-f Mailbox Database
MB001\Storage Group g-k\g-k Mailbox Database
MB001\Storage Group l-p\l-p Mailbox Database
MB001\Storage Group q-z\q-z Mailbox Database
```

As for the user CSV input file, there is no need to include a value for `Database` because this is worked out by the script.

All other features of `bulk-newmailbox.v3.ps1` remain the same as those found in previous versions of the mailbox creation script. The messages and progress indicator displayed during processing and the success and error messages written to the log file are the same.

Creating a Public Folder for the New Users

Exchange public folders offer a convenient method for storing and sharing information among mailbox-enabled users. Most organizations take public folder administration out of the hands of users and rest the responsibility on the shoulders of the Exchange administrator. Public folder creation and administration are tasks suitable for automation via scripting.

This section explores a script that is used to create a public folder for a mailbox-enabled user, and then set permissions suitable for that user to maintain their own content without allowing them to delete the folder or create sub-folders. The folder when created is named using the full name of the user. The script also confirms if the user is actually mailbox-enabled, and if the user actually needs a folder created in case one already exists.

The script uses these cmdlets:

- ❑   Write-Host
- ❑   Get-PublicFolderDatabase
- ❑   Get-PublicFolder
- ❑   Get-Mailbox
- ❑   Get-MailboxDatabase
- ❑   New-PublicFolder
- ❑   Add-PublicFolderClientPermission

The following lists the contents of script file `newuser-publicfolder.ps1`:

```
# newuser-publicfolder.ps1
#
# Synopsis: This script creates a Public Folder based on a mailbox enabled user
#           account used as an input value to the script. This script has to
#           be run by an administrator who is a member of the Exchange Recipient
#           Administrators group.
#
#           This script checks to see if the user is mailbox enabled and if a
#           Public Folder already exists for the user. If not, a folder is
#           created named for the user in the default Public Folder database
#           specified by the user's mailbox database. The folder client
#           permissions are set to allow the user full control over the folder
#           contents, and the user running the script is set as the folder owner.
#
# Usage: newuser-publicfolder.ps1 <mailbox enabled user>
#
# Example: newuser-publicfolder.ps1 user1@exchangeexchange.com

param([string]$user)

# Turn off error reporting to the display
$ErrorActionPreference = "SilentlyContinue"

#This function validates the user specified
function validateUser
{
    $notValidUser = $false

    if ($user -eq "")
    {
        $notValidUser = $true
        Write-Host -fore yellow "`nYou must enter a mailbox enabled user account as
input to this script.`n"
        return $notValidUser
    }

    if (!($usermb))
    {
        $notValidUser = $true
        Write-Host -fore yellow "`nThe account specified is not mailbox enabled or
could not be found in Active Directory.`n"
        return $notValidUser
    }

    if ($usermb.RecipientTypeDetails -ne "UserMailbox")
    {
        $notValidUser = $true
        Write-Host -fore yellow "`nThe mailbox enabled account specified is not a
user mailbox.`n"
        return $notValidUser
    }
```

(continued)

(continued)

```
        return $notValidUser
}

# This function checks the public folder database availability
function validatePFStore
{
    $databaseNotUp = $false

    if (!(get-publicfolderdatabase -identity:$PFDatabase -status).mounted)
    {
        $databaseNotUp = $true
        Write-Host -fore yellow "`nPublic Folder Database
'$($server.name)\$($PFDatabase.name)' is not available. Please check it's
status.`n"
        return $databaseNotUp
    }

    return $databaseNotUp
}

#This function validates the need to create a folder for the user specified
function validatefolder
{
    $hasFolder = $false

    if (get-publicfolder -identity:"\corporate\$($usermb.name)" -server:$server
    {
        $hasFolder = $true
        Write-Host -fore yellow "`nA Public Folder for this user already exists.`n"
        return $hasFolder
    }

    return $hasFolder
}

# Get the mailbox information for the specified user
$userMB = Get-Mailbox -Identity:$user

# Validate the user is mailbox enabled and the mailbox is a user mailbox
if (validateUser) { exit }

# Figure out where to create the folder
$PFDatabase = (Get-MailboxDatabase -Identity:$userMB.Database).PublicFolderDatabase
$server = (Get-PublicFolderDatabase -Identity:$PFDatabase).server

# Check if the public folder database is available
if (validatePFStore) { exit }

# Validate the user needs a folder created
if (validateFolder) { exit }
```

```
# Create the folder, exit if folder creation fails for any reason
$newFolder = New-PublicFolder -Name:$usermb.name -Path:"\corporate" `
-Server:$server -ErrorVariable err

If ($err -ne $null) { $err; exit }

$newFolder

# Set permissions on the folder
Add-PublicFolderClientPermission -Identity:$newFolder `
-User:$usermb.alias -AccessRights:Editor -Server:$server
```

Examining the newuser-publicfolder.ps1 Script

After the usual lines of comment, the script starts by defining the input parameter variable $user to hold the name of the mailbox-enabled user account entered when the script is run.

```
param([string]$user)
```

As was the case in previous scripts described in this chapter, the automatic variable $ErrorActionPreference is set to SilentlyContinue so default error messages are not displayed. Instead, the script generates its own error messages as appropriate.

```
# Turn off error reporting to the display
$ErrorActionPreference = "SilentlyContinue"
```

The first function definition called validateUser is used to check the user specified in $user to see if it is indeed a mailbox-enabled user account. The script assumes the administrator only wants to create public folders for users and not contacts or mail-enabled users. To keep track of whether the user is valid, the $notValidUser variable is set to $false. This is the value that is returned to the command that called validateUser if all tests pass and the user is valid.

```
#This function validates the user specified
function validateUser
{
    $notValidUser = $false
```

The next code segment uses an if statement to test if a value was passed at the command line when the script was run. If $user is null, $notValid is set to $true and an error message is displayed on the screen to instruct the administrator to supply a valid user account. The value of $notValidUser is returned to the command that called validateUser and all processing for the function is complete.

```
    if ($user -eq "")
    {
        $notValidUser = $true
        Write-Host -fore yellow "`nYou must enter a mailbox enabled user account as
input to this script.`n"
        return $notValidUser
    }
```

The next code segment uses another `if` statement to test if a value held in $userMB holds an object that is the result of running `Get-Mailbox` with $user as input. This command is used later in the script before the function is called, so should hold a value when tested at this point. Supplying a valid mailbox-enabled user to `Get-Mailbox` would result in populating $userMB with a mailbox user object that evaluates as true when tested. If the account is not mailbox-enabled, or cannot be found in Active Directory, then $userMB is false and the conditional test would ultimately result in true thanks to the `NOT` operator.

If the user is not mailbox-enabled, $notValidUser is set to $true and an error message is displayed to inform the administrator the account is not valid. The value of $notValidUser is returned to the command that called `validateUser` and all processing for the function is complete.

```
if (!($userMB))
{
    $notValidUser = $true
    Write-Host -fore yellow "`nThe account specified is not mailbox enabled or
could not be found in Active Directory.`n"
    return $notValidUser
}
```

The last `if` statement in this function tests to see if the mailbox-enabled user object held in $userMB represents a user mailbox or something else. Exchange Server 2007 provides for other types of mailboxes such as shared, equipment, and room. The script assumes that administrators only want to create public folders for user mailboxes using the script. The `RecipientTypeDetails` property holds the value that determines the mailbox type.

This `if` statement tests the value of `RecipientTypeDetails` to see if it is not equal to `"UserMailbox"`. If it is, the user is mailbox-enabled and is good to go for public folder creation, so the `if` statement is skipped. If it is not, the condition is then true and the statement is processed. $notValidUser is set to $true and an error message is displayed to inform the administrator the account is not a user mailbox-enabled account. The value of $notValidUser is returned to the command that called `validateUser` and all processing for the function is complete.

```
if ($userMB.RecipientTypeDetails -ne "UserMailbox")
{
    $notValidUser = $true
    Write-Host -fore yellow "`nThe mailbox enabled account specified is not a
user mailbox.`n"
    return $notValidUser
}
```

The last command in the function only executes if all three `if` statements evaluate false and returns the value stored in $notValidUser, which was set to $false at the beginning of the function.

```
return $notValidUser
```

The second function definition called `validatePFStore` is used to determine the current status of the public folder store that acts as the default public folder store for the user as determined by the mailbox database where the user's mailbox is located. The errors generated when the public folder store is unavailable are ambiguous, so this function serves as a more friendly way to inform the administrator that a problem exists with the public folder store.

To keep track of whether the public folder database is up or down, the $databaseNotUp variable is set to $false. This is the value that is returned to the command that called validatePFStore if the test passes and the public folder store is available.

```
# This function checks the public folder database availability
function validatePFStore
{
    $databaseNotUp = $false
```

The if statement in this function uses the Get-PublicFolder cmdlet to check the status of the public folder database identified by the value stored in the variable $PFDatabase. Before this function is called, a segment of code is used to work out the default public folder store for the user based on the mailbox database where the user's mailbox is located. From this information the name of the server holding the public folder store is determined and stored in variable $PFDatabase.

This value is passed to Get-PublicFolderDatabase, and the Status parameter is used to cause the command to actually contact the server where the database is located to see if it is mounted. The results of this query are returned in the Mounted property, which is de-referenced at the end of the command. If the database was valid, and the server reports that it is mounted, then the value stored in the property Mounted is true. The NOT operator changes the results to false and the if statement is skipped.

However, if the database is not mounted, the condition evaluates as true and the if statement executes. $databaseNotUp is set to $true and an error message is written to the display to tell the administrator to check the status of the public folder store. The value of $databaseNotUp is returned to the command that called validatePFStore and all processing for the function is complete.

```
    if (!(get-publicfolderdatabase -identity:$PFDatabase -status).Mounted)
    {
        $databaseNotUp = $true
        Write-Host -fore yellow "`nPublic Folder Database
'$($server.name)\$($PFDatabase.name)' is not available. Please check it's
status.`n"
        return $databaseNotUp
    }
```

The last command in the function executes only if the if statement evaluates false and returns the value stored in $databaseNotUp, which was set to $false at the beginning of the function.

```
        return $databaseNotUp
```

The last function called validateFolder is used to validate the need to create a public folder for the user. The script assumes that if a public folder already exists for the user, there is no need to create a new folder. To keep track of whether the user is valid, the $hasFolder variable is set to $false. This is the value that is returned to the command that called validateFolder if the test passes and the need to create a folder is valid.

```
#This function validates the need to create a folder for the user specified
function validateFolder
{
    $hasFolder = $false
```

The only `if` statement in this function uses the `Get-PublicFolder` cmdlet to see if a folder with a name that matches the name of the user already exists. The script assumes that all user-related public folders are to be created under a top level folder named `corporate`. Therefore the value used to identify the public folder for which the test is checking is constructed using the text `\corporate` and the value stored in the Name property of the user mailbox object stored in `$userMB`.

The same segment of code that works out the default public folder store for the user later in the script is also used to determine the name of the server holding the public folder store, which is stored in the variable `$server`.

If the `Get-PublicFolder` command returns a public folder object, then the condition evaluates true and the statement executes. `$hasFolder` is set to `$true` and an error message is displayed to inform the administrator that a public folder for this user already exists. The value of `$hasFolder` is returned to the command that called `validateFolder` and all processing for the function is complete.

```
if (get-publicfolder -identity:"\corporate\$($userMB.name)" -server:$server)
{
    $hasFolder = $true
    Write-Host -fore yellow "`nA Public Folder for this user already exists.`n"
    return $hasFolder
}
```

The last command in the function only executes if the `if` statement evaluates false and returns the value stored in `$hasFolder`, which was set to `$true` at the beginning of the function.

```
return $hasFolder
```

The next code segment does the work that must be completed before calling the `validateUser` function. This is the point where `$userMB` is populated with the results of `Get-Mailbox` using `$user` as the identity.

```
# Get the mailbox information for the specified user
$userMB = Get-Mailbox -Identity:$user
```

Now that `$userMB` is set, the `validateUser` function is called. If the returned results are false, this `if` statement is skipped and processing continues. If the results are true, then processing is complete and the script is exited.

```
# Validate the user is mailbox enabled and the mailbox is a user mailbox
if (validateUser) { exit }
```

The next code segment does the work that must be completed before calling the `validatePFStore` function. First the `Get-MailboxDatabase` cmdlet is used to get information for the mailbox database where the user's mailbox is located. All mailbox databases have a property called `PublicFolderDatabase` that as the name implies, identifies the default public folder database for those mailbox users. This is where the public folder should be created.

The identity of the mailbox database is determined using the Database property from the user mailbox object stored in `$userMB`. The `PublicFolderDatabase` property is then de-referenced from the results of `Get-MailboxDatabase` at the end of the command. That value is then set on the variable `$PFDatabase`.

The next command in this segment uses `Get-PublicFolderDatabase` to determine the server that holds the public folder database stored in the variable `$PFDatabase`. The server property is de-referenced at the end of the command to supply the value to `$server`. This variable is used in several other places in the script to supply the name of the server.

```
# Figure out where to create the folder
$PFDatabase = (Get-MailboxDatabase -Identity:$userMB.Database).PublicFolderDatabase
$server = (Get-PublicFolderDatabase -Identity:$PFDatabase).server
```

Now that all the prerequisite work is done, it's time to call the other functions. First, the `validatePFStore` function is called to see if the public folder store is available. If the test in the `validatePFStore` function determines the store is not available, a true value is returned. The `if` statement executes and the script exits. If the store is available, the results returned by `validatePFStore` are false and the `if` statement is skipped.

```
# Check if the public folder database is available
if (validatePFStore) { exit }
```

Next, the `validateFolder` function is called to see if the user really needs a public folder. If the user already has a folder, the result returned by `validateFolder` is true. The `if` statement executes and the script exits. If the user does not already have a folder, the result returned by `validateFolder` is false, and the `if` statement is skipped.

```
# Validate the user needs a folder created
if (validateFolder) { exit }
```

If the script has made it to this point, then the user is a valid mailbox-enabled user, the default public folder for the user is available, and the user does not already have a public folder.

The next code segment creates the public folder using the `New-PublicFolder` cmdlet. The input value for the `Name` parameter is taken from the full username stored in the `Name` property of the object stored in `$userMB`. The `Path` parameter value uses a static value that assumes all new user folders are to be created under the root folder `corporate`. The `Server` parameter value is taken from the server name stored in `$server`.

The results of running `New-PublicFolder` are stored in the variable `$newFolder` as a public folder object.

```
# Create the folder, exit if folder creation fails for any reason
$newFolder = New-PublicFolder -Name:$usermb.name -Path:"\corporate" `
-Server:$server -ErrorVariable err
```

At this point if the public folder fails creation, there is no need to continue and attempt to set permissions on a public folder that does not even exist. The next code segment uses an `if` statement to check if an error message has been stored in the variable `$err` by `New-PublicFolder`. This will be the case only if there was a problem creating the folder.

If so the `if` statement displays the error message stored in `$err`, then exits the script. The error messages generated by `New-PublicFolder` are sufficient to use in this case to tell the administrator there was a problem creating the folder.

```
If ($err -ne $null) { $err; exit }
```

If the folder was created successfully, then the next code segment sends the contents of $newFolder to the display. When the variable $newFolder is used in this way, the information displayed takes the form of the default output from New-PublicFolder.

```
$newFolder
```

The last code segment uses Add-PublicFolderClientPermission to set the permissions for the user on the new folder. The identity of the folder is taken from the public folder object stored in $newFolder. The User parameter input value is taken from the user alias as derived from the mailbox object stored in $userMB. The AccessRights parameter input value is a static value of Editor. This access right allows the users to create and delete their own content in the folder, but does not allow them to delete the folder or create sub-folders. The Server parameter value is taken from the server name stored in $server.

```
# Set permissions on the folder
Add-PublicFolderClientPermission -Identity:$newFolder `
-User:$usermb.alias -AccessRights:Editor -Server:$server
```

Running the newuser-publicfolder.ps1 Script

Running newuser-publicfolder.ps1 is really quite simple: the name of the script followed by the name of a mailbox-enabled user. The name supplied can be in the form of the full name encapsulated in quotes, the alias, the user principal name, or even the user's Global Unique Identifier (GUID). This is possible because the underlying Exchange Management Shell cmdlet used in the script accepts these forms of identity.

As with any good script, newuser-publicfolder.ps1 incorporates some simple validation and error control. The following examples demonstrate what happens when validation fails in preliminary testing before any main script processing is attempted.

When no mailbox-enabled user identity is specified, this error message is generated:

```
[PS] C:\>newuser-publicfolder.ps1

You must enter a mailbox enabled user account as input to this script.
```

When the mailbox-enabled user identity is either not mailbox-enabled or does not exist, this error message is generated:

```
[PS] C:\>newuser-publicfolder.ps1 bogus

The account specified is not mailbox enabled or could not be found in Active
Directory.
```

When the mailbox-enabled user identity is for a resource mailbox and not a user mailbox, the following error message is generated:

```
[PS] C:\>newuser-publicfolder.ps1 confrm1

The mailbox enabled account specified is not a user mailbox.
```

When a public folder for the mailbox-enabled user already exists, the following error message is generated:

```
[PS] C:\>newuser-publicfolder.ps1 user1

A Public Folder for this user already exists.
```

If the default public folder store for the mailbox-enabled user is not available, the following error message is generated:

```
[PS] C:\>newuser-publicfolder.ps1 user3

Public Folder Database 'MB001\Public Folder Database' is not available. Please
check it's status.
```

When a mailbox-enabled user who does not already have a public folder is used as the identity, the script executes and creates the folder. The output is standard for the `New-PublicFolder` and `Set-PublicFolderPermission` cmdlets.

```
[PS] C:\>newuser-publicfolder.ps1 user3

Name                                    Parent Path
----                                    -----------
User Three                              \Corporate

Identity     : \corporate\User Three
User         : exchangeexchange.local/Corporate/User Three
AccessRights : {Editor}
```

One aspect of a script like `newuser-publicfolder.ps1` is that it can be used as a maintenance task. Because the script validates the need to create a public folder for the given user, if the script is presented a group of mailbox-enabled users for processing, it is able to create folders as needed while ignoring users that already have folders.

To accomplish this, `Get-Mailbox` can be used to gather a collection of mailbox-enabled users based on some common property, then pass this collection by pipeline to a `foreach` command that calls the script for each user in the collection in turn.

For example, the following command gathers all the mailbox-enabled user accounts in the Organizational Unit "team," and then passes them to the foreach block for execution:

```
Get-Mailbox -OrganizationalUnit exchangeexchange.local/team | foreach {newuser-
publicfolder.ps1 $_} > c:\results.txt
```

The results of each cycle of the script in the foreach command are normally displayed at the command line, which may be awkward to follow when there are a large number of users to process. To address this, the command uses a redirection to a text file that can be reviewed for errors by the administrator once the command completes.

Summary

Administrators know scripts automate everyday tasks and ensure consistent results. The scripting capabilities of Exchange Management Shell offer a level of control unavailable in previous versions of Exchange Server. Any feature provided by Exchange Server 2007 can be administered via scripting.

One of the best examples of an administrative task that is easily accomplished via scripting is the bulk creation of objects, such as mailbox-enabled user accounts. A simple script needs only the minimum property values required for creation as input. The structured information stored in a comma-separated value (CSV) input file provides an ideal method for delivering input data to a script. Administrators may find simple scripts lack certain desirable features.

More evolved scripts take advantage of functionality already provided by built-in Management Shell commands. These scripts often include features like error control and logging to present a more complete solution.

Scripts often combine multiple administrative tasks into one solution for maximum results with a minimum of effort. Scripts are capable of employing logic to make complex decisions based on property values and conditions. These scripts truly maximize the effectiveness of automation.

16

Reporting, Maintenance, and Administration

By this point in reading this book you probably have a list of scripts that you want to put together because you want to try them out in your messaging environment. As you can imagine, once you really begin to harness the power of PowerShell you are going to have more and more ideas that you want to try out. In this chapter we discuss using PowerShell to create some reports and to help automate some administrative tasks. Because the sheer breadth of what you can accomplish with PowerShell scripting is immense, we are going to pick just a few examples to give you the tools you need to create your own scripts.

This chapter covers:

❑ Reading in files for processing

❑ Advanced output techniques

❑ Examples for using these techniques

Reading in Files

This section discusses the following cmdlets:

❑ Import-Csv

❑ Get-Content

One of the basic functions you will want to perform is to read in a file and work with the data that you find. You might wish to read in a file with a list of mailboxes that need to be created, or you might need to update a list of mailboxes with new office information. If you have been using

Exchange since version 5.5 you might remember all of the account modifications that could be done by importing and exporting CSV files. If you long for those days, you can relive them using PowerShell!

The basic command for reading in a file is Get-Content. You can open a file and read it by running Get-Content and specifying the file you want to read in:

```
Get-Content [-path] <string[]> [-totalCount <long>] [-readCount <long>] [-include
<string[]>] [-exclude <string[]>] [-filter <string>] [-force] [-credential
<PSCredential>] [-encoding {<Unknown> | <String> | <Unicode> | <Byte> |
<BigEndianUnicode> | <UTF8> | <UTF7> | <Ascii>}] [<CommonParameters>]
Get-Content [-literalPath] <string[]> [-totalCount <long>] [-readCount <long>] [-
include <string[]>] [-exclude <string[]>] [-filter <string>] [-force] [-credential
<PSCredential>] [-encoding {<Unknown> | <String> | <Unicode> | <Byte> |
<BigEndianUnicode> | <UTF8> | <UTF7> | <Ascii>}] [<CommonParameters>]
```

Get-Content requires that a file is provided to read from. The totalCount parameter specifies the number of lines that are retrieved. To retrieve the contents of the file with the list of databases in it the syntax would look like the following:

```
Get-Content C:\data\Databases.txt
```

Now that the data has been read in you can loop through each of the lines in the file by using a foreach loop, which would look like the following:

```
$dbs = Get-Content C:\data\Databases.txt
foreach ($line in $dbs)
{

}
```

Sure, this is okay for simple files but what if you need to import a spreadsheet that has multiple columns of data? This is a very common scenario because when you create mailboxes you need at a minimum the User Principal Name (UPN), name, and alias of the user. It would be a hassle to read in three different text files and then try to keep the data together. Thankfully, there is a way to do this with the Import-Csv cmdlet. A comma-separated value (CSV) file is a text-based file with the data separated into columns with commas and can be created with Notepad or Microsoft Office Excel. When you create the CSV file that you want to read in, be sure that the first line in the CSV has the name of the columns, because this makes the information easier to reference. Import-Csv has the following syntax:

```
Import-Csv [-path] <string[]> [<CommonParameters>]
```

This is a relatively simple command only requiring a path specified to the CSV file that will be imported. The cmdlet will return an object with the data read in from the file that can be used in a pipeline or script.

An example that we have used previously in the book can also be used to show how to use Import-Csv. This time, however, more detail will be given to describe how and why it works. First you need to start with a simple CSV file named `mailboxes.csv` that has the information you need to create the mailboxes. The file is created in Notepad and looks like the following list:

```
UPN,Name,Alias
jstidley@exchangeexchange.local,JoelStidley,jstidley
bkeane@exchangeexchange.local,BrendanKeane,bkeane
jcarpenter@exchangeexchange.local,JimCarpenter,jcarpenter
```

To use this file `Import-Csv` is used to read in the contents of the file and assign it to a variable. Once the data is assigned to a variable, access to the data is as simple as working with a dataset. A `foreach` loop can be used to step through each of the items in the object. Each column from the spreadsheet will be a property of the items; this makes working with the values of the properties just like working with any other object, and very easy.

```
@newUsers = Import-Csv Mailboxes.csv

foreach ($objItem in $newUsers)


{



}
```

Passwords are a special case when working in PowerShell. Passwords are stored as a special secured string value in memory. This means that this string is not stored in plain text and thus requires special handling. To streamline this process you can prompt for the user to add the password that will be used for all of the accounts:

```
$password = Read-Host "Enter password" -AsSecureString
@newUsers = Import-CSV Mailboxes.csv

foreach ($objItem in $newUsers)

{


New-Mailbox -alias $objItem.Alias -name $objItem.Name -UserPrincipalName
$objItem.UPN -Database "MB001\SG03\MB01" -OrganizationalUnit Users -Password
$Password -ResetPasswordOnNextLogon:$true
}
```

You pass the data from the file, specifying the appropriate values from the CSV in the spaces in the `New-Mailbox` cmdlet. Using the `foreach` loop you are stepping through the values that have been read in from the CSV file, line by line. To obtain the value for the current item, all you need to do is look at the property of the current item that is assigned to the `$objItem` variable.

You could take this example a step further by adding in more columns in this spreadsheet so that you can assign the street address or maybe even the group membership of the new accounts.

Exporting Data

This section discusses the following cmdlets:

❑   Out-File

❑   Export-Csv

No doubt, it is a requirement to be able to save data for reference at a later time. Natively, PowerShell provides for outputting data in text format or as a CSV file. Exporting data as it would appear onscreen to a text file is as simple as piping the data to Out-File and specifying the filename:

```
Out-File [-filePath] <string> [[-encoding] <string>] [-append] [-width <int>] [-
inputObject <psobject>] [-force] [-noClobber] [-whatIf] [-confirm]
[<CommonParameters>]

The filePath parameter is positional so without any switches Out-File expects to
have information piped to it and a filePath value provided which will be the file
written. The noClobber switch specifies that if there is a file with the name
specified in the filePath it will not overwrite the contents as is the default
behavior for the cmdlet. Using the encoding parameter the file being written can be
encoded in several different format by choosing Unicode, UTF7, UTF8 or ASCII.
```

To write a file with a list of all mailboxes in an Exchange organization you would simply run:

```
Get-Mailbox | Out-File C:\data\allmailboxes.txt
```

You could then open that file in a text editor for reference. But what if you have a complex set of data that you want to perform analysis against? You could take that text file and massage it until it worked in Excel or you could use simply the Export-Csv cmdlet. The Export-Csv file has the following syntax:

```
Export-Csv [-path] <string> -inputObject <psobject> [-force] [-encoding <string>]
[-noTypeInformation] [-noClobber] [-whatIf] [-confirm] [<CommonParameters>]
```

Export-Csv has syntax similar to the Out-File cmdlet except it has the noTypeInformation switch, which removes the first line of the exported CSV file which, by default, is the type of object that was exported to the file.

To get a list of all the attributes for all of the mailboxes in the Exchange organization you would simply run:

```
Get-Mailbox | Export-CSV C:\data\allmailboxes.csv
```

Most likely you would select specific objects to include in the export, which you could do by using select-object before the Export-Csv cmdlet.

A number of excellent third-party products can be used to export data. Most of these third-party products function just like Export-CSV and Out-File in that they allow for exporting data by piping the data at the command line to the third-party cmdlets.

One note when working with this: make sure that you are exporting data in the right format. Many of the mailbox sizes and statistics are typed as byte quantified size and most cmdlets that you would pipe this data to would expect the data to be a string or an integer. If these controls receive the byte quantified size typed data, they can't properly format it. You can find an example of working with byte quantified size values and third-party products later in this chapter.

Sending Email from PowerShell

When writing a monitoring PowerShell script it is essential for the script to be able to email an alert when something falls outside of a normal condition. Of course I know what you are thinking, "Why would you send an email if email was down?" or perhaps you are thinking, "Isn't that just like sending an email to the users to let them know that they can't get to their email?" Most likely you would send the email through a separate system, perhaps even to a mobile device through text messages.

Sending an email through PowerShell is pretty straightforward to those familiar with the .NET Framework. To be able to create a new SMTPClient object you use the New-Object cmdlet and specify the name of the class used to create the object. After creating the $smtp object, the Send method can be used with specific parameters called overloads to specify the information needed to send an email. The following lines of a PowerShell script are all you need to send a message:

```
$smtpServer = "relay.exchangeexchange.local"
$smtp = new-object Net.Mail.SmtpClient($smtpServer)
$smtp.Send("fromaddress@exchangeexchange.com","administrators@exchangeexchange
.com","Message Subject","Message body is typed here")
```

In this example the sender, recipient, message subject, and body are all set to a specific string. You can make this code snippet a little more sophisticated by putting variables in place so that you can send the error message or even the report directly from PowerShell using a script.

Real-World PowerShell Examples

Now that we have covered some of the more advanced PowerShell techniques, let's try to apply these in some real-world examples.

Applying Default Settings

System policies allowed an administrator to set mailbox defaults on mailbox stores just by creating a policy with the required settings and then choosing which stores would inherit the policy settings. This saved hours of work and also reduced the possibility of an administrator modifying the standard. System policies don't exist in Exchange Server 2007. There isn't any specific feature that fills that need either. However, using PowerShell you can create a very flexible system policy alternative.

Essentially the process involves creating a couple standard PowerShell scripts for each of the standards, providing a list of stores that these standards should be applied to, and then scheduling to run the scripts with Windows Scheduler (AT) or another scheduler program.

The first line of the script adds the Exchange snap-in. If you run a PowerShell script from the command line you don't get the Exchange management snap-in, so you need to add it manually. The second line of the script grabs the parameter that is passed to the script on the command line. The $args special variable is an array of the arguments that were passed to the script on the command line. The first item in the array is the first parameter specified on the command line. The following example uses a single argument in the script to specify the file to open and parse the contents of it so that you can determine which mailbox stores the script needs to modify:

```
Add-PSSnapin *Exchange* | out-null

$MBItems = get-content -path $args[0]
```

You use the Get-Content cmdlet to open the filename that you passed on the command line. Next, for each line read in from the file, you are going to run a Set-MailboxDatabase cmdlet to set the defaults that have been defined for your Exchange users. For a detailed discussion of the Set-MailboxDatabase cmdlet please reference Chapter 8. You will want to construct a Set-MailboxDatabase command that sets all relevant settings to meet your standard.

```
foreach ($objItem in $MBItems)
{
Set-MailboxDatabase $objitem -IssueWarningQuota 300MB -ProhibitSendQuota 400MB -
ProhibitSendReceiveQuota 600MB -ItemRetention 21.00:00:00 -MailboxRetention
21.00:00:00 -RetainDeletedItemsUntilBackup:$true
}
```

Next you need to create the text file that will have a list of the mailbox stores that you want to apply this policy to. In this file you should list each store's identity on its own line.

The identity for the mailbox stores are in this format: server name\storage group\mailbox store. A sample list of mailbox stores would look like this:

```
MB001\SG01\MB01
MB001\SG03\MB03
MB002\SG10\MB10
MB010\SG30\MB30
```

Now you have a script named SetStandardPolicy.ps1 that is custom tailored to set the standard. You also have a text file called StandardStores.txt. To make sure that these standards get applied and stay applied no matter what changes are made to the environment, you need to schedule the policy script to be applied periodically. I would suggest having these run at least once a day, if not more often. Now, create a scheduled task using Windows Scheduled Tasks or other task scheduler that runs every two hours or perhaps an interval that better fits your business environment:

```
PowerShell.exe -Command 'SetStandardPolicy.ps1 StandardStores.txt'
```

This ensures that each store listed in the StandardStores.txt file gets your standard settings. If you need to add or subtract a store from the list, all you need to do is adjust the text file; no need to modify the script when a database needs to be added or removed.

In order to adapt this for all of your database standard profiles in your organization you can create a corresponding script and text file for each. For instance, you may create a script for the executive or contract worker mailbox size limits and then schedule those scripts to be run as well. Similar scripts can be created to set standards to specific mailboxes, public folder databases, and even server configurations.

Reporting Tasks with PowerShell

In previous versions of Exchange it was always frustrating trying to create reports that told what was happening in your organization. If your manager asked you to create a report of all the mailbox sizes for your 100 Exchange servers you would either be creating a VBScript that used at least three different methods of getting information (CDO, WebDAV, ADSI, and so on) or you were doing a lot of clicking and exporting to a comma-separated values (CSV) file to import and massage in Microsoft Office Excel. We are going to cover a couple scenarios to get you started down the path of creating simple and powerful scripts to report on what is going on in your Exchange organization.

It seems like every few weeks a new PowerShell utility or tool is coming on the market. This is really good news for those of you who want to keep improving your reports and reduce the time it takes to troubleshoot and develop new scripts.

One of the many excellent tools that are available and the one that I have been able to spend the most time with is PowerGadgets, which enables you to create nice looking charts easily as you pipe your data to the gadget.

Reporting on Online Defragmentation and Backups

One of the more important factors to keep an eye on in your environment is whether online defragmentation is completing in a satisfactory length of time on all of the databases in the environment. This is important because if online defragmentation isn't completing at about once every two weeks, the database is going to grow larger than it needs to and it isn't going to perform as well as it can. If maintenance is not running often enough you may need to increase the length of the maintenance period or make sure that the maintenance period isn't overlapping with the backups.

The first thing you need to do is to get a list of each of the mailbox stores on the local server and assign the list to the variable $db. There are a number of methods of determining the name of the local server; this example obtains the MachineName property from the System.Environment object. You need to select only the local server because Get-EventLog doesn't provide access to remote event logs through PowerShell. You can, however, use Get-WMIObject to query a remote event log. This example sticks with Get-EventLog:

```
$servername = [System.Environment]::MachineName
$db = Get-StorageGroup -Server $servername | Get-MailboxDatabase
```

Now that you have retrieved the mailbox store list, you need to start looking for the right information from the event logs for each of these mailbox stores. When a database completes an online defragmentation pass either an event with an event id of 701 or 703 with a source of ESE is written to the event log. As you can see from Figure 16-1 the event provides information about the online defragmentation including the number of times it has completed. This level of detail in the event log is new to Exchange Server 2007 Service Pack 1.

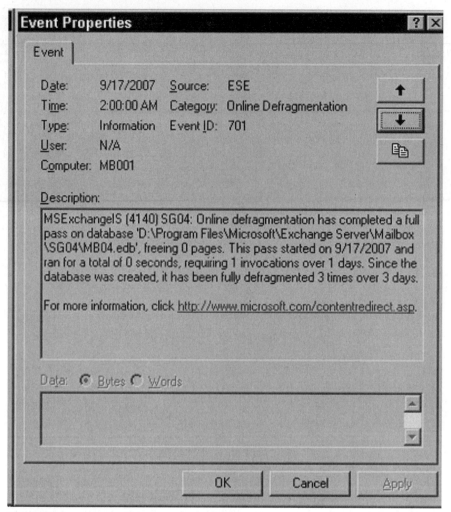

Figure 16-1

To find this event for each database you need to filter out all non-essential events. To do this you can use `Get-EventLog` and specify that you want to look only at the Application Log. You then need to look at only the events that have an event ID of 701 or 703 and have a source of ESE.

```
$EventLogs = get-EventLog -LogName Application | where-object {$_.EventID -eq 703 -
or $_.EventID -eq 701 -and $_.Source -eq 'ESE' }
```

As you can see in Figure 16-2 this returns a list of all the events in the event log with this critera. This is still too much data to be useful. Because you are interested in whether all databases have been completing the online defragmentation you need to pass in the database variable that you got earlier.

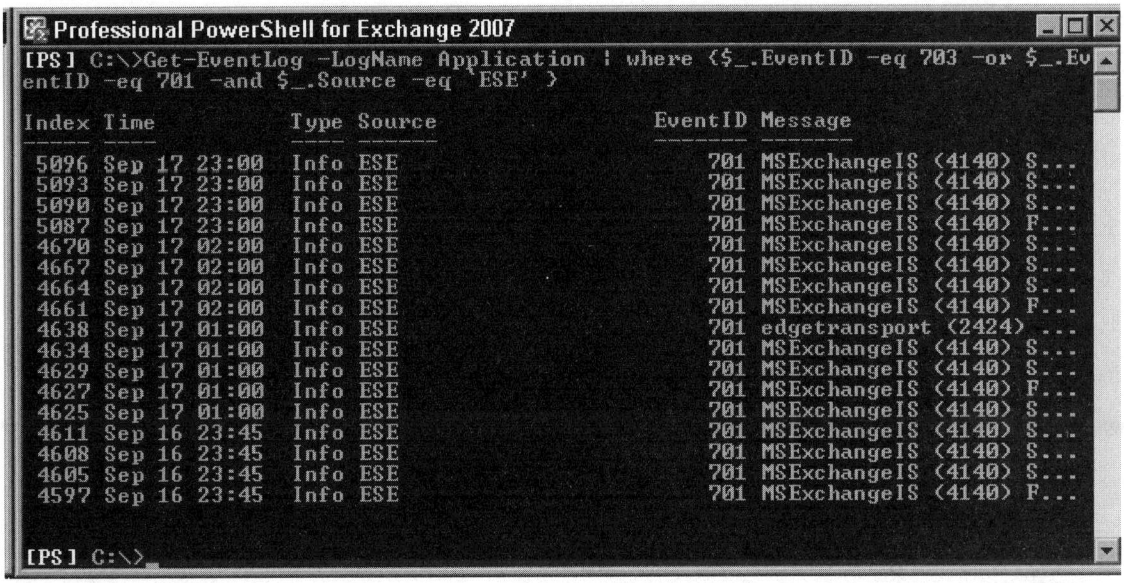

Figure 16-2

Because the database name does not have to be be unique on a single server you need to look for the database path that is listed in the event. So for every item in the storage group list you need to run the previous line of code, however you are also going to look for the database path as one of the variables that are plugged into the standard message text. You can do this by piping the output of `Get-EventLog` to another `Where-Object`. This `Where-Object` would need to use the `$objItem` variable to enumerate through your list of mailbox stores. In particular you are going to look at the `EdbFilePath` property because this is listed in the event.

```
Where-Object { $_.ReplacementStrings -like $objItem. EdbFilePath} | Select-Object
-first 1
```

Notice too that after you narrow down your list of events there is still the possibility of having more than one event returned, so this example used `Select-Object -first 1` to return only the first event from the list, which by default is the newest. You are now all set; you can add a couple `Write-Host` cmdlets to display the information that you are looking for. And you end up with the following script:

```
$servername = [System.Environment]::MachineName
$db = Get-StorageGroup -Server $servername | Get-MailboxDatabase

foreach ($objItem in $db)
{
$EventLogs = get-EventLog -LogName Application | Where-Object {$_.EventID -eq 703 -
or $_.EventID -eq 701 -and $_.Source -eq 'ESE' } | Where-Object
{$_.ReplacementStrings -like $objItem.EdbFilePath} | select-object -first 1
Write-host ' Mailbox store: ' $objItem.Identity
Write-host '   Last Defrag Completed: ' $EventLogs.TimeGenerated
Write-host ' '
}
```

Notice in Figure 16-3 that if maintenance hasn't run within the period of time that the server has event logs for, it shows up as a blank value for the last time the defrag was completed. In that case either maintenance hasn't completed in a sufficient amount of time or the event log size is too small and should be increased in size to keep more data.

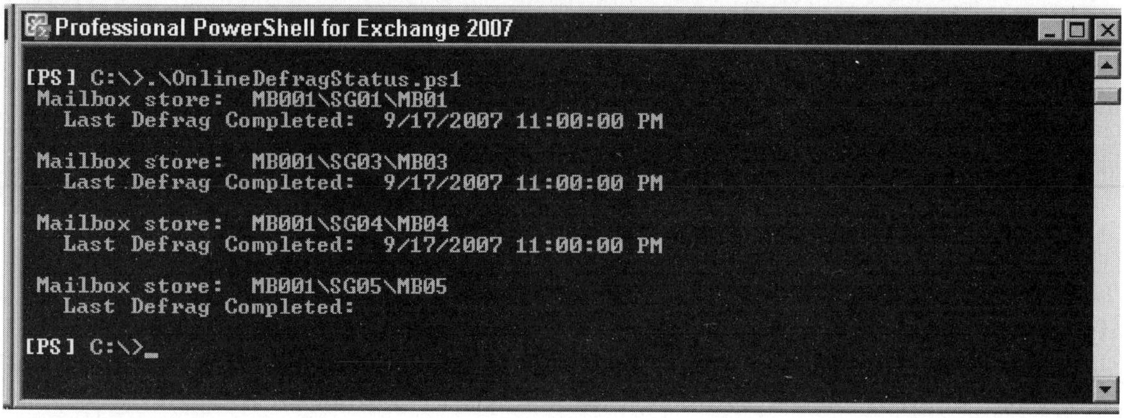

Figure 16-3

This report would also be an excellent place to report when the last time a backup was run on each of the stores. With the work you have already done to get this report it is a really easy task. In fact, the new script would look like the following:

```
$servername = [System.Environment]::MachineName
$db = Get-StorageGroup -Server $servername | Get-MailboxDatabase -status

foreach ($objItem in $db)
{
$EventLogs = get-EventLog -LogName Application | Where-Object {$_.EventID -eq 703 -
or $_.EventID -eq 701 -and $_.Source -eq 'ESE' } | Where-Object {
$_.ReplacementStrings -like $objItem.EdbFilePath} | Select-Object -first 1

Write-Host ' Mailbox store: ' $objItem.Identity
Write-Host '    Last Defrag Completed: ' $EventLogs.TimeGenerated
Write-Host '    Last Full Backup: ' $objItem.LastFullBackup
}
```

What was changed to get this information? You add the status switch to the Get-MailboxDatabase cmdlet because this is required to query the backup, mount, or online maintenance status. If you do not specify this switch the cmdlet will return $null for those properties. The last modification to the script was to add another Write-Host to be able to write the LastFullBackup property to the console. The output for this script looks like that in Figure 16-4.

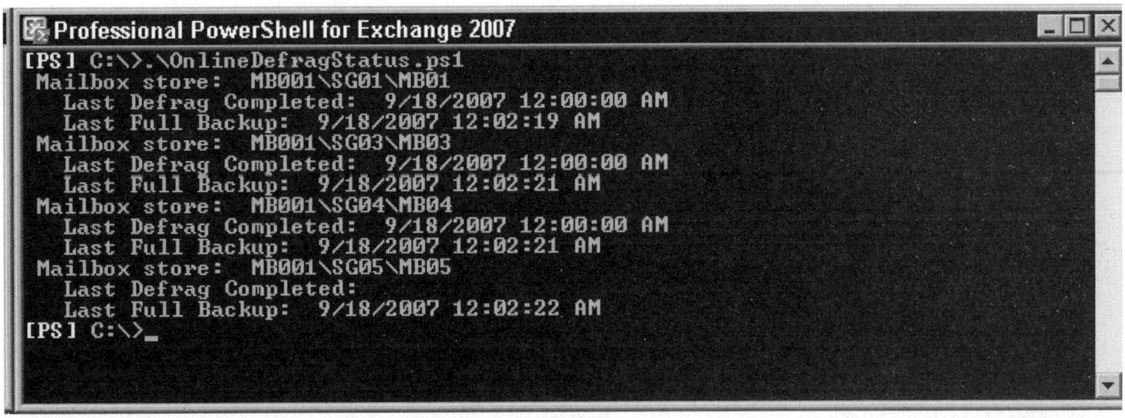

Figure 16-4

If you wanted to take this script even further you could put some logic in the report so that if maintenance hadn't run in two weeks or perhaps a backup hasn't run in two days, the report would highlight the problematic mailbox store in red to make it easier to distinguish. Rather than outputting the data to the screen you could also create an object and store the data in it for additional parsing later. You see an example of this later in this chapter.

Reporting Mailbox Size

A common task a messaging administrator performs is to report on the mailbox size of the user population. This example shows how to report which mailboxes are close to the limit, and capture a list of users who do not have limits assigned. `Get-MailboxStatistics` returns a list of mailboxes and statistics about those mailboxes.

`Get-MailboxStatistics` returns all mailboxes and the statistics for each. The results look something like those in Figure 16-5.

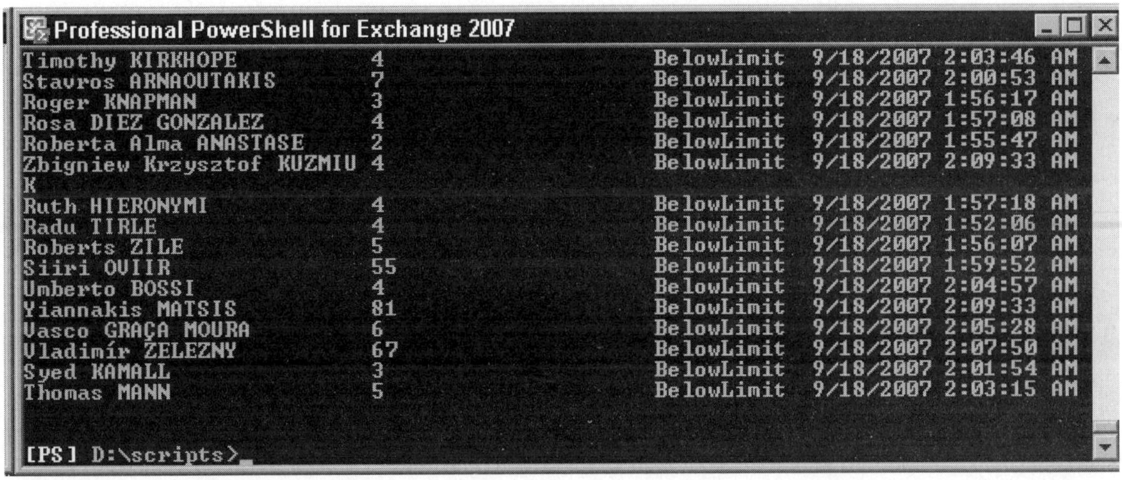

Figure 16-5

This may be useful if you want to manually go through a large list of mailboxes and the statistics. In this case, you are looking for mailboxes that are approaching the limit or have not been set, so you need to create a filter. To filter you can look at the StorageLimitStatus field. The valid values for this are NoChecking, BelowLimit, IssueWarning, ProhibitSend, or MailboxDisabled depending on where the mailbox size falls within the limits that have been set. A list of all mailboxes that are flagged with IssueWarning, ProhibitSend, or MailboxDisabled tells you which mailboxes have crossed one of the set limit thresholds. Also, to make sure that none of the Exchange administrators has disabled limits on any of the mailboxes you can add NoChecking to the filter as well. To do this, you pass the results of Get-MailboxStatistics to the Where-Object cmdlet as follows:

```
get-MailboxStatistics | Where-Object {
"IssueWarning","ProhibitSend","MailboxDisabl ed","NoChecking" -Contains
 $_.StorageLimitStatus }
```

Figure 16-6 shows the resulting list of all mailboxes that fit this criterion; however, this is still not as effective as it needs to be.

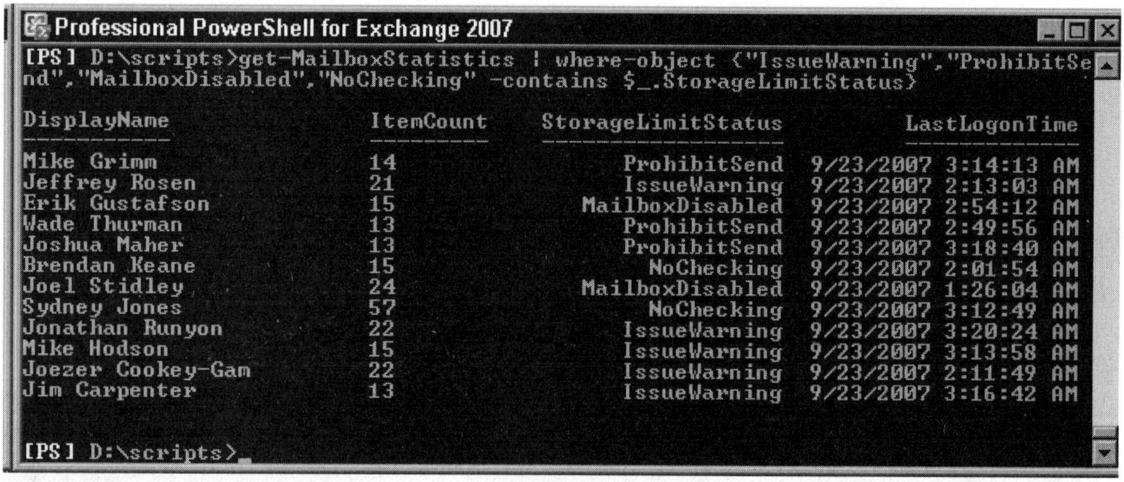

Figure 16-6

If this list were much longer it might be difficult to determine which user falls into each group. As shown in Figure 16-7, you can pipe this list to Sort-Object and arrange this list by the StorageLimitStatus and the TotalItemSize properties:

```
Sort-Object StorageLimitStatus, TotalItemSize
```

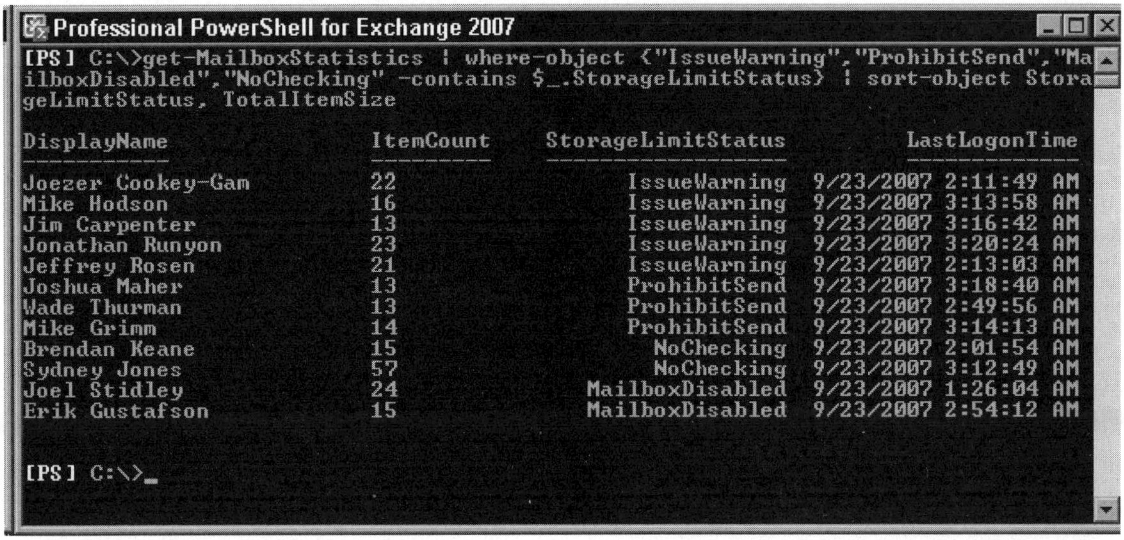

Figure 16-7

The standard columns that are shown are not very helpful. Use the following code to show `DisplayName` and `TotalItemSize` by piping the results. Figure 16-8 shows the outcome.

```
Format-Table DisplayName, StorageLimitStatus TotalItemSize
```

Figure 16-8

That is making some progress, however the TotalItemSize column is very unfriendly. Could you imagine handing this report to your supervisor? Does your supervisor want to see the size of the user mailboxes in bytes? As you recall from earlier in this book, PowerShell is based on the .NET Framework, which means that certain functions of the Framework are available within PowerShell. You can actually convert the value of TotalItemSize to kilobytes, megabytes, gigabytes, or terabytes from within the command by modifying the last Format-Table command to modify this value:

```
Format-Table DisplayName, @{expression = {$_.TotalItemSize.Value.ToMB()}} -Auto
```

This produces the result shown in Figure 16-9.

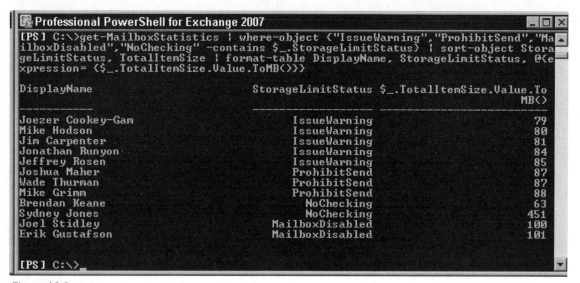

Figure 16-9

There is promise here. You have a readable number and a nice ordered list, however the title of the converted column is pretty ugly. You can assign a different label to a value column when using Format-Table by adding a semicolon, the keyword label, and then the new name. The following example shows how to change the label to TotalItemSizeMB, however any suitable title can be chosen:

```
Format-Table DisplayName, @{expression =
{$_.TotalItemSize.Value.ToMB()};label="TotalItemSizeMB"} -Auto
```

Now you have a final report. To save this so that you can review it later or send it to others you should pipe this data out to a file. You can do this by using the Out-File cmdlet as was discussed earlier in this chapter:

```
out-file C:\Data\MailboxReport.txt
```

The final script when added together looks like this:

```
get-MailboxStatistics | where-object
{"IssueWarning","ProhibitSend","MailboxDisabled","NoChecking" -contains
$_.StorageLimitStatus} | sort-object StorageLimitStatus, TotalItemSize | format-
table DisplayName, StorageLimitStatus,
@{expression={$_.TotalItemSize.Value.ToMB()};label="TotalItemSize(MB)"} | out-file
-filepath C:\data\MailboxReport.txt
```

What if you want to export this to a chart, perhaps using PowerGadgets? Chances are you would just want to list the sizes of the largest mailboxes near the quota. To do this you modify the script above so that rather than piping the data to the Format-Table cmdlet, you pipe the data to a Select-Object cmdlet. Select-Object doesn't accept changing the label so you also have to remove the label on your converted TotalItemSize value. Be sure to run this on a server that has the PowerGadgets client installed.

```
Add-PSSnapin PowerGadgets
get-MailboxStatistics | where-object
{"IssueWarning","ProhibitSend","MailboxDisable d","NoChecking" -contains
$_.StorageLimitStatus} | sort-object  TotalItemSize | select-object DisplayName,
@{expression={$_.TotalItemSize.Value.ToMB()}} |out-chart
```

You will get a chart very similar to the one in Figure 16-10.

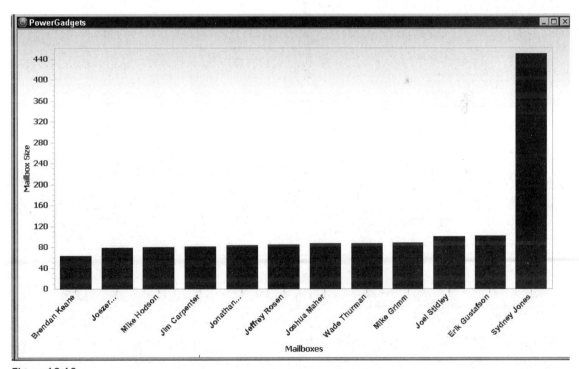

Figure 16-10

Why did I say *similar* to Figure 16-10? Well, to get this printed in the book I had to change the font sizes and colors. If you were to run this, you would still get a nice looking chart. Of course, you could also spend five minutes modifying the colors, sizes, and other formatting options to make it look just like you want it to.

You can obtain more information about using PowerGadgets including a free trial of the software at powergadgets.com.

Creating reports for mailbox size has always been a center of contention in the Exchange administrators communities. The debate has now changed from *how to create the report* into *how detailed to make the report* now that the tools are available.

Getting the Database File Size

Another interesting script that can be used to show off some of these PowerShell techniques is getting the database file sizes on disk. This script would be useful when determining backup sizing, or storing the data to trend file growth:

```
$server = [System.Environment]::MachineName
$db = get-MailboxDatabase -server $server

foreach ($objItem in $db)

{
 $dbsize = get-childitem $objItem.EdbFilePath
 Write-Host "Server\StorageGroup\Database" $objItem.Identity
 Write-Host "Size(KB)" $dbSize.Length

}
```

The first thing this script does is obtain a list of all of the mailbox stores on the server. Then for each mailbox store you cycle through a foreach loop and get the file path for the database. Then you return the mailbox store identity and the length of the file. You are returned a result set like the one in Figure 16-11.

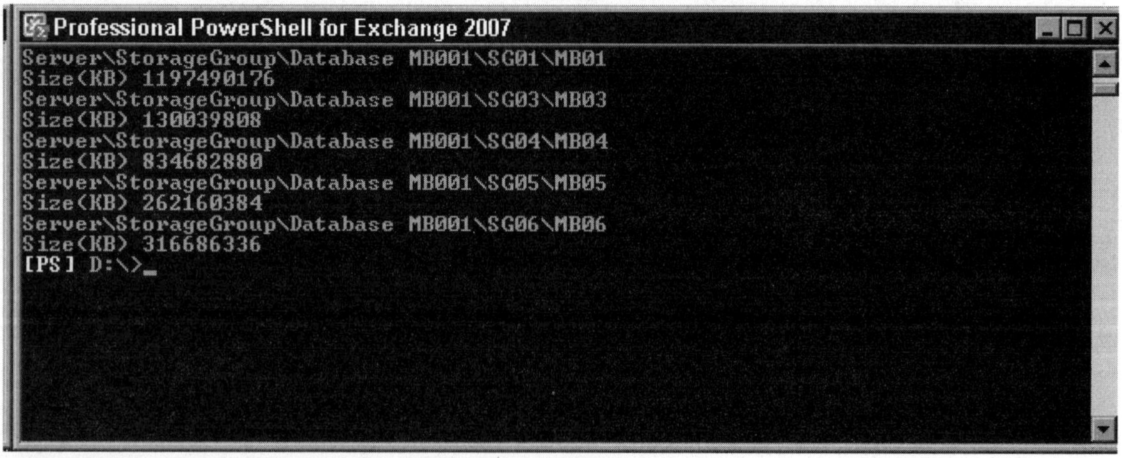

```
Professional PowerShell for Exchange 2007
Server\StorageGroup\Database MB001\SG01\MB01
Size(KB) 1197490176
Server\StorageGroup\Database MB001\SG03\MB03
Size(KB) 130039808
Server\StorageGroup\Database MB001\SG04\MB04
Size(KB) 834682880
Server\StorageGroup\Database MB001\SG05\MB05
Size(KB) 262160384
Server\StorageGroup\Database MB001\SG06\MB06
Size(KB) 316686336
[PS] D:\>_
```

Figure 16-11

The result set that is returned is pretty ugly and difficult to read. It would be better to return the result in a table. How can you do this when the identity and the file length are the results of two separate commands that are run? You can create a PowerShell object named $returnedObject using the New-Object cmdlet for each mailbox store and then you can display the results together. When using the Add-Member cmdlet to add values to the PowerShell object you need to define the type, name, and value of the property. In the following example you can see two NoteProperties added to the object, one named Server\StorageGroup\Database and the other named Size(KB), each with a value assigned to it from the respective command:

```
$server = [System.Environment]::MachineName
$db = get-MailboxDatabase -server $server

foreach ($objItem in $db)

{

 $dbsize = get-childitem $objItem.EdbFilePath

 $returnedObj = new-object PSObject
 $returnedObj | add-member NoteProperty -name "Server\StorageGroup\Database" -
value $objItem.Identity
 $returnedObj | add-member NoteProperty -name "Size(KB)" -value $dbSize.Length

 $returnedObj

}
```

The output, shown in Figure 16-12, is in a nice table format that you can easily read or output to a file for reference.

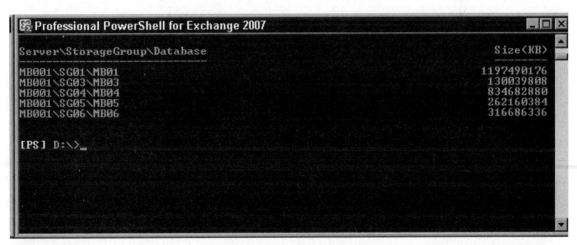

Figure 16-12

What can you do about formatting the file size so that it is shown in a more "user-friendly" number format? You can divide the length by 1024 kilobytes so that the size is represented in megabytes. Also, you can do some standard formatting as well. The following code shows modifying the format of the output value:

```
$server = [System.Environment]::MachineName
$db = get-MailboxDatabase -server $server

foreach ($objItem in $db)

{

$dbsize = get-childitem $objItem.EdbFilePath

$returnedObj = new-object PSObject
  $returnedObj | add-member NoteProperty -name "Server\StorageGroup\Database" -
value $objItem.Identity
  $returnedObj | add-member NoteProperty -name "Size(MB)" -value ("{0:n0}" -f
($dbSize.Length/1024KB))

  $returnedObj

}
```

Notice how the data looks in Figure 16-13. The size is represented in megabytes and with no numbers after the decimal point.

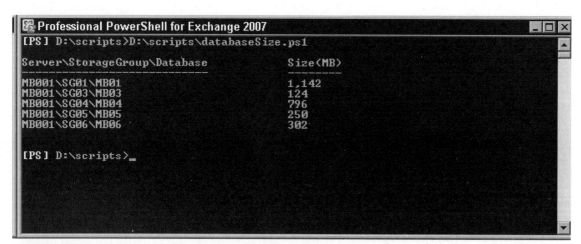

Figure 16-13

This formatting was done by using the filter {0:n0} when the value is added to $returnObject. This filter means that the data being entered is a number and should have the (n)umber followed by zero (0) digits after the decimal. If you wanted to have one number after the decimal you could change this filter to {0:n1}.

Simple Monitoring with PowerShell

Nowadays most enterprises have an in-place monitoring solution; however, at times you may need to create a simple script to monitor a condition that is temporary enough that developing a script for the monitoring tool would take too much time or effort. Look at a simple example of a script that you could schedule to run every morning to check whether full backups have run on all of the databases in the last two days.

The first line returns a file of all of the mailbox databases in the organization, however to be able to get information on the backup status you have to specify the Status switch parameters. That information is passed to the Select-Object cmdlet to reduce the amount of data passed to the $results; in this example the only two values that matter are the identity or the name of the database and LastFullBackup, which is the time the last full backup completed successfully.

```
$results = Get-MailboxDatabase -Status | Select-Object Identity, LastFullBackup
```

Most of this script you have seen in other parts of this book. The new cmdlets introduced here are Get-Date and New-TimeSpan. The Get-Date cmdlet simply returns the date and time when the cmdlet is run and has the following command syntax:

```
Get-Date [[-date] <DateTime>] [-displayHint {<Date> | <Time> | <DateTime>}] [-
format <string>] [-year <int>] [-month <int>] [-day <int>] [-hour <int>] [-minute
<int>] [-second <int>] [<CommonParameters>]
 Get-Date [[-date] <DateTime>] [-displayHint {<Date> | <Time> | <DateTime>}] [-
uFormat <string>] [-year <int>] [-month <int>] [-day <int>] [-hour <int> ] [-minute
<int>] [-second <int>] [<CommonParameters>]
```

The displayHint parameter can be used to specify what portion you want returned. You can have it return just the date or the time or both the date and the time. The format and the uformat parameters can be used to return a standard or customized formatted date and time.

The New-TimeSpan cmdlet returns the difference between the two times that are passed to it. The New-TimeSpan cmdlet has the following syntax:

```
New-TimeSpan [[-start] <DateTime>] [[-end] <DateTime>] [<CommonParameters>]
 New-TimeSpan [-days <int>] [-hours <int>] [-minutes <int>] [-seconds <int>]
[<CommonParameters>]
```

There are two ways to use New-TimeSpan. One is to create an object that represents a time span and the other is the way we are using it in our example, to determine the time span between two dates.

In the following script the current time is passed using Get-Date and then the date that the last backup ran is passed to determine the time that has elapsed since the last full backup completed. Finally, the script tests whether that time is greater than two days and if it is, it sends an email with information about the database that has not had a successful backup in the last two days.

```
$results = Get-MailboxDatabase -Status | Select-Object Identity, LastFullBackup

foreach ($objItem in $results)
{

  $timesincelastbackup = New-TimeSpan $($objItem.LastFullBackup) $(Get-Date)

  If ($timesincelastbackup.days -gt 2)
      {

        $messagesubject = "Backup Alert for " + $objItem.Identity
        $messagebody = "Warning " + $objItem.Identity + " has not completed a
backup in " + $timesincelastbackup.days + " days!"

        $smtpServer = "relay.exchangeexchange.local"
        $smtp = new-object Net.Mail.SmtpClient($smtpServer)

$smtp.Send("backupalerts@exchangeexchange.com","administrators@exchangeexchange.com
",$messageSubject,$messagebody)

      }
}
```

This script can be modified to send only one email with a list of all of the backups that are outside of the normal parameters by creating a variable that would have a list of all of the offending databases and then sending the email at the end of the process. Also, the same concept can be used to send alerts for message queues that are continuing to increase in size or for a variety of other conditions.

A number of other fairly simple monitoring scripts can be created to make sure you can keep a finger on the pulse of your Exchange organization:

❑   Monitor site link costs to make sure that the Active Directory administrators have not modified something that would affect Exchange message delivery.

❑   Monitor memory and storage I/O throughput.

❑   Monitor and trend Hub Transport queue lengths.

Summary

Windows PowerShell can be used for a variety of monitoring, reporting, and administrative tasks. The possibilities for what can be accomplished to reduce errors, increase productivity, and provide better information about an Exchange organization is endless.

This chapter went into a little more detail on reading in files, command-line arguments, as well as exporting data into files and email. You then went through a few real-world examples using these techniques that you can use and adapt in your organization today. You now should have an understanding of the main components needed to create your own scripts.

Using the .NET Framework to Automate Exchange PowerShell Tasks

In this chapter you'll see how to leverage Exchange PowerShell from within the .NET Framework and how to make a basic web-based page to run PowerShell cmdlets. We also discuss some ideas on what can be done to use .NET. This chapter involves some programming, so previous experience would be helpful.

PowerShell is built on the .NET Framework, and the only management interface exposed for Exchange Server 2007 is the PowerShell cmdlets, so running PowerShell from within something like C# or VB.NET would be easy. Because this is the only interface that is exposed, the Exchange product team uses the PowerShell cmdlets to provide the Exchange Management Console graphical management tool. You can run PowerShell cmdlets easily from within the .NET Framework, and you will work through a few examples in this chapter.

This chapter covers the following topics:

❏   Accessing PowerShell from the .NET Framework

❏   Solving problems with PowerShell and the .NET Framework

Accessing PowerShell from the .NET Framework

To be able to work with PowerShell from the .NET Framework, you need to first download the Windows PowerShell Software Development Kit (SDK) from Microsoft. To be able to run any of the Exchange cmdlets you will also need the Exchange Server 2007 management tools installed.

The Windows PowerShell SDK has been rolled into part of the Windows Software Development for Windows Vista and .NET Framework 3.0 Runtime Components. You can obtain the Windows Software Development for Windows Vista and .NET Framework 3.0 Runtime Components from Microsoft here: `microsoft.com/downloads/details.aspx?familyid=c2b1e300-f358-4523-b479-f53d234cdccf&displaylang=en`.

Although you can use C# and Visual Basic.NET to automate Windows PowerShell, this chapter focuses on C# examples. For those readers who are more comfortable with VB.NET, the following examples can be converted into usable VB.NET.

Starting a Web Project

This example leads you through the creation of several simple pages to demonstrate how to get started using Windows PowerShell to manage your Exchange servers from the .NET Framework. After installing the Windows SDK along with the required Windows PowerShell components, create a new C# ASP.NET web application project in Visual Studio 2005. Start Visual Studio and create a new C# web project.

Then you will need to add a reference to `System.Management.Automation.dll` in your web project. The Windows PowerShell SDK assemblies are installed by default in `C:\Program Files\Reference Assemblies\Microsoft\WindowsPowerShell\v1.0\`. To add a reference from within Visual Studio, click the Website menu, then click Add Reference. Click the Browse tab and then navigate to the location of the `System.Management.Automation.dll` and click OK.

In your newly created web project you will be able to open the `Default.aspx.cs` file and add several of the following directives to your code to reference the PowerShell libraries as well as the `Collections.ObjectModel` library:

```
using System.Management.Automation;
using System.Management.Automation.Host;
using System.Management.Automation.Runspaces;
using System.Collections.ObjectModel;
```

The following list describes what each of these namespaces does:

❑ `System.Management.Automation`: This is the root namespace, and it contains the classes, enumerations, and interfaces required to create customer cmdlets.

❑ `System.Management.Automation.Host`: This contains the classes, enumerations, and interfaces that a cmdlet uses to communicate with the host application.

❑ `System.Management.Automation.Runspaces`: This contains the classes, enumerations, and interfaces used to create a runspace. This allows for a Windows PowerShell pipeline to run cmdlets.

❑ `System.Collections.ObjectModel`: This contains classes that can be used as collections. This isn't specific to Windows PowerShell, however it proves useful to the examples used in this chapter.

After adding the directives, `Default.aspx.cs` should look similar to the file shown in Figure 17-1.

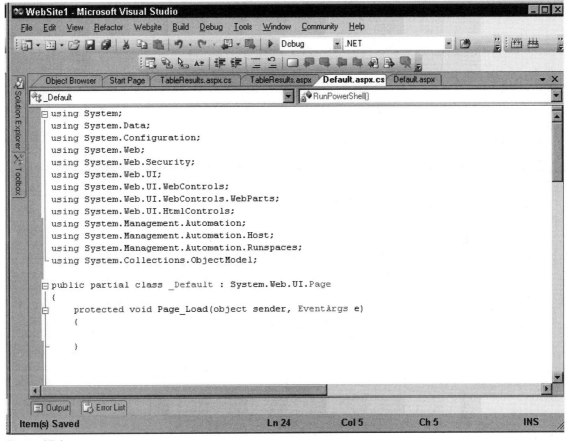

Figure 17-1

Now that the SDK is installed, the required library is referenced and the directives are added, so you can start accessing PowerShell from your web project.

The Windows PowerShell Runspace

If you aren't a programmer or have no experience with programming, you might find the next few paragraphs confusing. Here are a few definitions to help you out:

❑   A class is a container of properties, functions, and behaviors that describe an object.

❑   An object is created from a class and is assigned properties and values.

❑   A method is a piece of code that can be run. A method is usually a discrete action that can be run.

❑ Overloaded methods are methods that parameters are passed to modify how the action completes.

❑ Casting is the process of converting an object from one data type to another. For example, an integer can be converted to a string.

To be able to access PowerShell from the .NET Framework, a runspace must be created. A runspace object provides the ability for an application to be able to host or execute pipelines in a controlled manner. A runspace is created using the RunspaceFactory class. This class has only one method, CreateRunspace. This CreateRunspace method has four overloaded methods and the one of interest is the overload that requires a RunspaceConfiguration object as input. The RunspaceConfiguration object provides the ability to pass configuration parameters to the runspace. The following example creates a RunspaceConfiguration object and adds in the Exchange administration snap-in so that you are able to access the Exchange tools. If a runspace is created without passing a RunspaceConfiguration object, the runspace would not have access to the Exchange management tools. The RunspaceConfiguration object can be created with the number of PowerShell snap-ins that you require.

The code to create the runspace and add the Exchange snap-in looks like this:

```
RunspaceConfiguration EMSConfig =
    RunspaceConfiguration.Create(); PSSnapInException
    snapInException = null;
PSSnapInInfo info =
    EMSConfig.AddPSSnapIn("Microsoft.Exchange.Management.PowerShell.Admin",
    out snapInException);
Runspace EMSRunSpace =
    RunspaceFactory.CreateRunspace(EMSConfig);
    EMSRunSpace. Open();
```

To enable the running of commands, an instance of a pipeline object must be created from the runspace that you have already created. The pipeline object provides the ability to stream the output of one command into the next command in the list. To create the pipeline, use the CreatePipeline method of the runspace that you created. The CreatePipeline method has overloaded methods that enable you to pass single commands or an entire pipeline of commands that you want to run. A simple example would be to have the pipeline run Get-Mailbox, as follows:

```
Pipeline pipeLine = EMSRunSpace.CreatePipeline("Get-Mailbox");
```

Now that you have specified the command that the pipeline will execute, the Invoke method of your pipeline object can be used to return a PSObject collection of the results of the command you ran. The PSObject collection results can be cycled through and inspected or used elsewhere in your code. The following example uses a foreach loop to cycle through each of the items in the returning PSObject collection and temporarily assigns the Name property value to a string:

```
Collection<PSObject> cmdData = pipeLine.Invoke();

foreach (PSObject cmdlet in cmdData)
        {

string cmdletInfo =
    cmdlet.Properties["Name"].Value.ToString();

}
```

To provide useful information you will most likely need to provide more than just a single cmdlet without any parameters. To run a more complicated set of commands or even a full script, call the `CreatePipeline` method with the entire command text. The code would look something similar to the following:

```
Pipeline pipeLine = EMSRunSpace.CreatePipeline("get-mailbox
   | where-object -
filterscript {$_.DisplayName = \"Rivera\"}");
```

At this point it may be beneficial to mention the `CreateNestedPipeline` method. This method works much like `CreatePipeline` does in the previous example; however, it is used if you need to build another pipeline when you already have one running in your runspace. This allows you more flexibility in your application because you do not have to wait for the current pipeline to complete before creating the new pipeline.

Calling the method with the entire command text is a quick way to run a simple set of commands. But, what if you need to programatically build a conditional command list? Perhaps if certain conditions were met you might need to add specific cmdlets to the pipeline. The `CreatePipeline` method can also create a pipeline without first passing it a command or a list of commands. The commands or cmdlets and their parameters can be added on the fly to the pipeline. This is accomplished by instantiating command objects from the `Command` class and then adding the command to the pipelines collection of commands. The command object (which equates to a cmdlet or pre-written script) in turn might require a set of parameters. The way command parameters are added to a command is very simular to the way commands are added to the pipeline. First instantiate a `CommandParameter` object from the `CommandParameter` class, passing the list of parameters to its constructor. Then add the `CommandParameter` object to the command's parameters collection. This example shows how to create a runspace and then add the `get-mailbox` command without any parameters:

```
Runspace EMSRunSpace = RunspaceFactory.CreateRunspace();
EMSRunSpace.Open();
Pipeline pipeLine = EMSRunSpace.CreatePipeline();
Command MBXCommand = new Command("Get-Mailbox");
pipeLine.Commands.Add(MBXCommand);
Collection<PSObject> cmdResult = pipeLine.Invoke();
```

To add multiple commands to the pipeline, a new command object must be created for each command and then added to the pipeline. In the following example the `MBXCommand` object is created for the `Get-Mailbox` command and then added to the pipeline. After that the `FTCommand` object is created for the `Format-Table` command before it is added to the pipeline:

```
Runspace EMSRunSpace = RunspaceFactory.CreateRunspace();
EMSRunSpace.Open();
Pipeline pipeLine = EMSRunSpace.CreatePipeline();
Command MBXCommand = new Command("Get-Mailbox");
pipeLine.Commands.Add(MBXCommand);
Command FTCommand = new Command("Format-Table");
pipeLine.Commands.Add(FTCommand);
Collection<PSObject> cmdResult = pipeLine.Invoke();
```

This example takes the results of the `Get-Mailbox` command and pipelines it to the `Format-Table` command. But what if you wanted to select only mailboxes that are hosted on the MB001 server? You need to add a parameter to the `Get-Mailbox` command. For instance, if you need to run `Get-Mailbox -Server MB001`, you need to use the `pipeline.command.add` method to add in `Get-Mailbox` as the command that needs to run and then use the `command.Parameters.Add` method to add `Server` and `MB001` to modify that command. The `CommandParameter` class requires only a name in the case of a switch parameter and a name and a value for parameters that have additional values:

```
Runspace EMSRunSpace = RunspaceFactory.CreateRunspace();
EMSRunSpace.Open();
Pipeline pipeLine = EMSRunSpace.CreatePipeline();
Command MBXCommand = new Command("Get-Mailbox");
pipeLine.Commands.Add(MBXCommand);
CommandParameter verbParam = new CommandParameter("Server",
    "MB001");
EMSCmd.Parameters.Add(verbParam);
Command FTCommand = new Command("Format-Table");
pipeLine.Commands.Add(FTCommand);
Collection<PSObject> cmdResult = pipeLine.Invoke();
```

When adding commands to a pipeline this way, take care to ensure that the command is being passed correctly typed data. Most of the cmdlets accept standard Int64, string, or byte quantified size for their parameter values. However, a number of Exchange cmdlets have the `filterscript` parameter and this parameter requires a value typed as a `ScriptBlock` and will not accept a string value. Creating a `ScriptBlock` value isn't as straightforward as you might think. To create a script block you must create a new `RunspaceInvoke` object and then cast the script as a `ScriptBlock` type. The code looks something like this:

```
RunspaceInvoke rsi = new RunspaceInvoke();
ScriptBlock sBlock =
    (ScriptBlock)rsi.Invoke("{$_.DisplayName -match
    \"Br\"}")[0].BaseObject;
```

To create a `ScriptBlock` you cannot use a `RunspaceFactory` object like you are using to pipeline your commands. You must use an instance of `RunspaceInvoke` to create a ScriptBlock. The `RunspaceInvoke` `.Invoke` method returns a `PSObject` collection of the `filterscript` string you passed it. In the example only one item in the collection is passed back to you. You access this collection entry by specifying its index in the collection `[0]`. At this point you are looking at a `PSObject` and because the `PSObject` cannot be cast to a `ScriptBlock` object, another solution is needed. It just happens that the `PSObject` class has a `BaseObject` attribute, which is of type `Object`. An instance of type `Object` can be cast to an instance of type ScriptBlock. Now that the ScriptBlock has been properly cast you can use this in the pipeline as the value for the `filterscript` parameter, as you can see in the following code sample:

```
RunspaceConfiguration EMSConfig =
    RunspaceConfiguration.Create();
PSSnapInException snapInException = null;
PSSnapInInfo info =
    EMSConfig.AddPSSnapIn("Microsoft.Exchange.Management.PowerShell.Admin",
    out snapInException);
Runspace EMSRunSpace =
    RunspaceFactory.CreateRunspace(EMSConfig);
EMSRunSpace.Open();
```

```
Pipeline pipeLine = EMSRunSpace.CreatePipeline();

Collection<PSObject> cmdData = pipeLine.Invoke();

foreach (PSObject cmdlet in cmdData)
        {

        string cmdletnm =
  cmdlet.Properties["Name"].Value.ToString();
            TextBox1.Text += cmdletnm.ToString() + "\r\n";
            }

pipeLine=null;
```

To see the data returned from the PowerShell runspace, add a text box control named TextBox1 and a button control that runs the preceding code to Default.aspx of a test web site and you should get similar results to those in Figure 17-2.

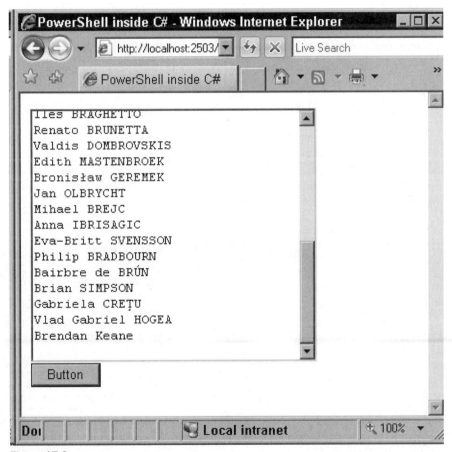

Figure 17-2

You can take this example a little further and allow the user to select a number of properties to filter by. As shown in Figure 17-3, add a drop-down list named `DropDownList1` to provide a list of properties to filter. Then add a text box named `TextBox2` so that the user can type the filter criteria. The drop-down list control should be pre-populated with values such as `DisplayName`, `ServerName`, `IsMailboxEnabled`, and `Database`.

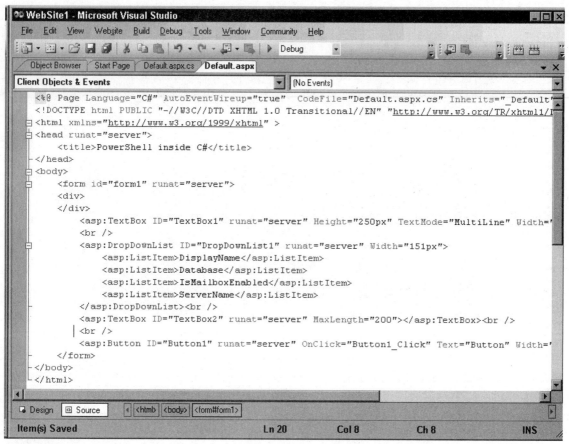

Figure 17-3

After you add the controls, you need to modify the code used to generate the `ScriptBlock` so that it will take input from the drop-down list and text box. The code would look something like this:

```
ScriptBlock sBlock = (ScriptBlock)rsi.Invoke("{$_." +
    DropDownList1.SelectedValue + " -match \"" +
    TextBox2.Text. Replace("\\","\\\\") + "\"}")[0].BaseObject;
```

The `Replace` method is used to allow a user to specify the full database path which includes the "\" character.; however, with any software development care needs to be taken to ensure that users are unable to input malicious code into the text box. This should be done with proper bounds checking and security best practices. The results of a search from the new page would look like Figure 17-4.

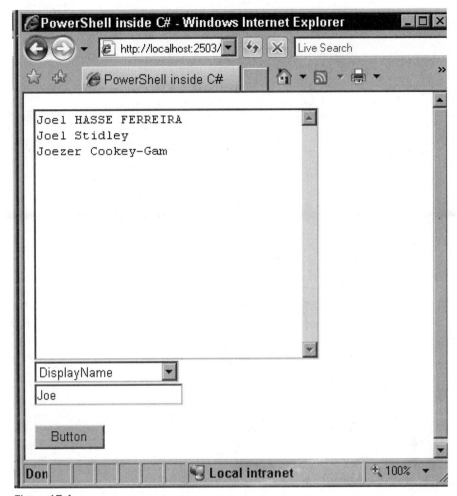

Figure 17-4

Several other options can be added to provide information to non-technical users via a website. For example, this page could return a table of the mailboxes, server name, and the mailbox store. To do this you can drop a `GridView` control onto the page to replace the `TextBox` control. To use the returned data, a dataset is created and each object from the pipeline is added the dataset.

```
RunspaceConfiguration EMSConfig =
    RunspaceConfiguration.Create();
PSSnapInException snapInException = null;
PSSnapInInfo info =
    EMSConfig.AddPSSnapIn("Microsoft.Exchange.Management.PowerShell
    .Admin", out snapInException);
```

(continued)

(continued)

```
Runspace EMSRunSpace =
    RunspaceFactory.CreateRunspace(EMSConfig);
EMSRunSpace.Open();

Pipeline pipeLine = EMSRunSpace.CreatePipeline();
Command EMSCmd = new Command("Get-Mailbox");
pipeLine.Commands.Add(EMSCmd);
CommandParameter verbParam = new CommandParameter("Server", "MB001");
EMSCmd.Parameters.Add(verbParam);
Command EMSCmd2 = new Command("Where-Object");
pipeLine.Commands.Add(EMSCmd2);
RunspaceInvoke rsi = new RunspaceInvoke();
ScriptBlock sBlock = (ScriptBlock)rsi.Invoke("{$_." +
    DropDownList1.SelectedValue + " -match \"" +
    TextBox2.Text.Replace("\\","\\\\") + "\"}")[0].BaseObject;

CommandParameter verbParam2 = new
    CommandParameter("FilterScript", sBlock);

EMSCmd2.Parameters.Add(verbParam2);

Collection<PSObject> cmdData = pipeLine.Invoke();

DataSet ds = new DataSet();

    ds.Tables.Add("Pipeline");
    ds.Tables["Pipeline"].Columns.Add("DisplayName");
    ds.Tables["Pipeline"].Columns.Add("ServerName");
    ds.Tables["Pipeline"].Columns.Add("Database");

foreach (PSObject cmdlet in cmdData)
{

    ds.Tables["Pipeline"].Rows.Add(cmdlet.Properties["Name"].Value.ToString(),cmdlet
    .Properties["ServerName"].Value.ToString(),cmdlet.Properties["Database"].Value
    .ToString());

}

GridView1.DataSource = ds.Tables["Pipeline"];
GridView1.DataBind();
pipeLine = null;
```

The results of running this modified page are shown in Figure 17-5.

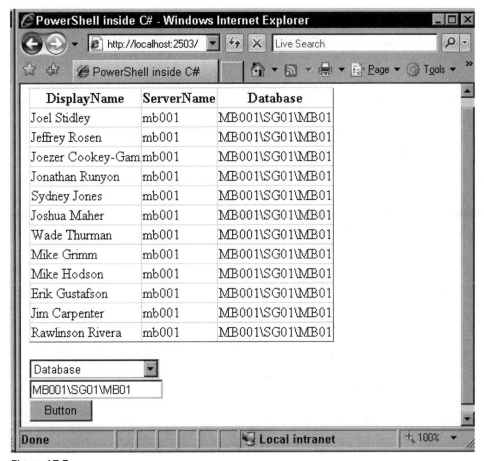

Figure 17-5

In this example, we haven't made any formatting changes to the table or any attempt to provide an esthetically pleasing interface. You can, however, see how simple it is to work with the data in PowerShell. With minimal effort you can create runspace and pipeline objects that can be used to retrieve data.

Solving Problems with PowerShell and the .NET Framework

After you understand the basics of Exchange Server 2007, Windows PowerShell, and how to work with them from the .NET Framework, a multitude of uses open up. Even though PowerShell scripts can be created for administrators to use, a web interface can be created for running these commands and to hold business logic around these tasks.

One example might be creating a web-based tool to use in the case of a disaster recovery scenario. One of the tasks in a disaster recovery scenario might be to failover the mailboxes to the standby continuous replication (SCR) target database. Each of the manual steps can be automated by creating business logic and creating code.

Another example of adding business logic with the .NET Framework is allowing an administrator to request a size increase for a mailbox, but before applying the changes a confirmation request can be sent to the user's supervisor to approve the quota increase.

Summary

The only programmatic management interface for Exchange Server 2007 is through PowerShell. A case in point is that the Exchange Management Console relies on the PowerShell cmdlets to be able to manage Exchange. This makes it important when creating complex and interconnected business processes to be able to leverage the .NET Framework.

This chapter covered creating a PowerShell runspace and modifying the configuration of that runspace to be able to access the Exchange management snap-in. Then an example was used to show how to create a pipeline and add commands to that pipeline in a number of ways.

Index